D1804858

REF
LB
2376.6
.G7   International guide
I58   to qualifications
1987 in education

$145.00

DATE			

THE CHICAGO PUBLIC LIBRARY
SOCIAL SCIENCES AND HISTORY DIVISION
400 NORTH FRANKLIN STREET
CHICAGO, ILLINOIS 60610

© THE BAKER & TAYLOR CO.

International Guide to
Qualifications
in Education

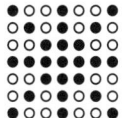 The British Council
National Academic Recognition
Information Centre

International Guide to Qualifications in Education

Second Edition

Mansell Publishing Limited

London   New York

SOCIAL SCIENCE & HISTORY DIVISION
EDUCATION & PHILOSOPHY SECTION

Mansell Publishing Limited
(A subsidiary of The H. W. Wilson Company)
6 All Saints Street, London N1 9RL, England
950 University Avenue, Bronx, New York 10452, U.S.A.
First published 1984. Reprinted 1985. Second Edition 1987.

© The British Council 1984, 1987

All rights reserved. No part of this
publication may be reproduced or
transmitted in any form or by any means,
electronic or mechanical, including
photocopy, recording or any information
storage or retrieval system, without
permission in writing from the publishers or
their appointed agents.

British Library Cataloguing in Publication Data

International guide to qualifications in
   education. — 2nd ed.
  1. Degrees, Academic
  I. National Academic Recognition
Information Centre
378'.013   LB2381
ISBN 0-7201-1848-4

Library of Congress Cataloging in Publication Data

International guide to qualifications in education

  1. Students, Foreign--Great Britain. 2. School
credits--Standards--Evaluation. 3. Universities and
colleges--Great Britain--Entrance requirements.
4. Comparative education. I. National Academic
Recognition Information Centre (Great Britain)
[DNLM: 1. Education--Standards. LB 2350 I61]
LB2376.6.G7I58   1987   378'.105   87-5589
ISBN 0-7201-1848-4

Printed in Great Britain

Contents

Introduction ix
The British Council and Its Work xi
Guide to Reading Transcripts of
  Educational Certificates xiii

Afghanistan 1
Albania 4
Algeria 7
Angola 11
Argentina 14
Australia 18
Austria 45
Bahamas 55
Bahrain 57
Bangladesh 61
Barbados 66
Belgium 69
Belize 78
Benin 81
Bermuda 84
Bolivia 86
Botswana 90
Brazil 94
Brunei 98
Bulgaria 101
Burkina 105
Burma 108
Burundi 113
Cameroon 116
Canada 120
Central African Republic 136
Chad 138
Chile 141

China 145
Colombia 149
Congo Brazzaville 153
Costa Rica 156
Cuba 161
Cyprus 164
Czechoslovakia 168
Denmark 173
Dominican Republic 183
Ecuador 187
Egypt 190
El Salvador 195
Ethiopia 199
Fiji 203
Finland 206
France 213
Gabon 225
Gambia 228
Germany, East 231
Germany, West 236
Ghana 245
Greece 251
Guatemala 256
Guinea 258
Guyana 262
Haiti 265
Holy See 268
Honduras 271
Hong Kong 274
Hungary 282
Iceland 286
India 291
Indonesia 296

Contents

Iran   301
Iraq   306
Ireland   310
Israel   315
Italy   320
Ivory Coast   326
Jamaica   329
Japan   334
Jordan   339
Kenya   344
Korea, South   352
Kuwait   357
Lebanon   363
Lesotho   367
Liberia   371
Libya   374
Luxembourg   377
Malawi   383
Malaysia   387
Mali   395
Malta   399
Mauritius   404
Mexico   408
Morocco   412
Nepal   416
Netherlands   419
New Zealand   428
Nicaragua   435
Niger   437
Nigeria   440
Norway   445
Oman   454
Pakistan   457
Panama   461
Papua New Guinea   463
Paraguay   466
Peru   470
Philippines   473
Poland   477
Portugal   484
Puerto Rico   490
Qatar   492
Romania   495
Rwanda   499
Saudi Arabia   502

Senegal   507
Seychelles   512
Sierra Leone   515
Singapore   518
Solomon Islands   524
South Africa   527
Spain   535
Sri Lanka   548
Sudan   553
Suriname   557
Swaziland   561
Sweden   565
Switzerland   573
Syria   582
Taiwan   586
Tanzania   589
Thailand   594
Togo   598
Tonga   602
Trinidad and Tobago   604
Tunisia   607
Turkey   610
Uganda   618
Union of Soviet Socialist
   Republics   622
United Arab Emirates   627
United Kingdom   631
United States   641
Uruguay   648
Vanuatu   651
Venezuela   655
Viet Nam   660
West Bank   667
Yemen   671
Yemen, Democratic   674
Yugoslavia   677
Zaire   681
Zambia   685
Zanzibar   690
Zimbabwe   692

Contents

Appendices
1. Cambridge Overseas School Certificate and Cambridge Overseas Higher School Certificate   697
2. London Chamber of Commerce and Industry   700
3. City and Guilds of London Institute   702
4. East African Examinations Council   704
5. West African Examinations Council   706
6. Caribbean Examinations Council   709
7. College of Europe   711
8. European Baccalaureate   712
9. International Baccalaureate   715
10. United Nations Relief and Works Agency   717
11. United Nations University   719

Introduction

Since the publication of the first edition of the *International Guide to Qualifications in Education* in 1984, the name of the British national centre has changed from the National Equivalence Information Centre (NEIC) — its Council of Europe title — to that of the National Academic Recognition Information Centre (NARIC) in line with European Community practice. It is now located in the Higher Education Division of the British Council. The *International Guide* is the Centre's main publication and the present edition covers some 140 countries from which students come to Britain in search of further study, training or employment.

Each country entry usually consists of the following sections:

a. a brief introduction;
b. *Evaluation in Britain*, which, taking the British system as the norm, discusses the recognition generally accorded to key qualifications by British institutions;
c. *Marking Systems*, which describe the marking systems used at secondary and tertiary levels;
d. a survey of the structure of education, level by level: *School Education, Further Education, Higher Education* and *Teacher Education*.

The country chapters are preceded by a note on the British Council and its work and by a guide to reading transcripts of educational certificates. They are followed by several appendices on international institutions and agencies and on examinations and examining boards.

All the information contained in the present edition has been thoroughly overhauled, updated and checked. It has not been possible, however, to obtain information about recent educational developments in the following countries: Afghanistan, Argentina, Burundi, Central African Republic, Chad, Iran, Libya, Rwanda, Yemen and Zaire.

From its beginnings in 1975, in response to a Council of Europe requirement that all member states should provide national information centres on academic recognition and mobility, the Centre has been maintained by the British Council and assisted in its work by the Council's overseas network and close working relationship with the higher education sector in Britain.

Introduction

In determining comparative evaluations for each country's diplomas, the Centre has benefited from the experience of the following bodies and the generous help of the officers named: Council for National Academic Awards (Mrs M. Farthing); Joint Matriculation Board (Mr F. G. Stewart and Mrs J. D. Theakestone); Scottish University Council on Entrance (Mr A. D. Mackintosh); City and Guilds of London Institute (Mr K. A. E. Sears); Plymouth Polytechnic (Dr C. S. Sparrow) and London University Entrance Requirements Division (Mr N. Mohammed).

It should be remembered that the British NARIC is an advisory body offering guidance on the recognition *likely to be accorded* a particular qualification by British institutions, based on collective past experience. It has no power to make authoritative statements or to give assurances which would challenge the right of individual institutions to make their own judgements.

Enquiry Service

If you are unable to find the information you require in the *International Guide to Qualifications in Education*, please contact:

National Academic Recognition Information Centre
The British Council
10 Spring Gardens
London SW1A 2BN
United Kingdom
Telephone: 01-930 8466

The British Council and Its Work

The British Council, which was established in 1934, is an independent non-political body incorporated by Royal Charter. Her Majesty The Queen is its Patron.

The Council is governed by a Board with representatives from Parliament, the universities, the arts and sciences, industry and commerce, the Foreign and Commonwealth Office and the Overseas Development Administration. The Board, with the approval of the Secretary of State for Foreign and Commonwealth Affairs, elects a Chairman and appoints a Director-General, who is responsible to the Board for the day-to-day management of the Council.

The British Council is a non-profit-making body, registered as a charity in Britain. It is funded largely by grants from the Foreign and Commonwealth Office and the Overseas Development Administration (ODA). In addition, the Council disburses large sums as agents for the ODA and for international organizations. The Council also earns revenue from English language teaching and paid educational services.

The aim of the British Council is to promote an enduring understanding and appreciation of Britain in other countries through cultural, educational and technical co-operation. It does this by:

a. teaching English and helping others to teach English;

b. helping people with professional and other interests in common, in Britain and in other countries, to meet and get to know one another;

c. providing information about Britain's cultural, educational and intellectual life through its offices, libraries and centres around the world, and through presentations of books;

d. organizing exhibitions of British art and books, and performances of British drama, dance, music and films abroad;

e. recruiting teachers, lecturers and consultants for educational programmes and projects overseas;

f. promoting exchanges between young people, and twinning of towns and regions;

g. fostering institutional links between British and foreign universities and institutes of higher education as a framework for collaborative projects in staff training, research and development;

h. arranging training programmes, specialist courses and study visits in Britain for people from overseas.

The British Council and Its Work

The Council's relations with other countries cover culture in its widest sense and embrace education, science, the arts and every kind of social and intellectual interchange. Activities are conducted on a basis of mutual respect and mutual benefit and the Council works in close co-operation with the relevant authorities and institutions in overseas countries. It is a cardinal principle that the Council's activities should be conditioned by the demands and circumstances of each particular country and therefore the pattern of work is different in each country.

The British Council has offices in over eighty countries and in seventeen towns in Britain. Its staff includes specialists in agriculture, the arts, education, English language teaching, librarianship, literature, medicine, physical sciences and technology. Specialist advisory committees help keep the Council in touch with British achievements and current issues. There are advisory committees for Scotland and Wales, the Committee for International Co-operation in Higher Education, and committees and panels for publishing, libraries, English teaching, law, medicine, science, engineering and technology, agriculture and veterinary science, drama and dance, fine arts, music and films, television and video.

The British Overseas Development Administration engages the Council as adviser and executive agent for much of the Government's aid to developing countries in the fields of education and training. The Council provides consultants and trainers for projects overseas and access to training institutions in Britain. Over 8,000 trainees are placed and administered each year under the Government's Technical Co-operation Training Programme, and thousands of others are handled on behalf of foreign governments, United Nations agencies and as part of projects financed by international lending agencies such as the World Bank.

The British educational system has a good reputation overseas and information on its teaching methods, materials and organization is readily available from the British Council. The Council also demonstrates recent innovations and experiments in education and, by arranging courses, study visits and training in Britain, it enables overseas teachers and educational administrators to see things for themselves. It also puts British teachers, academics and other education specialists in touch with their counterparts abroad. Postgraduate training is arranged for selected foreign students in British universities, colleges and polytechnics, and advice and information is provided for other applicants.

Guide to Reading Transcripts of Educational Certificates

Age cannot always be a guide to the level to which a person will have studied, particularly in third world countries where educational facilities may not be developed or widespread.

Translations, whether made by official translators or the holders of the qualifications themselves, should be treated with care: the word *diploma* is used to cover a wide range of qualifications, from the primary school-leaving certificate to a Master degree, and can give the wrong impression of the qualification actually obtained.

As it is essential to have sufficient information when checking the student's level, certificates and full transcripts should be requested giving the following details:

a. full name of institution issuing documents and town/city where the institution is situated;
b. name of qualification in the language of the country where obtained;
c. marks obtained;
d. length of period of study to obtain qualifications, with dates;
e. details of any previous educational qualifications.

It is essential to have a wide knowledge of the British education system when comparing British and other qualifications. In addition to the United Kingdom chapter in this work, *British Qualifications: a Comprehensive Guide to Educational, Technical, Professional and Academic Qualifications in Britain* 16th edition (London: Kogan Page, 1986) may be useful.

The United Kingdom, with the exception of Scotland, is perhaps the only country in the world that has early specialization. Hence, a difficulty arises when comparing a school-leaving certificate from overseas with GCE Advanced-level. Normally, students in other countries may take anything from four to ten subjects in their final certificate. It is usually considered that the student's overall standard in this certificate is comparable to that of a student who had taken GCE A-levels, that is to say, under the British system the student would have been capable of obtaining at least five GCE passes, two being at the Advanced level. Individual subjects may only be compared to GCE O-level since it is unlikely that any one subject could have been studied in the same depth as only two or three subjects taken at A-level.

Guide to Reading Transcripts of Educational Certificates

The subject of English in an overseas school-leaving certificate is not usually considered of GCE O-level standard, unless the medium of instruction was English. Neither is a degree in the subject of English likely to be of the same standard as a British degree in that subject (even if degrees from that country are normally compared to degrees from Britain) unless English was the medium of instruction and the examination was in English.

Because of early specialization, British university entrance requirements are correspondingly high and the Bachelor degree may be taken in three years instead of four (or more) as in most other countries.

The British Bachelor degree may cover a small range of subjects which are studied in depth (Honours) or be more wide-ranging (Ordinary or General).

Afghanistan

Democratic Republic of Afghanistan

Note - all information relates to the period before 1979

Educational policy has been developed in accordance with the Five-Year Plan - the first of these was 1957-62, with the emphasis on central control.

Under the new Education Policy of January 1975, the period of compulsory primary education was lengthened to eight years. However, it was not possible to enforce this owing to insufficient facilities.

The medium of instruction is one of the two national languages, depending on which is spoken by the majority. At the university, English is used as the medium of instruction in the Faculties of Engineering and Agriculture.

The academic year runs from March to December (colder regions), from August to May (warmer regions) from April to December (higher school).

EVALUATION IN BRITAIN

School

Baccaluria - generally considered to compare to GCE O-level standard.

Higher

Bachelor degree - generally considered to be below British Bachelor degree standard.

MARKING SYSTEMS

School

Until 1976:

Marking was on a scale of 0-10 (maximum); minimum pass mark is 3.5 and minimum average is 50% of the sum of the highest marks for all subjects.

Afghanistan

Since 1976:

Marking is on a percentage scale: 40% is the minimum pass mark for individual subjects; the minimum average is 50% of the sum of the highest marks for all subjects.

Higher

Marked on a percentage scale: 50% is the minimum pass; the minimum average is 55% of the sum of the highest marks for all subjects.

SCHOOL EDUCATION

Pre-primary

There are extremely limited facilities for children aged 4-6.

Primary

This covers 6 years for children aged 7, divided into two 3-year cycles. In rural areas the period is shorter. The lower cycle covers mother tongue, mathematics, religious instruction, arts, crafts and physical education. The upper cycle covers the same subjects plus a second language, social studies and science.

Secondary

There is an entrance examination for admission to this level. It covers 6 years, divided into two 3-year cycles: grades 7-9, studied at middle school, and grades 10-12 at high school/lycée. In the first cycle, the curriculum covers Dari, Pushtu, mathematics, Koran, theology, history, chemistry, physics, biology, Arabic, a foreign language (often English), economics, geography, and manual work. On completion of this cycle pupils take an examination to decide on admission to the second cycle. This cycle offers the same curriculum, with the addition of geology in grade 10 and religion and logic/psychology in grade 12. Girls study needlework in grades 7-9 and home economics in grades 9-12. On completion of this cycle, pupils take the examinations for the Baccaluria.

Technical secondary

In the lower secondary cycle at the middle schools, boys may specialize in commerce, theology, applied arts, mechanics, military training, or mechanics, and girls in teacher training or commerce. In the upper secondary cycle, boys may specialize in teacher training, Islamic law, aeronautics, technology, land surveying, agriculture, dentistry, and nursing, and girls in nursing, home economics, and teacher training.

3-year courses covering grades 8-10 (including an orientation year) are available to train plumbers, mechanics, etc.

The Afghan Institute of Technology, established in 1951, trains supervisors and assistant engineers on courses covering grades 10-12. The best students may then go on to the Faculty of Engineering at Kabul University.

Afghanistan

HIGHER EDUCATION

There is 1 university, the University of Kabul. Admission to first-degree courses is based on the **Baccaluria** and success in an entrance examination (concours) course leading to the award of the **Bachelor degree/Licence** lasting 3-4 years, with 5 years in engineering and veterinary medicine, and 7 years in medicine (including 1 year pre-medical and 1 year internship). A further 3-4 years study leads to the award of a **Master** degree (only in medicine). There are no other postgraduate facilities.

TEACHER EDUCATION

Primary

A 1-year course is required (at a teacher training college) on completion of upper secondary school.

Secondary

Lower/middle school: a 2-year course is offered from grade 14 at a higher teacher training college (first established in 1964).

Upper School/Lycee: a 4-year degree course is available at the university, selected graduates of the higher teacher training colleges being admitted to the last 2 years.

Albania

People's Socialist Republic of Albania

Education in Albania is state-controlled.

Education is compulsory from age seven to sixteen (before 1963 from seven to fifteen).

EVALUATION IN BRITAIN

School

Secondary School Leaving Certificate (obtained after 12 years of education) accorded GCE O-level status by some institutions.

Higher

Bachelor degree - generally compared to a British Bachelor degree.

MARKING SYSTEMS

School - continuous assessment.

University - examination.

SCHOOL EDUCATION

Schooling is divided into 3 cycles, each of 4 years. Basic schooling is provided in 8-year schools, the first 4 years concentrating on language (Albanian) and mathematics and the second 4 years on science. Geography and history are taught from the fifth and fourth years respectively. Pupils have to engage in practical work of social value as part of their education. The final examination is called 'Examination of Freedom' and is set by the Ministry of Education and Culture.

Albania

General secondary

Secondary education (middle school) lasts 4 years and provides an extension of basic education; it is broadly-based and vocationally orientated, including practical training. The school-leaving examination, the Examination of Maturity, gives access to higher education.

Technical-professional secondary

This is more vocational than general secondary education, though general studies are included. Courses last 4 or 5 years.

<u>Technical schools</u> (Teknikume) specialize in, for example, mechanics, engineering, agriculture, building. Courses last 4 years. The leaving certificate gives access to appropriate areas of study in higher education.

<u>Pedagogical schools</u> (Shkollat Pedagogjike) - see below under TEACHER EDUCATION.

There are also secondary-level schools providing 4- or 5-year courses in, for example, music, art, physical education, administration.

FURTHER EDUCATION

<u>Lower vocational schools</u> (Shkollat e Ulte Profesionale) provide training for skilled workers in various branches of industry, commerce and agriculture. Entry is on the basis of completion of compulsory education at age 16.

HIGHER EDUCATION

Access to higher education is by means of the Certificate of Maturity from a general secondary school/middle school or from a technical or vocational secondary school.

University

There is only 1 university, Tirana State University. The first degree is the Bachelor degree in most subjects and a professional title in pharmacy, engineering, technology, dentistry and medicine. Degree courses last 4 years, except in engineering, technology and dentistry (5 years), and medicine (6 years).

Institutes of higher education

These include an Institute of Fine Arts, Institutes of Agriculture, Institutes of Engineering, an Institute of Mechanics, and 5 Institutes of Education (1 of Physical Education). Courses lead to professional titles of degree status, and last 4 to 5 years.

Albania

TEACHER EDUCATION

Secondary

After completion of 8 years basic education pupils can take a 4-year secondary level course to obtain the necessary qualification to teach in the first 4 years of the basic school. The leaving certificate from the secondary teacher schools gives access to the Institutes of Education and to the University (except technological and medical studies).

Admission to Institutes of Education is on the basis of the Secondary School Leaving Certificate (following 12 years of education). Courses last 3 years (formerly 2 years) for teachers in the upper 4 years of basic school, and 4 years for teachers in secondary schools.

Teachers for secondary schools may also receive training as part of the 4-year Bachelor degree course at university.

University

After obtaining a Bachelor degree or professional title, a university graduate may follow a course lasting 3 years (5 years part-time) and take a competitive examination to teach at university level.

Algeria

People's Democratic Republic of Algeria

Education is compulsory from age six to fifteen.

The medium of instruction is Arabic whenever possible at all levels from Ecole Fondamentale to University. The National Policy has decreed that Arabic should be the language of instruction in all Algerian educational institutions.

The academic year is from September to July.

EVALUATION IN BRITAIN

Baccalaureat - generally thought to lie between GCE O- and A-level standards. For entry into higher education the host institution may require British GCE A-levels in addition.

Licence - awarded for high average marks, has been compared to British Bachelor (ordinary) degree standard (when obtained after 3 years study).

Doctorat de Troisieme Cycle - usually equated to the British research M.Phil. but has been replaced by the 3-year **Magister** degree, also equated with the research M.Phil.

Doctorat d'Etat - usually equated with the British Ph.D.

MARKING SYSTEMS

School

Marking in the Baccalaureat examinations is on a scale of 0-20 (maximum):

16-20	tres bien	very good
14-15	bien	good
12-13	assez bien	fair
10-11	passable/moyen	pass
0- 9	insuffisant	fail

Algeria

Higher

A uniform standard of grading is now being introduced using a 0-20 scale with 10 as the pass mark. Some university cohorts are still working on a 0-5 scale:

15-20	tres bien	very good
13-14	bien	good
12	assez bien	fair
11	passable	pass
10	moyen	borderline

Students at university may pass a course <u>avec mention</u> (with Honours) or <u>sans mention</u> (without Honours).

The 4 levels of Honours are: tres bien, bien, assez bien, and passable.

This type of grading does not indicate Honours degrees as compared with Pass degrees as in the British system but is only a differentiation of the standard of the pass.

SCHOOL EDUCATION

School education has been divided into 2 cycles in Algeria, primary and secondary.

Primary

The <u>Ecole Fondamentale</u> takes children from the age of 6+ for a 9-year teaching period. During this period the pupils are given a standard common-core education in which all subjects are taught in the same way throughout the country. Only in the last 2 years of the Ecole Fondamentale are pupils subjected to formal tests for selection orienting them either for work or further education. Programmes and syllabuses are being introduced on an annual basis. The medium of instruction is Arabic. At the end of the 9-year programme it is expected that the students will be awarded a **Brevet d'Etudes Fondamentales** (BEF), at which stage some will leave school to work while the more able will transfer to secondary education.

Secondary

This is provided in Lycees where students can choose from 3 options: humanities, mathematics and science. The Lycee cycle lasts 3 years, at the end of which the students take the **Baccalaureat** in the appropriate subjects.

The most gifted students often attend a Lycee Technique where they may be awarded a **Baccalaureat Technique Mathematique**. Students specializing in commerce at a Commercial Lycee sit for the **Baccalaureat Secretariat Comptabilite** at the end of a 3-year course.

Technical/vocational

Vocational training is provided by the <u>Instituts de Formation Professionnelle</u> in such fields as mechanics, car-body repair, hairdressing, secretarial work. After leaving the <u>Ecole Fondamentale</u> successful students of <u>Instituts de Formation Professionnelle</u> may be awarded the **Certificat d'Aptitude Professionnelle** (after 3 years) and the **Brevet de Maitrise** (after 4 years).

Algeria

Technological institutes

These are usually National Institutes under the auspices of one or other of the main ministries, i.e. light or heavy industries, agriculture, etc. These institutes offer a variety of courses aimed at the secondary, higher and graduate levels. Students are trained in a specific skill. Recruitment is at Baccalaureat level, and leads to an **Ingenieur** after a 5-year programme. At lower level, students who have reached **Baccalaureat** level but not passed the examination may follow a two-and-a-half year course leading to the **Diplome de Technician**. The **Diplome d'Ingenieur** is generally equated with a **Licence** in science or technology from a university.

HIGHER EDUCATION

The **Baccalaureat de l'Enseignement Secondaire** is the basic entrance requirement for university or an equivalent institution. Not all university departments, however, require the same average mark. For example, English and French sections of the Instituts de Langues Vivantes (ILVEs) require 12/20, while future doctors are required to average 15-18. There is a further selection hurdle after the end of the first year of medical studies (common core). These requirements vary from year to year and department to department, depending on such factors as availability of places or facilities.

The first degree is a **Licence**. The **Licence es Lettres**, currently a 3-year course, is being extended to 4 years. The **Licence es Sciences** is a 4-year course. There is no difference between a **Licence d'Enseignement d'Anglais** and a **Licence d'Anglais**, except that the holder of the **Licence d'Enseignement d'Anglais** will have signed an agreement with the Ecole Normale Superieure to enter the teaching profession.

The **Doctorat de Troisieme Cycle** and the **Doctorat d'Etat** are both postgraduate degrees. The Doctorat de Troisieme Cycle has been replaced by the 3-year **Magister** degree.

Certain agricultural and engineering institutes, as well as the Ecole Polytechnique, award the **Diplome d'Etat** in Agriculture and Engineering after a 5-year course.

TEACHER EDUCATION

Primary

Students holding the Brevet may follow a 2-year course at an Institut de Technologie de l'Education followed by a probationary year. This leads to the title of **Instituteur**. A 1-year course plus a probationary year leads to the title of **Instructeur**.

Algeria

Students holding the **Baccalaureat de l'Enseignement Secondaire** follow a 2-year course at an Institut de Technologie de l'Education, which leads to the title of **Professeur de l'Enseignement Moyen**. Teachers are inspected in their second year and if approved are awarded the **Certificat d'Aptitude a l'Enseignement Moyen** (CAPEM). These teachers operate at the higher levels of the Ecole Fondamentale. Changes are expected in teacher training following changes in the school system.

Secondary

No specialized training is provided for secondary and university teachers. Although there are some degree courses designed for prospective teachers (e.g. **Licence d'Enseignement d'Anglais** above), most have a degree and acquire experience in the job. In their second year of teaching they are inspected and may be awarded the **Certificat d'Aptitude a l'Enseignement Secondaire** (CAPES).

Angola

People's Republic of Angola

There are three levels of education: Ensino de Base, Ensino Medio and Ensino Superior. When the education system was reorganized in 1976 the existing Portuguese system was modified, the ninth and tenth years no longer being general education but work/vocational specific.

Education is compulsory from ages seven to eleven.

The medium of instruction is Portuguese.

The academic year runs from October to June.

EVALUATION IN BRITAIN

School

Secondary School Leaving Certificate - generally compared to GCE O-level standard.

Higher

Bachelor - generally considered to be between GCE A-level and British Bachelor degree standard.

Licenciado - generally compared to British Bachelor (Honours) degree standard.

MARKING SYSTEMS

Ensino de Base exams are marked out of 20. Students must have at least 10 in every subject to go on to Ensino Medio.

Ensino Medio has as yet no standardized exams; exams are set by individual teachers.

Angola

SCHOOL EDUCATION

Primary

Ensino de Base is divided into 3 levels:

1st level compulsory education starts at age 6 or 7 (often a lot later) and lasts 4 years

2nd level lasts 2 years and is the minimum qualification for state employment.

3rd level lasts 2 years and leads to a national examination which students must pass to go on to Ensino Medio.

Secondary

Ensino Medio is a 4-year vocational course. Students who complete this may, after working for the state for 2-5 years, go on to university.

There are also 2-year pre-university courses. These were an interim measure so that technicians and teachers could be trained quickly and are to be phased out by 1990.

HIGHER EDUCATION

There is 1 university, the Universidade de Augustinho Neto. It has 5 faculties in Luanda, 2 in Huambo and Instituto Superior de Ciencias e Educacao (ISCED) in Lubango. The Luanda Faculties are Medicine, Engineering, Science, Economics and Law. Huambro produces agronomists and students can also study the first 2 years of Medicine and Economics.

The entrance requirement is the Secondary School Leaving Certificate and successful performance in an entrance examination.

The first qualification to be obtained is the **Bacharel** on completion of 4 years study, with a further 2 years leading to the **Licenciado**. A **Doctorate** may be obtained after a further 2-3 years research.

Angola

TEACHER EDUCATION

Teachers are trained either at <u>Instituto Normal de Educacao</u> (INE) or at <u>Instituto Superior de Ciencias e Educacao</u> (ISCED), Lubango.

INE

These institutes train teachers for Ensino de Base, and are part of Ensino Medio. They offer 4-year courses. The first intake was in 1981 so the first students graduated in July 1985. Students in the eleventh and twelfth years specialize and their special subjects are the only subjects that they are allowed to teach at the 3rd level of Ensino de Base. Most of the teacher trainers are Co-operantes The INE's also give 2-year courses for teachers who have been teaching at Ensino de Base without any formal training.

There is a Distance Learning Programme to upgrade unqualified teachers. The first phase of the programme is aimed at raising the teacher's own level of education to Ensino de Base (3rd level) by 1990. The second phase is professional training including theories of education and methodology.

ISCED

This institute is part of the university. It trains teacher trainers for INE, and teachers for Ensino Medio. On paper anyone who graduates from this institute is a qualified teacher trainer. These graduates sometimes teach in ISCED itself. The courses are 5 years, the last year (Estagio, equivalent to a probationary year) being spent in classroom practice and writing a dissertation.

ISCED has also set up a distance-learning programme. The students on this course receive duplicated notes of the material given in lectures and sit exams at the university. There is no provision for seminars or tutorials, neither is there any set work.

Argentina

Argentine Republic

Education in Argentina comes under the control of the national government.

Education is compulsory for children aged six to fourteen.

Most students at all levels are part-time. In schools, pupils normally attend either from 8 a.m. - 12 p.m. or from 1-5 p.m.

The medium of instruction is Spanish. English and French are taught both at primary and secondary levels. There are public (i.e. state) and private institutions at all levels.

The school year runs from March to December. The university academic year varies, but in most institutions runs from April to December.

EVALUATION IN BRITAIN

School

Bachillerato - generally considered to compare to GCE O-level standard.

Higher

Licenciado - may be considered to compare to British Bachelor degree standard.

Argentina

MARKING SYSTEMS

The same marking system is used throughout the education system. Secondary school marks are generally given in numerals. University and other institutions of higher education use either number or concept marks. A scale of 0-10 is used:

10	sobresaliente	excellent
8-9	distinguido	very good
6-7	bueno	good
4-5	aprobado	pass
2-3	insuficiente	insufficient
1	reprobado	failure

SCHOOL EDUCATION

A new system was introduced in some schools involving 6 years at primary school, 3 at middle school and 3 at secondary school. However, the system described below, involving 7 years at primary school and 5 years at secondary school, is still dominant.

Primary (ciclo primario)

This lasts 7 years (ages 6-13) and is compulsory. Pupils are promoted from one grade to the next on the basis of continuous assessment and end-of-year evaluation.

Secondary (ciclo secundario)

Secondary education in state institutions is not compulsory. The course normally lasts 5 years (divided into the 3-year ciclo basico and the 2-year ciclo superior) but can last 6 or 7 years. The length of the course depends on the programme followed by the student. Students can opt for courses of general academic, commercial, teacher training, technical, vocational, art or social welfare education; those who obtain an average assessment mark of 7 (out of 10) or more during the year and pass their grade examinations (final-year examinations) are promoted from one grade to the next.

The **Bachillerato** is the final school-leaving certificate. Some schools provide a longer course leading to the **Bachillerato Especializado**. The extra year enables pupils to study certain subjects more intensively but not at a more advanced level.

Academic:

Academic secondary courses of 5 years are offered in the national Colegios or Liceos. These institutions prepare students for university entrance.

Commercial:

State commercial schools Escuelas Comerciales offer 6-year courses. The basic cycle is similar to that provided at the academic schools, but in the second cycle approximately 40% of the curriculum is devoted to commercial subjects. Graduates are awarded the title of **Perito Mercantil** (literally Expert in Commerce). Successful graduates are eligible to enter the Economics faculties of the universities.

Argentina

Technical:

Responsibility for technical and vocational training comes under CONET (Consejo Nacional de Educacion Tecnica) and is provided in <u>Escuelas Industriales</u>. Students can start at age 14. They follow a 6-year course and can specialize in particular fields. Successful graduates are eligible for higher education. Students can obtain a **Technical Auxiliary's Certificate** after completing the first cycle and a year's specialization. CONET works closely with industrial organizations in the design and teaching of its courses.

Escuelas Normales (normal schools):

Before 1971, students who graduated from these schools were awarded the title of **Maestro** or **Maestra** and were qualified to teach in primary school or to pursue studies in higher education or teacher-training institutes. In 1971 this stream was discontinued and all teacher training was made post-secondary.

Vocational:

Courses in vocational education (educacion profesional) can last 1-8 years, although most last 4 years. Vocational education is largely aimed at girls. Courses cover home economics, the clothing trade, clerical work and some technical subjects. Graduates are not eligible for higher studies.

Other:

Agricultural secondary schools offer a 7-year course. Students can also follow a 3- to 4-year paramedical course to qualify as a medical auxiliary. There are 4-year secondary courses for social workers and 'artistic' courses which can last up to 10 years.

HIGHER EDUCATION

Higher education is provided in universities and other higher institutions. Until 1975 possession of the **Bachillerato** ensured university entrance. Applicants are now required to take an entrance examination in some faculties before starting their degree courses.

University **Bachelor degree** courses vary from 2 to 7 years. (As there are only nominal university fees, students may choose to obtain a number of first degrees and may even, in exceptional cases, take 2 degree courses at the same time.) Most students attend university part-time and support themselves. Some first-degree courses lead to membership of a profession and a professional title (e.g. **Ingeniero**), as well as the normal academic qualification known as the **Licenciado**. In some fields the **Licenciado** is the second degree following the granting of a diploma. The postgraduate degree (**Doctorado**) is awarded on presentation of a thesis 1-2 years after the first degree. A foreign language is increasingly mandatory for a doctorate.

There are many short and long postgraduate courses run by universities, research institutes, and state bodies. These do not lead to formal qualifications, but the certificates are cited in curricula vitae.

Outside the university, professional courses are available in areas such as nursing, librarianship, higher technician training and administration.

Argentina

TEACHER EDUCATION

Primary

Before 1970, primary school teachers were trained in the secondary schools and pursued a 2-year course after completing the ciclo basico. Prospective primary school teachers must now be secondary school graduates and follow a 2-year teacher-training course at a higher teacher-training institute followed by 1 semester of practical experience. Successful graduates must be prepared to undertake in-service training and refresher courses.

Secondary

Prospective secondary school teachers receive 4-5 years training after obtaining the Bachillerato. The final qualification (**Profesorado**) is considered the equivalent of a university degree in Argentina. Students can attend independent teacher-training institutions called Profesorados. University graduates can obtain the teaching certificate after a 1-year course in departments attached to the universities. Students spend about 6 hours a week on teaching practice throughout the course.

ADULT EDUCATION

Adult literacy and evening secondary courses are available. Some of the new universities offer 2-year Bachillerato courses for those over 20 years of age.

Australia

Commonwealth of Australia

Each state government has the primary responsibility for all aspects of its school system; hence although the system is very similar throughout Australia, there are distinct differences between each state. In the Australian Capital Territory the education system is the direct responsibility of the Federal government.

GENERAL

School education

The school year runs from January/February to December.

Pre-primary Pre-schools are operated mainly by voluntary organizations, such as kindergarten unions, church and community groups, and to varying degrees by most state education departments.

Primary Progression to secondary school is automatic, and no certificate is awarded.

Secondary In general, the secondary school leaving certificate obtained on completion of the first cycle of secondary education gives access to vocational classes in technical colleges, secretarial courses or to junior posts in commerce, industry or public administration. The secondary school leaving certificate awarded on completion of the second cycle gives access to colleges of advanced education, and to universities.

Correspondence schools have been established in each state capital city to cater for the needs of children who cannot go to school daily because of distance or because of illness or physical disability. These schools cater for primary and secondary years up to matriculation standard. In Tasmania, correspondence courses are administered through the Hobart Technical College's External Studies Service. Teaching is provided at infant, primary, secondary and post-secondary levels.

Schools of the Air are an attempt to give children in the outback a little of the atmosphere of school life and to supplement their correspondence education by two-way radio equipment. First established in 1951 in the Northern Territory, 12 schools now operate in: South Australia (1), New South Wales (1), Queensland (3), Western Australia (5) and the Northern Territory (2).

Australia

Further education

Further education is provided by colleges of technical and further education, which are the responsibility of state governments, and which offer a wide range of courses mainly for trade qualifications.

Higher education

This is provided at universities and colleges of advanced education. The 19 universities are autonomous institutions. Most university courses are full-time day courses taking 3-6 years, but some may be done by part-time or external study. Postgraduate studies and research can be undertaken at all the universities.

In 1965 the Committee on the Future of Tertiary Education in Australia recommended the diversification and development of higher education outside the universities. Some existing technological institutions were thus developed as colleges of advanced education and some new colleges were also established. Between 1981 and 1983 many of these colleges (especially the teacher training ones) were amalgamated to form multi-campus institutions. There are now about 47 colleges of advanced education which, like the universities, are autonomous and degree-conferring. They offer courses oriented towards vocations such as teaching, librarianship and physiotherapy. While some colleges offer Master-level courses, most of the courses provided in colleges of advanced education lead to associate diploma, diploma, degree or postgraduate diploma awards, all of which are nationally registered.

Teacher education

All the former teachers colleges have now become accredited colleges of advanced education or have been absorbed into other colleges. They offer degree courses in early childhood, primary, secondary and special education.

Specialized education

<u>Conservatoria of Music</u>: 2 of these are affiliated to universities, and the remaining 3 are colleges of advanced education. Diploma courses are offered over 3-4 years, and also a range of degree courses (Bachelor, Master, and Doctorate). Music departments of universities also offer specialist study.

Educational training in the defence services

In January 1986 the Australian Defence Force Academy became the centre for tertiary education for the Armed Services, replacing the 3 colleges which had previously provided degree courses for the 3 services. The new Defence Force Academy is situated in Canberra, the national capital. Within the Academy, the University of New South Wales (located in Sydney) has established University College. This offers courses of undergraduate study to officer cadets who are in residence at the Academy, and higher degree courses to both military and civilian applicants. The undergraduate courses lead to the award of a Bachelor degree in arts, science or engineering.

Australia

Australian Scholastic Aptitude Test (ASAT)

This is a 3-hour objective test taken by students in some states in their final year at school. The usual format is 100 multiple items on different areas in roughly the following proportions: mathematics 20; science 30; humanities 30; social sciences 20.

A total score of scholastic aptitude is calculated, as well as verbal and quantitative sub-scores. The ASAT total score is used to scale teacher-assessed scores in the calculation of:

the Tertiary Entrance Score in the Australian Capital Territory

the Tertiary Entrance Score in the Tertiary Entrance Statement of Queensland

with the Tertiary Entrance Examinations results in Western Australia, to calculate the admission requirement for courses at the universities.

As the scores themselves are not directly comparable between subjects in the final certification, the ASAT results provide a guide on a state-wide basis. However South Australia, Victoria, Tasmania, the Northern Territory and New South Wales do not use ASAT for scaling their examination scores.

Special forms of ASAT are administered to mature students for entry into some tertiary institutions in most states. This administration, and the test development of all forms, is conducted by the Australian Council for Education Research in Melbourne.

From 1986 the ASAT has included a 2 hour written test, which is taken after the multiple choice paper.

EVALUATION IN BRITAIN

School

It is generally considered that a student qualified to enter university in Australia, would be qualified for admission to a degree course in Britain, although not all universities and polytechnics accept this.

Higher

Bachelor (Ordinary) degree - generally considered comparable to a British Bachelor (Ordinary) degree.

Bachelor (Honours) degree - generally considered comparable to a British Bachelor (Honours) degree.

AUSTRALIAN CAPITAL TERRITORY (ACT)

MARKING SYSTEMS

ACT Year 12 Certificate

This certificate is awarded in 2 parts, the **Secondary College Record** and the **Supplementary Information for Tertiary Entrance**. A student's attainments in units are reported on the Secondary College Record on a 5-point scale from A to E. This represents unit grades and course scores achieved during years 11 and 12.

The Supplementary Information for Tertiary Entrance includes, for each T-classified course, the course score and an adjusted course score, obtained by scaling the distribution of course scores to the distribution of the results obtained by the students in the Australian Scholastic Aptitude Test. The student's score in the aptitude test is also shown.

An aggregate is calculated for each student by taking the 3 best scaled course scores in T-classified major courses plus 0.6 of the next best major or minor T-classified course score. From a rank ordering of all students on their aggregates, each student's standing is expressed as a **Tertiary Entrance Score**, which is a percentile ranking, covering all students in the ACT.

SCHOOL EDUCATION

Attendance at school is compulsory for children aged 6-15.

Until 1974 schooling in the ACT was controlled by the education authorities of New South Wales. In 1974 the ACT Schools Authority was established and is now responsible for primary and secondary education in the ACT.

Primary

This caters for students aged 5-12 (kindergarten to year 6). There is no formal examination for entry to secondary schooling.

Secondary

This is conducted in 2 kinds of institution: high schools for the first 4 years, and secondary colleges for the final 2 years. At the end of high school, year 10 students receive a school report on their achievements, based on teacher assessment.

The education programme offered by secondary colleges consists of registered, accredited and Tertiary Entrance (T) classified courses. Accredited courses are those judged by the ACT Schools Accrediting Agency to be educationally sound and appropriate for students studying in years 11 and 12. Accredited courses which are considered sufficiently academically demanding are classified as T by the Australian National University. Registered courses, which provide a variety of recreational and less academic activities are approved by college boards and registered with the Accrediting Agency.

Course-work is not examined externally.

Australia (Australian Capital Territory)

The Accrediting Agency arranges for year 12 students to sit the Australian Scholastic Aptitude Test (ASAT), a test measuring verbal and quantitative reasoning processes in humanities, social sciences, science and mathematics, developed by the Australian Council for Educational Research. ASAT results are used to scale T-course scores, the best 3.6 of which are aggregated to form the Tertiary Entrance Score. This figure is reached by taking the 3 best scaled course scores in T-classified major courses (taken over 2 years), plus 0.6 of the best minor course (taken over 1 year). These scores are reported on the ACT Year 12 Certificate which is awarded in 2 parts, the Secondary College Record and the Supplementary Information for Tertiary Entrance.

The Secondary College Record reports the units and courses studied and the unit grades and course scores achieved during years 11 and 12. The Supplementary Information for Tertiary Entrance reports T-course and scaled scores, ASAT total and verbal and quantitative sub-scores, the Tertiary Entrance Score, student ranks and a rating in English comprehension and expression.

Secondary College Records are awarded to students who complete at least 1 unit in years 11 and 12. The Supplementary Information for Tertiary Entrance is awarded to students who meet the requirements for the award of a Tertiary Entrance Score.

Unit grades are reported on a 5-point letter scale, A being the highest grade, E the lowest. Course scores are reported on a scale which has a mean of 65 and standard deviation of 15.

FURTHER EDUCATION

In April 1977 New South Wales relinquished its control of Technical and Further Education(TAFE) facilities in the ACT. The office of ACT Further Education is now responsible for the administration of this sector of education, which is offered by the Canberra College of Technical and Further Education, Bruce College of Technical and Further Education, Woden College of Technical and Further Education, and Canberra School of Music.

The Schools of Art and Music provide degree courses in those fields, while the TAFE institutions provide courses in the following areas: professional, apprenticeship, trade, other skills, pre-employment ('preparators'), and adult education.

The TAFE colleges have the facility to provide degree units as well as apprenticeship, certificate, and trade courses, but few do. They also offer courses leading to the award of the New South Wales Higher School Certificate.

Admission requirements vary depending on the course but generally apprenticeship and below requires completion of 4 years of secondary schooling (i.e. completion of year 10) and more advanced courses require normal matriculation requirements (i.e. Higher School Certificate or ACT Year 12 Certificate).

TEACHER EDUCATION

2 institutions in the ACT offer teacher-training courses; Canberra College of Advanced Education and Signadou College.

Australia (New South Wales)

Canberra College of Advanced Education provides nearly all undergraduate and postgraduate work in education for the ACT (the Australian National University has no faculty of education). It offers 3- and 4-year courses in Early Childhood and Primary Education leading to a **B.Ed.**, and a 1-year course for graduates to become primary and secondary teachers, with a **Graduate Diploma of Education**. It also offers a 3-year BA course in Technical and Further Education Teaching, a 3-year **Bachelor of Applied Science** in Health Education and a 2-year **Diploma of Teaching** in Technical and Further Education. Additional postgraduate courses include 1-year graduate diplomas in either special education or curriculum and a 2-year M.Ed. programme or M.Ed. in School Counselling.

Signadou College is a denominational institution which offers a 3-year **Diploma of Teaching** for primary teachers and a 1-year **Graduate Diploma** in religious education.

Admission to both institutions is with the normal matriculation requirements.

For information on HIGHER EDUCATION, see end of chapter.

NEW SOUTH WALES

MARKING SYSTEM

Matriculation examination (until 1965) was graded pass/fail.

School certificate

1962-75	:	subjects at advanced level were graded pass/fail only
	:	subjects at ordinary level were graded credit and pass.
1975	:	subjects at advanced and ordinary levels were graded 1-5, on a distribution scale of 10%, 20%, 40%, 20%, 10%
	:	subjects at the modified level were graded only 1 or 2.
1976	:	subjects were graded on a scale of 1-10, with 10% of the candidature in the state being allocated to each grade; i.e. grade 1 means the student is placed in the top 10% of all students presenting the subject etc.
1977-	:	Students only take reference tests, which are common for all students in the state, in English and mathematics. The English test is graded 1-5, on a distribution scale of 10%, 20%, 40%, 20%, 10%. The mathematics test is divided into 3 levels: advanced, intermediate and general. Grades are distributed as follows:

advanced A-C (distribution scale 50%, 40%, 10%)
intermediate A-D (30%, 30%, 30%, 10%)
general A and B (60%, 40%).

The actual certificate states grades for English and mathematics and lists the subjects 'satisfactorily studied', according to internal teacher assessment.

Australia (New South Wales)

Higher School Certificate

1967-75:

1	pass at first level
2	pass at second level
2F	pass at second level (full course)
2S	pass at second level (short course)
3	pass at third level
P	pass in general studies
F	fail
X	absent

1975-85:

Awards were based on the student's performance in the examination and the estimate of that performance submitted by the school. The examination marks were scaled and the schools' estimates adjusted; together these formed a student's scaled mark in each course. This scaled mark was then used to determine a student's percentile band (i.e. performance in relation to other students) and aggregate mark, which was obtained by adding the candidate's 10 best unit scores. Each unit was worth 50 marks, so the maximum possible aggregate mark was 500. The aggregate mark formed the basis for both tertiary selection and entry to many areas of employment.

1986- :

The award of a Higher School Certificate will be based on a student's performance in the examination and a school assessment. The examination marks will be scaled using a common average for all 2-unit courses and the assessment marks will be adjusted for state-wide comparability. The examination mark and the assessment mark for each course will be reported separately. The marks in each course will not be aggregated.

SCHOOL EDUCATION

Education is compulsory for ages 6-15.

Primary

This stage lasts 6 years, normally from age 6; however most children attend a kindergarten for 1 year from age 5. On completion of year 6 pupils may transfer to year 7 in a secondary school; there is normally no secondary school entrance examination.

Secondary

A new system was introduced in 1962, following the Education Act of 1961. Pupils who commenced secondary education before 1962 completed their course under the former system; those who commenced in 1962 or a later year came under the new system.

Under the old system (pre-1962) secondary schooling lasted 5 years. The first year consisted of generalized study, followed by a 2-year course of approved studies, leading to the **Intermediate Certificate** (i.e. at the end of the third year). On completion of a further 2 years of approved studies, students were awarded the **Leaving Certificate**.

Australia (New South Wales)

In each subject in the Leaving Certificate examinations, passes were awarded at A and B levels and at 1st Class Honours and 2nd Class Honours standards as well. To qualify for honours the candidate had to sit for the Pass paper and also for an Honours paper, which was based on a more advanced study of the subject. For the award of a Leaving Certificate a student was required to gain a minimum of B pass in at least 4 subjects at one sitting or at two consecutive sittings of the examination. To qualify for matriculation on the basis of the Leaving Certificate, passes were required at one sitting in 5 subjects including English, and other subjects chosen from specified groups. The last examination for the Leaving Certificate was held in 1966. The last Intermediate Certificate in the third year of the 5-year secondary course was awarded in 1965, although an Intermediate Certificate continued to be issued in respect of the third year of the new 6-year secondary course until 1966. Until 1965 students could also take the **Matriculation Examination** of the University of Sydney in 5 subjects at the end of form 5.

From 1962 the length of secondary education was extended from 5 to 6 years. The course comprised 4 years leading to the **School Certificate** examination, with a further 2 years leading to the **Higher School Certificate**. Courses leading to the School Certificate examination were offered at modified, ordinary and advanced levels. The advanced level was designed to challenge the ability of the top 25% of the students studying that subject, while the ordinary level was to test the middle 50% and the modified level the lowest 25%.

The idea of levels was abandoned in 1976. A minimum of 6 subjects had to be studied, including English, mathematics, science and 1 of either history, geography or social studies. The minimum number of passes for the award was 4 at either level.

In 1975 the examination was phased out and the certificate is now awarded mainly on the basis of internal school assessment. Standards are maintained by externally prepared moderating tests.

Since 1977 all students take common examinations in English and mathematics and the results for all schools are compared with other schools in the state. Each school is allocated a certain number of each grade depending on their overall standard. The school then assigns the grades to the students according to their ranking, based on test results and teacher assessment.

Since 1967 the **Higher School Certificate** has been taken 2 years after the School Certificate, although the course was again changed in 1975. From 1967-75 the Higher School Certificate was offered at 3 levels:

First - an Honours course designed to challenge the ablest candidates.

Second - for candidates who may wish to study the subject beyond secondary school. Only in mathematics and science were students offered the choice between a 'full' course or a 'short' course. Full courses counted as 1-and-a-half subjects, which was important in the calculation of the aggregate marks in examination results of the Higher School Certificate.

Third - for candidates who will probably not continue the study of the subject beyond secondary school.

Passes in 5 subjects including English with at least 3 at second level, satisfied minimum entrance requirements for a first-degree course in Australia when this school system was in existence.

Australia (New South Wales)

The Higher School Certificate examination was restructured and a new syllabus came into operation in 1975. The idea of levels was abandoned and courses were organized on a basis of units of study. Each unit represented 3 periods of study per week and carried a possible examination mark value of 50. In general, there were 3 types of course in all subjects:

3 unit - offering suitable preparation for the study of that subject at tertiary level, as well as deeper and more extensive treatment than in the 2-unit courses

2 unit - offering suitable preparation for the study of that subject at tertiary level

other 2 unit - of more general content, not intended to lead to further study of that subject at tertiary level.

In mathematics there were 4 courses:

4 unit - defined as a 3-unit course in other subjects

3 unit - 2 unit in other subjects

2 unit - meeting general needs and suitable for those whose tertiary studies require some mathematical understanding

2 unit A.

In science there were 3 courses:

4 unit - involving study from at least 3 scientific disciplines

2 unit

2 unit A

In 1980 the Board of Senior School Studies adopted the redefinitions of courses, as listed below. These courses were first examined in the **Higher School Certificate** in 1983.

Courses are no longer defined in terms of their link with tertiary studies. The Board considers that the definitions should be more general, as its Higher School Certificate courses have to cater for a much wider range of interests and abilities. A course is defined in terms of the amount of school study, i.e. teaching and guided-study time at school. The current maximum possible mark of 50 per unit of all courses will continue to apply. The Board has adopted the following definitions of courses:

A 1-unit course requires two 2 hours of school study per week in year 11 and/or year 12.

A 2-unit course requires 4 hours of school study per week in years 11 and 12. There are 3 types:

> those related to the 3-unit course in that subject, e.g. English 2 unit/3 unit (related) course

> those not related to a 3-unit course in that subject; non-related 2-unit courses are known either as 2-unit (general) e.g. 2-unit (general) German or have been given a specific course descriptive title e.g. Geography (Australia and its Neighbours)

Australia (New South Wales)

2-Unit Z courses in certain foreign languages, which are also not related to 3-unit courses. They are designed for students commencing study of a particular language for the first time in year 11.

A 3-unit course incorporates all of a 2-unit course and requires 6 hours of school study per week in each of years 11 and 12.

A 3-unit course in mathematics incorporates all of a 2-unit course and requires 6 hours of school study per week in each of years 11 and 12. A 3-unit course in science incorporates some aspects of the 2-unit course and requires 6 hours of school study per week in each of years 11 and 12.

4-unit courses are available in only 2 subjects - mathematics and science.

A 4-unit mathematics course incorporates all of the 3-unit course and requires 8 hours of school study per week in year 12 following 6 hours of school study per week in year 11

A 4-Unit science course incorporates all of the 3-unit course and requires 8 hours of school study per week in each of years 11 and 12.

To be eligible for the Higher School Certificate a student must study subjects with course values totalling at least 11 units, including at least 2 units of English.

The Conservatorium High School offers music training and academic courses.

The Agricultural High Schools provide general education leading to the School Certificate and Higher School Certificate with special emphasis on agricultural courses, which include farm practice.

The Correspondence School offers education from pre-school to year 12 (Higher School Certificate) to students who are not able to enrol in regular government schools, usually because they live in isolated areas.

FURTHER EDUCATION

This state has over 100 colleges of Technical and Further Education (TAFE) offering some 1,400 courses, although not all colleges offer all courses. In remote areas, small centres and mobile units provide limited instruction. Some courses are available by external studies. In addition to the regular courses, colleges offer courses for special purposes - handicapped people, multicultural groups, women, and unemployed youth. Enrolment priorities, details of courses and colleges, are published in the annual Handbook and the State Guide to TAFE. Generally, courses are categorized as follows:

Pre-employment/pre-apprenticeship 1-year courses for holders of the School Certificate. On completion of the course students may enter apprenticeship training with advanced standing.

Trade courses offered concurrently with indentured or non-indentured employment, providing trade qualifications required for registration.

Certificate courses offering training for technicians and other middle-level occupations. Admission is generally completion of year 10 at secondary school.

Australia (Northern Territory)

Higher Certificate courses - same type of course as that leading to the Certificate, but intended for those who need a greater breadth and/or depth of knowledge and skill than would be obtained on the Certificate course. Admission is with the Certificate or the Higher School Certificate.

Associate Diploma courses offer para-professional training for student holding the Higher School Certificate.

Many special courses cater for both vocational skills (generally requiring a shorter training period than Certificate courses) and for leisure. These courses do not lead to a formal qualification but students receive a statement of their attainment.

General education courses, primarily for adults, ranging from basic literacy and numeracy to courses leading to the Higher School Certificate or special adult matriculation to colleges of advanced education and universities.

TEACHER EDUCATION

The present basic teacher-training qualifications require completion of a 3-year full-time Diploma or a 4-year full-time degree course, with 1 or more majors in specific secondary education specializations; or, for primary and early childhood teachers, a 3-year full-time Diploma course followed by 1 year of practical teaching experience and 1 year further study to complete requirements for the award of a Bachelor of Education. The final year for the Bachelor of Education, whether secondary, primary or early childhood, may be undertaken in part-time or external studies.

University graduates may be admitted to a 1-year full-time course leading to a Diploma in Education awarded by either a university or a college of advanced education.

For information on HIGHER EDUCATION see end of chapter.

NORTHERN TERRITORY

MARKING SYSTEMS

The Matriculation examination is marked on the scale 1-100: an aggregate of 295 from 5 subjects is needed for matriculation.

SCHOOL EDUCATION

Schooling is compulsory for children aged 6-15.

Schools may be broadly divided into 2 groups: those in predominantly European communities and those in predominantly Aboriginal communities.

Australia (Northern Territory)

Until the end of 1972, schools in the first group were administered by the South Australian Department of Education. South Australian syllabuses were used and examination procedures were similar to those followed in South Australia. Schools in the second group were administered by the Welfare Branch of the Northern Territory Administration. Courses of study and methods of assessment were those approved by the Welfare Branch.

In 1973, control of the entire education system in the Northern Territory was transferred to the Commonwealth Department of Education and administered by the Northern Territory Division of that Department.

In 1979 control of education in the Northern Territory was taken over by the Northern Territory Government based in Darwin. A Northern Territory Department of Education was created and this is now responsible to the Northern Territory Minister of Education for administering education throughout the Northern Territory.

While all the government schools are now controlled by a single authority, and have been so since 1973, the 2 broad groups referred to above still remain. In addition, there is a small number of independent schools in both urban and Aboriginal communities, run mainly by the Catholic and other education agencies.

Most schools in Aboriginal communities provide primary education only, although many also have courses for students of post-primary age. The primary students follow the same core curriculum as those in urban schools and, while there are common assessment programmes in English and mathematics at year 5 and 7 levels, there is no uniform external assessment.

Urban schools follow a 7/5 pattern, i.e. 7 years primary and 5 years secondary education. Common assessment programmes operate in English and mathematics in years 5 and 7 but there is no uniform external assessment. At the end of year 10 students receive a **Junior Secondary Studies Certificate**, based on school assessments, which are moderate in English and mathematics.

At senior secondary level, assessments in year 11 are school based, with moderation in English and mathematics. Most year 12 students follow courses of the Senior Secondary Assessment Board of South Australia. These courses fall into 2 groups: school assessed subjects, in which gradings are awarded on externally moderated school assessments; and publicly examined subjects, in which gradings are awarded on the basis of 50% external examination used as a moderating instrument.

All students who follow courses at senior secondary level receive a **Northern Territory Senior Secondary Studies Certificate**. Students who complete SSABSA courses receive in addition a **SSABSA Certificate of Achievement**.

FURTHER EDUCATION

The Darwin Institute of Technology offers a variety of courses to Bachelor degree level for students with qualifications to year 12 Certificate level.

The Community College of Central Australia at Alice Springs serves a vast area of Central Australia providing recreational, pre-trade, trade, post-trade and paraprofessional studies to the community. Graduate studies through Australian institutions are serviced by an External Studies Section of the College.

Australia (Queensland)

Batchelor College is the centre for Aboriginal teacher education in the Northern Territory. Courses conducted at the College include a 3-year **Associate Diploma of Teaching (Aboriginal Schools)**, an **Associate Diploma in Adult Education** and a **Certificate in Community Management**. Provision is available for graduates of the teacher education programme to proceed to degree studies with advanced standing status.

Katherine Rural College conducts certificate courses in general rural education, culminating in the award of the **Certificate in Rural Studies**.

The Territory Training Centre based in Darwin conducts a variety of pre-vocational and trade courses in metal fabrication, diesel, automotive, carpentry/joinery and refrigeration.

Courses conducted through TAFE colleges are designed in close consultation with industry, community and relevant interest groups. Courses undergo stringent accreditation procedures, coupled with regular reviews and re-accreditation ensuring constant monitoring.

TEACHER EDUCATION

Apart from Batchelor College (see above) the Darwin Institute of Technology is the only college in the Northern Territory to offer teacher training courses. At undergraduate level primary teacher training courses consist of a 3-year **Diploma of Teaching** or a 4-year **B.Ed**. No undergraduate courses are available for training secondary teachers. At postgraduate level there is a 1-year Graduate Diploma course for primary teaching and also for secondary teaching for students whose undergraduate majors are in mathematics, computing or science.

For information on HIGHER EDUCATION see end of chapter.

QUEENSLAND

MARKING SYSTEM

Junior Certificate

Awarded at the end of year 10, with 5 levels of achievement: very high to very limited.

Senior Certificate

Awarded at the end of year 12, with 5 levels of achievement: very high to very limited.

Interim Statement of Results

Tertiary entrance scores range from 990 downwards in intervals of 5, until all those eligible have been given a score. A given score applies to a band of students and indicates the relative position of that band of students in the order-of-merit test.

Australia (Queensland)

SCHOOL EDUCATION

Education is compulsory until age 15.

Primary

This is offered over 7 years.

Secondary

This is offered over 5 years, covering years 8-12. The minimum school-leaving age is 15, which often coincides with completion of year 10, when a student is awarded the **Junior Certificate**.

Until 1972, on completion of year 12, students took the **Queensland Public Examination**, administered by the University of Queensland.

In 1973 the Queensland final secondary school examination was superseded by a system of continuous internal assessment with external moderation. From 1986 all schools will follow the ROSBA (Review of School-Based Assessment) system of assessment, which uses criterion referencing. Students receive 2 separate statements on completion of year 12, based on assessment of courses they have taken in years 11 and 12: the **Interim Statement of Results** and the **Senior Certificate**.

The Interim Statement of Results is issued by the Board of Secondary School Studies. Students are assessed on their best 20 semester units over the final 2 years. The Statement records the Board subjects (those for which a syllabus has been provided by the Board) and Board-registered school subjects (those offered by the school and approved by District and/or State Review Panels prior to implementation) studied in years 11 and 12. It also records the number of semester units studied and the level of achievement on completion of each subject, as well as a score obtained by scaling assessments made at the end of year 12 against results of the Australian Scholastic Aptitude Test taken by all eligible students.

From these Tertiary Entrance (TE) scores, the Board of Secondary School Studies compiles an order-of-merit list which is available to tertiary institutions for use in selection. Schools may issue School Certificates at Junior and Senior levels, in addition to the Board certificates.

The Senior Certificate is issued by the school last attended by the student and is signed by the principal of that school. It records a student's achievements as listed in the Interim Statement of Results but does not include the Tertiary Entrance Score, if applicable.

TECHNICAL AND FURTHER EDUCATION

Technical and further education is provided by the Division of Technical and Further Education (TAFE). A wide range of trade courses for apprentices is available, as well as pre-vocational/pre-employment courses covering such areas as engineering/construction, business studies and catering and hospitality. Advanced trade and certificate courses at sub-professional level are also offered. Extension courses aimed at meeting

Australia (Queensland)

demonstrated community needs, including personal enrichment, are organized locally in such diverse subjects as craft activities, introduction to computers and navigation. In addition, many courses, including vocational and access courses, are designed to meet the needs of disadvantaged groups, such as illiterate adults, Aboriginal and Islander citizens and handicapped people. Tertiary-level studies leading to a Bachelor of Arts degree are offered at the Queensland College of Art.

TEACHER EDUCATION

Pre-service teacher education is provided at 11 tertiary institutions, 4 such institutions offer 3-year courses leading to a **Diploma of Teaching** for would-be early childhood, primary and secondary teachers. Students may also enrol in the 4-year **Bachelor of Education (Secondary)** degree course or the 2-year **Postgraduate Bachelor of Education (Secondary)** course offered at James Cook University, or in Griffith University's 4-year **Joint Bachelor Degree Graduate Diploma in Teaching** Programme, conducted in conjunction with the Brisbane College of Advanced Education (CAE). **Diploma of Education/Teaching** courses are available for students who have completed an approved degree or equivalent qualification. The **University of Queensland** and the Conservatorium of Music, in conjunction with Brisbane CAE, provide specialist Bachelor degree courses in music, agricultural science and human movement studies (the University only, in respect of the latter 2 areas). McAuley College offers pre-service and postgraduate courses in teacher education (primary) for those interested in the Catholic school system.

The fourth year of teacher preparation courses is considered as a postgraduate year. All applicants for teaching positions in either state or non-state schools must have completed an approved course of teacher education successfully. Teacher education in Queensland is under continuous review by the Board of Teacher Education.

For information on HIGHER EDUCATION see end of chapter.

SOUTH AUSTRALIA

MARKING SYSTEM

Intermediate Certificate (up to 1968) was graded 1 (highest) - 6.

Leaving Certificate (up to 1975) was graded 1 (highest) - 6.

The School Report (since 1975) is based on continuous assessment.

Australia (South Australia)

Matriculation Examination

1966-77	grades A-G, A-D being pass grades
1978-9	scale 1-100; aggregate of 225 from 5 subjects needed for matriculation
Since 1980	scale 1-100; aggregate of 295 from 5 subjects needed for matriculation

SCHOOL EDUCATION

Education is compulsory from aged 6 to 15.

Primary

Schooling is offered over 7 years.

Secondary

Until 1968 students normally took the **Intermediate Certificate** examination at year 10 after 3 years of secondary education. If students continued for a fourth year, they could obtain the **Leaving Certificate**. The Leaving Certificate served as a matriculation requirement until 1965. Many students intending to go to university stayed on at school for an additional year after taking the Leaving Certificate. This year was known as Leaving Honours and students could obtain the **Leaving Honours Certificate**

In 1966 the **Matriculation Examination** was introduced as a year-12 examination (i.e. after 5 years of secondary education), replacing Leaving Honours.

The Intermediate Certificate was abolished in 1966 and the Leaving Certificate was abolished in 1975, both being replaced by continuous school assessment.

As matriculation was designed specifically for students wishing to continue their education to the tertiary level, it did not serve the needs of students who wanted to remain at school for a twelfth year, but not continue their formal education beyond that. In 1979 the **Secondary School Certificate** (SSC), developed and approved by the Education Department 10 years earlier to replace internal certificates offered by schools, was expanded to include year-12 subjects. The SSC was administered by the SA Education Department and approved as being of a suitable standard for year 12.

SSC subjects were school assessed and externally moderated on a grading scale of A-D, with U being unsatisfactory. Students selecting subjects from both SSC and Matriculation groups received 2 certificates at the end of year 12, while students leaving school before the end of year 12 received a **School Leaver Statement** from the school.

Students wishing to matriculate needed to present 5 subjects accepted by the universities as suitable for tertiary entrance. Since 1978 they have been assessed on a scale of 1-100. Before 1978 they were reported as grades A-G.

Australia (South Australia)

In 1984 the organization administering the Matriculation Examination, the Public Examinations Board (PEB), was abolished. The **Senior Secondary Assessment Board of South Australia (SSABSA)** was subsequently established, with responsibility for the assessment and certification of students at year 12 level. This included responsibility for both the former PEB subjects and former SSC subjects.

Although there was a 2-year phase-in period in which both types of subject were taught and assessed, SSABSA issued a single certificate to year 12 students from its inception in 1984. Results on this certificate were reported either on a scale of 1-100, if the subjects was publicly examined, or as grade A-D or U, if the subject was school assessed. From 1986, all subjects will be reported on a scale of 1-20, with a statement explaining the student's achievement in each subject and an accompanying grade of A-E.

TECHNICAL AND FURTHER EDUCATION

The Department of Technical and Further Education, through a network of 22 colleges of TAFE, offers a variety of vocational courses leading to associate diploma, advanced certificate, certificate and statement of attainment, according to the nationally endorsed system of TAFE.

TEACHER EDUCATION

The South Australian College of Advanced Education offers a variety of courses for training teachers; in general 3-year diploma courses for prospective primary school teachers and 4-year degree courses for secondary school teachers. The Flinders University of South Australia also offers a 4-year degree for primary teachers.

For information on HIGHER EDUCATION see end of chapter.

TASMANIA

MARKING SYSTEMS

School Certificate and **Higher School Certificate** (since 1969); these are graded credit, higher pass, lower pass, fail. (The award of failure does not appear on certificates.)

SCHOOL EDUCATION

The minimum school-leaving age is 16.

Australia (Tasmania)

Primary

This lasts until the end of year 6.

Secondary

This lasts a minimum of 4 years, with the option of staying at school for a further 2 years to study for the **Higher School Certificate**. In 1969 the **Schools Board Examination** at the end of the fourth year of secondary study was replaced by the **School Certificate**, awarded on the basis of internal school assessments with external regional moderation. Students who leave school at the end of the third year may receive a **School Certificate** (preliminary award).

In 1969 the **Matriculation Examination** conducted by the University of Tasmania was replaced by the **Higher School Certificate** conducted by the Schools Board of Tasmania. Most subjects in the Higher School Certificate are offered at 2 levels. In most subjects a level II syllabus is provided for those wishing to undertake a preliminary study of a subject before attempting the level III syllabus. It is not necessary to attempt level II before attempting level III, nor do results obtained at level II count towards the level III award. The Board also offers 200+ level II units of study each of 40 hours. To obtain an award in one of the 16 level II subjects available in units, 3 units must be chosen from the list of units available for that subject.

FURTHER EDUCATION

There are 5 colleges offering further education courses: Hobart, Launceston, Burnie, Devenport and the West Coast Community College at Queenstown. Certificate courses are designed for specific occupational areas at the middle or sub-professional level. Students holding the School Certificate may undertake the technician or middle level certificate courses, which take them to a level beyond the matriculation qualification and overlap the work done in the early years of a university or college of advanced education course.

TEACHER EDUCATION

Students wishing to obtain teaching qualifications from the University of Tasmania may study for degrees in the Faculties of Arts, Economics, Commerce or Science, and then complete a further year of study in the Faculty of Education for a **Diploma of Education** or alternatively undertake the 4-year **Bachelor of Education** degree.

Infant/primary

Students holding the matriculation requirements may enter 1 4-year course (B.Ed. or BA/B.Sc. + 1 year Diploma of Education).

Secondary

As for primary teachers. Students are required to teach in 2 of the following areas: business studies, computer studies, mathematics, English, modern languages, general science, social science, or in either music or art.

Australia (Tasmania)

Each year the university allows a small number of outstandingly successful students to undertake Honours studies. Such students have an extra year added to their studies before proceeding to the Diploma of Education course.

The university offers postgraduate courses for those with teaching experience: **Bachelor of Special Education, Master of Special Education, Master of Education, Doctor of Philosophy.**

The Division of Teacher Education at the Tasmanian State Institute of Technology prepares students for teaching appointments in kindergartens and primary and secondary schools. The Division offers 3-year courses, leading to a Diploma of Teaching, the minimum teaching qualification, and a fourth year of study leading to the award of a Bachelor of Education.

For information on HIGHER EDUCATION see end of chapter.

VICTORIA

MARKING SYSTEM

Intermediate Certificate (until 1967) - graded pass/fail.

School Leaving Certificate (until 1972) - graded pass/fail.

Matriculation Certificate (Until 1969) - graded Honours 1, Honours 2 and pass.

Higher School Certificate (1970 to present) - graded A-F (satisfactory completion = A-D) or S/N (satisfactory completion = S).

Victorian Certificate of Education (1987-9) - graded A-F (satisfactoty completion = A-D) or S/N (satisfactory completion = S).

Victorian Certificate of Education (1990 onwards) - to be determined.

Intermediate Technical Examination Certificate (year 10 - form 4) - graded pass/fail (choice of systems).

Technical Learning Certificate (year 11 - form 5) - grade pass/fail (choice of systems).

Technical Year 12 Certificate (year 12 - form 6) - graded pass/fail (choice of systems).

SCHOOL EDUCATION

Education is compulsory to age 15.

Australia (Victoria)

Pre-school

Pre-school is an option provided for many children, although it is not a compulsory pre-requisite for the preparatory year.

Primary

Primary schools provide 7 years of education; the preparatory year followed by 6 years of primary education (i.e. to year 6). Entrance to the preparatory year requires a minimum age of 4-and-a-half. The usual range of ages in primary schools is from 4-and-a-half to 12. Pupils attending government schools can choose, on completion of primary education (i.e. year 6), to attend either a high school, a post-primary school or a technical school.

Secondary

Until 1967 students could obtain the **Intermediate Certificate** on completion of form 4, and until 1972 the **School Leaving Certificate** was obtained on completion of form 5. It is not now usual practice for high schools to award a certificate at the end of form 5 (year 11); however a high school may provide a student with a statement that he/she has satisfactorily completed an eleventh year of education.

Formerly, students were able to stay on for a further year to study for the **Matriculation Certificate**. From 1970 until 1986, the year-12 programme was called the **Higher School Certificate** (HSC).

All these examinations were administered by the Victorian Universities and Schools Examinations Board (VUSEB) until that organization was dissolved in early 1979, and by the Victorian Institute of Secondary Education (VISE) until mid-1986. In 1981 VISE implemented new assessment procedures. A greater diversity of subjects was offered and a combination of school-based and external assessment was established. Normal requirements for the successful completion of HSC were grade D or better in at least 12 units (equivalent to 4 subjects). English was compulsory.

In 1981 VISE accredited, as one of the courses offered under the Higher School Certificate, an Approved Study Structure known as **Schools Year 12 and Tertiary Entrance Certificate** or the 'STC' course. This whole course of study involved content and assessment procedures being developed at the school level, within the centrally accredited structure, and moderated by regional meetings of the teachers involved.

FURTHER EDUCATION

The operation of Technical and Further Education (TAFE) is the responsibility of the TAFE Board. Courses are available at a wide variety of levels, including some at technical secondary. In year 11, TAFE schools/colleges conduct Vocational Orientation Programme (VOP) courss for students who do not hold the appropriate prerequisite qualifications to begin TAFE certificate courses. In year 12, the schools/colleges offer Tertiary Orientation Programme (TOP) courses for students who do not hold the necessary qualifications to begin a diploma or degree course. The certificate qualification obtained at the end of the TOP courses is recognized in Australia as an alternative to the Higher School Certificate.

Australia (Victoria)

Technical

Technical schools provide a general secondary education to year 12 (form 6). The Technical Accreditation Programme covers the assessment and accreditation of courses for certification at:

Year 10 (form 4) - **Intermediate Technical Examination Certificate**

Year 11 (form 5) - **Technical Learning Certificate**

Year 12 (form 6) - **Technical Year 12 Certificate**.

These certificates are awarded by the Ministry of Education.

At year 12, 23 technical schools also offer the TAFE Tertiary Orientation Programme and others offer some of the subjects and courses towards a **VISE Higher School Certificate**.

Schools are responsible for their courses up to year 10 and can award the Ministry of Education Intermediate Technical Examination Certificate provided they comply with the requirements stated in the Assessment Instruction.

There are 2 types of course for which schools can award the Leaving Technical Certificate:

Code A courses are state-wide courses provided by the relevant State Curriculum Committees. In maths, the sciences, English, business studies and graphic communication, state-wide examinations and/or tests are also provided.

Code B courses are school-based and are submitted for approval annually. Code B accreditation is also given to schools with established whole-course structures at year 11.

The Technical Year 12 Certificate is awarded to students undertaking a school-devised course which meets the requirements laid down in the Technical Accreditation Programme assessment instruction and developed in the Technical Year 12 Study Structure Handbook. These are whole-course models focussed on student goals and requirements.

The Victorian Curriculum and Assessment Board (VCAB), the successor to VISE, was set up in July 1986 to determine curriculum, assessment and certification for the new Year 12 Certificate, the **Victorian Certificate of Education** (VCE).

The new certificate will report assessment obtained over a 2-year, semester-based course of study. The VCE year 11 and 12 curriculum will replace all current year 12 programmes and is planned to be introduced in 1989 at year 11 into all Victorian schools.

For the interim period 1987-9, a 1-year **Victorian Certificate of Education** will be awarded to those candidates who would previously have qualified for Higher School Certificate, or the certificates of either of the 2 other year-12 programmes currently offered, the Tertiary Orientation Programme and the Technical Year 12 Programme (T12).

Australia (Western Australia)

TEACHER EDUCATION

Pre-school and primary

Students take the 3-year **Diploma** course of teaching (primary or early childhood). The entrance level for the Diploma is usually successful completion of 6 years secondary (high) or secondary technical education. Following at least 1 year of approved teaching experience, students may then proceed to a fourth year of study (**Bachelor of Education** award) where they have the opportunity to specialize in such areas as educational planning, music, art, curriculum studies. Students who have completed a degree may take the **Diploma in Education (Primary)** at La Trobe University.

Secondary

Students trained to be high-school teachers are usually specialist teachers qualified to teach in 2 subject areas. They may take either a Bachelor degree at a university or a college of advanced education, and then a 1-year **Diploma in Education**, or a 4-year **Bachelor of Education** course. The entrance requirement for both options is the Higher School Certificate or equivalent.

Technical

These teachers have the opportunity to teach in the secondary technical area and/or the TAFE area of technical education. They must have completed either (a) an approved 3-year diploma or degree from a university or a college of advanced education, or (b) an approved trade qualification and 5 years work experience after obtaining the qualification. An approved course of teacher education is also required.

For information on HIGHER EDUCATION see end of chapter.

WESTERN AUSTRALIA

MARKING SYSTEMS

Leaving Examination (until 1974) - graded distinction and pass. Subjects offered at matriculation level graded pass and fail.

Leaving Certificate (1975) - graded A-F.

Certificate of Secondary Education (1975) - graded on a 7-point rating scale.

A	top 10% of students
B	next 10%
C	next 25%
D	next 25%
E	next 15%
F	next 13%
NA	the last 2%.

Australia (Western Australia)

Certificate of Secondary Education (since 1976) - graded on a 10-point rating scale at 10% intervals, i.e. grade 1 represents the top 10% of the students sitting the subjects.

SCHOOL EDUCATION

Schooling is compulsory from age 6 until the end of the year in which a student turns 15.

Primary

Education normally begins in February of the year the child turns 6, and lasts for 7 years. Children then transfer automatically to a secondary school or class.

Most children attend kindergarten for 1 year, some for 2 years, in a pre-primary class or at a pre-school centre.

Secondary

From 1967, this consisted of 2 phases, lasting 3 years and 2 years respectively. During the first phase the core subjects of English, mathematics, social studies and science were taught and assessed at several levels. In English, science and social studies there were 3 levels: advanced, intermediate and basic. In mathematics there were 4 levels: advanced, ordinary, elementary and basic.

At the end of this phase pupils were awarded the **Achievement Certificate**, on the basis of moderated internal assessments. The Certificate was issued by the Board of Secondary Education. Generally this stage coincided with the completion of compulsory schooling and students could leave with this qualification. A student who left before then was given a certificate showing achievements for every full year of secondary schooling worked. Before 1967 the **Junior Certificate**, based on an external examination, was awarded at the end of the first phase.

Until 1974 there was a **Leaving Certificate** examination at the end of the second phase (i.e. the end of the fifth year of secondary education), conducted by the Public Examinations Board. The Leaving Certificate was used not only as a school leaving certificate of secondary education, but also by the tertiary institutions for matriculation purposes. Most candidates took 6 or 7 subjects. For most subjects offered, 2 levels of paper were set, one being specifically for matriculation purposes. In 1974 the title of the Leaving Certificate examination was changed to the **Tertiary Admissions** examination. Responsibility for the issue of the school leaving certificate was then vested in the Board of Secondary Education. The 1975 School Leaving Certificate took account of both school assessment and examination results. To correspond with the introduction of school assessment the Board of Secondary Education changed the title of the certificate from Leaving Certificate to **Certificate of Secondary Education**. From 1977 the Certificate of Secondary Education was issued on the basis of 50% school assessment and 50% results of the Tertiary Admissions Examination. This examination formed the general basis of selection for entry into tertiary education institutions.

Australia (Western Australia)

The Tertiary Admissions Examination Board conducted the examination which was typically taken in 6 subjects. The Certificate of Secondary Education included some subjects which were 100% school assessed, in addition to the subjects examined by the Tertiary Admissions Examinations Committee. In calculating their entrance requirement each year, tertiary institutions in Western Australia used the Australian Scholastic Aptitude Test to scale the raw TAE scores and produce an admission aggregate.

Commencing in 1986, for years 8-10, students will study at least 1 unit in each of the following 7 areas: English, languages and communication, mathematics, science and technology, social studies, practical and creative arts, personal and vocational education and physical education. School reports will be issued 2 or 3 times per year, based on internal assessment moderated by the Secondary Education Authority, which has replaced the Board of Secondary Education. The new Authority will issue a **Certificate of Secondary Education** of grades obtained in year 9 through to the year of exit at year 10, 11 or 12. New tertiary entrance requirements have been introduced based on Secondary Graduation (year 12) performance in a range of subjects and a satisfactory level of literacy. The Tertiary Entrance Score is based on a 50-50 composite of scaled external examination marks and moderated school assessments.

FURTHER EDUCATION

Pre-apprenticeship courses provide a full year of instruction for students before they undertake an apprenticeship in their chosen career. Apprenticeship training is offered in 63 trades.

The Technical Extension Service provides a wide range of formal and vocational courses for students unable to attend lectures.

Full and part-time courses are offered in technical colleges in a variety of subjects. Students entering these courses should have completed year 10 with credit or advanced passes in particular subjects, depending on the course undertaken. Some courses lead to the award of a **Diploma** which is a professional/semi-professional qualification, and generally confers full or partial recognition by the various bodies concerned.

The Western Australian Academy of Performing Arts, and 3 country-based Community Colleges at Karratha, Hedland and Kalgoorlie also provide technical and further education courses.

The Western Australian Institute of Technology is a college of advanced education, which offers courses leading to the award of **Associated Diplomas**, **Bachelor degrees**, **Graduate Diplomas** and **Master degrees**. Admission is based on the Tertiary Admissions examination.

TEACHER EDUCATION

Until 1981, the Western Australian Teacher Education Authority was a statutory body of 5 constituent colleges; Churchlands, Claremont, Graylands, Mount Lawley and Nedlands. The colleges offered a variety of undergraduate and post graduate courses in teacher training but the basic course lasted 3 years and the minimum requirement for entry was satisfactory performance in the Tertiary Admissions Examination. The Western Australian Institute of Technology, the University of Western Australia and Murdoch University (constituted in 1975) also provided courses in teacher training, mainly 4 years.

From 1981, the Western Australian College of Advanced Education has operated from the Churchlands, Claremont, Mount Lawley and Nedlands campuses in replacing the constituent colleges of the Western Australian Teacher Education Authority. Recently, 2 new campuses have opened in Joondalup and Bunbury. All campuses, together with the 2 universities and the Institute of Technology, continue to provide courses in teacher training.

For information on HIGHER EDUCATION see below.

HIGHER EDUCATION

Universities

The first British colony in Australia was established in 1788 and its first 2 universities, Sydney and Melbourne, set up in the 1850s. The universities of Adelaide and Tasmania were established towards the end of the nineteenth century, and the universities of Queensland and Western Australia in the early years of this century. By the First World War, Australia had 1 university in each of the 6 states, and in the 1930s university colleges were established in Canberra and Armidale. Each of the 6 universities was closely involved with the life of its own state, training teachers for the state secondary schools and for the professions. Many of the academic staff were recruited from universities in the UK; most of the Australian teachers did their postgraduate training in British universities and some also went to the USA. Collectively the universities followed British traditions.

The years of immediate post-war reconstruction after the Second World War saw an era of unprecedented change and expansion in the Australian university scene. Total student enrolments, which by 1946 had reached 25,500, quickly increased until, in the 1980s, they reached almost 200,000. Accompanying this growth was an expansion in research and graduate work, for which institutions looked increasingly to the US for appropriate models, thus modifying the strongly British orientation of Australian universities. The Ph.D. degree was introduced soon after the Second World War, and over 20,000 students are now enrolled in higher degree programmes.

As part of the post-war reconstruction strategy, the Australian government established the Australian National University in Canberra, while in 1949 the New South Wales government founded the New South Wales University of Technology (later to become the University of New South Wales) with a special emphasis on applied science and engineering. 11 further universities followed between 1958 and 1975. Now every state has at least 2 universities, except Tasmania which has 1. There are a total of 19 universities in Australia.

Most university courses are full-time day courses, taking 3-6 years, but some may be completed by part-time or external study. Postgraduate studies and research can be undertaken at all Australian universities. The academic year runs from March to November. Arts and science faculties generally adhere to the tradition of a 3-year Pass degree and a 4-year Honours degree, the fourth year of study being only open to approved students who will already have specialized or performed particularly well in the early years of the course. In engineering and technical faculties, Honours degrees are generally awarded on the basis of merit in a single common course, though the Honours student may have undertaken a specified additional period of study within the same period. Where a 3-year scientific or technological degree exists, it is not the general practice to award it with Honours.

Pass degrees in architecture and dentistry generally take 5 years, and medicine 6 years, all with a possible additional year for Honours.

It is important to note that whereas most students in Britain automatically undertake Honours degree courses, the reverse is true in Australia. Most students enrol for Pass degrees, Honours degrees being the exception. It is usual for the student to decide at the end of a 3-year Pass degree whether to continue to an extra Honours year. It is unusual to enrol from year 1 on an Honours course. Many faculties do not offer Honours courses, so a Pass degree is much more acceptable in Australia than its counterpart in Britain.

A student who has qualified for a Bachelor degree at a sufficiently high level can proceed to study for a Master degree. This is obtained after 1 or 2 years of graduate studies leading to submission of a thesis. Some Master degrees are offered on a taught basis with qualifying examinations. In medicine and engineering a period of practical training is usually required before the student qualifies for the Master degree. Alternatively a student who has qualified for an Honours degree at a sufficiently high level can proceed to study for a Doctorate. The usual period of studies is 3 years and culminates in the submission of a thesis.

Bachelor (Honours) degrees are classified I, IIA, IIB, III.
Bachelor (Ordinary) degrees are not classified.

Colleges of Advanced Education

The advanced education sector was established in the 1960s to provide an alternative to university education which would offer courses of high standard but with special focus on applied teaching and preparation for employment. It has quickly developed as a strong and distinctive sector, with a dual concern for vocational and academic relevance, complementing the role of the universities. Currently attracting over 175,000 enrolments in either full-time, part-time or external study, the colleges offer a wide range of courses at **Associate Diploma**, **Bachelor degree**, **Graduate Diploma** or **Master degree** levels, spanning most academic and professional disciplines.

A Bachelor degree course normally extends over 3 years (in some cases 4 or more) if taken on a full-time basis; the Diploma course, 3 years; and the Associate Diploma, 2 years. Degree courses account for approximately two-thirds of college enrolments at undergraduate level.

Graduate Diploma courses are designed to enable graduates to acquire specific vocational qualifications through a short intensive programme of study - usually for 1 year, if full-time. These courses are particularly attractive to graduates already in employment who wish to acquire further qualifications in specialist areas to enhance their professional expertise or to prepare for new careers.

Master degree programmes are offered by course-work or research to graduates wishing to pursue in greater depth their academic specializations or professional studies.

Australia (Higher Education)

The length and dates of the academic year vary slightly between colleges but, in general, the academic year commences in February or early March and ends in November. Many colleges also accept new enrolments in mid-year.

The colleges offer a wide range of courses in fields such as science, engineering, technology, computing, health sciences, agriculture, teacher education, business studies, administration, art and design, information sciences, media, communications and language, and social sciences. The approach in many courses is interdisciplinary with an applied, problem-solving orientation. Courses are accredited on a college, state or territory basis and registered nationally by the Australian Council on Awards in Advanced Education. They are planned in consultation with employers and professional bodies and their awards enjoy a high level of acceptance in the community.

The college sector is extremely diverse. There are 47 colleges, located in all states and territories of Australia. There are large institutes of technology and multi-purpose colleges in the capital cities, and multi-purpose colleges and specialist institutions in the capital cities and multi-purpose regional colleges to serve country areas. In addition, there are small institutions specializing in such fields as agriculture, art, music, education, health sciences or pharmacy. In a country as large as Australia there has been scope for colleges to develop in response to the needs of the states, cities and communities in large interior regions.

All of the colleges are funded by the Australian Government for their central teaching function. They are not similarly funded for research activities, but the sector's standing in applied research and development is reflected in the increasing funding support it is receiving from industrial and commercial sources and from research grant bodies.

Austria

Republic of Austria

Education is compulsory between ages six and fifteen.

EVALUATION IN BRITAIN

School

The **Reifezeugnis** from a Gymnasium or Allgemeinbildende Hohere Schule (also known as the **Matura** or **Maturazeugnis**), may be considered to satisfy the general requirement of universities and polytechnics.

The **Reifezeugnis** from a Berufsbildende Hohere Schule has been compared to a BTEC National Diploma (formerly Ordinary National Diploma). This qualification gives access to technological subjects in higher education in Austria.

The qualification **Ingenieur** (Ing.) has been compared to a standard between a BTEC Higher National Diploma (formerly Higher National Diploma) and British Bachelor degree standard.

Higher

Most Austrian first degrees take a minimum of 4 years to complete (5 years in Engineering and related subjects) - they are generally compared to British Bachelor degree standard.

MARKING SYSTEMS

Marking is usually on a scale of 1-5 (minimum), with 4 as the minimum pass mark. The marks may also be classified as:

1	sehr gut	very good
2	gut	good
3	befriedigend	fair
4	genugend	poor
5	nicht genugend	failure

Austria

SCHOOL EDUCATION

Primary (Volksschule, Grundschule or Sonderschule) **and lower secondary** (Hauptschule or Sonderschule)

Primary education lasts 4 years from age 6 and is provided in <u>Volksschule</u> (also <u>Grundschule</u>) or for mentally or physically handicapped children at <u>Sonderschule</u>.

Upper compulsory education continues for another 4 years in <u>Hauptschule</u> or Sonderschule or in the lower bracket of academic secondary schools (for those aiming at higher education). A new Hauptschule curriculum began in September 1985 starting with the first forms. This discontinued the system of 2 streams and introduced one standard class for all pupils. There are now achievement groups for German, mathematics and a modern foreign language (usually English) and transfer to upper academic secondary schools is easier.

Pupils who do not wish to continue full-time education after Hauptschule attend the pre-vocational school (Polytechnischer Lehrgang) for the ninth year of compulsory education.

Secondary

Academic secondary schools are categorized as <u>Allgemeinbildende Hohere Schulen</u>. They are divided into different types according to subject specialization.

They have, as common core subjects, religious instruction, German, 1 modern foreign language, history and social science, geography, mathematics, biology, physics, music, art, handicrafts and physical education.

The first 4 years (grades 1-4) are called Unterstufe and the second 4 years (grades 5-8) are called Oberstufe. Generally, only those who achieve satisfactory marks in all compulsory subjects can be promoted to a higher class, although in the case of one fail with otherwise good marks the teacher's conference can decide to let the pupil go on to the next grade.

Grades 1 and 2 (fifth and sixth years of schooling) of all types of Allgemeinbildende Hohere Schulen have a common curriculum. In grades 3 and 4 a first differentiation into 3 types is introduced as follows:

<u>Gymnasium</u>, emphasizing Latin

<u>Realgymnasium</u>, emphasizing geometrical drawing, more mathematics and natural science

<u>Wirtschaftskundliches Realgymnasium fur Madchen</u>, emphasizing natural science, handicraft, music.

A second differentiation is made in the upper level with the <u>Gymnasium</u> splitting up into:

<u>Humanistisches Gymnasium</u>, with Greek and 1 modern foriegn language

<u>Neusprachliches Gymnasium</u>, with a second modern foreign language and Latin

Austria

Realistisches Gymnasium, with Latin and 1 modern foreign language, descriptive geometry (in grades 7 and 8), more mathematics and natural science.

The Realgymnasium continues as:

Naturwissenschaftliches Realgymnasium, with Latin and 1 modern foreign language, more mathematics, natural science or descriptive geometry (in grades 7 and 8)

Mathematisches Realgymnasium, with 2 modern foreign languages, more mathematics, descriptive geometry (in grades 7 and 8).

The Wirtschaftkundliches Realgymnasium fur Madchen continues with 1 modern foreign language and alternatively a second modern foreign language or Latin. Other new subjects are food science, home economics, psychology, philosophy, pedagogics.

In addition to the ordinary Allgemeinbildende Hohere Schulen form with 8 years, there is an upper cycle form (grades 5 to 8, entrance after completion of 8 years of compulsory schooling) called Oberstufen-Realgymnasium. There are 3 different branches specializing either in instrumental music, descriptive geometry or natural science.

All 3 types teach a modern foreign language and from grades 6 to 8 alternatively a second modern foreign language or Latin.

The Aufbaugymnasium and Aufbaurealgymnasium provide extension courses for students (mainly adults) who have completed Hauptschule and wish to have an academic secondary education. There is no age limit, courses begin with a transitional year and progress to a 4-year course. The curricula correspond with the Humanistische (or Neusprachliche) Gymnasium or the Naturwissenschaftliche Realgymnasium (with descriptive geometry) respectively.

The Gymnasium and Realgymnasium fur Berufstatige offer part-time evening classes for students over 17 in employment who have completed 8 years of compulsory schooling. They last 9 semesters (4 years). The curricula correspond to those of the Neusprachliche Gymnasium and the Mathematische Gymnasium respectively.

The school-leaving examination taken on completion of the Gymnasium or Realgymnasium is the **Matura** (or **Reifeprufung**). It consists of 2 parts: a written examination and an oral examination. The written examination is taken in 4 compulsory subjects, depending on the type of school. German, 1 modern foreign language and mathematics are always included. The fourth subject can be Latin, Greek, a second modern foreign language, descriptive geometry, biology or physics.

The oral examination covers 3 different subjects, according to the type of school. The candidate has to choose those subjects out of 3 groups of subjects.

The Reifeprufung gives access to higher education.

Technical/vocational

There are 3 types of institution: Berufsbildende Pflichtschulen, Berufsbildende Mittlere Schulen and Berufsbildende Hohere Schulen.

Austria

Berufsbildende Pflichtschulen:

These provide compulsory part-time education on day- or block-release for apprentices in trade, industry, commerce, craft, agriculture and forestry. They start after the Polytechnische Lehrgang. According to the type of training and the duration of apprenticeship, the courses last 2-4 years and finish with a 'termination of apprenticeship examination' (**Lehrabschlussprufung** or **Gehilfenprufung**).

Berufsbildende Mittlere Schulen:

These provide the basic professional training for employment in commerce, technology, arts and crafts, women's occupations, social work and agriculture. Most courses are full-time and last 1-4 years (grades 1-4) but do not give access to higher education. Admission is granted after the completion of 8 years of compulsory schooling and the passing of an entrance examination.

Some of these schools are:

Gewerbliche, Technische und Kunstgewerbliche Fachschulen

Trade, technical and arts and crafts schools providing full training in one or more occupations through theoretical and practica instruction. Courses last 2-4 years and end with the **Abschlussprufung** (final examination).

Handelsschulen

Commercial schools offering 3-year full-time training.

Buro und Verwaltungschulen

Women's vocational school offering 3-year full-time training in domestic science and commercial occupations as well as in certain aspects of tourism and catering.

Hauswirtschaftsschulen

Provides domestic science and basic commercial training over a 2-year coruse.

Haushaltungsschulen

A domestic science course lasting 1 year which gives access to teh Fachschule fur Sozialberufe.

Fachschulen fur Sozialberufe

Vocational schools for social workers offering 1-3 year training courses for youth leaders, family assistance workers, senior citizens assistance workers, marriage and family counsellors.

Hotelfachschule, Gastgewerbefachschule

Training in tourism and catering occupations, lasting 3 years.

Austria

Fachschule fur Tourismus

Training for administrative work in tourism, lasting 3 years.

Landwirtschaftliche Fachschulen

Vocational agricultural schools with the length of training depending on the type of school and the preliminary education of the student (from 2 winter terms up to 4 years). The main areas of training are gardening, agriculture, wine and food.

Forstliche Fachschulen

A course in forestry lasting 1 year.

There are also schools comparable in level to Berufsbildende Mittlere Schulen, which come under the auspices of the Ministry of Health. They include the nursing schools (Allgemeine Krankenpflegeschulen), schools for medical auxiliaries (Schulen fur den Medizinisch-Technischen Fachdienst) and midwifery schools (Bundeshebammenlehran-stalten).

Berufsbildende Hohere Schulen

Courses last 5 years (grades 5-9) and provide advanced general and technical/vocational education for occupations at middle management level. Admission requirements are the successful completion of 8 years of compulsory education plus the passing of a standardized aptitude test. Admission to upper classes is possible after passing an entrance test. Some schools provide evening classes for adults in employment. The school-leaving examination is the Reifeprufung (or Matura), which gives access to higher education.

The most important types of Berufsbildende Hohere Schulen are:

Hohere Technische und Gewerbliche Lehranstalten

Upper-level secondary technical and trade schools teaching technical knowledge and skills for technical, trade and engineering occupations. There are also schools offering 4-year part-time courses for people over 17 in employment. These schools also offer 1- and 2-year courses (Abiturientenlehrgange) for graduates of other types of school who wish to be trained in a particular area.

Hohere Lehranstalten fur Fremdenverkehrsberufe

Upper-level secondary schools offer training for prospective senior personnel in tourism and catering.

Handelsakademien

Upper-level secondary commercial schools provide training for all branches of business. There are 4-year evening courses for people over 17 already in employment.

Hohere Lehranstalten fur Wirtschaftliche Frauenberufe

Domestic and catering schools prepare students for jobs at executive level in domestic science, social work and economy. These schools are co-educational. Courses last 5 years and lead to the **Reifezeugnis**.

Austria

<u>Hohere Landwirtschaftliche Lehranstalten</u>

Courses in agriculture lasting 5 years.

<u>Hohere Lehranstalten fur Forstwirtschaft</u>

Courses in forestry lasting 5 years.

FURTHER EDUCATION

The following courses are available to holders of teh Reifezeugnis:

<u>Akademie fur Sozialarbeit</u>

Training in the field of social work for 2 years leading to a **Diploma**. Entry is by passing an aptitude test.

<u>Abiturientenlehrgange</u>

Vocational courses lasting 1-2 years at Berufsbildende Hohere Schulen give additional training to holders of the Reifezeugnis in particular branches of technology, trade, tourism and catering.

<u>Kollegs</u>

Courses lasting 4 semesters for holders of a Reifezeugnis of an Allgemeinbildende Hohere Schule. It provides additional training in tourism corresponding to courses at Hohere Technische und Gewerbliche Lehranstalten. These courses are run by Berufsbildende Hohere Schulen.

<u>Schulen fur Gehobene Medizinish-Technischen Dienste</u>

Courses for medical laboratory technicians and related occupations lasting 2-3 years.

HIGHER EDUCATION

This is provided by 18 institutions of university status, including 4 general universities, 8 specialized uiniversities (formerly called Hochschulen) and 6 fine arts colleges.

Access to university is free and open to holders of a Reifezeugnis though students may have to take additional examinations for certain types of study. Non-secondary school leavers without a Reifezeugnis may enter higher education by taking one of the following examinations:

Austria

Berufsreifeprufung (taken at all universities)

For candidates aged 25-45 who did not have an opportunity to obtain a Reifezeugnis when younger, or who wish to study a subject at university related to their profession in which they have to be highly qualified or in which they have acquired special knowledge through serious private study.

Studienberechtigungsprufung

Since 1978 some universities have offered 10-month preparatory courses leading to the Studienberechtigungsprufung which entitles the candidate to study only the subject(s) the examination(s) were taken in.

In order to attend the preparatory course the candidate must be at least 24 years of age and pass an aptitude test.

Courses and degrees

The Austrian universities offer 3 different types of studies:

Ordentliche Studien (normal degree courses)

Hochschulkurse und Hochschullehrgange (miscellaneous university courses)

Studium als Ausserordentlicher Horer und Studium als Gasthorer (non-degree courses)

Diplomstudien usually last 8-10 semesters (4-5 years) and are organized into 2 parts (Studienabschnitte), both of which lead to a Diplomprufung. The first is basic study of the subject and ends with the **1st Diplomprufung**; the second part involves specialization and ends with the writing of a paper (Diplomarbeit) and the **2nd Diplomprufung**. After passing this examination, the student is conferred the first academic degree called **Magister**.

After Magister, students may continue studying for 2-4 semesters to obtain a **Doktoratsstudium**. A dissertation (doctorate thesis) must be written and between 1-3 Rigorosen (examinations) passed. The title **Doktor** is then conferred, which is the highest academic qualification.

Alongside the full-length degree courses, some universities offer short courses (Kurzstudien) lasting 5-6 semesters. They do not lead to an academic degree but to a title of occupation. Presently there are 3 types:

Datentechnik (computation methods; Geprufter Rechentechniking)

Versicherungsmathematick (actuarial mathematics; Geprufter Versicherungs-mathematiker)

Kurzstuium fur ubersetzer (translating; Akademisch Geprufter Ubersetzer)

While the individual courses and lectures of the Urdenliche studien are strictly regulated, students have more freedom of choice with the so-called Studium Irregulare. These special courses incorporate elements of the Ordentliche Studien combined by the student to form a tailor-made course. These combinations are study experiments (Studienversuche) and must be approved by the academic authorities.

Austria

Hochschulkurse und Hochschullehrgange:

These are open to university students, university graduates and even students who do not hold a Reifezeugnis. These courses may offer practical or academic training and last from 3-4 weeks up to 6 semesters. Courses cover a variety of subjects including advertising and sales management, electronic data processing, medicine and veterinary medicine, social sciences, physics, Austrian language and culture.

Some of the Hochschulkurse and Hochschullehrgange can be considered postgraduate courses.

Apart from the universities, there are several non-university institutions which offer postgraduate courses. Among these are the Diplomatic Academy in Vienna (Diplomatische Akademie), the Institute for Advanced Studies and Scientific Research (Institut fur Hohere Studien und Wissenschaftliche Forschung), the American Medical Socient, Vienna Academy of Medicine for Postgraduate Training (Wiener Medizinische Akademie fur Arztliche Fortbildung), and the Austrian Latin America Institute (Osterreichisches Lateinamerika-Institut).

Studium als Ausserordentlicher Horer und Studium als Gasthorer:

All students who are a minimum of 17 years old and wish to attend university lectures or Hochschulkurse and Hochschullehrgange without having a Reifezeugnis may do so as Ausserordentliche Horer. University graduates from other countries who wish to have their foreign degrees validated in Austria may have to enrol for crtain coruses as an Ausserordentlicher Horer, too.

All those university graduates who want to attend lectures, Hochschulkurse or Hochschullehrgange for a certain period without beginning a second course of studies may do so as Gasthorer.

Ausserordentliche Horer and Gasthorer are free to take examinations with Hochschulkurse and Hochschullehrgange. They must not take examination, however, with ordinary university lectures.

TEACHER EDUCATION

Teachers undergo very different kinds of training, according to the level of teaching they intend to take up. Generally teacher training can be divided into university level and non-university level.

Non-university

Colleges provide training for teachers at compulsory schools. There are also colleges which train specialist teachers for various kinds of vocational school. The admission requirement is the Reifezeugnis.

Austria

Padagogische Akademien

Introduced in 1965, these provide training for teachers at Volksschule, Hauptschule, Sonderschule, Polytechnisher Lehrgang and also Arbeitslehrreinnen (home economics teachers). Students must pass an aptitude test. From 1985/6 onwards all courses take 3 years, and on completion students take the **Lehramtsprufung** (teachers' examination). Teaching practice is given in practice schools attached to the Akademien.

Technical teacher training colleges (Berufspadagogische Akademien) and agriculutural teacher training colleges (Land- und Forstwirtschaftliche Akademien).

These train teachers of domestic science, trade subjects, agriculture and forestry at Berufsbildende Mittlere Schulen and Berufsbildende Hohere Schulen, as well as teachers of shorthand and typing, and teachers at Berufsschulen. Admission requirements may either be a Reifezeugnis or a master craftsman's certificate plus professional experience. Courses last 1-3 years.

Institutes of Education (Padagogische Institute)

Originally designed for the further training of teachers at Volksschulen, Hauptschulen, Sonderschulen and Polytechnische Lehrgange these now also provide further training for teachers at Allgemeinbildende Hohere Schulen and Berufsbildende Schulen.

University

All teachers at Allgemeinbildende Hohere Schulen and teachers of certain subjects at Berufsbildende Hohere Schulen and Berufsbildende Mittlere Schulen must be university graduates. Students have to qualify in 2 subjects, combined in accordance with the relevant regulations.

Teacher training at university is undergoing a complete change. So far students have been trained according to the old regulations. On completion of a minimum of 8 semesters (4 years) of studies, the student passes **Lehramtsprufung** in both subjects and in pedagogics and is then conferred the academic degree of **Magister**. Without teaching experience, new teachers complete a probationary year (Probejahr) before they are fully qualified. The new regulations will include practical teaching as part of the studies, but it is not yet known when they will come into effect.

Kindergarten

Kindergarten teachers are trained at Bildungsanstalten fur Kindergartenpadagogik. Admission depends on the completion of 8 years of primary schooling and passing an aptitude test. Since September 1985 courses last 5 years and lead to the **Reifeprufung**.

Bildungsanstaltan fur Erzieher train teachers at schools and children's day centres.

Admission requirements and the duration of training are as for kindergarten teachers. There is a special 2-year coruse (Kolleg fur Erzieher) for those who hold a Reifezeugnis.

Religionspadagogische Akademien provide 2-year course for Catholic religious instructors and require the Reifezeugnis for admission.

Austria

Evangelische Frauenschule fur kirchlichen und sozialen Dienst provide similar training for Protestant religious instructors.

There are also Bundesanstalten fur Leibeserziehung which train Sportlehrer (sports teachers) and Schilehrer (skiing instructors).

ADULT EDUCATION

Distance education (Fernstudien)

This has been provided since 1979 by the Interuniversitares Forschungsinstitut fur Fernstudien located at the University of Klagenfurt. This institute has links to all major Austrian universities and offers special courses for adults in employment. Very few study programmes have been developed so far, such as coures for applied mathematics, solar energy, teacher training.

While these study programmes are still being developed, students may choose to study at the Fernuniversitat Hagen in the Federal Republic of Germany, which offers normal degree courses in economics, law, social science, pedagogics, mathematics, electronic engineering.

Studies for senior citizens (Seniorenstudium)

Austrian universities welcome senior citizens as students. Courses, degrees and conditions of admission are the same as for young students.

Bahamas

Commonwealth of the Bahamas

Education in the Bahamas is under the jurisdiction of the Ministry of Education.

It is compulsory for children aged five to fifteen.

Free education is available in Ministry schools, while the independent schools, which provide education at primary, secondary and higher levels, are fee-paying.

EVALUATION IN BRITAIN

Bahamas Junior Certificate - generally considered to be below GCE O-level standard.

GCE O- and A-levels - of the same standard as GCE O- and A-level examinations taken in Britain.

SCHOOL EDUCATION

Schools are categorized as follows:

Primary	ages 5-11
Junior High	11-14
Junior/Senior High	11-16
Senior High	14-16

There are also all-age schools, and special schools catering for students with learning disabilities.

On completion of 9 (sometimes 10) years of education, pupils take examinations leading to the award of the **Bahamas Junior Certificate** (BJC).

After 11 or 12 years, students may take the **GCE O-level examinations** of the University of London or the **Royal Society of Arts Certificates.** A few schools offer further 2- or 3-year courses leading to the University of London **GCE A-level examinations.**

Bahamas

FURTHER EDUCATION

Several schools of continuing education offer daytime and evening secretarial and academic courses, and the government-operated Princess Margaret Hospital offers a nursing course at 2 levels.

The College of the Bahamas was established in 1974 as a community college, and runs on a 2-semester system (September/December, January/April) with a summer session (May/June). The College provides a 2- or 3-year programme leading to an **Associate degree** in any of 6 academic divisions: natural science, social science, education, humanities, business studies, and technology. Several college programmes are offered in conjunction with the University of the West Indies, the University of Miami and Florida International University.

The Hotel Training College offers a range of subjects up to middle-management level. The College maintains relations with the University of Miami and Florida International University, and has an 'articulation' agreement with the College of the Bahamas. Courses offered are only to **Diploma** level.

HIGHER EDUCATION

The Bahamas has been affiliated to the University of the West Indies since the early 1960s. The University is regional, serving most of the English-speaking Caribbean, and has 3 campuses in the islands of Jamaica, Trinidad and Barbados. It maintains an administrative office and a full-time representative in Nassau, through whom Bahamian students may seek admission to any of the campuses.

Based in Nassau, the University of the West Indies Centre for Hotel and Tourism Management offers the final 2 years of the **B.Sc. Hotel Management** and the **B.Sc. Tourism Management** to both full- and part-time students. Additionally, in collaboration with the College of the Bahamas it offers the Part II **B.Sc. Management Studies** to part-time students. The Centre also offers postgraduate diplomas in both Hotel and Tourism Management.

TEACHER EDUCATION

The University's **B.Ed.** is offered in Nassau in collaboration with the Education Division of the College of the Bahamas, which provides 1- and 2-year courses of basic training for non-graduates, and in-service training.

The College of the Bahamas also trains technical teachers.

Bahrain

State of Bahrain

School education is centrally administered with central control of syllabuses etc.

Primary education is in theory compulsory but school attendance has not yet been enforced. This question is currently under discussion.

The medium of instruction is Arabic; English is introduced in the fourth year of primary education as the main foreign language and is compulsory to the end of secondary education.

The academic year runs from October to June.

EVALUATION IN BRITAIN

School

Secondary School Certificate - generally compared to GCE O-level standard on a subject-for-subject basis provided marks of at least 50% have been obtained in subjects which can be taken in the GCE examinations, except English language.

MARKING SYSTEMS

School

Secondary School Leaving Certificate (Tawjahiya): Marking varies per subject; maximum and minimum grades per subject are shown on the certificate.

Higher

Grade-point average:

4	excellent
3	good
2	satisfactory
1	minimum pass

Bahrain

SCHOOL EDUCATION

Pre-primary

There are a few private kindergartens.

Primary

This covers 6 years from age 6.

The curriculum covers Arabic, English (introduced in the fourth year), general science, religious instruction, arithmetic, geography and history. Pupils may proceed to intermediate education.

Intermediate

This covers 3 years. The curriculum covers religious instruction, Arabic, English, history, geometry, algebra, arithmetic, general science, physical education, home economics (girls), arts and crafts. Pupils take the examinations for the **Intermediate School Certificate** and, dependent upon the results, may proceed to some form of secondary education.

Secondary

This covers 3 years. Pupils may attend general, technical or commercial schools but there is no provision to switch from one to another.

General secondary

All pupils take religious instruction, Arabic, English, physical education and vocational education. In addition, they may specialize in either literary studies or science. Those in the literary stream also take history, geography, society and philosophy. Those specializing in science take arithmetic, physics, chemistry and natural history. In addition, the following small specialized section shave been introduced in general secondary schools: agriculture, health sciences, hotel and catering, printing and textiles. Those specializations all culminate in the examinations for the Secondary School Leaving Certificate (Tawjahiya).

Technical secondary

The 3-year course leading to the Technical School Leaving Certificate (Tawjahiya) covers the compulsory subjects (as in the general schools) and: workshop practice, technology, mathematics, chemistry, physics and engineering drawing. Pupils may also undertake courses leading to the qualifications of the City & Guilds of London Institute.

Commercial secondary

The 3-year course leading to the Commercial School Leaving Certificate (Tawjahiya) covers the compulsory subjects (as in the general schools) and: bookkeeping and accountancy, pure and financial mathematics, economics, practical secretarial work in English and Arabic, and English and Arabic typing.

Bahrain

FURTHER EDUCATION

Within Bahrain University (see note below) the Gulf Polytechnic (formerly known as the Gulf Technical College and established in 1968), offers a variety of courses, all taught in English. The entrance level is the Secondary School Certificate. Until recently, full-time courses lasting 4 years led to examinations for the **City & Guilds** of London Institute **Ordinary Technician Diploma** (2 years) and **Higher Technician Diploma** (2 years) in mechanical engineering, electrical engineering, building and civil engineering, and construction. The Polytechnic now runs its own technican courses on an American-style system. In secretarial and commercial subjects, courses usually last 2 or 3 years and may lead to examinations of the **Royal Society of Arts** and the **Business & Technican Education Council**.

The College of Health Sciences, established by the Ministry of Health in April 1976, offers vocational training for health personnel in nursing and a variety of allied health programmes primarily for medical technicians. All courses are taught in English.

HIGHER EDUCATION

In May 1986, a legislative decree announced the establishment and organization of Bahrain University, as a result of a merger of the existing University College of Science, Arts and Education founded in 1978 and the Gulf Polytechnic.

A transitional period is expected to ensue, during which the 2 founding institutions will retain something of their separate identities until the merger can be fully implemented.

4-year degree courses are offered in business and management, commercial studies, accounting, engineering disciplines (Gulf Polytechnic), mathematics, sciences (B.Sc.), Arabic, education, English, Islamic studies (BA, B.Ed.) and physical education (B PE) (University College).

The Arabian Gulf University was established in 1980 although the main campus is still under construction. The first department to accept students (in 1982) was the College of Medical Science which offers a 2-year pre-medical course followed by a 2-year pre-clinical stage after which is awarded a **B.Sc. in Medical Studies.** Then follows a 3-year clinical stage leading to the award of the MD certificate. The other departments in the University expect to start recruiting students very soon, when the building programme has been completed. It is expected that the University will develop almost exclusively postgraduate studies and research for the next 10 years, although a first-degree course in special education is envisaged. Priority will be given to 3 subject areas: desert sciences, bio-engineering and special education.

Bahrain

TEACHER EDUCATION

The Faculty of Education at the University College of Arts, Science and Education, offers qualifications in Education including **M.Ed.** in Science Education and a **Postgraduate Diploma in Education**. The college also undertakes in-service re-training of subject teachers at the intermediate and lower secondary levels. Graduates may be appointed to primary and intermediate schools, as well as to secondary schools.

Many teachers hold degrees obtained abroad.

Bangladesh

People's Republic of Bangladesh

Bangladesh seceded from Pakistan in 1971.

There is no compulsory education.

The official medium of instruction is Bangla.

The academic year varies according to the level of education: for primary and secondary levels it begins in January and ends in December. In educational institutions for study beyond class 10, courses begin in July and end in June. Most university courses are out of phase with the official academic year; some, for example, begin in October/November rather than in July. Internal political disturbances have delayed courses, with examination dates being deferred several times. Degrees have been referred to by the notional date of completion rather than by the year in which they were finally awarded.

EVALUATION IN BRITAIN

School

Secondary School Certificate (SSC) - generally considered to be below GCE O-level standard.

Higher Secondary Certificate (HSC) - generally considered to compare to GCE O-level standard.

Polytechnic diplomas - generally considered to be slightly above GCE O-level standard.

Higher

Bachelor degrees - Both Pass and Honours degrees are generally considered to compare to GCE A-level standard.

Engineering degrees have been known to be accepted for postgraduate study in Britain. Medical degrees granted after 1972 are not recognized by the British General Medical Council, except degrees granted by Dhaka Medical College from 1983 onwards and Sir Salimullah Medical College, Dhaka from 1984 onwards.

Masters degrees - have been known to be accorded British Bachelor degree standard.

Bangladesh

MARKING SYSTEMS

School

Secondary School Certificate and **Higher School Certificate** are group examinations graded (percentages) as follows:

60-100	1st division pass
45-59	2nd division pass
33-44	3rd division pass
0-32	fail

Further

Polytechnic Diplomas are group examinations graded (percentages) as follows:

60-100	first class
50-59	second class
0-49	fail

Although 50% is the official cut-off point, the pass/fail line is often 45%. Students must also gain a minimum of 45% in individual subjects.

Higher

Grades for degrees at the university are usually decided by examination. The grading system (percentages) used is that for the Secondary School Certificate:

60-100	1st class/division
45-59	2nd class/division
33-44	3rd class/division

Pass degrees are classified by division and Honours degrees by class.

SCHOOL EDUCATION

Primary

This begins at age 5 and lasts 5 years (classes 1-5). Children can join up to about age 8, and rural classes often cover a 3-year age range.

Secondary

For admission to the 3-year junior secondary cycle pupils usually have to pass an entrance examination conducted by individual schools. On completion of class 8 some pupils leave school, but most proceed to the senior secondary cycle. There is no public examination at the end of the junior secondary cycle. Most junior secondary classes are simply the lower end of high schools, which normally extend to class 10. Pupils proceed to the senior secondary cycle by passing the school's internal examination.

Bangladesh

The main courses are humanities, science and commerce. Other courses, mainly in agricultural subjects, are taken by very few pupils. In all courses, Bengali and English are compulsory subjects. On completion of class 10, students take the **Secondary School Certificate** examination, which is the first public examination and the only examination taken at this stage.

Students who pass this examination may apply for a 2-year higher secondary/intermediate course. These courses are mainly offered by intermediate colleges, although some high schools extend as far as class 12, and some degree colleges also offer courses for the **Higher Secondary Certificate** (previously called the **Intermediate Certificate**). English and Bengali are compulsory subjects for all courses.

A limited number of Cadet Colleges offer a curriculum for classes 7-12 similar to that taken for the Secondary School Certificate and Higher Secondary Certificate examinations. There are some courses in military studies and emphasis is placed on physical education and sport. Students agree to serve in the armed forces after their courses, but most proceed to university.

Madrasah schools traditionally concentrated on Islamic instruction, preparing boys for religious duties. In recent years however greater emphasis has been given to a more general education. The final examination at these schools is considered to compare to the Secondary School Certificate. Students who achieve satisfactory results can apply for admission to class 11 in a general college.

Technical/vocational secondary

Craft courses at the certificate level are organized by Vocational Training Institutes. These courses are for prospective car and farm mechanics, joiners, bricklayers, etc. Students must have reached at least class 8 standard. Other certificate courses are run by some of the polytechnics operating a 'second shift' system. Similar courses are offered by private vocational schools, technical training centres (2-year course) and the Bangladesh German Technical Training Centre. Some agricultural extension training institutes offer 2-year diploma courses.

FURTHER EDUCATION

Bangladesh has many polytechnics, which offer 3-year diploma courses in various branches of engineering and technology. The minimum entrance qualification is a 2nd division pass in the Secondary School Certificate. Three-year diplomas are also offered by monotechnics specializing in leather and textile technologies.

HIGHER EDUCATION

In arts, science and commerce, **Pass** degrees are obtained after 2 years study and **Honours** degrees after 3 years. The first degree in **Engineering** B.Sc.(Eng.) is obtained after a 4-year course and that in **Medicine** (MB BS) after a 5-year course.

Bangladesh

Holders of Pass degrees may proceed to a 2-year **Masters** course if their marks are good in the first degree, whilst holders of an Honours degree may complete a Masters degree in 1 year.

Most students taking Pass degree courses study at colleges (affiliated to universities) whilst those taking Honours degree courses study at one of the universities; however, a few colleges offer Pass and Honours degree courses and postgraduate courses. All universities in Bangladesh offer M.Phil. and Ph.D. courses.

The **Bachelor Degree in Law** involves a 2-year full-time course after a first degree in any subject offered by the affiliated colleges. Some universities have introduced 4-year **LL B** (Honours) and 1-year **LL M** courses.

The 4 general universities are Dhaka, Rajshahi, Chittagong and Jahangirnagar; the latter is still in the early stages of development. A new university called the Islamic University has been founded but as yet no courses have started. The 2 specialist universities are the Bangladesh University of Engineering and Technology (BUET) and the Bangladesh Agricultural University (BAU). The BUET developed from the East Pakistan University of Engineering and is the only technical university awarding degrees in mechanical, civil, electrical, chemical and metallurgical engineering. It has very strict entry requirements, including a special entrance examination.

From 1972-4 widespread political disturbances had an adverse effect on studies.

TEACHER EDUCATION

Primary

Primary school teachers are trained at the Primary Training Institutes. In 1975 the Ministry of Education decided that the course previously lasting 1 academic year should be condensed to 8 months, without any long break between successive courses. The course leads to a **Certificate**.

Instructors at these institutes usually have a first degree and a teaching certificate.

Secondary

From 1973-8 the colleges of education offered 3-year degree courses leading to a **BA in Education**. The minimum entry qualification was the Higher Secondary Certificate. Graduates were expected to be qualified to teach in junior secondary classes. The colleges of education offer 2-year degree courses which lead to a **B.Ed**.

Four of these colleges have been upgraded to teacher training colleges, and one has become the site of the Academy for Fundamental Education. The teacher training colleges train university graduates to teach in secondary schools during a 1-year course leading to a B.Ed. The B.Ed. courses are validated by the universities to which the colleges are affiliated.

Bangladesh

The specialist teacher training colleges offer 2 courses: a 1-year **Diploma in Technical Education**, and a 2-year degree course, leading to a **B.Sc. in Technical Education** which is validated by Dhaka University. Students of either course must have at least a Diploma in Engineering. There are 3 other specialist teacher training colleges in Dhaka; the <u>College of Physical Education</u>, the <u>College of Arts and Crafts</u>, and the <u>College of Home Economics</u> which offer BA, B.Sc and B.Com. Pass courses for 2 years. Some colleges have started BA (Hons) in a few subjects.

The <u>Institute of Education and Research</u> (IER) at Dhaka University offers **Diploma, M.Ed.** and **Ph.D.** courses. The Diploma courses are considered to be the equivalent of the B.Ed. courses at the teacher training colleges. Both Diploma and B.Ed. holders may be accepted for the 1-year M.Ed. courses.

Barbados

The education system is based on the British system.

There is no period of compulsory education.

The medium of instruction is English.

The academic year runs from September to June.

EVALUATION IN BRITAIN

School

GCE O- and **A-levels** - of the same standard as GCE O- and A-level examinations taken in Britain.

Caribbean Examinations Council Secondary Education Certificate - grades 1 and 2 at the general proficiency level have been equated to GCE O-level (grades A, B or C).

Higher

Bachelor degrees - generally considered to compare to British Bachelor degree standard.

MARKING SYSTEMS

School

GCE O- and A-levels are marked as in Britain.

Caribbean Examinations Council Secondary Education Certificate: subject examinations are taken at 2 proficiency levels:

Basic
General

Barbados

5 grades are awarded, defined as follows:

I   comprehensive working knowledge of the syllabus

II   working knowledge of most aspects of the syllabus

III working knowledge of some aspects of the syllabus

IV   limited knowledge of a few aspects of the syllabus

V   insufficient evidence on which to base a judgement.

Higher

Bachelor degrees are awarded with the following classifications:

first-class honours
second-class upper division
second-class lower division

If the performance has been insufficient for Honours, the degree is awarded as a Pass.

SCHOOL EDUCATION

Primary

This covers 6 years (generally from age 5). On completion, pupils take the **Common Entrance Examination** (11+), which decides admission to secondary education.

Secondary

This covers a possible 7 years, the last 2 being the sixth form.

On completion of 5 years secondary education, pupils take the examinations for the GCE O-levels of the London and AEB Boards, or, more recently, the **Caribbean Examinations Council** (see Appendix).

A number of 'all-age' schools offer both primary education and the first 3 years of secondary education, culminating in the **Barbados School-Leaving Certificate**, now replaced by the **Barbados Secondary School Certificate Part I** (there is no Part 2). This certificate may also be obtained by pupils who have completed 3 or 4 years secondary education at the 'newer' secondary schools (established since the mid-1950s on comprehensive lines).

On completion of the 2-year sixth-form course, pupils take the examinations for the GCE A-levels of the London and AEB Boards.

TECHNICAL SECONDARY/FURTHER EDUCATION

The Technical Institute opened in 1953 and offered pre-apprenticeship, apprenticeship and secondary technical courses leading to qualifications from the City & Guilds of London Institute. The Institute was absorbed into the Samuel Jackman Prescod Polytechnic, established in 1970. The Polytechnic now offers courses leading to qualifications from the City & Guilds of London Institute, RSA and GCE O- and A-level examinations. Admission to most courses is on the basis of the Barbados School-Leaving Certificate/Barbados Secondary School Certificate Part I.

The Barbados Community College was established in 1969 to provide courses at post-secondary level (i.e. from GCE O-level) in agriculture, commerce, liberal arts, and science and technology. Courses lead to examinations of overseas (normally British) professional bodies (e.g. London Chamber of Commerce), and most are based on the credit system. Courses are also available which lead to the GCE A-levels.

HIGHER EDUCATION

A campus of the University of the West Indies based in Barbados at Cave Hill opened in 1963. It houses the University's Faculty of Law; it also has facilities for education, natural science, social sciences, arts and general studies. The University became an independent degree-granting institution in 1962, although under its affiliation to the University of London it offered external degrees of that University until 1963.

The normal minimum entrance qualification for **Bachelor** degree courses is 5 GCE passes, 2 being at A-level. There is a lower matriculation level of 5 GCE O-levels; students who enter at this level take 4-year degree courses, the first year leading to the preliminary/NI examination. Bachelor degree courses normally last 3 years, with medicine taking 5 years.

Facilities are also available for study leading to **Master** and **Doctorate** degrees.

TEACHER EDUCATION

Erdiston College was established in 1948 as a teacher-training college; until 1954, it offered a multi-purpose 1-year course. This was then extended to 2 years. Since 1970, the college has offered a 2-year course for primary school teachers and a 2-year course for teachers for secondary comprehensive and all-age schools. Admission to both courses is by GCE O-levels.

Belgium

Kingdom of Belgium

Education in Belgium is a sensitive political matter, reflecting the linguistic and religious differences within the country, stemming from the existence of two main cultural communities, the Dutch-speaking area in the north and the French-speaking area in the south. There is also a small German-speaking area in the east. Brussels, the capital, is geographically in Flanders but largely French-speaking, and mainly surrounded by Flemish-speaking communes.

The linguistic differences within the country were legally acknowledged by the Act of July 1963 which established that French should be the medium of instruction in Wallonia, Dutch in Flanders, and German in the Cantons de L'Est. Since 1966 there have also been two Ministries of Public Education, one for the French-speaking area and one for the Dutch-speaking area. To combat the linguistic differences the curricula, syllabuses and courses in state schools are laid down by law, and certificates obtained at the same level but in different media schools have equal validity.

The sector of Roman Catholic Schools, which runs parallel with the state sector is subsidized by the State and caters for over 50% of the school and non-university higher education population.

Compulsory education was from age six to fourteen but was extended by the Law of 29 June 1983 to eighteen. Pupils must undertake full-time education between ages six to fifteen. This period is extended to sixteen if the pupil has not completed the first two years of secondary education, and by a period of part-time education for pupils ages fifteen/ sixteen to eighteen.

The academic year runs from September to June in primary and secondary schools and from October to June/July in higher education and universities.

EVALUATION IN BRITAIN

School

Certificat d'Enseignement Secondaire Inférieur generally considered to be
(Diplome d'Humanites Inférieures)* below GCE O-level standard.
Certificaat van Lager Secundair Onderwijs

Certificat Complementaire - generally considered to approach GCE O-level standard. It is not issued in the reformed system.

* Denominations in brackets only appear on older certificates.

Belgium

Certificat de Fin d'Etudes du Premier Degre du Secondaire or **Certificat de Fin d'Etudes du Deuxieme Degre du Secondaire** - generally considered to be below GCE O-level standard.

Certificat d'Enseignement Secondaire Superieur
(Certificat d'Etudes Moyennes Superieurs)*
(Certificat (Diplôme) d'Humanites)*
Getuigschrift van Hoger Secundair Onderwijs
(Getuigschrift van Hoger Middelbaar Onderwijs)*
(Humanioragetuigschrift)*

generally considered to be between GCE O- and A-level standards.

Maturite/Bekwaamheidsdiploma - may satisfy the general requirement for universities and polytechnics.

Higher

Candidat/Kandidaat - generally considered to be between GCE A-level standard and a British Bachelor degree standard.

Licencie/Licenciaat - has been known to be accorded British Master degree standard, but is more likely to be compared to British Bachelor degree standard.

* Denominations in brackets only appear on older certificates.

MARKING SYSTEMS

School

Before 1969: percentage scale.

Since 1969: various; details given on certificates.

Higher

In university-level education the following grades are accorded at the end of each academic year:

met voldoening avec mention	approximately 60%
met onderscheiding avec distinction	approximately 70%
met grote onderscheiding avec grande distinction	approximately 80%
met grotste onderscheiding avec la plus grande distinction	approximately 90%

The decision to award these grades is taken internally at each university by a Board of Professors. Degrees are graded according to performance in any one year's group and do not necessarily reflect the same performance between one year and the next.

Belgium

SCHOOL EDUCATION

Pre-primary

Widespread facilities are available for children between 2- and-a-half and six.

Primary

This covers 6 years from age 6, and is divided into three 2-year cycles. On conclusion of the third cycle pupils obtain:

Certificat de Fin d'Etudes Primaires/Certificat d'Etudes de Base
Getuigschrift van Lager Onderwijs/Getuigschrift van Basisonderwijs.

Secondary

Before 1969:

Pupils who wished to leave school on completion of compulsory education could take a 2-year course, now phased out (quatrieme degre primaire/vierde graad lager onderwijs/voortgezet lager onderwijs).

General secondary education covered 6 years, divided into two 3-year cycles. In the lower cycle pupils had to choose between the Latin section (classique) and the modern section. The former was again divided into 2 subsections after the second year; Latin/Greek or Latin/mathematics. The modern section included both science and economics and prepared pupils for the science and economics sections in the second cycle of secondary education. On completion of the second year of this cycle pupils were able to transfer to the commercial course for a further 2 years. Obligatory subjects in this lower cycle were history, geography, mathematics, the mother tongue, a first foreign language, biology, art, physical education and, for the Latin section, Latin. On completion of this cycle pupils obtained:

Certificat d'Enseignement Secondaire Inferieur
Getuigschrift van Lager Secundair Onderwijs.

Pupils had to choose between the following during the upper secondary cycle:

Latin/Greek, Latin/mathematics, Latin/sciences
Sciences A (based on mathematics and physics)
Sciences B (based on natural sciences)
Human sciences
Economics.

On completion of the first year of this cycle pupils obtained:

Certificat Complementaire
Certificat de Qualification de Quatrieme Annee
Kwalificatiegetuigschrift van Het Vierde Leerjaar

and on completion of the full cycle:

Certificat d'Enseignement Secondaire Superieur
Certificat d'Etudes Moyennes Superieures
Certificat (Diplome) d'Humanites
Getuigschrift van Hoger Secundair Onderwijs
Getuigschrift van Hoger Middelbaar Onderwijs
Humanioragetuigschrift.

The certificate had to be ratified by the Commission d'Homologation, set up by the government to supervise standards; without this certificates are not valid.

Pupils who wished to enter a university or other institution of higher education had to obtain an additional qualification in either 1 principal subject or 2 subsidiary subjects, the:

Maturite
Diplome d'Aptitude a Acceder a l'Enseignement Superieur
Bekwaamheidsdiploma dat Toegang Verleent tot Het Hoger Onderwijs.

The examination for this qualification was instituted in 1965 and taken at the school where the student sat the final school leaving examination. It could be taken at the same time, but certainly not later than 3 years after that examination.

Technical secondary

Before 1969:

This covered 6 years, divided into two 3-year cycles, and was considered to bring pupils up to the same level as pupils who had studied general academic secondary education. Pupils who wished to obtain a leaving certificate on completion of the first cycle had to stay at school for a further (fourth) year. An extra (fifth) year enabled the pupil to obtain a specialization certificate. On completion of the second 3-year cycle pupils obtained a technicians certificate or final vocational certificate and could go on to a higher technical school or technical teacher training college. They were also able to take the examinations for the Maturite, entitling them to university admission.

Pupils holding certificates from vocational schools could proceed to complementary secondary vocational education e.g. for assistant nurses.

Artistic education (music, dramatic art or plastic arts) was organized in different institutions and at different levels. Some certificates, especially in plastic arts, were accepted as equivalent to technical school certificates.

Since 1969 (Reformed System):

The new system introduced has now been adopted by most schools.

The 6 years are divided into three 2-year cycles:

Observation =   taken by all students irrespective of their
                later specialization in general academic,
                technical, artistic or vocational fields

Orientation/guidance
Determination/specialization.

Belgium

There are still 4 distinct types of secondary education:

General, with courses in	mathematics physics and natural science economics and social sciences modern languages Latin Greek technical sciences industrial chemistry electromechanics
Technical, with courses in	agriculture horticulture mechanics electricity woodwork
Artistic, with courses in	applied and decorative art interior design architectural drawing
Vocational, with courses in	steelwork building construction dressmaking hairdressing

Pupils may choose from one specialism to another until the fourth year. There are some restrictions in the vocational section; until 1985 students in this section could not change, now they can if favourably advised by an Admission Board. A pupil who has already completed 2 years in a vocational section, must start again in the second year in whichever new section is chosen. Students who have completed the full 6-year cycle in a vocational section may only change to a technical section by beginning again from the fifth year.

Each year pupils obtain an end-of-year report, (attestations d'orientation/ orienteringsattersten), based on continuous assessment, for streaming according to ability. On completion of the third year, students in the general technical and artistic section may still obtain:

Certificat d'Enseignement Secondarire Inferieur
Getuigschrift van Lager Secundair Onderwijs.

In the vocational section a similar qualification may be obtained, providing students have completed 4 years and passed the examen de qualification de quatrieme annee/ kwalificati eexamen van de vierde leerjaar.

On completion of the third cycle pupils obtain:

Certificat d'Enseignement Secondaire Superieur
Getuigschrift van Lager Secundaire Onderwijs

which states which section was followed, i.e. general, artistic or technical. From 1987 students who have completed the third cycle (6 year total) in a vocational section, may follow a more general seventh year and gain a similar certificate which gives access to short courses of higher education only.

Belgium

Since 1985-6:

Examinations for the Diplome de Maturite/Bekwaamheidsdiploma which give access to university or non-university higher education are no longer organized, except for students who, for whatever reason, did not pursue a normal course of study.

Now the

Diplome d'Aptitude d'Acceder a l'Enseignement Superieur
Bekwaamheidsdiploma dat Toegang Verleent tot het Hoger Enderwijs

is issued by a board of teachers following 1 year of evaluation of a pupil's work using criteria defined by a Royal Decree. Certificates still have to be ratified by the Commission d'Homologation to be valid.

With the extension of compulsory education from age 14 to 18, new forms of education systems had to be created. 15-year-olds may choose to follow:

Full-time secondary education (described above).

An apprenticeship with the self-employed, the craft industries, small and medium-sized businesses, organized by the Ministry for Small Firms and Trades (Ministere des Classes Moyennes) which comes under the authority of the linguistic community concerned.

An industrial apprenticeship organized by the Joint Committees in each industrial sector and the National Labour Council within the Ministry of Employment and Labour. These already exist in the diamond industry, inland water transport and clothing industry.

Reduced timetable schooling at 90 centres called Centres d'Enseignement a Horaire Reduit attached to secondary education establishments. This is organized by the Ministry of Education.

Work experience training organized by associations recognized by the Ministry for the linguistic community concerned.

Training offered in evening and weekend classes.

Outside the school system training is given by vocational and pre-vocational guidance training centres (Centres d'Orientation et d'Initiation Professionnelle) for unemployed people under 25 whose lack of basic training excludes them from the conventional vocational training systems. Courses lasting 6 weeks are organized to determine the appropriate level of training for each individual.

HIGHER EDUCATION

There were 3 types of non-university education (ingenieur commercial, ingenieur technicien, graduat). This has now been replaced by a 2-tier system. Short courses of at least 4 years at non-university level lead to a Graduat/Graduaat (certificates issued on completion of this course do not state Graduat/Graduaat). Long courses of at least 4 years at university level lead (according to discipline) to the following qualifications:

Belgium

Ingenieur industriel/Industrieel Ingenieur
Licencie-traducteur/interprete/Licentiaat-vertaler/tolk
Licencie en Sciences Commerciales/Licentiaat Handelswetenschappen
Licencie en Sciences Administratives/Licentiaat Bestuurswetenschappen
Ingenieur Commercial/Handelsingenieur
Architecte/Architect

The normal entrance qualification for a higher education course are the:

Certificate d'Enseignement Secondaire Superieur
Getuigschrift van Lager Secundaire Onderwijs

Diplome d'Aptitude Acceder a l'Enseignement Superieur
Bekwaamheidsdiploma dat Toegang Verleent tot het Hoger Onderwijs (Maturite/Maturiteit).

There is no system of numerus clausus (restrictions on numbers) except in applied sciences where prospective students have to take a special entrance examination, and for foreign students.

The first stage of university study leads to the qualification of **Candidat/Kandidaat** after 2-3 years of generalized study. The second stage is a further 2-3 years of specialist study, including the preparation of a thesis, and leads to the qualification of **Licencie/Licenciaat**. In certain subjects the final qualification is the professional qualification (e.g. engineer) and the course may be a little longer.

For the **Doctorate/Doctorat/Doctoraat**: there are no regulations as to duration but it may be obtained in not less than 1 year after the award of the Licence and consists of the presentation of an original thesis, defended in public.

The Candidat/Kandidaat in natural and medical sciences is obtained after 3 years, and the qualification of Doctor of Medicine or Surgery after a further 4 years, including several periods of probation in a clinic and 1 year as resident in a hospital. With this qualification, doctors enter the medical register in Belgium and may set up in general practice.

The Candidat/Kandidaat in veterinary medicine is obtained after 2 years study and the qualification of Doctor after a further 3 years.

In law the Candidat/Kandidaat is obtained in 2 years, and the Licencie/Licenciaat in 3 years.

There are 2 categories of degree: **state/legal degrees** and **academic degrees.** State degrees are a pre-requisite for practising certain professions or holding certain posts in professions, e.g. law (the Bar), teaching (to become a principal). Courses for which the entrance requirements and syllabuses are fixed by law lead to a state degree. For courses which lead to academic degrees the admission requirements and syllabuses are determined by the university (if private) or by the government (if a state university).

An important consequence of Belgium's linguistic differences has been the split of the two 'free' (i.e. non-state) universities: the University of Louvain split in 1973 into the Katholicke Universiteit te Leuven (which remains in the town of Louvain) and the Universite Catholique de Louvain (whose main campus is at Louvain la Neuve near Ottignies in Wallonia). There is another campus called Louvain-en-Woluwe (Brussels) where the University hospital is. The University of Brussels split into the Universite Libre de Bruxelles (ULB) and the Vrije Universiteit Brussel (VUB).

Belgium

The <u>College of Europe</u>, although heavily subsidized by the Belgian government and the City of Bruges, is separate from the Belgian education system, being a small postgraduate college with an international student body (see appendix).

TEACHER EDUCATION

Before 1967

Primary

Students who had completed the first cycle of secondary education undertook a 4-year course at a primary teacher training college. The syllabus included all the modern and classical courses normally taken in the second cycle of secondary education, and pedagogical training. On completion of the course students obtained a **Certificat d'Humanites** and the title of primary teacher.

1967-74

Pre-primary/nursery

On completion of the first cycle of secondary education pupils undertook a 4-year course at a nursery teacher training college. Students could also enter directly into the second year of this course on completion of the first year of the second cycle of secondary education or the first year of a primary teacher training course. The syllabus is the same as that of the second cycle of secondary education for the first 2 years. On completion of the course students obtained a **Diplome de Fin d'Etudes** allowing university admission, but not a Certificat d'Humanites.

Primary

The length of the primary teacher training course was increased by 1 year and divided into 2 cycles:

First cycle lasting 3 years, based on the old 4-year course, and leading to the **Certificat d'Humanites**

Second cycle lasting 2 years, including practical training, and leading to the **Primary Teachers Certificate**.

Since 1974

All types of teacher training (not just for secondary level as before) have been part of the higher education system and courses last 2 years.

Since 1985

Prospective teachers of pre-primary, primary and lower secondary level attend a 3-year course at a teacher-training college.

Belgium

Pre-primary

On completion of the course the teachers obtain the:

Diplome d'Institutrice (eur) 'Gardienne'/'Gardien'
Diploma van Kleuterleidster.

Primary

On completion of the course teachers obtain the:

Diplome d'Institutrice (eur) Primaire
Diploma van Lager Onderwijzer (van Lagere Onderwijzeres).

Lower secondary

On completion of the course teachers obtain the qualification of **Regent** with a:
Diplome Agrege de l'Enseignement Secondaire Inferieur
Diploma van Geagregeerde voor het Lager Secundair Onderwijs.

Upper secondary

At this level teachers must be university graduates, with an additional teaching qualification. Students may take the examinations for the teaching qualification

Agregation de l'Enseignement Secondaire Superieur
Agregaat van het Hoger Middelbaar Onderwijs

at the same time as their degree examinations, or later.

Higher

The qualification of

Agrege de l'Enseignement Superieur
Geaggregeerde voor het Hoger Onderwijs

cannot be granted until at least 2 years after the Doctorate has been obtained. The candidate must present an original dissertation, plus 3 theses, defend it in public and give a lecture.

Belize

Before 1960 most of the educational facilities were provided by missionary organizations, mostly from the United States. There are still many schools run by religious organizations and voluntary agencies but with government assistance.

Education is compulsory from age six to fourteen.

The medium of instruction is English.

EVALUATION IN BRITAIN

School

GCE O- and A-levels - of the same standard as GCE O- and A-levels taken in Britain.

Caribbean Examinations Council Secondary Education Certificate - grades 1 and 2 at the general proficiency level have been equated to GCE O-level (grades A, B or C).

Higher

Bachelor degrees - generally considered to compare to British Bachelor degree standard.

Master degrees - generally considered to compare to British Master degree standard.

MARKING SYSTEM

School

Subject examinations for the **Caribbean Examinations Council Secondary Education Certificate** are taken at 3 proficiency levels:

Belize

Basic
General
Technical

The 5 grades awarded are:

Grade I   comprehensive working knowledge of the syllabus

Grade II   working knowledge of most aspects of the syllabus

Grade III   working knowledge of some aspects of the syllabus

Grade IV   limited knowledge of a few aspects of the syllabus

Grade V   insufficient evidence on which to base a judgement

Higher

Bachelor degrees are awarded with the following classifications:

Class I
Class II upper division
Class II lower division

If the performance has been insufficient for Honours, the degree is awarded as a Pass.

SCHOOL EDUCATION

Primary

This covers 6 years, usually from age 6 but pupils may enter at 5. On completion of this cycle, pupils take the **Common Entrance Examination**, which determines entrance to secondary school.

Secondary

This normally covers 7 years divided into 2 cycles, the lower lasting 5 years and the upper 2. On conclusion of the lower cycle, pupils may take the examinations for the GCE O-levels of the British Boards (Associated Examining Board, London, Oxford, and Cambridge Overseas), or (since 1979) the Caribbean Examinations Council **Secondary Education Certificate**.

After a further 2 years, pupils may take the examinations for the GCE A-levels of the British Boards.

Some schools offer an accelerated form of the lower cycle, lasting 4 years instead of 5.

Pupils who do not wish to go beyond the period of compulsory school take a post-primary course lasting 3 years.

Belize

Technical/vocational secondary

Various courses are available, mostly leading to qualifications of the City & Guilds of London Institute, the London Chamber of Commerce, and the Royal Society of Arts.

HIGHER EDUCATION

The <u>University of the West Indies</u> has campuses at Cave Hill in Barbados, St Augustine in Trinidad, and Mona in Jamaica. Admission requirements are based on the British model of 5 GCEs, 2 being at A-level.

Courses leading to the award of the **Bachelor of Arts/Science** degree last 3 years.

Master degree courses generally last 2 years. Research leading to the award of a **Doctorate** takes a minimum of 3 years after the Bachelor degree.

<u>St John's College</u> offers courses based on the American pattern, with a 2-year post-GCE O-level course leading to an **Associate of Arts** degree.

TEACHER EDUCATION

Prospective teachers take 3-year post-GCE O-level courses (2 years study plus 1 year practical work) at 2 training colleges (the Government Training College and St John's Training College).

Benin

People's Republic of Benin

The People's Republic of Benin (known as Dahomey before 1975) became an independent republic within the French Community in 1958; full independence was proclaimed in 1960.

Education is free, universal and compulsory.

The official medium of instruction is French, but the government intends to implement a de-westernization policy involving a gradual shift to national languages.

The academic year runs from October to July.

The school curricula are modelled on those of France, but they are gradually being adapted to local needs and traditions.

EVALUATION IN BRITAIN

School

Brevet d'Etudes du Premier Cycle (BEPC) and **Brevet de Technicien** - generally considered to be below GCE O-level standard.

Baccalaureat/Baccalaureat de Technicien - generally compared to GCE O-level standard; these are the only pre-university courses which satisfy matriculation requirements in Benin.

Diplome Universitaire d'Etudes Litteraires (DUEL), **Diplome Universitaire d'Etudes Scientifiques** (DUES), **Diplome Universitaire d'Etudes Generales** (DUEG) - generally compared to GCE A-level standard.

Maitrise - generally considered to be below the standard of a British Bachelor degree.

Benin

MARKING SYSTEMS

Grades determined for course work and examinations are as follows:

A	14-20
B	12-13
C	10-11
D	9
E	0-8

There are no similar number or letter grades for the **Baccalaureat**. The quality of the examination results is specified in <u>mentions</u>, these being as follows:

passable	acceptable
assez bien	good
bien	very good
tres bien	exceptional

A student may have grades below 9 in one or more subjects and still receive the **Baccalaureat** as long as the overall grade average is 9 or higher.

SCHOOL EDUCATION

Primary

Primary education lasts 6 years and leads to the **Certificat d'Etudes Primaires Elementaires**.

Ruralized schools

In 1967 10 primary schools in central Benin were designated 'ruralized schools', where the teaching of agricultural skills and growing of cash crops would be stressed.

Secondary

Secondary education lasts 7 years, divided into 2 cycles. At the end of the first 4-year cycle, students are awarded the **Brevet d'Etudes du Premier Cycle**. The second 3-year cycle consists of the classe de premiere, classe de seconde and classe terminale. At the end of this cycle successful students obtain the **Baccalaureat**. (Students may choose 1 of 2 options to study in the **Baccalaureat**: either literature or science.

Technical secondary

Technical Lycees offer 6-year secondary courses leading to the **Baccalaureat de Technicien**; the **Certificat d'Aptitude Professionelle** (CAP) is taken after 3 years study and the **Baccalaureat de Technicien** after a further 3 years study.

HIGHER EDUCATION

This is provided in the Universite Nationale du Benin (formerly the Universite du Dahomey founded in 1970) and the College Polytechnique Universitaire.

The university has 5 departments: literary and linguistic studies; scientific and technical studies; agricultural studies; education; medical and paramedical studies. It also incorporates the National Training Institute of Administration and the Institute of Regional Development.

The first phase of studies lasting 2 years leads to the **Diplome Universitaire d'Etudes Litteraires** (DUEL) or the **Diplome Universitaire d'Etudes Scientifiques** (DUES). The DUEL involves specialized work in 1 of the following areas: philosophy, modern literature, foreign languages, linguistics or history and/or geography. In the first year of the DUES there are 2 main options: pure science (mathematics, chemistry, first year's preparation for teaching); and biological science and geology (chemistry, biology, physics). In the second year increased specialization leads to the DUES in mathematics and physics, physics and chemistry, or chemistry, biology and geology.

Students who have the DUES or DUEL may continue their studies for a further 2 years and obtain the **Maitrise**. A further 2 years of study after the Diplome Universitaire d'Etudes Generales (DEUG) is required for the Maitrise in law or economics.

For the Maitrise in the humanities or science, candidates must obtain 2 **Certificats d'Etudes Superieures**.

The **Diplome d'Ingenieur Agronome** is awarded after 5 years successful study of agronomy.

The qualification **Ingenieur de Conception** represents 4 or 5 years study post-Baccalaureat.

The **Doctorat de 3e Cycle** represents 2 or more years study beyond the **Maitrise**, which is obtained in France.

The **Doctorat en Medicine** is obtained after 7 years of university study.

TEACHER EDUCATION

Primary

School teachers are educated in teacher-training colleges of which there are 6 in Benin, 1 for each province. The entrance requirement is the **Brevet d'Etudes du Premier Cycle** (BEPC) and success in a competitive entrance examination. Successful students are awarded the **Certificat Elementaire d'Aptitude Pedagogique** (CEAP).

Secondary

Teachers of lower and upper secondary education are trained at the Ecole Normale Superieure of the University. After 2 years of study there is a competitive examination to enter the Ecole Normale Superieure, Porto Novo which trains teachers for upper secondary education. Those who are unsuccessful enter lower secondary education.

Bermuda

Bermuda is an internally self-governing colony of Britain.

Education is compulsory for children between the ages of five and sixteen, and free for all secondary school children up to the age of nineteen.

The school year runs from September to July.

EVALUATION IN BRITAIN

Bermuda Secondary School Certificate - generally considered to compare to GCE O-level standard, provided that a grade-point average of 2.5 is achieved.

Diploma of Arts and Science (awarded by Bermuda College) - may be accepted in lieu of GCE A-levels.

MARKING SYSTEMS

School

A	4.0	outstanding
B	3.0	very good
C	2.0	good
D	1.0	satisfactory
E	0.0	unsatisfactory

The grade-point average is the sum of grade points over 5 years, divided by the number of courses taken.

SCHOOL EDUCATION

Pre-primary

There are places available for approximately 60% of 4-year-olds.

Bermuda

Primary

This lasts 7 years from age 5.

Secondary

There are 5 government, 4 government-aided and 4 private secondary schools in Bermuda. All government and government-aided schools follow the same curriculum which lasts for 5 years and leads to the **Bermuda Secondary School Certificate**.

This was introduced in 1974 and the first holders gained the qualification in 1979. Previously children sat the Cambridge and London Overseas School Certificate (see Appendix). The Bermuda Secondary School Certificate is based on continuous assessment of the students and includes multiple-choice tests, essay questions, projects, oral examinations and practical work. Compulsory courses are English, mathematics, Bermudan history, Bermudan geography, civics, science and physical education.

FURTHER EDUCATION

Bermuda College is the only post-secondary institution. It has departments in academic studies, business studies, general studies, hotel technology and technology. It has about 3,000 students on both full-time, part-time and evening courses. Some are preparing for GCE A-levels or for a 2-year diploma which will enable them to go on to university education in Britain or the United States. Others are following 2-year vocational courses which are closely linked to the Bermudan economy.

Some evening classes are run by Americans at United States Naval Air Station in conjunction with the University of Maryland.

Queens University of Canada runs correspondence courses in conjunction with the Department of Education.

TEACHER EDUCATION

There are no teacher-training courses in Bermuda. Scholarships are provided annually to enable teachers to train abroad.

Bolivia

Republic of Bolivia

The Education Code of 1955 laid down the structure of the education system. Responsibility for education in urban and rural areas was separated under the Ministry of Education and the Ministry of Rural Affairs, respectively, until 1970 when they were combined. The reforms of 1968 were an attempt to standardize education in urban and rural areas.

Under the Constitution of 1961, education was compulsory for children aged seven to fourteen. Primary education is now compulsory, although there are insufficient facilities to enforce this.

The medium of instruction is Spanish.

The academic year runs from March to December.

EVALUATION IN BRITAIN

School

Bachillerato - generally considered to compare to GCE O-level standard.

Higher

Licenciatura - may be considered to compare to British Bachelor degree standard.

MARKING SYSTEMS

Until 1968:

School and Higher

Marking was on the scale 1-7 (maximum), with 3-6 as the minimum pass mark.

Bolivia

7	excelente
6	muy bueno
5	bueno
4	regular
3	deficiente
2	malo
1	pesimo

1968-72:

Marking was on the scale 1-5 (maximum), with 2.6 the minimum pass mark.

5	excelente
4	bueno
3	regular
2	deficiente
1	malo

Since 1972:

School

Marking is on the scale 1-7 (maximum), with 3.6 the minimum pass mark.

Technical schools and Higher

Marking is on a percentage scale.

SCHOOL EDUCATION

Pre-primary

Some facilities exist for 2-year courses for children up to age 7.

Primary

Until 1968:

This covered 6 years for children from age 7. The curriculum included language, mathematics, civics, natural science, religious instruction, music, handicrafts and physical education.

Since 1968:

This covers 8 years for children from age 7, divided into a basic cycle of 5 years and an intermediate cycle of 3 years. The curriculum of the basic cycle includes mathematics, language, natural science and social studies; physical education, religion and moral education for children in urban schools, health education, agriculture and home economics for children in rural schools. The curriculum of the intermediate cycle covers the same subjects.

Bolivia

Secondary

Until 1968:

This covered 6 years, divided into a lower cycle of 4 years and an upper cycle of 2 years. The curriculum covered language, mathematics, natural science, biology, chemistry, physics, technical drawing, social studies, history, culture, society, political theory, economics, geography, psychology, philosophy, foreign languages, religious instruction, physical education, music and art. Pupils could specialize in social science or physical sciences during the upper cycle.

Since 1968:

This now covers 4 years taken in general academic or technical/vocational courses. The academic course consists of two 2-year cycles. Some schools offer specialization in the second cycle in social studies/economics, chemistry/biology or physics/mathematics. On completion of this cycle pupils take the examinations for the **Bachillerato en Humanidades**.

Technical secondary

The first year of the 4-year course is common for all pupils and covers the same curriculum as that offered on the general academic courses. Pupils may then specialize in industrial, commercial, artistic or agricultural subjects. On successful completion of the course pupils obtain the qualification of **Tecnico Medio/Perito** (skilled worker). They may also obtain the Bachillerato en Humanidades even if they have studied purely science subjects (a Bachillerato en Ciencias used to be awarded).

Adults (students over the age of 18) may attend accelerated courses to complete the primary and secondary course in 6 years and obtain the **Bachiller por Madurez Suficiente**, or take examinations for the **Bachiller Autoensenanza**.

FURTHER EDUCATION

The qualification of **Tecnico Superior** may be obtained on completion of a course lasting 4 years (8 semesters) from the Tecnico Medio or Bachillerato.

HIGHER EDUCATION

Before 1983, to enter the degree courses, students required the Bachillerato or to pass the entrance examination. The curso vestibular, offered by some universities, is a pre-admission course. It is only compulsory at the Universidad Catolica de La Paz.

Students may take as long as they wished to obtain a qualification, although the average is 5-8 years. The first term (curso basico) is common for all pupils. The first qualification is the **Licenciatura**. The **Bachillerato** may be awarded after 4 years study of social science and economics. In 1972 the credit system was introduced. Credits are earned on the basis of the difficulty of a subject and vary from 1 to 6; full-time students usually earn 20-25 credits per semester.

The **Doctorado** may be awarded after a period of original research in law and philosophy. There are 2 other postgraduate courses: development sciences and public health. A **Master** degree may be granted in Medicine.

The duration of studies leading to a particular profession varies:

medicine - 6 years plus 1 year of professional experience leads to the **Doctorado**

dentistry - 5 years

law - 5 years.

Universities also offer courses of 2-4 years leading to the **Tecnico Superior** in nursing, physiotherapy and laboratory technician skills. From 1986, it will be possible to obtain the Tecnico Superior in engineering.

The universities were closed from August 1971 to August 1972 and underwent a series of reforms following the 1971 revolution.

TEACHER EDUCATION

Before 1970 there was no integrated system of teacher training because of the serious differences in the urban and rural parts of the country.

Before 1970:

Urban - Primary

On completion of 4 years secondary education students took a 4-year course leading to a **Diploma de Egreso**. A further 2 years teaching experience led to the title of **Maestra Normal de Educacion Primaria**.

Urban - Secondary

On completion of 6 years secondary education students took a 4-year course leading to a **Diploma de Egreso**. Holders of this could then enter a university or undertake 2 years teaching experience leading to the title of **Profesor de Ensenanza Secundaria**.

Rural - Primary and Secondary

Pupils who completed 6 years primary education undertook a 4-year course leading to a **Diploma de Egreso**. A further 2 years teaching experience led to the **Maestro Normalista Rural**. Pupils who completed 4 or 6 years secondary education took a 2-year course leading to the same qualification.

Since 1970:

Primary (basic and intermediate)

A 3-year course for holders of the secondary school Bachillerato.

Secondary

A 4-year higher education course, plus 2 years of professional experience.

Botswana

Republic of Botswana

Since independence in 1966 the education system of Botswana has been closely connected with those of Lesotho and Swaziland.

No sector of education is as yet compulsory.

The medium of instruction is English.

The academic year runs from January to December for schools and from August to May for universities.

EVALUATION IN BRITAIN

School

Junior certificate - below GCE O-level standard.

Cambridge Overseas School Certificate - grades 1-6 are generally equated to GCE O-level (grades A, B, C).

Higher

Successful completion of **Part 1** (i.e. the first 2 years) of a **Bachelor degree** at the University of Botswana, Lesotho and Swaziland or at the Universities of Botswana and Swaziland is generally considered to bring a student up to GCE A-level standard.

Successful completion of **Part 2** (i.e. a further 2 years) is generally considered to bring a student to a standard between GCE A-level and a British Bachelor degree.

MARKING SYSTEMS

School

Cambridge Overseas School Certificate is graded 1-9.

Botswana

Higher

Until 1967:

A pass with distinction
B pass
C fail

Since 1967:

Results for each Part 1 and Part 2 examination subjects are classified:

A outstanding   80-100%
B superior   70-79
C good   60-69
D pass   50-59
E fail, but may take a supplementary examination
                     40-49
F fail   below 40

The overall results for the examinations are classified:

1st class	average of A
2nd class 1st division	average of B
2nd class 2nd division	average of C
pass	average of D
fail	average of E or F

SCHOOL EDUCATION

Primary

Children begin between the ages of 6 and 8. The course used to last 8 years, divided into 6-year and 2-year cycles. It now lasts 7 years, covering standards 1-7. On completion of this phase of education pupils obtain the **Primary Leaving Certificate (PLC)**/Ministry of Education **Standard VII Primary Certificate**.

Secondary

This covers 5 years, divided into 2 cycles: intermediate (3 years, forms I to III); and senior secondary (2 years, forms IV to V). On completion of form V pupils may take the examinations for the **Cambridge Overseas School Certificate**. There are plans to change to a 7-3-2 structure in the near future and eventually to 6-3-3.

Technical secondary

The Botswana Training Centre, now the Botswana Institute of Administration and Commerce, offers a wide range of post-primary technical and craft courses. It also offers secretarial courses, usually with the junior certificate as the entrance requirement, and operates a range of in-service courses for higher executive officers, statisticians, prison wardens, etc.

Botswana

The Home Craft Centre offers a 2-year post-primary course in home economics and management, leading to a **Home Craft Certificate**; and a 1-year course for qualified teachers to specialize in home craft subjects, leading to a **Home Craft Teachers Certificate**.

St Joseph College runs commercial courses for pupils who have completed form II.

FURTHER EDUCATION

Botswana Polytechnic offers courses leading to the **BTEC National Certificate, National Diploma, Higher Certificate** and **Higher Diploma**.

HIGHER EDUCATION

The University of Basutoland (now Lesotho), Bechuanaland (now Botswana) and Swaziland was founded in 1964 at Roma in Lesotho, to provide facilities for higher education for all three countries. With the independence of Botswana and Lesotho in 1966 it became the University of Botswana, Lesotho and Swaziland. In 1973 a new campus was opened at Gaborone in Botswana with facilities for Part 1 courses (see below) and in 1974 instruction was also offered for Part 2 courses in humanities. When Lesotho withdrew from the arrangement in 1975, Botswana and Swaziland continued their co-operation and the University became the University of Botswana and Swaziland with campuses at Gaborone and Kwaluseni (Swaziland). In July 1982 the 2 constituent colleges of the University of Botswana and Swaziland became independent universities: the University of Botswana and the University of Swaziland.

Degree courses last 4 years (four-and-a-half years in Law) divided into two 2-year cycles, Part 1 and Part 2 (for the LL B there is an additional Part 3 examination). The normal entrance requirement is the Cambridge Overseas School Certificate in 1st or 2nd division, with credit in English language.

There are no facilities for studying engineering, architecture, medicine, pharmacy, dentistry or veterinary medicine. Courses are available leading to an MA, M.Sc. or M.Ed. A wide range of undergraduate certificate and diploma courses are also offered.

TEACHER EDUCATION

Primary

Two courses used to exist to train primary school teachers: the **Primary Lower** and **Primary Higher Certificates**. Since 1973 these courses have been condensed into a 2-year course to be taken at a teacher training college and leading to a **Primary Teachers Certificate**. The entrance requirement for the Lower and Higher Certificates used to be the Primary Leaving Certificate; students must now hold the Junior Certificate although some will also hold the Cambridge Overseas School Certificate. The teacher training colleges are now affiliated to the university.

Secondary

A 2-year advanced teachers course for students holding the Cambridge Overseas School Certificate at the Gaborone campus of the University of Botswana, Lesotho and Swaziland, UBLS, (until 1976) or at the University of Botswana and Swaziland UBS (until 1982) and at the University of Botswana since 1982, leads to a **Teachers Certificate** of the university. Students may also take a 4-year degree course at university leading to a **BA or B.Sc. in Education**.

Brazil

Federative Republic of Brazil

Education in Brazil has traditionally been centrally organized and controlled. The Basic Law of 1961 defined the structure of the system, although the 1971 reform laws radically reorganized the school system both at primary and secondary level.

The official medium of instruction is Portuguese.

The academic year runs from March to December.

EVALUATION IN BRITAIN

School

Certificado de Conclusao de 1° Grau (known before 1971 as the Certificado de Curso Ginasial - generally considered to be below GCE O-level standard.

Certificado de Conclusao de 2° Grau (known before 1971 as the Certificado de Curso Colegial) - generally considered to compare to GCE O-level standard.

Higher

Bacharel (Bacharelado), **Licenciado** (Licenciatura) and **Professional Title** - may be considered to compare to British Bachelor degree standard.

MARKING SYSTEMS

School

Marking is usually on a scale of 1-10 (maximum), with 5 as the minimum pass mark.

Higher

There is a great variety of grading scales (e.g. alphabetical, numerical and percentage), even within the same institution.

Brazil

SCHOOL EDUCATION

In 1971 the Brazilian government enacted legislation promoting extensive reforms in primary and secondary education. All primary and secondary schools now come under direct supervision of the Secretariat of Education, thus providing central control to ensure consistency in standards and to equalize the value of the various secondary level specializations.

Pre-1971:

Primary (ensino primario):

This covered grades 1-4, and was compulsory. On completion, children sat the entrance examination for secondary education.

Secondary (ensino medio):

This lasted 7 years, divided into the primeiro ciclo/curso ginasial, covering grades 5-8, and the segundo ciclo/curso colegial, covering grades 9-11.

It was sometimes possible to stay on for a twelfth year. On completion of the curso colegial pupils obtained the **Certificado do Curso Colegial**. During this cycle pupils could specialize in 1 of 3 branches:

academic (classical and scientific)

technical (industrial, commercial, agricultural and artistic studies, home economics and nursing)

teaching ('normal' schools provided instruction for prospective elementary teachers).

All pupils who completed this course were eligible to sit the university entrance examination (**Concurso Vestibular/Concurso de Habilitacao**).

Post-1971:

Primary (1° grau):

This covers grades 1-8 and is compulsory for children aged 7-14. The selection examination previously required to proceed from grade 4 to grade 5 has been abolished.

Secondary (2° grau):

This covers grades 9-11, with the possibility of staying on for a further year. There is often a local selection examination for entry to this cycle, as there is some competition for the available places.

Pupils no longer specialize in 1 of the previous 3 branches as all schools are required to give an all-round education. Compulsory subjects are: Portuguese language; Brazilian literature; a modern foreign language (normally French or English); history; geography; mathematics; physics; chemistry; biology; art; moral, civil and health education; and physical education. Until 1982 each school had to provide a form of professional education (habilitacao), including a period of practical training for technical students. The option to specialize in teacher training during the cycle of secondary education can now be taken as the professional training during this cycle. At the end of this phase of education, pupils are awarded a **Certificado de Conclusao de 2º Grau** or a **Diploma de Tecnico de Nivel Medio** and may then take the university entrance examination, the **Concurso Vestibular**.

Technical secondary:

Since the 1971 reforms, during the phase of secondary education, pupils may take a course ranging from 2 to 5 years in a variety of technical and vocational fields leading to the qualification of **Certificado de Auxiliar Tecnico** (assistant technician) or **Diploma de Tecnico de Nivel Medio** (technician). Holders of these qualifications may take the university entrance examination.

In 1975, 10 new training fields were established to enable all pupils to receive some basic vocational training (habilitacao basica). Some pupils may leave school having completed this training with the **Certificado de Habilitacao Basica**.

HIGHER EDUCATION

Access to higher education is on the basis of success in the university entrance examination, Concurso Vestibular. A high failure rate in this examination has led to the establishment of 1-year courses, cursinhos, which prepare students specifically to take this examination. The schools offering these courses are also called cursinhos and are privately owned and operated.

There is a numerus clausus (restricted entry) for each faculty, with engineering and medicine being the most prestigious and hence most popular faculties in any institution.

Courses of higher education may be taken at universities, federations or 'isolated' institutions. Federations are groups of independent institutions which have joined together, thus hoping to provide better structured courses of study. The 'isolated' institutions/faculties are usually institutions specializing in a limited range of fields. Within each type, institutions may be federal, state, municipal or private.

Courses vary from 3 to 5 years. After the reforms of 1972 all universities introduced a basic cycle of at least 1 year in either the humanities or science. On completion of a full academic course, students may obtain the **Bacharel**, **Licenciado** or a **Professional Title** (e.g. engenheiro - engineer). In departments where both the **Bacharel** and **Licenciado** are offered, the Bacharel is normally taken by those not considering a teaching career. The **Licenciado** is offered only in fields where a student might wish to undertake secondary or tertiary-level teaching. However it is possible and quite usual for a student to work for and complete the 2 degrees simultaneously; their academic standard would not be raised by obtaining both qualifications.

Students who wish to proceed to postgraduate study must first take an entrance examination. The first level of study usually takes 2 years beyond the undergraduate degree and leads to the qualification of **Mestre/Mestrado**. The **Doutor/Doutorado** requires an additional minimum of 2 years study beyond the Mestre. Under the reforms of 1971 each tertiary-level institution had to adopt the semester credit system, whereby each course carries a fixed number of credits and is completed in 1 semester.

The first qualification to be obtained in medicine is the **Doutor em Medicina** after a 6-year course, which includes a 2-year basic cycle, a 3-year course in clinical sciences and 1 year of practical experience.

TEACHER EDUCATION

Primary

Pre-1971:

During the second cycle of secondary education (curso colegial) pupils could take the teaching specialization.

Post-1971:

During the phase of secondary education (i.e. de 2° grau) pupils can undertake teacher training during the period of professional training. Training taken over 3 years qualifies the person to teach in grades 1-4, and training taken over 4 years qualifies the person to teach in grades 1-6. The qualification obtained is the **Diploma de Professor do Ensino de 1° Grau**.

Secondary

The requirement for teaching at the secondary level and for the seventh and eighth years of primary schools (since 1971) is completion of the course leading to the **Licenciatura**.

Higher

The first level is **Auxiliar de Ensino**, for which teachers must hold a Bacharel/Licenciatura/Professional Title. Teachers must remain in this post for at least 2 years and usually no more than 4 years.

The position of **Professor Asistente** requires the degree of Mestre, and that normally of **Professor Adjunto** the degree of Doutor, although promotion to a higher rank is possible as a result of long service. The rank of professor was known as **Catedratico**, but is now **Professor Titular**.

ADULT EDUCATION

Facilities are available for people who left school before completing their primary or secondary education to return to school to further or complete their education (ensino supletivo). There are no age limits for entering supletivo courses but students must be 18 to receive the **1° Grau Diploma** and 21 to receive the **2° Grau Certificate**. The diploma or certificate awarded is of equal value to that obtained by students under the normal system. Students may then go on to take the university entrance examinations.

Brunei

Education has only been widely available since 1954, but it is free and available to all.

There are two media of instruction, either English or Bahasa Malay.

The school year runs from January to December.

EVALUATION IN BRITAIN

Cambridge Overseas School Certificate - grades 1-6 are equated to GCE O-level (grades A, B or C).

Cambridge A-levels - grades A-E are equated to GCE A-level.

Matriculation - from 1986 ex-Malay medium school pupils take a matriculation course at the Sixth Form Centre, followed by an examination designed and validated by Brunei University.

Chinese schools offer a **1-year post O-level course** as preparation for entry to the University of Taiwan.

MARKING SYSTEMS

See Appendix on Cambridge Overseas School Certificate.

SCHOOL EDUCATION

Primary

About 70% of children attend government primary schools where the medium of instruction is Malay for the first 3 years. The remainder attend private schools where the medium of instruction is English or Chinese (Mandarin). The private schools follow the same system as government schools.

Brunei

After 3 years in primary school all pupils sit standardized tests, and take the **Primary Certificate of Education** at approximately age 11.

All pupils entering the primary school system after 1984 follow 6 years primary education of which the final 3 (after the standardized tests) are bilingual: English and Malay.

Secondary

After 3 years in secondary schools, students take the **Brunei Junior Certificate of Education** in Malay or English. Subjects covered include: Malay, English, mathematics, integrated science, history, geography and Islamic studies. For some this is the school leaving certificate. A further 2 years is required to sit the **Cambridge O-levels** in Malay or English.

All pupils entering the secondary school system from 1985 follow the 3-year bilingual programme leading to the **Junior Certificate of Education** which is a qualifying examination for entry to upper secondary level, academic or technical streams.

Academic courses lead to the **Cambridge Overseas School Certificate** examinations, although most enter privately for **University of London GCE** examinations. Technical courses lead to **City & Guilds**, RSA, or BTEC examinations.

Those who continue their education go to the Sixth Form Centre and take **Cambridge A-level examinations**.

The private schools only teach to O-level standard and most of their pupils continue their education overseas.

FURTHER EDUCATION

The Institute Teknologi Brunei (ITB) offers courses in business studies, computer studies and electrical/electronic engineering. Courses last 2 years plus 6 months industrial placement. The entry qualification is 4 O-levels plus 1 A-level or BTEC.

An Institute of Nursing is being developed under a link with the Welsh School of Medicine.

City & Guilds craft-level courses are offered to lower secondary school leavers. BTEC National Certificate/Diploma technician courses are offered after O-level.

Sinaut Agricultural College offers its own technician's award.

HIGHER EDUCATION

The University Brunei Darussalam (UBD) opened in October 1985, with assistance from University College Cardiff and Leeds University.

Brunei

The following 4-year Honours bilingual degree programmes are offered to matriculants (those holding 2 A-level passes):

BA in Education (currently Malay-medium only) - Islamic studies, Malay language and literature, education studies and teaching practice

B.Sc. in Education - maths, physics, chemistry and biology majors, education studies and teaching practice

BA in history/geography; history/economics; geography/economics

BA in Business Management and Public Administration

BA in Social Policy and Planning.

TEACHER EDUCATION

The Sultan Hassanal Bolkiah Teacher's College has been upgraded to an <u>Institute of Education</u>.

It runs several courses:

1. 3-year **Certificate in Education** course with an entry requirement of 4 O-levels

2. In-service courses for primary school teachers

3. 2-year in-service course leading to the **Bachelor of Education** in conjunction with University College Cardiff and validated by the University of Wales

4. From 1986 a **BA (Primary Education)** awarded by the University Brunei Darussalam will be offered on a pre-service basis.

Bulgaria

People's Republic of Bulgaria

National programmes for the implementation of educational reform covering the period of 1979 to 1993, include changes in the content of instruction, the organization of instruction, an emphasis on creativity, and polytechnic vocational training.

Education is free and compulsory for children aged seven to sixteen (grades 1-8). However, primary education usually starts at age six. By 1993 compulsory education will comprise the first ten grades.

The medium of instruction is Bulgarian. Specialized secondary schools provide training in some foreign languages (English, French, German or Russian) between the so-called preparatory grade and grade 9.

The school year runs from September to June and consists of two terms.

EVALUATION

Diploma Za Zavarsheno Sredno Obrazovanie - (Diploma for Completed Secondary Education) - may be considered to satisfy the general requirement of universities and polytechnics; some institutions may require passes in 2 approved subjects at GCE A-level and students must satisfy the English language requirement.

Diploma Za Zavarsheno Visshe Obrazovanie (Diploma for Higher Education) - generally compared to British Bachelor degree standard.

Diploma za Kandidat na Naukite - Ph.D.

Diploma za Doctor na Naukite - D.Sc.

MARKING SYSTEM

The grading system (1-6 with a minimum pass mark of 3) is the same for all levels:

1 poor
2 insufficient
3 fair
4 good
5 very good
6 excellent

Bulgaria

SCHOOL EDUCATION

Pre-school

This caters for children aged 3-6. It is conducted in specialized, half-day, full-day and weekly kindergartens (Detski Gradini). These often operate with nurseries for children aged 1-3, though the nurseries are under the Ministry of Public Health. About 85% of all children receive pre-school education.

Secondary

This comprises 3 stages and as many cycles of the general-education and polytechnical training.

The first stage (general-education) consists of 3 cycles: initial (grades 1-3), primary (grades 4-8), and basic secondary (grades 9-10). The general education programme includes natural science, mathematics, social and humanitarian studies.

The second and third stages combine general education and vocational training; studies are conducted in the schools, while practical training takes place in specialized centres. This covers grade 11 and, for some more complex occupations, there is an additional grade 12.

Successful completion leads to a **Diploma za Zavarsheno Sredno Obrazovanie** (Diploma for Secondary Education) and a document of occupational proficiency. A certificate of education and document of occupational proficiency are also available for those who have not completed secondary education.

Almost all students complete primary education and 97% undergo secondary education. The forms of training after the compulsory period of education include regular, extramural and evening courses. Extramural and evening courses are popular mainly for post-secondary and higher education, and cater for about 25% of the students.

There are 4 types of school and college:

<u>Unified secondary polytechnical schools</u> of the general type.

<u>Unified secondary polytechnical schools</u> with provisions for teaching in foreign languages. Students are admitted on the basis of competitive examinations in Bulgarian language and mathematics after grade 7; the leaving certificate after grade 7 is also taken into account. The first school year is a preparatory one.

<u>Technical colleges</u> provide 4-years training in economics, various branches of technology, agriculture, applied arts, music, sports, etc. Admission is competitive. The arts schools admit students of different age-groups, depending on what they specify.

<u>Secondary vocational-technical schools</u> provide 3-years training in various technical branches, in services, etc.

All secondary schools award the **Diploma za Zavarsheno Sredno Obrazovanie** (Diploma for Secondary Education) required for entry to higher education.

Bulgaria

Special

There is a network of boarding schools, entirely supported by the state, for children with physical or mental disabilities.

HIGHER EDUCATION

<u>Technical colleges</u> admit secondary school graduates for a 2-year course. They usually train medical personnel (human and veterinary), economists and technicians.

<u>Semi-higher institutes</u> (Poluvisshi Instituti) offer a 3-year course. They are primarily for teachers for pre-school institutions and certain disciplines at primary level, such as labour education, music and drawing. In 1985, it was decided to abolish them after students had finished their studies. They will become faculties of the higher pedagogical institutes and of the universities, to conform with the requirement for higher education for all teachers.

There are 3 universities, 10 higher schools of technology, 2 higher pedagogical institutes, 3 economic, 2 agricultural and 5 medical institutes, and 1 institute for physical education and sports. There are also 2 institutes for foreign students studying the Bulgarian language, which include courses in foreign languages for Bulgarians.

Entry to higher education institutions is on the basis of competitive examinations and the Diploma za Zavarsheno Sredno Obrazovanie. The examinations, vocational trends, number of first-year students and other conditions are determined each year by the Ministry of Education.

The period of training at higher education institutions varies from 4-and-a-half to 6 years, depending on speciality. Undergraduates also undertake relevant research. Over 50% of students receive state scholarships.

Those who complete higher education by submitting a diploma paper or a thesis, or by passing the necessary state examination, can begin a postgraduate course or get a job.

A scientific degree known as **Candidat na Naukite** is awarded to those who successfully defend a dissertation. A still higher degree is that of **Doctor na Naukite**, awarded for notable contributions to science.

Higher education institutions have special departments for postgraduate professional training which include courses in advanced areas of science and technology. These courses are usually full- or part-time but there are extramural courses. Diplomas are awarded for successful completion.

Bulgaria

TEACHER EDUCATION

Universities and pedagogical institutes provide opportunities for advanced teaching qualifications. The system also includes specialization abroad, scholarships, and research work.

Research workers and lecturers at higher education institutions undergo an obligatory course of pedagogical training. Centres for pedagogical studies and for professional qualifications have been set up at these institutions. Sofia University plays a leading role in this respect.

There are specialized research institutes at the Ministry of Education, such as the Research Institute in Higher Education, the Research Institute in Vocational Training and the Research Institute in General Education. Other institutes cover modern methods and educational materials.

MILITARY EDUCATION

Military Service is obligatory for young men after the age of 18. They can take their competitive entrance examination before their military service which lasts 3 years in the navy and 2 years for all other services. The period of training at the higher military educational establishments is recognised as normal military service. These establishments are under the Ministry of Defence.

Burkina

Burkina Faso

This chapter covers the period since independence was gained in 1960. The education system is based on the French pattern.

There is no compulsory education.

The medium of instruction is French.

The academic year runs from October to June.

EVALUATION IN BRITAIN

School

Baccalaureat/Diplome de Bachelier de l'Enseignement du Second Degre - generally compared to GCE O-level standard.

Higher

Licence - generally considered somewhat above GCE A-level standard.

MARKING SYSTEMS

School and Higher

Marking is on a scale of 0-20, with 10 as the minimim pass mark.

16-20	very good
14-15	good
12-13	quite good
10-11	average

SCHOOL EDUCATION

Primary

This covers 6 years.

Secondary

This covers 7 years, divided into a 4-year lower cycle followed by a 3-year upper cycle. The lower cycle may be taken at a <u>College d'Enseignement General</u> or a <u>Lycee</u> and culminates in the **Brevet d'Etudes du Premier Cycle**. The upper cycle may be taken only at a Lycee and leads to the examinations for the **Baccalaureat/Diplome de Bachelier de l'Enseignement du Second Degre**. This is available in a variety of series depending on the student's specialization:

A   philosophie-lettres, options A1-A5
B   economique et social
C   sciences mathematiques et physiques
D   sciences mathematiques et naturales
E   mathematiques et technique

Technical secondary

The **Certificat d'Aptitude Professionnelle** (CAP) is taken in place of the **Brevet d'Etudes du Premier Cycle** (BEPC) in Colleges d'Enseignement Technique (i.e. after 4 years).

On completion of the upper cycle in a technical specialization, pupils take the examinations for the **Baccalaureat de Technician/Diplome de Bachelier de Technicien** available in 3 series:

E   mathematics and technical
F1   mechanical construction
F2   electrical
G1   administration
G2   accounting/management

HIGHER EDUCATION

There is only 1 university, the <u>University of Ouagadougou</u>. It was established in 1965 as the Ecole Normale Superieure, became the Centre d'Enseignement Superieur in 1969, and obtained its present status in 1974.

The entrance requirement to degree courses is the Baccalaureat/Diplome de Bachelier de l'Enseignement du Second Degre.

2 years study in the humanities leads to the **Diplome d'Etudes Universitaires Generales** (DEUG). After a further year in the humanities, students obtain the **Licence**, and after a fourth year the **Maitrise**. A similar pattern is followed in all the university institutes (Law, Medicine, Economics, Technology, Sciences, Mathematics, Engineering, Film Production).

TEACHER EDUCATION

Primary

Teachers are trained at secondary-level training colleges.

Secondary

Teachers are trained in the appropriate department or institute. English teachers are trained in the Department de Langues Vivante by means of a teacher-training option in the third year.

Burma

Socialist Republic of the Union of Burma

Since the establishment in 1962 of the Revolutionary Government, the Higher Education Law of 1964 and the Basic Education Law of 1966 have been promulgated and constitute the fundamental educational legislation.

Education is not compulsory.

With independence in 1948 Burmese became the official language, though English was permitted and was the official medium of instruction in schools. Since the military coup of 1962 Burmese has become the medium of instruction at all levels except in professional institutes (such as medicine and technology) where English is also used.

The school year officially begins in June and ends in March, but variations of a month or more are frequent.

EVALUATION IN BRITAIN

School

Basic Education High School Examination (Matriculation) - generally considered to compare to GCE O-level standard.

Higher

Bachelor (Honours) degree - generally considered to compare to British Bachelor (Ordinary) degree standard.

MARKING SYSTEMS

School

Marking is on a percentage scale; a minimum average of 45% is required for university entrance.

Higher

Until 1964/5:

5 excellent
4 good
3 satisfactory
2 unsatisfactory
1 poor

For the first year of study the minimum pass mark for individual subjects was 2, although the minimum mark for the sum of 6 single subjects was 15.

For the second, third and fourth years of study the lowest pass mark for the main subject was 3, for the other subjects 2.5, and the minimum average 2.5.

Since 1964/5:

A percentage scale has been used. The minimum mark required for admission to the second, third and fourth years of courses is 45%; 50% in medicine.

SCHOOL EDUCATION

Primary and secondary

Before the changes implemented in the system by the new government, school education was arranged as follows:

primary standards	I - IV
middle	V - VII
high	VIII - IX.

There was no fixed age for entry at the primary stage, although most children started at 7.

From 1952 to 1961 the **Matriculation** examination was held on completion of standard IX in conjunction with the **High School Final Examination** (HSF). From the academic year 1961/2 an extra year of high school was introduced for the **Matriculation** examination which then became a separate examination. From 1961 to 1963 it was conducted by the Joint Matriculation Board of the Universities of Rangoon and Mandalay.

In the early 1970s primary education was extended to cover standards I-V inclusive. Many children will previously have attended pre-schools from age 3 or 4, and kindergarten at age 5 before proceeding to primary school at age 6. All schools are state-controlled except the Phone Gyi Khaungs, monastery schools run for small children by the Burmese clergy.

Middle schools cover standards V-VIII, and high schools standards IX and X. At the end of middle school the annual examination is now an internal examination conducted by the heads of the state schools. At the end of standard X, students may take the **Basic Education High School Examination** (Matriculation). According to their aggregate mark for all subjects, successful candidates were placed in merit order on the 'A' or 'B' lists. Those on the 'A' list could proceed to Regional Colleges and thence to professional institutes or universities; those on the 'B' list became e.g. primary teachers after professional training. The 'A' and 'B' lists were amalgamated in 1980.

English is introduced at standard V, and both English and Burmese are compulsory subjects in the Matriculation examination.

Technical secondary

The State Technical High School prepares students for admission to the government technical institutes, for employment in industry as apprentices, and for admission to the study of engineering at the higher education level.

A few trade schools (formerly called artisan training centres) provide 2 years of training for middle school leavers.

A number of agricultural schools provide training either at middle or high school levels.

FURTHER EDUCATION

2 government Technical Institutes at Insein and Mandalay offer 3-year courses in: building construction; railway, highway and municipal technology; machine tool design technology; diesel power and heavy equipment; electric power; electronics; and mining. Entry is with the Matriculation and success in an entrance examination.

The Agricultural Institute at Pyinmana offers post-secondary training for agricultural extension workers and for teachers of vocational agriculture in the high schools. Entrants must have passed the Matriculation and **Regional College Final Exams** or be junior assistant teachers.

HIGHER EDUCATION

Before 1964

Rangoon University was re-established on a unitary basis following the end of the Second World War. By 1963 it comprised the Central University in Rangoon and constituent colleges in Moulmein and Bassein, the Engineering Faculty being the Rangoon Institute of Technology.

The University of Mandalay, formerly a constituent college of Rangoon University, consisted of the main university at Mandalay and constituent colleges in Taunggyi, Magwe and Myitkyina.

Students who passed the Matriculation examination and were admitted to the university followed a 2-year course of foundation studies, including both their major field and general education terminating in the intermediate examinations. Those who passed these examinations were awarded the **Intermediate Certificate**, which represented 12 years schooling. (11 years for students who entered the university before 1962). An additional 2 years of study led to the award of a **Bachelor of Arts** or **Bachelor of Science** degree. Students who passed their intermediate examinations with sufficiently high marks could opt for a somewhat more concentrated 2-year arts or 3-year science course, leading to a BA or B.Sc. Honours degree.

1-2 years study was required beyond an Honours degree for the award of a **Master of Arts** or **Master of Science**. Normally holders of BA or B.Sc. Pass degrees were not admitted to study for the Master degree unless they had completed an additional 2-year qualifying course.

The **Bachelor of Medicine and Surgery** (MBSS) represented completion of a 7-year course of pre-medical and medical study beyond the intermediate level. The **B.Sc. Engineering** represented 6 years of study, and agriculture and forestry usually required 5 years.

The University for Adult Education in Rangoon was not a degree-granting institution.

There was extensive unrest and agitation at the universities in 1963.

Since 1964

With the promulgation of the Union of Burma University Education Law in 1964, the new government undertook the reorganization of the universities and higher institutes of learning. The reorganization decentralized the Universities of Rangoon and Mandalay and transformed many of their component parts into separate institutions. The University for Adult Education achieved degree-granting status as the Workers' College. Admission is still on the basis of matriculation results, but, depending on performance in this examination, students are admitted to either their first, second or third choice of institution.

Pass degrees are now obtained on successful completion of a 4-year course, and **Honours degrees** after a 5-year course.

In 1977 the Regional Colleges were established: these offer courses for the first 2 years of tertiary education. A further examination is then taken as a leaving qualification from the regional college and yet another as entrance to university. Those with the best marks proceed to the final parts of their course. Usually students with the best marks go to the socially prestigious Institutes of Medicine and Technology.

TEACHER EDUCATION

Primary

1 year of training after successfully completing middle school at a teacher-training institute or college (the latter has a higher status) is required for certification as a primary assistant teacher (PAT).

Burma

Middle school

Originally a 1-year course, this was extended in 1961/2 to a 2-year course for students holding the **High School Final Examination**. The course is taken at a teacher-training college and leads to the student being certified as a junior assistant teacher. If a PAT certificate is already held (as is often the case), the middle school training course is only 1 year.

High school

Teachers are trained at the Institute of Education, Rangoon (formerly Faculty of Education at Rangoon University). 3 courses are available: **BA in Education (BA Ed.)** awarded after 2 years beyond the **Intermediate Certificate; Diploma in Education** awarded after 1 year beyond the BA or B.Sc.; and **B.Ed.** awarded after 1 year beyond the Diploma in Education.

Burundi

Republic of Burundi

Since the country's accession to independence in 1962 there has been a number of educational reforms, in particular the reforms of secondary education in 1964 and of primary education in 1970.

Free schooling was introduced when the Republic was proclaimed, in November 1966, although as yet no sector is compulsory.

French is one of the official media of instruction; the others are the indigenous languages.

EVALUATION IN BRITAIN

School

Diplome des Humanites Completes - generally considered to compare to GCE O-level standard.

Higher

Bachelor degree - generally compared to British Bachelor (Ordinary) degree standard.

MARKING SYSTEMS

School

90-100%	excellence
80-89	la plus grande distinction
70-79	grande distinction
60-69	distinction
50-59	satisfaction
below 50%	failure

Burundi

Higher

As above.

SCHOOL EDUCATION

Primary

Some primary schools also offer facilities for pre-primary classes (classes gardiennes).

Primary education covers 6 years from age 6 and is divided into three 2-year cycles. There is now officially a seventh year of primary education which is intended as preparation for secondary school. Some schools still offer only the first 2 cycles.

Kirundi is the medium of instruction, with French as a compulsory subject each year.

Secondary

General secondary education covers 6 years, divided into 2 cycles, the lower 2 years, and the upper 4 years. In the first year of the upper cycle pupils choose 1 of 2 streams (modern or Latin); there are 4 divisions in the second and third years (modern, classical, scientific and economic). In the final year of this cycle there are 5 divisions; modern, classical, science A, science B and economics. Only pupils who specialize in the Latin division in the first year of this cycle may be admitted to the classical division in the second year. Only pupils who specialize in the science division in the third year may take science A or B in the final year. The second cycle leads to the **Diplome des Humanites Completes**.

Technical/vocational secondary

Pupils wishing to undertake a technical specialization during secondary education may attend a 7-year course leading to the qualification of **Technician**.

Craft schools offer 2-, 3- and 4-year courses in a variety of fields, beyond primary school.

The intermediate social schools provide a 4-year general course in the humanities specifically for girls.

HIGHER EDUCATION

The <u>Universite Officielle de Bujumbura</u> was established in 1964 by a Royal decree, which transformed the former College du Saint-Esprit, founded by the Roman Catholic Society of Jesus in Bujumbura in 1960, into a joint enterprise between the Government and the Church. The University now comprises 4 faculties (philosophy and arts, economic and social sciences, science, and law). The first stage of study lasts 1-2 years and is generally based. A further year in the faculty of law leads to the **Baccalaureat en Droit**, and a further 2 years to the **Licence**. In other subjects, students may obtain the **Candidature** if they complete 2-3 years study after the first stage of 1-2 years. They must then complete their studies abroad.

Burundi

The entrance requirement for a course at the University is the Diplome des Humanites Completes, which must be validated by a commission of the Ministry of National Education and Culture. For courses in civil engineering, mathematics and physics pupils must also pass a special entrance examination.

TEACHER EDUCATION

Primary

Teachers are trained on 7-year secondary-level courses. On completion of the full course pupils obtain a secondary school certificate and the ordinary teachers diploma.

Secondary

The higher teacher-training school (Ecole Normale Superieure) was established in 1965 and trains teachers for the lower and upper cycles. The entrance level is the secondary school certificate or successful completion of the course at the primary teacher-training school.

Cameroon

Republic of Cameroon

Cameroon was a German colony from 1884 to 1916. France administered the former East Cameroon from 1916 to 1959. It became independent in January 1960 as the Republic of Cameroon and was joined in October by the former British-administered territory of the Southern Cameroon, after which it was known as the United Republic of Cameroon until 1984 when 'United' was dropped.

Two different education systems operate in Cameroon, one in the former British south-west and north-west provinces and the other in the eight former French provinces. The former British provinces follow broadly the British model of education, while the former French provinces follow that of France.

Education is compulsory from age six to eleven.

The medium of instruction is English in the two anglophone provinces and French elsewhere.

The academic year runs from September to June in the east and from October to June in the west.

EVALUATION IN BRITAIN

School

Anglophone:

Cameroon **GCE O-** and **A-level** examinations - generally compared to British O- and A-level standards.

Francophone:

Baccalaureat - generally considered to lie between GCE O- and A-level standards.

Higher

Licence (from the University of Yaounde) - awarded with high average marks, has been compared to British Bachelor degree standard.

Maitrise - may be compared to British M.Phil. standard.

Cameroon

MARKING SYSTEMS

School

Anglophone:

The GCE O- and A-levels are marked as in Britain.

Francophone:

Marking for the Baccalaureat is on a scale of 0-20 (maximum) with 10 as the pass mark:

16-20	tres bien	very good
14-15	bien	good
12-13	assez bien	fair
10-11	passable	pass
0- 9	fail	fail

Higher

The same marking score is used as for francophone secondary education. The degrees of Master and Doctorate may be awarded with the following classifications:

Tres honorable avec felicitations du jury
Tres honorable
Honorable

SCHOOL EDUCATION

Primary

Anglophone:

After 7 years of primary school, students take the **First School Leaving Certificate Examination** and the **Government Common Entrance Examination**. Students can leave school with the First School Leaving Certificate, but success in both is essential for entry to secondary school.

Francophone:

After 7 years of primary education students take 2 national examinations to determine their entry to secondary school. These are the **Certificat d'Etudes Primaires Elementaires (CEPE)**, also called the **Concours d'Entree en Sixieme**. Only enough students are passed to fill the places available in the first year of secondary school (sixieme).

Cameroon

Secondary

Anglophone:

The first cycle of secondary education consists of a 5-year course leading to the Cameroon GCE O-level. The Cameroon education authorities are assisted in the setting and marking of GCE O- and A-levels by the London Board.

The Cameroon College of Arts, Science and Technology offers 2-year courses leading to GCE A-level examinations.

Francophone:

General secondary education is provided by Colleges d'Enseignement General (CEG), Colleges d'Enseignement Secondaire (CES) and Lycées. The premier cycle covering the first few years leads to the Brevet d'Etudes du Premier Cycle (BEPC). At the Lycees only, the second cycle leads to the Baccalaureat.

Technical and vocational secondary

Anglophone:

Secondary technical pupils take the City and Guilds Craft examinations or the Certificat d'Aptitude Professionelle (CAP). In commercial schools, students can enter for the Royal Society of Arts (RSA) Stage 2 examinations or the CAP after the first cycle. Those who continue to the second cycle take the RSA Stage 3 or GCE A-levels. For more vocationally oriented students there are Sections Artisanales Rurales (SAR) as well as the Manual Arts Centre (for boys only) which operate on a day-release basis. Sections Menageres (homecraft centres) also offer some basic academic courses, but without formal examinations.

Francophone:

First-cycle education leading to the Certificat d'Aptitude Professionelle in industrial and commercial subjects is available in the Colleges d'Enseignement Technique (CETI). Second-cycle education is covered by the Lycees Techniques and some private CETIs which offer a 3-year course leading to the Baccalaureat or the Brevet de Technicien (technician's diploma). The Brevet provides the opportunity for specialization in surveying, manufacturing engineering, automobile engineering, or metalwork. The Baccalaureat can be taken in the following options: mathematics and technology; general mechanics; electronics; electrotechnology; civil engineering; or industrial cooling systems.

Sections Artisanales Rurales and Sections Menageres offer 2-year post-primary courses in vocational subjects. No certificates or diplomas are awarded.

HIGHER EDUCATION

Access to the University of Yaounde is based on the first Baccalaureat or GCE A-level examinations. The first stage of higher education leads after 2 years to the Diplome d'Etudes Scientifiques Generales (DESG) or the Diplome d'Etudes Litteraires Generales (DELG). The second phase of 1-2 years study leads to the Licence (either

Libre or **d'Enseignement**) and to a **Diplome d'Etudes Superieures** after a further year. A second cycle of 1-2 years leads to the **Maitrise** or a further professional qualification. A third cycle of 2 or more years culminates in the **Doctorat du Troisieme Cycle**, or the highest qualification, the **Doctorat d'Etat**.

The Ecole Nationale Superieure Polytechnique is part of the University. It offers 3-year courses in electronic, electromechanical or civil engineering, leading to the qualification of **ingenieur de travaux** (site engineer) and 5-year courses in either civil or industrial engineering, leading to the qualification of **ingenieur de conception** (design engineer).

The Ecole Nationale de Technologie offers 2-year courses for foremen, 4-year technician courses (the entrance requirement for both being the CAP) and a 3-year site engineers' course for applicants holding the Baccalaureat.

Agricultural education is provided by various government institutions.

Medical training is provided by the Centre Universitaire des Sciences de la Sante.

TEACHER EDUCATION

Primary

Anglophone:

Students with the Primary School Leaving Certificate and 3 years teaching experience are eligible for the Grade III teachers' **Certificat d'Aptitude de Maitre d'Enseignement General**. For the Grade II **Certificat d'Aptitude Pedagogique d'Instituteur Adjoint**, 3 or more O-levels are the entrance requirement. GCE A-levels are required for the **Certificat d'Aptitude Pedagogique d'Instituteur**.

Francophone:

Ecoles Normales d'Instituteurs Adjoints (ENIA) offer 1-year courses after the BEPC. The Ecoles Normales d'Instituteurs (ENI) offer 2-year courses after the Brevet d'Etudes du Premier Cycle and 3-year courses after the Baccalaureat. Students who complete ENIA courses do not receive certificates but are registered as **Instituteurs Adjoints**.

Secondary

Before 1979:

Students with the Baccalaureat or GCE A-levels used to take the **Diplome d'Etudes Superieures** after a 3-year course. With this qualification they were eligible to take the **Certificat d'Aptitude Pedagogique d'Enseignement Secondaire**.

Since 1979:

The qualification obtained after the first 3-year cycle has been renamed the **Diplome de Professeur des Colleges d'Enseignement General**. Entry to the second cycle is now restricted to graduates with experience.

Canada

Responsibility for the organization and administration of public education in Canada is exercised by the ten provincial and territorial governments: Alberta, British Columbia, Manitoba, New Brunswick, Newfoundland, Nova Scotia, Ontario, Prince Edward Island, Quebec and Saskatchewan. The Federal government is directly concerned only with schools for Indian children and certain special schools, although it does exercise exclusive jurisdiction over education in the Yukon Territory and the Northwest Territories.

All children must attend school from age six or seven to fifteen or sixteen.

French and English are the official languages of Canada, but the predominant medium of instruction is English, except in Quebec.

EVALUATION IN BRITAIN

School

It is generally considered that a student qualified to enter university in Canada would be qualified for admission to a degree course in Britain, although not all universities and polytechnics accept this.

Diplome d'Etudes Collegiales (from Quebec) - generally considered comparable to GCE A-level standard.

Higher

Bachelor (Ordinary) degree - generally considered comparable to a British Bachelor (Ordinary) degree.

Bachelor (Honours) degree - generally considered comparable to a British Bachelor (Honours) degree.

Master degree - generally compared to a British Master degree.

MARKING SYSTEMS

School

Alberta

High School Achievement Statement:

departmental examinations - percentage scale
performance in non-examinable subjects - letter grading

Before 1969:

H	80-100%
A	65-79
B	50-64
C	40-49
D	0-39

After 1969:

Marks for subjects in grades X, XI and XII are reported in percentages. For physical education and fine arts taken in grades X and XI, schools may use either letter grades or a percentage scale.

A	80-100%
B	65-79
C	50-64
D	40-49
F	below 40
P	pass

Effective 1983:

Government examinations were re-introduced in 7 grade XII subjects. Transcripts indicate 3 grades for such courses: a teacher grade, a departmental mark and a final grade, which is the average of the other 2 grades. The final grade is used for determining entrance to post-secondary institutions. The pass grade in grade XII courses was changed to 50%.

British Columbia

Senior Secondary School Statement:

A	86-100%
B	73-85
C+	67-72
C	60-66
P	50-59
F	below 50
I	incomplete
CS	secondary school subject taken by correspondence study

Canada

Manitoba

High School Graduation Diploma/Statement of Standing:

A+	90-100%	honours
A	80-89	excellent
B	70-79	good
C	56-69	average
D	50-55	pass
F	below 50	fail

New Brunswick

High School/Grade 12 Diploma: a percentage scale.

Newfoundland

Pass Certificate: 36 credits including 21 'core' credits.

Graduation Diploma with Distinction:
satisfies minimum graduation requirements, + 550 or more marks in 7 level III courses.

Graduation Diploma with Honours:
satisfies minimum graduation requirements, + 550 or more marks in 7 university preparatory level III courses, as specified by the Department of Education.

Nova Scotia

High School Diploma: a percentage scale.

Ontario

Secondary School Graduation Diploma (SSGD) - grade XII

Secondary School Honours Graduation Diploma (SSHGD) - grade XIII

Ontario Secondary School Diploma (OSSD) - from 1986

One credit is granted on successful completion of a course for which a minimum of 110 hours has been scheduled. No credit is assigned to courses completed before the introduction of the credit system.

Achievement:

A	80-100
B	70-79.9
C	60-69.9
D	50-59.9
P	Pass

Equivalent standing toward the SSGD and the OSSD may be granted for:

Maturity - on the basis of age and length of time out of school.

Equivalent education - equivalent courses not normally identified as secondary education, but not post-secondary education. Equivalent secondary education courses completed outside Ontario.

Canada

Apprenticeship training - on the basis of successful completion of each period of appropriate apprenticeship training.

Music - standing toward the SSGD, SSHGD, OSSD and OAC (Ontario Academic Courses) may also be granted for appropriate work completed at a recognized conservatory, college or school of music.

Level of difficulty - no level of difficulty has been assigned for courses completed before 1979/80.

B   Basic-level courses focus on social and personnel skills, as well as preparation for direct entry into employment.

G   General-level courses are appropriate preparation for employment or further non-university education.

A   Advanced-level courses are appropriate preparation for grade 13 and OAC courses, and focus on theoretical knowledge as well as fundamental knowledge and practical applications. All grade-13 courses are at the advanced level of difficulty and are preparation for university entrance.

OAC   Ontario Academic Courses are at the advanced level of difficulty and are preparation for university entrance.

Prince Edward Island

High School Diploma: percentage scale.

Quebec

High School Diploma/Secondary Grade V Certificate: unit credit system.

A unit represents the measure of the value of a course. A course which requires the equivalent of 1 period of instruction per day throughout the school year yields 2 units. On the certificate this is indicated by the last digit of each subject code (a 6-digit code).

CEGEP Diploma: (see under Quebec school education):
percentage scale, 60 being the lowest pass mark. The mark received is reported with the average of the section of the course in which the student is registered.

Saskatchewan

Record of High School Standing: credit system.

Further education

Community colleges use a percentage scale or letter grades, which are then computed to a yearly average. The average is based on a 4-0 scale.

Higher education

Depending on the individual institution, 1 of 3 systems may be used:

percentage
alphabetical (A-F)
pass/fail.

ALBERTA

School education

Education is compulsory to age 16.

Primary lasts for 6 years, covering grades I-VI, and is sometimes referred to as Division 1 (years 1-3) and Division 2 (years 4-6).

Secondary lasts for 6 years, divided into junior high school - 3 years (grades VII-IX, Division 3), and senior high school - 3 years (grades X-XII, Division 4).

Compulsory subjects in junior high school are language arts, social studies, mathematics, science, physical education and health.

All courses in senior high school are numbered in decads: numbers 10-19 represent grade X courses, 20-29 grade XI and 30-39 grade XII. All courses have a certain credit value, which may vary from course to course, but is usually 5. Each credit denotes that a minimum of 25 hours has been assigned for that subject. A minimum of 40% or grade D is required to receive the credit in grade X and XI courses, and a minimum of 50% in grade XII courses. Normally a student is limited to attempting only 40 credits in any one academic year. Compulsory subjects are language arts, mathematics, science, social studies and social sciences.

For the award of the **General High School Diploma** students must obtain 100 credits, which must include 15 credits in language arts (5 must be obtained in grade XII), 10 credits in social studies and social sciences, 2 credits in physical education in grade X, a minimum of 5 credits in mathematics (with a maximum of 10 in grade X and 15 in grades X and XI), a minimum of 3 credits in science, and a minimum of 10 credits in other grade XII courses, in addition to the 5 for English (language arts) in grade XII.

Since September 1983, an **Advanced High School Diploma** has been awarded to students who have completed the General High School Diploma, with a minimum final mark of 50% in the following grade XII courses: English 30, social studies 30, mathematics 30, one of biology 30, chemistry 30 or physics 30. All 6 of these grade XII courses require completion of a government examination. In addition, English 33 (not used for university entrance) also has a government examination. Students who complete the 4 required grade XII courses for an Advanced High School Diploma with a minimum mark of 65% and an average of 80% will be awarded the **Diploma with Excellence**.

Students wishing to proceed to university are usually required to obtain a minimum mark of 50% with an average of 60% in the 5 or 6 grade XII subjects necessary for entrance. The Advanced High School Diploma is not required.

Teacher education

Prospective teachers both at the primary and secondary school level may register for the 4-year **Bachelor of Education degree** course, offered by the Universities of Alberta, Calgary and Lethbridge. The entrance requirement is the High School Graduation Diploma.

Canada (British Columbia and Manitoba)

BRITISH COLUMBIA

School education

Compulsory education is from age 7 to 15.

Primary lasts for 7 years, grades I-VII.

Secondary lasts for 5 years, divided into junior secondary (3 years) and senior secondary (2 years).

The minimum secondary school graduation requirements include the successful completion of at least 12 courses, numbered 11 or 12. Core requirements include English 11, English 12, social studies 11, physical education 11, and a course in consumer education. A student must also successfully complete 3 provincially authorized 12-level courses, in addition to English 12. Transcripts of grades are issued by the Ministry of Education. Final grades for grade 12 provincially examinable courses are based on the school percentage (50%) and the final exam percentage (50%). A **Dogwood Diploma** is issued by the Ministry of Education for each student who has completed graduation requirements.

An average of at least C+ (67-72%) is required for admission to undergraduate courses at universities in British Columbia.

The figure 11 against a subject on the **Senior Secondary School Statement** signifies that a subject was studied in grade XI, and 12 that it was studied in grade XII.

Teacher education

Primary teachers have to undertake a 3-year post-secondary course, which leads to the **Standard Certificate**.

Most secondary teachers undertake either a 4-year Bachelor degree in Arts or Science, followed by 1 year of teacher training, or a 5-year **Bachelor of Education (Secondary)** degree course. Both types of training will lead to the **Professional Certificate**.

MANITOBA

School education

Compulsory education is from age 6 to 16.

Primary, from age 6, covers grades K-III or IV.

Middle is usually from grades V-VIII or IX.

Secondary lasts 4 years, covering grades IX to XII. Many schools organize themselves in grade groupings of K-VI, VII-IX, X-XII.

Canada (Manitoba and New Brunswick)

Students take a general course, which is common for all, to the end of grade IX. Compulsory subjects are language arts, mathematics, science, social studies, and physical education and health. Art and music are compulsory to the end of grade VI. Optional courses begin in grade VII, and by grade X students may specialize.

There are 4 high school course patterns in addition to a mature students' programme:

university entrance course

general course - which also leads to high school graduation, and possible admission to a community college

vocational/industrial/business

occupational entrance (slower learners).

Courses are identified by a 3-digit number, e.g. 100, 201, 302, 103, 204, 305. The 10, 20, 30 refer to courses taken in grades X, XI and XII respectively. The suffix 0 signifies a subject taken in the university entrance course, 1 the general course, 2 the commercial course, 3 the industrial course, 4 an occupational entrance course, and 5 other courses.

All courses at the senior high school level are assigned a certain credit value. A student may earn 1 credit by successfully completing a course of study for which a minimum of 110 hours tuition has been taken. Most courses carry a credit of 1; English 300 is a 2-credit course.

The final secondary school leaving certificate, the **High School Graduation Diploma**, is obtained on successful completion of grade XII, i.e. on obtaining 20 credits. These must include credits obtained for English, social studies, mathematics and science in each of grades X and XI, English in grade XII, physical education, and 9 or 10 credits selected from other courses. A minimum overall average of 60% is generally required for admission to university in Manitoba. The Diploma (or Statement of Standing) is awarded on the basis of work completed during the last 3 years of the secondary school course.

Teacher education

To teach at both primary and secondary level students may undertake 1 of several types of training of which the more common are:

4-year **Bachelor of Education** degree course

3-year BA or B.Sc. degree course, followed by a 1-year teacher training course, leading to a **Teaching Certificate**.

NEW BRUNSWICK

School education

Primary lasts for 6 years.

Secondary lasts for 6 years, divided into 3 years junior high school and 3 years senior high school. In senior high school students may choose 1 of 3 types of course:

Canada (New Brunswick and Newfoundland)

The college preparatory programme designed to prepare students for specific courses at college or university; the programme is subdivided into regular and enriched courses, the latter offered to students with considerable interest and ability in a particular subject

the general educational and occupational programme for students who do not wish to progress beyond senior high school to university, or to undergo specialized training

a practical course, including remedial training.

Couses are numbered with 3 digits: the first 2 indicate the grade in which the subject has been studied. The third digit signifies the type of course; 1 represents an enriched college preparatory course, 2 a regular college preparatory course, 3 a general educational and occupational course, 4 a practical course. Second language courses end in 5 for enriched courses, 6 for regular courses, 7 for general educational and occupational courses, and 8 for practical courses.

The **High School Graduation Diploma** is awarded on successful completion of 1 of the following:

College preparatory programme. 15 credits, to include 10 compulsory credits; 3 in English, 1 in French, 2 in history, 2 in mathematics, 1 in science and 1 in physical education, and 5 electives.

General education and occupational programme. Business education students. 15 credits, to include 7 compulsory credits; 3 in English, 2 in mathematics, 1 in social studies, 1 in physical education, and 8 electives.

Industrial education and home economics. 15 credits, to include 7 compulsory credits; 3 in English, 2 in mathematics, 1 in social studies, 1 in science, and 8 electives, plus non-credit physical education.

Practical programme. 15 credits, to include 8 compulsory credits; 3 in English, 1 in social education, 1 in physical education, 3 in mathematics, and 7 electives.

A minimum overall average of 60%, usually in 6 subjects, in the High School Graduation Diploma is normally required for admission to degree courses at the universities in New Brunswick.

Teacher Education

The formal training required to be a teacher at elementary or secondary level us a 4-year course leading to a **B.Ed. degree.**

NEWFOUNDLAND

School education

Primary and elementary (grades I-VI)
Junior high (grades VII-IX)
High school (grades X-XII)

Canada (Northwest Territories and Nova Scotia)

There are 3 types of graduation diploma:

Graduation Pass Certificate
Graduation with Distinction
Graduation with Honours

Minimum graduation requirements include successful completion of 21 'core' credits, with an overall attainment of 36 credits.

Graduation with Distinction has satisfied minimum graduation requirements and attained 550 or more marks in any 7 level III (grade XII) courses.

Graduation with Honours has satisfied minimum graduation requirements and attained 550 or more marks in 7 university-preparatory level III courses (grade XII), as specified by the Department of Education.

The pass mark in all subjects is 50%.

The grade XII High School Diploma admits the holder to Memorial University in Newfoundland, provided all courses required for admission are successfully completed, with an overall average of not less than 60%. Most other Canadian universities accept Newfoundland grade XII High School Diploma for entrance to the first year of a 4-year degree programme.

Teacher education

The minimum qualification for permanent certification is 3 years of university training in education, beyond grade XII graduation. However, most new teachers entering the profession have university degrees.

It should be noted that preference is given to teachers with a minimum of 5 years university training (or more) for teacher certification purposes.

NORTHWEST TERRITORIES

The education system is modelled on that of Alberta, i.e. 6 years primary followed by two 3-year cycles of secondary education.

NOVA SCOTIA

School education

Compulsory education is from age 5 to 16, a total of 13 years.

Primary covers 6 years, grades 1 to VI, following a preparatory year of full-time school attendance where reading and writing skills are introduced.

Secondary covers a further 6 years, divided into 3 years junior high school and 3 years senior high school.

Canada (Nova Scotia and Ontario)

After junior high school, or after the first or second year of senior high school, students may enter a programme in 1 of the province's vocational schools.

Students in the senior high school programme may complete either a University Preparatory programme or a General Academic programme: both lead to the **Nova Scotia High School Completion Certificate**. A minimum of 16 full-year courses are required for this certificate, including 3 in English and 1 in Canadian studies. Local school boards may award their own graduation certificates on the completion of 17 courses, including additional specified courses in mathematics, sciences and social studies. A few secondary schools are francophone and students are instructed in both French and English, depending on the subject matter.

Some post-secondary institutions still admit students to some programmes after grade 11, but most universities require a minimum average of 60% in the final year of studies, grades 12, in 5 appropriate academic subjects. Mathematics 442 is a terminal academic course and Mathematics 441 is a pre-calculus course.

At senior high school each course is referred to by its subject's name followed by 3 digits. The first digit indicates the type of course: 2 - high school leaving; 3 - open category; 4 - university preparatory; 5 - Honours university preparatory. The second digit indicates the year in which the course is taught: 2 - grade 10; 3 - grade 11; 4 - grade 12. The third digit distinguishes different courses of the same subject area, type and grade level: e.g.g ENG441 - English literature; ENG442 - Canadian literature.

Teacher education

Teacher training is provided at the universities. Admission to the 1-year Bachelor of Education programmes requires completion previously, or concurrently, of an undergraduate degree. Since 1975 the **Nova Scotia Teacher College** has offered a 3-year teacher training programme, leading to the **Associateship in Education**. Some graduates of this programme then proceed to one of the Nova Scotian universities and obtain a **Bachelor of Education** degree after a further year.

ONTARIO

School education

Compulsory education is from age 6 to 16.

Primary/elementary lasts 8 years, covering grades 1-8.

Secondary lasts 4 years, covering grades 9-12 with a possible extra year in grade 13. Occasionally this cycle is referred to as years 1-5 (i.e. including grade 13).

Following a re-organization of the secondary school system in the early 1960s, the **Secondary School Graduation Diploma** was granted (from 1965-72) to students who successfully completed grade 12 of a 4- or 5-year secondary course. The fourth year of the 5-year course indicated that a student could be admitted to grade 13 courses; the 4-year course indicated that a student was not normally admitted to grade 13 classes without completing work additional to that required for the Secondary School Graduation Diploma of the 4-year course.

Canada (Ontario)

In 1968 some secondary schools were re-organized on a credit system, and a **Secondary School Graduation Diploma** (SSGD) was granted to a student who obtained 27 credits in the first 4 years of secondary school. Since 1973 all secondary schools have been organized on the credit system, a credit being awarded when a student successfully completes a course for which a minimum of 110 hours of classroom study has been taken. From 1973-86 the **Secondary School Graduation Diploma** was granted to students who had successfully completed 27 credits in a secondary school on the following basis:

at least 1 credit from each of the 4 areas of study in each of the first 2 years in a secondary school (8 credits)

at least 1 further credit after the first 2 years from each of the 4 areas of study (4 credits)

a further 15 credits from any area in any year.

Areas of study:

Communications (e.g. languages)
Social and environmental studies (e.g. geography and history)
Pure and applied sciences (e.g. mathematics)
Arts (e.g. art, music, physical and health education).

From 1977-86 students entering secondary school must have included the following 9 compulsory credit courses within the 27 credits:

grades 9 and 10 -   2 credit courses in English
                     2 in mathematics
                     1 in science
                     1 in Canadian history
                     1 in Canadian geography

grades 11 and 12 -   2 credit courses in English studies.

Students holding the Secondary School Graduation Diploma could stay on for a further year to obtain the **Secondary School Honours Graduation Diploma** (SSHGD), formerly called the **Senior Matriculation**. The SSGD was formerly the **Junior Matriculation Certificate**. Before 1972 the SSHGD was granted to a student who had standing in 7 grade-13 credits. From 1972-86 the Diploma was granted to students who had obtained at least 6 credits in grade 13. This qualification was generally required for entrance to universities in Ontario.

In 1984, implementation of a new secondary school curriculum commenced. The Secondary School Graduation Diploma hitherto awarded to grade 12 graduates, and the Secondary School Honours Graduation Diploma awarded to grade 13 graduates will be replaced by a single certificate called the **Ontario Secondary School Diploma** (OSSD).

Students entering grade 9 in September 1984 commenced study for the OSSD, which has been awarded to graduating students from June 1986. Although the Secondary School Honours Graduation Diploma (the grade 13 diploma) will be retained for some students until 31 August 1990, no diploma other than the Ontario Secondary School Diploma will be awarded to graduating students after that time. During the transition period, all current courses taught for credit will be acceptable for the new diploma.

Canada (Prince Edward Island)

Students entering secondary school programmes on or after 1 September 1984 must earn a minimum of 30 credits to receive the Ontario Secondary School Diploma. 16 of the 30 credits are compulsory and 14 are elective. A credit is earned by successfully completing a course that involves a minimum of 110 hours of classroom work. Short courses may be available to students and fractional credits may be given.

Credits (total 30) required for the Ontario Secondary School Diploma:

Compulsory - English/Francais 5, French/Anglais 1, mathematics 2, science 2, Canadian history 1, Canadian geography 1, arts 1, physical and health education 1, business/technological studies 1, senior social science 1 = 16 credits.

Elective - 14.

Students who plan to go to university will be required to take 6 **Ontario Academic Courses** (OACs), which are the new prescriptive, provincially designed university-entrance courses that will be offered by the secondary schools in Ontario. (The OACs will replace the grade 13 programme by 1988.)

OACs may be taken after successful completion of the 30-credit Ontario Secondary School Diploma or they may be counted as credits towards the OSSD.

Teacher education

Since the Education Act in 1974, Ontario has had 1 certificate for teachers, the **Ontario Teacher's Certificate** (OTC). All new graduates from teacher-education programmes and all practising teachers and others who hold existing basic teaching certificates - elementary, secondary, vocational or occupational - now hold the OTC. All new and old qualifications are included on a Teacher Qualification Record Card issued to each teacher by the provincial Ministry of Education.

Faculties of Education or Schools of Education (Teachers Colleges) in Ontario are now all affiliated with universities. The duration of the basic Ontario Teacher's programmes is 1 year, leading to a B.Ed. and OTC. Candidates must hold a university degree and must declare 1 of 3 grade divisions acceptable to teach: primary/junior (K-6), junior intermediate (4-10), or intermediate senior (7-13). Prospective teachers for the junior/intermediate programme should have at least 3 full courses in a subject taught in the school system, and those for the intermediate senior division should have a major and minor in 2 subjects taught in the school system.

PRINCE EDWARD ISLAND

School education

Primary lasts for 6 years, although in rural areas it may be 8.

Secondary lasts a further 6 years divided into two 3-year cycles.

To obtain the **High School Graduation Diploma** on completion of grade XII, students must gain a minimum of 15 credits over grades X, XI and XII, to include 3 courses in English, and 2 in mathematics. Each credit represents 140-150 hours of instruction.

A minimum overall average of 60% is normally required in the high school graduation for admission to the University of Prince Edward Island, with at least 5 subjects, including English and maths, at the grade XII academic level.

Canada (Quebec)

The college preparatory programme is designed to prepare students for certain courses at colleges or universities. The programme is subdivided into regular and enriched courses, the latter offered to students with considerable interest and ability in a particular subject.

The general educational and occupational programme is for students who do not wish to progress beyond senior high school to university, or to undergo specialized training.

Teacher education

4 types of qualification are available:

Certificate 4 is granted to students who have successfully completed a 4-year Bachelor of Education degree.

Certificate 5 is granted to students who have successfully completed a 4-year Bachelor degree and in addition a 1-year Bachelor of Education degree.

Certificate 5A is granted to students who have completed an approved year of study beyond Certificate 5.

Certificate 6 is granted to those who have completed an approved academic Master degree plus a 1-year Bachelor of Education or a Master degree in Education (minimum of 6 years post-secondary study).

QUEBEC

School education

Primary is usually from age 6, for 6 years.

Secondary lasts 5 years, covering grades VII-XI or secondary forms I-V.

The **Grade XI Secondary V Certificate** is awarded on attainment of 18 credits in grades X and XI. 10 units must be in courses taken in the fifth year of secondary education and include at least 2 units in the second language. Generally, the compulsory subjects in forms IV and V are English, French, history and, in Catholic schools, religion. Each paper in the grade XI certificate examinations is given a value of unit credits, usually 2 for each.

The General and Vocational College Act of 1967 led to the establishment of the **Colleges d'Enseignement General et Professionel** (CEGEPs). These institutions offer 2-year academic courses preparing students for entry to university, and 3-year terminal technical/vocational courses, which prepare students directly for employment. Admission to both types of course is by the Secondary V Certificate.

If a student takes the 2-year pre-university course he or she is required to complete 24 credit courses to qualify for the **Diploma of Collegial Studies (DCS)/Diplome d'Etudes Collegiales (DEC)**:

Canada (Saskatchewan)

	Total credits

Core courses
    4 English/French
    4 humanities
	8

plus field of concentration
    12 courses from 3 or 4 disciplines
    within 1 of 3 groups (maximum
    6 courses in the same discipline)
	12

plus complementary courses
    to ensure a diversified programme of
    studies, 4 courses ought to be
    selected outside the field of concentration
	4

	24

The curriculum of this 2-year course was previously offered in the first year of the university degree courses.

Teacher education

To qualify to teach at either the elementary or secondary level it is necessary to obtain certification from the Ministry of Education. Certification can be obtained either by completing a 3-year university **Bachelor of Education** programme, or a 1-year **Diploma** programme, after the award of a Bachelor degree.

SASKATCHEWAN

School education

Until the early 1970s compulsory education was to age 15; it is now to age 16.

Primary schooling covers 8 years, grades I-VIII. In the early 1970s a divisional system was introduced, covering Divisions I to IV; each division represents the work of a 3-year period under the previous grade system. Primary education now covers Divisions I-III (i.e. years 1-9).

Secondary used to cover grades IX to XII and now covers Division IV (years 10 to 12).

The final secondary school certificate, and that required for university matriculation, is **Complete Division IV Standing**, i.e. 21 credits. These must include 7 credits from year 10, a minimum of 7 from year 11, and a minimum of 5 from year 12. Course numbers identify the year-level and type of course taken; the first digit represents the year of the course (1 means taken in year 1 of Division IV), the second digit indicates the type of course. Every course in Division IV is assigned a certain credit value, usually 1, which represents 100-120 hours of study.

Teacher education

Until 1964 prospective teachers undertook a 1-year course at a normal school, later called a teachers college.

Canada (Yukon Territory)

In 1964 the teachers college became part of the university and students now undertake a 4-year **Bachelor of Education** degree.

YUKON TERRITORY

The education system is modelled on that of British Columbia, i.e. 7 years primary, followed by 5 years secondary.

TECHNICAL SECONDARY EDUCATION

The pattern of vocational education varies from province to province. Many secondary schools provide technical and vocational courses as part of their programme.

Trade and occupational training schools are available for those students who have passed the provincial school-leaving age and have left the regular school system. Courses at the trade level do not usually require high school graduation; the grade level required varies according to trade and province and ranges from grade 8 to 12.

FURTHER EDUCATION

There are many institutions offering instruction at this level as well as public and private specialist colleges and institutes: Colleges of Applied Arts and Technology, Institutes of Technology, and Community Colleges (in addition to Colleges of Trades and Technology, Forest Ranger Schools, Land Survey Institutes and so on).

Colleges of Applied Arts and Technology

These are located mainly in Ontario. They were originally conceived as terminal institutions, with few possibilities for transfer to universities. Their scope has now been widened to include a broader range of courses.

Institutes of Technology

The general entrance requirement at these institutes is high school graduation or at least high school standing in relevant subjects. Diplomas in applied arts or technology are awarded on successful completion of the 2-3 year courses.

Community Colleges

Many of these colleges have been established since the late 1960s; others grew out of existing colleges. They do not award degrees, and are oriented more towards community service. Hence, the types of course vary according to the institution and its locality. However, in general, full and part-time courses are available in a variety of subjects in career, remedial and general education. Some colleges also offer 1- and 2-year preparation courses for university entrance or advanced university entrance.

Canada (General)

HIGHER EDUCATION

In general the English language universities offer 3-year courses leading to a **General/Pass degree**, a 4-year course with a specialization, and 4-year courses leading to an **Honours degree**. Until the late 1960s and the introduction of the CEGEPs the French language institutions in Quebec offered a 4-year degree course. They now offer a 3-year course leading to a BA or B.Sc. from the level of the Diploma of Collegial Studies.

Most universities in Nova Scotia now require 3 years for a general Arts or Science degree and for degrees in subjects such as secretarial administration, and 4 years for all other degrees.

Students holding an Honours degree or a 4-year specialized degree may proceed to undertake a further year of study leading to a **Master degree**. Those holding only a Pass degree must first complete a qualifying year. The qualification of **Master of Philosophy** may be awarded after 2 years of study, but only in arts subjects.

The award of the **Ph.D.** requires a minimum of 2 years study post-Master level or 3 years post-Honours degree.

A wide variety of postgraduate certificates and diplomas are also offered.

Honours degrees may sometimes be unclassified. If degrees are classified it may be either:

    1st Class Honours, Honours,
or 1st Class Honours, 2nd class Honours.

The academic year runs from September to April/May.

The number of universities per province varies. There are several other types of institution affiliated to the universities.

An affiliated college is one that is administratively independent, but whose academic affairs are governed by the senate of the university to which it is affiliated. Instruction is given in the college, but degrees are awarded by the university.

A constituent college is an integral college of a particular university.

A federated college or university is an institution that holds its degree-granting powers in abeyance during the term of federation with another university.

A degree in **Architecture** is normally obtained on successful completion of a course lasting 5 years (after senior matriculation). In many provinces the programme is 2-3 years and may only be entered on completion of a Bachelor degree.

The **Bachelor of Law** (LL B) is normally obtained after 5 years, the first 2 years comprising general studies.

The **Doctor in Medicine** is normally obtained after 6 years, the first 2 years comprising more general studies.

Central African Republic

The Central African Republic was formerly the French colony of Ubangi Shari. In 1958 Ubangi Shari elected to remain within the French community and adopted its present title. The education system, unified in 1962, is based on the French system. All education is the responsibility of the Ministry of Education.

The medium of instruction is French.

EVALUATION IN BRITAIN

School

Baccalaureat - generally considered to be GCE O-level standard.

Higher

Licence - has been compared to British Bachelor Pass degree standard.

MARKING SYSTEMS

No information available.

SCHOOL EDUCATION

Primary

This lasts 6 years: at the end of the course pupils are awarded the **Elementary Primary School Leaving Certificate**. At the end of the sixth year, pupils take a competitive examination which grants access to the first year of secondary education (concours d'entree en sixieme).

Central African Republic

After primary education, pupils may be directed into general and technical secondary education, apprenticeship centres, the Ecole des Arts et Metiers (school of arts and crafts), the College d'Enseignement Technique Feminin (technical school for girls) or to agricultural education.

Secondary

This is divided into 2 cycles. The first is a 4-year course which leads to the **Brevet Elementaire du Premier Cycle** (BEPC). The second cycle consists of a 3-year course ending in the Baccalaureat examination or **Diplome de Bachelier de l'Enseignement du Second Degre**. This gives access to higher education.

Technical secondary

Courses of technical education are also available. They lead to various **Certificats d'Aptitude Professionnelle** (CAP), and the **technical Baccalaureat**.

HIGHER EDUCATION

Universite de Bangui, consists of the Faculty of Law and Economics, the University Institute of Technology, the University Institute of Mining and Geology, the Institute of Mathematical Studies and Research, the Institute of Research for Higher Education, and the Ecole Normale Superieure (higher teacher-training college).

TEACHER EDUCATION

Primary

The teacher-training school for primary school teachers offers a 2-year course. Candidates are selected after obtaining the Lower Secondary School Certificate.

Secondary

Secondary school teachers are trained at the Ecole Normale Superieure.

Chad

Republic of Chad

Before the early 1960s education was offered only by mission and Koranic schools. Since then compulsory schooling has been from age six to twelve but lack of facilities prevents this being fully implemented. There is standard national curricula at school level.

French is the official medium of instruction; at early primary level many children have to learn the language.

The school year runs from September to June.

EVALUATION IN BRITAIN

School

Baccalaureat - generally considered to compare to GCE O-level standard.

Higher

Diplome Universitaire de Lettres Modernes (DULMO), Diplome Universitaire de Sciences (DUS) - generally considered to compare to GCE A-level standard.

Licence - generally considered to be between GCE A-level and British Bachelor degre standard.

MARKING SYSTEMS

No information available.

Chad

SCHOOL EDUCATION

Primary

This lasts 6 years, leading to the **Elementary School Certificate.** Some schools offer courses only lasting 2-3 years and these do not lead to a formal qualification. The standardized curriculum includes reading, writing, spelling, grammar, mathematics, history, geography, science and drawing.

There is a competitive entrance examination (concours d'entree en sixieme) for admission to secondary education.

Secondary

Secondary is divided into 2 cycles; the lower, lasting 4 years, leading to the **Lower Secondary School Certificate,** and the upper lasting a further 3 years, leading to the examinations for the **Baccalaureat.** During this cycle pupils may specialize in the mathematics, science or literature options.

Technical secondary

Technical lycees offer the full 7-year secondary courses leading to a Baccalaureat.

Technical schools offer courses starting from the quatrieme classe (i.e. third year of lower secondary), lasting 5 years, and leading to the different certificates of vocational aptitude.

Apprenticeship centres offer 3-year courses leading to an apprenticeship certificate.

FURTHER EDUCATION

Holders of the Lower Secondary School Certificate may enter:

Postal and Telecommunication School (Fort-Archambault) for a 4-year course

Institute of Zootechnical Studies (Fort Lamy) for a 5-year course. At the end of the first 3-year cycle, students are certified as superintendents (controleurs); completion of the second cycle leads to certification as ingenieurs. Those who hold the Baccalaureat may directly enter the second cycle.

HIGHER EDUCATION

No facilities were available until the University of Chad opened in Ndjamena in 1972. There are now also specialist institutes and national schools.

The first stage of studies comprising 2 years leads to the **Diplome Universitaire de Lettres Modernes (DULMO)** in humanities, to the **Diplome Universitaire de Sciences (DUS)** in science, or to the **Diplome Universitaire de Sciences Juridiques, Economiques et de Gestion (DUSJEG)**. After a further year of study students may obtain the **Licence** in humanities and law.

TEACHER EDUCATION

Primary

Those who had completed primary education could enter a teacher-training school for a 6-year course (the first 4 years were generally based, with the last 2 being the professional training), leading to a primary school teachers certificate.

Those who completed the 4-year lower secondary cycle at a lycee could undertake a 2-year course of training as moniteurs (teacher aides).

The training courses for this level have now been lengthened to 3 years from the entrance level of completion of the lower secondary cycle. Certificated moniteurs may also undertake retraining on this course.

Secondary

The university trains teachers on degree courses.

Chile

Republic of Chile

The Chilean education system has undergone extensive change since 1973, especially higher education, which is no longer solely provided by the universities.

Education is compulsory for children aged six to thirteen.

The medium of instruction is Spanish.

The academic year runs from March to December and is divided into three terms.

EVALUATION IN BRITAIN

School

Licencia de Educacion Media obtained after 4 years of secondary education - generally considered to compare to GCE O-level standard.

Higher

Licenciatura - may be considered to compare to British Bachelor degree standard.

MARKING SYSTEMS

The same grading system is used both for secondary and higher education. The maximum mark available is 7, and the minimum pass mark is 4.

Before 1973:

7	muy bueno	very good
6	bueno	good
5	mas que suficiente	above average
4	suficiente	average
3	deficiente	
2	malo	failure
1	muy malo	

Since 1974:

6.0-7	muy bueno	very good
5.0-5.9	bueno	good
4.0-4.9	suficiente	average
1.0-3.9	insuficiente	failure

In higher education a percentage system is commonly used. In the Faculty of Medicine a point scale is used.

SCHOOL EDUCATION

Primary (Educacion Basica)

This covers an 8-year compulsory period (ages 6-13). Each school devises its own internal examinations. Marks are awarded on a scale of 1-7 (maximum). Children who successfully complete all 8 grades of primary education are awarded a primary school-leaving certificate which grants access to secondary education.

Secondary (Educacion Media)

The state secondary schools are known as Liceos. Private secondary schools are called Colegios or Institutos. The secondary education course lasts 4 years. Students choose to specialize in 1 of 2 categories: humanistic-scientific or technico-professional.

Humanistic-scientific:

Most pupils choose to enter the humanistic-scientific branch of education provided in the Liceos. These offer a 2-year common course of studies and 2 years of specialization in literacy, historical and social sciences, or natural sciences and mathematics.

Technico-professional:

This branch of education is intended to be less academic and more vocational. It is divided into 4 categories:

Industrial
Agricultural
Commercial
Special services and techniques.

After a common year of general studies, students specialize in one of these categories. Although these courses were intended to provide technicians for industry, agriculture and commerce, most graduates (like the graduates of the humanistic-scientific secondary schools) apply for university education.

Students of both branches who successfully complete their secondary education are awarded the **Licencia de Educacion Media**.

Chile

FURTHER EDUCATION

Apart from the vocational opportunities offered within the sphere of school and university education, various non-academic courses are available for those in employment.

INCAP (Instituto Nacional de Capitacion) provides practical courses in motor mechanics, machine repairs, building construction, mining, agriculture and cottage industries. Students attend regional centres which offer courses suited to the particular area. Many of these demand no more than 3 years of primary education to satisfy the entrance requirements. Courses are composed of 3 stages, each of which lasts approximately 400 hours, designated formacion, capacitacion and especializacion. Each stage lasts approximately 4 months. Shorter courses are offered. Most trainees attend on a part-time basis. There are no formal examinations. The instructors decide whether the student has been successful; 100% attendance is required.

The Instituto Tecnologico of the University of Santiago and the Instituto Politecnico of the Federico Santa Maria Technical University offer a limited number of similar courses.

The Departamento Universitario Obrero Campesino (DUOC), part of the Catholic University, offers part-time courses at centres throughout the country. Most of the courses are offered at evening classes and cover technical and arts and crafts subjects, as well as health and education.

HIGHER EDUCATION

Students holding the **Licencia de Educacion Media** sit a national university entrance examination called the **Prueba de Aptitud Academica** (PAA). This is a multiple-choice examination valid for all universities, professional institutes and academies in Chile. Candidates compete nationally in the examination, which consists of 2 papers: language aptitude (mostly comprehension) and mathematical aptitude. Each candidate may be required to take an additional **Prueba de Conocimientos Especificos** (test of specific knowledge) in 1 of 5 or more areas (mathematics, natural sciences, social sciences, physics and chemistry) relevant to the subject the candidate wishes to pursue at university. The student's average marks obtained in secondary school are also taken into account.

Higher education is provided by the universities, academies, institutes and military and police academies. 12 subjects (carreras) are available only at the universities: architecture, medicine, law, civil engineering, dentistry, veterinary medicine, forestry, agronomy, psychology, biochemistry, commercial engineering, and pharmacology.

Undergraduate courses vary from 2-and-a-half years to 7 years, with a 5-year degree course as the norm; they generally lead to the **Licenciatura** or **Professional title**.

Chile

Postgraduate studies are offered mainly by the University of Chile and the Catholic University. These range from 1-year diploma courses to 3-year courses leading to doctorates. Students holding the **Licenciatura** may be awarded a **Magister** after 2 years further study. The **Doctorado** (doctorate) is awarded after the submission of a thesis.

TEACHER EDUCATION

Primary

Before 1973, prospective pre-primary, primary and secondary school teachers were trained in the Escuelas Normales at the level of secondary education. Pre-primary and primary teachers are now required to take a 3-year university degree course.

Secondary

Prospective secondary school teachers follow a 5-year university course in which they cover education and a specialized subject. Successful students receive the qualification of **Profesor**.

Part-time courses are being made available for unqualified and semi-qualified teachers. In-service courses for state teachers have been offered since 1966.

China

People's Republic of China

The period from the founding of the People's Republic of China in 1949 to the late 1950s was one of reliance on Soviet assistance and loans; the education system was patterned on that of the Soviet Union, with Russian as the second language at school. Educational facilities were expanded and great importance was attached to examinations.

After the 1950s the Soviet pattern was rejected. In the period known as the Great Leap Forward, beginning in 1958, the concept of manual labour was introduced to the education system.

In the mid-1960s the education system lapsed into chaos and disorganization, as education was one of the most important issues of the Cultural Revolution. In 1966 all schools and universities were closed to prepare for a reorientation and restructuring of the whole system (for example the period of schooling to be decreased, abolition of college entrance examinations). Some institutions began to reopen in 1967, but teachers often had no formal qualifications, students entered university without having taken any examinations, and there was no form of assessment during the university course. Great importance was given to manual labour and the link between production and education. Many institutions remained closed until the early 1970s.

During the early 1970s, the so-called Educational Revolution of 1971-5, a number of 'colleges' and 'universities' were established offering spare-time and short-term highly vocational courses. The curriculum was changed at all levels to make it more relevant to the needs of society. Courses were shortened, and students had to work before going on to university, normally for a minimum of two years.

The reform of the education system has continued since the death of Mao Tse Tung in 1976. Academic merit is again emphasized, rather than solely political consciousness. It is difficult to generalize about the present situation, as progress is happening at different rates throughout China, but since 1978 the school curriculum has again become centrally regulated, and five years primary education is compulsory.

EVALUATION IN BRITAIN

School

1952-8:

School-Leaving Certificate - generally considered to compare to GCE O-level standard.

China

Since 1978:

Chinese University Entrance Examination - generally compared to GCE O-level standard on a subject-for-subject basis, where marks of 50% and over have been obtained in subjects which have counterparts in the GCE examinations (except English language).

Higher

Enquirers should contact the National Academic Recognition Information Centre.

MARKING SYSTEMS

School

The Chinese University Entrance Examination is marked on a percentage scale per subject, with no minimum pass mark and a maximum mark for examinations of 500. The minimum usually required for entry to university or teacher-training college in China ranges from 280 to 370, although some major universities may require as high a figure as 380.

The maximum mark does not include the mark obtained for the test in the foreign language, except for students wishing to study foreign languages at higher education level. In this case the mark for the foreign language test is counted, but the mathematics result is not included.

Higher

No information available.

SCHOOL EDUCATION

Pre-primary

In the past, facilities for children aged 3-6 years were limited, but these are now being expanded. Kindergartens are divided into 3 grades: 3-4 year olds, 4-5 year olds and 5-6 year olds.

Primary

1952-1967:

This period generally covered 6 years for children aged 6-and-a-half to 7; it was divided into two cycles of 4 and 2 years respectively. Some schools operated an experimental system of 5 years. There was an entrance examination to decide entry to secondary education.

China

Since 1967:

This period covers 5 years. The curriculum includes Chinese language, mathematics, general knowledge, foreign languages, physical education, music, painting, agricultural work and industrial work.

Secondary

Until 1966 (Cultural Revolution):

This covered 6 years (divided into two 3-year cycles, junior middle school and senior middle school respectively). The emphasis of the curriculum was on the sciences and political training.

All schools closed in 1966, and some began to reopen in the spring of 1967.

From 1967 to mid-1970s:

This period initially covered only 2-3 years of combined junior and senior middle school; it was then expanded to 4 years, divided into two 2-year cycles.

From 1967-77 the end-of-course examination was internally set and controlled by the Revolutionary Committee in each school without any form of external moderation.

Since the mid-1970s:

This period covers 5-6 years, divided into two cycles of 3 and 2-3 years in junior and senior middle school respectively. The curriculum covers: Chinese language and literature; mathematics; politics; physics and chemistry; history; geography; a second language (often English); culture; physical training; and foundations of agriculture (including biology) - plus a period of work study in a school workshop, often combined with sessions at a regular factory.

In 1977 the first external examinations since before the Cultural Revolution were introduced at the end of the course to decide entrance to a course of higher education: National College Entrance Examinations. The examinations are standardized and taken nationwide. Compulsory subjects are Chinese, mathematics and politics. In addition, pupils take either chemistry and physics or geography and history, according to specialization. A foreign language may also be included: there is a choice of English, French, Spanish, Russian, and German.

Technical secondary

Some courses are available at this level and generally last 3 years.

HIGHER EDUCATION

Until the beginning of the Cultural Revolution in 1966, students could enter university on completion of secondary school and success in an entrance examination. When the institutions began to reopen in 1967, places on higher education courses were allocated by regional revolutionary committees to communes and factories, which then decided to whom they should be awarded on the basis of good socialist consciousness and activity. Normally students would have completed secondary school, but some entered university with little previous education. In the early 1970s students were generally expected to work for at least 2 years before entering university. In 1977, entrance examinations were again instituted which are now taken by pupils on completion of secondary education.

Until the Cultural Revolution, courses lasted from 3 years (humanities) to 6 years (science). When the institutions reopened, courses were reduced to 3-4 years and the curriculum was orientated towards the practical application of subjects studied, labour practice, political education and community work. Since the late 1970s, most courses have again been lengthened to 4 years (6 years in medicine and dentistry). The curriculum still contains a small element of political-ideological training, military-physical training, and productive work (besides the main area of specialization).

From 1949 to 1980, only certificates and diplomas were awarded. Since February 1980, **Bachelor degrees** have been awarded for particularly good results.

Until 1955 no postgraduate study facilities were available, and students mostly went to the Soviet Union. In 1955 the qualification of **Associate Doctor** was established, but few were awarded. After the closure of the universities in 1966, postgraduate study was re-instituted in 1978, and since 1981 students have been able to obtain a **Master** degree after 2 years successful study. An Academic Council has been appointed to arrange supervision of **Ph.D.** work and to approve the granting of Ph.D. degrees. Since 1982 the Chinese government has instituted a number of educational development programmes to raise academic standards and introduce a wide range of research courses in universities.

The People's University offers special classes to enable students to make up any deficiency in their secondary education; these normally last 2-4 years.

A number of spare-time colleges have been established by factories and trade unions. These offer 4-year courses in various fields and/or short advanced courses. In China these institutions are regarded as offering the same standard of education as the universities.

The Central TV University was established in 1979. (In the early 1960s TV universities had been set up in Peking, Tianjin, Shanghai, Shenyang, but these were all closed during the Cultural Revolution. The CCTV offers numerous 3-year courses, including mathematics, physics, engineering and electronics and Chinese language. Graduates are granted a **Diploma.** There are also 28 provincial TV universities.

TEACHER EDUCATION

Primary

Lower: 3-4 years at a junior teachers training school for pupils having completed primary school.

Upper: 3 years at a senior teachers training school for pupils having completed junior middle/lower secondary education.

Secondary/middle school

3-4 years at a teachers training college/institute for pupils having senior middle/upper secondary education.

Colombia

Republic of Colombia

State education is free and compulsory for children aged seven to eleven.

The medium of instruction is Spanish.

Owing to climatic conditions, the academic year runs from September to June in the southern departments of Valle, Cauca and Narino, and from February to November elsewhere.

EVALUATION IN BRITAIN

School

Bachillerato (sometimes called **Diploma de Bachiller**) awarded on successful completion of secondary education - generally considered to compare to GCE O-level standard.

Higher

Bachiller and **Licenciado** or **Professional Title** - may be generally considered to compare to British Bachelor degree standard.

MARKING SYSTEMS

School

Pupils are examined at the end of each year of secondary studies. The final yearly grade is arrived at from the examination mark (40%) and average marks for work done during the year (60%). Failure in more than 2 subjects means that the pupil concerned must repeat the year.

The examinations are conducted internally, but in the sixth year of the **Bachillerato** course the examination papers are corrected by the pupils' own teacher and a teacher delegated by the Ministry of Education.

Colombia

Before 1974 the Bachillerato was marked on a scale of 1-5 (maximum), with 3 as the minimum pass mark.

During 1975-8 it was marked on a scale of 1-10 (maximum), with 5 as the minimum pass mark.

Since 1978 the Bachillerato has been marked on a scale of 1-100 (maximum), with 50 as the minimum pass mark. Some certificates are still marked on the old 1-10 (maximum) scale.

Higher

The degree structure at Colombian universities is based on the United States. Students must follow a programme of unit courses, some compulsory and others elective. Each course has a unit value, and a prescribed number of units is required for graduation. Student performance on each course is indicated by a grade point on the scale 0.0-5.0, where 3.0 is usually the minimum acceptable. At the end of the whole course, grade-points are averaged to show general level of achievement. An average of 5.0 is rare.

SCHOOL EDUCATION

In 1975 and 1976 major educational reforms were announced which involved the restructuring of the education system according to the periods of basic education covering primary (grades 1-5), secondary (grades 6-9) and middle and intermediate education (grades 10-11 and 12-13 respectively). The system is, however, only slowly being introduced, and many institutions still operate on the lines of the traditional 5-year primary and 6-year secondary courses.

Within the public (i.e. state) system, education is provided by national, muncipal and departmental schools. Private schools are run by the Catholic Church, other religious organizations, secular concerns and co-operative groups. All private schools must conform to the state's curricular models.

Pre-primary

Most kindergartens are located in the larger towns and run by private organizations, but the Instituto Colombiano de Bienestar Familial (Colombian Institute of Family Welfare), a government agency, is also beginning to provide such facilities.

Primary

This is compulsory and covers grades 1-5 (ages 7-12).

Secondary

Many secondary institutions offer the traditional 6-year course (ages 12-18), culminating in the **Bachillerato** or final school-leaving certificate. This course is tailored to satisfy university entrance requirements. Diversification within the secondary system is also encouraged, and students can choose from various modalidades, or specializations, including: commerce, industry, primary teacher training and agriculture.

Colombia

In the early 1970s several large comprehensive secondary schools with a vocational bias were established under the Ministry of Education. Called <u>Institutos Nacionales de Educacion Media</u> (INEM) or National Institutes of Middle Education, they can also equip students for university entrance. They provide courses in the humanities, domestic science, commerce, industry and agriculture. Similar institutions with a specific agricultural bias called <u>Institutos Tecnicos Agropecuarios</u> (Agricultural Technical Institutes) run parallel to <u>INEM</u>.

Technical secondary

Technical secondary schools offer courses leading to the **Bachiller Tecnico**. After some years of approved industrial experience, this can be converted to the level of **Tecnico Intermedio**. The INEM produce school-leavers holding the **Bachiller Tecnico** who have some technical training. The <u>National Apprenticeship Service</u> (SENA) provides most of the technical secondary training. Students who pursue apprenticeship schemes must have completed at least 4 years of formal secondary education. They are seconded from their work in industry for periods varying from 18 months to 3 years. These courses are not oriented towards university entrance.

FURTHER EDUCATION

Apart from the normal first-degree programmes, universities offer vocational courses lasting up to 3 years, providing training for, among others, laboratory technicians, nurses, dental assistants, physiotherapists, managers, and the various types of engineer. In addition, several <u>Institutos Tecnologicos</u> (technological institutes) provide courses leading to the qualifications of **Tecnico de Alto Nivel** or **Tecnologo**.

HIGHER EDUCATION

University entrance is based on the **Bachillerato**. A national university entrance examination is also used by some universities, but this is not compulsory.

Most Bachelor degree courses take 4-5 years. Some courses take only 3 years. Full medical qualifications can take 6-7 years. Students can frequently attend university on a part-time basis. In this case courses can take 8 or more years to complete. The degree structure follows that of the United States.

TEACHER EDUCATION

Primary

Teachers (normalistas) are trained in Escuelas Normales, which are on the level of secondary institutions.

Secondary

Teachers are trained either in the pedagogic universities or in the other universities, where they take courses in their specialist topics as well as in education. There are some university-level courses in pre-school and primary education.

NON-FORMAL AND ADULT EDUCATION

The Ministry of Education sends out teams which provide courses in different parts of the country.

The Ministry of Communications provides primary and secondary education by means of specially devised radio and television programmes on INRAVISION. Courses are approved by the Ministry of Education and lead to qualifications at primary or secondary level which have equal recognition to those obtained in the formal system.

The National Apprenticeship Service (SENA) is another agency which contributes greatly to non-formal education. It provides training centres for the whole of Colombia as well as mobile training programmes.

Accion Cultural Popular (Popular Action for Culture) promotes the education of Colombia's rural population and runs courses by radio on literacy, numeracy, health, agriculture, economics and rural development, supplemented by specially produced literature and a correspondence service.

The Colombian government has also developed the CAMINA project to help illiterate people.

Congo Brazzaville

Formerly the French colony of Middle Congo, Congo Brazzaville has followed a basically French system of education since independence in 1960.

The medium of instruction is French.

The academic year runs from October to June.

EVALUATION IN BRITAIN

School

Baccalaureat - generally compared to GCE O-level standard.

MARKING SYSTEMS

School

Subjects are marked on a scale of 0-20 (maximum), with no official minimum pass mark.

Overall grades of **Baccalaureat** are passable, assez bien, bien, tres bien (maximum).

A student may have subject grades below 9 in 1 or more subjects and still obtain the Baccalaureat, if he/she attains an overall average grade of 9 or higher.

SCHOOL EDUCATION

Primary

This covers 6 years numbered in reverse order (i.e. classes 12-7), leading to the **Certificat d'Etudes Primaries Elementaires** (CEPE).

Congo Brazzaville

Secondary

This covers 7 years, divided into a 4-year lower cycle and a 3-year upper cycle, with classes numbered in reverse order (i.e. 6 to classe terminale). On completion of class 3, pupils obtain the **Brevet d'Etudes du Premier Cycle** (BEPC). During the second cycle pupils may specialize in mathematics, science or literature. On completion of this cycle pupils take the examinations for the **Baccalaureat**, available in a variety of options, depending on specialization:

A humanities and philosophy
B economics
C mathematics and physical science
D natural science
E science and technology.

Pupils who do not take the examinations (or fail) are given a **Certificat de Fin d'Etudes Secondaires**, a record of attendance and performance in the final year at school.

Technical secondary

On completion of lower secondary education, pupils may take a 'short' technical secondary course (2-3 years), leading to the qualification of **Brevet de Technicien**, or a 'long' course (3-4 years) leading to the **Baccalaureat Technique**, a qualification available in 2 options, depending on specialization:

F technology
G commerce.

HIGHER EDUCATION

There is 1 university - founded in 1959 as the Centre d'Etudes Administratives et Techniques Superieures, it became the University of Brazzaville in 1971 and acquired its present title of <u>Universite Marien Ngouabi</u> in 1977.

The entrance requirement is the **Baccalaureat**.

The University is made up of the following faculties and departments:

<u>Faculte des Lettres</u> and <u>Faculte des Sciences</u>

The first stage of studies after 2 years leads to the **Diplome Universitaire d'Etudes Litteraires** (DUEL) in arts and humanities and **Diplome Universitaire d'Etudes Scientifiques** (DUES). A further year of study leads to the **Licence**, and a further 2 years (including the submission of a thesis) to the **Maitrise**. The **Doctorat de Troisieme Cycle** may then be obtained on completion of 2 or more years research.

<u>Faculty of Law and Management</u> - INSSEJAG (Institut Superieur des Sciences Economiques, Juridiques, Administratives et de Gestion)

As above, leading to the Licence, Maitrise and Doctorat of Law or Economics.

Congo Brazzaville

A 2-year training course leads to **Brevet de Technicien Superier** (BTS) in secretarial and management duties.

<u>Faculty of Medicine and Pharmacy</u> - INSSSA (Institut Superieur des Sciences de la Sante)

6 years study with thesis leads to MD (Doctorat en Medicine ou Pharmacie).

3 year study is required to become a trained nurse (Infirmier Diplome d'Etat).

TEACHER EDUCATION

Primary

Training is undertaken at secondary education level.

Secondary

A 2-year post-secondary course at the Institut Superieur des Sciences de l'Education (INSSED), a teacher-training college which forms part of the Universite Marien-Ngouabi, leads to the qualification of **Certificat d'Aptitude au Professorat dans les Colleges d'Enseignement General** (CAP de CEG). A further year of study leads to the title of **Professeur de Lycee** with the qualification of **Certificat d'Aptitude au Professorat de l'Enseignement Lycee** (CAPEL), formerly called the **Certificat d'Aptitude au Professorat de l'Enseignement Secondaire** (CAPES).

<u>ENSET</u> (Ecole Normale Superieur de l'Enseignement Technique):

This institute trains technical teachers for the **Certificat d'Aptitude au Professorat de l'Enseignement Technique** (CAPET). As INSSED.

<u>ISEPS</u> (Institut Superieur d'Education Physique et Sportive - Higher College of Physical Education):

4 years training leads to the **Certificat d'Aptitude au Professorat d'Education Physique et Sportive** (CAPES)

3 years training is required for the Assistant Teacher qualification.

Costa Rica

Republic of Costa Rica

Education is the responsibility of the Higher Council of Education (Consejo Superior de Educacion). Many private institutions exist, but are subject to state inspection.

State education is free and compulsory for children aged six to fourteen.

The medium of instruction is Spanish.

EVALUATION IN BRITAIN

School

The certificate of completion of secondary studies/cycle IV (sometimes referred to as the **Bachillerato**) - generally considered to compare to GCE O-level standard.

Higher

Bachiller/Licenciado obtained after 4-5 years full-time study - may be considered to compare to British Bachelor degree standard.

MARKING SYSTEMS

School

Cycles I-III:

100	S	sobresaliente	excellent
80	N	notable	very good
60	Suf.	suficiente	pass
below 60	I	insuficiente	fail

Cycle IV:

Marking is on the scale 1-100, with 65 as the minimum pass mark.

Higher

The grading scale is 0-10 (maximum); with 7 as the minimum pass mark.

The symbols used are:

A   Curso Aprobado (course passed). It is only used when the course does not carry credit and therefore is not marked on the above numerical scale.

P   Reprobado (failed). This generally applies to practical courses, e.g. laboratory work where some of the requirements have not been fulfilled. P generally equates to 5.

RJ   Retiro Justificado. Used when a student has been authorized to withdraw from a course without penalty.

E   Escolaridad Ganada. Used in cases where the student has not passed a course, but has no marks below 6. The student is permitted to undertake further examinations and enrol in the following course even if the course in which an E has been obtained is a prerequisite.

SCHOOL EDUCATION

Pre-primary

Kindergarten courses are generally only 1 year. The number of pre-primary schools is increasing although they are mainly situated in urban areas.

Primary

Basic education consists of 3 cycles of 3 years which are compulsory. These 9 years plus the fourth 3-year cycle replaced the old 6+6 system of elementary and secondary education.

The curriculum in cycles I and II (the first 6 years of school education) includes language and social studies, science and maths, aesthetics (e.g. art, music, dance and drama) and practical activities (e.g. agriculture, physical education, family life and religion).

Promotion to each successive grade is based on continuous assessment marks of 60 and above. On successful completion of cycle II, the student is awarded a certificate.

On entering cycle III, the last 3 years of basic education, students have a choice of course: they may either continue academic studies or, if they intend to leave school at the end of the cycle and enter employment or undertake further technical training, follow a technical programme which has been in existence since 1971. The course provides training in agriculture in rural areas, crafts in certain urban areas and domestic industries for women in both areas. The course also contains an element of general academic studies. Students completing the technical course successfully are awarded a **Certificate of Aptitude**. Able students may also enter cycle IV. Students completing the general academic course are also awarded a **Certificate**.

Secondary

The final cycle of school education is also known as cycle IV or the diversified cycle. Students choose an area of specialization which may last 2 or 3 years. The specializations offered are:

Sciences and Letters (academic)	2 years
Fine Arts: Music, Drama, Dance	2 years
Technical: Industrial, Commercial, Agricultural	3 years
Health	Shortly to be introduced
Media	

The curriculum for all specializations is divided into 3 parts: the study of certain core subjects such as Spanish, social studies, maths, science, and foreign languages; the chosen specialization; and complementary studies which might include art, physical education and religious studies.

To be promoted to the second year in cycle IV and third year where it exists, students must pass all subjects with a minimum mark of 65. Students who successfully complete the Science and Letters course receive an **Academic Certificate** from the Ministry of Education specifying the level of achievement or a **Diploma** indicating the branch of study selected and the specialization within that branch if they have completed any of the other programmes.

HIGHER EDUCATION

Access to higher education is based on the diploma or certificate, called the **Bachillerato**, indicating completion of cycle IV. In addition students must pass an entrance examination and satisfy faculty and course requirements.

There are 3 state universities in Costa Rica: the University of Costa Rica (UCR), founded in 1940, the National University (UNA), founded in 1973, and the Instituto Tecnologico de Costa Rica (ITCR).

There is also a private university, the Universidad Autonoma de Centro America (UACA) and the Universidad Estatal a Distancia (UNED), which was modelled on the British Open University.

First degree studies are also offered at institutions of higher education outside the university sector.

There are 3 levels of academic study: pregrado, grado and posgrado. At the pregrado level, short courses (carreras cortas) are offered on completion of which a **Diploma** is awarded, but this does not give the holder professional status. Graduates of courses of at least 4 semesters (2 years) are known as **diplomados**.

Costa Rica

Titles obtainable at the grado level are the **Bachillerato** or **Bachiller** degree which is normally awarded after 4 years study and the **Licenciatura** after 5 years. The first year of the course leading to these qualifications is a general one at all 3 state universities.

At posgrado level, the qualification of **Maestria** normally entails 2 years study after the Bachillerato whereas the **Doctorado** follows 2 years after the Maestria.

Professional titles such as Profesor de Ensenanza Media (secondary teacher) or ingeniero (engineer) merely indicate the area of professional competence. Individual institutions decide whether to emphasize the title or the degree level.

To complete the academic requirements of a degree course, students must obtain the prescribed number of credits. For example, the requirements are for Bachillerato 120-144 credits, Licenciatura 30-36 credits beyond Bachillerato, Maestria 60-72 beyond Bachillerato, and Doctorate 100-120 also beyond the Bachillerato. A credit is defined as a course of work equivalent to 3 hours per week for 15 weeks.

The Autonomous University of Central America follows its own system of academic units; e.g. to qualify for the Bachiller, students must complete at least 72 units. Each 4-month period (3 per academic year) comprises 12 units. The Maestria requires at least 48 more units.

The Instituto Tecnologica de Costa Rica which has university status, offers courses for those aiming at professional and middle-level technical careers in agriculture, industry, mining, computer sciences and business administration. The Bachiller degree normally lasts 3 years, the exception being the 4-year technical teachers' course, run in conjunction with the University of Costa Rica, which provides the pedagogical content. On completion of the course, students receive the title **Profesor de Educacion Tecnica**. The grading scale runs from 0-100, with 70 as the minimum pass mark.

In the non-university sector, institutions are usually privately run and specialize mainly in business courses. The degrees and diplomas awarded by such institutions are not recognized in the formal education system.

TEACHER EDUCATION

Teacher training takes place solely at the higher education level at 1 of the 3 public universities.

Teachers may be either:

Profesores Titulados, who possess a recognized degree or professional title in education

Profesores Autorizados, who do not possess a title or specific degree in teaching but have qualifications in other fields

Profesores Aspirantes, who are not qualified but are employed as teachers because of the lack of qualified personnel.

Costa Rica

The universities therefore train teachers in the first category and provide up-grading courses for those in the other 2 categories.

Generally the Bachelor degree in Education at all levels requires 4 years full-time study comprising approximately 145 credits. The Licenciado represents a further years study and involves completion of an extra 33 credit courses. All degrees involve periods of practical training.

ADULT EDUCATION

Special provision is made for this. At all levels (cycles I-IV) there are night schools, multipurpose rural centres (centros polivalentes rurales), literacy training projects, Saturday schools and music training available. In the private sector, opportunities exist for adult study in commercial, technical and craft subjects.

Adults may qualify for academic certificates by completing a course of study entitled Educacion Basica por Suficienza which is considered the equivalent of completion of cycles I and II; and the **Bachillerato por Madurez** which is equivalent to the certificate awarded on completion of cycles III and IV of the formal system.

Cuba

Republic of Cuba

Since Fidel Castro came to power in 1959, education in Cuba has undergone major changes, with emphasis on education for the population as a whole and the development of skills necessary for the country's economy.

Primary education is compulsory.

The medium of instruction is Spanish.

The academic year runs from September to July.

EVALUATION IN BRITAIN

School

Secondary School Completion Diploma - generally considered to be below GCE O-level standard by at least 1 year.

3-year Pre-University Course - may be compared to GCE O-level standard.

Higher

Licenciados (from the University of Havana) - generally considered to compare to British Bachelor degree standard.

MARKING SYSTEM

The following grades are used throughout:

90-100	sobresaliente	excellent
80-89	aprovechado	above average
70-79	aprobado	passing
Below 70	desaprobado	failure

Cuba

SCHOOL EDUCATION

Primary

This covers grades 1-6.

Secondary

After primary school, pupils have 3 options: basic secondary school; lower secondary technical school; and teacher training.

Basic secondary school:

This 4-year course involves academic and practical studies. Apart from academic studies, students regularly work a period of 45 days in agricultural production at the <u>Escuelas Campo</u> (schools in the countryside). These are being replaced by co-educational lower secondary boarding schools in rural areas (<u>Escuelas en el Campo</u>).

Those who complete basic secondary school are awarded the **Secondary School Completion Diploma** and may go on to various kinds of upper secondary institution.

Technical schools:

<u>Escuelas Tecnologicas</u> (technical schools) offer general education and training in various technical subjects. Training leads to 2 levels of qualification - skilled worker and middle-level technician. These correspond, respectively, to the completion of the second and third year of the basic secondary course. Successful completion of technical school grants access to the technological institutes.

FURTHER EDUCATION

Courses at the pre-university institutes (<u>Institutos Pre-Universitarios</u>) normally cover 3 years. Successful students may enter the university faculties relevant to their pre-university studies. There are also 13 vocational pre-university institutes (<u>Institutos Pre-Universitarios Vocacionales</u>), the most important of which is the <u>Lenin Vocational Institute, Havana</u>.

Alongside the pre-university institutes, colleges like the Technological Institutes, Language Institutes, Technical Institutes of Economics, and Advanced Schools of Physical Education offer 4-year courses. Success in these courses grants access to the relevant university faculty.

Cuba

HIGHER EDUCATION

The 1962 Education Act consolidated all university courses into 3 national universities, the University of Havana, the Universidad Central de Las Villas and the Universidad de Oriente. University admission requirements are standardized and demand success in the pre-university secondary education course and the university entrance examinations.

Higher education courses are also offered at the Institute of Economics, the Andres Gonzalez Higher School of Fishing, the University Centre at Camaguey and university branches at agricultural, mining and industrial work centres.

TEACHER EDUCATION

Primary

A scheme has been set up to ensure that all primary school teachers have a degree in primary school teaching by 1990. They will be allowed sabbatical years to concentrate on degree studies. It is hoped that once primary school teachers have degrees, they will be able to take a sabbatical every 7 years to maintain and improve their standards.

Secondary

Teachers are trained at 3 institutes of education (within the Universities of Havana, Las Villas, and Oriente) which offer 5-year courses to qualify students for basic secondary and upper secondary teachers' certificates. The admission requirement is the Secondary School Completion Diploma.

Cyprus

Republic of Cyprus

Under the 1960 Constitution, education is the responsibility of the Greek-Cypriot and Turkish-Cypriot communities separately, a separation made absolute by the de facto division of the island since 1974. At secondary level in particular, identification with the education systems of Greece and Turkey, respectively, is strong.

In the south (Greek-Cypriot) there are many private educational institutions at all levels, but there are few in the north (Turkish-Cypriot).

In the south, primary education has been compulsory since 1962. In the north, it is not yet compulsory.

Greek and Turkish are the media of instruction in most schools in the south and north respectively. Most private schools are English-medium. There is one public English-medium school in the north. Almost all further education, apart from teacher-training, is in English.

The academic year runs from September to June.

EVALUATION IN BRITAIN

School

Apolytirion/Apodeiktikon/Lise Bitirme Diplomasi/Cyprus Certificate of Education - generally compared to GCE O-level standard on a subject-for-subject basis (where a pupil has obtained marks of over 50% in subjects which may be taken in the GCE examinations, except English language).

MARKING SYSTEMS

School

Greek-Cypriot system:	1-20, minimum pass mark 10
Turkish-Cypriot system:	1-10, minimum pass mark 5

Cyprus

SCHOOL EDUCATION

Pre-primary

Public provision has expanded considerably on the Greek-Cypriot side in recent years. There are now nursery schools and classes in ordinary schools. Provision is starting on the Turkish-Cypriot side. Private facilities exist on both sides.

Primary

This covers 6 years in both systems for children aged 5-and-a-half (Greek-Cypriot) and 6 (Turkish-Cypriot). The curriculum consists of Greek or Turkish, English (in the last 2 years), religious instruction, mathematics, natural science, history, geography, handiwork and art, music, agriculture and domestic science, physical education and general education (including hygiene).

Secondary

Public education is comprehensive and co-educational and covers 6 years in both systems, divided into two 3-year cycles.

Greek Cypriot: 3 years Gymnasium, followed by 3 years Lykeion.

Turkish Cypriot: 3 years middle school (Ortaokul), followed by 3 years Lise.

Most pupils complete all 6 years.

Entrance to the first cycle at the neighbourhood school is automatic in both systems, except the English-medium school Turk Maarif Koleji and English-medium streams at 2 other schools, which have a highly competitive entrance examination in Turkish and mathematics.

In both systems the first cycle is common for all pupils and consists of:

Greek-Cypriot	ancient and modern Greek, English, mathematics, general science, history, civics, geography, religious instruction, music, art, craft (for boys) and home economics (for girls), and physical education
Turkish-Cypriot	Turkish, English, mathematics, general science, social studies (history, civics, geography), ethics, music, art and physical education; optional subjects are religious knowledge, agriculture, home economics, craft and (in some schools) French and/or German

In the second cycle, the Greek-Cypriot system offers a scheme of options, the 5 main fields of specialization being classical (humanities), science, economics, commercial/secretarial, and foreign languages. Two-thirds of the teaching periods are still, however, devoted to the compulsory core-curriculum, consisting of ancient and modern Greek, English, French, mathematics, physics, chemistry, history, civics, religion and (fourth year only) general science, music and art.

On completion of this cycle, pupils take the examinations for the **Apolytirion**, in which English is a compulsory subject.

Cyprus

In the Turkish-Cypriot system, the curriculum in the first year of the Lise is very similar to that of the first cycle. Specialization begins in the second year, when pupils with good grades in science and mathematics may choose to enter the science stream while the remainder go into the arts stream. In the third year the science stream subdivides into natural sciences (with the emphasis on biology and chemistry) and mathematics (mathematics and chemistry). The compulsory core-curriculum is Turkish, English, history, civics, ethics, physical education and (second year only) psychology, mathematics, (third year only) philosophy. The English-medium school Turk Maarif Koleji, in common with other Lises, prepares pupils for the **Lise Bitirme Diplomasi**, in which English is a compulsory subject, and for the entrance examination to universities in Turkey. In addition, Turk Maarif Koleji prepares pupils for TOEFL, British O-levels and to a very limited extent A-levels. The English-medium streams established at 2 provincial Lises in 1980 will follow the same dual-purpose curriculum.

Before 1951, the examinations held at the end of the secondary cycle were the **Colony of Cyprus Ordinary** and **Distinction Examinations**. They were superseded by the **Cyprus Certificate Examinations** until 1959. Since independence, all examinations have been school-based and therefore have no general validity; in consequence many Greek-Cypriot public school pupils study privately for outside examinations such as Greek university entrance, GCE (6,165 entrants for one or more subjects in 1984) and TOEFL. Almost all the private schools work towards GCE as well as towards their internal diploma.

Technical/Vocational

Greek-Cypriot:

Only about 11% of pupils attend these schools, including those at Gymnasium level. The curriculum for the first 3 years is the same as in the Gymnasia, and pupils can transfer from one to the other at age 15. Specialization begins in the fourth year, and there are 3 main sections: electrical, mechanical and building, although some schools have dressmaking sections and there are now hotel and catering sections in all schools close to tourist areas. The sections are divided into 2 streams: vocational, which places more emphasis on practical work and lasts for 2-3 years; and technical, which is more academic and lasts the full 3 years.

Turkish-Cypriot:

About one-third of pupils at upper secondary level attend these schools. All but one cater for upper secondary level only and offer 3-year courses either in commercial or technical subjects; there are also 2 vocational schools for girls. In the technical schools, pupils choose a combination of subjects from the following: plumbing, sanitary engineering and metal work, electronics, electrical engineering, welding, technical drawing, woodwork and carpentry, fitting, autoengineering, and building (one school).

FURTHER EDUCATION

Greek-Cypriot:

A large number of students who continue their education do so abroad. In Cyprus the Higher Technical Institute offers 3-year English-medium courses, training technician engineers (civil, electrical and mechanical) for industry, and the merchant marine and teachers for the technical schools. Other public sector institutions offering full-time courses of 1-3 years are the Hotel and Catering Institute, the Forestry College and the Schools of Nursing and Midwifery. There is a rapidly growing number of students, including foreign entrants, at institutions in the private sector, most of which concentrate on secretarial or business studies and work towards internal diplomas and British professional qualifications.

Turkish-Cypriot:

Most students continue their education abroad. In Cyprus, as they no longer have access to the Higher Technical Institute (which was bi-communal before 1974) a Higher Technological Institute was established in Famagusta in 1979 to offer English-medium technician engineering courses at a similar level. There are also small agricultural, hotel and catering, and nursing and midwifery schools.

HIGHER EDUCATION

There is no university in Cyprus, but in 1985 the Government declared that one would be established within 3 years.

The Higher Technological Institute, Famagusta since 1986, has been upgraded and renamed The University of Eastern Mediterranean.

TEACHER EDUCATION

Primary and pre-primary

All teachers in the public sector must have attended a 3-year course from the end of upper secondary education at the Pedagogical Academy in the south and the Turkish Teacher Training College in the north.

Secondary

Greek-Cypriot:

All general secondary teachers must be graduates but few have any initial teacher training. The Pedagogical Institute runs in-service training courses which are compulsory for probationers, but voluntary for others.

Turkish-Cypriot:

All teachers must be graduates of a university or a teachers' training college, usually in Turkey. New entrants from universities must now also have a teaching qualification and most Turkish universities offer a pedagogical course which can be taken concurrently with the specialist subjects. There is little formal in-service training.

Czechoslovakia

Czechoslovak Socialist Republic

There are two National Ministries of Education: one in Prague for the Czech Socialist Republic and one in Bratislava for the Slovak Socialist Republic. However the content and duration of courses is fixed for all pupils nationwide.

The education system has undergone a number of changes, in particular those from the following Education Acts: 1948 which established nine years basic compulsory education; 1953 which lowered basic education to eight years, but established the eleven years 'unified' school system; 1960 which again increased basic education to nine years, expanded vocational and technical education and increased the emphasis on polytechnical studies; 1968 the Law on the Reorganization of Secondary General Education; 1978 introducing the new system; 1966 the Law on Higher Education Institutions; and 1980 the Law on Higher Education.

Education is now compulsory for ten years (under the Law of 1978) from ages six to sixteen. During 1948-53 it was compulsory for nine years from age six; 1953-60 eight years; and 1960-78 nine years.

The medium of instruction may be Czech or Slovak depending on the Republic in which an institution is situated, as the Constitution guarantees all citizens the right to education in their mother tongue.

The academic year is from September to August.

EVALUATION IN BRITAIN

School

Maturitni Zkouska/Maturita - may be considered to satisfy the general requirements of universities and polytechnics.

Higher

Absolvent Vysoke Skoly (university diploma or first degree) - generally compared to British Bachelor degree standard.

Ph.Dr. - generally considered to be between a British Master degree and a Ph.D.

Candidate of Science - generally compared to a British Ph.D.

Dr.Sc. - generally compared to a D.Litt/D.Sc.

Czechoslovakia

MARKING SYSTEMS

School

vyborny	1	excellent
chvalitebny	2	very good
dobry	3	good
dostatecny	4	pass
nedostatecny	5	fail

Higher

vyborne	excellent
velmi dobre	good
dobre	pass
nevyhovel	fail

SCHOOL EDUCATION

Pre-primary

Facilities are available in creches (Jesle) for children aged 1-3, and in nurseries (Materska Skola) for children aged 4-6.

Primary/Basic (Zakladni Skola)

1948-52:

This covered 9 years, divided into a 5-year lower cycle, followed by 4 years at middle school.

1953-60:

This covered 8 years, divided into a 4-year lower and 4-year upper cycle.

1961-76:

This covered 9 years, divided into a 5-year lower and 4-year upper cycle. From 1976 onwards it covered 8 years, divided into a 4-year lower cycle and a 4-year upper cycle.

Compulsory subjects are: mother tongue, Russian language, history, geography, mathematics, civics, general science, physical education, art and music. Some specialization is possible from grade 5. Progress to each grade is by continuous assessment.

Pupils may proceed if performance in 1 or 2 subjects is unsatisfactory, provided it is not in mother tongue or mathematics.

Czechoslovakia

Since 1978:

Under the new system basic education has been reduced to 8 years (i.e. the first cycle has been shortened to 4 years), and is followed by 2 years compulsory secondary education.

Secondary (Stredni Vseobecna)

This covered 3 years until 1969 when, under the Law of 1968 on the Reorganization of Secondary General Education, it was increased to 4 years. The transition was completed in 1973/4. Pupils specialized, until the mid-1960s in 1 of 3 options: humanities, mathematics and physics, biology and chemistry; and now in 1 of 2 branches: science, and humanities. However most of their time is spent on general core subjects: Czech language and literature, Russian, one modern language, mathematics, history, geography, physics, chemistry, biology and physical education. All pupils learn Russian as the first foreign language. On completion of this cycle pupils take the examinations for the **Vysvedceni o Maturitni Zkouska (Maturita)** (Czech)/**Skuske** (Slovak). The examinations are taken normally in only 4 subjects: Czech, Russian, mathematics (by pupils who specialized in science) or history (by pupils who specialized in the humanities), and 1 subject of their choice.

Technical (Stredni Odborna Skola)

A 4-year course of vocational training and general education leads to an occupational qualification with the opportunity for pupils to take the examinations for the **Maturitni Zkouska (Maturita)** (i.e. in Czech, Russian, technical subjects, and the preparation of a project). A 2-year course is available for pupils already holding the **Maturitni Zkouska (Maturita)** - it does not contain the element of general education. These schools offer courses in: agriculture, economics, fine arts, forestry, health services, library work, teacher training, and technical training.

Apprentice schools (Ucnovska Skola)/training centres (Odborne Uciliste) run by major industrial concerns, offer courses of 2-4 years for pupils who have 8 years basic education. The courses contain an element of general education, and train pupils to become skilled workers; they may then apply to technical universities.

Secondary schools for workers (Stredni Skola pro Pracujici) offer courses of evening study for pupils who have left school after 8 years basic education. These last 5 years and lead to the examinations for the **Maturitni Zkouska (Maturita)**.

HIGHER EDUCATION

There are approximately 40 institutions of higher education (Vysoke Skoly) including 5 traditional universities, 4 technical universities, and many specialized institutions (e.g. the Schools of Mining and Transport) with university status. Traditional universities offer courses mainly in the humanities, pure sciences, economics, law and medicine. The University of the 17th November, founded in the late 1960s and closed in 1974, specialized in courses for students from developing countries.

Admission is on the basis of the Vysvedceni Maturitni and an entrance examination. Admission quotas are determined annually by the 2 Ministries of Education.

Czechoslovakia

Until 1950 a first-degree course lasted 4 years but was then increased to 5 years. Under the Higher Education Act of 1966 the period of study is 4-6 years, according to subject. A first-degree course leads to the status of **absolvent vysoke skoly** (graduate) and the qualification of **Diploma** or **Degree**. Arts graduates with a Diploma do not add letters to their names but science graduates with a Degree use a prefix. The two are equivalent and Diploma does not signify an award for a shorter course, as in Britain.

Engineering	4-5 years, leads to qualification of **Inzenyr** (ing.)
Medicine	6 years, leads to qualification of **Doktor Mediciny** (MUDr.)
Dentistry	5 years, leads to qualification of **Doktor Mediciny** (MUdr.)
Veterinary medicine	5 years, leads to qualification of **Doktor Veterinarstvi** (MVDr.)
Pharmacy	4-5 years, leads to **Pharm.Dr.**
Architecture	5 years at technical universities, leads to qualification of **Inzenyr Architekt** (Ing.Arch.) or 6 years at a Faculty of Art leads to qualification of **Akademicky Architekt**.

Graduates may sit an additional examination, examen rigorosum/rigorozni zkouska. This leads to the qualification of **Doktor** (i.e. Doktor of Philosophy, Ph.Dr.; Doktor Prav; JUDr. - law; RNDr. - natural sciences, Pac.Dr., Pharm.Dr., Rs.Dr. According to the 1980 Law on Higher Education, no minimum time is prescribed and the preparation of a thesis is not obligatory. In many cases the qualification 'Doktor' is obtained a very short time after the Diploma. Before 1966 the first qualification in these subjects was the **Promovany**, e.g. **Filolog, Biolog, Provnik** etc.

A minimum of 3 years full-time study (or 5 years part-time) and the preparation of a thesis (vedecka aspirantura) leads to **Candidate of Science (Kandidat Ved/Candidatus Scientiarum/C.Sc.)**. At this level a working knowledge of 2 world languages is required.

A further period of research, which may vary in length, leads to **Doctor of Science (Doctor Ved/Doctor Scientiarum/Dr.Sc.)**.

At postgraduate level students must study Marxism-Leninism and languages.

TEACHER EDUCATION

Kindergarten

Teachers follow a 4-year course after 9 years basic education, or 2 years for holders of the Maturitni Zkouska (Maturita). Also a 5-year part-time course at a university may be taken.

Czechoslovakia

Primary and lower secondary

Teachers follow a 4-year course for holders of the Maturita in a Faculty of Education.

Secondary

A 4- or 5-year course at a university or Pedagogical Faculty, i.e. training alongside the normal degree studies, or a course comparable to B.Ed. at institutions of teacher education responsible only for the further education of teachers.

Denmark

Kingdom of Denmark

The Folkeskole Act of 1975 is the basis of the present primary and lower secondary education, organized as nine years comprehensive education, combined with an optional pre-school class and an optional tenth year.

Compulsory education was from age seven to fourteen until 1972, when it was increased to fifteen. It was increased again in 1973 to sixteen.

The medium of instruction is Danish, but English is compulsory from the fifth to the tenth form in the Folkeskole, and is provided or required by schools offering upper secondary education for another one to three years.

The academic year runs from August/September to June.

EVALUATION IN BRITAIN

School

Folkeskolens Udvide de Afgangsprove - generally compared to GCE O-level standard.

(Bevis for) **Studentereksamen, Hojere Forberedelseseksamen** and (Bevis for) **Hojere Handelseksamen** - may be considered to satisfy the general requirement of universities and polytechnics.

Higher

Candidatus Philosophiac (Cand. Phil.) - generally compared to British Bachelor degree standard.

Candidatus Magisterii (Cand. Mag.) and **Magister Artium** (Mag. Art.) - generally compared to British Master degree standard (MA/M.Sc.).

MARKING SYSTEMS

School

1947-63:

Marking was on a scale 0-15 (maximum), with 5.33 as the minimum pass mark.

Denmark

14.83-15	ug (udmaerket godt)
14.50-14.82	ug-
14.17-14.49	mg+
13.67-14.16	mg (meget godt)
13.00-13.66	mg-
12.33-12.99	g+
11.33-12.32	g (godt)
10.75-11.32	g-
9.33-10.74	tg+
8.00- 9.32	tg (temmelig godt)
5.33- 7.99	tg-
2.66- 5.32	mdl+ (maadelig)

Since 1963:

Marking is on a scale 0, 3, 5, 6, 7, 8, 9, 10, 11, 13 (maximum); minimum passing grade has been 6.

To pass the upper secondary examinations, the sum of all the marks must be at least 5.5 multiplied by the number of marks, and the sum of the two lowest marks plus the average of the rest of the marks must be at least 13.

Higher

Until 1971:

Each faculty within a university or department within other institutions of higher education had its own marking scale, e.g. 0-16, 0-15, 0-10, etc. There is usually some explanation on the transcript of marks.

Since 1971:

Marking is on a scale of 0-13 (maximum); an average of 6 or, in some cases, at least 6 in each subject, is required for passing.

SCHOOL EDUCATION

Pre-primary/kindergarten (Bornehave)

Some facilities are available for children aged 2-and-a-half to 7 years.

Before 1958

Primary (Grundskole)

This begins at age 7 and runs for 5 years.

Denmark

Secondary

Lower:

4 years of middle school were divided into an examination department and a non-examination department. On completion of the 4-year course in the examination department pupils took the **Hellemskoleeksamen**. The non-examination department offered 2-, 3- and 4-year courses.

Pupils passing the Middle School Examination could proceed for a 1-year course in the Real-department, culminating in the **Realeksamen**.

Upper:

Success in this examination or the Middle School Examination entitled pupils to proceed to a 3-year course at a Gymnasium, culminating in the **Studentereksamen**. Pupils could specialize in 1 of 3 branches during their 3-year course: classics, science, or modern languages. Each branch offered basically the same curriculum, although the emphasis on each subject varied according to the branch taken.

1958-76

Primary

This was a 7-year course at a Hovedskole. Pupils were not streamed in years 1-5. At the end of class 5, pupils could be divided into 2 sections/lines:

line a - mainly for pupils proceeding to classes 8, 9 and 10 of General, vocationally-oriented education

line b - to prepare pupils for the Realafdeling (3-year academic lower secondary course).

Secondary

Lower:

There are 2 courses - the Realafdeling and the General.

Realafdeling

The 7-year course at a Hovedskole plus this 3-year course was sometimes referred to as the Folkeskole. The curriculum covered Danish, Norwegian, Swedish, English, German, mathematics, history/civics, geography, biology, music, physical education, religious instruction and physics with chemistry. There was no streaming or specialization, but an emphasis on the sciences was possible in the third year. French and Latin were optional in the second and third years. On completion of the 3-year course, pupils sat for the **Realeksamen**. This consisted of written and oral examinations in Danish, arithmetic and mathematics, and the first foreign language, and oral tests in a certain number of the above-mentioned subjects, excluding religious instruction and music. This number was fixed by the Ministry of Education.

Denmark

General

All pupils took Danish, arithmetic, religion, physical education, integrated studies (history, geography, biology) and vocational/educational guidance activities. In addition each pupil chose up to 4 subjects from English, German, typing, home economics, workshop, childcare, housecraft, needlework, dressmaking, bookkeeping, library work, building crafts, electronics, photography, French, mathematics, science, agriculture and nature study. At the end of the ninth class all pupils were entitled to leave and receive a certificate testifying to their performance in the subjects taken (**Afgangsprove**), and on completion of class 10 the **Hojere Afgangsprove**. Most pupils however sat for optional state-run examinations at the end of class 9 or 10 - **Statskontrollerede Prove efter 9. eller 10. Klasse**. The usual school grading system was used, but there was no pass mark.

Upper:

It was possible to enter the 3-year academic upper secondary course at a <u>Gymnasium</u> on completion of the second year of the <u>Realafdeling</u> (lower academic secondary), but some pupils completed the full 3-year course and took the examinations for the **Realeksamen** before proceeding to the <u>Gymnasium</u>. The first year was common to all pupils, and at the start of class 2 pupils might choose between 2 specializations/ lines:

languages (Sproglig Linie) - covering social studies (offered from 1967/8), modern languages and classical languages

mathematics (Matematisk Linie) - covering social studies, mathematics and physics and natural science.

The curriculum included Danish, Latin/Greek, English (which could be dropped in classes 2 and 3 for pupils taking the mathematics specialization), German, French/Russian, history, classical culture, mathematics, general science, religious instruction and geography. The emphasis on the subjects depends on the specialization. On completion of the 3-year course, pupils took the examinations for the **Studentereksamen**. These consisted of 4 written examinations and 6 oral tests. The School-Leaving Certificate showed the marks obtained in the examinations and in the final year's work. If a pupil was not examined in a subject, the year's course mark was also noted on the certificate under the main heading 'examination marks' and sub-section 'transferred'.

Since 1976

Primary and Secondary

Lower:

According to the education act (Folkeskolelov) of 1975, in force from 1976, there is 9 years basic comprehensive school (<u>Folkeskole</u>) and a voluntary 1-year (class 10). On completion of class 9 all pupils are entitled to leave after sitting the **Afgangsprove** (leaving examination). On completion of class 10 pupils can sit the **Folkeskolens Udvide de Afgangsprove** (advanced leaving examination). There is no pass mark.

There is a common curriculum for all pupils in classes 1-7:

Denmark

Basic syllabuses: Danish, arithmetic/mathematics, physical education, Christian studies, creative art and music. Plus the following subjects, depending on class: history, geography, biology, needlework, English, woodwork, home economics, physics, chemistry, German.

Classes 8 and 9: Danish, arithmetic/mathematics, physical education, Christian studies, contemporary studies, physics/chemistry, English; with German and Latin optional. Electives are: creative art, music, history, geography, biology, needlework, drama, film, motor knowledge, vocational studies, electronics, child care, woodwork, home economics, typing, and photography.

Class 10: Danish, physical education, contemporary studies, English. Schools must offer German, arithmetic/mathematics, Christian studies, religious studies, physics/chemistry and French; they may also offer the electives available in classes 8 and 9, plus history.

There is no overall examination; leaving examination may be taken on a single-subject basis, and the pupils decide whether they want to take an examination in a particular subject.

Upper:

Pupils who have completed classes 9 or 10 of the Folkeskole can be admitted to a Gymnasium on the basis of a Statement, issued by their previous school, that they are 'qualified' or 'perhaps qualified' for studies at this level. They must have passed the leaving examination of the Folkeskole. In the first form of the 3-year course there are 2 'lines': languages and mathematics. In the second and third forms the language line is divided into 4 branches:

modern languages
music/languages
social studies/languages
classical languages.

The mathematics line is divided into 4 branches:

mathematics/physics
mathematics/biology
mathematics/social studies
mathematics/music.

The examination taken on completion of the course is the **Studentereksamen**, which consists of oral and written tests arranged by the Ministry of Education.

Higher Preparatory Examination (HF)

Courses leading to the **Hojere Forberedelseseksamen** (Higher Preparatory Examination) were introduced in 1967 for persons who have done practical work for some years, but want further education.

The formal requirement for admission to courses is 10 years school attendance, with the **Folkeskolens Udvide de Afgangsprove** in Danish and the **Afgangsprove** in mathematics, English and German. Alternative qualifications corresponding to 10 years of school attendance may, however, be accepted.

Denmark

The HF course is a 2-year course with a nucleus of common-core subjects and a number of elective subjects that can be freely combined. To complete the examination, the student must pass in all subjects from the common-core nucleus, plus some of the elective subjects. The HF exam may also be taken subject-by-subject after day or evening courses under the Act on leisure-time education. The common-core subjects are: Danish, Christian studies, history, biology, geography, mathematics, English, German, social studies, music/art, and physical education/sport. The first 3 (and English) must be taken for both years, the others for one. The optional subjects for the second year are: biology, mathematics, German, social studies, music, art, physical education, French/Russian, Italian/Spanish, physics, chemistry, psychology, and English.

Technical secondary

On completion of the ninth year of the general course of lower secondary education, pupils may take the **Teknisk Forberedelseseksamen**, and on completion of the tenth year the **Hojere Tekniske Forberedelseseksamen**. Success in either examination gives access to upper secondary schools and to schools which provide vocational education and training of a practical/theoretical nature, and to firms, companies and public institutions which provide a practical/theoretical education and training.

Under the new system of the post-1977 reform, technical secondary courses will be available (approximately 1 to 1-and-a-half years of education plus 1 to 1-and-a-half years of practical training) for pupils completing the basic 9 years of education. See below.

Vocational

Apprenticeship training (Laerlingeuddannelse):

Under the Apprenticeship Act of 1956 anyone below the age of 18 who is recruited for skilled work must become an indentured and registered apprentice. The minimum age to begin such training is now 16, and the person must have completed the compulsory period of education. The training period is separately fixed for each field and sector, and ranges from 2-4 years. In industry and crafts either a test is held with the award of a **Svendeprove** (journeyman's certificate), or a certificate of training is awarded after internal and external assessment. Commercial apprenticeships for employment in shops and offices lasts 2-4 years from the end of class 9. The theoretical instruction is given at Handelsskoler. The courses culminate in the **Handelsmedhjaelpereksamen** (shop and office assistants examination). A 1-year full-time course from the end of the ninth or tenth year at a Handelsskole leads to the **Handelseksamen**. Handelsgymnasier offer 2-year courses for holders of the Handelseksamen or a 1-year course for holders of the Studentereksamen. Both lead to the **Hojere Handelseksamen**. The **Hojere Teknisk Eksamen** (advanced technical examination) is a 2-year course. Year 1 is the same for all students; in year 2, they have 4 lines to choose from, all technical. The examination enables the student to take up higher education courses.

Basic vocational education (EFG):

This has existed as an alternative to apprenticeship training since 1972; and the Act on Basic Vocational Education was passed in 1977.

The first part (basic year) is common to all students in a particular sector and takes place in a school. The subjects taught comprise both general and vocational subjects. The student subsequently specializes and at the same time applies for a practical job in that field. The second part, which may take up to 3 years, alternates between school attendance at the technical school and practical work. A certificate is awarded after completion of the course of training. It is equivalent to the certificate issued on completion of apprenticeship training.

<u>Vocational Youth Schools</u> (Ungdomsskoler) provide courses for unskilled workers who have completed compulsory schooling and are aged under 18.

<u>Folkehojskoler</u> and <u>Folkeuniversitetet</u> offer full-time residential courses of all-round general education. There are no formal entrance requirements, but students should normally have completed Hovedskole and be 18 years old. There is no fixed syllabus or length of course, but courses normally contain Danish (literature and language), social and foreign affairs, foreign languages, psychology, musical appreciation, mathematics and science. There are no leaving examinations.

FURTHER EDUCATION

The <u>Teknika</u> offer 4-year courses leading to the qualification of **Teknikum Ingenior**. The entrance requirements are either the **Studentereksamen** (mathematics branch), Higher Preparatory Examination (HF), including the optional subjects mathematics and physics, or the special entrance examination for an engineering college. To be admitted to an engineering college the candidates are required to have practical training, either as an apprentice or on a specially prepared course of education at a workshop training school. At least 1 year of previous practice is required for candidates with upper secondary school leaving examinations, and for candidates with an entrance examination the training period must be at least 2 years. The first year is common for all students. They may then choose 1 of 5 lines/specializations: civil and construction engineering, electrical, mechanical, production engineering, or shipbuilding. Students who enter holding the **Studentereksamen** may first undertake the 3 years of specialization. Besides the purely technical subjects, students study Danish, foreign languages, accounting, law, and the principles of management.

HIGHER EDUCATION

The normal entrance qualifications for most faculties are the **Studentereksamen, Hojere Forberedelseseksamen** (HF) or **Hojere Handelseksamen** (HH). A system of numerus clausus (restricted entry) has operated since 1977 for faculties.

Students enjoy a certain amount of academic freedom and are free to decide when to take their final examination. Certain faculties (e.g. Science) lay down detailed syllabuses to be followed.

The <u>universities</u> confer both graduate and postgraduate degrees. There are no so-called undergraduate degrees. There are various types and levels of graduate degrees.

Denmark

Graduate degrees

The most usual is the **Candidatus degree**. The title is usually shortened to **Cand.** followed by the abbreviated Latin term for the discipline. The candidate degrees can be taken in the following disciplines: Theology (Cand. Theol.), Law (Cand. Jur.), Economics (Cand. Polit.), Statistics (Cand. Stat.), Actuarial Science (Cand. Act.), Sociology (Cand. Scient. Soc.), Humanities - 2 subjects (Cand. Mag.), Humanities - 1 subject (Cand. Phil.), Psychology (Cand. Psych.), Science (Cand. Scient.), and Medicine (Cand. Med.).

Before 1985

The Faculty of Arts offered different types and levels of degrees: **Cand. Phil. (Candidatus Philosophiac)** the degree awarded for a hovedfag (major subject), **Cand Mag. (Candidatus Magisterii)** awarded for hovedfag plus bifag (major plus minor), **Mag. Art. (Magisterkonferens)**, an advanced graduate degree in a single subject or a group of related subjects. It is scheduled to take 6 years. The last students are scheduled to pass this exam in 1992.

The bifag is the minor subject. It carries the title Examen Artium but does not constitute a degree/qualification or qualify for permanent posts. The minimum length of the course for the bifag is 2 years.

The hovedfag or major subject - Cand. Phil. - takes 4 years. Of these 4 years, the bifag takes up the first 2 years, after which the students continue with the course for the hovedfag for a further 2 years. A minor thesis, the so-called speciale, completes the hovedfag.

The Cand. Mag. degree comprises a hovedfag and a bifag in another subject. The subjects combined may be chosen from those offered by the Faculty of Arts or some subjects under the Faculty of Science. The course for the Cand. Mag. degree is thus at least 6 years.

Magister degrees take 6-8 years. The full title is Magister followed by the Latin term for the discipline. There are 2 Magister titles: **Magister Artium, Mag. Art.** (humanities, cultural sociology, and psychology); **Magister Scientiarum, Mag. Scient.** (science).

After 1985:

The bifag is substituted by a 2-year grunduddannelse. The Candidatus degrees are then as follows:

Cand. Phil. awarded after 2 years grunduddannelse and a supplementary 2 years in a related subject.

Cand. Mag. awarded after 4 years (2 years grunduddannelse and a combination of courses lasting 2 years) plus 1-2 years in another subject.

The **Mag. Art.** awarded after the Cand. Phil. plus 2 years study in the main subject (a total of 6 years).

Postgraduate degrees

The **Licentiate degree** is the first advanced postgraduate degree. Persons with a Danish Candidate (or Magister) degree are eligible for admission as Licentiate students provided that the Faculty concerned has approved their project. Licentiates are offered in the following fields: theology, medicine, law, economics, sociology, arts, psychology, and science.

Denmark

Doctoral degrees

These are awarded solely for a thesis submitted by the candidate. The requirements are such that several years intensive and independent research is necessary to produce a thesis of a sufficiently high standard to be accepted for the doctorate, and only persons of exceptional merits can expect to receive this degree.

Doctoral degrees are conferred in the following fields: theology (**Dr. Theol.**), social sciences (**Dr. Jur.**/law, **Dr. Polit.**/economics, **Dr. Scient.**/sociology), medicine (**Dr. Med.**), humanities (**Dr. Phil.**), science (**Dr. Scient.**), psychology (**Dr. Phil.**). The usual qualification for a Doctoral candidate is a Candidate, Magister, or Licentiate degree.

Specialist qualifications are obtained at other institutions of higher education.

Danish universities do not normally have faculties of pharmacy, dentistry, architecture and veterinary medicine. These are usually studied in specialized universities or institutions of higher education:

Dentistry - **Candidatus Odontologiae**, 5 years

Pharmacy - **Candidatus Pharmaciae**, 5 years

Architecture - **Arkitekt**, 5 years

Veterinary medicine - **Candidatus Medicinae Veterinariae**, 3-6 years.

These institutions (excluding the School of Architecture) also confer Licentiate and Doctoral degrees.

Engineering:

The education of Civilingeniorer takes place at Denmark's Tekniske Hojskole (the Technical University of Denmark) and at the Aalborg University Centre. The entrance requirements are the Studentereksamen (mathematics/physics branch) or the Hojere Forberedelseseksamen (including the optional subjects mathematics and physics). The duration of study is generally 5 years.

The degree of **Civilingenior** is conferred on the student after the final examination has been passed.

Civilingenior (graduates from Denmark's Technical University and Aalborg University Centre) may continue their studies another 2-3 years to obtain the degree of **Lic. Techn.** (Licentiatus Technices). These postgraduate studies consist of research work which forms the basis for a thesis constituting the final examination work. The Doctor's degree (Dr. Techn.) can also be obtained at these institutions.

The engineering degree (**Akademiingenior**) may be obtained after a course lasting 3 years at the Denmark's Ingeniorakademi. The entrance requirements are the **Studentereksamen** (mathematics/physics line) or Hojere **Forberedelseseksamen/Teknikumingenior**. A special entrance examination for engineering college is applicable for candidates who do not hold the above mentioned examinations.

Beside the universities, 2 university centres were established in the 1970s; at Roskilde in 1972 and at Alborg in 1974. Courses at these institutions are shorter than the traditional courses and more practical.

Denmark

Folkehojskoler and Folkuniversitet offer full-time residential courses of all-round general education. There are no formal entrance requirements, but students should normally have completed Hovedskole and be 18 years age. There is no fixed syllabus or length of course, but courses usually contain Danish (literature as well as language), social and foreign affairs, foreign languages, psychology, musical appreciation, mathematics and science. There are no leaving examinations.

TEACHER EDUCATION

Before 1968:

Bornehave (pre-primary/kindergarten) - teachers at this level follow a 2-and-a-half year upper secondary course.

Folkeskole (i.e. primary and lower secondary) - teachers followed a 3-year course for holders of the Studentereksamen, or a 4-year course for holders of the Realeksamen.

Since 1968:

Bornehave (pre-primary/kindergarten) - teachers must follow a 3-year upper secondary course from the Studentereksamen or completion of Folkeskole, Hojere Forberedelseseksamen, Hojere Handelseksamen education, plus 2 subjects in the Hojere Forberedeseksamen, plus 2 years practical experience.

Folkeskole (primary and lower secondary basic education) - teachers follow a 3-and-a-half to 4-year course from the Studentereksamen or Hojere Forberedelseksamen or Hojere Handelseksamen at a university-level training institute/school (Laererseminarium).

Gymnasium (upper secondary) - teachers at this level are university graduates holding the **Candidatus Magisterii** who have passed the **Paedagogicum**. The Paedogogicum is a postgraduate course lasting 5 months conducted by the Ministry of Education's Directorate for Upper Secondary Education. It includes teaching practice at an upper secondary school and a concurrent theoretical course comprising general education, didactics, educational psychology and school hygiene.

Dominican Republic

Education is compulsory from age seven to fourteen.

The medium of instruction is Spanish.

The academic year runs from September to June.

EVALUATION IN BRITAIN

School

Bachillerato en Ciencias y Letras - generally considered to compare to GCE O-level standard.

Higher

Licenciatura - generally considered to be below British Bachelor degree standard.

MARKING SYSTEM

School

Primary (years 1-6)

85-100	A	
70-84	B	
55-69	C	Pass mark C
40-54	D	
0-40	F	

For the Bachillerato, marking is on a percentage scale applied to the average of the monthly grades at the end of the academic year.

Dominican Republic

```
80-100    course passed with no final examination required
60-79     referred to a final examination
0-59      fail
```

Higher

```
90-100    A
80-89     B     Pass mark 70
70-79     C
60-69     D
0-59      E
```

SCHOOL EDUCATION

Pre-primary

Very few facilities are available. However, most private schools offer a 4 year pre-primary programme.

Primary

This extends over 6 years and on completion pupils are awarded the **Primary School Certificate**.

Secondary

This is divided into two different systems. The traditional system extends over 6 years.

Until 1967/8:

The 6-year period was divided into a 2-year cycle of intermediate education at a <u>Liceo Intermedio</u>, followed by a 4-year cycle of secondary education. On completion of the first cycle pupils were awarded the **Certificado de Suficiencia en los Estudios Intermedios**, and on completion of the second cycle the **Bachillerato**. In the final year of the second cycle students could specialize in 1 of 3 areas: physics and sciences, mathematics and physics, or humanities and philosophy. Students wishing to specialize in commercial fields could take a 3-year upper secondary course leading to the **Bachiller Comercial**.

1970 - present

The second system belongs to 'Reforma Educativa' which was initiated in 1970, but due to the lack of facilities most public and private schools were unable to adopt this system.

The 6-year period is made up of a 4-year cycle of intermediate secondary education - the 'ciclo comun', followed by a 2-year cycle, during which pupils specialize - 'ciclo superior'. On successful completion of this cycle pupils obtain the **Bachillerato** and if they wish to attend university immediately, they must take the academic specialisation: **ciencas y letras**. If students specialise in commercial fields, agriculture, home economics or industrial arts they are awarded the **bachiler tecnico**, which enables them to seek employment, rather than continue their education.

Dominican Republic

Technical secondary

A number of technical and vocational schools offer courses in agriculture, commerce, home economics and various trades. Entrance requirements vary from completion of grade 6 to completion of grade 10, and courses last 1-4 years. The usual qualification obtained is **'Perito'** ('expert in...'). Courses are now being standardized to form the ciclo superior, and to lead to the award of a **Bachiller Technico**.

The Instituto Politecnico Loyola (IPL) offers a 4-year course, covering grades 8-12, and leading to the qualification of **Perito**. The qualification awarded by this Institute is usually considered to be of a higher standard than that obtained elsewhere.

HIGHER EDUCATION

Courses of higher education last 3-5 years and lead to a **Tecnico, Profesorado, Licenciatura** or professional qualification. A 5-year course in dentistry, law and veterinary medicine leads to the qualification of **Doctorado**, with an extra year in medicine.

After a further year of study students obtain the **Magister** or **Doctorado**.

There are 19 universities:

Universidad Autonoma de Santo Domingo (UASD)
Universidad Catolica Madre y Maestra (UCMM)
Universidad Nacional Pedro Henriquez Urena (UNPHU)
Universidad Asociacion Pro-Educacion y Cultura (UNAPEC)
Universidad Central del Este (UCE)
Instituto Tecnologico de Santo Domingo (INTEC)
Universidad Tecnologica de Santiago (UTESA)
Universidad Dominicana O & M (O & M)
Universidad Nordestana (UNNE)
Universidad Iberoamericana (UNIBE)
Universidad Adventista (UNAD)
Universidad Interamericana (UNI)
Universidad Tecnologica del Cibao (UTECI)
Instituto Tecnico Comercial (ITECO)
Instituto Tecnologica del Sur (UTESUR)
Universidad Eugenio Maria de Hostos (UNIREMHOS)
Universidad Catolica de Santo Domingo (UCSD)
Universidad CDEP
Universidad Odontologica (UOD)

The entrance requirements for degree courses is the bachillerato, and, for some universities, since 1972, the **Academic Aptitude Test**.

TEACHER EDUCATION

Primary

Before 1966 a 3-year upper secondary course led to a **Diploma de Aptitud a la Ensenanza** at an Escuela Normal, with the title of **Maestro Normal Primario** or **Maestro Normal de Primera Ensenanza**.

Since 1966/7 on completion of grade 10 (the ciclo comun) students take a 2-year course leading to the qualification of **Maestro Primario**. All students take the following subjects: Spanish, mathematics, civics, science and professional education.

Secondary

Before 1966 a 3-year course at an Escuela Normal for holders of the Bachillerato, led to the qualification of **Maestro Normal de Segunda Ensenanza** (not a degree-level course).

Since 1966 - a 2-year course at university has led to the qualification of **Profesorado**, or a 4-year course to a **Licenciatura en Educacion**, with a major in mathematics, social studies, biology, physics, language (English, Spanish or French), chemistry or philosophy.

Ecuador

Republic of Ecuador

The Government through the Ministry of Education exercises central control of all aspects of primary and secondary education. The National Council for Higher Education controls higher education institutions. There are public (i.e. state) and private institutions at all levels.

The first nine years of education, up to the end of the basic cycle (first cycle of secondary education), are compulsory.

The medium of instruction is Spanish.

The academic year varies from October to July, to April to January.

EVALUATION IN BRITAIN

School

Bachillerato (humanidades, ciencias or tecnico) - generally considered to compare to GCE O-level standard.

Higher

Licenciado or **Professional title** obtained after 5-6 years study - may be considered to compare to British Bachelor degree standard.

MARKING SYSTEMS

School

At secondary level there are usually 3 examinations during the academic year (at the end of each term), each marked on a scale of 0-20.

Ecuador

19-20	excellent
16-18	very good
12-15	good
10-11	pass
0-9	fail

In order to take the final examination each year pupils must obtain over half marks in each of the 3 (i.e. a total of over 30 in each subject). The only mark to appear on transcript is that obtained in the final examination, on a scale of 0-20.

Higher

There is no standard system of grading common to all institutions of higher education, and it may even vary within the constituent faculties of an institution. The most common systems used are the percentage scale and a scale of 0-10, with 6 or 7 being the pass mark.

SCHOOL EDUCATION

Primary

This begins at the age of 6 for 6 years, divided into three 2-year cycles.

Secondary

This may take up to 8 years depending on the chosen specialization. The period is divided into a 3-year basic cycle, followed by a cycle of 3-5 years. The basic cycle is common for all pupils. In the diversified cycle, pupils may specialize in:

Academic studies, leading to the examinations for the **Bachillerato en Humanidades** or **Ciencias** after 3 years

Technical studies, leading to the examinations for the **Bachillerato Tecnico** after 3 years

Vocational studies, leading to a qualification after 1-2 years.

HIGHER EDUCATION

In theory all students holding a Bachillerato with a particular specialization may proceed to university, although in practice only those with an academic specialization may do so. Some of the private institutions also require prospective students to sit an entrance examination.

Ecuador

Students may take courses over 4 years leading to the award of the **Licenciado**, or 5-6 years leading to the award of a professional qualification (e.g. electrical engineer, economist, architect, veterinary surgeon, etc.; the latter 3 confer the title of **Doctor**), with 7 years for medicine.

Very few institutions offer postgraduate courses although some are available in technical fields, leading to the qualification of **Masterado**.

Short courses of between 2-4 years lead to an advanced vocational qualification, e.g. librarian, nurse, etc.

The Escuela Politecnica Nacional is a degree-awarding institution.

TEACHER EDUCATION

Primary

Teachers are trained in 2-year post-Bachillerato courses.

Secondary

Teachers are trained in 4-year courses at university leading to a **Profesor de Educacion Media**.

Egypt

Arab Republic of Egypt

There are two parallel systems of education in Egypt: a modern secular system that comprises both public and private schools and the Al-Azhar Islamic education system.

'Basic education' is compulsory.

Public education is free at all levels.

The medium of instruction is Arabic.

The academic year runs from September to May.

EVALUATION IN BRITAIN

School

School Certificate of General Secondary Education - generally compared to GCE O-level standard on a subject-for-subject basis, provided marks of at least 50% have been obtained in subjects which can be taken in the GCE examination, except English language.

Higher

Bachelor degree - not generally compared to British Bachelor degree standard students with a high final classification may be accepted for post-graduate work.

MARKING SYSTEMS

School

Individual subjects in the General School Certificate examination have different maximum and minimum pass marks. All subjects require a minimum of 40% of the maximum pass mark apart from Arabic and Religion, which require a minimum pass mark of 50%.

Average grades of 60-65% are required to satisfy Egyptian matriculation requirements, although some faculties may demand higher average grades. The Faculties of Science, Engineering and Medicine, for example, may demand average grades of 90%.

Egypt

Higher

Marking systems vary from faculty to faculty.

Arts	90-100%	excellent
	80-89	very good
	65-79	good
	50-64	pass
Medicine	85-100%	excellent
Dentistry	75-84	very good
Veterinary Medicine	65-74	good
Pharmacy	60-64	pass
Other science	85-100%	excellent
faculties	75-84	very good
	65-74	good
	50-64	pass

A first-class Honours degree is awarded if a student obtains grades of 'excellent' in the last year's work and 'very good' in each of the preceding years.

A second-class Honours degree is awarded if a student obtains grades of 'very good' in the final year's work and 'good' in each of the previous years.

No Honours recognition is awarded if a failure has been indicated at any time during course work.

The American University in Cairo operates the American marking system.

SCHOOL EDUCATION

Primary

This covers a 6-year compulsory period (ages 6-12). Pupils take examinations each year in order to be promoted to the next grade. At the end of the sixth grade, pupils take the **Primary School Certificate** examination, which ensures promotion to the preparatory level.

Preparatory

This lasts 3 years (ages 12-15) and has now been made compulsory, giving a 9-year system of 'basic education'. This is divided into general and vocational streams, although it has been decided to delay specialization until the beginning of secondary education. Pupils are promoted to the next grade by examination and at the end of the course take the **General Preparatory Education Certificate** examination. According to the results obtained in the examination, students enter the secondary general schools, secondary technical schools, primary teacher training colleges or vocational training schools.

Egypt

Secondary

This lasts 3 years (ages 15-18). Pupils enter the general or technical schools.

General secondary

These schools offer an academic course which prepares pupils for university. During the first year pupils follow a common curriculum. In the second and third years pupils choose between sciences, mathematics and literature.

At the end of the course pupils take the **School Certificate of General Secondary Education** or Thanawiya Amma in 13 subjects within the chosen branch. Marks of at least 50% in each subject are needed to obtain a Certificate. This Certificate also gives access to university.

Technical secondary

The 1956 Educational Act established Special Consultant Councils to promote industrial, agricultural and commercial schools.

Technical secondary schools prepare students for work in skilled trades in industry, agriculture and commerce. Applicants must have the Preparatory School Certificate and not exceed 18 years of age. These schools offer a 3-year technical course. Students who are successful in the national examination are awarded the **Technical Secondary School Certificate**, which makes them eligible for higher education. The programme of the technical secondary schools covers 4 subject-areas: general education, industrial education, agricultural education and commercial education. Students follow the general education course and choose 1 of the other subjects as their specialization.

Industrial:

During the first year, students cover a general course involving metal lathe work and blacksmith work, carpentry and joinery, masonry, weaving and spinning. In the second and third years students may specialize in general mechanic training, automechanics, electricity, masonry, weaving and spinning. Students may take the final state secondary examinations at the end of the industrial course. This gives access to **Bachelor degree** courses at the Institutes of Higher Learning in Industrial Technology.

Agricultural:

A 3-year programme serves as a general introduction to agriculture, providing knowledge of modern agricultural methods and some field experience. At the end of the course students can take the final state examination. This gives access to the Institutes for Higher Learning in Agriculture which offer Bachelor degree courses.

Commercial:

Students take a general 3-year course. Those who gain high marks in the final examination may enter the Higher Institutes of Commerce and pursue a **Bachelor degree** course.

Vocational:

Many more students are involved in vocational training courses, offered by private industry, religious foundations and the Ministry of Industry. The Ministry of Industry has training centres and supervises the training of apprentices in 101 trades. Students who hold the Preparatory School Certificate and are not over 18 years of age can follow a 5-year course at the end of which they receive the **Vocational Diploma**.

HIGHER EDUCATION

Entry to university in Egypt is extremely competitive and is based upon a student's score in the General Secondary or the Technical Secondary Certificate. Students would normally need an average of 70% or above.

A **Bachelor degree** normally takes 4 years (5 years for engineering and pharmacology and 7 years for medicine). After 3 years further study, students may obtain the **Majistair** (1-year full-time study and 2 years set aside for the dissertation); 4 (occasionally 3) further years study lead to the **Doctorate**.

Higher institutes

Some 2-year industrial and commercial institutes and 2- and 4-year private institutes exist on the post-secondary level, although many higher institutes were integrated into the university system after 1975. These were established after the 1952 revolution had called for higher education to be made available to the masses.

TEACHER EDUCATION

Primary

Students who wish to teach in primary schools must hold the Preparatory School Certificate. They follow a 5-year course which provides a general education for the first 3 years while students may specialize in a particular area during the fourth and fifth years. Successful students are awarded the **Elementary Teaching Certificate** after the final examination. Graduates who score in the top 25% in the final examination can apply for admission to the second year of a university faculty of education to follow courses leading to the Bachelor degree and the Preparatory or Secondary Teaching Certificate.

The Al-Azhar teacher institutes also provide 3-year scientific and literary courses with religious orientation for students who will teach in primary schools supervised by Al-Azhar.

Secondary

University faculties of education provide 4-year secondary school teacher training courses for holders of the General Certificate of Secondary Education. Both preparatory and general secondary teachers follow the same course which leads to the **Bachelor degree**.

Graduates who hold a 4-year university degree in an academic field can also teach on the secondary level after undergoing 1 year of postgraduate training at the Faculty of Education when they are awarded the **General Diploma**.

Egypt

Students who have completed the technical secondary school course may pursue a 2-year course at a technical teacher-training institution which enables them to teach in the 3-year technical secondary school. Alternatively they may enrol for the 5-year **Bachelor of Science** degree course at the Faculty of Technology and Education in Matarey and go on to teach at the vocational-technician secondary school.

Some higher institutes train general secondary school graduates as teachers of art, domestic science, music and physical education. These are 4-year courses.

There are facilities for in-service teacher training in some university faculties of education.

El Salvador

Republic of El Salvador

Education in El Salvador is controlled by the Ministry of Education and is free.

In the 1960s and 1970s reforms and full-scale expansion plans were initiated to improve facilities which were almost non-existent in rural areas. Teacher training programmes were also expanded to provide the teaching force for the new schools.

Basic or primary education is compulsory for all children where facilities are available.

The medium of instruction is Spanish.

The school academic year runs from February to October. At the National University of El Salvador the year runs from January to October; the year at the Universidad Centro Americana Jose Simeon Canas runs from March to December. Both institutions operate on two semesters, each of five months.

EVALUATION IN BRITAIN

School

Bachillerato (academic) - generally considered to compare to GCE O-level standard.

Higher

Licenciado and **Professional Titles** (obtained after 5-6 years) - may be considered to compare to British Bachelor (Honours) degree standard.

MARKING SYSTEMS

School

Subjects are graded on a scale of 1-10 (maximum) as follows:

El Salvador

10	sobresaliente	excellent
9	muy bueno	very good
8	bastante bueno	quite good
6-7	bueno	good
5	regular	pass
1-4	malo	fail

Higher

The grading scale is the same as that used for school qualifications, except at the Universidad Centro Americana Jose Simeon Canas where 6 is the minimum pass mark.

SCHOOL EDUCATION

Pre-primary (parvulario)

Kindergarten lasts 3 years, for children aged 4-6, where facilities exist. The state-run institutions, Escuelas de Parvulos, prepare children for primary studies.

Primary (basico)

This lasts 9 years and is compulsory for students aged 7-15. It is composed of 3 cycles, each of 3 years. Level 1 consists of cycles 1 and 2 (grades 1-6) and level 2 consists of the third cycle (grades 7-9).

State-run primary schools, Escuelas de Educacion Basica, curriculum covers studies in the humanities, which includes Spanish and social sciences, and science, which includes maths and physical education. In the third cycle students begin the study of a foreign language.

Pupils who pass in all subjects and fulfil the requirements of each cycle receive a certificate. Transcripts showing grades achieved are issued at the end of each year throughout primary and secondary education.

Secondary (medio)

The secondary cycle for students of 16-18 years lasts 3 years covering grades 10-12, culminating in the **Bachillerato** which gives access to higher education provided that the appropriate entrance examination has been passed. State secondary institutions are called Institutos.

The secondary curriculum entails the study of certain core subjects in the fields of language, social studies, foreign languages, maths, natural sciences, art and sport. In addition to these basic subjects, which must be studied by all, pupils can choose to specialize in certain areas. The **Bachillerato** is then awarded in the corresponding specialization.

El Salvador

The following specializations and options within those areas are possible:

Academic	natural sciences mathematics and physics humanities
Agriculture	
Arts	plastic arts painting music
Commerce and administration	bookkeeping secretarial skills
Hotel management, catering and tourism	
Seamanship and fishing	naval engineering) fishing) not offered seamanship) since 1976
Health	nursing environmental health
Vocational	beauty art and decoration fashion and design
Industrial	engineering automobile engineering electrical engineering electronic engineering
Pedagogical	nursery education special education

HIGHER EDUCATION

Access to higher education is on the basis of success in the Bachillerato and an appropriate entrance examination.

There are 15 universities, including the National University of El Salvador and the Universidad Centro Americana Jose Simeon Canas. In the non-university sector, there are several specialized institutions.

The University of El Salvador, founded in 1841, is a state institution which offers degree courses leading to the professional titles of **Ingeniero** and **Arquitecto** in the fields of engineering and architecture, and to the qualification of **Licenciado** in most other fields. The length of the course varies according to subject and may last from 5 to 7 years, although 5 years full-time study is normal. Graduation is followed by a period of professional work in the service of the state. The title of **Doctor** is awarded in medicine, chemistry and pharmacy after 7 years full-time study. The **Doctorado** is awarded after a further 2 years study following the Licenciado or professional title.

El Salvador

University education is based on the American pattern in that the first 2 or 3 years of the course are general, preparing students for specialization in the later stages of the degree. Graduation occurs when a certain number of credits have been accumulated. Credits are earned on completion of a series of courses which are to a certain extent complete in themselves. A student who has completed the academic requirements of the course, i.e. has obtained sufficient credits, is known as an **Egresado**. Students must then present a thesis and they graduate when it has been approved.

The <u>Universidad Centro Americana Jose Simeon Canas</u> is a private university which began teaching in 1966. Studies lead to the Licenciado, awarded after 5 years in economics and humanities, after 6 years in administrative studies, and after 5 years for the title of Ingeniero.

Higher education courses outside the universities may be followed at specialized institutions such as the <u>School of Social Work</u>, the <u>Higher Teacher Training Institute</u>, the <u>School of Physical Education</u> and the <u>Central American Technical Institute</u>. Institutions in other fields, e.g. nursing, agriculture, art, tourism, are generally known as Higher or National Schools. Courses may be of 2 or 3 years.

TEACHER EDUCATION

Teacher training courses may vary from 9 months to 3 years. At the end of the course, students receive a **Certificate**.

Primary teachers are trained in normal schools (Escuelas Normales), an alternative to grades 10-12 of the secondary cycle. The certificate received after 3 years also gives access to certain areas of higher education, e.g. the Faculty of Humanities at the University of El Salvador, the School of Social Work, or other similar institutions.

Training courses for secondary teachers and teachers of higher education are run at the universities or at the Higher Teacher Training Institute.

ADULT EDUCATION

The <u>Adult Literacy Programme</u> attracts many young people who have either never had the opportunity of attending schools or who finished school prematurely because existing facilities were insufficient.

Adult Study Centres (Centros Escolares de Adultos) give the opportunity to improve on existing education by offering an accelerated first cycle of 3 years (normally 6 years) and a second cycle of 3 years which is identical to the third cycle of primary education. Those completing each cycle will receive the same certificates as students who complete their education normally. These centres also offer vocational training programmes.

Ethiopia

Since the 1974 revolution and the establishment of Ethiopia as a socialist state, the military government has attempted to introduce wide educational reform with the accent on non-formal and adult education and in-service teacher training.

Education is free from primary to college level.

The medium of instruction is Amharic in primary schools and English in secondary schools and university.

The academic year runs from September to July.

EVALUATION IN BRITAIN

School

School Leaving Certificate - generally considered comparable to GCE O-level standard when a mark of C or above has been achieved.

Higher

An Ethiopian **Bachelor degree** is unlikely to be considered comparable to a British Bachelor degree.

MARKING SYSTEMS

School

Marks are out of 100, with 50 as the pass mark.

A	90-100	excellent
B	80- 89	very good
C	60- 79	satisfactory
D	50- 59	poor
E	Below 50	failure

Ethiopia

Higher

Marks are out of 100; the lowest pass mark is 60.

90-100	excellent
80- 89	good
70- 79	average
60- 69	pass
0- 59	failure

SCHOOL EDUCATION

Primary

Primary schooling lasts 6 years. At the end of grade 6 pupils take the Primary School Certificate.

Secondary

The Government intends to change the secondary school system from a 2-year lower and a 4-year higher to a 4-year lower and a 2-year higher format.

Lower:

Schooling covers grades 7-10 (ages 13-16). Schools offer a practical education. All instruction is theoretically in English from grade 7. There is a national examination at grade 8.

Higher:

The Ministry of Education plans eventually to postpone higher secondary education until pupils have undertaken a period of practical experience. At present, grades 11-12 offer general academic courses. At the end of this period pupils take the **School Leaving Certificate**.

FURTHER EDUCATION

Technical and vocational

This is provided by secondary school-level courses and specialist institutions. These include the Polytechnic Institute in Bahir Dar, the Commercial School in Addis Ababa, the Veterinary School in Debre Zeit, the Wondo Guenet Forestry Resources Institute, the Technical School at Addis Ababa, the Technical School in Asmara, the Institute of Telecommunications, and the Institute of Civil Aviation.

In-service training is provided by several government agencies.

Ethiopia

Agricultural

The Agricultural Institutes at Ambo and Jimma and the Junior Agricultural Colleges at Debre Zeit and Aswassa offer a 2-year diploma in general agriculture.

Military

The Ethiopian Military Academy in Harar aims to offer courses which are broadly comparable to the first and second years of Ethiopian degree courses.

HIGHER EDUCATION

The entry qualification for all higher education institutions is the School Leaving Certificate. Higher education is provided by several post-secondary institutions (see FURTHER EDUCATION and TEACHER EDUCATION) and also by Addis Ababa University and the University of Asmara.

Addis Ababa University was founded in 1961 and has 10 campuses. It was closed in 1974 and reopened in 1976.

The University of Asmara was founded in 1959 as a private Catholic university. It no longer has any private status and like Addis Ababa University is now administered by the Higher Education Commission.

TEACHER EDUCATION

In the past, teacher education involved pre-service training: for primary, 1 year after grade 11; for lower secondary, 2 years after grade 12; and for senior secondary, 4 years after grade 12. Emphasis is now on in-service training.

Primary

Primary school teachers take 1-year training courses after grade 12 at the regional teacher training institutes coordinated by the Ministry of Education. The Ministry hopes to initiate 4-year pedagogy courses in lower secondary schools.

Secondary

Lower:

Lower secondary school teachers receive instruction at the College of Teacher Education in Kotebe. The College offers a 2-year course.

Science teachers are trained at the Alameya College of Agriculture and the Bahir Dar Science Teachers' Junior College.

Bahir Dar Teachers' College offers a 4-year degree course for secondary school teachers, leading to the degree of **B.Ed**.

The Ministry is also planning to open 2-year pedagogy courses in selected higher secondary schools which will provide trained lower secondary school teachers.

Ethiopia

Higher:

Higher secondary teachers are trained in the Faculty of Education of Addis Ababa University.

Technical

The College of Pedagogical Sciences at Addis Ababa University offers a 2-year diploma programme for prospective technical education teachers.

ADULT AND NON-FORMAL EDUCATION

The Adult Education Department offers adult literacy courses. The Community Skill Training Centres offer basic education and literacy courses for adults. The Ministry of Education is extending correspondence-course education.

Fiji

The education system is closely related to that of New Zealand, and students take some examinations administered by the New Zealand Examinations Board, but increasingly modified to Fijian needs. The New Zealand examinations will be replaced by the Fiji School Leaving Certificate in 1989.

There is no compulsory period of education, but most children complete at least eight years of primary education.

The medium of instruction is English, although in the early years of primary education one of the Fijian/Indian languages may be used.

EVALUATION IN BRITAIN

School

Fiji Junior Certificate - generally considered to be below GCE O-level and Certificate of Secondary Education standard.

Form 7 Examination - generally considered to be between GCE O- and A-level standard. Passes in 5 separate subjects, with grade B in 4 of them, would satisfy University of London entrance requirements.

New Zealand University Entrance Examination - generally considered to be between GCE O- and A- level standard (see corresponding section in chapter on New Zealand).

Higher

Foundation Year of the University of the South Pacific - generally considered to compare to GCE A-level standard.

Bachelor degrees - generally considered to compare to British Bachelor degree standard.

Fiji

MARKING SYSTEMS

School

New Zealand University Entrance Certificate - no marks are shown on the certificate.

Form 7 Examination - percentage scale, minimum pass is 50%; the pass marks are then transferred into grades:

A	80-100%
B	65-79
C	50-64

Higher

Degrees of the University of the South Pacific are unclassified.

SCHOOL EDUCATION

Primary

This normally lasts 8 years from age 6. At the end of this period pupils sit the **Fiji Eighth Year Examination**. Some schools take in pupils at the end of the sixth year of primary school. These pupils sit the **Fiji Intermediate Schools Examination**.

Secondary

This covers a possible 7 years: 4 years junior secondary and a possible 3 years senior secondary. At the end of form IV all pupils sit the **Fiji Junior Certificate** examination. This is used as a qualifying examination for admission into form V in any kind of secondary school. At the end of form V, pupils sit for the **New Zealand School Certificate** examination. This is mostly set and marked in New Zealand, but is increasingly being modified by the New Zealand Examination Board to include topics in certain subjects relevant to Fiji. At the end of the form VI pupils sit for the **New Zealand University Entrance Examination**, set and marked in New Zealand (for further information see the chapter on New Zealand). This certificate is a prerequisite for entry into the preliminary class at the University of the South Pacific (a year preceding the degree course).

From 1957 to 1967 form VII was available in a few schools, but with the opening of the University of the South Pacific in 1968 form VII in secondary schools was abolished. The University instituted the Preliminary II course (now called the **Foundation Year**) which is comparable in standard and scope to the course previously offered in form VII. Form VII was reintroduced in secondary schools in 1980. Students can follow the form VII course in school or the Foundation Year at the University of the South Pacific. In the examinations at the end of form VII pupils must take 4 or 5 subjects, including English and Fiji studies. A certificate is awarded to a pupil in respect of a subject in which 50 or more marks have been obtained.

Technical secondary

Some facilities are available, including trade courses and courses in office skills leading to examinations of the **Royal Society of Arts**.

FURTHER EDUCATION

In 1978 the Derrick Technical Institute and Western Division Technical Centre at Ba were amalgamated into the Fiji Institute of Technology. This offers post-trade and apprenticeship courses, also courses leading to the **Ordinary Technicians Diploma** in engineering and a **Diploma in Business Studies**. The Institute also offers courses leading to several City & Guilds of London Institute examinations.

HIGHER EDUCATION

The University of the South Pacific was established in 1968 with campuses in Suva, Fiji, and in Western Samoa. Admission is on the basis of the university entrance examination, but students may also successfully complete the Foundation Year or a 1-year course beyond New Zealand University Entrance or form VII of secondary school.

Courses leading to the **Bachelor of Arts/Science degree** last 3 years.

Postgraduate courses in selected areas are offered.

TEACHER EDUCATION

Primary

A 2-year course is available for students who have passed the New Zealand University Entrance Examination.

Secondary

A training course may be taken concurrently with a degree at the University, which takes 4 years after the Foundation course. This trains teachers for forms V and VI.

Finland

Republic of Finland

The Law of Principles of Public Education of July 1968 required that the school system be developed in accordance with the main principles of comprehensive education. Both teacher and higher education have undergone substantial changes.

Compulsory education starts at age seven and lasted for eight years until 1972, nine years since then. After comprehensive school most pupils continue either in senior secondary education of three years (fifty per cent in 1985) or various kinds of vocational education.

The national languages are Finnish and Swedish, and both are used as media of instruction. Both language groups have their own schools.

The academic year runs from August to May in schools and from September to May at university level.

EVALUATION IN BRITAIN

School

Ylioppilastutkinto Studentexamen - may be considered to satisfy the general requirement of universities and polytechnics.

Higher

Kandidaatti/Kandidat - generally compared to British Bachelor degree standard.

Licentiate (Lisensiaatti/Licenciat) - generally compared to a British Master degree.

Doctorate (Tohtori/Doktor) - generally compared to a British PhD.

MARKING SYSTEMS

School

Marking is on a scale 4-10 (maximum), with 5 as the minimum pass mark.

Finland

Matriculation examination:

Before 1969 - 0-3 (maximum)

0 improbatur (fail)
1 approbatur
2 cum laude approbatur
3 laudatur

Since 1970 - 0-6 (maximum)

0 improbatur (fail)
2 approbatur
3 lubenter approbatur
4 cum laude approbatur
5 magna cum laude approbatur
6 laudatur
N.B. 1 is not used.

Higher

Approbatur, cum laude approbatur, laudatur (maximum)

N.B. The system of marking at the matriculation examination refers to grades, i.e. laudatur is better than magna cum laude approbatur. At tertiary level the terms laudatur etc. refer to the length of study completed, e.g. for the basic degree (Hum.Kand.) it was only necessary to study up to cum laude approbatur.

SCHOOL EDUCATION

Pre-primary/kindergarten (Lastentarha)

Private facilities are available for children aged 3-6.

Before 1977

Primary (Kansakoulu/Folkskola)

There were 2 systems for children aged 7. Under one system primary schooling lasted 6 years and was called Kansakoulu/Folkskola. Under the second system children who would eventually want to go to an academic secondary school went to this school for only 4 years. There was a competitive examination to decide entry to lower secondary at 11+.

Junior/lower secondary (Kansalaiskoulu/Medborgarskola or Keskikoulu/Mellanskola)

Following primary education, pupils took a 2-year course if they had completed 6 years primary, or a 5-year course if they had completed 4 years, at a civic school, the period being referred to as Kansalaiskoulu/Medborgarskda or Keskikoulu/Mellanskola in the case of the 5-year course. During the latter course pupils studied religious education, mother tongue, the second national language, natural sciences, geography, mathematics, a first foreign language, history, social and economic sciences, home economics, music, art, technical and textile work, and physical education in years 2-5. On completion of this course pupils got the intermediate school certificate or **Keskikoulunpaastotodistus/Mellanskolans Dimissionsbetyg**.

Finland

Since 1977

Basic school (Peruskoulu/Grundskola)

Although the law introducing the basic school system was passed in 1970, transition to the new system was gradual, commencing in 1972 and only reaching completion in 1979/80. Basic education now consists of 2 cycles:

lower (ala-aste/lagstadium) lasts 6 years, and covers grades 1-6

upper (ylaaste/hogstadium) lasts 3 years and covers grades 7-9 (some schools also offer grade 10).

Before 1982:

Lower cycle - the curriculum covered the mother tongue, the second national or first foreign (usually English) language (from grade 3), religious instruction, environmental studies (grades 1-4), mathematics, natural history and geography (grades 3-6), history, social studies and civics (grades 5 and 6), music, art and handicrafts, and physical education.

Upper cycle - the curriculum covered mother tongue, religious instruction, history, social studies and civics, physics and chemistry, natural history and geography, physical education, home economics, music, art and handicrafts, mathematics (2 levels of courses in grade 7 and 3 levels in grades 8 and 9), first foreign language (3 courses) and second national language (2 courses). The choice of level in the last 3 subjects was made by parents and was important because intermediate courses in mathematics and the first language and the 'long' course in the second national language were required for entry to senior secondary school (Lukio/Gymnasium). In grades 8 and 9 optional courses were offered in technical subjects, home economics, commercial subjects, agriculture, forestry and (one more) foreign language.

Since 1982:

Lower cycle - the curriculum covers the mother tongue, the second national or first foreign language (most frequently English) from grade 3, religious instruction, mathematics, environmental studies, natural history and geography, history, social studies and civics (grades 5 and 6), music, art and handicrafts, physical education and pupil counselling. Total number of lessons weekly amounts to 21 in grades 1 and 2, 25 in grade 3 and 26 in grades 4 to 6.

Upper cycle - the curriculum covers mother tongue, religious instruction, history and social studies, physics and chemistry, natural history and geography, physical education, home economics, music, art and technical/textile crafts, mathematics, the first foreign language, the second national language and pupil counselling. Total number of lessons weekly amounts to 30.

Senior secondary school (Lukio/Gymnasium)

This has always been a 3-year course. Throughout, pupils receive marks during the school year for each subject. Pupils with marks of 5 or more in all subjects may proceed to the next grade, and if only 1 or 2 subjects are marked 4 they can proceed on passing a supplementary examination. Pupils with marks of 4 in 3 or more subjects must repeat the year.

Finland

Before 1982:

The curriculum covered religious instruction, mother tongue, second national and first foreign language (usually English), second foreign language (German, French or Russian), mathematics (short or long course), geography (for those following the short course in mathematics), biology, history and social studies, physical education and health education, art or music. Optional subjects include physics, chemistry (short or long), philosophy and psychology, geography (for those following the long course in mathematics), third foreign language (German, French, Russian or Latin), art or music.

Since 1982:

Teaching is now organized into a system of 38-hour course units called kurssi.

The curriculum covers religious instruction, mother tongue, the second national and the first foreign language, a second foreign language (German, French or Russian), mathematics (a short or long course), chemistry, geography, biology, history and social studies, physical education and health education, art or music and pupil counselling. Optional subjects include physics, philosophy and psychology, a third foreign language (German, French, Russian or Latin), art, music and automatic data processing. Remedial courses are also offered.

On completion of the 3-year senior secondary school pupils can obtain the **Secondary School Leaving Certificate/Lukionpaastotadistus/Dimissionsbetyg fran Gymnasiet**.

The matriculation examination

Since 1958 the cycle has culminated in the **matriculation examination/Ylioppilastutkinto Studentexamen**. It consists of 4 compulsory written tests, in the mother tongue (i.e. composition in Finnish or Swedish), a second national language (i.e. Finnish or Swedish), a first foreign language (French, German, Russian, or English), and either mathematics or a general paper (reaalikoe/realprov). It is also possible to take tests in 2 of the following optional subjects: reaalikoe (general paper), mathematics, and foreign languages. The general paper includes questions on religious instruction and religious history, philosophy and psychology, history, social and economic sciences, physics, chemistry, biology and geography. The foreign language tests also include listening comprehension.

A fail in the mother tongue or composition means that the student has failed the complete examination. A student who fails, or wishes to improve grades or obtain extra passes, has 2 chances of resitting the examination within 2 years of the original attempt. A student who is successful and has got the School Leaving Certificate obtains the **Matriculation Board Certificate/Ylioppilastutkintotodistus/Student Examensbetyg**.

Technical secondary

The reform of the basic school organization was accompanied by equally significant reform of the technical secondary syllabus. Before 1972, vocational training was divided into 660 separate, narrowly defined study programmes. Because of the changing needs of business and industry, it was felt that training had to be broadened and, at the same time, the continuation from the secondary school level to the institute level had to be encouraged.

Finland

The resulting rationalization has created a system which offers 24 basic study programmes each consisting of a core of general studies, common to all, together with one specialization. The successful completion of a programme culminates in the examination of vocational proficiency, the final examination in secondary vocational education. The certificate thus gained qualifies the student to enter any one of several related jobs in a given field. It also provides the foundation for further studies.

Several specialized occupations are not included in the basic programmes and provision for training in these fields is given separately or through apprenticeship contracts.

Secondary-level vocational training is offered in various institutions. The emphasis at school level is on performance and practical skills; at institute level the emphasis is on training for planning and supervision.

<u>Vocational schools</u> (Ammattikoulut/Yrkesskolor) 20% are state-owned and the rest are communal. Both general and specialized schools exist. The former have departments of, for example, metal work, machine repairs and electrical work. The latter provide education in, for example, the mechanical and chemical wood-processing industries, the food production industry and the graphical industry.

Training periods in schools last 2-3 years. The <u>state-owned vocational schools</u> (Valtion Keskusammattikoulut/Statliga Centralyrkesskolorna) offer courses which are not generally available at municipal vocational schools.

<u>Vocational institutes</u> (Ammattiopistot/Yrkesinstitut) provide training at a higher level and are often specialized, e.g. the School for Dental Technicians. Pupils who have completed the matriculation exam may also enter this level and the training period lasts 4-5 years.

<u>Technical schools</u> (Teknilliset Koulut/Tekniska Skolor) admit basic school leavers who have some work experience and offer 3-year courses to train technicians, leading to a **Lower Diploma**.

<u>Technical institutes</u> (Teknilliset Opistot/Tekniska Institut) admit graduates of technical secondary schools and a course leading to a qualification as an engineer lasts 4 years. Secondary school graduates with a pass in the matriculation examination need only 3 years but must have taken the long course in mathematics. The courses lead to a **Higher Diploma**, close in standard to the former lower first degree.

Since 1972 pupils at both vocational and technical institutes have been able to take the matriculation examination at the end of their course.

<u>Commercial schools and institutes</u> (Kauppaoppilaitokset/Handelslaroanstalter) The 2-year full-time commerce and administrative courses give the qualification of commercial school graduate (Merkantti/Merkantexamen) and the 3-year full-time courses lead to the qualification of commercial college graduate (Merkonomi/Merkonom). Courses include marketing, accountancy, secretarial work, civics and economics, foreign trade, COMECON trade, etc.

<u>Agricultural schools and institutes</u> (Maatalousalan Oppilaitokset/Lantbrukslaroanstalter) aim to offer the opportunity of acquiring a versatile knowledge of food production and a good command of the technical and economic know-how that goes with it. Courses at school level last 2 years and at institute level 4-5 years.

Finland

<u>Schools and institutes for health personnel</u> (Terveydenhuoltoalan Oppilaitokset/ Laroanstalterna i Halsovardsbranschen). Studies at school level for nursing auxiliaries last 1 to 1-and-a-half years. The institute level education conferring professional qualifications as nurse, laboratory technician, etc. requires 2-and-a-half to 4 years.

<u>Hotel and restaurant schools and institutes</u> (Hotelli- ja Ravintola-alan Oppilaitokset/ Laroanstalterna i Hotell- och Restaurangbranschen) offer training in the preparation of food and in general hotel and restaurant work at school level (for workers) lasting 2-3 years and at institute level (for supervisory staff) lasting 3-4 years.

HIGHER EDUCATION

There are 20 universities and institutions of higher education. The normal entrance requirement for degree-level courses is the matriculation certificate, plus entrance examinations run by the individual institutions. A system of numerus clausus (restricted entry) operates for all faculties.

There were 2 levels of first degree (there is now only 1 basic degree) and 2 of post-graduate degree.

Lower first degree - this was not available at all institutions, and has now been phased out. The course lasted 3-4 years.

Upper or 'basic' first degree (Kandidaatti/Kandidat) - students take a major and 2 or 3 minor subjects. The degree usually takes 5-7 years.

Holders of the Kandidaatti/Kandidat may apply for the **Maisteri** which confers certain voting rights at the university but is not a qualification in itself.

The **Licentiate (Lisensiaatti/Licenciat)** is a lower postgraduate degree. Students have to study 2 subjects, and the major may be different from the one taken at Kandidaatti level. They must also present a thesis. The average age of obtaining a Doctorate (Tohtori/Doktor) is 35 years.

Medicine and dentistry - the Licentiate is the first qualification in these subjects.

The **Doctorate (Tohtori/Doktor)** is a higher postgraduate degree and requires a full dissertation.

For the basic degree and the Licentiate, subjects may be studied at 1 of 3 levels: approbatur, cum laude approbatur and laudatur. A certain number of passes at each level is required to gain the appropriate certificate.

Since 1980, most courses have been based on the credit system. In general, the average amount of work of a full-time student in an academic year is equal to 40 credits, implying an average of 40 weeks of study during the academic year. The Kandidaatti requires approximately 160-180 credits, depending on the discipline studied. For the lower first degree (now phased out) students had to include studies in at least 3 and at most 5 subjects (there was no major subject), the minimum number of credits per subject being 10.

Finland

TEACHER EDUCATION

Until 1980

Primary

A 4-year course from the end of junior secondary education or 2 years from the matriculation examination, is taken at a Seminaarit/Seminariet. (This is now mostly covered by the courses for the basic school.)

Basic school

A 3-year course is taken from the end of senior secondary school. The class teacher's certificate is considered in Finland to be comparable to the former 'lower' first degree.

Senior secondary

A 1-year postgraduate course leads to a subject teacher's diploma, for holders of the Kandidaatti/Kandidat and Licensiaatti/Licentiat.

Since 1980

Pre-primary

A 2-year course at a Lastentarhaopettajaopisto, leads to a pre-primary teachers certificate. The entrance requirement is the matriculation examination or completion of basic/junior secondary education and professional training in the field.

Basic school and senior secondary

A basic university degree is taken, requiring 4-5 years of study (approximately 160 credits).

France

French Republic

There has always been a tendency towards great centralization within the education system in France, although moves were made from the late 1950s to reverse this trend. In recent years, decentralisation has increased.

School education was reorganized in 1959, in 1966 (according to the Fouchet reforms), and in 1975 (under the Haby reforms).

The outbreak of violence in May/June 1968 indicated dissatisfaction with the higher education system, and led to the Loi d'Orientation d'Education of November 1968, which radically altered the system.

The curricula and teaching methods at school level are still laid down by the Ministry of Education; universities now have more freedom.

Until 1959 the compulsory minimum school leaving age was fourteen. It was raised in 1959 to sixteen for all children reaching age six after that year (effective from 1967).

The school year runs from September to June.

EVALUATION IN BRITAIN

School

Certificat d'aptitude professionel (CAP) - generally compared to City and Guilds of London Institute (CGLI) Craft Certificate Part 2.

Brevet d'apprentissage/Brevet d'etudes professionelles (BEP) - generally compared to CGLI Craft Certificate Part 2/3.

Brevet de technicien (BT) - generally compared to CGLI Technician Certificate Part 2.

Brevet professionel (BP)/**Brevet de Maitrise** - generally compared to CGLI Craft Certificate Part 3.

Brevet d'Etudes du Premier Cycle - generally considered to be below GCE O-level standard. Its title was changed in 1981 to **Brevet de College**.

France

Baccalaureat de l'Enseignement du Second Degre (former Baccalaureat Parts I and II, and Diplome de Bachelier de l'Enseignement du Second Degre) - may be considered to satisfy the general requirement of universities and polytechnics.

Baccalaureat de Technicien - generally compared to BTEC National Diploma standard (formerly Ordinary National Diploma), may be considered to satisfy the general requirement of universities and polytechnics.

Further

Brevet de Technicien Superieur and **Diplome Universitaire de Technologie** - generally compared to City and Guilds of London Institute Full Technological Certificate (Technician Scheme)/BTEC Higher National Diploma standard (formerly Higher National Diploma).

Higher

Licence - generally compared to British Bachelor degree standard.

Maitrise - generally compared to a taught Master degree (MA/M.Sc.), although part of it consists of a short thesis of about 100 pages.

Magistere (introduced in 1985) - will probably be compared to British Master degree standard, or just above.

Doctorat de Troisieme Cycle (last awarded in the academic year 1984-5) - generally compared to a Master degree by research (M.Phil.).

Docteur de l'Universite - generally compared to a British Ph.D.

Habilitation a Diriger des Recherches - generally compared to a British D.Phil.

MARKING SYSTEMS

School

Baccalaureat: individual subjects are marked on a scale of 0-20 (maximum), 10 being the minimum pass mark.

16-20	tres bien	very good
14-15	bien	good
12-13	assez bien	fair
10-11	passable	pass

Higher

The Licence is classified: passable, assez bien, bien and tres bien.

If no classification (mention) is given, the Licence is awarded with the grade passable.

No classification or marking is given for qualifications from the <u>Grandes Ecoles</u>.

France

ABBREVIATIONS

Qualifications

Note: some qualifications have the same abbreviations; check institution where obtained to ascertain nature of qualification.

Bac(c)	-	Baccalaureat
BC	-	Brevet de College
BEP	-	Brevet d'Etudes Professionnelles
BEPC	-	Brevet d'Etudes du Premier Cycle
BP	-	Brevet Professionnel
BT	-	Brevet de Technicien
BTn	-	Baccalaureat de Technicien
BTS	-	Brevet de Technicien Superieur
CAP	-	Certificat d'Aptitude Pedagogique
CAP	-	Certificat d'Aptitude Professionnelle
CAPEGC	-	Certificat d'Aptitude au Professorat de l'Enseignement General de College
CAPES	-	Certificat d'Aptitude au Professorat de l'Enseignement du Second Degre
CAPET	-	Certificat d'Aptitude au Professorat de l'Enseignement Technique
CEP	-	Certificat d'Etudes Primaires
CEP	-	Certificat d'Education Professionnelle
DEA	-	Diplome d'Etudes Approfondies
DES	-	Diplome d'Etudes Superieures
DESS	-	Diplome d'Etudes Superieures Specialisees
DEUG	-	Diplome d'Etudes Universitaires Generales
DUEL	-	Diplome Universitaire d'Etudes Litteraires
DUES	-	Diplome Universitaire d'Etudes Scientifiques
DUT	-	Diplome Universitaire de Technologie

Institutions

CEG	-	College d'Enseignement General
CES	-	College d'Enseignement Secondaire
CET	-	College d'Enseignement Technique
CFA	-	Centre de Formation d'Apprentis
LEGT	-	Lycee d'Enseignement General et Technologique
LEP	-	Lycee d'Enseignement Professionnel
IUT	-	Institut Universitaire de Technologie
UER	-	Unite d'Enseignement et de Recherche

France

SCHOOL EDUCATION

Pre-primary

Facilities are available in <u>Ecoles Maternelles</u> for children aged 2-6.

Primary

This covers 5 years from age 6, divided into 3 cycles:

preparatoire (preparatory)	1 year
elementaires (elementary)	2
moyens (intermediate)	2

The curriculum covers reading, writing, French, arithmetic, moral guidance, history, geography, observation exercises, drawing, singing, handiwork and games.

Pupils proceed automatically to secondary education, without an entrance examination, unless they come from a private school or have an unsatisfactory report from the primary school. The final certificate, the **Certificat d'Etudes Primaires** (CEP), reports only class marks.

Before the compulsory minimum school-leaving age was raised to 16 in 1969, pupils not wishing to proceed to a general academic secondary course took a 2-year primary terminal course on completion of the normal 5-year course. On completion of the 2-year course, they were awarded the **CEP** and could take an entrance examination for admission to a technical school.

Secondary

This is divided into 2 stages covering 7 years: lower and upper.

Lower:

The lower cycle (enseignement secondaire du premier cycle) covers 4 years, and classes are numbered in reverse order; i.e. the first year of secondary education is the sixth class, the second year is the fifth class, etc.

Since 1959 the first 2 years have been known as the observation cycle. The core subjects are: French, mathematics, history/geography, 1 foreign language, physical education, and, since 1975, experimental sciences, artistic activities (including music and drawing) and manual and technical education. There has been no streaming since 1975.

The second cycle of 2 years is known as the orientation cycle. Pupils may continue their general education with the same core subjects plus 1 obligatory subject from the following: an additional foreign language, the reinforced study of the foreign language, Latin, Greek, or 1 of 3 technical subjects. Pupils not wishing to do this may begin a course with a vocational bias.

France

From 1959 pupils attended Colleges d'Enseignement General for lower secondary education; these were renamed <u>Colleges Uniques</u> in 1977/8. In the mid-1960s, schools called <u>Colleges d'Enseignement Secondaire</u> were established, which covered all the various types of lower secondary course, i.e. classical (Latin, with optional Greek), modern I (including 2 modern languages), modern II (including 1 modern language), and transition classes. These were reclassified as <u>'Colleges Uniques'</u> in 1977/8 and are now all referred to simply as <u>Colleges</u>.

Until 1976 pupils could take an examination in 6 subjects on completion of the full 4-year course of lower secondary education, to be awarded the **Brevet d'Etudes du Premier Cycle** (BEPC); now called **Brevet de College**.

Pupils going on to take the course of upper secondary education culminating in the examinations for the Baccalaureat did not normally take these examinations for the BEPC. However, it is now awarded without examination to pupils going on to some form of upper secondary education. Other pupils must take the examinations. Pupils who have completed this 4-year cycle but have not reached the minimum school-leaving age (16) undertake a 1-year course leading to a **Certificat d'Education Professionnel** (CEP) and may then leave school.

Upper:

This includes long and short courses.

Short courses

Under the decree of 8 July 1968 these courses provide further general and vocational training lasting not more than 2 years. Courses are taken in the <u>Colleges de Second Cycle</u> (formerly the <u>Colleges d'Enseignement Technique</u>) and in the <u>Colleges d'Enseignement General</u>, both now reclassified <u>Colleges Uniques</u>. Pupils obtain a **Brevet d'Enseignement General**, with a particular specialization.

Long courses

These last 3 years in the <u>Lycees d'Enseignement General et Technologique</u> (formerly the <u>Lycees Classiques</u>, <u>Lycees Modernes</u> and <u>Lycees Techniques</u>), leading to the examinations for the **Baccalaureat**. In the first year of this cycle, i.e. the second class (fifth year of secondary studies), there are 4 sections:

A	literary
AB	literary and economic
C	scientific
E	technical.

The following subjects are common to all 4 sections: history, French, geography, civics, one modern language, mathematics, physical sciences, and physical education. There is no streaming in the first 2 years of this cycle. In the second year of the cycle, i.e. sixth year/classe premiere, there are 5 sections:

A	literary studies
B	economics and social science
C	mathematics and physical science
D	natural sciences
E	industrial science and technology.

France

The final year of this cycle is known as the classe terminale.

Until 1966:

The examinations for the Baccalaureat were taken in 2 parts. At the end of the second year of the 3-year cycle, the **Part I** examinations were taken in the 3 compulsory subjects (French, history and geography) plus 3 other subjects. On completion of the final year, pupils took the examinations for the **Baccalaureat Part II**, which is more specialized and concentrates on mathematics, science and philosophy. The examinations are now all taken at the end of the 3-year cycle, although the examinations in French - both written and oral (epreuve anticipee de francais) - may still be taken 1 year earlier. There are now 21 different specializations in the Baccalaureat, depending on the subjects taken. French, mathematics and a modern foreign language are common to all.

General

Series A	philosophy, arts; subdivided A -A with varying options
Series B	economics and social sciences
Series C	mathematics and physics
Series D	mathematics and natural sciences
Series D	agricultural and technical sciences
Series E	mathematics and technical sciences

Technical

Series F subdivided into:

F1	mechanical construction
F2	electronics
F3	electrotechnology
F4	civil engineering
F5	physics
F6	chemistry
F7	biological sciences
F8	medical and social sciences
F9	building engineering
F10	microtechnics
F11	music technology

Series G subdivided into:

G1	public administration
G2	business management
G3	commerce
Series H	computer science/information science

There are now 2 sets of examinations for the Baccalaureat. The first group is compulsory and includes 2 written and 2 oral examinations in 4 different subjects. Pupils who obtain an average mark of 12 or more out of 20 for these 4 subjects are awarded the Baccalaureat and need not sit the second group of examinations. Pupils who obtain only an average mark of 8-12 out of 20, have to take the second group of examinations. This group consists solely of oral examinations and includes 2 subjects (known as the epreuves orales de controle) already examined in the first group of written papers as well as a couple of subjects not already tested. Pupils who then obtain an overall average for the 2 groups of examinations of 10 or more out of 20 are awarded the **Baccalaureat**. Pupils who still fail the examinations but have completed a full course of study obtain the **Certificat de Fin d'Etudes Secondaires** (CFES). An alternative name for the Baccalaureat is the **(Diplome de) Bachelier de l'Enseignement du Second Degre**.

The technical and economic specializations of the Baccalaureat lead to the **Baccalaureat de Technicien**, introduced in 1968. An increasing number of Lycees Agricoles, are awarding the **Baccalaureat Agricole**. Although the Baccalaureat in any specialization used to entitle the holder to university admission in any faculty, a decree of 6 August 1986 defined the list of Baccalaureat specializations which would entitle the holder to university admission.

Pupils who wish to proceed to the Grandes Ecoles d'Ingenieurs (see HIGHER EDUCATION) take a 2-to 3-year course after the Baccalaureat, culminating in highly competitive entrance examinations (concours d'entree). Students generally take 1-5 of these examinations and if successful are entitled to access to certain institutions and may then choose which one they wish to attend. The academic year for these courses is longer than at the lycees/universities, and the timetable is very heavy. Normally only students with first-class Baccalaureats are admitted. In theory, courses in commercial subjects and veterinary medicine last 1 year, and courses in literary and scientific subjects last 2 years. However, most students take longer and have to resit the examination.

Technical secondary

Short:

On completion of 4 years lower secondary education, pupils can take a technically biased 2-year course leading to the qualification of **Certificat d'Aptitude Professionnel** (CAP) and the position of Agents Techniques. The courses were taken originally at the Centres d'Apprentissage, which became the Colleges d'Enseignement Techniques in 1959 and later the Lycees Techniques.

Pupils may also obtain this qualification by way of a 3-year apprenticeship, beginning at the end of the third year of lower secondary education, which includes part-time attendance at a Lycee d'Enseignement Professionnel (LEP), formerly Colleges d'Enseignement Technique.

Pupils undertaking the apprenticeship in small-scale craft industries take a final examination (examen de fin d'apprentissage artisanal), and obtain the qualification **Brevet d'Apprentissage**.

Pupils wishing to undertake a more general vocational upper secondary course may take a 2-year craft course at a Lycee d'Enseignement Professionnel (LEP), on completion of 4 years lower secondary education, leading to the qualification of **Brevet d'Etudes Professionelles** (BEP). Holders of this qualification may enter directly the second year of the 3-year course for the **Brevet Technicien** (see below, under Long).

Holders of the **CAP** or **BEP** may then undertake a 2-year specialization course in a limited number of subjects, leading to the qualification of **Brevet Professionnel** (BP). The corresponding qualification for holders of the **Brevet d'Apprentissage** after a similar specialization course is the **Brevet de Maitrise**.

France

Long:

On completion of 4 years lower secondary education pupils may undertake a 3-year course at an <u>Ecole National Professionnel</u> (now <u>Lycee Technique</u>) leading to the qualification of **Brevet de Technicien** (BT). This qualification will admit the holder to university under certain circumstances.

Pupils who reach the compulsory school-leaving age (16) before completing the normal 4-year lower secondary course are offered a 1-year intensive course of vocational training in a <u>Centre de Formation d'Apprentis</u> (CFA).

FURTHER EDUCATION

Before 1966, holders of the Baccalaureat or Brevet Technicien could undertake a 2-year specialized and practically oriented course at a <u>Lycee Technique</u> leading to a **Brevet de Technicien Superieur** (BTS).

In 1966 a number of university institutes of technology (<u>Instituts Universitaires de Technologie</u> - IUT) were established; these offer 2-year courses leading to the **Diplome Universitaire de Technologie** (DUT). These courses and the DUT are intended to replace the courses leading to the BTS, but are less specialized. Each institute constitutes a <u>Unite de l'Enseignement et de Recherche</u> (UER) of the university to which it is linked.

HIGHER EDUCATION

Entry is on the basis of success in the Baccalaureat. However, options A and B no longer give direct admission to medical and science faculties for which students must also successfully pass a special entrance examination.

University studies may be divided into 3 cycles.

First cycle

Before 1966:

All students undertook a common first year (l'annee de propedeutique). Successful performance in the end-of-year examinations led to the **Certificat d'Etudes Litteraires/Scientifiques Generales** (CELG/CESG), but this was abolished, mainly because of a high failure rate. Until the 1966 reforms students often took longer than the usual 3 or 4 years to obtain a Licence.

1966 reforms:

The qualifications **Diploma Universitaire d'Etudes Litteraires** (DUEL) and **Diploma Universitaire Scientifiques** (DUES) were introduced and awarded on completion of the first cycle (usually 2 years) of the Licence course in the humanities and sciences respectively.

France

Since 1966:

The first cycle of university study in the sciences and humanities has been limited to 3 years and only one re-examination permitted.

Since 1973-4:

The first cycle became more specialized and now leads to the **Diplome d'Etudes Universitaires Generales** (DEUG) normally after 2 years study.

Second cycle

1973-4:

One year of study after the DEUG, students could obtain a **Licence** in arts and science subjects (3 years total) or after a further 2 years study in law and economic subjects (4 years total).

Since 1976:

The Licence in law and economics may be obtained 1 year after the DEUG (3 years total).

A **Maitrise** was created in law and economics.

To obtain a Licence (or any other Higher Education qualification) students must obtain a certain number of **Certificat d'Etudes Superieures** (CES) (called Certificat de Licence until the mid-1960s).

Until 1978 there were 2 types of Licence (differing in course content):

Licence Libre
Licence d'Enseignement.

A student who prepared a Licence Libre had a freer choice of subjects than a student preparing a Licence d'Enseignement, who was and is bound by a number of regulations, compulsory subjects, etc. (e.g. a second foreign language is necessary for the Licence d'Enseignement d'Anglais).

In management and technology, students may, after obtaining the DEUG, study for a Maitrise directly, which is awarded after a 2-year course: MST, MIAGE, MSG.

In arts and science subjects, 1 further year of study after the Licence now leads to the **Maitrise**. There is no official time limit to obtain the qualifications of the second cycle (Licence and Maitrise). The **Magistere**, which was first introduced in 1985, is awarded after a 3-year course. The entrance requirements are the DUT or the DEUG. Admission is selective. This qualification is intended to be high-level and vocational.

Third cycle

Until July 1984:

The qualifications obtained in the third cycle were the **Doctorat de Specialite de Troisieme Cycle** and the **Doctorat d'Etat**.

To obtain the former, students took a 1-year course after the **Maitrise** leading to the **Diplome d'Etudes Appropendies** (DEA); followed by 1-2 years research and submission of a thesis.

The **Diplome d'Etudes Superieures Specialisees** (DESS) is obtained after 1 year of specialized training directly related to a profession. The entrance requirement is a Maitrise.

The **Doctorat d'Etat** was the highest qualification in arts and sciences, but could also be obtained in pharmacy, law, economic science and medicine. There was no maximum time limit for research for the thesis but the minimum was 2 years after the Maitrise. In literary subjects the thesis usually took at least 5 years to prepare. In law, students had to hold the Licence and the Diploma d'Etudes superieures (DES) before being admitted to research for this qualification. The DES was obtained after 1 year of research in law and economics if the student was successful in written and oral examinations and the presentation of a thesis.

Since 1984:

The Law on Higher Education (5 July 1984) created a new Doctorate which replaces the Doctorate de Troisieme Cycle and the Doctorate d'Etat.

The new Doctorate is preceded (as were former Doctorates) by 1 year's study for the DEA, and followed by 2-4 years research to doctoral title. The standard of the new Doctorate is higher than the former Doctorate de Troisieme Cycle.

The new doctoral title is: **Docteur de l'Universite X** and the diploma will include the title of the thesis and names of titles of Jury members.

This Doctorate is delivered by universities on their own responsibility, and by certain other higher education institutions.

The **Habilitation a Diriger des Recherches** is of a higher level than the previous Doctorate d'Etat. An applicant must already hold the Doctorate and demonstrate an ability to plan and direct research work. An assessment is made of the candidate's entire scientific work and there is no time limit.

Medicine, dentistry, pharmacy

The first 2 years of the course in medicine cover basic biology. The first year is also followed by students of pharmacy and dentistry. The examination at the end of the first year may only be taken twice; but, even if a student passes, promotion to the second year is not automatic, as it depends on the number of hospital training places available.

The **Diplome d'Etat de Docteur en Medecine** is obtained after a further 7 years of specialized study. The **Diplome d'Etat de Docteur en Chirurgie Dentaire** is obtained after 4 years following the basic first year, and the **Diplome d'Etat de Docteur en Pharmacie** after 4 years following the basic first year.

The **Diplome d'Etudes Specialisees** (DES) is a specialist qualification obtained after 4-5 years training following a competitive examination at the end of the sixth year of medical studies. After the sixth year, medical students may also undertake research and prepare a DEA and then a Doctorate.

France

In dentistry and pharmacy, the Diplome d'Etat is a prerequisite to specialization. In dentistry, students obtain the **Certificats d'Etudes Specialisees** (CES) A and B 2 years) or the **Certificat d'Etudes Cliniques Speciales Mentien Orthodontive** (CESMO). In pharmacy, they undertake 4 Diplomes d'Etudes Specialisees (DES) which will take another 4 years. Both dental students and pharmacists may undertake research and prepare a DEA and a Doctorat. A DES is also available in pharmacy (1 year).

Universities and other institutions

The state has a monopoly on conferring degrees. Students studying at private institutions often enrol concurrently at a national university so that they may sit the state examinations, which are usually necessary to practise a profession.

One effect of the 1968 law on higher education was the decentralization of the institutions. The large faculties were broken up into small 'education and research units' (Unites d'Enseignement et de Recherche), some of which were then regrouped to form new universities. Besides universities, other types of institution offer courses at this level; these are national institutions providing advanced training for senior government and civil posts in the ministries and the services: e.g. <u>Ecoles Polytechniques</u>, <u>Ecoles Nationales d'Administration</u>, <u>Ecoles Superieures des Mines</u>; higher national colleges of engineering (<u>Ecoles Nationales Superieures d'Ingenieurs - ENS</u>).

Grandes Ecoles d'Ingenieurs

These are specialist institutions whose administration falls under individual ministries. They may be private and responsible to the Paris Chamber of Commerce, for instance. They have no parallel in Britain. They are highly selective, classified in different groups of decreasing prestige and recruit their students by competitive examination (concours d'entree) organized centrally and taken throughout France.

Admission is at 2 levels:

After the Baccalaureat, either by internal examination or 'Sur Dossier', according to the marks obtained at the Baccalaureat, during the final year at school. The course is 4-5 years.

After the Baccalaureat, candidates prepare in 'classes preparatoires' (2-3 years) a highly competitive examination to enter the Grandes Ecoles. The course is then 3 years. The most prestigious schools recruit students according to the second type of admission.

Courses generally lead to the award of the qualification **Diplome d'Ingenieur**. So prestigious is this award of the top-ranking Ecoles that holders generally go on to become high-level civil servants or industrial managers rather than professional engineers, who generally come from the remaining Ecoles. A recent development has been the establishment of the postgraduate **Diplome de Specialisation** which can be awarded by some of the Grandes Ecoles, although holders of the Diplome d'Ingenieurs can also transfer to a university for postgraduate research leading to a Doctorat after completion of a DEA.

France

TEACHER EDUCATION

Pre-primary and primary

Before 1972:

Students holding the Baccalaureat were trained on a 2-year course at an Ecole Normale leading to the **Certificat d'Aptitude Pedagogique** (CAP), which included 1 month of teaching practice each term for the 2 years. There was also provision for students to undertake a 4-year course if they had completed only 5 years of general secondary education.

1972-8:

Students were recruited to the 2-year course by competitive examination after the Baccalaureat. At the end of the course, students were awarded a **Certificat de Fin d'Etudes Normales** (CFEN), which also qualified them for the Certificat d'Aptitude Pedagogique (CAP), necessary for teaching.

Since 1979:

The course now lasts 3 years from the level of Baccalaureat and leads to the **Diplome d'Enseignement Superieur** as well as the CAP.

Secondary

Because the present Colleges may be former Colleges d'Enseignement General, former Colleges d'Enseignment Secondaire or the former first 5 years of a Lycee, teachers may hold 1 of a variety of qualifications, depending on the type of subject and the age of the pupils taught. Those holding the **Certificat d'Aptitude au Professorat d'Enseignement General de College** (CAPEGC) usually teach 2 (sometimes 3) subjects at the lower levels; at the higher levels, most teachers hold the **Certificat d'Aptitude a l'Enseignement du Second Degre** (CAPES) and usually teach only 1 subject. The latter title is obtained after a competitive Civil Service examination, success in which is dependent on the number of posts available each year, of which the first part is prepared in the universities. The second part (a 1-year teacher-training course) is prepared in the Centres Pedagogiques Regionaux (CPR) and comprises practical teaching work under supervision. Some teachers may hold the Agregation. In the Colleges et Lycees Techniques, most teachers are holders of the **Certificat d'Aptitude au Professorat d'Enseignement Technique** (CAPET), the technical education equivalent of the CAPES.

In the Lycees, most teachers are holders of the CAPES, and a few hold the **Agregation**. Like the CAPES, the Agregation is a competitive Civil Service examination, of a very high academic standard, prepared in the universities and the Ecoles Normales Superieures; success also depends on the number of posts available each year. The teacher-training element is, however, much shorter, consisting of a 6-week period. Candidates must be holders of the Maitrise or CAPES. Very few candidates succeed in obtaining the **Agregation** at their first attempt, and many prepare for it whilst already in teaching posts.

Higher

Teachers at this level receive no formal professional training, but there are minimum qualifications laid down for each grade, according to discipline.

Gabon

Gabonese Republic

Formerly a French colony in French Equatorial Africa, Gabon has continued to follow a basically French pattern of education since independence in 1960.

The medium of instruction is French.

The academic year runs from October to June.

EVALUATION IN BRITAIN

School

Baccalaureat - generally compared to GCE O-level standard.

Higher

Licence - generally considered to be between GCE A-level and British Bachelor degree standards.

MARKING SYSTEMS

School

Marking is on a scale of 0-20 (maximum) per subject, with no official minimum pass mark.

Overall grade at **Baccalaureat** is classified

tres bien	very good
bien	good
assez bien	fair
passable	pass

A student may have grades below 9 in one or more subjects and still receive the Baccalaureat if the overall grade average is 9 or higher.

Higher

The **Licence** is classified as:

tres bien	very good
bien	good
assez bien	fair
passable	pass

SCHOOL EDUCATION

Primary

This covers 6 years. The classes are known as: maternelle (ages 3-5); class CP (cours preparatoire), for which the child must be 6-years-old; classes CE1 and CE2 (cours elementaire); and classes CM1 and CM2 (cours moyen). At the end of this period pupils obtain the **Certificat d'Etudes Primaires Elementaires (CEPE)**.

Secondary

This covers 7 years, divided into a lower (premiere) cycle lasting 4 years and an upper (deuxieme) cycle lasting 3 years. Classes are numbered in reverse order: classe septieme to classe terminale. On conclusion of the lower cycle, pupils obtain the **Brevet d'Etudes du Premier Cycle**. During the second cycle, pupils may specialize in mathematics, science or literature. On completion of the cycle, pupils take the examinations for the **Baccalaureat**, which may be obtained in 1 of the following options:

A	humanities and philosophy
B	economics
C	mathematics and physical sciences
D	natural science
E	science and technology

Pupils who do not qualify for the Baccalaureat are awarded the **Certificat de Fin d'Etudes Secondaires**, a record of attendance and performance in the final year.

Technical secondary

On completion of the lower cycle pupils may opt to take a 'short' course (2-3 years) or 'long' course (3-4 years) of technical secondary education. The former leads to the **Brevet de Technicien**, and the latter to the **Baccalaureat Technique** which may be obtained in 1 of 2 options:

F	technology
G	commerce

Some apprenticeships and short vocational courses are available.

Gabon

HIGHER EDUCATION

There is one university, the National University of Gabon, founded in 1970, and now called the Universite Omar Bongo.

The entrance requirement for degree studies is the Baccalaureat.

The first cycle of studies lasts 2 years and leads to:

Diplome Universitaire d'Etudes Litteraires (DUEL)	arts and humanities
Diplome Universitaire d'Etudes Scientifiques (DUES)	science subjects
Diplome Universitaire d'Etudes Juridiques (DUEJ)	law
Diplome Universitaire d'Etudes Economiques (DUEE)	economics.

Most of these qualifications now come under the overall title of **Diplome d'Etudes Universitaires Generales** (DEUG).

A further 1 year of study in the arts and sciences and a further 2 years in economics and law lead to the **Licence**. Students may then proceed for a further year which includes the preparation of a thesis and leads to the **Maitrise**.

Students who wish to study law but do not hold the Baccalaureat, may undertake a 2-year course leading to the **Capacite en Droit**.

TEACHER EDUCATION

Secondary

Lower:

2-year post-secondary course at an advanced teacher-training college leading to the **Diplome de Professeur de Premier Cycle de l'Enseignement Secondaire**.

Upper:

Teachers are normally graduates.

Gambia

Republic of the Gambia

The basis of the education system is the Education Ordinance of 1963.

There is no compulsory education.

The medium of instruction is English.

EVALUATION IN BRITAIN

School

Secondary IV Certificate - generally considered below GCE O-level standard.

West African School Certificate - grades 1-6 are equated to GCE O-level standard (grades A, B, C).

West African Higher School Certificate - grades A-E are equated to GCE A-level standard.

MARKING SYSTEMS

School

West African School Certificate is graded 1 (maximum) - 9, 9 is a fail.

1, 2	credit
3, 4, 5, 6	very good
7, 8	pass

West African Higher School Certificate is graded A (maximum), B, C, D, E, O or S (subsidiary pass), F (fail).

Gambia

SCHOOL EDUCATION

Primary

This covers 6 years from age 8. On completion of this period, pupils take the **Common Entrance Examination** administered by the West African Examinations Council; the results determine whether pupils go on to Secondary Technical Schools or Secondary High Schools.

Secondary

Secondary Technical Schools offer 4-year courses leading to the **Secondary Technical Leaving Certificate** at the completion of form 4, set locally and administered by the West African Examinations Council.

The Secondary High Schools offer a 5-year course leading to the examinations for the **West African School Certificate**, followed by a further 2 years in the sixth form leading to the examinations for the **West African Higher School Certificate**.

FURTHER EDUCATION

Technical and vocational

Gambia Technical Training Institute offers a range of courses leading to the examinations of the **City & Guilds of London Institute** and the **Royal Society of Arts**.

Gambia College has 4 constituent schools:

> The School of Agriculture runs courses for extension workers and a certificate course for Agricultural Assistants, examination set and examined locally.
>
> The School of Education awards the Gambia Primary Teachers Certificate which is a local qualification.
>
> The School of Nursing and Midwifery conducts courses leading to the award of State Registered Nurse; State Enrolled Nurse; State Certified Midwife; and Community Health Nursing Certificate.
>
> The School of Public Health offers courses leading to the examinations of the **West African Health Examination Board Diploma** (Royal Society of Health), and a locally set and examined diploma.

The Hotel Catering School conducts courses leading to locally set and examined awards in various areas of hotel work.

The Management Development Institute, newly established, runs short courses and seminars mainly for middle- and upper-level officers in Government service.

Gambia

The National Vocational Training Centre conducts courses of 1 or 2 years in such areas as masonry, carpentry and welding, mainly at a basic level and locally examined.

HIGHER EDUCATION

There are no institutions of higher education. Students at this level go to a broad range of countries, including the United Kingdom, United States of America, Canada, Australia, New Zealand, Sweden, France, Soviet Union, Federal Republic of Germany and West and East African countries.

TEACHER EDUCATION

Gambia College School of Education offers a 3-year course for primary school teachers. Students enter with the Secondary IV examination or the West African School Certificate. The School of Education awards the **Gambia Primary Teachers Certificate**.

East Germany

German Democratic Republic

Since the establishment of the Republic in 1949 the education system has been totally controlled by the State; there are no private schools. The Ministry of Public Education (Ministerium fur Volksluldung) is responsible for schools and teacher training. The Ministry for Higher and Specialized Education (Ministerium fur Hoch-und-Fachschulweren) is responsible for universities, special institutes and technical schools. A Pedagogical Congress is held every 5 years to review previous achievements and to set the goals for the next period. The system has been structured mainly in accordance with the Law on the Socialist Development of Education in the German Democratic Republic of 1959 and the Law on the Integrated Socialist Education System of 1965.

Compulsory education was for 8 years (ages 6-14) until 1969, and is now for 10 years (ages 6-16) covering the period of basic education.

The medium of instruction is German.

The academic year runs from September to June.

EVALUATION IN BRITAIN

School

Abschlusszeugnis/Mittlere Reife - generally compared to GCE O-level standard.

Abitur/Reifezeugnis - may be considered to satisfy the general requirement of universities and polytechnics.

Higher

Diplom - generally compared to British Bachelor degree standard, sometimes compared to a Master degree.

Doktor eines Wissenschaftweiges - generally compared to a British Ph.D.

MARKING SYSTEMS

School and Higher

Marking is on the scale 1-5 (1 is maximum, 4 is the minimum pass mark).

East Germany

1	sehr gut	very good
2	gut	good
3	befriedigend	sufficient/fair
4	gerugend	satisfactory
5	ungenugendnicht bestanden	poor/failed

SCHOOL EDUCATION

Pre-primary

Creches (Kinderkrippen) are available for children aged 1-3, and there are numerous Kindergartens for children aged 3-6.

Basic

Until 1959:

Basic education (Grundschule) covered 8 years and led to the **Abschlussprufung**, followed by 4 years secondary education which led to the **Abitur** examination, or by 3-5 years at a trade or technical school.

1959-65:

This compulsory period of basic education was increased to 10 years for children aged 6 to 16 years. It was divided into 2 stages: Unterstufe (lower) classes 1-4, and Oberstufe (upper) classes 5-10.

Since 1965:

Basic education still covers 10 years for ages 6-16. It is divided into 3 cycles:

First cycle (Unterstufe) - classes 1-3. The curriculum covers German, mathematics, manual training, singing, music, drawing, painting and modelling, and physical education

Second cycle (Mittelstufe) - classes 4-6. The curriculum covers German language and literature, mathematics, natural science, social science, Russian, singing, music, painting and modelling, physical education, manual training and polytechnic instruction (e.g. instruction in the principles of socialist production)

Third cycle (Oberstufe) - classes 7-10. The curriculum covers mathematics, natural sciences (physics, astronomy, chemistry, biology and physical geography), social science, German, Russian, physical education, civics, optional foreign language (usually English or French), and polytechnic instruction (e.g. instruction in the principles of socialist production); at this stage great importance is attached to practical instruction, often 1 day per week will be spent in a factory for example.

There is no streaming, although some specialization may be available in classics, modern languages or science/mathematics. The **Abschlusszeugnis/Mittlere Reife** is awarded at the end of the tenth grade.

East Germany

Secondary

1959-65:

This covered 4 years for pupils aged 14 to 18, thus involving some form of selection 2 years before the end of the basic schooling. At this stage pupils could choose to enter a Berufsschule (vocational school), some of which offered examinations for the Abitur. Pupils who entered a Berufsschule which did not offer the Abitur, could either take up employment on completion of their courses and attend an evening secondary school (i.e. the part-time equivalent of a secondary school) leading to examinations which would enable them to enter a course of higher education, or they could go to a higher vocational school.

Since 1965:

Secondary education now covers 2 years. It is called <u>Erweiterte Allgemeinbildende Polytechnische Oberschule</u> and covers classes 11 and 12: upon completion, pupils take the examinations for the **Abitur/Reifezeugnis**. Compulsory subjects are mathematics, physics, chemistry, biology, Russian, English or French, history, geography, German, art or music, civics and polytechnical education.

Some Berufsschulen also offer the examinations for the **Abitur**. These courses last 2 years, and also lead to the **Facharbeiterprufung** (skilled worker diploma). Essentially the vocational schools are of 2 kinds: state-run, and operated by employers (Betriebsberufsschule). These offer apprenticeships leading to the qualification of **Facharbeiterprufung** and a lower-level version of the Abitur - the **Fachschulreife**. Holders of this latter qualification may proceed to a <u>Fachschule</u> (technical school) for a 3-year course leading to a professional qualification and the **Abitur**. Courses may be taken by full-time, part-time (evening) or correspondence study.

'Olympiads' are national competitors in mathematics, science, foreign languages and German at the end of the class 10. Children who are particularly gifted at music or sport may be chosen to receive intensive training in these areas alongside their general education.

HIGHER EDUCATION

Courses of higher education are offered by universities, technical universities and specialized institutes (Hochschulen).

Access is based on success in the Abitur and an aptitude test (Eignungsprufung). A system of restricted entry (numerus clausus) is in operation; the numbers of students to be admitted is decided according to the National Economic Development Plan. Preference is also given to those who have been employed in a productive occupation or army or social service for at least a year. For certain subjects (e.g. medicine, dentistry, agronomy, mining or metallurgical engineering) previous practical experience is necessary.

Studies are undertaken in stages:

Grundstudium - during which students acquire the basic knowledge of their subject. Students have to take **Vorprufung** on conclusion of this stage; this is not a qualification in itself, but students must pass to proceed with their studies.

East Germany

Fachstudium - this covers the specialist study and with the Grundstudium takes approximately 4 years (5 in theology and medicine), leading to the **Diplomprufung** and the qualification of **Diplom** + specialization (e.g. Diplom-Ingenieur - degree in engineering). This qualification entitles the holder to practise a profession.

Spezialstudium (postgraduate study) - this is only open to students who have the Diplomprufung. The course (aspirantur) is in 2 stages:

Promotion zum Grad - leading to the qualification of **Doktor eines Wissenschaftszweiges,** after 3-4 years original research

Doktor der Wissenschaft after a minimum of 4 years highly specialized research.

All courses include compulsory non-specialist studies, i.e. physical education, Russian, another foreign language, and the study of Marxism-Leninism.

Besides full-time study students may also take their courses by correspondence or by evening study.

TEACHER EDUCATION

Kindergarten

Training involves a 2-year course at Oberstufe (secondary) level (i.e. on completion of grade 10) at a pedagogical school; teachers must then work under supervision for 2 years. Nursery auxiliaries who have not completed a full course of education undertake a corresponding course lasting 3 years.

Basic

Teachers at the Unterstufe (grades 1-3) undertake a training course lasting 3 years at secondary level at a teacher-training institute (Institute fur Lehrerbildung) which is comparable in standard to the Fachschulen (technical schools) and leads to the qualification of **Lehrbefahigung.** Compulsory subjects are German language and literature, new mathematics and 1 elective from sport, music, art or handiwork. Before the introduction of the polytechnic school the course was taken on completion of 8 years Grundschule.

Teachers at the Mitteloberstufe (grades 4-10) undertake a 4-year course at a training college (Padagogische Hochschule/Institute) for holders of the Abitur/Reifezeugnis, leading to a state diploma. The course includes the preparation of a thesis and teaching practice; students study a major and a minor subject (the former for the full 4 years, the latter for 2 years only).

Secondary

Until 1960:

Teachers at grades 11 and 12 undertook a course of higher education lasting 4 years.

Since 1960:

Teachers at grades 11 and 12 undertake a 5-year course of higher education. They take the Staatsexamen and are awarded a **Diplomlehrer/Lehrerhefatzigung.**

East Germany

Headteachers

Teachers have to undertake a 1-year full-time course followed by 6 months part-time study including the preparation of a thesis, leading to a qualification in educational administration.

Retraining and refesher courses

Teachers are legally required to retrain in their subject specialization, methodology and Marxism-Leninism on a short course every 4 years.

ADULT EDUCATION

A number of people continue general and vocational education in some kind of centre: Abendoberschulen and Betriebsoberschulen (evening and factory schools), Arbeiter-und-Bauern-Fakultaten (Workers' and Peasants' Faculties). Courses are available for particular qualifications, including entrance examinations to courses of higher education.

West Germany

Federal Republic of Germany

Under the Basic Law (Grundgesetz) of the Federal Republic of Germany the legislative and administrative responsibility for education rests with the 11 Lander (states). Only a fixed number and range of duties are attributed to the Federal Government; the legislative responsibilities cover the enactment of a framework of provisions for the general principles in the higher education sector, for the advancement of scientific research, and for vocational training provided outside the formal school system and vocational guidance.

The basic structures of the Lander education systems (e.g. length of compulsory education, beginning and end of the school year, designation of the various educational institutions and their organizational form, essential elements of curricula) were standardized by Agreements between the States for the Standardization of the School System from 1954-64. There is broad uniformity between the systems of the Lander, the instruction offered and the qualifications gained, but sometimes nomenclature and periods of study vary.

Education is compulsory from age six. It lasted 8 years until 1964, when it was increased to nine years (ten years in three states) full-time plus a further three years part-time (i.e. regardless of whether a person has taken up full-time employment, he/she must attend a Berufsschule, vocational school, part-time or continue full-time at a Berufsfachschule).

The medium of instruction is German.

The academic year varies but is generally from September/October to June/July.

EVALUATION IN BRITAIN

School

Gesellenbrief Facharbeiterbrief - generally compared to the City & Guilds of London Institute Craft Studies Part 3.

Mittlere Reife - generally compared to GCE O-level standard on a subject-for-subject basis, where marks of sehr gut, gut, befriedigend or ausreichend have been obtained.

West Germany

Abitur/Zeugnis der Allgemeinen Hochschulreife/Reifezeugnis - generally compared in overall standard to GCE A-level and may be considered to satisfy the general requirement of universities and polytechnics. The comparison is not normally made on a subject-for-subject basis because, although since 1976 pupils have been examined in 4 subjects only in the final examinations, they study a much wider range of subjects than students preparing for GCE A-levels.

Abschlusszeugnis - a certificate awarded on the basis of performance in school examination (i.e. Mittlere Reife, Abitur, Fachhochschulreife).

Abgangszeugnis - a certificate that may be given to pupils on leaving school at any age (e.g. parents move to another part of Germany). It includes such information as attendance record and last examination marks.

Higher

Enquirers should contact the National Academic Recognition Information Centre.

Doctorate - generally compared to a British Ph.D.

MARKING SYSTEMS

School

1	sehr gut	very good
2	gut	good
3	befriedigend	satisfactory
4	ausreichend	pass
5	mangelhaft	fail*
6	ungenugend	

* In the normal school year, a fail is one 6 or two 5s but in examinations 5 is a fail.

Abitur examinations since 1976:

15, 14, 13	very good
12, 11, 10	good
9, 8, 7	satisfactory
6, 5, 4	fair
3, 2, 1, 0	fail

The marks obtained for term-time work are converted to the marking scale now used for the Abitur as follows:

15	1+
14	1
13	1-
12	2+
11	2
10	2-

West Germany

Each grade (except grade 6) covers 3 points. Achievement/main/intensive courses carry triple weighting, giving a possible maximum per subject of 45. For admission to the examinations for the Abitur, a minimum of 200 points (100 in achievement courses, 100 in basic courses) is required. On the leaving certificate (Zeugnis der Allgemeinen Hochschulreife) entitling the holder to general admission to higher education are given the marks accumulated in the last 4 semesters of the course and those of the Abitur examination. To pass the Abitur a minimum of 300 out of 900 points is required, (although the marks for the Abitur examinations themselves are out of 300).

Higher

1	sehr gut	very good
2	gut	good
3	befriedigend	satisfactory
4	ausreichend	sufficient (pass)
5	mangelhaft	fail

SCHOOL EDUCATION

Pre-primary

Facilities are available for children aged 3 - 6 at <u>Kindergarten</u>.

Primary

This generally covers 4 years for children from age 6 in a <u>Grundschule</u> (that is, the first level of <u>Volksschule</u>), but in some Lander it may be 6 years. The curriculum generally covers German, religious instruction, local studies, history, geography, science, arithmetic, music, art, craftwork and physical education. Normally no examinations are taken at the end of the cycle, and some pupils may stay at this type of school until completion of compulsory schooling.

Secondary

This may cover 9 or 10 years. The school attended depends on parental choice and the recommendation of the primary school teachers. In many Lander the first 2 years are referred to as the orientation phase (orientierungsstufe) and the type of schooling is not decided until completion of this phase.

There are 4 main types of secondary school covering the period of compulsory schooling:

1. <u>Volksschule</u> (until 1963); <u>Hauptschule</u> (from 1964)

In 1964 the <u>Volksschule</u> was reorganized, and the second cycle renamed <u>Hauptschule</u>; compulsory schooling was extended to cover 9 years.

It covers grades 5-9 in most Lander and grades 5-10 in some, with the possibility of a tenth year in the other Lander so that pupils may take the examinations for a certificate equivalent to the **Realschulabschlusszeugnis**.

West Germany

The course includes instruction in 1 foreign language (usually English), and the curriculum covers German, a foreign language, mathematics, physics/chemistry, biology, geography, history, social affairs, religious instruction, music, art, civics and physical education. On completion of the course, pupils take the examination (Qualifizierter Hauptschulabschluss) and obtain a **Qualifikationsvermerk**, which may give entry to a course of upper-secondary education at a gymnasium. The certificate awarded is the **Hauptschulabschluss** (HSAS). In Bavaria, pupils do not sit examinations at this stage for the award of the certificate. The **Hauptschulabgangszeugnis** may be given to a pupil who leaves the school at any stage during the course, and is not based on examination performance.

2. Realschule/Mittelschule/Progymnasium

This covers grades 5-10 in most Lander (grades 7-10 in Lander where primary schooling covers grades 1-6). One foreign language (English) is compulsory. On completion of the course, pupils take the examinations for the **Realschulabschlusszeugnis/Mittlere Reife**. The curriculum covers the same subjects as at the Hauptschule, but they are taught at a more advanced level.

3. Gymnasium/Hohere Schulen (before 1955)

This covers the full 9 years secondary schooling (grades 5-13), or 7 years (grades 7-13) where primary schooling lasts 6 years, but pupils may leave at the end of grade 10.

The curriculum in grades 5-10/7-10 covers German, mathematics, biology, geography, music, art, physical education, at least 2 foreign languages, history, social studies, physics and chemistry. On completion of grade 10, the **Mittlere Reife** is awarded (no examinations are taken).

Pupils wishing to continue their studies could, until 1976/7, specialize in 1 of 3 options:

mathematisch naturwissenschaftliches	mathematics - natural science
neusprachliches	modern languages
altsprachliches	classical languages

Compulsory subjects common to all 3 options included German, civics, chemistry, physics, mathematics, physical education, music and art.

Following the resolution of the Conference of Ministers of Education of July 1972 the re-organized upper level of the Gymnasien (reformierte gymnasiale oberstufe) was introduced in 1976/7 (in Baden-Wurttemberg and Bayern 1977/8). The course of instruction covers 3 broad subject areas:

language/literature/art
social sciences
mathematics, natural sciences/technology.

Compulsory subjects include German, foreign languages, art, music, philosophy, and/or religious instruction, civics or history/geography/social studies, economics, mathematics, physics, chemistry and biology. In addition pupils study elective subjects, which comprise approximately one-third of the course. Electives include the subjects mentioned as being compulsory, plus e.g. education, psychology, sociology, statistics, geology, data processing, technology, etc. Both elective and compulsory subjects are taught at basic (Grundkurse) and intensified/main/achievement (Leistungskurse) level. The latter comprise 5-6 lessons per week, and basic courses only 2-3 lessons a week. Pupils must take 2 intensified courses, of which one must be either a foreign language, mathematics or a natural science.

On completion of grade 13, pupils take the examinations for the **Abitur/Zeugnis der Allgemeinen Hochschulreife/Zeugnis der Reife**:

a. In the 'traditional' form of Gymnasium (normally pre-1972) pupils took 4 written examinations: German, mathematics, a foreign language, and a subject related to the specialization (i.e. physics for the mathematics/natural science option, a further language from the original choice of languages - English, French and Latin - for the modern languages specialization, Latin for the classical option); and oral examinations in these subjects. Pupils received the **Abitur** certificate if they obtained the classification of ausreichend or above in all subjects).

b. In the reorganized upper level of Gymnasium (post-1972) pupils take 3 written examinations and 1 oral. The first and second written examinations are in the subjects taken as achievement/main/intensive courses; the third written examination is taken in one of the elective subjects. The oral examination is chosen from: language, literature, arts, social studies, mathematics, science, religious studies and history, but must not be in 1 of the subjects already tested in a written examination. The complete set of examinations must include 1 living foreign language, mathematics, natural science and German. One of the compulsory subjects may be taken at the end of grade 12. The final grades on the **Zeugnis der allgemeinen Hochschulreife** are based on marks obtained in the final examinations and on class performance in the basic and achievement/main/intensive courses during grades 12 and 13.

c. There is still a limited number of specialist Gymnasien (see under Berufliches Gymnasium). On completion of the 3-year course, pupils take the examinations for the **Abitur** and, if successful, are awarded the **Zeugnis der Fachgebundenen Hochschulreife**. This may be transformed into the **Zeugnis der Allgemeinen Hochschulreife** by passing supplementary examinations.

d. There is a limited number of Gesamtschulen (comprehensive schools), and some are not truly comprehensive. Some cover only grades 5-9/10; others cover the full period of secondary schooling (grades 5-13). There are 2 types of school:

ko-operativ - offering facilities for the 3 other types of school (i.e. Hauptschule, Realschule and Gymnasium) on the same site, but with different classes

integrierte - each subject is taught at 3 levels, and students choose their own level according to ability within each subject.

Pupils at the comprehensive schools take the same examinations as at the other types of secondary school.

e. Aufbaurealschule, Aufbauhauptschule and Aufbaugymnasium - students aged 28 and upwards normally transfer from industry (not school) to these institutions.

Technical and vocational secondary

All children who leave full-time schooling at age 15 must attend part-time (1 day a week minimum) school for 3 years. (This applies to all school leavers between 15 and 18, whether in training apprenticeships or under contract.)

West Germany

A great variety of institutions offer this type of course, and there are variations between the individual Lander. However, some major types may be identified:

Berufsschule (part-time vocational school/day continuation school)

These offer courses mainly for those who leave school at 15 or 16 and then proceed to vocational training in industry, as well as for those who are employed but receive no on-the-job training. Courses consist of practical and vocational training (about 60%) and a programme of general subjects such as German, civics/social affairs, economics, English, religion and sport (about 40%). At the end of the course, trainees take a final examination administered by the local Chamber of Commerce (Industrie- und Handelskammer, see under Apprenticeships). They receive a leaving certificate from the Berufsschule, issued without a preceding examination.

Berufsaufbauschule (part-time continuation, vocational school)

These offer courses for students who have already completed 6 months at a part-time vocational school (Berufsschule). The teaching both of the general and of the vocational courses is at a higher level than at Berufsschule. General subjects covered are German, a foreign language, history and social affairs, geography (including economic geography, mathematics, physics and chemistry). The courses vary from 1 year full-time to 3 years part-time. There are 5 areas of specialization, all of which incorporate economics and business management: general commercial/industrial; industrial/technical; home economics/nursing; social work; and agriculture. Courses lead to the **Fachschulreife**, considered in the Federal Republic of Germany to be comparable to the **Realschulreife**. With this qualification students may enter a Fachschule or the second year of a Fachoberschule.

Fachschule (advanced technical school)

These offer courses of 6 months to 2-and-a-half years for students who have completed a vocational training course. Courses are available in a variety of fields, e.g. remedial gymnasia. Personnel for middle management are trained in a variety of fields (e.g. at Technikerschulen). The entrance requirement for courses at Fachschulen and Technikerschulen is the Mittlere or Fachschulreife.

Berufsfachschule (full-time specialized vocational school)

These train lower-level technicians, at the same time improving their general education. The various specializations sometimes lead to a complete change in an institution's name: e.g. Handelsschule is a Berufsfachschule specializing in commerce. The entrance requirement is successful completion of Hauptschule (grade 9) or Realschule (grade 10). Courses vary from 1 to 3 years. At schools requiring a Hauptschul-leaving certificate for admission, a qualification considered equivalent in the Federal Republic of Germany to the leaving certificate of a Realschule, may be obtained on conclusion of a course lasting 2 years.

Hohere Berufsfachschule (full-time specialized higher vocational school).

Students completing a course at a Berufsfachschule may go on to this type of school, which prepares them for positions in lower and middle management as well as for entry to a course at a Fachhochschule (see under Further Education). Such students have to undergo an additional year of practical training. Courses vary in length according to the specialization.

West Germany

Fachoberschule (senior full-time technical school)

This type of school was first established in 1969. It offers a course at grades 11 and 12 for students who have completed the course at a Realschule or an apprenticeship. Courses include an element of practical training in grade 11 as well as some general education. (Compulsory subjects for all students include German, social studies, mathematics, natural sciences, a foreign language and physical education.) The specializations include: engineering, economics and administration, domestic science, design and navigation. Success in the final examination leads to the **Fachhochschulreife**, the entry qualification for colleges of technology (Fachhochschulen, see under **Further Education**). Written examinations are taken in 4 subjects: German, mathematics, a foreign language and 1 subject taken from the particular subject area taught at the Fachoberschule. Oral examinations are also given in all subjects of the written examination, and 1 career-oriented subject.

Apprenticeships

These normally last approximately 2 to 3 and a half years for those who have completed compulsory schooling (grade 9). The apprentice must attend a part-time vocational school (Berufsschule). At the end of the apprenticeship an examination is taken. The examination is supervised by the committee of the professional organization (Handwerkskammer). If the apprenticeship has been contracted by a master craftsman, the certificate issued is the **Gesellenbrief**. If the apprenticeship has been contracted by an industrial organization, the examination is supervised by a committee of the Chamber of Commerce and Industry (Industrie- und Handelskammer), and the certificate issued is the **Facharbeiterbrief**. A skilled worker who wishes to obtain a higher qualification, may undertake a course lasting 3-4 semesters (1-and-a-half to 2 years) at a Technikerschule (see under Fachschule) after gaining at least 2 years experience in the respective fields. Among the qualifications which may be obtained is **Staatlich Geprufter Techniker**.

Berufliches Gymnasium (vocational grammar school)

Pupils who complete a course at Realschule may take a course lasting 3 years, specializing in a particular field (e.g. agriculture, economics, textiles, music/art, social studies) which will prepare them for entry to specific faculties at institutions of higher education. Vocational subjects are taught instead of a foreign language. The qualification obtained is the **Fachgebundenes Abitur**.

FURTHER EDUCATION

Courses of advanced technical education are offered by Hohere Fachschulen, Akademien, and Fachhochschulen (until 1968 called Ingenieurschulen; then reclassified as institutions of higher education and renamed).

The entry requirement to courses at these institutions is the Fachhochschulreife/Abitur/Realschulreife (+2 years vocational experience). Courses normally last 3-4 years (inclusive of practical training, the duration of which varies, depending on the course and the lander in which the person is studying) although students may take longer if they wish. The qualification obtained on completion of the course, which emphasizes the practical orientation and application of the subjects studied, is the specialization **Graduiert**, e.g. **Betriebswirt** (grad.), **Sozialpadagoge** (grad.).

West Germany

Until 1979, the qualification obtained in the field of engineering was the **Ingenieur graduiert** (Ing.grad.). However, following from the 1976 Framework Act for Higher Education (Hochschulrahmengesetz), the Fachhochschulen have been given the same legal basis as the universities. Thus, since 1979 students studying at these institutions receive a qualification with the same name as students studying at a university, **Diplom Ingenieur** (Dipl.Ing.). In certain states it is required that certificates supply the initials FH after the title of the qualification to show that it has been awarded by that type of institution. The standard of the course has not been altered. Holders of the Ing.Grad. may request the title of Dipl.Ing. which in certain Länder requires an additional examination.

HIGHER EDUCATION

The entrance qualification to courses of higher education is the Abitur/Zeugnis der Allgemeinen Hochschulreife. The qualification obtained on completion of the course at a specialist gymnasium, the Zeugnis der Fachgebundenen Hochschulreife gives access to courses only in certain relevant fields. However, students may sit a further set of examinations (Erganzungsprufungen), and success in these would entitle the holder to access to all faculties; owing to limited places, a system of restricted entry (numerus clausus) has been introduced to decide admission to courses in medicine, veterinary medicine, dentistry, pharmacology and psychology. The system may also operate in other fields, depending on the demand for places, and this can change from year to year.

Courses are offered by universities, technical universities (Technische Hochschulen, now mostly called technical universities) and comprehensive universities (Gesamthochschulen, formed recently by grouping existing institutions of higher education).

The first qualification to be obtained is the **Diplom/Staatsexamen** (in subjects covered by arts as well as certain professional fields, except engineering and science - see also under **Teacher Education**). The minimum period to obtain either qualification is 4 years (8 semesters). Most students take longer (on average 5 years/10 semesters), and apart from restrictions on courses in certain professional fields (e.g. medicine, science and technology faculties), students can decide when to take their final examinations. The principle of academic freedom is the underlying feature of this sector of higher education. Students may normally attend the university of their choice, have the right to change universities part of the way through their studies or for a semester, and are responsible for planning their studies (apart from courses for which there are professional requirements and in which students have little choice because of the many prescribed courses). In most fields there is an intermediate examination, **Vordiplom** (science, economic and social science, and technology)/ **Zwischenprufung** (humanities) after 4-5 semesters, during which the studies are more generally based than in the second period, when they specialize. In medical, scientific and technological faculties, many institutions bar from further study students who fail these intermediate examinations.

Until the early 1960s students of the humanities had to continue studying for the doctorate as there was no earlier qualification to be obtained. The **Magister Artium** was then introduced as a qualification which could be obtained after the same period of study as the Diplom/Staatsexamen in fields that did not lead to the Diplom for those who did not wish to teach or fulfil requirements for other professional fields.

West Germany

The **Doctorate** may be obtained after a minimum of approximately 2 years research after the award of the **Diplom/Magister Artium/Staatsexamen**. The process of obtaining the doctorate is known as Promotion, and the oral examination taken on completion of the research is the Rigorosum.

TEACHER EDUCATION

Primary (Grundschule)
Lower secondary (Hauptschule)
Comprehensive school (Gesamtschule, grades 5/7-10)

From the entrance requirement of the Abitur/Zeugnis der Allgemeinen Hochschulreife/Zeugnis der Reife, students take a course which lasts a minimum of 6 semesters (3 years), plus 1 examination semester, at a Padagogische Hochschule (teacher training college); in Bavaria, Berlin, Bremen, Hamburg, Hesse, Lower Saxony, North Rhine - Westphaliaand Saarland all training is undertaken at universities. On completion of the course, students take the examinations, **Erste Staatsprufung fur das Lehramt an Grundschulen/Hauptschulen/Gesamtschulen**. This is followed by a probationary period of 2 years, known as the Referendarzeit. During this period the probationary teacher has a light teaching load but has to attend seminars and write a dissertation. It culminates in a second set of examinations, **Zweite Staatsprufung**.

Lower Secondary (Realschulen)
Upper Secondary (Gymnasien)

From the entrance requirement of the Abitur/Zeugnis der allgemeinen Hochschulreife/Zeugnis der Reife, students take a course lasting a minimum of 8 semesters (4 years), although in practice few prospective teachers take the examination in less than 10, at a university. On completion of this period, pupils take the first set of examinations, **Erstes Staatsexamen**, followed by the probationary period (Referendarzeit), lasting 2 years - see under Primary. At the end of this period, students take the second set of examinations, **Zweites Staatsexamen**.

The names of the examination, Staatsprufung and Staatsexamen, are interchangeable at lower secondary (Realschulen) and upper secondary level. It is therefore strongly recommended that the type of institution at which the student studies, and the level of education for which the prospective teacher has been trained, should be checked.

Ghana

Republic of Ghana

In general, education in Ghana is centrally administered and almost totally government financed.

In theory, primary education is compulsory.

English is the official medium of instruction at all levels, although since 1971 the local language has been used for the first years of primary school.

The academic year runs from September/October to June/July.

EVALUATION IN BRITAIN

School

West African School Certificate (WASC) - grades 1-6 are generally equated to GCE O-level standard (grades A, B, C).

West African Higher School Certificate (WAHSC) - grades A-E are generally equated to GCE A-level grades.

Middle School Leaving Certificate - generally considered to be below GCE O-level standard.

Post-Middle School Certificate A - likely to be considered to lie below GCE O-level standard.

Post-Secondary Certificate A - may be compared to a standard between GCE O- and A-levels.

Further

Tarkwa School of Mines Diploma - may be considered comparable to a standard between B/TEC National and Higher National Diploma (formerly OND and HND).

Higher

Bachelor degree - generally considered to compare to British Bachelor degree standard.

Ghana

MARKING SYSTEMS

School

West African School Certificate — graded 1 (maximum) to 9.
West African Higher School Certificate — graded A (maximum) - F.

Higher

The 3 universities record their letter grades according to slightly different scales, which are usually noted on the transcript:

Legon		Kumasi		Cape Coast	
A	70+	A	75+	A	69+
B	50-69	B	65-74	B	50-68
C	40-49	C	55-64	C	40-49
D	30-39	D	40-54	D	30-39 (fail)
E	below 30	E	below 40 (fail)	E	below 30

SCHOOL EDUCATION

During the last 30 years there have been 3 main patterns of school education, affecting both primary and secondary education:

1. The Accelerated Development Plan for Education of the early 1950s established the system of:

i. 6 years primary education from age 6. The **Secondary Common Entrance Examination** was taken on completion of grade VI to determine secondary school entry, as places were limited.

ii. 4 years middle school, at the end of which pupils obtain the **Middle School Leaving Certificate**.

2. In 1963 there was radical reorganization, which led to the following changes:

i. 8 years primary education from age 5.

ii. Pupils could then take the Secondary School Common Entrance Examination (SSCEE), and begin the 5-year secondary course leading to the examinations for the **West African School Certificate/GCE O-levels**.

Syllabuses are provided by the West African Examinations Council. A limited number of schools offer the 2-year course in lower and upper sixth forms, on completion of which students take the examinations for the **West African Higher School Certificate/GCE A-level**.

Ghana

Pupils who fail the Common Entrance Examination after class 6 or are not selected by a secondary school may enrol in a middle school after passing an entrance test. The middle school consists of forms 1-4 and provides basic general education. Pupils in middle school forms 1-3 can again attempt the Common Entrance Examination to enrol in forms 1-5 of a secondary school. If unsuccessful, they take the Middle School Leaving Certificate examination at the end of middle school form 4. A pass in this examination entitles the student to the **West African Middle School Leaving Certificate.**

3. The 1974 plan for the New Structure and Content of Education was to be fully implemented by 1980/1; however, many schools still follow an older system. The Plan envisaged radical administrative and curricular reform as follows:

First cycle education provides for 6 years primary from age 6, followed by 4 years middle school. These 10 years of basic education are free and theoretically compulsory. At the end of middle school (form 4) there is a Middle School Leaving Certificate examination for those who have not moved to secondary school via the Common Entrance Examination.

Entry to secondary school is by competitive examination (the CEE) taken in primary 6, or in the middle school forms 1-4. The secondary school course is 5 years leading to the West African School Certificate or GCE O-level. Secondary form 5 leavers who attain a certain level in the School Certificate/GCE O-level examination do a 2-year course in a limited number of sixth-form schools, leading to the GCE A-level examination.

Financial constraints have prevented the implementation of this plan, though approximately 100 experimental junior secondary schools have been established.

Technical

There are 5 secondary technical schools offering O-level and sometimes A-level courses in various subjects, with a special emphasis on technical subjects and technical drawing.

Entry is as for ordinary secondary schools. On completing middle school forms 3 or 4 it is possible to enter 1 of 16 <u>technical institutes</u> offering a 3-year craft course based on City & Guilds qualifications or RSA for secretarial subjects.

Before 1963 there were 4 junior technical institutes and 4 technical institutes. The junior technical institutes were then upgraded to technical institutes and 3 of the technical institutes (at Accra, Kumasi and Takoradi) were designated polytechnics. Since then both junior technical and technical institutes have been established.

Girls who complete middle school may undertake a 3-year catering course at a technical institute culminating in the examinations for a City & Guilds qualification. Secretarial and commercial courses of 3-4 years are also offered to middle school leavers without any preliminary or pre-vocational training. Examinations for the GCE O-level in commercial and secretarial subjects are taken at the end of the course, but students who fail these may take the single-subject examinations of the RSA. Students undertaking a 5-year course take examinations for the **Ghana Business Certificate** of the West African Examinations Council.

FURTHER EDUCATION

The 3 former technical institutes in Accra, Kumasi and Takoradi were designated polytechnics in 1963 for training technicians. Entry is based upon completion of secondary school, provided the subjects of English, mathematics and science have been passed at ordinary level or on completion of the general engineering or general building course at the technical institutes. The polytechnics offer the following courses:

Technician Certificate in electrical, mechanical and building trades - 3 years

Advanced craft courses in engineering and in building trades and building - 2 years

Ordinary Technician Diploma in mechanical and electrical engineering; and other subjects (textiles, tailoring, photography) - 3 years

Course in institutional management - 3 years

Course in catering and domestic subjects - 3 years; fashion and dressmaking - 2 years

Course in business studies - 2 years.

Tarkwa School of Mines offers a 3-year course leading to a diploma, with the entrance requirement of GCE O-level in mathematics, physics, chemistry, and engineering. In 1978 this institution became the Institute of Mining and Mineral Engineering of the University of Science & Technology, Kumasi, and now offers degree-level courses in mining engineering.

Trade training centres

The Canadian Government has assisted with the establishment of technical training centres in Accra and Kumasi and the Japanese financed the establishment of the Tema Textile Training Centre attached to the Tema Technical Institute.

The National Vocational Training Institute (NVTI) was set up with ILO assistance in 1969. It co-ordinates industrial and vocational training by establishing standards and certifying courses, setting up pilot training centres and assisting local communities to establish their own vocational centres. It deals with craft, technical, clerical and domestic science skills.

The University of Science and Technology offers 2-year courses in the Faculty of Science leading to the award of the Higher National Diploma (HND). 1- and 2-year courses are offered in e.g. land survey.

HIGHER EDUCATION

This is offered by 3 universities:

University of Ghana at Legon - founded 1948, granted full university status in 1961.

Ghana

<u>University of Cape Coast</u> - founded as a University College in 1962; designated University College of Science Education in 1964-6, resumed its former title in 1966 and achieved full university status in 1972.

<u>University of Science and Technology</u> (UST), Kumasi - founded as Kumasi College of Technology in 1952 and achieved university status in 1961 as the Kwame Nkrumah University of Science and Technology. It was given its present title in 1966. Before the accession of the college to university status the Faculty of Engineering provided courses leading to the external B.Sc. (Eng.) degree of the University of London.

The usual minimum entrance requirement for Bachelor degree courses is 5 GCEs, 2 or 3 being at A-level. The University of Cape Coast however will accept students with a number of passes at GCE O-level, if in suitable subjects, for entry to a 1-year preliminary course before the normal degree course.

Most Bachelor degree courses may be taken as General or Honours; the latter are classified: I, II division i, II division ii, or pass.

Bachelor degree courses at the University of Ghana normally take 3 years and at the other 2 universities 4 years (at the University of Cape Coast only since 1975/6). First degrees in medicine take 5 years. Master degrees generally require 2 years study (including the presentation of a thesis) after the award of the Bachelor degree.

TEACHER EDUCATION

Non-graduate teachers

There are presently 3 types of teacher-training college:

Certificate A (post middle-school) colleges

The basic teacher-training course for primary school teachers is 4 years, leading to the **Teacher's Certificate A**. This was originally subdivided into a 2-year course leading to a **Teacher's Certificate B,** and a further 2-year course leading to the **Post 'B' Teacher's Certificate**; this subdivision has now been abolished. The entry requirement is the Middle School Leaving Certificate or completion of middle school form 4. Alternatively, entry may be gained by completion of at least 2 years of the secondary school academic stream (i.e. form 2). Pupil-teachers who may have finished middle school up to 7 years ago and have been teaching untrained may also undertake these courses. Admission, is also dependent on the results of a combined examination for entry to 4-year courses at teacher-training colleges and, for pupil-teacher selection, an examination conducted by the West African Examinations Council on behalf of the National Teacher Training Council.

Post-secondary colleges

These colleges were established in 1975 to provide a 3-year post O-level course to train teachers for the new junior secondary schools, but because of the delay in the establishment of the junior secondary programme they have produced teachers for classes in various types of school covering the first 9 or 10 years of education. The programme has been reviewed, the quasi-specialist aspects of the course have been abandoned and it has become a general teacher-training course. However, some of the colleges have retained a bias for 1 of several subjects: home science, agricultural science, business studies, technical subjects and science. English, mathematics and education remain the externally examined subjects.

Advanced teacher-training colleges

These accept experienced teachers who already have a teacher's certificate (usually Certificate A) to specialize in 1 subject, normally for 3 years, to enable them to teach at secondary schools and at teacher-training colleges and thus supplement the Cape Coast graduate specialist. Subjects studied include music, Ghanaian languages, technical education, agricultural sciences, as well as the usual academic subjects. The qualification given is a diploma and these colleges are often referred to as 'diploma-awarding institutions'.

Graduate teachers

The University of Cape Coast, primarily a teacher-training university, provides undergraduate courses in all the main academic disciplines, the study of which is combined with education. On completion of the 4-year course, which includes teaching practice, graduates are qualified to teach in secondary schools.

Cape Coast also offers a 1-year PGCE (for graduates of University of Ghana and University of Science and Technology, Kumasi), but many graduates go straight into teaching.

Unqualified teachers

There are many unqualified teachers at all levels of the school system, including pupil-teachers and national service personnel (graduates doing compulsory national service on completion of their degree courses).

Technical teachers

There are 2 Technical Teachers Colleges.

Greece

Hellenic Republic

Education in Greece has traditionally been centralized and state controlled.

Until the late 1950s, emphasis in the school curriculum was on classics; since then the balance with science and technology has been restored.

Official education begins at the age of five-and-a-half, and primary education is taken over six years. Secondary education caters for the age range eleven-and-a-half or twelve to eighteen. Compulsory education terminates at age fifteen.

Higher education is offered at universities and university-level institutions (generally known as AEI) and institutions of further education (known as TEI). Education at all levels is tuition-free to all Greek citizens.

The academic year runs from September/October to June.

EVALUATION IN BRITAIN

School

Apolytirion of Gymnasio - generally considered below GCE O-level standard.

Apolytirio of Lykeion - generally considered comparable to GCE O-level standard on a subject-for-subject basis where a pupil has obtained marks of at least 11 out of 20 in subjects which may be taken in the GCE examinations (except English language).

Higher

Bachelor degree - generally considered comparable to British Bachelor degree standard.

MARKING SYSTEMS

Secondary

Marking is on a scale of 1-20 (maximum), with 10 as the pass mark.

Greece

Higher

Marking is on a scale of 1-10 (maximum), with 5 as the minimum pass mark.

SCHOOL EDUCATION

Pre-primary (Nipiagogeio)

Extensive facilities are available for children aged four-and-a-half to five-and-a-half in the state school system. Law 1566, recently passed, makes provision for expansion of pre-primary education in the state school system to allow for admission of children aged 3-and-a-half for 2 years, but this has not been implemented yet.

Some schools in the private sector already offer facilities for children aged 3-and-a-half.

Primary (Demotiko Scholio)

This covers 6 years for children from age 5-and-a-half. The curriculum covers: religious instruction, Greek language, environmental studies, history and elements of civics, arithmetic, elements of science (natural science, physics and chemistry), geography, handicrafts, music, physical education, drawing. On completion of this cycle, pupils obtain the primary leaving certificate.

Secondary (Gymnasio and Lykeio)
Before 1977:

Secondary education consisted of one 6-year cycle in establishments called Gymansio. To continue their education at secondary level, primary school leavers had to take an entrance examination consisting of tests in Greek, mathematics, physics, geography, religious instruction, and history.

Since 1977:

The former 6-year Gymnasio has been divided into two 3-year cycles to form Gymnasio (lower cycle) and Lykeio (upper cycle). At the same time entrance examinations from primary education to Gymnasio (average age 12) were abolished and entrance examination was introduced from Gymnasio to Lykeio (average age 15). The 6-year primary and the 3-year lower cycle secondary (Gymnasio) constitute now the statutory 9-year compulsory education. In 1983 entrance examinations to Lykeio were abolished.

Lower cycle (Gymnasio) leavers may continue their education at General Lykeio, Technical Vocational Lykeio (TEL), or Technical Vocational School (TES). There are also ecclesiastical Lykeia which prepare boys for the priesthood. All the above comprise the upper-secondary cycle. The length of studies at all types of Lykeia is 3 years (4 years at evening Lykeia), while at Technical Vocational Schools it is 2 years (3 years at evening TES).

The curriculum of the first cycle covers ancient Greek in translation, modern Greek, mathematics, history, physical education, science, French or English, religious knowledge, geography, domestic science, handicrafts, music, biology, anthropology, hygiene, and civics. On completion of this cycle, pupils are awarded the **Apolytirio of Gymnasio**.

Greece

The curriculum of the General Lykeio consists of academic subjects similar to those offered in the Gymnasio, plus Latin, philosophy, sociology, ancient Greek and economics.

The curriculum of the Technical Vocational Lykeio (TEL) consists of a selection from the subjects of General Lykeio, and specialist subjects including engineering, economics, agriculture, etc., according to the chosen orientation.

On completion of the upper secondary cycle, pupils have to sit examinations for the school-leaving certificate (**Apolytirio**). On the basis of the marks obtained, they may apply for admission to higher education institutions. The examinations are held once a year, May-June, and are administered and controlled by the Ministry of Education on a national basis. <u>Desmes</u> is the name of the group of subjects which are taken at the general examinations after completion of the 3-year Lykeio school (upper secondary). While success in a Desmi is required for the Apolytirio award (the school-leaving certificate) it is also the necessary academic requirement (except Desmi 5) for admission to universities, TEI (formerly KATEE), and similar institutions including now the Army Academies.

Until last year there were 4 Desmes of subjects: each Desmi to correspond to a strictly specified group of university schools, departments or faculties to which candidates are permitted to apply for entry. Only recently the Ministry announced that in addition to the existing 4 Desmes, a fifth Desmi will be introduced this year for Lykeio leavers who need an Apolytirio, i.e. for employment, but do not wish to apply for university. Candidates may choose only 1 Desmi and are not allowed to change in the same academic year. Applications for university places are submitted in March. Each of the 4 Desmes of the general examinations consists of 4 compulsory written papers. The modern Greek paper (composition) is common to all 4 Desmes:

Desmi	1 (or A)	composition, mathematics, physics and chemistry
	2 (or B)	composition, physics, chemistry and biology - anthropology
	3 (or C)	composition, ancient Greek, Latin and history
	4 (or D)	composition, mathematics, history and sociology.

The mathematics paper in Desmi 4 is different from that in Desmes 1 and 2. The Desmes subjects are taught intensively in the third year of Lykeio school together with the other subjects provided in the school curriculum. The Desmes courses are called preparatory courses. The new fifth Desmi course is called course of General Usefulness (**Genikis Ofelimotitas**) and includes: language (modern Greek), applied economics, a foreign language (English or French), principles of office skills, environment and health, introduction to sociology, study of work (production) environment and administration.

The marking system used for assessment is the numerical scale 1-20, where 20 is the highest attainment.

The grades obtained in each paper of the appropriate Desmi (1, 2, 3 and 4) together with the grades obtained in the certificates of progress (**Endiktiko**) in the first, second and third (final) year of Lykeio schooling (the third-year certificate is called **Apolytirio**), determine the place of a Lykeio-leaver on the list of candidates for university admission.

Greece

The number of places to be offered in each school or department is usually known by spring every year. The places available are offered in descending order to candidates on the results lists. The lists of successful candidates are normally published in September. Those whose marks do not earn them a place may return to the state post-Lykeio departments to repeat their Desmi courses, or some of them, and try again in the next year.

FURTHER EDUCATION

In 1973 Anotera (post-Lykeio) technical educational institutions were established under the name of KATE. In 1977 these were renamed KATEE (Kentra Anoteras Technikis Epangelmatikis Ekpethefseos) to include vocational professional courses in a wide range of subjects. Candidates had to be holders of the Lykeio Apolytirio and to have passed entrance examinations conducted by the Ministry of Education nationwide. The length of studies was 3 years, including practical training. Upon graduation, students were awarded the **Ptychion of KATEE**.

Following Law 1404 of 1983, the KATEEs were restructured to upgrade the courses offered, and were renamed TEI (Technologika Ekpedeftika Idrymata). New courses were introduced, and the length of the courses was extended. There are cases where hours of instruction increased by 15-55%, and an additional semester of study has been added. Additionally, there is a new feature in the TEIs, which is a period of compulsory practical training after the course of study. The final award is called **Ptychion of TEI**.

HIGHER EDUCATION

There are 11 universities and a number of 'graduate' schools offering courses at this level. Since 1959, admission has been by competitive entrance examination, open to all students who have successfully completed any course of secondary education. Courses last a minimum of 4 years, with 5 years in engineering, agriculture, veterinary medicine, and dentistry, and 6 years in medicine. All courses at the National Technical University last 5 years. Under the University Law of 1978, there was a limit on the number of times students could resit examinations and the number of additional years they could take to complete their degrees; this limit has now been lifted.

Postgraduate courses are available in a limited number of fields and last 2 years (leading to a postgraduate diploma). There are facilities for research leading to the award of a doctorate.

Higher education is under state control, in accordance with the Greek Constitution.

There are foreign institutions offering courses at this level but qualifications awarded by such institutions are not recognized by the State.

Greece

TEACHER EDUCATION

Pre-primary and primary

Before 1984:

Pre-primary and primary school teachers were trained at pedagogical academies; 1 year for pre-primary teachers, and 2 years for primary teachers.

Since 1984:

Pedagogical academies for teachers of pre-primary and primary education have been incorporated into existing universities as Department of Pedagogics. The duration of studies is now 4 years and the degree awarded is equivalent to a Greek university degree.

Secondary

University graduates may take a 3-month course in education. After 3 years teaching they take a 2-year refresher course.

Guatemala

Republic of Guatemala

Compulsory education extends from age seven to fourteen, but it is not possible to enforce this owing to insufficient facilities.

The medium of instruction is Spanish.

The academic year runs from January to October.

EVALUATION IN BRITAIN

School

Certificado de Graduado/Bachillerato en Ciencias y Letras - generally considered to compare to GCE O-level standard.

Higher

Licenciatura - may be considered to compare to British Bachelor degree standard.

MARKING SYSTEMS

School

61% is the minimum pass mark.

Higher

51% is the minimum pass in the state university and 1 of the private universities; 61% is the minimum pass in the other 3 private universities.

SCHOOL EDUCATION

Pre-primary

Some facilities are available for children aged 4-6.

Guatemala

Primary

This covers 6 years, from age 7, and is divided into three 2-year cycles. The curriculum covers Spanish, mathematics, geography, history, science, handicrafts, art and music, health and safety, agriculture, industrial arts and home economics.

Secondary

This covers 5 years, divided into a 3-year ciclo prevocacional of general education, followed by a 2-year ciclo diversificado. During the first cycle, common to all pupils, the curriculum includes mathematics, Spanish, sociology, natural science, drawing and painting, music, handicrafts or domestic science, electives (e.g. a foreign language - usually English or French, typing, etc.). In the second cycle, pupils may specialize. On conclusion of the second cycle, pupils take the examinations for the **Bachillerato**.

Technical secondary

A course of 3 years upper secondary education leads to the **Perito Industrial**, **Agricola** or **Contador** (commerce).

HIGHER EDUCATION

There are 5 universities, of which only 1 is state-run. The entrance requirement is the **Bachillerato en Ciencias y Letras** or equivalent certificate at Bachillerato level, plus an entrance examination.

The **Licenciatura** takes 5-6 years, of which the first 1-2 years are devoted to general studies. A further 1-year course followed by a minimum of 1 year of research leads to the **Doctorado** in law, the humanities, education, and the economic and social sciences.

Medicine - the title of **Doctor** generally takes 8 years to obtain.

In 1964 the School of General Studies was established, and all students had to attend this for 2 years before entering specific faculties for their specialist studies. It was closed in 1968.

The National School of Nursing offers a 3-year course leading to the qualification of **Enfermera Graduada**.

TEACHER EDUCATION

Primary

A 3-year upper secondary-level course leads to a **Trained Teacher's Certificate**.

Secondary

Teachers for this level are graduates.

Guinea

Revolutionary People's Republic of Guinea

Before 1960 almost all education in Guinea was provided by mission and Koranic schools but, during the 1960s, a series of reforms and implementations altered the nature of the schooling. A major reform was the replacement of French with the various vernaculars as the principal media of instruction; however this was only effectively achieved in the early 1970s and reversed in the 1984 reforms. At all levels, educational facilities are limited.

The school year runs from September to July.

EVALUATION IN BRITAIN

School

Baccalaureat - generally considered to be overall GEE O-level standard.

Higher

Licence - may be considered below British Bachelor degree standard.

MARKING SYSTEMS

School

The marking system is out of 10.

Higher

As above.

Guinea

SCHOOL EDUCATION

1961-7

Primary

This covered 4 years until 1964 when it was increased to 5 years. It was referred to as the first cycle.

Secondary

This was divided into 2 parts:

lower (2nd cycle) covering 3 years, which was soon increased to 5 years.

upper (3rd cycle) covering 5 years, which was then correspondingly decreased to 3 years.

Due to the very limited facilities, few children actually proceeded to secondary education.

1968-84

Primary

This covered 6 years and was referred to as the first cycle. Children studied French, history, the indigenous language, geography, arithmetic, natural sciences, drawing, music, sewing, physical education and civics.

Secondary

This was divided into 2 cycles (the second and the third), each of 3 years. During the lower cycle pupils studied philosophy and ideology, national and French languages, history, geography, mathematics, sciences (biology, chemistry and physics), administrative accounting and instruction in techniques of teaching. On completion of the cycle pupils took the examinations for the **Brevet**, necessary to proceed to the third cycle.

During the higher cycle pupils in the academic lycees continued to study the same subjects as during the lower cycle, plus statistics and business administration, although they could specialize in the literary or scientific options. On completion of the cycle pupils took the examinations for the Baccalaureat. In 1973/4 the cycle was lengthened to 4 years.

Technical secondary

Lower:

Since the late 1960s there have been 2 types: vocational/technical and rural (the School of Rural Education/Centre d'Enseignement Rural - CER). In 1968 this was changed to the Centre d'Education Revolutionnaire. The Centre is primarily concerned with agricultural practices and land use.

Guinea

Upper:

During this cycle pupils could attend a technical lycee for the 3-year course or a vocational school which could offer courses of various lengths.

Ecoles Professionnelles

These offer intensive vocational/technical training. They include the National Arts and Trades School, the National Health School and the National Telecommunications School. These 3 professional schools became university faculties in 1975.

Since 1984

Primary

French became the language of instruction. The study of indigenous languages was dropped. English is to be introduced as a subject from the third year.

Secondary

The second cycle is now 4 years. National languages and ideology have been dropped. English has been added.

The third cycle has been reduced to 3 years, leading to the **1st Bac.** in grade 12 and the **2nd Bac.** in grade 13 (terminale). Students specialize in 1 of the following options from grade 11.

Bac. Sciences Experimentales
Bac. Sciences Mathematiques
Bac. Sciences Sociales

Technical secondary

With the elevation of the 3 Ecoles Professionelles to University faculties, it is intended that there be 'Centres de Formation Professionelle in each region to train qualified workers (ouvriers qualifies). Candidates are recruited mainly from grade 10.

HIGHER EDUCATION

The main change from the reform of 1984 is a drastic reduction in the number of 'Facultes Agronomiques' and their redeployment; the system was producing too many theoreticians and not enough practitioners. The current position is as follows:

The fourth cycle normally consists of 5 years followed by a practical year and a dissertation.

Institutes des Sciences Agro-zootechniques, recruit after the 2nd Bac. These are situated at Faranah, Kankan and Kindia.

Institut Geo-Mines at Boke, recruits after the 2nd Bac.

Guinea

Ecole Normale Superieure at Maneah and Ecole Normale Superieure Technique at Matoto (Conakry) each recruit after the 2nd Bac. and an entrance examination.

University of Conakry comprises the following Faculties and recruits after the 2nd Bac.:

Faculte des Sciences (old ENAM)
Faculte des Chimie
        Electromecanique
        Mechanique
        Pharmacie
        Genie Civile

Faculte des PTT
        Sciences Sociales et de la Nature
        Sciences Administratives et Juridiques
        Sciences Biologiques
Faculte de Medicine

University of Kankan still offers courses in both social sciences and science; but some courses have been transferred to the University of Conakry.

The following recruit students from 'le niveau Bac.', essentially Bac. failures who are expected to take an entrance test:

Ecole Nationale de la Sante (3)
Ecole Nationale d'Agriculture (Tolo-Mamou, Macenta and Dubreka)
Ecole Normale Secondaire (Dubreka and Pita)

These are designed to train middle-level personnel, nurses and primary school teachers.

TEACHER EDUCATION

Primary and secondary

Primary normal schools offer 2-year courses from the entrance level of grade 9, leading to the **Primary Schoolteachers Certificate.** A more advanced course from grade 10 and lasting for 3 years leads to the qualification of **Secondary Schoolteacher.**

Higher

Teachers at the Polytechnical Institutes are usually graduates of these institutes or from abroad.

Guyana

Republic of Guyana

This chapter covers the period from independence in 1966 for the area previously known as British Guyana.

Education is compulsory for children aged five to sixteen.

The medium of instruction is English.

The academic year runs from September to July.

EVALUATION IN BRITAIN

School

Cambridge Overseas School Certificate - grades 1-6 are equated to GCE O-level (grades A, B or C).

Caribbean Examinations Council Secondary Education Certificate - grades 1 and 2 at the General Proficiency level have been equated to GCE O-level (grades A, B and C).

GCE A-levels - of the same standard as GCE A-level examinations taken in Britain.

Higher

Bachelor degrees - generally considered to be below British Bachelor degree standard.

MARKING SYSTEMS

School

Cambridge Overseas School Certificate: graded 1 (maximum) - 9 (fail).

Guyana

Caribbean Examinations Council Secondary Education Certificate: subject examinations are taken at 3 proficiency levels:

basic proficiency
general proficiency
technical proficiency

5 grades are awarded:

I comprehensive working knowledge of the syllabus

II working knowledge of most aspects of the syllabus

III working knowledge of some aspects of the syllabus

IV limited knowledge of a few aspects of the syllabus

V insufficient evidence on which to base a judgement.

Higher

Bachelor degrees:

Subjects are graded A (maximum) - F
Degrees are classified: pass with distinction
                          pass

SCHOOL EDUCATION

Primary

This covers 7 years from age 5. On completion of grade 7, pupils take the **Secondary School Entrance Examination** (SSEE) which determines admission to secondary education.

Secondary

Pupils are placed into Sixth Form Schools, Junior Secondary Schools and Community High Schools. The Sixth Form Schools prepare students through the Caribbean Examination Council Secondary Education Certificate for A-level over a period of 7 years. The Junior Secondary School prepares children for the Caribbean Examination Council Secondary Education Certificate over a period of 5 years. The Community High School prepares students for the Caribbean Examinations Council basic proficiency-level examination over a period of 5 years.

Technical secondary/Further

The Government Technical Institute offers courses leading to various diplomas, **BTEC National Certificate** and **BTEC Higher National Certificate** (formerly Ordinary National Certificate/ONC and Higher National Certificate/HNC). The Industrial Training Centre and the School of Home Economics also offer courses at this level.

Guyana

HIGHER EDUCATION

The <u>University of Guyana</u> was established in 1963, based to a large extent on the American system. The entrance requirement to **Bachelor** degree courses is 5 GCE O-levels. Bachelor degree courses generally last 4 years; they include courses in architecture and engineering. There are now facilities for study in law, medicine, dentistry and pharmacy.

Master degrees generally take a further 1-2 years.

At first most students studied on a part-time (evening) basis and degrees generally took 5 years to obtain; but since 1971 most courses have been available full-time.

TEACHER EDUCATION

Primary

A 2-year course at the <u>Government Training Centre</u> leads to a **Trained Teachers Certificate**.

Secondary

A 3-year course leads to a **Certificate**; there is also a 2-year part-time **Postgraduate diploma** course at the university.

Haiti

Republic of Haiti

The Haitian school system is centralized under the Department of National Education. Although private schools exist, the pupils take nationally administered examinations.

The six-year primary cycle of education is compulsory.

French is the official medium of instruction, although Creole may be used in the first two years of primary school.

The academic year usually runs from October to July.

EVALUATION IN BRITAIN

School

Brevet d'Etudes du Premier Cycle - generally considered to be below GCE O-level standard.

Baccalaureat (Philosophie) - generally considered to compare to GCE O-level standard.

Higher

Licence - generally considered to be slightly below British Bachelor degree standard.

MARKING SYSTEMS

School

Marking is on a scale of 1-10 (maximum), with 5 as the pass mark.

Haiti

Higher

Marking is on a percentage scale, with 60% as the minimum pass.

Students must obtain a minimum average of 65% at the end of each year for every course taken; if they do not, they must retake the whole year.

SCHOOL EDUCATION

Pre-primary

This is not compulsory, but facilities do exist for children to attend 1 year of pre-primary schooling.

Primary

This extends over 6 years, divided into three 2-year cycles: preparatory, elementary and intermediate. On completion of the sixth year pupils take the examinations for the **Certificat d'Etudes Primaires.**

Secondary

This extends over 7 years, divided into a 3-year lower cycle and a 4-year upper cycle. On successful completion of the lower cycle pupils obtain the **Brevet Elementaire du Premier Cycle**, and on passing the examinations at the end of the 7 years students obtain the **Baccalaureat.**

As in France, successive classes are numbered in descending order, i.e. pupils enter the sixieme classe, and proceed to cinquieme and quatrieme, making up the first cycle, and then the troisieme, seconde, premiere or rhetorique, and the final year is known as philosophie.

At the end of the third year of upper secondary education pupils take the examinations for the **Baccalaureat (Rhetorique)**, and after the final year the examinations for the **Baccalaureat 2 (Philosophie).**

Students may specialize from the beginning of the lower secondary cycle in 1 of 3 options:

A   Latin/Greek

B   Latin/science

C   science/modern languages

They may not change their specialization after the troisieme classe.

Technical secondary

Holders of the Brevet Elementaire du Premier Cycle (BEPC) may take a 4-year course in commercial training, accounting, and hotel management for the **Brevet d'Aptitude Professionelle**, or a 2-year course for the **Brevet Superieur**. Holders of the latter qualification may do the 3-year nursing certificate course. Students who have the Baccalaureat 1 may do the 3-year nursing diploma course.

Haiti

HIGHER EDUCATION

Most facilities for higher education are offered by the state-run <u>University of Haiti</u>, although there are specialized institutions (e.g. Schools of Law), some privately run.

Courses usually last 3-5 years, and lead to a **Licence** or **Diplome d'Etudes Superieures**.

A **Licence** in law takes 4 years; the **Baccalaureat en Droit** is obtained after the first 2 years.

In arts or science the **Certificat d'Etudes Superieures** is obtained after 3 years.

The professional qualification in engineering is obtained after 4 years, in agriculture and pharmacy after 5 years, and in medicine after 7 years.

The admission requirement for entry to such courses is the Baccalaureat 2, and in addition students wishing to enter the prestigious courses of law, medicine, dentistry, economic sciences, agriculture and veterinary medicine, must take a competitive entrance examination.

No facilities are available for postgraduate study.

TEACHER EDUCATION

Primary

Holders of the **Brevet d'Etudes du Premier Cycle** (BEPC) may take a competitive entrance examination for entry to a teacher-training college for a 4-year upper secondary course. On successful completion students obtain the **Diplome de Fin d'Etudes Normales**.

Secondary

Students holding the Baccalaureat 2 may take a competitive entrance examination for entry to an advanced teacher-training college for a 3-year course in humanities, philosophy, social science, languages, mathematics and natural science. On successful completion students are awarded the **Certificat d'Etudes Superieures Licence** by the Faculty of Letters and Pedagogy of the University of Haiti.

Holy See

Vatican City State

Many of the institutions dependent on the Holy See (at present 138) are located in extraterritorial buildings in Rome. The majority of schools are located throughout the world.

The medium of instruction for ecclesiastical studies used to be Latin, but this is disappearing; and, except for subjects with a strong Latin component, all the others are taught in the language requested by the majority of students.

In Europe the academic year runs from October to June; in the rest of the world the time varies according to geographical factors.

EVALUATION IN BRITAIN

School

Maturitas/Testimonium Maturitatis e Lyceo - in Italy is considered equivalent to the **Maturita Classica** for entry into Italian state universities and may be considered to satisfy the general requirement of British universities and polytechnics.

Further and Higher

Licentia - generally compared to British Bachelor degree standard.

Doctoratus - represents a 1 year period of post-graduate research which may be accepted for further post-graduate study in Britain.

MARKING SYSTEMS

School

The marking system adopted in state schools is used.

Higher

Marking systems vary from country to country and university to university.

Holy See

Ecclesiastical universities in Rome adopt the following grading system:

magna cum laude probatus	honour
cum laude probatus	credit
probatus	pass
non probatus	insufficient

Numerical marks assigned to each of these vary from institution to institution.

SCHOOL EDUCATION

Primary

In ecclesiastical schools this conforms to educational provisions offered under the state system of the country and is not designed for future church ministers.

Secondary

This is designed for future church ministers. It is provided in the educational cycle known as Seminarium Minus whose course of study consists of a 3-year lower secondary cycle, followed by a 5-year upper secondary cycle which is organized and denominated differently in each nation. At the end of the 5-year upper secondary cycle, pupils sit an examination for the award of **Maturitas**, whose certificate is known as **Testimonium Maturitatis**.

FURTHER AND HIGHER EDUCATION

Ecclesiastic education continues with 2 different courses of study:

Non-academic

Normally offered in Seminarium Maius, this leads to priesthood but gives no legally recognized qualifications. The course of study lasts 6 years and is known as **Sexennium Philosophico-theologicum** (consisting of a 2-year period of philosophical studies followed by a 4-year period of theological studies). This pattern is applied throughout the world and, although a diploma may be awarded on completion, it has no legal value.

Academic

This is provided in ecclesiastical faculties, universities and university institutes. Two-thirds are devoted to theology, philosophy and canon law. The curriculum is organized on a 3-cycle basis. The first cycle, lasting 2-3 years, depending on the subject of study, is a foundation course at the end of which the **Baccalaureatus** is awarded. The second cycle, normally 2 years, is a period of specialization, at the end of which the **Licentia** (until 1929 corresponding to a degree) is awarded. The third cycle, lasting a minimum of 1 year, is a period of original research leading to a doctoral thesis and the award of **Doctoratus**. Thus, academic studies take 6-9 years, depending on the subject of study.

Institutions offering courses at the higher education level consist of ecclesiastical and Catholic universities and faculties (colleges). The institutions offer courses only in sacred subjects and subjects in the humanities related to these (in some or all of the following: theology, philosophy, religious sciences, civil and canon law, social sciences, psychology, and biblical and oriental studies).

TEACHER EDUCATION

Holders of the qualifications of the ecclesiastical institutions above (**Baccalaureatus, Licentia,** and **Doctoratus**) are allowed to teach religious instruction in state schools in Italy and in all religious secondary schools; the Doctoratus also entitles the holder to teach in ecclesiastical universities.

Honduras

Republic of Honduras

Compulsory education covers six years (primary education).

The medium of instruction is Spanish.

The academic year runs from February to December.

EVALUATION IN BRITAIN

School

Bachillerato en Ciencias y Letras obtained on completion of the academic secondary course - generally considered to compare to GCE O-level standard.

Higher

Licenciatura - may be considered to compare to British Bachelor degree standard.

MARKING SYSTEMS

School

Marking is on a percentage scale (lowest pass 61) or a numerical scale of 1-5 maximum (lowest pass 3).

100-96	5	sobresaliente	excellent
95-76	4	muy bueno	very good
75-61	3	bueno	good
60-40	2	aplazado	referred/fail
39-1	1	insuficiente	fail

SCHOOL EDUCATION

In addition to the state system, there is a flourishing private sector. Instruction is in Spanish and English and these schools are required to conform to standards laid down by the government.

Pre-primary

Limited facilities are available.

Primary

This covers 6 years from age 7.

Secondary

This covers 5 years divided into a lower cycle/ciclo comun de cultura general, of 3 years, and an upper cycle of 2 years. The lower cycle covers general education; pupils may then specialize in the upper cycle, on the completion of which they take the examinations for the **Bachillerato en Ciencias y Letras**.

Technical secondary

A variety of specializations is available during the upper cycle of secondary education which in these fields lasts 3 years, leading to, for example, **Perito Mercantil**, a qualification in business/office skills. These qualifications also entitle the holder to university admission.

HIGHER EDUCATION

This is offered by one university and a number of specialized institutes. The admission requirement is the Bachillerato en Ciencias y Letras (or technical equivalent). All students spend the first year (for medical students 2 years) in the Centre of General Studies. Successful completion of the specialized course leads to the **Licenciatura/ professional qualification**. In addition to the common first-year, courses last as follows:

medicine	6 years, leading to the **Doctorado**
pharmacy dentistry	5 years, leading to the **Doctorado**
law economics engineering	5 years

Honduras

TEACHER EDUCATION

Primary

Teachers are trained during the upper secondary cycle, on courses lasting 3 years and leading to the **Maestro de Educacion Primaria**.

Secondary

Teachers are trained at the higher teachers training school on courses lasting 4 years for holders of the **Bachillerato**.

Hong Kong

No stage of education was compulsory until 1971 when the six-year cycle of primary education became obligatory. With the recent expansion in facilities the three-year junior secondary cycle has also become compulsory.

Medium of instruction - see individual sections.

EVALUATION IN BRITAIN

School

Certificate of Education (English) - generally considered to compare to GCE O-level standard if grades of distinction or credit have been obtained.

Certificate of Education (Chinese)	sometimes considered
Chinese School Certificate	comparable to GCE O-level
Chinese University Matriculation Certificate	standard.

Higher Level Certificate - generally considered to be between GCE O- and A-level standard.

Advanced Level Certificate - grades A-E are generally considered to compare to GCE A-level standard, grade O or a Subsidiary pass is generally considered to compare to GCE O-level standard.

<u>Hong Kong Polytechnic</u>

Ordinary Certificate - generally considered to compare to BTEC National Certificate (formerly Ordinary National Certificate ONC).
Ordinary Diploma - generally considered to compare to BTEC National Diploma (formerly Ordinary National Diploma OND).

<u>City Polytechnic of Hong Kong</u>

Diploma - generally considered to compare to BTEC National Diploma.

Hong Kong

Technical Institutes

Craft and technician-level qualifications generally compared to an appropriate qualification of the City & Guilds of London Institute, the London Chamber of Commerce and Industry and BTEC.

Higher

Higher Diplomas and Higher Certificates (from Hong Kong Polytechnic and City Polytechnic) - generally considered to compare to a standard between BTEC Higher National Certificate and BTEC Higher National Diploma.

Professional Diplomas (from the Polytechnics) - deemed to be comparable to those of the academic requirements for corporate membership of professional institutes.

Bachelor Degrees (from University of Hong Kong, Chinese University of Hong Kong and Hong Kong Polytechnic) - Honours degrees generally compare to British Bachelor (Honours) degree standard and Pass degrees to British Bachelor (Pass) degree standard.

From 1986 it is anticipated that Bachelor degrees of a similar standard will also be offered by Hong Kong Baptist College and City Polytechnic of Hong Kong.

MARKING SYSTEMS

School

Certificate of Education (English)

A	pass with distinction
B,C	pass with credit
D,E	pass
F	fail

Chinese School Certificate 1952-65

pass with distinction
pass with credit
pass
fail

Chinese School Certificate 1966-7

A	pass with distinction
B,C	pass with credit
D,E	pass
F,G	fail

Chinese School Certificate 1967

A	pass with distinction
B,C	pass with credit
D,E	pass
F,G,H	fail

Hong Kong

Chinese (Middle) School Certificate

Marks usually on a percentage scale;

either: excellent   over 90
         good   over 80
         fair   over 70
         pass   over 60
         poor   less than 60

or: pass   40
         credit   no fixed marks but usually credit represents top 25% of the
         distinction marks of candidates in that subject in a given year, and
                      distinction represents the top 2-3%

Hong Kong School Leaving Certificate 1946-8

    pass/fail

Hong Kong School Certificate Examination 1949-61

    pass with distinction
    pass with credit
    pass
    fail

Hong Kong English School Certificate 1961-5

1	pass with distinction
2,3	pass with credit
4,5,6	pass
7,8,9	fail

Hong Kong English School Certificate 1966-8

A	pass with distinction
B,C	pass with credit
D,E	pass
F,G,H	fail

Hong Kong Certificate of Education (English/Chinese) 1968-

A	distinction
B,C	credit
D,E	pass
F,G,H	fail (G, H grades not offered after 1985)

Hong Kong Higher Level Certificate (English/Chinese) 1979-

A	distinction
B,C	credit
D,E	pass
F,G,H	fail

Hong Kong Advanced Level Certificate 1980-

A	distinction
B,C	credit
D,E	pass
O	subsidiary/ordinary level pass
F,G,H	fail

Chinese University Matriculation 1970-8

A-E	pass
F-H	fail

Higher

See under HIGHER EDUCATION.

SCHOOL EDUCATION

Primary

Most primary schools use Chinese as the medium of instruction, with English being studied as a second language from the second year of the course. With the exception of the junior English schools, the 6-year course of primary education normally begins at age 6. On completion of this course suitable pupils were chosen on the results of the **Secondary School Entrance Examination** for places in secondary schools. As sufficient places have been available since 1978 for every primary school-leaver to proceed to 3 years junior secondary education, selection for entry to this cycle is no longer necessary, and the secondary school entrance examination has been replaced by a system of allocating secondary school places - the Secondary School Places Allocation (SSPA) - based on internal school assessments scaled by a centrally administered academic aptitude test, parental choice of secondary school and the division of the territory into 24 school 'nets' or districts.

Secondary

After 6 years primary education pupils may enter

Anglo-Chinese grammar school
Chinese middle school
Secondary technical school
Pre-vocational school

for a further 3 years junior secondary followed by 2 years secondary and possibly 2 years higher secondary (forms 6 and 7). In order to select pupils in the 15-16 age group to proceed to subsidized senior secondary education, the junior secondary examination was introduced in 1981.

Hong Kong

On completion of 5 years secondary schooling at the Anglo-Chinese grammar schools pupils took the leaving examination, which has undergone certain changes in name:

1946-48	Hong Kong School Leaving Certificate
1949-61	Hong Kong School Certificate
1961-67	Hong Kong English School Certificate.

After a further 2 years pupils took the examinations for the **Higher School Certificate**.

From 1968-74 there were 2 public examinations at the end of form 5: the **Hong Kong Certificate of Education** (English), conducting its examinations in the medium of English (except for Chinese subjects), and the **Hong Kong Certificate of Education** (Chinese), conducting its examinations largely in the medium of Chinese. These examinations were conducted by separate Boards under the authority of the Director of Education.

In 1974 a new **Certificate of Education** was introduced, awarded by the Hong Kong Certificate of Education Board to students who have completed a recognized secondary school course, normally 5 years, and passed the necessary examinations. These examinations can be taken either in English or Chinese, with the syllabuses, examination papers, marking schemes and grading system common to both media. The University of London is involved in the moderation of the examination question papers. The Hong Kong Examinations Authority took over the responsibility for the conduct of these examinations in 1978.

In 1968 the University of Hong Kong took over the administration of the **Advanced Level Certificate Examinations**, open to students with satisfactory grades in the Hong Kong Certificate of Education. The University of London was involved in the moderation of the examination papers. The Hong Kong Examinations Authority took over the conduct of the **Chinese University Matriculation Examination** in 1979, and took over that of the **Hong Kong University Advanced Level Examination** during 1980. These examinations became known as the **Hong Kong Higher Level Examination** and the **Hong Kong Advanced Level Examination** respectively.

The Chinese middle schools offer a 5-year course (leading to Middle 3 or Middle 5) which until 1974 culminated in the **Chinese School Certificate**. Since 1974 these schools have offered the **Hong Kong Certificate of Education** (Chinese). Some schools also offer a 1-year sixth-form matriculation course to prepare students for entrance into the Chinese University of Hong Kong.

Technical/vocational secondary

Technical secondary schools offer a 5-year course leading to the **Hong Kong Certificate of Education**. Instruction is in English, with Chinese taught as the second language. Students who wish to continue their studies may do so in the sixth form or at the technical institutes.

Pre-vocational education is a 3-year post-primary course, about half of which is general education and the rest practical training in technical fields. The curriculum usually covers at least 3 major fields of industrial or commercial activity, including mechanical and electrical engineering, printing, textiles and clothing, commerce, retailing and merchandizing, hotel work and catering, and home economics, the aim being to give pupils a grounding in a range of basic skills. These schools also offer an introduction to craft apprenticeship. Pre-vocational school-leavers may continue their studies at technical institutes.

Hong Kong

Until 1978 the secondary modern schools provided a 3-year course in general subjects, together with woodwork and metalwork for boys, and housecraft and commercial subjects for girls at junior secondary level. They have now been expanded to offer senior secondary courses.

FURTHER EDUCATION

Colleges offering further education may be registered under the Post-Secondary Colleges Ordinance of March 1970, which affords a status below that of a university institution but above that of a secondary school. The institutions at present registered under this ordinance are Lingnan College and Shue Yan College. With government financial aid and a student grant scheme offered to Lingnan College, its 4-year course has been restructured to a 2+2+1 year Course (i.e. 2-years course at form 6 level, followed by further 2-years at post-form 6 level and an additional 1-year course). However, Shue Yan College opted to retain its existing structure of 4-year courses.

The Hong Kong Baptist College also registered under this ordinance and adopted a similar pattern to Lingnan College. However, in 1983, a new ordinance took the College into the orbit of the Hong Kong University and Polytechnics Grants Committee (UPGC) similar to the 2 universities and 2 polytechnics, and so it became the fifth fully government-funded institute of higher education.

There is also a number of private day and evening colleges which receive no government aid but offer post-secondary courses of varying standard. If a college is registered under the Education Ordinance and offers degrees, this will not be recognized as post-secondary qualifications in Hong Kong, as the college is not recognized under the Post-Secondary Colleges Ordinance.

Technical further education is offered by a number of technical institutes and the Hong Kong Polytechnic. The 7 technical institutes offer training for craftsmen and lower-level technicians by full- and part-time courses. On completion of 3 years secondary education students may begin the craft courses, and on completion of 5 years secondary education the technician courses, which culminate in a technician diploma in various specialities. A number of programmes have already been validated by the BTEC in Britain.

The Hong Kong and City Polytechnics offer full- and part-time courses leading to their own ordinary and higher diplomas, and to the membership examinations of many British professional institutions, some of which have granted exemption from certain parts of their examinations to students on the higher diploma courses.

HIGHER EDUCATION

Higher education is offered by the 2 universities and Hong Kong Polytechnic. From 1986 first degrees are also being offered by Baptist College and City Polytechnic.

Hong Kong

University of Hong Kong

This offers 3-year courses leading to the award of Pass or Honours degrees in the Arts, Sciences or Engineering. Honours degrees are classified as follows: Class I, Class II Division I, Class II Division II, Class III. Students whose achievement is insufficient for Honours may be awarded Pass degrees. **Master degrees** may be obtained after 1-2 years of full- or part-time study. English is the medium of instruction and examination. Chinese is used only for courses in Chinese language and literature, Chinese history and Chinese translation.

Chinese University of Hong Kong

This was inaugurated in 1963 as a federal university. It has 3 constituent colleges. 4-year courses are offered leading to **Bachelor degrees** in Arts, Business Administration, Science and Social Science. Degrees are awarded with Honours (1st class, 2nd class upper division, 2nd class lower division, 3rd class), and as Pass degrees. A 5-year programme is offered in the Faculty of Medicine leading to the degrees of **Bachelor of Medicine and Bachelor of Surgery**. Postgraduate programmes are also offered leading to **Master and Doctoral degrees**. The principal medium of instruction is Chinese but both Chinese and English may be used as students are required to be proficient in both languages.

The Departments of Extra Mural Studies of the 2 Universities run many short courses covering a very wide range of subjects.

Hong Kong Polytechnic

This offers 4-year sandwich courses leading to the award of Honours degrees in Engineering and Textile and Clothing Marketing. There is a part-time Honours degree in Combined Maths and Science Studies (up to 6-and-a-half years), and a Pass degree in Design (3 years full-time) and Social Work (2 years full-time). Honours degrees are classified as follows: Class I, Class II Division I, Class II Division II, Class III and as a Pass degree. The medium of instruction and examination is predominantly English.

The 2 Polytechnics also offer the postgraduate **Diploma in Management Studies**.

TEACHER EDUCATION

Teacher training is offered by the 3 Colleges of Education and the Technical Teachers Colleges.

Colleges of Education

A 2-year full-time course for A-level entrants is offered in 2 colleges. It is designed to train teachers for primary schools and the junior forms of secondary schools. All 3 colleges offer a full-time 3-year course in English, while Grantham also offers a course in the medium of Chinese; the minimum academic entry requirement is 6 passes in the Hong Kong Certificate of Education, and admission is dependent on the recommendation of the Colleges of Education Joint Selection Board.

A third-year full-time course, introduced in 1968, offers more advanced training for teachers on completion of the 2-year course. This is for teachers of cultural and practical subjects up to Hong Kong Certificate of Education standard.

A range of special refresher courses is available for primary and secondary school teachers.

A 1-year full-time course is available for qualified teachers of Art and Design, Physical Education and Music.

2- and 3-year part-time in-service courses (Chinese and English) are offered to train unqualified teachers in aided and primary schools. Applicants must be full-time teachers, with a minimum academic qualification of passes in the Certificate of Education examinations and 2 years approved teaching experience.

2-year part-time in-service courses are run for kindergarten teachers and teachers of handicapped children.

Technical Teachers College

A 1-year full-time course is offered to train mature persons, with a recognized technician or equivalent qualification and several years experience, to teach specialized subjects in a technical institute or in a pre-vocational school.

A 2-year full-time course is offered to train teachers for technical or commercial subjects in junior secondary schools. Most students are secondary technical school leavers with passes in the Certificate of Education.

In-service technical teacher training is also offered:

1-year full-time supplementary third-year course - designed as an upgrading course for in-service secondary school teachers teaching technical or commercial subjects. The course participants will already have undergone the 2-year course above.

2-year full-time retraining course - specifically designed to retrain mature primary school teachers, with some experience in handicraft teaching, to become teachers of technical subjects in junior secondary schools.

2-year part-time day-release course - designed for serving technical teachers who, though academically qualified, may not have been teacher-trained.

2-year part-time evening course - for serving or intending teachers teaching part-time evening classes run by the technical institutes.

Hungary

Hungarian People's Republic

The Public Education Act of 1985 defines the system, including aims, structure and organization of education.

Education is compulsory from ages six to sixteen.

The medium of instruction is Hungarian (except in certain nursery, primary and secondary schools for ethnic minorities).

The academic year runs from the beginning of September to the end of June.

EVALUATION IN BRITAIN

School

Erettsegi/Matura - may be considered to satisfy the general requirement of universities and polytechnics.

Higher

Oklevel (diploma) - obtained after successful performance in the Allamvizsga and generally compared to British Bachelor degree standard.

MARKING SYSTEMS

School

5	jeles	excellent
4	jo	good
3	kozepes	average
2	elegseges	pass
1	elegtelen	fail

Higher

In subjects of instruction the same marking system is used as in schools. For the doctor's degree (physicians, dentists, vets and lawyers) and the university doctorate the grades are:

4.51-5.00	summa cum laude
3.51-4.50	cum laude
2.00-3.50	rite (pass)

SCHOOL EDUCATION

Pre-primary/kindergarten

Nursery schools (Bolcsode) are available for children aged 1-3 and kindergartens (Ovoda) for those aged 3-6.

Primary and lower secondary/elementary

This covers 8 years from age 6, divided into two 4-year cycles, undertaken in general schools (Altalanos Iskola). The curriculum covers Hungarian language and literature, Russian, history, geography, arithmetic - geography, physics, chemistry, biology, technics, drawing, singing - music and physical education.

Secondary

There are 4 types of secondary school:

Grammar school (Gimnazium) pupils follow a 4-year course terminating with the qualification **Erettsegi**. The curriculum covers Hungarian language and literature, history, introduction to socialist ideology, Russian, a second foreign language, mathematics, physics, chemistry, biology, drawing and fine arts, physical education, technics, occupational guidance and optional courses. The Erettsegi examination is taken in only 4 subjects: written and oral examination in Hungarian language and literature, mathematics, an oral examination in history, and a written or oral examination in 1 subject chosen by the pupil.

Secondary technical school (Szakkozepiskola) pupils follow a 4-year course, terminating with the qualification **Erettsegi**. The curriculum covers general subjects (Hungarian language and literature, history, Russian, mathematics, physics) and vocational subjects. The Erettsegi examination is taken in Hungarian language and literature, history, mathematics, and a vocational subject.

School for vocational skills (Szakmunkaskepzo Iskola) pupils follow a 2-3 year course, terminating with the qualification **Szakmunkas** (skilled worker). The general subjects studied are the same as in secondary technical schools but with fewer weekly lessons and a greater emphasis on vocational training.

Vocational schools: these give skilled worker qualifications in a particular field and prepare pupils for their chosen professions.

FURTHER EDUCATION

Evening and correspondence schools are available for adults and those who did not attend a secondary school after leaving the Altalanos Iskola.

HIGHER EDUCATION

The normal requirement for entry to higher education courses is the Erettsegi plus an entrance examination in 2 subjects, as required by the faculty in which the student wishes to study. Students should be aged 18-35, and the actual numbers admitted is decided by the government in accordance with the needs of the national economy. Even if a student passes the entrance examination, a place is not necessarily guaranteed. Those with the best results are awarded a place but a certain level of achievement must always be attained. Students unsuccessful in one year may re-apply, or choose to obtain some work experience before applying. A course of studies lasting 4-6 years and including the preparation of a thesis usually leads to the state examination (Allam-vizsga), and the qualification of **Oklevel**. This normally enables students to practise a profession. In the following fields the qualification of **Doktor** is awarded on completion of the corresponding course of studies but is considered a professional qualification, not an academic degree:

law	5 years
medicine	6 "
veterinary medicine	5 "
dentistry	5 "

In other subjects, after the Oklevel, the university qualification of **Doktor** can be awarded after a minimum of 1 year, but usually takes 2-3 years.

In addition to the chosen subject(s), all students must take Russian, another foreign language, physical education and political studies.

The **Kandidatus** is a post-university academic qualification awarded after not less than 3 years research after the Oklevel by a Committee of the Academy of Sciences on successful submission of a thesis and an oral examination which includes the use of foreign languages.

The **Tudomanyok Doktora** is the highest post-university academic qualification awarded by the Academy. Students must already have the Kandidatus, and at least 4 years experience of original research.

Besides the 8 universities there are 5 institutions of university status.

TEACHER EDUCATION

Pre-primary/kindergarten

This is a 2-year course on successful completion of 4 years at Gimnazium or 4 years at a specialized vocational secondary school (Ovonoi Szakkozepiskola).

Primary/Elementary

First cycle:

This is a 3-year course at a teacher training college (Tanitokepzo Foiskola) after the 4-year course at a Gimnazium leading to the **Erettsegi**.

Second cycle:

This is a 4-year course at a college of education (Tanarkepzo Foiskola), specializing in 2 subjects, on completion of the 4-year course at a Gimnazium leading to the **Erettsegi**.

Secondary (gymnasium and technical)

Students follow a 5-year course at university. A pedagogic element is built into all university courses, regardless of whether the particular student is intending to take up teaching.

Iceland

Republic of Iceland

The education system is highly centralized, with a consequent high degree of standardization. Comprehensive schooling at primary level was introduced by legislation in 1974, and it is intended to widen this to include secondary schooling in the near future.

Compulsory education was for eight years from age seven but was increased to nine years by the 1974 law. It has only been enforced since 1985.

The medium of instruction is Icelandic, with English being compulsory from grade 7.

The academic year runs from September to June.

EVALUATION IN BRITAIN

School

Studentsprof - may be considered to satisfy the general requirement of universities and polytechnics if obtained from a Gymnasium; compared to BTEC National Diploma (formerly Ordinary National Diploma) if from a technical/vocational school.

Higher

Bachelor degree - generally compared to British Bachelor degree standard.

Kandidatsprof/Candidatus Mag. - generally compared to British Bachelor degree standard.

MARKING SYSTEMS

School

Marking is on a scale 0-10 (maximum), with an average of 5 needed to proceed to the next year of school and an average of 6 needed to proceed to (upper) secondary.

Higher

Marking is on a scale 0-10 (maximum), with 5 as the pass mark.

Iceland

SCHOOL EDUCATION

Pre-primary

There are day-care centres for children aged 0-6 and pre-school classes for children aged 5-6.

Before 1974/6

Primary

This was a 6-year course from age 7 at a <u>Barnaskoli</u>, leading to the **Barngorof** (leaving examination). All pupils could proceed to lower secondary eduction, but the results of this examination determined which stream (i.e. general or vocational) a child should enter. Danish was the first compulsory foreign language, and was begun in the fourth or fifth year.

Lower secondary (unglingaskoli)

This covered 2 years, and was offered in 2 streams: boknamsdeild (general) and verknamsdeild (vocational). Both streams led to the **Unglingaprof**. Pupils could then leave school, or enter the landsprofdeild for 1 year to prepare for the **Landsprof** which gave entrance to the Gymnasium (Menntaskoli), or stay at a secondary school (Gagnfraeoaskoli) for 2 more years leading to the **Gagnfraeogorof**.

Since 1974/6

Although the law on the Comprehensive Primary School was passed in 1974, the system was only fully implemented in 1976.

Primary

This now covers 9 years, of which grades 1-8 are compulsory. In grades 1-3, compulsory subjects are Icelandic, mathematics, social studies, religious studies, domestic science, arts and crafts, music, and physical education. From grade 4, science and Danish are added, with English from grade 6.

National Comprehensive Primary School (NCPS) examinations are administered at the end of grade 9 in a limited number of subjects, e.g. in 1981 in Icelandic, Danish, English and mathematics. Depending on the results of these examinations and internal school assessments, pupils may proceed to (upper) secondary education. In 1980/1 the entry requirements for study at (upper) secondary level were as follows:

A student who completes comprehensive primary school is eligible to study at a secondary school if he/she obtains grade A, B or C in the NCPS examination subjects, and grade 4 or higher in the school examination subjects.

If a pupil does not fulfil these requirements he/she may undertake a preparatory course giving no credit (O-course) at a secondary school.

(Upper) Secondary

This continues to cover 4-years. The first year covers a common curriculum for all pupils, and specialization begins in the second year. There were originally only 2 specializations/lines: maladeild - languages, and natturufraeoideild - natural sciences. There are now 4, i.e. modern and ancient languages, social sciences, physics, mathematics and natural sciences, music and business studies. The content of instruction is based on the unit-credit system (i.e. 1 unit equals 1 hour of instruction a week over 1 school year). The aggregate over the 4 years will be approximately 144 (i.e. average of 36 per year). A course comprises a combination of 3 subject groups:

compulsory	up to 100 units
specialization/line	not less than 24
elective	not less than 14

At the end of the 4-year course pupils take the **Studentsprof** (matriculation examination).

Since 1973 a number of comprehensive schools have been established. Each school is divided into several divisions, each of which covers several related lines already existing at the secondary level. The courses of study vary from 1-4 years, and are based on the unit-credit system.

Technical/vocational secondary

The Commercial College of Iceland (Verzlunarskoli) and the Co-operative Commercial College offer 2-year business-orientated courses on completion of lower secondary or comprehensive primary education. This may be followed by a 2-year advanced course leading to the **Verzlunarskoliu Islands Studentsprof** (matriculation examination).

The framhaldsdeild offers pupils who have completed the lower secondary or comprehensive primary course, a 2-year course leading to a diploma. With this qualification pupils may then enter the adfaranam (pre-teachers university course).

Students can make a contract with a master or a company of masters. The master sees to all practical instruction in the subject and the theory is provided by the vocational school.

Students can also enrol at a trade school, or department, in connection with other vocational schools or secondary comprehensive schools. At present there are 6 departments: metalwork, woodwork, hairdressing, electricity, book-binding and tailoring. This course takes 1 year and is divided equally between theory and practice. Those who complete trade school can go on to make a contract with a master or they can continue their education in departments for advanced students at the trade schools.

FURTHER EDUCATION

The Technical College (Taekniskoli) offers a 3-4 year diploma course in engineering technology. For admission, students should possess a general education equivalent to that offered by a vocational school and a certain amount of practical experience. The

Iceland

College also offers full degree courses in electrical and mechanical engineering technology. These courses are modelled on corresponding courses in Danish technical colleges, and must be completed abroad, normally in Denmark. The College offers a variety of lower level courses lasting 1-2 years to train technicians in various fields including electricity, construction mechanics, fisheries and laboratory science.

HIGHER EDUCATION

There is only 1 university, the University of Iceland at Reykjavik, although the Technical College, Agricultural School and Teacher Training College offer courses at this level. Entrance to degree-level courses is with the Studentsprof (matriculation examination).

The first qualification in the arts and humanities is the **Bachelor degree** obtained after approximately 3 years. A 2-year postgraduate course for holders of this qualification leads to the **Kandidatsprof/Candidatus Mag**.

Engineering - 4 year courses lead to the **Bachelor degree** in civil engineering, electrical engineering, mechanical engineering, and nautical engineering.

Law - a 5-year course leads to the qualification of **Cand. Juris**.

Theology - a 5-year corse leads to the qualification of **Cand. Theol.**; a 3-year course leads to the **Bachelor degree in Divinity**.

Medicine - a course lasting 6-7 years leads to the **Cand. Med**.

Dentistry - a course lasting 5-6 years leads to the **Cand. Odoent**.

On obtaining their first formal qualification students may then be admitted to study for a doctorate **(Doktorsprof)**.

TEACHER EDUCATION

There is 1 teacher-training college, the University College of Higher Education, which since 1971 has been classified as a higher education institution.

In the general teacher-training section of secondary schooling (almenn kennaradeild) pupils who had passed 1 of the middle/intermediate school examinations (e.g. Landsprof) could take a 4-year course leading to the **Almennt Kennarprof**, with which they could teach at primary and lower secondary levels. This section was disbanded in 1973.

Holders of the Studentsprof could undertake a 2-year course leading to the Almennt Kennarprof with the same status as above.

Holders of the Almennt Kennarprof could undertake a 1-year course in the menntadeild, and proceed to the Teachers College.

Iceland

The adrafanam is a 2-year course for graduates of the framhaldsdeild (upper technical secondary education), preparing them for admission to the Teachers College.

Teachers for the comprehensive primary school now have to undertake a 3-year B.Ed. degree course at the University College of Higher Education.

Teachers at the (upper) secondary level have to hold a university degree in their subjects of specialization, and complete a 1-year course in pedagogy and didactics, which includes practical training, at the University of Iceland.

India

Republic of India

The system of education in India has been based largely on the British pattern. Changes are planned to come into effect by the academic year 1987. It appears that central government will be asked to set and evaluate national standards.

Education is the responsibility of the individual state; in most states it is compulsory from ages six to eleven.

Hindi (or the regional language) is spoken in the primary grades of state schools and in most secondary schools. English is the main medium of instruction in most universities. Students can often opt for the local language in examinations.

The school year varies from one region to another; usually July to April.

EVALUATION IN BRITAIN

School

Certificates awarded on completion of standard X:

Matriculation Certificate	generally considered to be below GCE O-level standard
Secondary School Certificate	
All India Secondary School Certificate	
Indian Certificate of Secondary Education	

Certificates awarded on completion of standards XI or XII:

Indian School Certificate (ISC)	often considered comparable to GCE O-level standard
Intermediate Certificate	
Higher School Certificate (HSC)	
Higher Secondary Certificate	
Senior School Certificate	

Higher

Bachelor of Arts	generally considered to compare to GCE A-level standard.
Bachelor of Science	
Bachelor of Commerce	

India

Bachelor of Science (Engineering)
Bachelor of Engineering
Bachelor of Technology

when awarded from an Indian Institute of Technology (IIT), or the Indian Institute of Science, Bangalore, comparable to British Bachelor (Honours) degree standard

Master of Arts
Master of Science
Master of Commerce

comparable to British Bachelor (Honours) degree standard

Master of Technology
Master of Science (Engineering)

when awarded from an Indian Institute of Technology (IIT), or the Indian Institute of Science, Bangalore, comparable to British Master degree standard.

MARKING SYSTEMS

School

School examinations are often graded on a percentage basis. Subjects in papers may have different minimum and maximum pass marks.

Higher

65-100%	First Division/Class
50-65%	Second Division/Class
40-50%	Third Division/Class

SCHOOL EDUCATION

The 'new' 10+2+3 pattern of education, first recommended in 1917, has been adopted by most states and union territories. The pattern consists of 10 years schooling plus 2 years higher secondary education (either in schools or in colleges) and a 3-year period of higher education for a first degree.

Primary

Primary education generally covers an 8-year period (7 in some states). Students enter the lower primary stage at age 6 and complete it at 11 (standards I to V). The upper primary stage consists of a 3-year course for the 11-14 age group (standards VI to VIII). The syllabus covers traditional subjects such as reading, writing and arithmetic, supplemented by elementary history, geography and general science. Pupils begin to study English in standard III or later. Examinations are set either by schools or by the Municipal Boards and are usually held at the end of each term and school year.

Secondary

Secondary education may cover 2, 3 or 4 years, depending on the state. Many schools do not go beyond the standard X examination. (The term 'higher secondary' is often used for standards XI and XII.) Curricula are determined by the State and Central Boards of Secondary Education and include subjects such as mathematics, science, history and geography. English is also studied. These examining boards issue various school-leaving certificates, including the **Secondary School Leaving Certificate** (SSLC), the **Higher Secondary Certificate** (HSC) and the **Indian School Certificate** (ISC).

Technical/vocational secondary

Many states offer vocational courses at secondary school, concentrating on agriculture, commerce, technology, paramedical services and home science. Most vocational training, however, is still carried out at the Industrial Training Institutes. These offer training of 1 to 2 years, often followed by a period of apprenticeship. The entrance requirement depends on the trade to be followed. For technical subjects, students may have to have a pass in standard X with mathematics and science as a compulsory requirement. The medium of instruction in the Institutes of Technology is the local language; however, in the more technical areas, English terminology is widely used.

Technical Vocational Diploma courses are also offered by the polytechnics and rural institutes, most of which are financed and controlled by state governments. The courses, of 1-3 years, aim to produce foremen, skilled technicians and supervisors. The engineering programmes generally require 3 years full-time study (possibly with an additional year of practical training). The normal admission requirement is a standard X certificate, but some courses require the Higher Secondary Certificate or equivalent.

FURTHER EDUCATION

The Central Board of Secondary Education (CBSE) established its Open School, which offers CBSE school-leaving qualifications. It also plans non-formal technical, vocational and life-enrichment courses.

Recently most state governments agreed to set up similar Open Schools.

Many universities offer a wide variety of correspondence courses for certificates, diplomas and degrees.

1986 marks the beginning of some courses in the Indira Ghandi National Open University. It is planned that a wide choice of subjects will be available and credit transfer will be linked with the formal education system.

HIGHER EDUCATION

Higher education is offered in universities, institutes of higher learning 'deemed to be universities' and institutions declared of national importance (including the Institutes of Technology).

India

First-degree courses are generally conducted in affiliated colleges, i.e. a network of private and state-sponsored institutes recognized by a specific university which takes direct responsibility for postgraduate studies. Curricula and examinations are controlled by the universities.

Students wishing to enter higher education must have completed either **standard XI or XII** and hold an appropriate certificate. Students who have completed standard X only must attend a 1-2 year **pre-university course** at the university.

The Institutes of Technology (IIT) and other centrally sponsored institutes and universities conduct the **Joint Entrance Examination** (JEE) for admissions to degree courses in engineering, pharmaceutics and architecture.

The term **first degree** describes the degree obtained after the first stage of higher education. It covers the **Bachelor of Arts, Science** and **Commerce degrees.** First degrees generally require 3 years full-time study. Entrance to an Honours course may require a higher pass mark in the pre-university course or appropriate school-leaving certificate. An Honours degree does not normally involve longer study but does indicate greater specialization.

The **Master degree** in Arts, Science and Commerce is a 2-year course. Students take an external examination at the end of each year: Previous (Part 1) and Final (Part 2). The Master of Philosophy requires a year's study and research after the MA degree.

Applicants for a Master degree are generally required to have a Division II Bachelor degree. A Pass or Division III is sometimes acceptable. Candidates for the 5-year integrated Master degree courses in Science need to sit the Joint Entrance Examination. Admission to all postgraduate courses in Engineering and Technology is restricted to those who qualify through **Graduate Aptitude Test in Engineering** (GATE).

An **All-India Entrance Examination** for medical colleges should be introduced from the 1987 session. At present, state governments/universities hold entrance examinations in their respective jurisdictions.

The **Ph.D.** degree is taken by research at least 2 years after the Master or 3 years after the Bachelor degree. It is now standard practice for all aspirants to Ph.D. courses to hold a Master degree.

TEACHER EDUCATION

Primary

Lower primary school teachers take a 1-2 year course at Teacher Training Institutes attached to the State Departments of Education leading to a **Teacher Training Certificate.** The entrance requirement is a pass in the standard X examination.

Upper primary school teachers must have a pass at standard XII and take a 2-year diploma course.

India

Secondary

Secondary school teachers are usually graduates who have taken a 1-year Bachelor of Education course at a college affiliated to a university.

The Regional Colleges of Education offer a 4-year course leading to a subject degree and a **Bachelorship of Education**.

A number of universities offer M.Ed. and Ph.D. courses. Teachers of technical and vocational subjects are trained in separate Technical Teacher Training Institutes.

Indonesia

Republic of Indonesia

Overall responsibility for education rests with the Ministry of Education and Culture, in which there are four main divisions: basic and secondary education, higher education, culture, and out-of-school education and sports. Each of the twenty-seven provinces has its own department of education, which reports directly to Jakarta. There are also many private institutions at every level.

There is no period of compulsory education, but primary education is available to all.

The medium of instruction is Bahasa Indonesia.

The academic year used to run from January to December. The 1978 academic year was then extended by 6 months to run through to June 1979, and the academic year now runs from mid-July to mid-June, divided into two semesters.

EVALUATION IN BRITAIN

School

SMA Leaving Certificate (senior academic high school) - generally considered to compare to GCE O-level standard in subjects which may be taken in the GCE examinations (except English language) where marks of 50% and above have been obtained.

Higher

Before 1981:

Sarjana Muda (often referred to as 'bachelor') - generally considered to compare to GCE A-level standard, or slightly above.

Sarjana - generally considered to compare to British Bachelor degree standard.

Pasca Sarjana - generally considered to compare to British Master degree standard.

Indonesia

After 1981:

S1 **Sarjana**
S2 **Magister** - generally considered to compare to British Bachelor degree standard.
S3 **Doktor** - generally considered to compare to British M.Phil. standard.

MARKING SYSTEMS

School

SMA Leaving Certificate is marked on a scale 1-10 (maximum). Grades 1-6 on the 7 point scale are generally regarded as pass grades.

Higher

A credit system is used and it is essential to see the academic transcript in addition to the degree certificate.

SCHOOL EDUCATION

State schools, religious schools and private schools (Sekolah Swasta) operate side-by-side with the core curriculum controlled by the Ministry of Education.

Primary (Sekolah Dasar - SD)

This is a 6-year course from age 6 or 7. Children are promoted from one year to the next depending on performance.

Secondary

Junior secondary:

Entry to this 3-year cycle is by competitive examination. This was originally organized centrally, but since 1971 some elements have been set and organized provincially. According to the results of this examination the pupil may enter 1 of 4 types of junior secondary school (Sekolah Menengah Tingkat Pertama - SMTP):

academic	Sekolah Menengah Pertama (SMP)
commercial	Sekolah Menengah Ekonomi (SMEP)
home economics	Sekolah Kejuruan Kepandaian Putri (SKKP)
technical	Sekolah Teknik (ST)

Most pupils proceed to the academic junior secondary schools, and some of these schools set their own entrance examination. Students begin to learn English at this stage and continue to the end of their secondary studies.

Indonesia

Senior secondary:

Students may proceed to the senior high schools (Sekolah Menengah Tingkat) for a further 3-year course if they are successful in the competitive examination. There are 7 types of school:

<u>Sekolah Menengah Atas</u> (SMA) offer a continuation of the academic course taken at the SMP schools of junior secondary level. There are several streams from the second year of the 3-year course, so that students may specialize in arts, science, social studies or technical/vocational studies. The curriculum is broader than O-level studies in Britain.

<u>Sekolah Menengah Ekonomi Atas</u> (SMEA) offer a continuation of the commercial courses taken at junior level.

<u>Sekolah Kejuruan Keputrian Atas</u> (SKKA) offer home economics.

<u>Sekolah Pendidikan Guru</u> (SPG) provide training for future primary school teachers.

<u>Sekolah Guru Olahraga</u> (SGO) are sports teacher schools.

<u>Junior Academies</u> may be sponsored by government departments or are sometimes private institutions. They offer courses in e.g. administration, commerce, police work.

Technical secondary

The <u>Sekolah Menengah Teknik</u> (SMT) provide a 4-year post-junior secondary course to train students up to the level of a trade technician, i.e. above the tradesman level to which the Sekolah Teknik aspire. There are also agricultural secondary schools.

There are senior secondary vocational schools, run by different ministries, e.g. legal schools, police schools, nursing schools, and schools for junior pharmacists.

HIGHER EDUCATION

Students holding a leaving certificate from a senior high school (SMA) are entitled to proceed to some form of higher education, although in practice they will also take a selection examination. There is fierce competition for places at the 5 top-ranking universities: the <u>University of Indonesia</u>, the <u>Institute of Technology at Bandung</u> (ITB), the <u>Agricultural University Bogor</u> (IPB), <u>Gajah Mada University Jogyakarta</u>, and <u>Airlangga University Surabaya</u>. These institutions have recently joined together to set one combined entrance examination for their own institutions (**Sipenmaru**).

Before 1981:

Courses leading to the first qualification, the **Sarjana Muda**, were taken over 3 years, with a further 2 years, during which students wrote and presented a thesis, leading to the **Sarjana**. This latter qualification conferred the title of **Doctorandus** (Drs). Courses in certain subjects (e.g. medicine) were slightly longer. There was an intermediate qualification between the Sarjana and Doctorate (Ph.D.), the **Pasca Sarjana**. This was supposed to take 2 years study after Sarjana while a Ph.D. took a further 2 years.

Indonesia

After 1981:

The system is similar to the American system with semesters and credits.

The **S1 Sarjana** is awarded after 4-and-a-half years (9 semesters) of uninterrupted full-time study at a recognized university. For medicine and other professional courses the period of study is normally at least 1 year longer. Degree certificates usually bear the inscription 'Sarjana' followed by the subject e.g. Sarjana Teknik (engineering). Holders of the qualification use the title Doktorandus (men) or Doktoranda (women).

The **S2 Magister** (new style 'masters') is awarded after 2 years of courses plus research.

The **S3 Doktor** should take another 2 years of research, but in practice there is little opportunity to continue direct from a Magister course to a Doktor in the minimum theoretical time. Most awards are given to established, mature academics and other researchers.

There are 5 main types of institution:

Universities - these have semi-autonomous faculties, and offer courses leading to the award of the Magister, Doktor and various diplomas. There are also private universities which may award their own degrees. These are either fully recognized by the Ministry of Education and Culture or the private degree is converted into a recognized degree by taking a supplementary Ministry examination.

Technical institutes - there are 3: the Bandung Institute of Technology (ITB), the Bogor Institute of Agriculture (IPA), and the newer Institute of Technology Surabaya (ITS).

Institut Keguruan dan Ilmu Pendidikan (IKIP) - these institutions rank as universities with full degree-granting status. Their function is to train teachers for the junior and senior secondary schools. They also award sub-degree diplomas for primary, junior secondary and technical teachers (D1, D2 and D3).

Akademi and Sekolah Perguruan Tinggi - single-faculty academies which offer diploma/certificate technician-level courses.

Polytechnics - these are attached to universities but will provide sub-degree junior technician training. These are being expanded. They award diplomas relating to the number of years of study (D1, D2, D3; D4 is about to be introduced).

TEACHER EDUCATION

Primary

Teachers for this level are trained at the Teacher Training College (SPG) which offers a 3-year course at the senior secondary level.

Indonesia

Junior secondary

Some teachers at this level have been trained in the Pendidikan Guru Sekolah Lanjutan Pertama (PGSLP), which offered a 2-year course for students graduating from the senior high schools. However these have now been phased out. The Teacher Training College for Secondary School Teachers (IKIP) trains teachers for junior secondary schools.

Senior secondary

Teachers for this level are trained on 4-and-a-half year courses at the IKIPs, leading to the award of the Sarjana.

Technical secondary

Faculties for technical teacher training (FKIT) exist at several IKIPs, awarding diploma and Sarjana qualifications.

Iran

Islamic Republic of Iran

The predominant feature of the education system in Iran is the high degree of centralization. A number of reforms were introduced in the mid-1960s, with the major emphasis being at primary and secondary level. Although the changes in the system have been fully effected at primary level, many secondary schools are still following the old system.

Under the old system the first 6 years of schooling were compulsory, with the first 8 years being compulsory under the new system.

EVALUATION IN BRITAIN

School

National High School Diploma (on completion of sixth grade of secondary or fourth grade of intermediate secondary education) - generally accorded GCE O-level status on a subject-for-subject basis when marks of at least 50% are obtained in subjects which can be taken in the GCE examinations, except English language.

Fogh Diplom (higher technical diploma, technician 1st class) - generally accorded BTEC National Diploma status (formerly known as the OND).

Higher

Licence (on completion of a 4-year course) - generally considered to approximate to a standard between GCE A-level and the British Bachelor degree. Degrees obtained after a longer course of study (i.e. in pharmacy, dentistry, medicine and veterinary medicine) usually require a longer period of study than usual in Britain, but no information is available on the comparative standard.

MARKING SYSTEMS

School

End-of-term examinations are graded on a scale 0-20, with 10 as the minimum pass mark. The end-of-year examinations in June are the most important. The grades are multiplied by a coefficient of 2.

In the final year of secondary education (sixth year or fourth year of intermediate secondary) a student is considered to have passed if the average of all the final examination results is not less than 10, the total yearly average is not less than 10, and a zero has not been received in any examination. The total yearly average is determined by dividing the sum of the first, second and third term grades by 4.

Higher

The grades are:

A (distinction), B, C, D (low pass), F (fail), N (incomplete). Some faculties still work on the numerical scale 0-20, 10 being the minimum pass mark.

SCHOOL EDUCATION

Old system (theoretically pre-1965)

Primary

This was offered over 6 years, usually beginning at age 6. At the end of the sixth year all pupils took an examination administered by the provincial education authorities. Pupils who passed were permitted to continue their studies in secondary schools.

Secondary

This covers 6 years consisting of two 3-year cycles. In the first cycle, students follow a uniform curriculum. Students who pass the examination at the end of the first cycle are eligible to continue their studies in 1 of the 3 branches of academic secondary education (mathematics, science or literature), or at a technical school. The total number of hours and subjects studied is the same for all branches, but the emphasis varies according to the subject specialization. On completion of this cycle students take a national school leaving examination.

Vocational/technical secondary

<u>Vocational schools</u> admit students who have completed 6 years of primary education and offer a 3-year programme of study designed to train skilled workers with a specialization in 1 of the following: automechanics, building, cabinet-making, carpentry, masonry, metalwork, smelting, or tinwork. If students successfully complete the course they either leave school to seek employment or continue their training at a technical school.

<u>Technical schools</u> offer 3-year programmes to train technicians in specialized fields. A student who has completed the first cycle of secondary education or the 3-year vocational course is eligible for admission to a technical school. There are 4 types of technical school:

Boys' technical (industrial) schools, offering courses specializing in automechanics, building, casting, construction, electrical work, metalwork, welding and woodwork. The curriculum is similar to that of the vocational schools.

Girls' technical schools, offering courses in assistant nursing, decorating, dressmaking, dyeing, home economics, secretarial work, and spinning.

Agricultural secondary schools, training agricultural specialists. For the first 2 years of the 3-year course students follow a uniform course which emphasizes agricultural and related subjects. During the third year they specialize in 1 of the following: animal husbandry, field crops, rural industries, and use of farm machinery.

Business secondary schools, training technicians for business and commercial fields, offering courses which include specialized study in accounting, bookkeeping, business correspondence, business law, economics, labour law, statistics and the use of business machines.

New system (theoretically post-1965)

Primary

Primary education is now offered over 5 years. At the end of the fifth year pupils take an official examination; success in this entitles a student to proceed to the guidance cycle of secondary education.

Secondary

The curriculum for the 3-year guidance cycle is general, and uniform for all schools. On completion of this cycle, students take a national examination. Those who pass are eligible to continue their education in 1 of the 4 branches of the cycle of intermediate (secondary) education, subject to the student's ability and interests, and the needs of the country. A student who wishes to follow a course of study other than the one considered most suitable is required to pass a special entrance examination.

The 4 branches of intermediate (secondary) education are academic, industrial, rural and agricultural, and services. The first 3 years of the academic branch cover a generalized curriculum, while the final year offers specialization in: literature and the arts, natural science, physics and mathematics, social science and economics.

On completion of this 4-year cycle, students take the National High School Diploma examinations which is the secondary school leaving examination, and also the university entrance examination (see EVALUATION IN BRITAIN). Students who fail in any subject in these examinations, retake the subject in August/September.

Vocational/technical secondary

Students tending towards vocational/technical secondary education enter either a 4-year technical course or a 2-year vocational or agricultural course. The 4-year course aims to produce lower grade technicians (higher grade technicians are trained at the post-secondary institutes of technology), whilst the 2-year course aims to produce skilled workers and farmers. The services branch is intended for students wishing to enter the civil or public services (including for example banking, insurance, accountancy, etc.).

Until the guidance cycle becomes compulsory in practice, semi-skilled workers will be admitted to schools which offer simple vocational training and which admit graduates of the 5-year primary cycle. Depending on the requirements of the particular skill, training may last up to 2 years.

FURTHER EDUCATION

The Institutes of Technology offer a 2-year post-secondary school course leading to the qualification of **Fogh Diplom** (higher technical diploma/technician 1st class/technician 1). Post-secondary colleges with particular specializations also offer similar 2-year courses.

HIGHER EDUCATION

Since the Revolution a number of institutions have changed their names. Many have been closed. Information on the current situation is limited.

Entrance to higher education is on the basis of success in the National High School Diploma. However, as there are normally more applicants than places available, students usually sit a competitive university entrance examination.

Until 1964, courses leading to the **Licence** in letters, science, theology, law, economics and political science lasted 3 years. The first degrees in engineering and medicine were the **Fogh Licence** (a 4-year course) and the **Doctorate** respectively.

In 1964 certain reforms in the university sector were instituted; the **Licence** was changed to a 4-year degree course, and semester, credit and letter-grade systems were introduced. The first degree in engineering is now the Licence. Degree courses are modelled rather more on the American pattern, and students tend to specialize less than they would in Britain. Under the credit system the Licence requires 140 semester hours, of which at least 60 must be in a major field.

The postgraduate qualification of **Fogh-Licence** generally requires an additional year of study above the Licence, except in architecture which requires 2 years.

Programmes leading to a **Doctorate** in the arts or sciences usually require 2 years of study above the Fogh-licence, 3 or more years above the Licence in faculties which offer no Fogh-licence. In dentistry, medicine and veterinary medicine the Doctorate is the first degree; for dentistry and pharmacy it requires 5 years, for medicine 7-9 years and for veterinary medicine 5 years.

Besides the universities there are many other state and private institutions of higher education. These do not have university status but offer a 2-year **Associate degree** (AA degree) - in some cases a **Bachelor of Arts degree**. They include institutions such as technical colleges, schools of nursing, colleges of commerce, drama, music, computer science, management and business studies, paramedical studies, and training institutions for specific organizations such as banking and insurance.

TEACHER EDUCATION

Primary

Girls who have completed the first cycle of secondary school enter <u>Normal Schools</u> for a 2-year course aimed at training teachers for rural areas.

Graduates of the second cycle of secondary schools follow a 1-year course at one of the teacher-training centres.

Secondary

There are 2 main types of course available at teacher-training colleges:

A 4-year course leading to the qualification of **Licence** (taken in 2 stages of 2 years each and open to students who have completed a full course of secondary education). The first 2-year stage prepares teachers for the first cycle of secondary education. Students who complete the second 2 years receive the Licence and are eligible to teach in the second cycle of secondary education.

A 1-year course open to holders of the university **Licence** to train teachers for both cycles of secondary education. The first of these colleges was the National Teacher's College of Tehran (now the Teacher Training University); it has been followed by the establishment of similar colleges within other universities.

Regional teacher-training colleges have been established to train teachers for the guidance cycle of secondary education. These colleges run 2-year courses for students who complete their secondary education and pass an entrance examination. The students may specialize in 1 of 4 fields: science and mathematics, Persian and social studies, foreign languages, and pre-vocational courses.

Vocational/technical secondary

The vocational teachers' training college admits students who have completed academic or technical secondary education. The 4-year course is in two 2-year stages leading to a **Licence**. The first stage trains teachers for vocational schools, the second stage for technical schools. Teachers for secondary business schools are trained in the College of Business.

Iraq

Republic of Iraq

The education system is highly centralized, all levels of school education coming under direct control of the Ministry of Education. Tertiary education is under the control of the Ministry of Higher Education. There is a rigid system of examinations; continuous assessment is not practised.

The medium of instruction is generally Arabic.

The academic year runs from September to June.

EVALUATION IN BRITAIN

School

Baccalaureat (sixth form) - Generally accorded GCE O-level standard on a subject-for-subject basis where a student has obtained marks of at least 50% (regardless of the pass marks) in the final examinations in subjects that can be taken in the GCE examinations (except English language).

Further

Diploma - from technical institutes. The Diploma is generally compared to BTEC National Diploma (formerly OND) particularly if the grades of very good and/or excellent have been obtained.

Higher

Bachelor degrees - not always considered to compare to their British counterparts. Most British universities may consider an Iraqi Bachelor degree with a grade of good or above for admission to a Master degree course but will require the successful completion of a qualifying year for a research degree.

It is important to note that the Iraqi system of education allows those who reach the highest marks in the Iraqi **Baccalaureat** to study medicine, architecture, engineering, science subjects, and so on to arts, educational and administrative subjects at the bottom of the scale.

Iraq

MARKING SYSTEMS

School

The **Baccalauréat** is graded on a percentage scale; pass mark 50.

Further

Diploma courses (in technical institutes) are graded on a percentage scale:

90+	excellent
80-89	very good
70-79	good
60-69	medium
50-59	pass
below 49	fail

Higher

Degrees - percentage scale:

90-100	distinction/excellent
80-89	very good
65-79	good
50-64	pass/fair
below 49	poor/fail

SCHOOL EDUCATION

Primary

This covers 6 years from age 6. Promotion from class to class is based on examinations culminating in the **Primary Baccalauréat** examination conducted by the Ministry of Education. This qualification was suspended in 1978 but has since been reinstated. The medium of instruction is Arabic - except in the Northern Autonomous Region, where it is Kurdish, though Arabic is taught at all stages.

Secondary

Arabic is the medium of instruction throughout. Secondary education is divided into 2 cycles, intermediate and preparatory.

Intermediate:

This lasts 3 years and all pupils follow a common curriculum. The course culminates in a general examination, held by the government. A **Certificate of Intermediate Studies** (more commonly known as **Third-Form Baccalauréat**) is awarded.

Preparatory:

Before 1966-7, this involved 2 years study, leading to the examinations for the **Baccalaureat**. It now covers 3 years. In the general academic schools a degree of specialization is introduced: scientific or literary studies for the last 2 years, culminating in the **Sixth-Form Baccalaureat** examination in the appropriate section. This is the basic qualification for university courses. Students who fail part of or all the examinations in June may resit in September; if any subjects are failed in September, the year must be repeated. In the final examinations, however, up to 2 subjects only may be failed and retaken in September; if 3 or more subjects are failed in June, the year must be repeated.

Vocational secondary

There are 4 types of vocational secondary school:

agricultural
industrial
home economics
commercial

For admission to any of these 3-year courses, pupils must hold the intermediate school-leaving certificate. All courses lead to a **Baccalaureat** in a particular speciality.

FURTHER EDUCATION

Offered by <u>Technical Institutes</u> specializing in administrative, technical, agricultural and medical subjects (governed by the Foundation of Technical Institutes). Courses normally last 2 years, leading to a **Diploma** or **Technician Diploma**.

HIGHER EDUCATION

Competition is keenest for entry to Bachelor degree courses in the faculties of medicine, architecture, engineering and science; however steps have been taken to limit the number of students admitted to courses in the humanities. Most first-degree courses last 4 years (5 for architecture, dentistry and pharmacy; 6 for medicine).

Examinations are held at the end of each year, but there are also internal monthly and/or mid-year examinations contributing approximately 40% to the final marks.

Tuition is mainly in Arabic.

Of the 6 universities, the largest and most important is the University of Baghdad, established in 1956, reorganized as a state university in 1958, and made independent in 1963. Originally it incorporated 13 separate colleges and institutions, established between 1908 and 1955. In 1967 the Universities of Basrah and Mosul (formerly colleges of the University of Baghdad) were established as separate universities, each originally with 6 faculties. The University of Technology, Baghdad, founded in 1975, was formerly the College of Engineering Technology at Baghdad University. Al-Mustansiriyah University in Baghdad was founded in 1963 and at first ran evening classes leading to degrees; it became a state university in 1974. The University of Salahuddin (formerly Sulaimaniyah University) opened in 1968 in the Kurdish homeland as a state institution and moved to Erbil in 1981. Al-Hikma University, a private university run by the American Jesuit Fathers, was incorporated in the University of Baghdad in 1970.

Bachelor degrees are also awarded by Al-Bakr University (a military college in Baghdad), by Basrah Naval College (also military) and by Baghdad Police College. The academic value of these institutions has yet to be convincingly demonstrated.

There is also a medical college at Kufa.

TEACHER EDUCATION

Primary

Primary school teachers take a 5-year course, after secondary intermediate school, at one of the teacher training institutes, leading to a **Diploma**.

Secondary

Secondary school teachers are trained at the Colleges of Education, the constituent colleges of the Universities of Baghdad, Mosul, Basrah, Al-Mustansiriyah and Salahuddin. They offer a 4-year **Bachelor of Arts** course for prospective secondary teachers.

Ireland

Education was compulsory from age of six to fourteen until 1972, when it was raised to six to fiteen.

The medium of instruction in post-primary schools is English and Irish.

EVALUATION IN BRITAIN

School

Intermediate certificate - generally considered below GCE O-level and Certificate of Secondary Education (CSE) standards.

Leaving certificate - generally considered between GCE O and A-level standard as long as passes at grades A-C are obtained in subjects which may be taken in GCE examinations; passes at ordinary/standard level would generally be compared to GCE O-level, whilst passes at the higher/honours level would be considered higher than this, but not fully up to GCE A-level.

Further

National Certificate (of the NCEA) - generally compared to BTEC National Certificate/Diploma (formerly Ordinary National Certificate/Diploma) standard.

National Diploma (of the NCEA) - generally compared to BTEC Higher National Certificate/Diploma (formerly Higher National Certificate/Diploma) standard.

Higher

General degree - generally compared to British Ordinary degree standard.

Bachelor Honours degree - generally compared to British Bachelor (Honours) degree standard.

Master degree - generally compared to taught Master degree standard.

Ireland

MARKING SYSTEMS

School

Intermediate and Leaving Certificate:

A	85-100%	(Applies to subjects taken at both higher and ordinary levels.)
B	70- 84	
C	55- 69	
D	40- 54	
E	25- 39	
F	10- 24	

Before 1975 a candidate had to achieve grade D to pass in a subject, and to achieve this grade in at least 5 subjects to qualify for the award of the Leaving Certificate. Since 1985 each candidate has been issued a certificate showing the grades awarded at the examination. Thus the terms 'pass' and 'fail' no longer apply.

Matriculation examination - the marking system varies among institutions.

<u>University of Dublin, Trinity College</u>

Subjects are graded A, B, C, D, E, F and these grades are equivalent to those used in the Leaving Certificate. In the mathematics examination the results are expressed in 3 grades:

O	credit
P	pass
F	fail

<u>National University of Ireland</u>

A	75-100%
B	60- 74
C	45- 59
D	35- 44
Pass	35
E	25- 34
F	20- 24
No grade	below 20

Higher

A Bachelor degree may be conferred as either a General degree or an Honours degree.

Bachelor (Honours) degrees are classified:

First Class Honours; Second Class Honours, grade 1; Second Class Honours, grade 11; and Third Class Honours.

An undifferentiated Class II grade is awarded in some degrees.

Ireland

SCHOOL EDUCATION

Primary

Children may be admitted at age 4, and schooling normally covers 8 years.

There is no formal entrance test for secondary level, although schools may set an entrance examination.

Secondary

This covers 5-6 years divided into a junior cycle of 3-4 years, and a senior cycle of 2 years. On completion of the junior cycle, pupils take the **Intermediate Certificate** examination. Students normally take Irish, English and mathematics (at either higher or lower level), history and geography; they then choose not less than 2 subjects from Latin, Greek, classical studies, Hebrew studies, French, German, Spanish, Italian, science, home economics, music and musicianship, art, woodwork, metalwork, mechanical drawing and commerce. Civics is also studied in the lower cycle. Pupils make take the examination after 3 years secondary education, provided they are at least 14 years of age by 1 January in the year they are taking the examination and have followed an approved course of not less than 3 years.

Pupils generally take the **Leaving Certificate** examination after a further 2 years study. There are 2 syllabuses per subjects: higher and ordinary level. The higher papers cover the same ground as that of the ordinary course, but with greater depth and broader detail. Pupils normally take 6-9 subjects; they also study religious instruction and are taught physical education. Irish is not a compulsory examination subject for the Intermediate and Leaving Certificate; if a candidate fails to pass Irish in either of these examinations it no longer means failure of the overall examination. It is however, compulsory to study it.

Children whose primary education up to age 11 was received in Northern Ireland or outside Ireland may substitute any subject from the approved list for Irish in the certificate examinations.

In place of (or in addition to) the Leaving Certificate examination pupils may take the **Matriculation examination**; it is quite common for pupils to take both examinations, both represent the same level of attainment.

To obtain the Matriculation Certificate of the National University of Ireland, students must pass 6 subjects of the Matriculation examination which must include Irish, English, a third language and 3 other subjects of the programme for the Matriculation examination. Candidates not required to present in Irish must present in an alternative subject, to a total of 6, according to faculty groupings.

Specific subjects may be required for entry to different faculties.

The University of Dublin Trinity College Matriculation examination is in the following subjects only: biblical studies, geology, mathematics and Russian. The examination does not qualify for admission to courses for primary degrees.

The matriculation requirements of the University of Dublin Trinity College based on the results of the Leaving Certificate are a pass in English, a pass in mathematics and a pass in a language other than English or a pass in Latin and a pass in another non-linguistic subject, and a pass in 2 further subjects; 3 of the 5 subjects must be passed at grade G, higher level.

Ireland

For matriculation in the National University of Ireland on the results of the Leaving Certificate, the minimum requirement is a pass in 2 acceptable subjects at grade C, higher level and a pass in 4 other subjects at grade D, ordinary level. The passes must include the specified subjects for the faculties, i.e. Irish (unless exempt), English, and a third language plus 1 or 2 other specified subjects. Students may also matriculate on the joint results of the Matriculation and Leaving Certificate examinations.

If GCE examinations are presented, the general and specific faculty requirements must be satisfied, and at least 2 of the subjects must have been obtained at grade C, A-level.

For candidates presenting for Matriculation in the University of Dublin Trinity College on the results of the GCE examination, the requirements are: pass in English language, pass in mathematics and pass in a language other than English or a pass in Latin and a non-linguistic subject, and a pass in 3 further subjects. At least 2 of the 5 subjects (not including English language) must have been obtained at grade C, A-level.

There are comprehensive schools which combine secondary academic and secondary vocational education.

Technical/vocational secondary

Vocational schools provide full-time post-primary courses with emphasis on practical or vocational subjects. Pupils aged 13-16 follow courses lasting 2 years for the award of the **Day Group Certificate**. The courses are designed so that by remaining at school for a further year pupils may sit for their Intermediate Certificate. Some of these schools also provide courses, lasting 2 years, leading to the award of the Leaving Certificate.

ANCO, the Industrial Training Authority, lays down rules for school/college attendance for apprentices. Junior and senior trade certificate courses are available for apprentices on day- or block-release at the regional technical colleges. These colleges also offer courses for the Leaving Certificate in technical and commercial fields.

Agricultural colleges and colleges of rural domestic economy offer courses lasting 1-2 years for prospective farmers normally with an entrance level based on the Intermediate Certificate.

HIGHER EDUCATION

Admission to university education is on the basis of the Matriculation Certificate or certain grades in the Leaving Certificate, although neither entitles the holder to admission as competition for places is extremely keen.

There are 2 universities: The National University of Ireland (NUI) and the University of Dublin. The National University has 3 constituent colleges (University College Dublin, University College Cork and University College Galway). St Patrick's College, Maynooth is a recognized college of the National University of Ireland. It offers NUI degree courses in arts and science subjects and it is a Pontifical University. The college is also the national seminary for priests of the Roman Catholic Church. Trinity College is the only college of the University of Dublin.

Ireland

There are 2 National Institutes for Higher Education (NIHE), at Limerick and Dublin. NIHE Limerick admitted its first students in 1972 while NIHE Dublin admitted its first students in 1980.

The 9 Regional Technical Colleges offer a variety of post-Intermediate Certificate and post-Leaving Certificate courses:

1-year certificate courses
2-year **National Certificate** courses - post-Leaving Certficate
3-year **National Diploma** or National Certificate plus 1 year
4-year **degree** courses.

Most courses are validated by the National Council for Educational Awards (NCEA), established in 1972 to grant recognition to courses of higher education outside the university system (cf CNAA in Britain).

At the constituent colleges of the National University there are 2 types of Bachelor Degree: **General degree** and **Honours degree**, obtained on completion of 3 or 4 years study. However, for veterinary medicine and architecture, the first qualification is obtained on completion of a 5-year course. Degree courses in medicine and dentistry take 6 years.

A **Master degree** can be awarded after a minimum of 1 year's study following the Bachelor degree.

At Trinity College, students may obtain a **Bachelor (Honours) degree** on completion of 4 years study. After a further 3 years and payment of a fee, graduates with the Bachelor degree in Arts may proceed to a Master degree. Earned Master degrees require research/courses for specified terms.

The award of the **Doctorate** (Ph.D.) is on completion of at least 2 years original research after the award of the Bachelor degree.

TEACHER EDUCATION

Primary

The qualification for recognition as a primary teacher is a 2-year diploma - NT - awarded before 1976 or the B.Ed. degree of the National University of Ireland or of the University of Dublin. In the National University of Ireland, the B.Ed. degree may be awarded with Honours. In the University of Dublin Trinity College, an Honours degree requires a fourth year of study wholly within Trinity College Department of Education.

Secondary

Graduates take a 1-year university course leading to a Higher Diploma in Education. Training for teachers of specialized subjects is also available in 4-year degree programmes at Thomond College of Education, Limerick.

Teachers of home economics pursue a 4-year Bachelor of Education (Home Economics) degree course while art teachers pursue a degree or diploma course at a recognized college followed by a 1-year post-diploma/degree course.

Israel

State of Israel

The national system of education covers state secular schools, state religious schools, the independent ultra-orthodox Agudat Yisrael schools (non-Zionist), and Arab schools (Christian and Moslem). The state and state religious schools are supervised by the Ministry of Education and Culture. The schools operating within the Agudat Yisrael system are independent. Some privately run schools (extreme religious orientation) operate independently of both the state and Agudat Yisrael systems.

Education is compulsory from age five to sixteen.

The media of instruction are Hebrew at Jewish schools and Arabic at Arab schools.

The school and teacher training college academic year runs from 1 September to 30 June and the university academic year from November to July. Schools have three terms. Most higher-level institutions have a two-semester system.

EVALUATION IN BRITAIN

School

Bagrut - has been compared to overall GCE A-level standard when grades of 7 or better are obtained in 6 subjects, including English language.

Higher

Bachelor degree - generally compared to British Bachelor degree standard.

MARKING SYSTEMS

School

The Bagrut examinations are marked on a scale of 1-10 (maximum), with 6 as the minimum pass mark.

10	excellent
9	very good
8	good
7	fairly good
6	pass
5	borderline pass
4	
3	
2	fail
1	
0	

To be awarded the Bagrut certificate the student must pass (i.e. at grade 6 or above) each of the 5 compulsory Ministry subjects and 2 or more internal school subjects set by the secondary school and approved by the Ministry. Students may acquire one mark of 5 (almost satisfactory) as long as the subject is not Hebrew for Jewish students or Arabic for Arab students.

These 7 subjects are the minimum requirement. As many as 13 subjects may be listed on the matriculation certificate.

External candidates must pass in 6 subjects, although one grade of 5 may be tolerated.

Higher

The grading scales at Israeli universities may use letters, numbers or words. Usually the numerical scale is 0-100, with the pass mark at 50, 55 or 60.

SCHOOL EDUCATION

Before 1969, education was divided into 8 years primary and 4 years secondary. In 1969 a new pattern was introduced involving 6 years primary and 6 years secondary (3 years junior and 3 years senior). The new system obtains in most of the country.

Pre-primary

At age 5 children must attend 1 year of pre-primary education.

Primary

Jewish, Arab and Druze students attend separate schools. The basic curriculum is the same. The first 2 years cover reading, writing and arithmetic. In the following years children study such subjects as geography, history, science, handicrafts, art, music, foreign languages, physical education, agriculture, home economics, science and civics. Jewish students study a foreign language from the fourth year of schooling. English is the first compulsory foreign language. In Arab and Druze schools all students study Hebrew from the third year and English from the fourth or fifth grade. In grade 7, most children transfer to junior high schools where they follow a 3-year course.

Special primary schools

Special education is provided for physically, mentally, and emotionally handicapped children.

Secondary

Before 1969, this covered 4 years - it is now changing to 3 years in junior high (or intermediate) school and 3 years in upper (or senior) high school. There are 4 types of secondary school: academic, vocational, agricultural, and comprehensive. Working youth between 14 and 17 attend day-release centres where they study English, mathematics and Hebrew.

Academic

The academic high schools are based on the pattern of Central European education. Students follow a general course of academic studies during the first 2 years and specialize in the subjects to be taken in the Bagrut during the last 2 years. Before 1975 all pupils were examined in a set number of subjects at the same level. Under the new system, there are 3 levels of examination. Each level carries a different number of points so that a pupil can choose to take a subject at the 2-, 4- or 5-point level. There is also a 6-point level for very gifted children.

To obtain a matriculation certificate (Bagrut), a pupil must accumulate 21 points in 6 subjects which must include Jewish studies, general studies, science and a modern language. To enter higher education a student must have considerably more than 20 points.

Students who are not awarded matriculation certificates or who do not take the Bagrut examinations may be given certificates of completion of post-primary (or secondary) studies.

Religious schools

There is a separate structure of religious education within the state education system. The religious schools are under the direction of the Religious Education Department in the Ministry of Education. They offer the same basic curriculum as the state schools, but religious subjects predominate.

Kibbutz schools

Although these are part of the state system, they have several distinctive features. All children are expected to remain at school until age 18.

Schools in the occupied territories

Gaza Strip:

All schools follow the Egyptian school system (see chapter on Egypt).

Golan Heights:

All schools follow the Israeli system.

Israel

West Bank:

See chapter on West Bank.

Vocational

There are many vocational schools. Most are provided by voluntary agencies such as the Organisation of Rehabilitation through Training (ORT). The technical high schools offer 3 levels of course. The highest level leads to the examinations of the **Technical Bagrut** and a matriculation certificate which satisfies university entrance requirements in Israel. Other courses, prepare students for lower-level qualifications for work in trades and business. In general, the vocational schools offer 20 hours per week of practical training and 24 hours of general and technical subjects.

Agricultural

Most of the agricultural schools are boarding schools which prepare their pupils for work in agriculture. They also offer courses on horticulture.

FURTHER EDUCATION

Various institutions such as the ORT junior colleges provide engineering training for post-secondary students. They offer 2-year courses for students who have completed 12 years of education and hold the matriculation certificate, although some colleges have flexible entrance requirements. At the end of the first year (grade 13), students are awarded the qualification of 'technician', and at the end of the second year (14th grade 14) the qualification of Handassai (licenced practical engineer). The students take external examinations for these qualifications. In all, 11 different courses are available, leading to the Handassai Diploma. During the Diploma course, students spend 1 year in industry and submit a thesis based on their work experience. Most Handassai Diploma courses take 2 years (4 years if evening classes).

Students holding the Handassai Diploma and the matriculation certificate are eligible for university entrance but are unlikely to obtain more than 1 year's exemption, if that. The Diploma is issued by the Ministry of Labour and by various Community Colleges.

There is an extensive network of evening classes, offering vocational and recreational subjects. The Jewish Agency and other bodies organize courses in Hebrew for new immigrants.

HIGHER EDUCATION

The basic admission requirement for university is the matriculation certificate based on the Bagrut examination. Graduates of Kibbutz schools or vocational institutions who do not hold the matriculation certificate may have to undertake a year's preparatory course.

Israel

The basic first degree is the **Bachelor degree**. This normally takes 3 years; but in some subjects, such as engineering, architecture and law, 4 years is necessary. Medical and dental courses last 6 years. **Master degrees** require 1-2 years. The **Ph.D.** requires 3 years or more of course work and research.

Although Israeli universities were modelled on the European university system, their present structure is similar to that of American universities and colleges. Students must obtain a certain number of credits to be awarded a degree.

TEACHER EDUCATION

Prospective teachers are trained either in the teacher-training colleges or the university Faculties of Education.

Primary and intermediate

Kindergarten and primary teachers take a 2-year course; intermediate teachers a 3-year course. Many colleges offer both the 2- and 3-year courses. The minimum admission requirement is generally 4 (sometimes 3) subjects in the Bagrut examinations. Some colleges provide special 'bridging' courses for students without this. The religious teacher-training colleges (state religions and Aguda) stress the religious aspects of education. Their graduates can normally teach only in ultra-orthodox schools.

Most students are required to teach at least once a week throughout the course to complete their teaching practice.

Secondary

The Ministry of Education aims to require all secondary school teachers to be graduates. Students can either obtain a **B.Ed. degree** (over 4 years) or a degree in another subject and follow this with a teaching qualification. The basic entrance requirement for university teacher training is the matriculation certificate.

In-service

There are extensive opportunities for in-service teacher training, and teachers are encouraged to take advantage of the courses available. There are also full-time courses leading to certification for unqualified employed teachers.

Italy

Italian Republic

The education system is centralized under the Ministry of Public Instruction.

The main reforms were the Education Reform Act of 1963 and 1974 (Reform of the Scuola Media); the Law of November 1970 which liberalized the conditions of university entrance; the Presidential Degree number 382 of 11 July 1980 which redefined and reduced the categories of university staff.

Education is compulsory from age six to fourteen (i.e. primary to lower secondary).

The medium of instruction is Italian.

The academic year runs from September to June in schools, and November to October in universities.

EVALUATION IN BRITAIN

School

Diploma di Licenza della Scuola Media - generally considered to be below GCE O-level standard.

Diploma di Qualifica Professionale - generally compared to the City & Guilds of London Institute Craft Certificate Part 2.

Diploma di Maturita Classica/Scientifica/Tecnica/Linguistica/Professionale/Magistrale/Artistica - may be considered to satisfy the general requirement of universities and polytechnics.

Higher

Laurea - generally compared to British Bachelor degree standard.

Italy

MARKING SYSTEMS

School

Until 1968:

Marking was on a scale 0-10 (maximum); 6 was the minimum pass grade.

Since 1969:

A variety of marking systems has been adopted, as follows:

In the primary school at the end of each year a global assessment is made. In the lower secondary school the final assessment is expressed in 4 grades:

sufficiente	pass
buono	good
distinto	distinction
ottimo	excellent

In the upper secondary school, final marks are on a scale 0-60 (maximum); 36 is the minimum pass grade.

Higher

The final standard of degree is shown as the aggregate of the individual marks out of 110. Exceptionally, the degree may be awarded <u>cum laude</u>. Individual subjects are graded on a scale of 0-30 (maximum).

SCHOOL EDUCATION

Pre-primary (Istruzione del Grado Preparatorio)

Facilities are available for children from age 3. State nursery schools (<u>Scuola Materna Statale</u>) were formally established in 1968 from already existing pre-primary schools.

Primary (Istruzione Elementare)

This covers 5 years from age 6, divided into a 2-year lower cycle followed by a 3-year upper cycle. The first cycle covers general studies.

The curriculum of the second cycle covers: religious instruction, civil and moral education, physical education, history, geography, sciences, arithmetic, geometry, Italian, drawing and writing, singing, handiwork.

Until 1974 this cycle culminated in the tests for the **Primary School Leaving Certificate/Licenza Elementare,** and the results of this decided promotion to secondary school. Pupils now pass automatically from primary to secondary school.

Italy

Secondary

This covers 8 years, divided into 3 years lower secondary, followed by 5 years upper secondary.

Lower:

Until 1963, pupils could attend either a Scuola Media or Scuola d'Avviamento Professionale (more vocationally-oriented studies); in that year the 2 types of institution were combined to form the Scuola Media Unica. Compulsory subjects in the curriculum are religious instruction, Italian, history and civics, geography, mathematics, nature study and elementary science, a foreign language, art education, handiwork and physical education; Latin was compulsory until 1977; music was compulsory for only the first year, but now replaces Latin as a compulsory subject for the full cycle. However, students who wish to enter the classical branch of academic upper-secondary school must have studied Latin.

Pupils obtain the **Diploma di Licenza della Scuola Media** (or until 1962 the Diploma di Licenza di Avviamento Industriale/Professionale) on completion of the cycle.

Upper:

The upper-secondary courses are: classical, scientific, artistic, technical, vocational, and teacher training. The classical and scientific options are purely academic, intended for pupils wishing to go on to university.

Classical secondary school/Liceo Classico - a 5-year course divided into a 2-year course at Ginnasio and 3 years Liceo, with emphasis on the humanities, but with science subjects in the second cycle:

2-year Ginnasio - Italian, Latin, Greek, a foreign language, history and civics, geography, mathematics, religious instruction, physical education

3-year Liceo - Italian, Latin, Greek, history and civics, philosophy, natural science, chemistry, geography, mathematics, physics, art, history, religious instruction, physical education.

Scientific secondary school/Liceo Scientifico - more specialized preparation for those wishing to study science at university. The course lasts 5 years, divided into a first general year followed by a 4-year specialization course.

The curriculum covers:

First year/classe di collegamento - Italian, Latin, a foreign language, history and civics, geography, mathematics, drawing, religious instruction, physical education.

years 2-5 - Italian, Latin, a foreign language and literature, history and civics, philosophy, natural science, chemistry, geography, physics, mathematics, drawing, religious instruction, physical education.

On completion of the 5-year course, pupils take the examinations for the **Maturita** in a particular specialization (i.e. **Maturita Classica, Maturita Scientifica**), which allows entry to all faculties of Italian universities. Until the Reform of 1969 final examinations were taken in all subjects studied and included written as well as oral tests. After the Reform, final examinations for all types of secondary school consist of two written papers (an essay in Italian on any given subject and a paper on the specialist subject) and two oral examinations. Each year in April-May the Ministry of Education offers 4 subjects for the oral examinations; of these, one is chosen by the student and one by the examining board.

Technical secondary

The full 5-year technical upper secondary course is offered by the istituti tecnici. The areas of study include: industry, commerce, agriculture, nautics, aeronautics and each offers a number of specializations.

The 5 years are divided into a 2-year general course followed by 3 years (or 4 years in the case of special courses in agriculture) specialization. On completion of the course pupils take the examinations for the **Diploma di Maturita Tecnica** with the appropriate suffix, e.g. **industriale**. It allows entry to industry with the title **Perito**. Until the mid-1960s pupils could not proceed to university holding only this qualification; however students may now enter technical universities.

Vocational secondary

Before the Reform Act of 1963, vocational education was offered by the Scuola di Avviamento Professionale with a 4-year lower secondary course which included an element of workshop training, and led to the qualification of **Operaio Qualificato** (skilled worker). Shorter courses of 1-2 years (corsi di avviamento professionale) were available for pupils from age 11. These courses have now been incorporated in the general course offered by the Scuola Media. The Scuola Tecnica (trade schools) offered a 4-year course following on from the Scuola di Avviamento Professionale/Scuola Media.

These institutions have now been merged into the Istituti Professionali (vocational training schools). Pupils enter on completion of the Scuola Media, but pupils without the certificate from that cycle, the **Diploma di Licenza della Scuola Media**, may be accepted on passing an entrance examination. The 2- or 3-year courses (depending on the subject) lead to the **Diploma di Qualifica Professionale**. They are more practical than those of the technical secondary schools and aim to produce skilled workers for industries of importance to the economy. 5 fields of study are offered: industry, commerce, agriculture, hotel and catering, secretarial skills. In 1969 experimental post-qualifying courses (corsi sperimentali post-qualifica) were established in some of the Istituti Professionali offering a 2-year course following on from the first course (i.e. from the Diploma di Qualifica Professionale). Thus a total of 5 years leads to the **Diploma di Maturita Professionale** needed for university entry. (Despite being called 'experimental' these courses are now fully established.)

The Liceo Artistico offers foundation courses for further studies at an Academy of Fine Art or at a university. Pupils are admitted for a 4-year course on completion of lower secondary education. After the first 2 years the course is divided into 2 sections: one specialization enables the pupil to later pursue artistic studies at an Academy of Fine Art, and the other enables the pupil to enrol in the Faculty of Architecture (only) of a university; pupils wishing to enrol in other faculties must complete a further year of study. The final examination leads to the **Diploma di Maturita Artistica**.

Italy

HIGHER EDUCATION

Higher education is offered by universities and 2 polytechnic universities, specializing in architecture and the sciences.

Except for the Universita della Calabria at Cosenza, there is no system of numerus clausus (restricted entry), and since 1970 all students holding an upper secondary school diploma may enter a course of higher education if they have completed a full 5-year secondary course. The Maturita Classica gives admission to all courses, the Maturita Scientifica to all faculties; students holding a diploma on completion of a 4-year secondary course at one of the Istituti Magistrali or Licei Artistici may attend any course once they have completed a 1-year pre-university course (corso integrativo).

The first degree is the **Laurea** which carries with it the title of **Dottore**. The courses last 4-6 years, with 5 years in chemistry, architecture and engineering, and 6 years (plus 1 year training in a hospital) in medicine. To practice a profession students also have to pass a state examination (esame di stato).

There were no specific postgraduate degrees until 1981 when the first candidates for a postgraduate degree, **Dottorato di Ricerca**, were enrolled. Graduates undertake a programme of not less than 3 years. The doctorate is awarded by the Ministry of Education on the successful presentation of a final thesis. Post-lauream courses of specialization (corsi di perfezionamento) are available, varying from 1-5 years. They lead to the **Diploma di Specializzazione**, which is not an academic qualification, only proof of professional skills.

In certain subjects (e.g. statistics, interpreting, translating) a diploma is awarded after a course lasting 2-3 years; the holder is not entitled to the title of Dottore.

The title of **Libera Docenza** used to be awarded to holders of the **Laurea** who were well qualified and wished to teach in universities.

TEACHER EDUCATION

Pre-primary/kindergarten

A 3-year course (2 years theory, 1 year methodology) at a Scuola Magistrale (after completion of the Licenza Media) leads to the **Diploma di Abilitazione all'Insegnamento nelle Scuole del Grado Preparatorio**.

Primary

A 4-year upper-secondary course at one of the Istituti di Magistero leads to the **Diploma di Abilitazione Magistrale**.

Secondary

There is no formal pre-service training, but teachers are university graduates.

Italy

The competitive state examination (concorso) is the method of competition used at all levels of schooling for teachers to enter the profession (concorso abilitante), and to obtain a chair (concorso a cattedra) after gaining a university degree.

Ivory Coast

Republic of the Ivory Coast

The education system is based mainly on the French system.

The medium of instruction is French.

The academic year runs from October to June.

EVALUATION IN BRITAIN

School

Diplome de Bachelier de l'Enseignement du Second Degre/Baccalaureat - generally compared to GCE O-level standard.

Further

Diplome Universitaire de Technologie - generally compared to the BTEC Higher Diploma (formerly HND) standard.

Higher

Licence - generally considered to be between GCE A-level and British Bachelor degree standards.

MARKING SYSTEMS

School and higher

Marking is on the scale 0-20; minimum pass is 10

16-20	very good
14-15	good
12-13	quite good
11	average

Ivory Coast

SCHOOL EDUCATION

Primary

This covers 6 years from the age of 6, divided into 2-year cycles:

cours preparatoire	CP1, CP2
cours elementaire	CE1, CE2
cours moyen	CM1, CM2

On completion of the final year, pupils take an examination leading to the **Certificat d'Etudes Primaires Elementaires (CEPE)**.

Secondary

This covers 7 years, with classes numbered in reverse order. It is divided into a 4-year lower cycle followed by a 3-year upper cycle. The first cycle may be taken at a College d'Enseignement General or Lycee, and culminates in the examinations for the **Brevet d'Etudes du Premier Cycle (BEPC)**.

In the upper cycle pupils may specialize in a general/academic or technical course. The former is available only at a Lycee, and in 2 options: classical or modern (i.e. specializing in mathematics, modern languages or science).

After this cycle, pupils take the examinations for the **Diplome de Bachelier de l'Enseignement du Second Degre** in 1 of 6 options, depending on the specialization already studied:

A	philosophy - letters
B	economics and social studies
C	mathematics and physical sciences
D	mathematics and natural sciences
D	agricultural sciences
E	mathematics

Technical secondary

After 2-years lower secondary, pupils undertake a 3-year course at a <u>College d'Enseignement Technique</u>, leading to a **Certificat d'Aptitude Professionnelle (CAP)**.

After 2-years upper secondary, pupils may obtain a **Brevet d'Etudes Commerciales/Industrielles**.

The **Baccalaureat/Bachelier Technicien/Technique** may be obtained on completion of the 3-year upper-secondary technical course.

FURTHER EDUCATION

The <u>Institut Universitaire de Technologie</u> offers courses for holders of the Baccalaureat, leading to **Diplome Universitaire de Technologie**.

Ivory Coast

HIGHER EDUCATION

The only university, the <u>University of Abidjan</u>, originated in the Centre d'Enseignement Superieure established in 1958. It acquired university status in 1964 and adopted its present title in 1976.

2 years of study lead to:

Diplome Universitaire d'Etudes Litteraires (DUEL)	arts
Diplome Universitaire d'Etudes Scientifiques (DUES)	sciences
Diplome Universitaire d'Etudes Economiques Generales (DEEG)	economics
Diplome Universitaire d'Etudes Juridiques Generales (DEJG)	law

A further year of study leads to the **Licence** in the humanities and science subjects, or 2 years for law and economics. The period can vary, depending on the length of time spent by the students in obtaining the requisite number of **Certificats d'Etudes Superieures**.

The **Maitrise** in arts and science subjects takes 1 year.

The **Diplome d'Etudes Approfondies** (DEA) is obtained after a 1-year taught course. A minimum of 1 year's research then leads (in science, law and economics) to the **Diplome d'Etudes Superieures** or to the **Doctorat de Specialite de Troisieme Cycle**. In medicine and technology this stage leads to the professional qualification (i.e. **Doctorat** and **Ingenieur** respectively).

The qualifications of **Ingenieur-Docteur** and **Doctorat d'Etat** may be obtained after many more years of original research. The **Doctorat d'Universite** is only awarded to foreign students but is similar in standard to the Doctorat d'Etat.

TEACHER EDUCATION

Primary

Training is at upper secondary level and leads to the qualification of **Instituteur**.

Secondary

Lower:

A 1-year course for holders of the Baccalaureat leads to the **Certificat d'Aptitude Pedagogique pour l'Enseignement du Second Degre**. A 3-year course leads to the **Certificat d'Aptitude Pedagogique pour les Colleges d'Enseignement General de Premier Cycle du Second Degre** (CAPCEG). Holders of this qualification may then go to university for a further year to obtain the Licence.

Upper:

Teachers for this level may do a **Licence d'Enseignement** or a 1-year course if they already hold a degree. This leads to the **Certificat d'Aptitude Pedagogique pour l'Enseignement Superieur** (CAPES).

Jamaica

Compulsory education is being introduced in areas where conditions permit.

The medium of instruction is English.

The academic year comprises three terms and runs from September to June.

EVALUATION IN BRITAIN

School

Jamaica School Certificate (JSC) - generally considered to be below GCE O-level standard.

Secondary School Certificate (SSC) - may be considered to compare to Certificate of Secondary Education (CSE) standard.

Cambridge Overseas School Certificate - grades 1-6 are equated to GCE O-level (grades A, B or C).

The Caribbean Examinations Council Secondary Education Certificate - grades 1 and 2 at the general proficiency level have been equated to GCE O-levels (grades A, B or C).

Cambridge Overseas Higher School Certificate - grades A-E are equated to GCE A-level.

Higher

Bachelor degrees - generally considered to compare to British Bachelor degree standard.

MARKING SYSTEMS

School

The Cambridge Overseas School Certificate is graded 1 (maximum) - 9.

Jamaica

1-2	very good
3-6	credit
7-8	pass
9	fail.

Caribbean Examinations Council Secondary Education Certificate subject examinations are taken at 3 proficiency levels:

basic proficiency
general proficiency
technical proficiency.

The 5 grades awarded have been defined:

I	comprehensive working knowledge of the syllabus
II	working knowledge of most aspects of the syllabus
III	working knowledge of some aspects of the syllabus
IV	limited knowledge of a few aspects of the syllabus
V	insufficient evidence on which to base a judgement.

The Cambridge Overseas Higher School Certificate is graded A-F:

A-E	pass
O	subsidiary pass
F	fail
X	absent.

Higher

Bachelor degrees are awarded with the following classifications:

Class I
Class II upper division
Class II lower division

If the performance has been insufficient for Honours, the degree is awarded as a Pass.

SCHOOL EDUCATION

Pre-primary

There are a few public and private schools which offer 2- and 3-year courses for children aged 4-6. Basic schools, run by community and religious bodies, receive government assistance and provide day-care and some rudiments of schooling.

Primary

Primary education, which originally lasted 5 years, now begins at age 6 and lasts for 6 years (grades 1-6). At the end of grade 6, pupils take the **11+ Common Entrance Examination** which forms the basis of selection for secondary education.

Jamaica

Pre-independence school education was principally undertaken in 'all-age' schools which offered both primary (grades 1-6) and lower secondary education (grades 7-9). In the late 1960s, the pattern changed as new secondary schools were established.

Secondary

This covers grades 7-11 with an additional 2 years (grades 12-13) for those wishing to proceed to university.

The first stage of secondary education (grades 7-9) is offered in the new secondary schools, 'all-age' schools and the first 3 years of high schools and comprehensive high schools. Comprehensive schools are in theory integrated secondary, high and technical high schools, allowing for mobility between grades, subjects and programmes according to individual needs. These schools prepare students for the Jamaica School Certificate and GCE examinations. The new secondary schools, which cover grades 7-11, replaced the junior secondary schools, which offered courses in grades 7-9 only.

Pupils from 'all-age' and secondary schools can take the **13+ Common Entrance Examination** and enter a technical high school. Alternatively, on completion of grade 9, they may enter a high or comprehensive high school by passing the **Grade 9 Achievement Test** or they may be admitted to a vocational school by passing the appropriate entrance examination.

The second stage covers grades 10-11 at technical and comprehensive high schools, new secondary schools and high schools which also offer the opportunity for a further 2 years of study (grades 10-13).

On completion of grade 10, students may sit for the **Jamaica School Certificate**. This examination is also taken by those outside the formal education system who, because of insufficient places at secondary schools and other reasons, have been continuing their education through correspondence courses.

At the end of grade 11 in the new secondary schools, students are awarded the **Secondary School Certificate** which is based partly on continuous assessment over grades 10 and 11 and is partly nationally assessed. Also on completion of grade 11, those students at high schools sit for the **Cambridge Overseas School Certificate**.

In 1972, Jamaica joined a number of other Caribbean states in establishing the Caribbean Examinations Council (CXC). The **Secondary Education Certificate** set by the CXC will eventually replace the Cambridge Overseas Certificate (see Appendix).

In high schools, students may continue their studies for a further 2 years to grade 13, at the end of which they sit for the **Cambridge Overseas Higher School Certificate** or A-levels set by the GCE Examination Boards.

Community colleges are being developed to replace the sixth forms in high schools. They aim to prepare students not only for university but also for work. Students are admitted from high schools, secondary schools, technical and comprehensive high schools. Courses are offered in business (including secretarial studies), teacher education, pre-nursing, etc. These colleges also act as evening institutes and non-formal education centres.

Jamaica

Technical secondary

Technical secondary education in technical high schools consists of 4 years (grades 8-11). The first 2 years are general, specialization occurring in grades 10-11. Admission is normally on the basis of the 13+ Common Entrance Examination but students may also transfer from high schools. Courses are also offered part-time and lead to the **GCE, Royal Society of Arts, City & Guilds of London Institute** and other similar examinations.

Apart from the vocational education programmes offered in technical high schools and most secondary schools, vocational training is offered in vocational schools and trade centres which offer courses of 1-2 years depending on the trade or level of skill required. These courses prepare students for employment.

FURTHER EDUCATION

This is offered mainly at the Jamaica School of Agriculture, the Cultural Training Centre, the College of Arts, Science and Technology and certain community colleges. Admission is usually on the basis of completion of grade 11.

The Jamaica School of Agriculture (JSA) offers **Diplomas** (2 years) and **Associate degrees** (3 years). It also trains specialist agricultural teachers.

The College of Arts, Science and Technology (CAST) offers courses of 1-5 years on a full-time, part-time day release or evening basis culminating in college **Certificate** (2 years), **Diploma** (3 years) or professional qualifications, including the training of teachers for technical and vocational schools. Entrance requirements vary according to course but full-time students must pass the College Entrance Examination or possess the required number of GCE O-level passes.

The Cultural Training Centre (CTC) comprises the National Schools of Arts, Dance, Drama and Music. The courses are 2-3 years full-time and also part-time. Graduates are recognized as trained specialist teachers in their respective fields.

HIGHER EDUCATION

The University of the West Indies (UWI) is a regional institution with campuses at Mona in Jamaica, Cave Hill in Barbados and St Augustine in Trinidad. It is supported by and serves 14 territories in the West Indies. Students from participating territories may enrol at any campus.

Degree courses are offered at both undergraduate and postgraduate levels. There are also 1-year full-time and 2-year part-time (post-grade 13) certificates in education, agriculture, nursing, management studies, etc.

Diplomas are normally 1-year full-time postgraduate courses.

Jamaica

TEACHER EDUCATION

Entrance to teacher training colleges which train teachers mainly for primary and the new secondary schools is generally based on completion of grade 11. The courses are normally 3 years (2 years study and 1 year practical training). Upgrading courses are available for practising teachers and for those who do not meet the normal entrance requirements.

Training for teachers of specialized subjects takes place in teacher-training departments within institutions such as the College of Arts, Science and Technology.

Undergraduate and graduate training is offered in the School of Education at the University of the West Indies. Graduate teachers are usually employed in high schools, technical and comprehensive high schools and in vocational and secondary schools.

Japan

Japan established a new education system in 1946 following World War II, modelled on the American pattern of 6+3+3+4 cycles.

In 1947 the School Education Law and the Fundamental Law of Education were enacted, and a period of nine years compulsory education established to cover the ages of six to fifteen.

The academic year runs from April to March.

EVALUATION IN BRITAIN

School

Chugakko/Lower Secondary School Certificate - generally considered to be below GCE O-level standard.

Kotogakko/Upper Secondary School Certificate - generally considered to compare to GCE O-level standard.

Higher

Bachelor degree - generally considered to be below British Bachelor degree standard. Bachelor degrees from Tokyo and Kyoto Universities would generally be considered to compare to British Bachelor degree standard.

MARKING SYSTEMS

School

Grading is on the following scale:

A	5	maximum
B	4	
C	3	
D	2	minimum pass mark
F	1	fail

Higher

A variety of grading systems are used, but the most common is the scale of:

A	80-100
B	70-79
C	60-69
F (fail)	0-59

SCHOOL EDUCATION

Pre-primary

Mostly institutions at this level are private, but under the supervision of the national education authorities. They admit children aged 3,4 or 5 to 3-, 2- and 1-year courses respectively.

Primary

All children reaching age 6 are required to attend a 6-year course of primary education. The leaving certificate gives admission to the cycle of lower secondary education.

Lower secondary

Children attend these schools for 3 years, from age 12-15. Instruction is departmentalized and the majority of teachers are specialists. There is no selection procedure for entrance to municipal lower secondary schools, but children intending to enter private or national ones must take an entrance examination. Children may leave school at 15, but most continue their education. At this stage they take the **Chugakko/Lower Secondary School Certificate**.

Upper secondary

Entry to the 3-year upper secondary cycle is competitive, but 98% of those who apply are successful. Achievement tests are set by local authorities, while the national and private schools set their own entrance examinations.

The upper secondary schools offer both specialized and general courses. Since 1973 all students must cover Japanese language, social studies, mathematics, science, health and physical education, fine arts and a foreign language. Girls also have to study homecraft.

The specialized courses include vocational courses such as agriculture, fishery, home economics and nursing.

There are 3 types of upper secondary school: full-time, part-time and correspondence. The part-time and correspondence courses last 4 years or more. About half the students in the upper secondary cycle will be on part-time or correspondence courses.

All courses lead to the **Kotagakko/Upper Secondary School Certificate**.

Miscellaneous schools

Various types of course are offered ranging from 3 months to 4 years, but the normal period is 1 year. Most courses require only completion of the lower secondary cycle, although some may also require completion of upper secondary schooling.

FURTHER EDUCATION

Since 1962 a number of technical colleges have been established, offering 5-year courses to produce medium-level technicians. Entrance level is completion of the first cycle of secondary education, and admission is usually competitive. Students who complete the course successfully may apply for admission to the second 2-year cycle of study at a university, but few do so. The courses are based on the number of class-hours studied.

HIGHER EDUCATION

Following the reorganization of the education system in 1947 junior colleges were established as a new type of institution. They were started on a temporary basis to increase the opportunities for higher education. Some developed from the old technical or specialized colleges which did not meet the requirements to be upgraded to universities under the new system. The colleges were established as a permanent part of the system in 1964. Most are privately sponsored. All national junior colleges are attached to national universities as 'evening faculties'. Some of the colleges are also connected with secondary schools. There is no accreditation of junior colleges, although the Committee for Establishing Junior Colleges (a subcommittee of the University Chartering Committee) makes recommendations to the Ministry of Education on the standards to be met and kept. The colleges offer 2- and 3-year courses: on the 2-year course students must obtain 62 credits, of which 12 are achieved in general education and 2 in physical education; on the 3-year course students must obtain 93 credits, 18 being in general subjects and 3 in physical education. Although the credits obtained at junior colleges count towards those needed for a first degree at a university, few students transfer. As the emphasis and content of the first 2 years of university study is different from that of the 2-year courses at a junior college, students attempting to transfer may have to spend an additional 3 years to obtain a Bachelor degree.

There are national, local and private universities in Japan.

A national university entrance preliminary examination, the **Unified Primary Test**, was instituted in 1979, and aspiring entrants to all national and public universities sit for this before taking the entrance examinations of the individual institutions.

Japan

The universities established or approved since 1949 are similar to American universities. Undergraduate courses leading to the award of a **Bachelor degree** last 4 years and graduation requires 124 credits. Courses are classified as general education, foreign language, health and physical education, and professional subjects. Students must acquire the prescribed number of credits in each group of subjects. In the faculties of medicine and dentistry, courses last 6 years: 2 years of general education (64 credits) followed by 4 years of professional training.

The **Postgraduate Diploma/Shushi** is obtained after a 2-year course (4-years in medicine and dentistry) where the student has obtained 30 credits and prepared a research thesis.

The **Doctorate** may be awarded after a student has obtained at least 50 credits after the Bachelor degree, defended a research thesis and sat a final examination. It may also be awarded on the submission of a thesis based on original research or as a recognition of outstanding scholarship in a publication.

Most Japanese universities are private institutions. The Japanese University Accreditation Association (JUAA) is a voluntary association of national, public and private universities. The JUAA does not accredit junior colleges or technical institutes; its sphere is limited to institutions offering 4 or more years of education. As membership of the JUAA is voluntary, it is possible for institutions of good standing to remain outside the association. The JUAA lists a university as accredited if it has at least one faculty which has been approved for accreditation.

TEACHER EDUCATION

All primary and secondary teachers are trained on 4-year courses, mostly at universities, although some private colleges offer similar courses. A few colleges offered 2-year courses for prospective primary school teachers, but most of these had been discontinued by 1960. Prospective secondary school teachers are awarded the teaching qualification if they obtain the minimum number of credits (124) in each of the following subjects: general education, teaching subjects and professional subjects.

Teaching certificates are classified as regular and 'deputy' teachers certificates. Those who hold the **Regular Teachers Certificate** are qualified for full teaching duties, whilst holders of the **Deputy Certificate** may be assistant teachers only and the certificate is valid for only 3 years. The regular certificates are subdivided into first- and second-class certificates. School principals must hold the first-class certificate.

Kindergarten/primary/lower secondary

regular certificates:	first class awarded to university graduates second class awarded to junior college graduates.
deputy certificates:	awarded to those holding the leaving certificate of the second cycle of secondary education.

Japan

Secondary (upper)

regular certificates: first and second classes awarded to university graduates

deputy certificates: awarded to junior college graduates.

Technical

3-year courses are taken at institutes attached to university faculties of engineering. Teachers seeking higher class certificates must earn the additional credits and must have served for the prescribed number of years. The required credits may be acquired through in-service training or by attending regular university courses.

University

The grades of university academic staff are: **Professor, Assistant Professor, Lecturer,** and **Assistant**.

Jordan

Hashemite Kingdom of Jordan

This chapter covers the period from 1950, when the East and West Banks were unified (the latter only till 1967).

The education system in the West Bank continues to follow the Jordanian system; for full information since 1967, see the separate chapter. See also the appendix on Unrwa (United Nations Relief and Works Agency for Palestine Refugees), which took over responsibility for the education of the many refugees of the West Bank. The education provided had to comply with the minimum standards and curricula of the Jordanian Ministry of Education.

There are some private schools, but according to the 1964 Education Act Number 16 all schools must follow the same centrally authorized curricula, administer the same examinations and maintain standards. They must prepare students for the General Secondary Education Certificate examinations unless equivalent examinations are being pursued.

Some secondary schools (both government and private) are called 'colleges'.

There are nine years of compulsory education: six years of elementary education followed by a three-year preparatory cycle (junior high school).

The medium of instruction in schools is Arabic. At the University of Yarmouk and in all faculties of the University of Jordan, except the Arts faculties, instruction is in English.

The academic year runs from August to May in schools, and October to June in the universities.

EVALUATION IN BRITAIN

School

General Secondary School Certificate (Al Tawjihiyya) - generally compared to GCE O-level on a subject-for-subject basis where marks of at least 50% have been obtained in subjects which may be taken in the GCE examinations (except English language).

Jordan

Higher

Bachelor degrees - generally considered below the standard of a British Bachelor degree.

MARKING SYSTEMS

School

General Secondary School Certificate (since 1962), is usually marked on a percentage scale (minimum pass 40-50%), but the system used is clearly marked on the transcript of marks.

Higher

Percentage scale, with minimum pass 50% (until 1961 minimum overall pass was 60%).

SCHOOL EDUCATION

Pre-primary

There are a number of private kindergartens supervised by the Ministry of Education.

Primary/elementary

This covers 6 years from age 6. The curriculum covers Islamic education, mathematics, science, Arabic language, social studies, drawing, music, physical education and art education; English is introduced in the fifth year in the public schools and at an earlier stage in the private schools.

Secondary

This covers 6 years (divided into 3 years preparatory and 3 years secondary).

Preparatory:

The curriculum covers Islamic education, Arabic, English, mathematics, social science, physical science, art education, vocational training and physical education. Between 1975 and 1985 the cycle culminated in the nationally run examinations for the **General Preparatory Education Certificate**. Depending on the results of this, pupils could transfer to some form of secondary education. In 1985, the **Secondary School Entrance Examination** was introduced. Entrance to secondary schools or trade centres depends on the needs and results of students and the facilities available at both the Ministry and the school in the districts.

Jordan

Secondary:

Until 1961, this cycle consisted only of 2 years, but in 1961 it was extended to 3 years. (As a result, there was no final examination that year.) Pupils may undertake a course at 1 of 3 types of school (academic, vocational, comprehensive) but there is no facility for pupils to transfer once they have begun a course.

Academic schools

There is a general first year for all pupils; and since 1962 there has been specialization in grades 11 and 12 in literary or scientific streams. In the first year, pupils study Islamic education, Arabic, English, mathematics, physical sciences, biology, history, geography, art education, civil defence, vocational education, or home economics. In the literary stream the special subjects are general science, history, geography and economics; and in the science stream biology, physics, chemistry and additional mathematics; besides the compulsory subjects of Islamic education, Arabic, English, mathematics, art education, vocational education and defence. At the conclusion of this cycle, pupils take the examinations for the **General Secondary School Certificate** (Al Tawjihiyya). The examinations are taken in 2 parts; some subjects at the end of the first semester of year 3, and the rest at the end of that year.

Comprehensive schools

Comprehensive education was introduced on an experimental basis in 1975. Comprehensive schools begin with grade 10 and end with grade 12. At the beginning of their second year, students choose one of the available kinds of education in the school: academic, commercial, nursing, industrial, etc. Academic students in addition to general courses, have 4-6 periods of study in vocational skills a week.

Vocational schools

There are 6 specializations that can be pursued at vocational schools, as follows:

Industrial - for craft-level jobs. Each pupil spends the first year in general vocational training, and is then assigned to a trade. Pupils also study Arabic, English, mathematics, physical education, safety and organization of industry, religious instruction, physics and mechanics, industrial chemistry, engineering, drawing and workshop practice. There are also 2-year courses with a more practical bias.

Commercial - business correspondence, accounts and bookkeeping, financial mathematics, economics, mercantile law, Arabic typing and typing in one foreign language.

Agriculture - pupils study Arabic, English, mathematics, religious instruction and agricultural specialist subjects.

Nursing - 2- and 3-year courses.

Hotel administration.

Postal.

The **General Vocational Secondary Education Certificate** may be obtained in any of these specialities after a 3-year course.

Jordan

Trade Centres

These are open to students who successfully complete the preparatory cycle. Students can choose between Ministry of Education Trade Centres, the Vocational Training Corporation and the Jordanian Armed Forces Centres. The aim is to graduate skilled workers in various crafts and industrial specializations, such as electricity, utilization, automechanics, welding and blacksmithing, carpentry, plumbing and central heating, office machines mechanics, building. There are some Trade Training Centres for girls which cover dress making, beauty culture, ceramics, weaving. The course lasts for 2 years and includes cultural, technical and practical subjects.

FURTHER EDUCATION

Community Colleges of which there are currently 52 (including 23 private colleges), aim to provide wider access to higher education, thereby reducing the cost of university education, in fields of study which include technology, commerce, banking, agriculture, nursing, paramedical subjects, catering, institutional management, and education.

Courses are for 2 years and open to holders of the General Secondary Education Certificate or its equivalent.

Teacher Training Institutes are now included in the Community College system and the former Polytechnic is now called the Amman Polytechnic Community College. A 2-year course with a minimum of 75 credit hours leads to a **Diploma in Education**, which qualifies teachers for primary and preparatory levels.

Amman Polytechnic offers 2-year courses in engineering, architecture, surveying and laboratory technology for students holding the Secondary School Entrance Examination (science stream) or the General Vocational Secondary Education Certificate (industrial section).

Agricultural Institute offers 2-year courses for students holding the general vocational secondary education certificate (agricultural section).

Students in Community Colleges have to sit for the **Community College Comprehensive Examination**, set by the Ministry of Higher Education.

HIGHER EDUCATION

There are 3 universities: the University of Jordan in Amman, established in 1962; the University of Yarmouk, established in 1976; and the University of Mu'tah, established in 1981, which specializes in military education.

The entrance requirement is the General Secondary Education Examination. A minimum pass mark is set annually by the Council for Higher Education (65% in 1986).

Bachelor degrees generally last 4 years, depending on the subject of study, and are based on the credit system. The University of Jordan requires a minimum of 132 credit hours for graduates, and individual courses offered are worth 3 credit hours. Of the 132 minimum credit hours, 18 are university requirements (military training, Arabic, English, etc.). At the University of Yarmouk, the minimum number of credit hours is 122, of which 18 are university requirements.

At the Universities of Jordan and Yarmouk **Master degrees** can be obtained by completing 30 credit hours, of which 6 are for a thesis. Master degrees take a minimum of 2 years (usually 3-4 years).

TEACHER EDUCATION

Primary and intermediate secondary

A 2-year course is taken from the General Secondary Education Certificate, with a minimum of 75 credit hours, leading to a **Diploma of Education** (see under **Further Education**).

Secondary

Teachers must be graduates and undertake a 2-year **Postgraduate Diploma** course.

Kenya

Republic of Kenya

Kenya has implemented a highly centralized system of education since its independence in 1963.

In 1967 it co-operated with Tanzania and Uganda to form the East African Examinations Council (EAEC) to administer (at first with the University of Cambridge Local Examinations Syndicate, and from 1974 independently) the school examinations. However, Kenya withdrew from the EAEC in 1980 and has established its own Examinations Council (Kenya National Examinations Council) offering essentially the same examinations.

There are a number of private (religious and Harambee) schools; Harambee schools are self-help schools which have been created solely by voluntary contributions and are maintained by fees and donations.

Primary education is nominally free and compulsory.

The medium of instruction is English, but Swahili was used until 1970 in primary standards 1-4.

The academic year runs from:

October to July	university
May to April	primary teachers colleges and sub-degree secondary teacher education
January to December	primary and secondary schools.

EVALUATION IN BRITAIN

School

Kenya Junior School Certificate (KJSC) - generally considered below GCE O-level standard.

Cambridge Overseas School Certificate (COSC) East African Certificate of Education (EACE) Kenya Certificate of Education (KCE)	grades 1-6 are generally equated to GCE 'O' level (grades A, B, C) on a subject-for-subject basis;

the 'division' of the certificate indicates a student's overall examination performance and is not important in ascertaining a pupil's performance in individual subjects.

Kenya

Cambridge Overseas Higher School Certificate (COHSC) grades A-E are
East African Advanced Certificate of Education (EAACE) generally compared
Kenya Advanced Certificate of Education (KACE) to GCE A-level standard.

Higher

Bachelor degree - generally considered comparable to British Bachelor degree standard.

MARKING SYSTEMS

School

Kenya Certificate of Primary Education (KCPE) - taken after 8 years of primary education and examined for the first time in November 1985 - replaced Kenya Primary Examination (KPE) and Certificate of Primary Examination (CPE). There are 4 major subject areas examined and graded A, B, C, D.

Kenya Junior School Certificate (KJSE) is graded A, B, C, D, E.

Kenya Certificate of Education (KCE) is graded 1 (maximum) - 9 (fair):

1-2	very good
3-6	credit pass
7-8	pass
9	fail

The certificate also shows a classification in 1 of 4 divisions, which reflects overall examination performance.

Division 1: 6-23 points - pass in 6 or more subjects, including a humanities subject (group II), a mathematical subject (group IV), and a science subject (group V); pass with credit in at least 5 subjects, including 1 language (group I or group III), and a high general standard, as judged by aggregate performance in the 6 best subjects. Candidate must pass maths and English.

Division 2: 24-33 points - pass in 6 or more subjects, including a language from either group I or group III; pass with credit in at least 4 subjects and a certain general standard, as judged by aggregate performance in the 6 best subjects.

Division 3: 34 to 45 points - pass in at least 6 subjects with credit in at least 1 of them; or pass in 5 subjects with credit in at least 2 of them, and a satisfactory standard, as judged by the aggregate performance in the 6 best subjects.

Division 4: 46-51 points - at least 1 pass with credit in any 1 subject; or at least 2 passes at grade 7 in any 2 subjects; or at least 3 passes at grade 8 in any 3 subjects.

Kenya Advanced Certificate of Education (KACE) is taken 2 years after KCE:

Kenya

Graded Principal passes 'A' level and Subsidiary General Paper.

A 6
B 5
C 4
D 3
E 2
0 1
    (Subsidiary pass not Principal pass)

Higher

Bachelor degrees are classified:

First Class Honours
Second Class Honours (upper division)
Second Class Honours (lower division)
Pass

SCHOOL EDUCATION

Pre-primary

There is relatively little government provision and pre-school education in urban centres is provided by the private sector.

Primary

Before 1963: this covered 8 years.

From 1964-84: this covered 7 years (standards I-VII) from age 6.

Until 1967: pupils took the **Kenya Preliminary Examination** (KPE) on completion of standard VII; and until 1984 they took examinations for the **Certificate of Primary Education** (CPE).

In November 1985 the pupils (after standard VIII) took examinations for the **Kenya Certificate of Primary Education** as the first group of primary pupils who will go through the new 8:4:4 education system launched in 1985.

In this examination there are 9 papers in mathematics, science, English, Kiswahili, geography, history, music, home science, arts and crafts.

Pupils may proceed to secondary school depending on the results of these examinations, those who do not qualify for secondary education will have been equipped for craft training. This is a major aim of the 8:4:4 system.

Secondary

Until 1989 the secondary course will last for 6 years, covering 4 years lower secondary followed by 2 years upper.

Kenya

Lower secondary:

From 1966, pupils could obtain the **Kenya Junior Secondary Examination** in non-government aided schools (private and Harambee) at the end of the second year of secondary school.

After the Kenya Junior Secondary Examination some pupils leave school for employment but most continue to complete 4 years of secondary education.

To obtain the Kenya Junior Certificate, pupils have to pass in at least 5 of 7 subjects, and have at least 1 pass in each of 3 groups of subjects:

English, Swahili
Mathematics, general science, biology
Geography, history.

After 4 years students are entered for the **Kenya Certificate of Education** offered by the Kenya National Examinations Council. All candidates are required to sit 6-9 subjects at their first attempt. The subjects are divided into 8 groups: English language, humanities, mathematics, science subjects, languages, cultural subjects, technical subjects, and business studies. All candidates have to enter for at least 1 subject from each of the first 4 groups.

Successful candidates are classified into 4 divisions, based on a point system (see **MARKING SYSTEMS**).

2 years after Kenya Certificate of Education, students may enter for the **Kenya Advanced Certificate of Education**. Candidates sit a general paper designed to test their ability to express themselves in continuous prose and to analyse, interpret and draw conclusions from data. There are papers in either 3 or 4 subjects, of which at least 2 must be attempted at Principal level and up to 2 at Subsidiary level. Some candidates are entered by private schools for the **University of London GCE examinations** in January and February each year.

Brief history of the examination system in secondary schools

Until 1968: On completion of form 4 pupils took an externally set examination known as the Joint Examination for the **School Certificate and General Certificate of Education of the University of Cambridge**. The certificate was awarded in divisions I, II or III, reflecting overall performance.

1968-70: The **East African Certificate of Education**, was administered by the University of Cambridge in collaboration with the newly established East African Examinations Council. Pupils had to take English language and 5 and 8 other subjects. Those who achieved at the same examination a pass with credit (grade 6 or better), 2 passes (grade 7) or 3 passes (grade 8) were awarded an East African Certificate of Education which incorporated a General Certificate of Education. (The certificate was not awarded in divisions.)

1971: The **Joint Examination for the East African Certificate of Education and School Certificate**, was administered by the University of Cambridge in collaboration with the East African Examinations Council.

1974-80: In 1974 the East African Examinations Council took sole control of the examinations for the **East African Certificate of Education**.

Kenya

From 1980: The examinations for the **Kenya Certificate of Education** were first held in November 1980, and are based on the same syllabuses as those in use under the East African Examinations Council. Pupils take a maximum of 9 subjects. The curriculum of forms 1-4 covers mathematics, physics, chemistry, biology, Kiswahili, English, French, history, geography, religious instruction, physical education, art, music, home science, agricultural science, industrial education and business education.

Upper secondary:

This covers forms 5 and 6. There are 2 streams in form 6 - arts and science. On completion of form 6, pupils take examinations (usually in 3 subjects) plus a general paper. Until 1974, pupils took the **Cambridge Overseas Higher School Certificate** (COHSC) examinations; from 1974 to 1980, those for the **East African Advanced Certificate of Education** (EAACE); and from 1980, those for the **Kenya Advanced Certificate of Education** (KACE).

With the implementation of the new 8 years of primary education, the pattern of examinations will be as follows:

From 1985, after 8 years of primary education, a pupil will sit for the **Kenya Certificate of Primary Education**.

In 1989, pupils who enter form 1 in 1986 will sit for the **Certificate of Secondary Education** after 4 years of secondary education.

Both examinations will be administered by the **Kenya National Examination Council**.

In 1990, those who sat for CSE will enter the University to commence 4 years of degree studies for general degrees.

There will be no forms 5 and 6 in 1991.

Technical secondary

There are 14 secondary technical schools. These offer courses which consist of a group of basic general and scientific subjects, together with options in engineering, building, tailoring or business studies. These subjects are examined at **Kenya Certificate of Education** and the skill level demanded is equivalent to a Grade III trade test.

Classes are from forms 1 to 6. Forms 5 and 6 pupils are accepted for pure science subjects in physics, mathematics, chemistry and biology.

There are no technical subjects at the Kenya Advanced Certificate of Education examination level. Students who complete 4 years of secondary technical education may enter the polytechnics for the **Ordinary Diploma** in various options.

Craft training centres

Craft training centres, also known as village polytechnics, provide low-level craft training, largely for those in rural areas who have completed primary education.

On passing the government trade test, students may take up an apprenticeship or begin technician training at one of the 2 polytechnics.

Kenya

FURTHER EDUCATION

Harambee Institutes of Technology

These institutes provide training for school leavers with Kenya Certificate of Education, equipping them for employment in medium- and large-scale industry. As Harambee institutes, they have been set up through local initiative. There are 15 institutes registered with the Ministry of Education, and 11 offer examinable courses.

Courses last 2-4 years and cover such subjects as construction, mechanical engineering, business studies, textiles, agriculture, electrical engineering, home management. On completion, students receive a recognized technician/skill certificate.

Polytechnics

At present there are 2 polytechnics: the Kenya Polytechnic in Nairobi and the Mombasa Polytechnic, but plans are well advanced to develop a third polytechnic at Eldoret, opening in 1987.

The polytechnics offer a wide range of technical and business courses at post-Kenya Certificate of Education level, leading to certificates and diplomas in subjects such as accounts, business administration and institutional management. Most courses taken at the Kenya Polytechnic are examined by the Kenya National Examinations Council and Kenya Accountants and Secretaries Examination Board. Some courses are run by the City and Guilds of London Instiute (they may be taken in conjunction with locally run examinations).

HIGHER EDUCATION

There are 3 universities: the University of Nairobi, Kenyatta University and Moi University at Eldoret.

University of Nairobi

Known before independence as the Royal Technical College of East Africa, and the Royal College of Nairobi - later became a constituent College of the University of East Africa as University College Nairobi; attained full independent status through an Act of Parliament in 1970 as the University of Nairobi.

The entrance requirement for a Bachelor degree is a minimum of 5 Ordinary-level passes at Kenya Certificate of Education and 2 Principal passes at Kenya Advanced Certificate of Education.

Bachelor degrees with Honours (there are no Ordinary degrees) are generally obtained after 3 years, including those in law and engineering; veterinary medicine takes 4 years, and architecture and medicine 5 years

Master degrees in architecture, humanities, law, commerce, science, engineering, medicine and education take 1-3 years.

Holders of a Master degree take a minimum of 2 years research to obtain a **Ph.D**.

Kenya

The University has faculties of Agriculture, Architecture, Design and Development, Arts, Commerce, Engineering, Law, Medicine, Science and Veterinary Medicine. There are also Institutes of Adult Studies, African Studies, Computer Science, Development Studies, Population Studies and a School of Journalism. All faculties award undergraduate and postgraduate degrees and diplomas. The University Institutes offer postgraduate degrees through research, except the Institute of Adult Studies which runs a 1-year diploma course in Adult Education and the Institute of Computer Science which offers a 1-year (4 term) diploma course in Computer Science. The School of Journalism awards a postgraduate diploma in Mass Communications.

Kenyatta University

From 1978 to 1985, Kenyatta University College was a constituent college of the University of Nairobi, incorporating the University's Faculty of Education.

In September 1985, it achieved independent status as a university, and its major function is the training of teachers, largely for the secondary sector, at undergraduate, diploma and postgraduate levels.

Most students at Kenyatta University read for a B.Ed. The entry requirement for this 3-year course is a minimum of 2 principal subjects at Kenya Advanced Certificate of Education. The entry requirement for all the universities will change in 1991, when a new group of 8:4:4 will complete secondary education after 4 years, and not proceed to forms 5 and 6.

One third of the students' time is spent on educational studies, and the rest on the 2 Principal subjects they will teach at Kenya Certificate of Education level.

The University also offers a 2-year **Master degree** and a 1-year **Postgraduate Diploma in Education**.

Moi University

This new university opened in September 1984 with the transfer of the Department of Forestry from Nairobi University, now called the Faculty of Forestry Resources and Wildlife Management. Plans exist for 11 more faculties, with a concentration on scientific and technological subjects.

TEACHER EDUCATION

Primary

There are 15 primary school teachers colleges. All students admitted to teacher training colleges hold the Kenya Certificate of Education and have completed 4 years of secondary education. The teacher training course lasts 2 years, at the end of which students are awarded a P1, P2 or P3 certificate, depending on their success in centrally set examinations.

Kenya

Secondary

Kenya Technical Teachers College

This college was established with Canadian aid in 1978 to train technical teachers at **Diploma** level. It offers a 1-year course for the technically experienced and a 3-year course for those with no technical background. Teachers are trained for teaching technical, industrial and business studies in secondary and technical schools and institutes of technology.

Kenya Science Teachers College

This college trains science teachers for secondary schools. Before 1983, it admitted students with Kenya Certificate of Education for a 3-year course leading to an S1 qualification, and those with Kenya Advanced Certificate of Education for a 2-year course leading to a diploma. The S1 course was phased out in 1983, and the college now admits only the Kenya Advanced Certificate of Education students for a 2-year **Teaching Diploma**. The college was established by Swedish aid in 1966 and is now staffed entirely by Kenyans.

There are 4 other colleges for teacher training established in 1983, and all admit students after the Kenya Advanced Certificate of Education for a 2-year course: they are Kagumo, Kisii, Siriba and Moi Eldoret.

Kenyatta University

Formerly known as Kenyatta University College, a constituent college of the University of Nairobi, incorporating the University's Faculty of Education, Kenyatta University achieved independent status in 1985. A major function of the Kenyatta University is training teachers, largely for the secondary sector, at undergraduate, diploma and postgraduate levels (see HIGHER EDUCATION).

Agricultural training institutes

There are 5 such institutes: Egerton College, which admits students after the Kenya Advanced Certificate of Education diploma; Jomo Kenyatta College of Agriculture and Technology; Embu Institute of Agriculture; Bukura Institute of Agriculture; and the Animal Health and Training Institute at Kabete. The first 2 colleges run **3-year Diploma** courses and the last 3 **2-year Certificate** courses. Training is designed to produce a middle-level workforce and to provide teachers for schools and farmers' training institutes. The minimum entry requirement for all courses is the Kenya Certificate of Education.

South Korea

Republic of Korea

From 1910 to 1945 Korea was a Japanese colony. In 1945 the country was liberated by US and Soviet forces and subsequently divided into the Republic of Korea in the south and the Democratic People's Republic of Korea in the north. The system of education in the Republic of Korea has been influenced recently by the USA. It was previously modelled on the Japanese education system.

Education is compulsory from age six to twelve.

The medium of instruction is Korean. English is a compulsory subject at secondary school.

The academic year runs from March to December.

EVALUATION IN BRITAIN

School

High School Leaving Certificate - generally considered to compare to GCE O-level standard.

Higher

Bachelor degree - generally considered to be below British Bachelor degree standard.

MARKING SYSTEMS

School

There are no uniform grades in Korean secondary schools. The marking system may be lettered:

A	pass
B	pass
C	pass
D	pass
E	fail

South Korea

or numerical:

1 - 100 (maximum)

Higher

90-100%	A
80- 89	B
70- 79	C
60- 69	D
0- 59	F

SCHOOL EDUCATION

Primary

Compulsory elementary education lasts 6 years. Pupils concentrate on basic literacy and mathematical skills. The curriculum also covers moral education, Korean, social ethics, arithmetic, natural science, physical education, music and fine arts. English may be taught in grades 4-6 of elementary school. Success in the **Middle School Entrance Examination** granted access to middle school until it was abolished in 1968. A lottery system was then adopted to assign grade 6 children to middle school.

Elementary civic school

5 civic schools offer an elementary curriculum to those who are unable to obtain an elementary education. These used to cater mainly for illiterate adults, but now most of the students are children. After the third year, students can take the **Elementary School Equivalence Examination**. Successful candidates may continue their education in middle school or higher civic school.

Lower secondary education

Middle school

Middle schools offer a 3-year course (grades 7-9).

The curriculum concentrates on English and mathematics, although 11 academic subjects are covered.

Higher civic school

These offer a 3-year course of study, catering for employed students who can only attend at night. Volunteer or part-time teachers are often employed. At the end of the third year, students can take the **Middle-School Equivalence Examination**, success in which grants access to high school education.

South Korea

Upper secondary education

This is provided in academic high schools and vocational schools. The competitive high school entrance examinations were abolished in 1973. At present, students take a single qualifying examination. Those who are successful are allocated to a local school by means of a lottery system, designed to deter parents from choosing prestigious high schools for their children.

Academic high school

During the second year, students may choose to specialize in humanities or sciences. Studies are organized according to the credit system, each subject being allocated a number of credits on successful completion. Students must accumulate 200-214 credits for graduation.

Vocational high school

These are divided into 8 categories: trade, marine, arts, consolidated, agriculture, technical, commercial, and fisheries.

Although most vocational high-school graduates follow a vocational course, they may complete a course of study similar to that offered by the academic high schools. Such students are eligible to apply for higher education and teacher training. Those who follow a purely vocational course are eligible for higher education.

Technical high school

These should be distinguished from the ordinary academic and vocational schools. They offer courses equivalent to a high school education (with little emphasis on academic subjects) to graduates of middle schools and higher civic schools.

Students who fail to reach a certain standard of education may receive a certificate of attendance (Chulsuk Chung).

HIGHER EDUCATION

There are 5 categories of higher education:

1. colleges and universities (4-year undergraduate courses, except for 6-year medical colleges)
2. junior colleges for elementary teacher training (now being updated from 2 to 4 years)
3. junior vocational colleges (2 years)
4. miscellaneous schools of collegiate standing (2- or 4-year courses)
5. Air and Correspondence College.

Institutions of higher education are supervised by the Ministry of Education.

South Korea

Four-year colleges and universities

Students wishing to enter the 4-year colleges and universities must take the preparatory qualifying examination, the mark in which is considered along with the candidate's high school record. Students who are successful can apply for a second group of universities.

Subjects studied in the 4-year colleges and universities are marked according to the credit system. 1 credit hour is awarded for 1 hour of class a week (except in laboratory training, physical education and military training, which require 2 hours per week for 1 credit). Before 1973, 160 credits were required for graduation; this was then reduced to 140.

To graduate in dentistry and in medicine, 180 credits are needed. The course lasts 6 years full-time.

A minimum of 8 semesters residence is needed to satisfy graduation requirements, regardless of whether the required number of credits is obtained before this time.

Progression to postgraduate study is by graduation (accumulation of 140 credits) and a qualifying test.

Master degrees are obtained by satisfactory completion of 24 credits over 2 years and the submission of a thesis. Students can sit no more than 12 credits per year.

A further 36 credits over 3 years are required for a **Ph.D.**

A Ph.D. candidate must also demonstrate fluency in 2 foreign languages, pass an oral examination and submit a doctoral dissertation.

Junior technical colleges and **Junior vocational colleges**

Until 1966, Korean junior technical colleges were known as 'vocational higher schools'. They offer 2-year courses, as do the junior vocational colleges, and concentrate on technology, nursing and agriculture.

The junior technical colleges accept high-school graduates who have taken the preparatory examination. The junior vocational colleges are open only to high-school graduates.

Junior college

The Korean Ministry of Education considers the courses offered in the junior colleges as an introduction to the 4-year courses offered at the universities and 4-year colleges. The junior colleges must dedicate 40% of the curriculum to general studies (comparable to the first 2 years of the 4-year tertiary college course).

TEACHER EDUCATION

Before 1961, teachers were trained in normal schools, junior teachers' colleges and 4-year colleges of education. The normal schools, which were abolished in 1961, offered prospective elementary teachers a 3-year course of post-middle-school training. The junior teachers' colleges, which provided training for middle-school teachers, became junior teacher-training colleges.

Elementary

The system of teacher training was radically altered in 1961. Elementary school teachers needed a minimum of 2 years higher education. 2-year colleges of education were created, now known as junior teacher-training colleges; these are now being upgraded to 4-year colleges. Thus, teachers in elementary, middle and high school undergo the same period of training.

Prospective elementary school teachers must pass the **Preparatory Examination** (see **HIGHER EDUCATION**). Successful graduates must teach in the elementary school to which they are assigned for a minimum of 2 years after graduation if they have attended a national college.

Middle

Middle-school teachers must have a 4-year Bachelor degree and be qualified in a particular field.

High

High-school teachers must be graduates of a 4-year college and be adequately trained in a particular subject.

ADULT EDUCATION

The Air and Correspondence College

This institution was created in 1972. There are a number of radio and correspondence high schools. Students follow courses either by listening to broadcasts or through 4 weeks of regular class attendance.

Saemaul school

The Saemaul (New Village) Movement was launched in 1970. These schools, generally attached to vocational high schools or middle schools, offer 3-day training courses to the local inhabitants.

Adult education classes are also provided at primary school during the winter vacation.

Kuwait

State of Kuwait

The education system of Kuwait is highly centralized, including central control of curriculum at school level. Although there are private schools, under the Private Schools Law of 1968, they may open only with Ministry approval. Private Arab schools must prepare pupils for the Ministry-run examinations and use textbooks chosen by the Ministry. In foreign schools, Arabic language and religion must be taught.

Private English-medium schools prepare students for British O- and A-level examinations, and sometimes for the International Baccalaureat.

Compulsory education is from age six for eight years.

The medium of instruction is Arabic, although English is used in the Faculties of Science, Engineering, Medicine and Graduate Studies. English is compulsory at school from the beginning of the intermediate stage to the end of the secondary cycle.

The academic year runs from September/October to June and consists of two semesters.

EVALUATION IN BRITAIN

School

General Secondary Education Certificate (Shahadat-al-thanawia-al-a'ama) - generally compared to GCE O-level standard on a subject-for-subject basis, for marks of at least 50% in subjects which may be taken in the GCE examinations (except English language).

Further

Diploma in Applied Business Studies - is generally compared to the BTEC National Diploma (formerly OND).

Diploma in Applied Technology - is generally compared to the BTEC National Diploma (formerly OND).

Higher

Bachelor degree - generally considered to fall between GCE A-level and a British Bachelor degree standards; some students have been accepted for postgraduate study in Britain.

Master degree - comparable to British Bachelor (Honours) degree standard.

Kuwait

MARKING SYSTEMS

School

This varies according to subject; minimum and maximum marks are noted on the transcript. The column headed '2nd session' on a transcript of marks refers to marks obtained in examinations retaken.

Higher

Before September 1975:

90-100%   distinction/excellent

(first-class honours if the grade of distinction was obtained in the final year and no yearly grade was below very good; second-class honours if the grade of distinction was obtained in the final year and no yearly grade was below good)

80-89%   very good

(second-class honours if the grade of very good was obtained in the final year, and no yearly grade was below good)

70-79%   good
60-69%   pass
below 60%   fail

Since September 1975:

The grade determination is based 50% on the semester's work and 50% on the final examination.

A	9	excellent
A-	8	excellent
B+	7	very good
B	6	very good
B-	5	very good
C+	4	good
C	3	good
D+	2	pass
D	1	pass
F		fail

SCHOOL EDUCATION

Pre-primary

Some facilities are available for the 2-year courses for children aged 4-5.

Kuwait

Primary

This lasts 4 years from age 6. The curriculum includes Islamic religion, Arabic, music, arithmetic, elementary science, drawing, physical education and (for girls) needlework.

Intermediate

The curriculum includes Arabic language and history, social studies (including geography), science (including physics, chemistry and biology), physical education, Islamic religion, mathematics, and English as a foreign language. Practical studies (e.g. woodwork and needlework) are optional. Those who achieve 50%+ in Arabic and religious studies and 40%+ in the other academic subjects go on to the secondary cycle. Assessment is school-based and consists of formal examinations amd continuous assessment. Pupils obtain the **Intermediate School Certificate**.

Secondary

Pupils continue with the same subjects as in the intermediate school for the first 2 years, specializing in literature (arts) or science for the final 2 years. Literature streams study French as a foreign language in addition to English. In the **Shahadat-al-thanawia-al-a'ama** (General Secondary School Certificate), subjects are marked on a percentage basis and various averages on the whole examination are specified as part of the entry requirements to tertiary education.

A student who fails to achieve the minimum pass mark in up to 2 subjects in any year, can retake in September. If 3 or more examinations are failed, the whole year is repeated.

Since 1973, 6 intermediate and secondary schools have followed an experimental unit/credit-based syllabus and assessment programme. At the time of writing the programme was being evaluated and no decision to extend this experiment to other schools had been taken.

Technical secondary

This has been phased out, but the following were available:

Technical College

This was established in 1954 to provide technical education for Kuwaiti and other Gulf boys who had completed primary education. It offered a 2-year course leading to the **Technical Intermediate Certificate** and a 4-year course leading to the **Technical Secondary School Certificate**. In 1960, admission was restricted to those who had completed 3 years intermediate education.

In 1960, 2 streams were introduced. Pupils entered on completion of the intermediate cycle. After a common first-year they might take a 3-year course leading to pre-technician status in mechanics, electricity and building, or to craft proficiency. Neither entitled the pupil to go on to university.

Girls Technical Secondary School

In 1956 the Training Centre for Girls was established. It became the Girls' Technical Secondary School in 1968, offering a 4-year course. Pupils could specialize in secretarial, clerical and commercial work, social service, domestic economics, child-care or laboratory assistant work.

Kuwait

Commercial

Commercial education was offered at intermediate level until 1972. In 1962 the Commercial Secondary School opened, replacing an evening institute established in 1955 to provide instruction (for boys only) in accountancy, banking, secretarial skills, business administration and general studies.

Vocational

For Kuwaiti and Arab Gulf students only:

Telecommunications Training Institute, established 1966

Institute of Applied Engineering, established 1968

(Both offer 2-year technician courses from the entrance requirement of the **Secondary School Certificate**, and 1-year assistant technician courses from the level of the **Intermediate School Certificate**.)

Vocational Training Centre, established in 1971 to provide accelerated artisan training for intermediate school-leavers. Courses consist of 6 months general studies followed by: 1 year of studies in auto/diesel, machine shop fitting, air-conditioning/refrigeration, welding/sheet metal or heavy/light electricity; or 2 years study of radio/television or instrumentation.

FURTHER EDUCATION

This consists of a 2-year (4-semester) cycle at the following institutes:

Kuwait Institute of Applied Technology (men only), established 1968 to train technicians in mechanics, construction, electricity, electronics and chemical technology. The qualification obtained is the **Diploma in Applied Technology**.

Kuwait Business Institute, established in 1975 to train middle-level executives in courses leading to a **Diploma in Applied Business Studies**.

Health Institute, established in 1974 to train nurses and allied health technicians. The qualification obtained is the **Major in General Nursing**.

Kuwait Business School for Girls.

All the institutes teach and assess students through the unit/credit system, and courses/semesters may be repeated up to a maximum enrolment period of 8 semesters (4 years).

Kuwait

HIGHER EDUCATION

The <u>University of Kuwait</u> was founded in 1966 with Colleges of Science, Art and Education, and a residential University College for Women. Colleges of Law and Shari'a (Islamic Law) and of Commerce, Economics and Political Science were added in 1967. The first students of the College of Engineering and Petroleum were admitted in 1975, and the College of Medicine opened in 1976. The College of Higher Education (Graduate Studies) was established in 1977, and the College of Education was separated from Arts and began its own degree courses in 1981. The College of Medicine uses a system of assessment involving external examiners. A proposal to extend this system to all the colleges is under discussion.

The entrance requirements to undergraduate courses are the **General School Certificate**, with minimum average marks laid down by each department (e.g. 75% for medicine), and a competitive university entrance examination in which applicants exceed available places.

The unit/credit system for courses has been followed since 1975 in all departments. A **Bachelor degree** takes 4 years for all departments, except for Engineering (5 years) and Medicine (7 years).

The **Master degree** (2 years full-time or up to 4 years part-time) is available in course-plus-thesis form for chemistry, mathematics and physics. Other Master programmes are in preparation. There is no Ph.D.

Credits required for graduation (departments' requirements varying) are:

Colleges of Arts, Education, Law and Commerce	120-126
College of Science	132-137
College of Engineering	144
College of Medicine	121 (during the 4-year academic programme plus final examinations in the second and third clinical years)
College of Graduate Studies	30 credits (including 9 for thesis)

Study load is usually 12-16 credit-hours per semester (with minima of 10-13). The minimum and maximum periods for graduation are 7 and 14 semesters respectively. The system considers students with the following credit-hours:

less than 24	first academic year
24-56	second academic year
57-89	third academic year
90+	fourth academic year

A student whose grade-point average falls below 3 at the end of a semester, may be put on probation for up to 2 semesters and asked to withdraw if the required improvement has not occurred.

TEACHER EDUCATION

Primary

Before 1972: a 4-year course at secondary level from the entrance requirement of the **Intermediate School Certificate** was available at 1 of the 2 teacher-training institutes. The first 2 years were spent on general education.

Since 1972: a 2-year course from the **General Secondary Education Certificate** is available at the Teacher Training Institute for Men or the Teacher Training Institute for Women.

Intermediate

Before 1972: holders of the **General Secondary Education Certificate** could take a 2-year course at an intermediate teacher-training college.

Since 1972: teachers must be graduates.

Secondary

Teachers are graduates. The College of Arts of Kuwait University has courses leading to the **General Diploma in Education** and **Special Diploma in Education** in addition to the BA for students who want a teaching degree.

The College of Education of Kuwait University began its undergraduate teaching programme in 1981, offering 4-year courses leading to **teaching degrees** at all levels of general education (kindergarten to secondary), with majors in each subject in the intermediate and secondary school curriculum.

Lebanon

Lebanese Republic

There are three kinds of school in Lebanon today: public, private tuition-free, and private fee-based. Private tuition-free education is available only at the pre-primary and primary levels, and schools in this category are most often sponsored by religious and philanthropic institutions.

The Lebanese school system is based on the French system.

Education is not compulsory.

The media of instruction are Arabic, French and English in private schools and Arabic and French or Arabic and English in state schools.

The academic year runs from October to June.

EVALUATION IN BRITAIN

School

Baccalaureat (Part 2) - generally compared to GCE O-level standard.

Higher

Bachelor degree - unlikely to be considered comparable to British Bachelor degree standard.

MARKING SYSTEMS

School

The grading system is usually based on a scale of 1-20, with some private schools using a 0-100 or A-F scale.

18-20	excellent
15-17	very good
12-14	good
10-11	pass
0-9	fail

Higher

The American University of Beirut uses the following scale:

90-100%	A	excellent
80- 89	B	good
70- 79	C	fair
60- 69	D	weak
0- 59	F	fail

The grading systems used by the other institutions of higher education are not known.

SCHOOL EDUCATION

Primary

This lasts 5 years (grades 1-5). At the end of this period students used to take the **Certificat d'Etudes Primaires**, success in which granted access to secondary education; in 1970 this examination was abolished.

Intermediate

3 different tracks are offered:

lower secondary is a 4-year academic course designed to prepare students for the Baccalaureat

upper primary consists of 3 years similar to lower secondary and a fourth year of preparation for entering vocational schools or teacher-training institutes

vocational study is a 3-year practical course for lower grades; at the end of this cycle, students receive an academic, technical or professional **Brevet**, depending upon the track.

Secondary

Upper secondary education covers a 3-year cycle. 3 tracks are available:

3-year training programme for prospective primary and intermediate school teachers leading to a **Teaching Diploma**

vocational track for such trades as business, tourism, electronics, advertising, nursing, and mechanics; students take the **Technical Baccalaureat II** exams

academic track leading to the **Baccalaureat I** at the end of the eleventh school year and the **Baccalaureat II** at the end of the twelfth school year. The **Baccalaureat II** is necessary for government employment and institutions of higher education. It represents an additional year of secondary school.

General

Students who follow a general academic course of education take the **Baccalaureat (Part 1)** after 2 years of the 3-year cycle. The **Baccalaureat** examinations are general examinations involving 7 or 8 subjects. In the **Baccalaureat (Part 1)**, students choose 1 of 3 options: science, literature or ancient languages. At the end of the 3-year cycle, students take the examinations for the **Baccalaureat (Part 2)** in 2 of 3 specializations: experimental sciences, mathematics, or philosophy. Success in these examinations satisfies university entrance requirements.

Technical and Vocational

There is no technical or vocational education in general schools. The Directorate of Technical Education runs separate technical and vocational schools. Agricultural Colleges are run by the Ministry of Agriculture. The government examinations are the only recognized technical qualifications. Both private and state technical and vocational schools are authorized only to issue **Attestations** (stating that students have attended and successfully completed courses). The official certificates are awarded by the Ministry of Education (Directorate of Technical Education) to students who take the official government examinations.

Technical education is provided at upper secondary level; the **Baccalaureat Technique II** is awarded to students completing a 3-year course. Vocational education is offered at intermediate level; students follow a 3-year cycle leading to the **Brevet Professional**. Before 1980 the **Baccalaureat Technique I** was taken after 2 years study and the **Baccalaureat Technique II** after a further 2 years. The **Technicien Superieur** is awarded to students who are at least 20 years old and have completed 2 years of training past Baccalaureat Technique II.

HIGHER EDUCATION

There are 16 colleges and universities, and all but the Lebanese University are privately owned and run.

Some institutions offer short courses (2-3 years) leading to professional qualifications. Where longer studies are involved, the first stage leads after 3-5 years study to the **Licence**, Bachelor degree or **Maitrise** (in science) or **Diploma**, depending on the institution attended. In medicine the first degree and professional qualification is called the **Doctorat** and is awarded after 7 years study. The second stage involves more specialized work and leads to the **Maitrise** (in non-scientific subjects), the **Master degree** at the American University, the **Diplome d'Etudes Superieures**, the **Attestation d'Etudes Approfondies** (engineering), the **Doctorat de Troisieme Cycle** or the **Doctorat d'Universite**.

The third stage of higher education involves writing a thesis, followed by the award of a **Doctorate**.

Lebanon

The Lebanese University offers a 4- to 5-year **Licence** course. Teaching is in Arabic, French or English, depending on the faculty.

The Beirut Arab University operates on a charter from the University of Alexandria, with which it closely collaborates. It offers a 4-year degree course. Arabic is the medium of instruction in all but the Departments of English and Architecture, where courses are in English.

The American University of Beirut is affiliated to New York State University. Entrance requirements are satisfied by the Baccalaureat (Part 2) and an English language test. Some applicants must take the AVB Scientific-Quantative General Test. The university offers a 4-year Bachelor degree and postgraduate courses (based on the credit system). The medium of instruction is English.

The Universite St Joseph is administered by the Society of Jesus and has strong links with the University of Lyons. French is the primary language of instruction. Degrees awarded include 2-year Diplomas, the Licence, Maitrise, Higher Diplomas and Doctoral degrees.

Holy Spirit University of Kaslik was founded as a Maronite seminary in 1808, and in 1962 was recognized by the Lebanese Ministry of Education. Its curriculum has slowly expanded to include subjects other than theology. French is the primary language of instruction, although English is increasingly important.

The most important degree colleges include: Beirut University College (mainly for women, affiliated to New York State University and offering American-type courses up to Bachelor degree level), the Armenian Haigazian College (an English-medium institution offering Bachelor degrees), and the Centre d'Etudes Superieures (affiliated to the University of Lyons and offering a 4-year **Licence**).

TEACHER EDUCATION

Primary

Prospective primary school teachers take a 3-year diploma course, leading to the **teacher-training Baccalaureat**. The Brevet d'Etudes Elementaires satisfies entrance requirements.

Secondary

At the lower secondary level a preliminary experimental course to produce mathematics and science teachers began in 1971 with Unesco assistance.

The Faculty of Education at the Lebanese University offers 5-year courses for prospective secondary school teachers leading to the **Certificat d'Aptitude Pedagogique de l'Enseignement Secondaire** (CAPES). **Postgraduate Diplomas** in Education are offered by the American University of Beirut. **Bachelor degrees in Education** are offered by Beirut University College. There is no provision for teaching practice during the diploma courses.

Lesotho

Kingdom of Lesotho

Educational facilities are limited, and no sector is compulsory. Many schools are run by missions or are private. Lesotho was closely connected with Botswana and Swaziland until it established its own university in 1975; the links are now more informal.

English is the medium of instruction and examination.

The academic year runs from mid-August to mid-May.

EVALUATION IN BRITAIN

School

Cambridge Overseas School Certificate - grades 1-6 are equated to pass grades in GCE O-level (grades A, B, C).

Higher

Part 1 (i.e. the first 2 years) of a degree course at the University of Botswana, Lesotho and Swaziland or the National University of Lesotho is generally considered to compare to GCE A-level standard.

Part 2 (i.e. the remaining 2 years) of a degree course is generally considered to compare to a standard between GCE A-level and a British Bachelor degree.

MARKING SYSTEM

School

Cambridge Overseas School Certificate is graded 1 (maximum) to 9 as follows:

1 excellent, 2-3 good, 3-6 credit, 7-8 pass, 9 fail.

Higher

Before 1967:

A	pass with distinction
B	pass
C	fail

Since 1967:

Part 1 and Part 2 examinations are classified:

80% +	A	excellent
70-79%	B	very good
60-69%	C	good
50-59%	D	pass
40-49%	E	fail (but can take supplementary examination)
below 39%	F	complete fail

The degrees are classified:

First class	A average
Second class first division	B average
Second class second division	C average
Pass	D average
Fail	E, F average

SCHOOL EDUCATION

Primary

This covers 7 years, leading to the **Standard 7 Leaving Certificate**. Lesotho is the medium of instruction for the first 2 years and sometimes 3, with English being used for the remaining 3 or 4 years.

Secondary

Pupils who pass the standard 7 examination are eligible to enter secondary school, although places are limited.

Pupils may enter either a <u>junior secondary school</u> which offers 3 years of secondary schooling up to the level of the **Junior Certificate**, or a <u>high school</u> which offers 5 years to the level of the **Cambridge Overseas School Certificate**. The examination for the Junior Certificate is set and marked by the Examinations Council of Lesotho and Swaziland. Compulsory subjects are English, Sesotho, mathematics, science and development studies. The medium of instruction is English.

Technical/vocational secondary

Various home economics and craft schools and former training centres offer courses for standard 7 leavers.

Lesotho

Two trade schools offer courses for holders of the Junior Certificate.

FURTHER EDUCATION

Nurse-training schools offer courses for holders of either the Junior Certificate or Cambridge Overseas School Certificate.

The Agricultural College offers two-and-a-half-year courses in agriculture, agricultural engineering and rural domestic economy for holders of the Junior Certificate, and leads to the **Certificate in Agriculture** and the **Certificate in Home Economics**. It recently introduced a 2-year **Diploma** course in agriculture for holders of the Cambridge Overseas School Certificate.

The Lesotho Institute of Public Administration provides training for civil servants. Senior civil servants attend courses at the Institute of Development Management.

Lerotholi Polytechnic consists of a Technical Institute, a Technician Training Institute and a Commercial Training Institute, all of which accept school-leavers with either the junior certificate or the Cambridge Overseas School Certificate. The Polytechnic offers 3-year courses in building trades, mechanical, civil and electrical engineering, and courses of varying length in typing, bookkeeping, accounting and business studies, the former leading to the qualifications of the **City and Guilds of London Institute** and the latter being similar to **Royal Society of Arts** (RSA) courses. There is also a German project on the training of automobile mechanics.

HIGHER EDUCATION

Originally only one institution of higher education covered Lesotho and the neighbouring states of Botswana and Swaziland. The University of Botswana, Lesotho and Swaziland (UBLS) was founded as the Pius XII College in 1945. The administration of the college was assumed by the Missionary Oblates of Mary Immaculate, who established a link with the University of South Africa. The status of the College was then changed by royal charter to the University of Basutoland, Bechuanaland Protectorate and Swaziland (UBBS). When these territories became independent the institution became in 1966 the University of Botswana, Lesotho and Swaziland on a campus at Roma in Lesotho. The first degrees were conferred in 1967. In 1970 it was decided to decentralize the university and establish separate campuses in Botswana and Swaziland. In 1975 the campus at Roma became the National University of Lesotho.

The entrance requirement for degree courses at the University of Botswana, Lesotho and Swaziland and now the National University of Lesotho is the Cambridge Overseas School Certificate (1st or 2nd division) with credit in English language and mathematics. Courses leading to the award of a **BA**, **B.Com.** or **B.Sc.** last 4 years, and are divided into two 2-year parts, Part 1 and Part 2.

The **LL.B** takes a further 2 years (Part 3) for holders of a BA degree from that university, or 3 years for holders of other degrees or degrees from other institutions.

Lesotho

The University also offers diploma and certificate courses.

Taught courses of 2 years may lead to the award of an **M.Sc.** or **MA**, the MA may also be obtained by research.

TEACHER EDUCATION

Primary

The **Primary Teachers Certificate** (PTC) is obtained after 3 years study at the National Teachers Training College (NTTC). The entrance requirement is the Junior Certificate.

The **Advanced Primary Teachers Certificate** (APTC), intended to train headteachers of primary schools, is also obtained after 3 years study. The entrance requirement is the Cambridge Overseas School Certificate (Third class).

Secondary

The **Secondary Teachers Certificate** (STC), intended for those who have been trained as non-specialist teachers for the junior classes of secondary schools, is obtained after 3 years study for those holding the Cambridge Overseas School Certificate.

One year of these 3-year courses is spent on supervised teaching practice.

A 2-year in-service course for practising teachers leads to the **Lesotho In-Service Education for Teachers Certificate** (LIET). It is recognized in Lesotho only for salary purposes, not as raising a person's academic standard to any significant extent.

The **B.Ed.** degree obtained after 4 years study at the University qualifies teachers for higher secondary classes. Experienced teachers who already hold the Primary Teachers Certificate may obtain the degree after only 2 years study.

All students obtaining a degree at the University get a Concurrent **Certificate of Education** (CCE).

Liberia

Republic of Liberia

The curriculum and syllabuses at school level are controlled by the Ministry of Education. The system of higher education is modelled on the American system.

The medium of instruction is English.

The academic year runs from March to December.

EVALUATION IN BRITAIN

School

Senior High School Certificate - may be compared to GCE O-level standard.

Higher

Bachelor degree - unlikely to be considered comparable to British Bachelor degree standard.

MARKING SYSTEMS

School

Marking is on a percentage scale, pass mark 70%.

Higher

A	90-100
B	80-89
C	70-79
D	60-69
F	fail

Liberia

SCHOOL EDUCATION

Primary

This covers 6 years from age 6. From 1961 to 1973, pupils took the National Examination at the end of grade 6, but this has been abolished. Promotion to secondary school is now automatic.

Secondary

This covers 6 years, divided into 3-year cycles. The first cycle is the guidance cycle taken by all pupils, and during the second cycle pupils may specialize slightly.

In 1961, the Ministry of Education instituted the **National Examination** to be taken at the end of grades 6, 9 and 12 (now only 9 and 12) as a uniform means of comparing secondary school pupils. The examination is taken in 4 basic subject areas: mathematics, science, social studies, and language. At the end of grade 9 it leads to the **Junior High School Certificate** and at the end of grade 12 to the **Senior High School Certificate**. In awarding these certificates, some account is taken of marks obtained for course work.

Technical secondary

The Booker Washington Institute and the Liberian-Swedish Vocational Training Centre offer a variety of courses for holders of the Junior High School Certificate.

HIGHER EDUCATION

There are 3 institutions of higher education: the University of Liberia in Monrovia, Cuttington College (private, and linked to the Episcopalian Church), and Wm V.S. Tubman College of Technology in Cape Palmas. Entrance to degree courses is provided by the Senior High School Certificate plus an entrance examination in English and mathematics.

Bachelor degrees normally last 4 years, the first 2 years being spent on general studies and the liberal arts, and the last 2 on specialization. Degrees in law require 3 years of specialization.

Medical - degrees take 7 years: 3 years in natural sciences (i.e. 1 year of specialization) and 4 years in medical studies.

English and mathematics are compulsory during the first 2 years of the Bachelor degree.

There are no facilities for postgraduate study.

TEACHER EDUCATION

Primary

A 3-year upper secondary course at a teacher-training institute, leads to a **Lower Primary Teachers Certificate/Grade C Teaching Certificate**.

Secondary

Teachers are graduates; they may do a **B.Sc. in Education** (at William Tubman Teachers College, but awarded by the University), or undertake a 2-year course if they already hold a degree in another subject leading to a **Grade A Teaching Certificate**.

Libya

Socialist People's Libyan Arab Jamahiriya

Education is compulsory to age fifteen.

The medium of instruction is mainly Arabic, although English is sometimes used at higher education level.

The academic year runs from October to June.

EVALUATION IN BRITAIN

School

General Secondary Certificate - generally compared to GCE O-level on a subject-for-subject basis where marks of at least 50% have been obtained in subjects which can be taken in the GCE examinations, except English Language.

Higher

Bachelor degree - generally considered to be between GCE A-level and British Bachelor degree standards.

MARKING SYSTEMS

School

For every subject the minimum and maximum marks are shown on the certificate. In the literary branch of the secondary school, the maximum mark to be obtained is 260, the pass mark being 130. In the natural science branch the maximum is 330, and the minimum pass mark is 165.

Higher

Marking is on a percentage scale, with 50% as the minimum pass mark.

Libya

SCHOOL EDUCATION

Primary

This covers 6 years and pupils are tested annually.

Secondary

This covers 6 years divided into a 3-year preparatory/intermediate cycle and a 3-year secondary cycle. The curriculum for the first cycle covers religious education, Arabic, English, mathematics, science and health, art, agricultural education and home management, physical education, music.

The first year of the secondary cycle is common for all pupils, and covers religious education, Arabic, English, French, history, geography, physics, chemistry, biology, mathematics, art, physical education and military education. Pupils may then specialize in the literary or science branches. The literary branch covers history, geography, philosophy, sociology; the scientific branch covers physics, chemistry, biology and mathematics; the common subjects to both branches are: religious education, Arabic, English, French, physical education and military education. On completion of this cycle, pupils take the examinations for the **General Secondary Certificate**.

Technical secondary

This is offered at 2 levels:

Lower - a 4-year course for pupils who have completed primary education only, leading to a lower certificate.

Upper - a 4-year course for pupils who have completed intermediate education, leading to a higher certificate.

In both cases the 4-year course consists of 2 years general education followed by specialization in a particular field in the last 2 years.

The courses are offered by schools and specialist institutions.

The Institute of Petroleum in Tobruk was established in 1971 and trains skilled technicians on 2-year courses for pupils who have completed intermediate education.

HIGHER EDUCATION

The University of Libya was established in 1955. Since 1974 there have been 2 universities: the University of Garyounis at Benghazi and the University of Al Fateh at Tripoli. The University of Garyounis also has a campus at Beida, sometimes referred to as the Islamic University, founded in 1971 as a specialist religious institution, which also controls its own primary and secondary schools.

Libya

A 4-year course leads to a **Bachelor degree**, and a further 2 years to a **Master degree**. A **Doctorate** may be awarded after a further 2 years of research.

The <u>Higher College of Technology</u> was established in 1961 and offers 5-year courses in engineering and technological fields, leading to a professional qualification and a **Bachelor of Science** degree. The first year is common for all students.

TEACHER EDUCATION

Until the late 1960s teachers were mostly trained on completion of only 6 years primary education.

Primary/Preparatory/Intermediate

A 4-year secondary-level course is provided.

Secondary

A 4-year course at higher education level is provided.

Luxembourg

Grand Duchy of Luxembourg

During the 1960s a number of Acts were passed which affected almost every field of education. Under an Act of 1969, degrees and diplomas obtained at foreign universities are recognized in Luxembourg, as there is no institution offering a full course of higher education.

Compulsory education lasted eight years until 1963 when it was extended to nine years. Children now attend one year of compulsory education at pre-primary level.

The medium of instruction is Luxembourgeois at pre-primary and early primary level and is then replaced by German. French is taught intensively as a foreign language throughout the primary course.

The academic year runs from mid-September to mid-July.

EVALUATION IN BRITAIN

School

Diplome de Fin d'Etudes Secondaires - may be considered to satisfy the general requirement of universities and polytechnics.

MARKING SYSTEMS

School

On a scale of 1-60 (maximum)

Until 1970:

55-60	distingue
45-54	grand
30-44	satisfaisant
20-29	insuffisant
10-19	faible
1-9	tres faible

Luxembourg

Since 1971:

50-60	tres bien
40-49	bien
30-39	satisfaisant
20-29	insuffisant
1-19	mauvais

SCHOOL EDUCATION

Pre-primary

Some facilities are available for children aged 4-6 in kindergartens (<u>Jardins d'Enfants</u>. There is a compulsory 1-year course before primary school.

Primary (premier cycle de l'enseignement primaire)

This lasts 6 years. The curriculum covers religious instruction, Luxembourgeois, French, German, arithmetic, national history, geography, study of local environment, natural science, drawing, music, and physical education. On completion pupils obtain the **Certificat de Fin d'Etudes Primaires.**

Upper primary (deuxieme cycle de l'enseignement primaire/classes complementaires)

This covers 3 years for pupils who do not wish to proceed to secondary education but who must stay at school for a minimum of 9 years. In addition to general subjects, the curriculum covers metalwork and woodwork for boys, and home economics for girls, and includes some practical training. On completion, students obtain the **Certificat de Fin d'Etudes Complementaires.**

Further primary (enseignement primaire superieur)

This also covered 3 years for pupils not wishing to proceed to some form of secondary schooling. It was more academic than the classes complementaires, and the pupil was required to pass an entrance examination. These schools have been closing down since 1965 and replaced by intermediate schools (see below).

Secondary (l'enseignement secondaire)

Academic secondary school covers 7 years.

Before 1970:

Three types of course were available:

1. Classical education for boys, covering 7 years divided into 2 cycles of 2 and 5 years respectively. In the second cycle, pupils could specialize in Greek/Latin or Latin. From the fifth year, pupils specializing in Latin could once more specialize in Subsection A (languages/literature), Subsection B (mathematics) or Subsection C (natural science). From the sixth year, pupils in Subsection A could transfer to Subsection C.

Luxembourg

2. Modern education for boys, covering 6 years, was divided into 2 cycles of 3 years. Pupils had to pass an entrance examination to the second cycle, called the **Examen de Passage**. In this cycle they could specialize in the industrial section (bias towards science and mathematics) or commercial section (bias towards economics, commerce, and administration).

3. Secondary education for girls, covering 7 years divided into 2 cycles of 3 and 4 years respectively. Pupils had to pass an entrance examination to the second cycle, during which they could specialize in Latin or modern languages/commerce or modern languages (which was again subdivided into domestic science and commerce).

Since 1970:

Only 1 course is available. It lasts 7 years, and is divided into 2 cycles of 3 and 4 years respectively. Classes are numbered in descending order. Pupils must pass entrance examinations in German, French and arithmetic. The curriculum in the first year (classe d'orientation) is identical with the curriculum of the first year of the intermediate and technical schools. At the beginning of the second year (sixth class), pupils may specialize either in the classical branch (including the study of Latin) or in the modern (including the study of English). In the second cycle, pupils in the classical branch may specialize further in Latin and languages or Latin and sciences (with the option of taking mathematics or sciences or economics); pupils in the modern branch may specialize in modern languages (they must study a fourth modern language) or modern languages and sciences (with the option of mathematics, sciences or economics). The entrance examination to the second cycle (**Examen de Passage**) was abolished in 1974.

At the end of both cycles, pupils take the **Examen de Fin d'Etudes Secondaires** in the language in which each subject was taught in the last year of second cycle. Most pupils take examinations in French, German, English and philosophy. Pupils who specialize in mathematics or science are required to take only 2 modern languages. Depending on the specialization, pupils also take 3-5 subjects from: Greek, Latin, history, political economics, another modern language, mathematics, physics, chemistry, biology and economic science. Success in these examinations leads to the award of the **Diplome de Fin d'Etudes Secondaires**. The examinations may be retaken twice.

Intermediate

A 5-year intermediate course was introduced in 1965 which was divided into 2 cycles of 3 and 2 years respectively, the first cycle replacing the further primary courses. These courses are taken at the newly created <u>Colleges d'Enseignement Moyen</u>. The curriculum of the first cycle covers religious instruction, German, French, English (from the beginning of the second year), arithmetic, algebra, geometry, history, geography, natural science, civics, art, music, physical education and commercial practice. In the second cycle, pupils may specialize in the biological and social sciences (biology, anatomy and chemistry), commerce (bookkeeping, data-processing and typing), or technical studies (mathematics, physics and technical drawing). On completion of the course, pupils take examinations (in all subjects studied) for the **Certificat de Fin d'Etudes Moyennes**.

Technical secondary

Until 1979:

The Trade and Crafts School (<u>Ecole des Arts et Metiers</u>) ran a 4-year course for pupils who had completed 2 years of complementary classes. Pupils could specialize in building, mechanics, electrotechnics, and industrial machine tools.

Luxembourg

The technical schools offered a 5-year course for those who had completed primary school and who wished to become skilled workers or technicians. The course was divided into a 2-year cycle (d'orientation et d'observation), followed by 3 years of specialization (formation professionnelle), leading to the **Certificat d'Aptitude Professionnelle** (CAP). From 1970/1-79 pupils were able to follow a further 2-year cycle leading to the technicians certificate **Diplome de Technicien**.

Since 1979:

Under the new system technical secondary school is divided into 3 cycles:

Cycle d'observation et orientation

This is a 3-year course, following the sixth grade of primary school. The curriculum may be adapted according to the ability and needs of the individual. Pupils receive a certificate which confirms they have completed compulsory education.

Cycle moyen

This normally lasts 2-3 years and includes vocational training (regime professionnel) and technical courses (regime technique). Vocational courses are mainly apprenticeships and pupils normally study for 2 years and take 1 year of practical training. The qualification obtained on completion of the course is the **Certificat d'Aptitude Technique et Professionnelle** (CATP).

Cycle superieur

This lasts 2 years and leads to the following qualifications: **Certificat de Fin d'Etudes Secondaires Techniques** (in sciences, administration and technological subjects), the **Diplome de Technicien** (in agriculture, geology, chemistry, electrotechnics, mechanics and hotel business). These qualifications enable students to pursue their studies at a higher level in Luxembourg and abroad, or to begin work.

Vocational secondary (see **Technical secondary**, Cycle Moyen)

On completion of compulsory schooling apprenticeships in craft subjects last 2 to 2-and-a-half years, or 3 years in industry. They lead to the **Certificat d'Aptitude Technique Professionnelle** (CATP) or the **Certificat de Capacite Practique** (CCP), for those who do not pass the theoretical component of the course.

Full-time courses are available in business management, secretarial skills, retailing, hotel and catering, agriculture, and paramedical professions. Courses last 2-3 years (5 years for the paramedical professions) for pupils aged approximately 14.

FURTHER EDUCATION

Until 1979

On completion of 5 years intermediate secondary/technical studies, pupils could take a 4-year course leading to a **Higher Technician Diploma (Ingenieur Technicien)** at the Ecole Technique. The course was divided into a 1-year preparatory course, followed by

3 years specialization in civil engineering, mechanics, and electrotechnics. Before 1970, this course could be taken by holders of the Trade and Crafts School Leaving Certificate or on completion of 4 years secondary education.

Since 1979

The Grand-Ducal regulation concerning the establishment of the <u>Institut Superieur de Technologie</u> (IST) came into effect in September 1979. The IST, which replaces the <u>Ecole Technique</u>, is divided into 3 technical subject areas: mechanics, electrical engineering and civil engineering. Students with the following qualifications are admitted to IST: the Certificat de Fin d'Etudes Secondaires and the Certificat de Fin d'Etudes Secondaires Techniques. The studies at the IST last 3 years and lead to the **Diplome d'Ingenieur-Technicien (Higher Technician Diploma)**. This diploma usually allows students to enter professional life; but they may also continue their studies at a foreign university.

HIGHER EDUCATION

There is no university in Luxembourg, only a University Centre established in 1969. This offers a 1-year course (cours universitaires, formerly called cours superieurs) and leads to one of the following qualifications depending on the student's chosen specialization:

Certificat d'Etudes Litteraires et de Sciences Humanitaires
Certificat d'Etudes Scientifiques
Certificat d'Etudes Juridiques et Economiques

These certificates are considered by all Austrian, Belgian and French (and most German) universities as completion of the first year of an undergraduate course.

EUPED

At the Department of Law and Economics (Departement de Droit et de Sciences Economiques) of the Centre Universitaire in Luxembourg, students may take a 2-year course in applied economics and law (Cycle Court d'Etudes Universitaires Pratiques d'Economie et de Droit, EUPED), which prepares them for professional life.

The Centre also offers postgraduate professional training (cours complementaires) in such subjects as teaching and law. Although no qualification is obtained, students must attend to qualify for certain professions.

TEACHER EDUCATION

Primary

On completion of secondary school, students follow a 3-year course at the pedagogical institute, to obtain the **Brevet d'Aptitude Pedagogique**.

Luxembourg

Secondary

To teach at intermediate/lower school, students must take 2 years of a degree course abroad, followed by 2 years professional training in Luxembourg. Successful completion leads to the **Brevet d'Enseignement Moyen**.

To teach at upper secondary school, students must complete 4 years at a university, normally by taking 1-year cours universitaire in Luxembourg and a degree abroad, followed by 2 years postgraduate professional training (stage pedagogique) and an examination. To become a foreign language teacher the degree must be taken in the country where the language concerned is spoken. To be appointed, a teacher may have to pass a special examination (concours de recrutement) and the final grade accorded to the teacher includes an assessment of the concours de recrutement, the examen de fin d'etudes secondaires and any studies taken at the Centre Universitaire (compulsory for teachers of foreign language and science only).

Malawi

Republic of Malawi

Before independence in 1964, Malawi was known as Nyasaland. Its educational system was closely modelled on the British pattern. However it possessed few secondary schools and no institutions of higher education. Since independence the country has expanded its educational facilities. The University of Malawi was established in 1964.

The medium of instruction is Chichewa at primary school and English in all secondary and tertiary education.

The school year runs from October to August.

EVALUATION IN BRITAIN

School

Cambridge School Certificate and Malawi Certificate of Education — grades 1-6 are generally equated to GCE O-level standard (grades A, B, C).

Cambridge Higher School Certificate - generally equated to GCE A-level.

Higher

A **Degree** from the University of Malawi is unlikely to be considered comparable to a British degree.

Malawi

MARKING SYSTEMS

School

The Malawi Certificate of Education is graded as follows:

1, 2	pass with distinction
3, 4, 5, 6	pass with credit
7, 8	pass
9	fail

From 1971 to 1981, certificates were issued only to candidates who fulfilled certain requirements about groups of subjects passed. From 1982 onwards, the Malawi School Certificate of Education has been issued to candidates who meet the grouping requirements at one sitting, and the Malawi General Certificate of Education to candidates who obtain a pass with credit in one or more subjects but fail to fulfil the grouping requirements.

Higher

Students are assessed throughout the academic year and sit termly and yearly examinations. Course-work may constitute up to 50% of the final result. Students are generally obliged to pass in all subjects. The grading system is as follows:

6	pass with distinction
5	pass with marginal distinction
4	pass with credit
3	pass
2	pass (marginal)
1	fail (marginal)
0	fail

SCHOOL EDUCATION

Primary

Primary education lasts 8 years. At the end of standard VIII pupils take the **Primary School Leaving Certificate** (PSLC). Secondary school places are available only for the top 14% of those who take the PSLC.

Secondary

Secondary education lasts 4 years. At the end of the second year, pupils take the **Junior Certificate of Education Examination** (JCE). This gives access to certain jobs, some types of non-formal education and the apprenticeship scheme. Successful pupils may also enter form III.

Malawi

At the end of form IV, pupils take the **Malawi Certificate Examinations** (MCE). Before 1972, most pupils took the Cambridge Overseas School Certificate, while a few took the GCE examinations of the Associated Examining Board. From 1972 to 1981, MCE certificates were issued jointly by the Board in Malawi and by the Associated Examining Board in the UK, which was providing the professional aid for the development of the Board in Malawi. From 1982 onwards, certificates are issued in the name of the Malawi Certificate Examination and Testing Board only, but the Associated Examining Board will continue to monitor the equivalence of standards. The Kamazu Academy, Kasungu, and one school in Blantyre offer facilities for children who obtain good results in the MCE to sit for the **Cambridge Higher School Certificate**. Holders of this Certificate are admitted to the University of Malawi with 1 year of advanced standing.

FURTHER EDUCATION

Technical

Various facilities exist for craft and vocational training. Primary and junior secondary school graduates undergo training at trade training centres for various trade certificates, City and Guilds of London Institute examinations and internal diplomas.

The Malawi Government is gradually to replace examinations of the **City and Guilds of London Institute** by its own, beginning in 1986 or 1987. The new examinations will be validated by the City and Guilds of London Institute.

At a higher level the Malawi Polytechnic, linked to the University of Malawi, offers technician training courses to students who hold the **Junior Secondary School Certificate**. Employed people may upgrade their skills at evening classes. Most of these courses would be below O-level standard. Students can take preparatory courses for the **Junior Secondary School Certificate** and the **Malawi Certificate of Education**.

Agricultural

The Ministry of Agriculture runs 2-year courses.

HIGHER EDUCATION

The University of Malawi, founded in 1964, is composed of 4 colleges:

Bunda College of Agriculture, Lilongwe
Chancellor College, Zomba
Malawi Polytechnic, Blantyre
Kamazu College of Nursing, Lilongwe

Admission is based on the **Malawi Certificate of Education**, with 5 passes. Older candidates take a special entrance examination. The University offers 3-year **Diploma-level** courses and 4-year **General Degree** courses. Students can stay on for a fifth **Honours** year. Bunda College offers a 5-year degree in **Agriculture**.

Malawi

TEACHER EDUCATION

Primary

There are 2 types of teacher training college: for T3 teachers (junior primary) and T2 teachers (senior primary). T2 colleges admit students with the **Malawi Certificate of Education**. T3 colleges admit students with the **Junior Certificate of Education**. These colleges run 2-year courses at the end of which students sit the T2 or T3 Teachers Certificate.

The Malawi Institute of Education was established as an In-Service Training College and Curriculum Development Centre to provide teacher upgrading. 'Introduction courses' based at the Centre are intended to give school-leavers the basic skills to act as 'assistant' or 'pupil' teachers.

Secondary

Secondary teacher training is provided at the University School of Education. It offers a 3-year **Education Diploma** and selected graduates may, after a further 2 years study, receive a **B.Ed. degree**. The B.Ed. degree is being restructured so that the first 4 years will be taken in common with the general degree, the fifth year consisting of professional studies and teaching practice.

The **University Certificate of Education** course currently offered for graduate teachers with 1 or more years teaching experience will be integrated with the fifth-year B.Ed. programme.

ADULT EDUCATION

Malawi Polytechnic supervises evening class courses at Lilongwe Technical School. Many courses are aimed at assisting community development.

The Ministry of Agriculture and Natural Resources runs short courses (1-12 days) for farmers, to encourage better agricultural practice.

The Ministries of Agriculture, Community Development, Education, and Health provide home economics training at village level.

Plans exist for the establishment of a rural education centre in each district to provide the basis for various kinds of adult education programme.

Malaysia

This chapter deals with the education system of the twelve mainland states of Peninsular Malaysia.

Owing to the diversity of races, cultures and languages in Malaysia, the government imposes strict control over all areas of education with the aim of fostering Malaysian nationalism.

No sector of education is compulsory.

In 1956 the Razak Report recommended the establishment of a national system of education in which the national language(s) would be the medium of instruction, and a national system was then established by the Education Ordinance of 1957. Until 1967, under the terms of the Federal Constitution, English and Malay were the joint national languages; however, under the National Language Act of 1967, Bahasa Malaysia became the official language and medium of instruction at all levels.

The school year normally runs from January to November, and the university academic year from July to March.

EVALUATION IN BRITAIN

School

Sijil Rendah Pelajaran (SRP, formerly Lower Certificate of Education) - generally considered to be below GCE O-level standard. It has no counterpart within the British system.

Certificate of the Unified Examination for Independent Chinese Secondary Schools (formerly Senior Middle III). This is an internal examination in Chinese-medium schools. It is not recognized in Malaysia, and students often take the SPM (below) in addition unless they intend to continue their education overseas, e.g. in Taiwan. It may be considered to compare to GCE O-level standard on a subject-for-subject basis. The University of London has agreed to accept this exam in lieu of the O-level component of the general entry requirement for university, provided good grades have been obtained. Two Scottish universities are taking students with good grades in relevant subjects directly on to degree courses.

Malaysia

Sijil Pelajaran Malaysia (SPM, formerly Malaysia Certificate of Education) - equated to GCE O-level if grades 1-6 have been obtained (except in English language).

Sijil Pelajaran Vokesyenal Malaysia (SPVM)/ - Malaysian Vocational Certificate of Education - may be considered to be on a par with the SPM (academic), and the same guide to evaluation would apply.

Cambridge Overseas School Certificates and **Higher School Certificates** - see separate section.

Sijil Tinggi Persekolahan Malaysia (STPM)/ - Malaysian Higher School Certificate - equated to GCE A-level on a subject-for-subject basis. The STPM has now replaced the Cambridge Higher Overseas Certificate.

Further

Ungku Omar Politeknik/Kuantan Politeknik Technician Certificate - generally considered to approximate to BTEC National Diploma (formerly Ordinary National Diploma OND) standard.

Universiti Teknologi Malaysia post-SPM Diploma - generally considered to be slightly above BTEC National Diploma but below BTEC Higher National Diploma (formerly HND) standard.

Institut Teknologi MARA post-SPM Diploma - generally considered to be at the same standard as the Universiti Teknologi Malaysia Diploma.

Tenku Abdul Rahman College Diploma - generally considered to be slightly above BTEC National Diploma but below BTEC Higher National Diploma.

Higher

Bachelor degree - generally considered to compare to British Bachelor (Honours) degree standard.

MARKING SYSTEMS

School

Sijil Pelajaran Malaysia - is graded on a scale of 1 (maximum) to 9.

1		
2	distinction	camerlang
3		
4		
5		
6	credit	kepujian
7	pass	lulus
8		
9	fail	gagal

Malaysia

Sijil Tinggi Persekolahan Malaysia (STPM) is graded (like A-levels) on a scale A-E.

A
B
C   principal pass
D
E

R   subsidiary (O-level) pass

G   fail (gagal)

Further

Mara Institute of Technology Diploma is a 4-point cumulative grade system is used by all schools:

A	4	excellent
B	3.99-3.0	good
C	2.99-2.0	average
D	1.99-1.0	weak
E	0.99-0.0	fail
X	absent with permission or incomplete with permission	
Y	absent without permission.	

Each course earns a specified number of credits, depending on the work involved. Academic achievement is measured by grade points. On the 0-5 point scale, each credit-hour with A earns 4 grade points, B earns 3, C earns 2, D earns 1, and F earns none. The student's grade-point average (GPA) is calculated by dividing the total number of grade points (reached by multiplying the grade point for each course by the credit-hours of the course and then adding all) by the total number of credit-hours of enrolment. Students must normally maintain a minimum GPA of 2.0 to remain in good academic standing.

The cumulative grade-point average is the sum total of credit points obtained for all semesters divided by the total number of credit hours attempted for all semesters.

Ungku Omar Polytechnic, Kuantan Polytechnic

Marks are awarded on the following basis in each subject studied at the end of each year of study:

A,B,C,D	lulus	pass
E	gagal	failure
K	dikecualikan	exempted

University of Technology Diplomas

All diplomas are now awarded on the basis of grade-point averages, which follows the system used at Institut Teknologi MARA.

75% +	1st class
40-74	2nd class

Malaysia

Higher

Degrees are awarded with Honours and the following classifications:

class 1
class 2   division i
              division ii
class 3

Students whose achievement is insufficient for Honours may be awarded Pass degrees.

All universities now follow the semester system, and each student is graded in each subject taken at the end of each semester, using the same grade system as Institut Teknologi MARA.

SCHOOL EDUCATION

Primary

This begins for most children at age 6 and continues for 6 years (standards 1-6). There is a national syllabus in each subject. Children are promoted automatically at the end of each year, but a national assessment examination is held at the end of standards 3 and 5.

English as a medium of instruction was finally phased out of primary schools in 1975. The former English-medium schools have converted to Malay-medium, but Chinese (Mandarin) and Tamil schools remain. Students from Chinese or Tamil schools have to attend a 'remove class' before entering lower secondary level to prepare them for study in Malay. English continues to be taught as a compulsory second language in all schools.

In 1964 the **Secondary School Entrance Examination** (MSSEE) was abolished. Children now proceed automatically to secondary schooling at the end of standard 6.

Secondary

This covers a possible 7 years, divided into 3 stages:

lower (forms I-III)
upper (forms IV and V)
lower and upper sixth forms

Lower:

In 1965 the principle of comprehensive education was introduced in the lower secondary cycle of schools. These schools offer pupils the chance to study subjects in at least 1 vocational area (commerce, agricultural science, domestic science and industrial arts) in addition to the general subjects. At the end of form III pupils take the Malay-medium **Sijil Rendah Pelajaran** (SRP), formerly the English-medium **Lower Certificate Examination** (LCE). The SRP is essentially the same paper translated into Bahasa Malaysia, except for the lower level English language paper. The examinations are run by the Federal Examinations Syndicate. Since 1978 only 1 examination (SRP) has been taken in Bahasa Malaysia by all students.

Malaysia

Upper:

There is selective admission to this cycle: only candidates with the best results in the SRP are offered places in academic fourth forms, while those with minimum qualifications may go into technical or vocational schools. The growth of white-collar unemployment, however, has increased the popularity of vocational schools among the abler students. Until 1970 the examinations taken at the end of form V were those for the **Cambridge Overseas School Certificate**. This was succeeded by the **Malaysia Certificate of Education** (MCE), which has now given way to its Malay-medium equivalent, the **Sijil Pelajaran Malaysia** (SPM). Both MCE and SPM were drawn up by the Cambridge Local Examinations Syndicate; since 1978, however, responsibility has been given to the new Malaysian Examinations Syndicate, and Cambridge involvement is minimal. A new English language syllabus emphasizing communication skills has been introduced recently. This syllabus, known previously as English 122 and now as English 322, is not recognized outside Malaysia. Students can still take the Cambridge English language O-level (previously English 121, now English 1119) as an additional subject, and many opt to do so.

Children in Chinese-medium schools used to take the **Senior Middle III** examination set by the Ministry of Education until the 1960s. Nowadays most children from Chinese-medium schools take the same examination as their counterparts in the Malay-medium schools, i.e. the SPM.

There are independent Chinese secondary schools offering 6 years secondary schooling, leading to the examinations for the **Certificate of Unified Examination for Independent Chinese Secondary Schools**. The Malaysian Ministry of Education is not involved in any way with the examination, and the certificate is not recognized by them. It is usually taken by those children who intend to continue their studies in Chinese universities in Hong Kong and Taiwan.

Sixth forms:

There is selective admission to the lower sixth form, decided on the results of the SPM. Pupils now take the Malay-medium **Sijil Tinggi Persekolahan Malaysia** (STPM) at the end of the upper sixth, usually in 4 major subjects, and a general paper (Kertas Am). The Cambridge Board is still involved in an advisory capacity with these examinations.

Technical/vocational secondary

On completion of form III, students not obtaining good enough marks or not wishing to proceed to the secondary high schools, may go on to secondary vocational school, secondary agricultural school or secondary technical school.

The secondary vocational schools provide a general education with the opportunity to choose at least 1 vocational course in engineering trades, commerce, home science or agriculture. Courses culminate in the **Sijil Pelajaran Vokesyenal Malaysia** (SPVM), the Malaysian Vocational Education Certificate.

The secondary technical schools also provide a general education, with a strong technical bias, particularly in engineering. Courses in both types of school generally last 2 years.

Malaysia

FURTHER EDUCATION

There are post-secondary colleges offering courses with the entrance requirement of credits in various subjects in the Malaysian Certificate of Education. These include the following:

<u>MARA Institute of Technology</u> (Institut Teknologi MARA)

This runs a wide range of courses, some leading directly to the examinations of various professional bodies, but most to internal qualifications awarded by MARA. A number of courses lead to diplomas after 3 years from the comparable standard of GCE O-level. In a few subjects MARA offers 'advanced' diplomas, 2-year courses leading on from the Diploma up to Honours degree level. Continuous assessment is the main feature of student evaluation. The **Diploma in Law** is a 3-year post-STPM course, and some other Diplomas run for 4-years post-SPM.

<u>Tunku Abdul Rahman College</u>

This was founded as a pre-university college in 1968 and is funded by the Malaysian Chinese Association. It runs 2-year certificate courses from GCE O-level and 3-year **Diploma** courses from the comparable standard of GCE A-level. British examinations such as the <u>Institute of Building</u> and <u>CEI</u> are taken concurrently with the Diploma.

<u>Ungku Omar Polytechnic</u> (at Ipoh)

This was established in 1969; it aims at producing middle-level engineers and technicians on 2-year **Technician Diploma Courses**.

<u>Kuantan Polytechnic</u> offers similar courses, and other polytechnics are planned.

<u>Universiti Teknologi Malaysia</u> (UTM)

This was formed in 1972 by upgrading the Kuala Lumpur Technical College. This college offered 3-year post-SPM **Diploma** programmes in technical and professional subjects. These continue to be the major activity of the University, but **Degree** programmes are now also offered.

Private

There are private institutions of further education offering 3-year post-SPM **Diploma** courses in engineering and technological subjects, broadly equivalent to those offered by ITM. The best established are:

<u>Federal Institute of Technology</u>
<u>Institut Teknologi Jaya</u>
<u>Worker's Institute of Technology</u>.

Run by the trade union movement, they offer courses based on the syllabus of <u>Singapore Polytechnic</u>.

Students from these institutions often apply for, and are admitted to, degree courses in the UK.

Malaysia

HIGHER EDUCATION

This is offered by the 7 institutions of university status:

Universiti Malaya (UM) - established 1959
Universiti Sains Malaysia (USM) - University of Science, established 1969
Universiti Kebangsaan Malaysia (UKM) - National University, established 1970
Universiti Pertanian Malaysia (UPM) - Agricultural University, established as a university in 1971 by the merger of Serdang Agricultural College and the Faculty of Agriculture at UM
Universiti Teknologi Malaysia (UTM) - established as a University in 1972
International Islamic University - established in 1983
Universiti Utara Malaysia (UUM) - the Northern University, established in 1984.

Bachelor degrees are generally obtained on completion of 3 years study, except at the Universiti Teknologi where admission is usually on the basis of success in the SPM with credits in 5 subjects and degree courses last 5 years (6 for architecture). This institution also offers 3-year diploma courses, the entrance requirement being the SPM. The medium of instruction and examination is mainly Bahasa Malaysia, but English is used for certain subjects.

Universiti Pertanian also offers both diploma and degree courses: the degree courses last 4 years from the level of the STPM and the diploma courses are taken over 3 years from the entrance level of credits in the SPM. The diploma is of a much lower standard than the degree. A diploma holder who wishes to go on to the degree course gains exemption from the first year only.

Degrees at the Universiti Malaya are generally taken over 3-4 years and are classified as follows: first, second: upper division, second: lower division, third (students whose achievements are insufficient for Honours may be awarded Pass degrees). 1-year diploma courses are offered in certain subjects; 1- and 2-year courses leading to the award of a Master degree are also available.

Universiti Kebangsaan Malaysia was established in 1970 to cater for Malay speakers, but English is a compulsory subject. It offers 3-year degree courses and 4-year Honours degree courses in a variety of subjects. Courses leading to Master degrees are awarded over 2-5 years.

Universiti Sains Malaysia offers 3- and 4-year **General** and **Honours degree** courses, as well as 1-3 year courses leading to **Master degrees**.

International Islamic University offers 3 degree programmes: **Bachelor of Laws, Economics** and **Business Administration**.

TEACHER EDUCATION

Until 1973

Primary

Students entered a day training college for a 2-year course following Cambridge Overseas School Certificate.

Malaysia

Secondary

Students entered a Malaysian teachers' college for a 2-year course following Cambridge Overseas School Certificate.

Since 1973

Entrance to teacher training for primary and secondary school teachers alike is based on the Malaysia Certificate of Education. Students took a 2-year course leading to the **Certificate in Education**, which since 1981 has become a 3-year course.

Mali

Republic of Mali

The medium of instruction is French.

The academic year runs from October to June.

EVALUATION IN BRITAIN

School

Baccalaureat and
(Technical) Baccalaureat

Part II is generally compared to GCE O-level standard.

MARKING SYSTEMS

School

Baccalaureat (both options) and school education is graded on a scale of 0-20 (maximum), with 10 as the minimum pass mark.

16-20	tres bien	very good
14-15	bien	good
12-13	assez bien	quite good
10-11	passable	satisfactory
8-9	mediocre	mediocre
6-7	faible	weak
3-5	tres faible	very weak
0-2	nul	zero

Higher

Generally the same grading system as above, except that the pass mark is 12.

Ecole Nationale des Ingenieurs

0-5 (maximum), with 3 as the minimum pass mark.

Mali

SCHOOL EDUCATION

Primary

Primary education (enseignement fondamental) covers 9 years. This is divided into 2 cycles of 6 years (classes 1-6) and 3 years (classes 7-9). On completion of class 6, pupils sit for a test instituted in 1970 which determines whether they continue into the general academic or vocational streams of the second cycle of primary education or terminate education. Pupils are awarded the **Certificat de Fin d'Etudes du Premier Cycle de l'Enseignement Fondamental (CFEPCF)** which has replaced the **Certificat d'Etudes Primaire** awarded on completion of class 6 (then known as CM2).

Pupils who successfully complete the full 9 years of enseignement fondamental receive the **Diplome d'Etudes Fondamentales (DEF)**. In 1962 the DEF replaced the **Brevet d'Etudes du Premier Cycle** (BEPC) which was awarded on completion of class 10 (then known as 3e). Primary education previously consisted of 10 years instead of 9, and the secondary cycle consisted of only 2 years.

According to the results of the Diplome d'Etudes Fondamentales and certain other factors, students are streamed into academic, technical, agricultural or teacher-training institutions; they may also leave.

Secondary

Academic:

This covers 3 years (classes 10-12); it formerly consisted of classes 11-13 (then known as 2e, 1ere and terminale). This cycle is known as 'enseignement secondaire'.

In class 10, pupils are divided into an Arts stream (Serie 10e Lettres) and a Science stream (Serie 10e Sciences). Arts stream subjects are: French language; French and Negro-African literature; English; German or Russian or Arabic; history; geography; and some minor subjects. In the final 2 years of the secondary cycle (classes 11 and 12), pupils may opt for one of the following specializations culminating in the corresponding Baccalaureat:

sciences humaines (SH)	social sciences
langues litterature (LM)	modern languages
sciences biologiques (SB)	biological sciences
sciences exactes (SE)	physical sciences

Four major subjects are studied in each stream, depending on the specialization, but French and mathematics are common to all specializations.

On completion of class 11, students sit for the Mali **Baccalaureat Part I**, and **Part II** is taken at the end of class 12 (generally in June). Students must be successful in both parts to be awarded the full Baccalaureat.

Before 1985 there were 2 Arts options in classes 11 and 12:

lettres classiques (LC - class 11)	philo-lettres (PLE - class 12)	classics
lettres modernes (LM - class 11)	philo-langues (PLA - class 12)	modern languages

Mali

There are 2 types of Baccalaureat: the **Baccalaureat Option Malienne** and the **Baccalaureat Option Etrangere**, which is intended for foreigners and for Malian children who have had a large part of their education outside Mali. It is taken in one part only at the end of class 12, in 1 of 4 specializations (series).

A	lettres et langues	literature/languages
B	sciences economiques et sociales	economics and social sciences
C	mathematiques et sciences physiques	mathematics and physical sciences
D	mathematiques et sciences de la nature	mathematics and natural sciences

Technical/vocational

As an alternative to the academic schools, students may enter the Lycee Technique which prepares them for the technical **Baccalaureat** in 1 of 3 fields:

Mathematiques techniques et industrie (MTI)
Mathematiques techniques et genie civil (MTGC)
Mathematiques techniques et economie (MTE)

The technical **Baccalaureat** is taken in 2 parts at the end of classes 11 and 12.

Holders of the Diplôme d'Etudes Fondamentales may also attend a Centre de Formation Professionelle where 2-year courses lead to the qualification of **Certificat d'Aptitude Professionelle** (CAP).

The technical lycees no longer offer technician-training programmes. These are offered instead by the Ecole Centrale pour l'Industrie, le Commerce et l'Administration. Courses take 4 years, and lead to the qualification of **Brevet de Technicien**.

Holders of the Baccalaureat Part II may attend the Ecole des Hautes Etudes Pratiques for 2 years; there they receive the qualification of **Technicien Superieur**.

There is also an agricultural lycee which offers 3 to 4 year courses.

HIGHER EDUCATION

Mali has no university but has plans to open one before 1990. Post-secondary education is continued at 6 institutes of higher education, according to specialization.

Ecole Normale Superieure (see TEACHER EDUCATION)
Ecole Nationale d'Ingenieurs
Ecole National de Medecine et de Pharmacie
Institut Polytechnique Rural
Ecole des Hautes Etudes
Ecole Nationale d'Administration

Students entering the Ecole Normale Superieure (see also TEACHER EDUCATION) choose to specialize in a number of subjects. Because most of those who complete the course will enter the teaching profession, all students undertake some teacher training.

Mali

The Ecole Nationale d'Ingenieurs formerly known as the Ecole Technique Superieure, was created in 1939 and offers 4-year courses in electro-mechanical engineering, civil engineering, geology and topography, for holders of the Baccalaureat Part II in Science or of the technical Baccalaureat. Successful graduates are awarded the **Diplome d'Ingenieur** in the appropriate field.

The medical school, the Ecole National de Medecine et de Pharmacie, offers a 5-year course for holders of the Baccalaureat. It is affiliated to the Faculty of Medicine, Marseilles University, France.

The Institut Polytechnique Rural provides 4-year courses in agriculture, animal husbandry, water and forests and rural engineering. There are also technician-level courses for holders of the Diplome d'Etude Fondamentales.

The Ecole des Hautes Etudes Pratiques offers 2-year courses in secretarial work, accountancy and business management.

The Ecole Nationale d'Administration provides 4-year courses to train senior administrators for government service, in economics, public administration and management/legal science.

TEACHER EDUCATION

Teacher training for teachers of the first 6 classes takes place at regional Instituts Pedagogique d'Enseignement General (IPEG). The course runs for 4 years (full-time) for holders of the Diplome d'Etudes Fondamentales and consists of general education, pedagogy, child psychology and teaching practice. Before 1969 this was a 1-year course.

Training for teachers of classes 7-9 takes place in the Ecoles Normales Secondaires which run 4-year courses for holders of the Diplome d'Etude Fondamentales. Students specialize in 1 of 4 areas: French, history and geography; mathematics, physics and chemistry; natural sciences, agriculture and animal husbandry; languages (English), art and music.

Intending teachers of classes 10-12 attend the Ecole Normale Superieure, which runs 4-year courses for holders of the Baccalaureat Part II who have passed an entrance examination. Graduates of the course receive a **Diplome de l'Ecole Normale Superieure**. Mature students who are already Enseignement Fondamental teachers may gain entry by way of a competitive entrance examination, the **Concours Professionnel d'Entree**.

The Centre Pedagogique Superieur created within the Ecole Normale Superieure for postgraduate research offers 3-year courses leading to the **Doctorat de Specialite**, open to holders of the Diplome from the Ecole Normale Superieure. At the end of the first year, students sit for the **Diplome d'Etudes Approfondies** (DEA). The second and third years are devoted to a research dissertation, supervised in part by an overseas university.

Malta

Republic of Malta

Education in Malta is centrally organized. The University has its own constitution. There are private schools which require a licence for recognition.

Educational reforms launched in 1974 altered the character of Maltese education, previously similar to the British system, to make it more sensitive to local development needs and to provide facilities according to the ages, abilities and aptitudes of students.

Education is compulsory for all children aged six to sixteen, but the primary school course begins at age five by which time all children are enrolled in schools.

Maltese and English are the official languages and are the media of instruction from primary level.

The school year runs from mid-September to mid-July in the government sector, while the University year starts in mid-February.

EVALUATION IN BRITAIN

School

Students in secondary schools and technical institutes take UK GCE examinations at O- and A-level as well as their University of Malta Matriculation counterparts, and City & Guilds of London Institute examinations. There are also local certificates (generally in the technical sector) for trade school students.

Higher

Degrees (from the University of Malta) - generally compared to British degrees.

Malta

MARKING SYSTEMS

School

GCE O- and A-levels, City & Guilds of London Institute examinations, RSA and LCC certificates, Royal Schools of Music and Trinity College certificates, as well as all UK examinations taken in Malta are marked as in Britain.

Malta Matriculation Ordinary (M) Level: pass marks are 1-5 (1 = maximum). F indicates a failure.

Malta Matriculation Advanced (AM) Level: pass grades are A-E (A = maximum). F indicates a failure.

Other school leaving certificates (issued by schools) may contain marks of the last examination taken (in per cent or distinction, credit, pass).

The successful completion of courses in the Secretarial School, the Fellenberg Training Centre in Industrial Electronics and the Architects' Assistants and Draughtsmen course are considered by the University of Malta for university entry purposes as equivalent to a Malta Matriculation pass at advanced level.

Higher

First degrees are generally classified 1st class, 2nd class upper, 2nd class lower and 3rd class/pass.

SCHOOL EDUCATION

Pre-primary

There are government kindergarten classes for 4-year-olds. Private school nurseries enrol children at an earlier age.

Primary

Up to 1970 (when secondary education for all was introduced) this consisted of 2 years for infants and up to 7 elementary standards from age 5/6.

Since 1970, primary school lasts 6 years (Years 1 to 6) from age 5, roughly divided into two 3 year cycles. The curriculum consists of Maltese, English, mathematics, religion, civics, geography, history, science, physical education, art and handiwork, music and singing, and (for girls) needlework. Annual examinations, on a national level from Year 3 upwards, generally determine promotion and/or educational stream.

In 1985, preparatory secondary schools and opportunity centres were set up for pupils who would have finished their 6-year primary programme but are not yet considered able to pursue a secondary school course. Opportunity-class pupils are the very weak who generally need a special education curriculum.

Secondary

There are 2 types of secondary school: Junior Lyceums (selective) and secondary schools (area based). They offer 5-year courses roughly divided into: a 2-year cycle of orientation (common general curriculum) for Group 2 students not preparing for GCE; and a 3-year cycle of determination (common core plus 2 or 3 optional subjects) for Group 1 students studying for GCE. Annual examinations are set on a national level. These, together with half-yearly results and teacher's assessment, generally determine promotion and choice of subjects/stream.

New Lyceums and Private Schools Sixth Forms provide 2-year courses leading to GCE A-level (Oxford, London, AEB, local Matriculation). Entry into Government New Lyceums is based on at least 6 GCE O-level passes to include Maltese, English, maths, physics and Arabic. There is a scheme whereby students receive a monthly remuneration for work carried out during the summer holidays and on completion of the course.

Technical Secondary

Trade schools and Junior Craft Centres

There are trade schools which recruit boys from the end of form II and girls from age 14. Boys' trade schools run 4-year courses which end with a specialization in a trade (electrical, mechnical, automobile, marine plumbing, etc). Girls' trade schools run 2-year courses (which may be extended to 3 years) in 'women's' trades. Junior Craft Centres provide 2- to 3-year courses in a trade for students of lower educational ability. This training may be continued to semi-skilled level in Senior Craft Centres.

Technical institutes and other specialized centres

Technical institutes, which generally recruit students after form 5 of secondary education, provide craft and technican courses leading mainly to **City & Guilds of London Institute examinations**. There are also several specialized training/vocational institutions which issue their own certificates; some belong to Government Departments. Courses include industrial electronics, art and design, nursing, hotel management and catering.

HIGHER EDUCATION

1978-80

During this period there were 2 universities, the Old University and the (New) University of Malta. The Old University dated from 1592 and received royal patronage in 1937 as the Royal University of Malta. Up to 1978 it offered the following:

Bachelor degrees - for general degrees, students studied 3 subjects for 3 years; for Honours degrees, students studied 1 subject for 2 years, 1 subject for 3 years, and 1 subject for 1 year.

Malta

Master degrees - 1 year in science subjects; 2 years in architecture; 5 terms in arts subjects.

Law and medicine - the qualification of **Doctor** in both subjects took 5 years.

Dentistry - 4 years.

Theology - the first qualification was the **Licentiate**.

Doctorate (Ph.D.) - obtained after a minimum of 8 terms of research, following a Master degree in Theology (a minimum of 1 year after the Licentiate).

The Malta College of Arts, Science and Technology which was established in 1961 with departments of engineering, business management, and hotel management and catering, offered a variety of courses from GCE O- and A-level standard to college diplomas, university degrees, and City & Guilds of London Institute examinations. In 1974 the teacher-training colleges were transferred to the Malta College of Arts, Science and Technology as the department of educational studies.

In 1978 a law as passed to upgrade the Malta College of Arts, Science and Technology to a degree-granting institution to be called the New University, with the Royal University being called the Old University. This law was further amended in 1980; the Old University was phased out and the New University became the University of Malta.

Since 1980

The University of Malta grants the following degrees:

Faculty of Law:	**Doctor of Laws** (LL D)
Faculty of Medicine and Surgery:	**Doctor of Medicine** (MD), **Bachelor of Pharmacy** (Hons), (B.Pharm.Hons); **Bachelor of Pharmaceutical Technology** (B.Ph.Tech.Hons)
Faculty of Engineering & Architecture:	**Bachelor of Engineering and Architecture** (B.E. & A.); **Bachelor of Mechnical Engineering** (B.Mech.Eng.); **Bachelor of Electrical Engineering** (B.Electr.Eng.)
Faculty of Dental Surgery:	**Bachelor of Dental Surgery** (B.Ch.D.)
Faculty of Management Studies:	**Bachelor of Arts** (hons) in
	Public Administration Accountancy Business Management
Faculty of Education:	**Bachelor of Education** (Hons)

Entry for Maltese students is based on a system of sponsorship and employment by Government Departments, parastatal organizations and private firms on a points basis as determined by a Students Selection Board. The selected 'worker-students', who are paid a salary, alternate period of study at the University with periods of work for their employers.

Foreign students are admitted to the University but not the worker-student scheme. Entry requirements are 7/8 passes at GCE, 3 of which must be at A-level.

The University of Malta also runs evening Diploma courses usually 3 semesters (1 semester = 6 months).

TEACHER EDUCATION

Pre-service teacher training was introduced in 1944/5. In 1956 the course was made residential, extended to 2 years and the final examinations were moderated by the University of London Institute of Education. In 1973 the course was extended to 3 years. In 1974, the pre-service training of teachers was transferred to the Malta College of Arts, Science and Technology as the Department of Educational Studies and made non-residential. A 1-year Postgraduate Teacher's Certificate was started. In 1978, the course was updated and raised to degree level. A Faculty of Education was also set up. The B.Ed. (Hons) course now runs for 5 years with alternating periods of study and work.

The Faculty of Education runs Diploma and in-service courses.

Teaching in Malta is carried out by teachers (college-trained or university graduates), instructors, and kindergarten assistants. There are 3 grades of teacher, 3 of instructor (Grade III equivalent to Teacher Grade II), and 2 of kindergarten assistant. Instructors (usually in the technical sector) and kindergarten assistants receive in-service training. The Teacher Grade III category comprises Assistant Heads of School, Heads of Department and Counsellors.

Mauritius

Although there is no compulsory period of schooling, attendance at primary level is almost universal.

The medium of instruction is mostly English, but French is used at some institutions.

The academic year at schools lasts from January to November, and at the university from September to July.

EVALUATION IN BRITAIN

School

Cambridge Overseas School Certificate (COSC) - grades 1-6 are equated to GCE O-levels (grades A B or C).

Cambridge Overseas Higher School Certificate - grades A-E are equated to GCE A-level.

O- and A-level GCE examinations of the AEB, London and Oxford Boards will be of the same standard as the examinations taken in Britain.

Brevet de Technicien - generally considered to compare to the BTEC National Certificate (formerly ONC) or Technician Certificate of City & Guilds of London Part 2.

Brevet d'Aptitude Professionelle - generally considered to compare to CGLI Craft Studies Part 3.

Higher

Bachelor degrees - generally compared to British Bachelor degree standard. However, Honours Bachelor degrees from the University of Mauritius are rather more general than is often the case in Britain. Applicants for higher degrees in Britain may need to take a postgraduate diploma in an area of specialization or do a qualifying year before being registered for a Master degree.

Mauritius

MARKING SYSTEMS

School

Cambridge Overseas School Certificate is graded on a scale 1 (maximum) - 9 (fail).

Cambridge Overseas Higher School Certificate is graded A (maximum), B, C, D, E.

Higher

Bachelor degrees are classified:

class I
class II division i
class II division ii
class III or pass.

SCHOOL EDUCATION

Pre-primary

There are just over 700 private registered pre-primary units.

Primary

This covers 6 years for children from age 5.

The curriculum covers English, French, mathematics, science, geography, hygiene, civics, physical education, and music. On completion of standard 6 pupils now take the examinations for the **Certificate of Primary Education**. This certifies successful completion of primary education and determines the placement of pupils at secondary schools. Until 1977, pupils were also selected to take the **Junior Scholarship Examination** in 4 subjects (English, French, geography and mathematics) to decide placement at the government secondary school. Until 1979, pupils took the **Primary School Leaving Certificate**.

Secondary

This covers a possible 7 years: forms I-V leading to the examinations for the **Cambridge Overseas School Certificate/GCE O-level**, followed by 2 years in form VI leading to the examinations for the **Cambridge Overseas Higher School Certificate/GCE A-level**. Form III examinations were to be introduced in 1982, but have not yet come into being.

Technical secondary

The Technical Institute was established in 1959. It offered pupils the opportunity to specialize from the third year in either a commercial stream (including shorthand, typing and accountancy) leading to the examinations of the **Royal Society of Arts**, or a technical stream (including general science, technical drawing, metalwork and woodwork). Compulsory subjects for each stream were English, French and mathematics. In 1965 the Technical Institute merged with a government secondary school to form the John Kennedy College offering 3 streams: science, commercial and technical.

Mauritius

The <u>Lycee Polytechnique Sir Guy Forget</u> was set up in January 1982 to train students from form III at technician or craft level. Technical courses last 4 years and lead to the **Brevet de Technicien**, while craft courses last 3 years and lead to the **Brevet d'Aptitude Professionelle**.

The <u>Mahatma Gandhi Institute</u> was set up in 1970 to promote Indian culture and to study education and culture in general. It has courses in languages, music, and fine arts. It runs teacher training courses with the <u>Mauritius Institute of Education</u>.

The <u>Industrial Trades Training Centres</u> (ITTCs) were established in the late 1960s to train apprentices and adult workers in trades such as mechanical engineering craft practices, electrical installation, automechanics, welding and sheet metalwork, plumbing and pipework, carpentry and joinery, masonry and concrete. The courses mostly lead to examinations of the **City & Guilds of London Institute**.

FURTHER EDUCATION

Courses are available in paramedical subjects (e.g. nursing, medical laboratory technology and engineering) leading to the **Ordinary Technicians Diploma** (OTD) after 2-3 years post-GCE O-level study.

HIGHER EDUCATION

There is 1 university, the <u>University of Mauritius</u>, established in 1965. The normal entrance requirement for degree courses is 2 GCE A-levels.

Courses leading to **Bachelor of Arts/Science** degrees with Honours last 3-years; those leading to **Bachelor of Technology** degrees with Honours last 4 years. Most courses at the previously existing colleges led to diplomas. The University now offers 2-, 3- and 4-year courses leading to a Diploma in a variety of fields from GCE O-level, and 2-year courses leading to a Certificate.

The **Master of Philosophy** is awarded after a minimum of 2 years postgraduate study and the **Doctorate** (Ph.D.) after a minimum of 3 years.

There are no postgraduate taught courses, except in agriculture.

TEACHER EDUCATION

<u>Mauritius Institute of Education</u> provides various training courses.

Primary

A 2-year course or a 3-year part-time course from the level of the Cambridge Overseas School Certificate/GCE O-level leads to a **Teacher's Diploma**. A 2-year part-time course leads to a **Teacher's Certificate**.

Mauritius

Secondary

Teachers must hold a university degree or a non-graduate professional qualification for teaching.

The Institute runs a 1-year full-time/2-year part-time **Postgraduate Certificate in Education** and a 2-year part-time **Certificate in Educational Administration**.

Mexico

United Mexican States

Education in Mexico is secular; the Church and religious organizations are forbidden to own or administer schools. Private schools do exist, but must be legally authorized and conform to standards laid down by the Federal Government. Private institutions of higher education do not require Federal authorization, but to obtain recognition must have Federal or State government validation of courses and degrees. The universities have formed a National Association of Universities and Institutions of Higher Education, to co-ordinate work and standardize examinations.

Compulsory education lasts six years from age six.

The medium of instruction is Spanish.

The academic year runs from September to June or February to November.

EVALUATION IN BRITAIN

School

Bachillerato en Ciencias or **en Humanidades** an academic school leaving certificate specializing in science or arts - generally considered to compare to GCE O-level standard.

Higher

Licenciado or **Professional Title** - may be considered to compare to British Bachelor (Honours) degree standard. Students with an average of 8 are generally considered capable of postgraduate study in Britain.

MARKING SYSTEM

School

Marking is on a percentage scale, with 60% as the pass mark; or a scale of 0-10, with 6 as the minimum pass mark.

Higher

1-10 (maximum), with 6 as the pass mark.

SCHOOL EDUCATION

Kindergarten

This officially covers 3 years from age 4, but if children do attend it is usually only for 1 year.

Primary

This covers 6 years, divided into three 2-year cycles, from age 6 and leads to the **Primary Certificate**. Since 1969 there has been a uniform curriculum throughout Mexico.

Secondary

This covers 6 years, divided into two 3-year cycles, the first being the secundaria/educacion secundaria, and the second the preparatoria/ciclo secundario. The preparatory cycle (preparation for higher education) was administered by the universities and other institutions of higher education. Most public universities also have their own preparatory schools offering courses of 2-3 years after which students may proceed automatically to first-degree courses. The first year of the preparatory cycle is usually spent on general studies, after which pupils specialize for 2 years. On successful completion pupils obtain the **Bachillerato**. English is a compulsory subject.

Technical secondary

At the level of educacion secundaria there are also a number of schools offering specialized education, and at the end of this cycle pupils obtain a **Certificate of Secondary Studies**.

Industrial and commercial schools

These offer 3-year secundaria courses and 3-year preparatoria classes. Courses at both levels prepare pupils for a trade. On completion pupils obtain a **Vocational** or **Commercial Diploma**.

Preparatory-level courses (3-year) are also offered by:

Naval and military schools, which have rigid entry qualifications; successful students obtain a commission as lieutenant

Nursing schools

Schools for social workers

Art schools

Agricultural schools, opened in 1970.

Mexico

FURTHER EDUCATION

There are many Regional Institutes of Technology, which offer a variety of courses, from the level of **Tecnico** up to **Industrial Engineer**, a qualification obtained after a 4-year course.

The professional schools, often attached to a university, also offer various courses at this level.

HIGHER EDUCATION

Courses leading to the **Licenciatura** normally last 4 years, 5 years being necessary for certain professional qualifications (e.g. engineer, dentist, architect) and 6 years for medicine.

The usual entrance qualification is the Bachillerato en Ciencias or en Humanidades, and, in addition, students normally have to take an entrance examination.

In the educational reforms of 1973 the credit system, as used in the United States, was introduced in certain institutions. Degrees are obtained by passing a stated number of credit courses, and the successful presentation of a thesis. Students may enrol each term for as many credit courses as they wish. There is no limit on the length of time a student may remain registered for a first or second degree. On completion of all taught credit courses, a student receives a certificate of completion of studies. Some students leave university with only this certificate as they do not submit the necessary dissertation and thus obtain the formal degree qualification.

Private institutions of higher education may be incorporated with a state or federal university or obtain semi-autonomous status, and thus be entitled to award their own degrees and use their own curriculum.

There are 2 technical universities:

The National Polytechnic Institute, which incorporates many undergraduate institutions and a few postgraduate research centres

The Institute of Technology and Higher Education in Monterrey.

There are also many federal specialized institutions, e.g. Escuela de Arte Teatral and Escuela Medico Militar.

Postgraduate facilities exist at most institutions: the **Maestria** is obtained after a further year of study (including the preparation of a thesis) and the **Doctorado** a minimum of 1 year (usually 2-3) after the Maestria.

Mexico

TEACHER EDUCATION

Pre-primary and primary

A 3-year upper-preparatory level course for pupils, completing the secondary cycle, at a teacher training college leads to the qualification of **Normalista/Titulado**. This qualification can be acceptable for entrance to university.

Secondary

Holders of the Bachillerato or a primary school teacher's certificate can enter a 4-year course at a higher teachers training college (Escuela Normal Superior), which leads to the Maestro and entitles the holder to teach the first cycle of secondary education.

The normal requirement for teachers of the upper secondary cycle is a first degree or, at least, a certificate of completion of university studies.

Morocco

Kingdom of Morocco

The French protectorate covered most of the territory and lasted from 1912 to 1956; the Spanish protectorates in the north and south were renounced in 1956 and 1958: Ifni was surrendered in 1969, but Spanish enclaves have been retained at Ceuta and Melilla.

The education system was originally modelled on that of France. Koranic and private schools exist alongside government schools.

In theory, education is compulsory between ages seven and fourteen; in practice, particularly in rural areas, many children do not attend for the whole of this period.

At primary school the medium of instruction is Arabic. French is taught at primary school. At secondary school, most subjects (except physics, chemistry, and technical/commercial subjects) are taught in Arabic; English is also taught.

For the schools, the academic year begins on 15 September and ends on 30 June and is made up of three terms. For higher education, the academic year begins on 1 October. In May and June, two sittings of examinations are held.

EVALUATION IN BRITAIN

School

Certificat d'Enseignement Secondaire - generally considered to lie below GCE O-level standard.

Baccalaureat - generally considered to lie between GCE O- and A-level standards. For entry into higher education the host institution may require British GCE A-levels.

Higher

Licence - when high average marks have been obtained, has been compared to British Bachelor degree standard.

Morocco

MARKING SYSTEMS

School

Marking is on a scale of 0-20 (maximum) with 10 as the pass mark.

16-20	tres bien	very good
14-15	bien	good
12-13	assez bien	fair
10-11	passable	pass
0-9	fail	fail

Candidates with 9/20 may be passed by the examination committee.

Higher

As for school.

Candidates with 9/20 will be considered by the Examination Board, who may pass them if term work and attendance are good.

SCHOOL EDUCATION

Pre-primary

An element of Koranic education is compulsory for children aged 5 to 7. For those not in 'modern' pre-primary schools, this means a traditional Koranic school.

Primary

This lasts 5 years from age 7. Instruction is in Arabic but French is taught as a subject from the third year. Some private primary education is provided by French, American and Spanish schools and religious missions. Some Koranic schools provide primary education (in Arabic) with the emphasis on religious education. At the end of primary school, pupils not considered for promotion to secondary school take the **Certificat d'Etudes Primaires** (CEP).

State secondary

Access to secondary education is based on success in an examination in Arabic and French (**Examen d'Entree en 6eme**).

Premier cycle (junior secondary):

This covers a 4-year period normally spent in a College, at the end of which students who are not proceeding to upper secondary school take the **Certificat d'Enseignement Secondaire** (CES).

Morocco

Deuxieme cycle (senior secondary):

The second cycle consists of 3-years study, usually spent at a Lycee. At the end of the second cycle, students take 1 of the following:

Baccalaureat - with emphasis on arts or science

Baccalaureat Lettres Originelles - awarded in Arabic studies

Diplome de Technicien Marocain (DTM) - for those specializing in accountancy, commerce, hotel work, or various branches of engineering and technology.

Private secondary

This is provided by the French and Spanish cultural missions in the big cities. Several Moroccan private schools offer 'Arabic' education, supervised by the Ministry of Education. Traditional secondary schools offer an education that stresses Islamic and Arabic studies. The 3 American schools cater largely for the international community.

Vocational

Various government ministries offer vocational courses usually open to **Baccalaureat** or DTM holders only. There is an entrance examination.

HIGHER EDUCATION

The Baccalaureat satisfies university entrance requirements in Morocco.

2 years university study (the premier cycle) leads to the **Diplome d'Etudes Universitaires Generales (DEUG)**; 2 more years study leads to the **Licence**.

There are limits on admission to the Grandes Ecoles (tertiary level), the Technical Institutes, and the Faculties of Medicine and Dentistry. To date, other faculties have not imposed entry restrictions.

Certificat des Etudes Superieures **Diplome des Etudes Approfondies**	- postgraduate diplomas
Doctorat de Troisieme Cycle	- a research degree
Doctorat d'Etat	- the highest university degree. In medicine this is the sole university degree and is awarded after 6 years. In other subjects the period of research may vary.

TEACHER EDUCATION

Primary

Until 1978, regional primary-school training institutes trained students who had passed the fifth, sixth, seventh year or **Baccalaureat**. Since 1979, regional <u>Centres de Formation des Instituteurs</u> admit Baccalaureat holders, following a <u>competitive</u> examination, to a 2-year training course.

Morocco

Secondary

Junior secondary (premier cycle) teachers are trained in <u>Centres Pedagogiques Regionaux</u>, where they follow a 2-year course.

Senior secondary (deuxieme cycle) teachers are normally graduates and hold a postgraduate teaching diploma from the <u>Ecoles Normales Superieures</u> (ENS) or a degree from the <u>Faculty of Education</u> in Rabat.

Higher

A new programme was introduced in October 1982 for holders of the **Licence**. After a competitive examination and interview, the successful student follows a 4-year course and must submit a satisfactory thesis in order to become a maitre assistant (lecturer). In certain subjects, a 2-year course (to which entry is highly competitive), followed by a thesis, qualifies graduates to become lecturers.

Nepal

Kingdom of Nepal

The Ministry of Education was first established in 1951, but comparatively little attention and resources were allocated to education until recently. In 1971 the government drew up the National Educational System Plan for a uniform system of education over the whole country; at present the Plan is under review and some modifications are expected.

Education is not compulsory, due mainly to inadequate facilities.

At school, Nepali is the medium of instruction but English may be taught where schools have the staff.

EVALUATION IN BRITAIN

School

(Secondary) School Leaving Certificate (SLC) - generally considered to be below GCE O-level standard.

Proficiency Certificate - generally considered to compare to GCE O-level standard (except English language).

Higher

Bachelor degree - generally considered to compare to GCE A-level standard.

Master degree - generally considered to compare to British Bachelor degree standard.

MARKING SYSTEMS

School

The **Nepalese School Leaving Certificate** is a group certificate examination with subjects organized into compulsory, vocational and optional groupings. Students must present 7 subjects: 3 compulsory, 1 vocational and 3 optional. The pass mark on each paper is 32% and students must pass all papers to obtain a certificate.

First Division	60% +
Second Division	45-59
Pass or Third Division	32-44

Higher

Distinction	80-100%
Division I	65-79
Division II	50-64
Division III	40-49

SCHOOL EDUCATION

Primary

Under the new Plan the primary level embraces grades 1-5. From grade 4 one of the languages of the United Nations is included as a compulsory subject and in practice this is usually English.

Secondary

This now covers 5 years, divided into 2 years lower secondary and 3 years upper secondary/high school. In the upper secondary cycle students may take a general academic, technical secondary or Sanskrit course concentrating on the Hindu classics. At the end of this cycle (grade 10) students take the examinations for the **Secondary School Leaving Certificate** (SLC). The Minister of Education appoints the SLC Board which determines the subjects and content of the examinations.

HIGHER EDUCATION

From the early 1940s until 1961 students at the various degree colleges in Nepal took the degrees of the University of Patna in India. In 1959 the autonomous <u>University of Tribhuvan</u> was founded, and the link with Patna was broken in 1961 when Tribhuvan awarded its own degrees for the first time. Tribhuvan is the only degree-granting institution in Nepal. The university is in the process of change. It consists of 4 technical institutes, 6 faculties and 3 research centres. Since 1981 the university has allowed for the establishment of private campuses covering the humanities and management.

Courses leading to a Bachelor degree are taken in 2 parts; after 2 years study students take the **Proficiency Certificate** (previously known as the Intermediate Examination), and after a further 2 years (3 years for medicine, technical subjects and agriculture) the examinations for the **Bachelor degree** (previously referred to as the diploma).

Nepal

The **Master degree** may be taken after a further 3 years including 1 year of national development service.

Standards are generally considered comparable to those at an average Indian university.

There are 5 Sanskrit colleges, affiliated to the university, in which Sanskrit is the medium of instruction. There are plans for a Sanskrit university.

TEACHER EDUCATION

In 1971 the existing College of Education was absorbed by Tribhuvan University as the Institute of Education.

Primary

A 1-year pre-service course is provided for holders of the School Leaving Certificate (SLC).

A 6-month in-service course is provided for practising teachers who do not hold the SLC.

Secondary

Lower secondary:

2 years pre-service training for SLC-holders
1-year pre-service training for Proficiency Certificate holders
6-months in-service training for practising teachers with the Proficiency Certificate
7-months pre-service training for SLC-holders from vocational schools.

Secondary:

2-years pre-service training for Proficiency Certificate holders
1-year pre-service training for Bachelor degree/Diploma holders
6-months in-service training for practising teachers with Bachelor degree/Diploma.

Netherlands

Kingdom of the Netherlands

Several education acts have changed the system at all levels since the mid-1950s. One of the most far-reaching was the Secondary Education Act of 1963 (also called the Mammoth Law), which came into force in August 1968. Its main purpose is to integrate the various types of secondary education.

Until 1969 education was compulsory for eight years, beginning no later than age seven. The Compulsory Education Law of 1969 increased this to nine years, from age six to fifteen. In 1975 it was extended to ten years, starting at age six or seven; in 1985 it is planned that the school-starting age be lowered to five years, thereby extending compulsory education to eleven years.

The medium of instruction is Dutch, except in the international institutions where it is mainly English. English is introduced in the fifth year of primary education.

The academic year runs from August/September to June.

EVALUATION IN BRITAIN

Abbreviations

Dr.	Doctor
Drs.	Doctorandus
HAVO	Hoger Algemeen Voortgezet Onderwijs
HBS	Hogere Burgerschool (before 1968)
HBO	Hoger Beroeps Onderwijs
HBS	Hogere Beroeps School
Ing.	Ingenieur
Ir.	Ingenieur
LAVO	Lager Algemeen Voortgezet Onderwijs
LBO	Lager Beroeps Onderwijs
LBS	Lagere Bereops School
MAVO	Middelbaar Algemeen Voortgezet Onderwijs
Mr.	Meester
MBO	Middelbaar Beroeps Onderwijs
MBS	Middelbaare Beroeps School
MULO	Middelbaar Uitgebreid Lager Onderwijs
VWO	Voorbereidend Wetenschappelijk Onderwijs

Netherlands

School

MAVO/MULO Certificate - generally considered to be below GCE O-level standard.

HAVO Certificate - generally compared to GCE O-level standard.

VWO (Gymnasium A/B and **Atheneum A/B) Diplomas** - may be considered to satisfy the general requirement of universities and polytechnics.

Higher

The **Kandidaats** is not a terminal qualification and is difficult to compare to a British qualification. In the new structure of university education the Kandidaats diploma has been abolished.

In 1982 a new Act on the structure of university education came into effect. The Act applies uniformly to all university courses, restricting both the duration of the course and the time permitted to complete the course. University study is divided into 2 phases: the first lasts 4 years, culminating in the **Doctoraal Examen**; and the second provides additional training for professional qualifications and a preparatory period for independent research.

Doctoral Examen (Doctorandus, Ingenieur, Meester) has been accorded British Bachelor degree standard but may be compared to taught Master degree standard.

MARKING SYSTEMS

School

Including general secondary and lower and intermediate vocational training.

10	uitmuntend	excellent
9	zeer goed	very good
8	goed	good
7	ruim voldoende	very satisfactory
6	voldoende	pass
5	bijna voldoende	fail
4	onvoldoende	unsatisfactory
3	zeer onvoldoende	very unsatisfactory
2	slecht	poor
1	zeer slecht	very poor

Higher

Including university and higher vocational education. As above.

Netherlands

SCHOOL EDUCATION

Pre-primary/nursery (Kleuteronderwijs)

Under the 1955 Pre-primary Education Act this is encouraged by the State and, although not compulsory, is almost universal. It is available between ages 4 and 6.

Primary (Gewoon Lager Onderwijs)

This covers 6 years and offers a common curriculum which includes: reading, writing, arithmetic, Dutch, geography, history, nature study, chemistry, art, music, handicrafts, and physical education.

Before the changes instituted after the Primary Education Act of 1970, children had to repeat a year if they failed the end-of-year examination. Since 1970, children have been evaluated by continual assessment. In 1985 the new Primary Education Act came into effect: this integrated pre-primary and primary education to form one comprehensive cycle of elementary education for the age group 4-12 (Basis Onderwijs). The first year is optional. Compulsory education is from age 5.

Secondary

Before 1968:

Children who did not wish to continue general education after primary school could attend 2 years of complementary primary education (Voortgezet Gewoon Lager Onderwijs), at the end of which they could leave school, having completed compulsory schooling. The curriculum covered the usual subjects taken at primary school but with the emphasis on practical skills rather than on theoretical studies.

For pupils who wished to continue their education, but not to university level, advanced primary education (Uitgebreid Lager Onderwijs - ULO) was offered in 3- to 4-year courses after the usual 6-year primary course. The leaving qualification of these courses was the **MULO Certificate**, with which pupils could either leave school or proceed to intermediate vocational training.

For pupils who wished to take a course of general/academic education with the eventual aim of attending a course of higher education, there were 2 types of school: the Gymnasium and the Hogere Burgerschool.

The Gymnasium offered a 6-year course: during the final 2 years pupils could specialize in Section A, with the emphasis on Greek and Latin, or Section B, with the emphasis on mathematics and science. The leaving certificate obtained on successful completion of the full 6-year course entitled the holder to admission to university.

The Hogere Burgerschool offered 5-year courses. After the first 3 years, pupils could specialize in Section A, with the emphasis on economic and social studies and languages, or Section B, with the emphasis on mathematics and science. Pupils who successfully completed a full 5-year course could enter university. The last examinations for the Hogere Burgerschool were taken in 1973.

Netherlands

Since 1968:

The 1963 Secondary Education Act, implemented in 1968, as well as the 1970 Primary Education Act, led to the following changes.

The **LAVO Certificate** replaced the certificate obtained at the end of complementary primary education.

The **MAVO Certificate** replaced the MULO Certificate.

The **VWO (Gymnasium/Atheneum) Certificate** replaced the former Gymnasium and HBS Certificates.

A new type of secondary education, HAVO, was created.

As an essential feature of the educational reforms was to integrate the various forms of secondary education, a common transition year (brugklas/gemeenschappelijk leerjaar) was introduced for all pupils who had completed the usual 6-year primary course and then wished to follow a general secondary course.

Some schools now offer the 2-year complementary primary course; in other areas the same course is taken in the first 2 years at secondary schools for lower vocational training. It culminates in the award of the **LAVO Certificate**.

The **MAVO Certificate**, which replaces the MULO Certificate, is now obtained after a 4-year course covering the last 4 years of compulsory education. The Certificate can admit the holder to the fourth year of the HAVO schools or to intermediate vocational training. Examinations are held in 6 subjects and can be taken at a (lower) C level or (higher) D level.

The **HAVO Certificate** is awarded on completion of a 5-year course of general secondary education. There is a common curriculum for the first 3 years. Pupils then choose 5 subjects from the following: English, German, French, geography, history, commercial studies, economics, mathematics, physics, chemistry, and biology. For the last 2 years, pupils study these 5 subjects, which must include at least one foreign language, plus Dutch, and the final examinations are taken in these 6 subjects. Pupils who wish to proceed to higher technical school should include mathematics, physics and preferably chemistry in their HAVO studies.

Since 1968 there have been 2 types of school, each offering 6-year courses of VWO (pre-university education): <u>Gymnasium</u>, <u>Lyceum</u>, and <u>Atheneum</u>.

The <u>Gymnasium</u> teaches Latin and Greek during the whole 6-year course. From the fourth or fifth year, pupils specialize in stream A, concentrating on the classics, or stream B, concentrating on mathematics and science.

The <u>Atheneum</u> does not include Greek and Latin, and there is greater emphasis on modern languages, history, geography, law and economics. The Athenea also divide from the fourth or fifth year into an A stream, concentrating on economics and social science, and a B stream, concentrating on mathematics and science.

A <u>Lyceum</u> is a school combining the <u>Gymnasium</u> and <u>Atheneum</u>, with the first year of the curriculum in common.

Netherlands

In 1973 the **undivided VWO (ongedeeld VWO)** was introduced. Initially pupils study 10 subjects - reduced in the fifth and sixth years to 7, which must include Dutch and one foreign language, these are tested in the final examination for the **VWO, Gymnasium or Atheneum Certificate**. The Certificate shows marks obtained in the state-regulated written examination and the oral and/or written examination set by the school. Failure in 1 subject may be compensated for by a high mark in another, but a pupil who fails in 2 or more subjects must repeat the final year and resit the examinations.

Vocational (Beroepsonderwijs)

There are various fields, training beginning at different levels. Courses of vocational education are normally referred to by their abbreviations, both in terms of level and of field. The HBO schools (Hoger Beroeps Onderwijs) since 1968 have offered various courses of higher vocational training.

The levels may be divided as follows:

Lager Beroeps Onderwijs/School (LBO/LBS)   - lower vocational training
Middelbaar Beroeps Onderwijs/School (MBO/MBS)   - intermediate vocational training
Hoger Beroeps Onderwijs/School (HBO/HBS)   - higher vocational education.

The 4 main fields are: technical, domestic science and the social services, economics and administration, and agriculture.

Technical:

The LBS used to offer mainly 3-year courses, but these have been extended to 4 years. Pupils enter directly from primary school for what is essentially basic trade-training. On completion of the course, they can take up an apprenticeship or begin work in a factory.

The MBS offer 4-year courses which include a year of practical training in industry, mostly in engineering. Entrance to these is with the LTS and MAVO Certificates. The MTS Certificate entitles the holder to be admitted to post-secondary vocational institutions and to the teacher-training courses for junior and senior vocational schools.

The HBS offer 4-year courses, which include a year of practical training and lead to the technician qualification of **Ingenieur** (abbreviated **Ing.**, not **Ir.**, which is awarded by the universities). Admission is through the MBS Certificate or HAVO Certificate.

Domestic science and social services:

Domestic science training (huishouden/nijverheidonderwijs) is offered at lower (LHNO), intermediate (MHNO) and higher (HHNO) levels. Social services training (Social Pedagogisch Onderwijs) is offered at intermediate (MSPO) and higher (HSPO) levels. As there may be considerable overlap between courses in these 2 sectors, they are grouped together. Most courses are connected with specific but widely different occupations. From 1984 onwards all courses in these fields at intermediate level have been brought together in schools of MDGO (Middelbaar Dienstverlenent en Gegondheidszorg.

Economics and administration:

This is offered at lower, intermediate and higher levels (LEAO, MEAO and HEAO levels respectively).

Netherlands

Agriculture:

This is offered at lower (LAO/LAS), intermediate (MAO/MAS) and higher levels. Like the HTS graduate, the HAS graduate is awarded the title of **Ingenieur** (Ing.).

HIGHER EDUCATION

Vocational (HBO - Hoger Beroeps Onderwijs)

The HBO offer various post-secondary courses of higher vocational education of 3-4 years, including 1 year of practical training. Admission is with the HAVO Certificate. Graduates of higher technical and higher agricultural education are awarded the title **Ingenieur**, abbreviated **Ing**. HBO Certificates give admission to university education in some cases (with some exemptions).

Universities and institutions of comparable level (WO - Wetenschappelijk Onderwijs)

In 1982 a new structure of university education was introduced (see below); the old structure is gradually being phased out.

The VWO Certificate is the entrance requirement for courses of higher education at universities and institutions of comparable level. In theory, all students holding this qualification have the right to a university place, and this has led to overcrowding: since 1972 a system of numerus clausus (limited admission) has operated in the form of a lottery (in the fields of medicine, dentistry, veterinary science and others) which may vary from year to year.

Courses under the old structure were normally taken in 2 stages, the first leading to the **Kandidaats Examen** and the second to the **Doctoraal**. The **Kandidaats Examen** is usually taken after 3 years (in some subjects after 2 or 4 years) but is not recognized as a professional qualification. In some subject areas the Kandidaats Examen is preceded by a preliminary examination, **Propedeutisch Examen**, after 1 year.

The termination of university study both under the old and the new structure is the **Doctoraal Examen**, which confers the title of **Doctorandus, Meester** (in law) or **Ingenieur** (in technology and agriculture); the respective abbreviations **Drs., Mr.** and **Ir.** may be used before the holder's name. The usual time required to obtain these qualifications is 4 years (total) in law and 5-6 years (total) in all other subjects, including technology and agriculture. These qualifications give the holder the legal right to practise a profession, except in dentistry (tandarts), veterinary science (dierenarts), pharmacy and medicine (arts), where a practical period of 1 or 2 years, culminating in a final examination, is required before entry to these professions.

Until the early 1980s, under the old structure, students were allowed to resit any examinations and indeed to delay taking the examinations until they considered they were ready to do so.

Following the **Doctoraal Examen**, students may prepare a dissertation after full-time research lasting a minimum of 3 years; successful submission leads to the qualification of **Doctor** (Dr.).

Netherlands

At present there are 14 universities and Hogescholen apart from a number of theological institutions offering courses of university-level education. Under the University Education Act of 1960, universities must have at least 3 faculties, of which one must be medicine, mathematics or physics. (The technological universities at Delft, Eindhoven and Twente have departments rather than faculties). In 1982 the business school Nijenrode was given university status a Hogeschool voor Bedrijfskunde. In addition to the **Doctorandus** degree, students receive the degree of **Master of Business Administration** (MBA). In 1984 the Open University will be established and operational.

The Open University

The Open University first admitted students in 1984. There is no specific entry requirement, but every candidate is interviewed intensively, and must be at least 18 years old. Students choose the length of course that they wish to follow and can work towards a secondary school qualification (the VWO Certificate is the most popular), a degree, or an Open University qualification.

TEACHER EDUCATION

Pre-primary/nursery (Kleuteronderwijs)

The courses are divided into 2 parts at the nursery teacher training colleges (Opleiding tot Kleuterleidster).

Part 1 takes 3 years and leads to the qualification of **Kleuterleidster (Akte A - Nursery School Teacher's Certificate)**.

Part 2 takes 1 year and leads to the qualification of **Hoofdleidster (Akte B - Head Teacher's Certificate)**.

For admission to Part 1, pupils must hold the MAVO Certificate or evidence that they have completed the first 3 years of the HAVO or VWO course.

Primary

Before 1968:

Training for prospective primary school teachers was at 3 levels in Kweekscholen.

The first level lasted 2 years from the entrance standard of the MULO Certificate on completion of 3 years classical secondary schooling. This phase covered general education as in the ordinary secondary schools but did not lead to any particular qualification.

The second level lasted 2 years and led to the **Primary School Teacher's Certificate**.

The third level lasted 1 year and led to the certificate of a fully qualified primary school teacher eligible to become head of a primary school and teach general subjects in ULO schools.

Netherlands

1968-72:

The training was divided into 2 parts, the entrance level to the first part being the HAVO Certificate or full Pre-Primary School Teacher's Certificate.

Part 1 lasted 2 years and led to the qualification of primary school teacher (**Akte van Bekwaamheid als Onderwijzer**).

Part 2 lasted 1 year and was optional, leading to the qualification which made the holder eligible to become a head teacher (**Akte van Bekwaamheid als Volledig Bevoegd Onderwijzer**).

Since 1972:

The Part 2 course, available from 1968-72, became compulsory; and there is now only 1 final examination at the end of Part 2, leading to the full qualification of primary school teacher, eligible to become a head teacher (**Akte van Bekwaamheid als Volledig Bevoegd Onderwijzer**) and teach the following subjects at a lower general secondary school: Dutch, arithmetic, history, geography, and biology.

Integrated pre-primary/primary

In 1984 the new Pedagogische Academie voor het Basisonderwijs (PABO) was introduced to replace training for pre-primary/nursery and primary school teachers. The PABO higher vocational training course lasts 4 years. The entrance requirement is the HAVO Certificate.

Secondary

Before 1970:

Training was divided into 2 distinct levels.

The first level was a 3-year course from the level of MULO or completion of 3 years general secondary education, leading to the qualification of the **MO-A Certificate** (**Middelbaar Onderwijs**), entitling the holder to teach in ULO schools, nursery teacher-training schools and technical schools of domestic economics. To teach in primary teacher-training institutes, students had to hold the MO-A Certificate in 2 subjects.

The second level was a 3- to 4-year course from the MO-A Certificate in the same subject, leading to the **MO-B Certificate** and entitling holders to teach in secondary schools and pursue their studies at university.

Since 1970:

Following the implementation of the Secondary Education Act in 1968, teacher-training courses were revised and experimental training begun in teacher-training institutes linked to universities, the New Secondary School Teacher Training Colleges (Nieuwe Lerarenopleidingen). The institutes offer training at 2 levels: third grade and second grade (teachers). Third-grade teachers may teach in LAVO, MAVO and LBO schools. The second grade includes the first 3 forms of HAVO and all MBO schools.

Netherlands

All students at the Nieuwe Lerarenopleidingen are required to take 2 subjects. In a 4-year course these subjects as well as educational theory and practice are studied. Practical training is given much attention, but this differs from one institute to another. After the 4-year course a student is qualified to teach in the 2 fields at third-grade level. The student can also choose to follow an additional course for 6 months in 1 subject, to qualify to teach that subject at second-grade level. Holders of the second-grade teacher qualification may enter university at a level determined at the discretion of the university concerned.

First-grade teachers are educated at university. They are able to teach in VWO schools (i.e. Gymnasium and Atheneum), the final 2 forms of HAVO, and all types of HBO school. Universities require prospective teachers to attend education lectures and practical training/classroom observation. This pedagogic and didactic training can be taken before or after obtaining the Doctorandus-, Meester- or Ingenieur-degree.

An extensive parallel system of part-time teacher education exists, leading to lower, intermediate and higher teacher certificates (**LO-Akte, MO-A-Akte** and **MO-B-Akte**, respectively), corresponding to third, second and first grade.

Third-grade teachers The course lasts 2 years, part-time, leading to the **Lager Onderwijs Akte (LO-Akte)**; it is also known as a 'C course'. Teachers of this grade may teach in LAVO, MAVO and LTS schools.

Second-grade teachers The course lasts 3 years, part-time, leading to the qualification of **MO-A-Akte**, entitling the holder to teach up to the fourth form at HAVO schools and all MBO schools. Holders of the second-grade teachers' qualification may enter university at a level determined at the discretion of the university concerned.

First-grade teachers One course lasts another 3 or 4 years after the MO-A-Akte, leading to the award of an **MO-B-Akte**. Holders of these can teach in VWO and HBO schools and the final forms of HAVO.

INTERNATIONAL EDUCATION

Since 1950, a number of institutions have existed alongside the formal university system offering international post-secondary and postgraduate courses. The medium of instruction is usually English, and the courses have been set up primarily for students from developing countries. The courses are normally short (4 weeks - 18 months) and offered in: aerial survey and earth sciences; agriculture; hydraulic and environmental engineering; social sciences; food science and nutrition; European integration; management; building and housing; telecommunications; broadcasting; electronics; local government; and industrialization.

New Zealand

The national state school system is administered by the Department of Education, but local authorities have direct control of primary, intermediate and secondary schools.

Compulsory education is from age six to fifteen.

The medium of instruction is English.

EVALUATION IN BRITAIN

School

School Certificate (awarded on completion of form V) - usually considered to be below GCE O-level standard.

Matriculation

It is generally considered that a student qualified to enter university in New Zealand would be qualified for admission to a degree course in Britain.

The following qualifications may be compared to approximately GCE O-level standard:

Sixth Form Certificate (awarded on completion of 1 year in form VI)

University Entrance Certificate (awarded on completion of form VI, until 1986)

The following qualifications may be compared to a standard above GCE O-level:

Higher School Certificate (awarded on completion of 1 year in form VII) - may be compared to approximately 1 year above GCE O-level.

University Bursaries Examination - may be compared to overall GCE A-level standard, but not on a subject-for-subject basis.

Technical qualifications

New Zealand Certificate (in various subjects) - usually considered comparable to BTEC Higher National Certificate, formerly HNC standard.

New Zealand

New Zealand Technicians Certificate - usually considered comparable to the City & Guilds Final/Full Technological Certificate.

Higher

The university system in New Zealand is considered to be very similar to that in Britain.

Bachelor (General) degree (3 years) - usually considered comparable to British Bachelor (Ordinary) degree.

Bachelor (Honours) degree (4 years) - usually considered comparable to British Bachelor (Honours) degree.

Master degree - considered similar to its British counterpart.

MARKING SYSTEMS

School

School Certificate

Until 1962: no grades.

1962-8: marks of over 50% were needed in 4 subjects, including English.

1969- : success in 1 or more subjects.

Sixth Form Certificate

1969-85: awarded in 3 grades (A, B, C) for any subjects in which marks of over 50% were obtained.

1986- : awarded in 7 grades (A1, A2, B1, B2, C1, C2, D) for all subjects entered.

University Entrance Certificate (until 1986)

Most students obtained this award by accreditation, not examination.

If a student obtained passes in only 1, 2 or 3 subjects, or did not include English, a credit by examination was granted for each subject in which 50 or more marks were obtained.

Bursaries examination

Marks are on a scale of 0-100 per paper. Students may gain an A award by aggregating 300 or more marks, a B award with 250-299, or the basic entrance qualification by aggregating 160 or more marks in 4 other subjects.

New Zealand

Higher

A+	high first	C+	sound pass
A	clear first	C	pass
A-	bare first	C-	marginal pass
B+	high second	D	failure; reasonable chance of passing repeat course
B	clear second	E	failure
B-	bare second		

Classification for Bachelor degree:

First class	A
Second class (Division I)	A-/B
Second class (Division II)	B/B-
Third class	C+

Degrees are awarded with Honours in:

class 1
class 2 div. i
class 2 div. ii

Students not awarded Honours may be awarded Pass degrees.

Where an Honours degree is awarded after an undergraduate course of study (e.g. in engineering, law or science) Honours are awarded in first or second class only, with no third class. This degree then has the status of a high quality Bachelor degree, enabling candidates to go directly into postgraduate courses.

SCHOOL EDUCATION

Primary

This may commence at age 5, at the discretion of parents, but is not compulsory until age 6. After the first 2 years of infant classes, children complete standards 1, 2, 3 and 4. The remaining 2 years are usually completed at an intermediate school, but if no such school is available, forms 1 and 2 are provided at the primary school.

Secondary

Entrance to secondary schools is non-selective. These schools are required to give all students a basic 2-year course in English, social studies, general science, elementary mathematics, physical education, music and art and crafts, together with optional subjects related to particular courses. Secondary schooling runs from form III (age 13), to form VII.

At the end of form V (i.e. the third year of secondary education) students take the **School Certificate** examinations. Until 1962, school certificates did not show subject grades. From 1962 to 1968 students had to score over 50% in 4 subjects, including English, to be credited with a pass in the examination. In 1968/9 changes were made which enabled students successful in 1 or more subjects to receive a certificate stating that they had completed a 3-year course and obtained a school certificate in those subjects.

New Zealand

From 1986 all candidates will have received a certificate recording their achievements in each subject. A 7-point grade scale is used, ranging from A1 = high achievement to D = limited achievement. The grade scale covers the full range of achievement.

This certificate is generally considered to be the secondary school leaving certificate, but students may stay on for a further year to obtain the **Sixth Form Certificate**, which is gained without examination.

The **Sixth Form Certificate** is awarded to students who have satisfactorily completed a course at sixth-form level. It may be awarded in any number of subjects up to a maximum of 6. To complete a course satisfactorily a student must:

show a satisfactory attitude to work, fulfil a homework requirement set by the school and complete any necessary practical course

remain at school until a course completion date, set annually by the Department of Education.

Until 1986 students wishing to enter university in New Zealand needed to obtain a pass in the **Universities Entrance Examination**. This was taken at the end of form VI, usually at age 17. The pass could be gained by taking the examination or by being accredited by the Universities Entrance Board. In either case the certificate stated that the named candidate 'has shown competence in the following subject ... of the above examinations and is academically qualified to matriculate at any university in New Zealand'. The certificate showed the subjects taken, but did not show grades or marks. Candidates took 4, 5 or 6 subjects, which must have included English, at one sitting.

Prospective university students are encouraged to stay at school for a fifth year of secondary education. In this year they normally take the **University Bursaries Examination** or the **Entrance Scholarships Examination**. Candidates for the University Bursaries Examination take 3, 4 or 5 subjects. Examination papers in 5 subjects include advanced papers in 3 of the subjects. Scholarships are awarded on the aggregate marks of all 8 papers.

In the final year of secondary education (form 7 or upper form VI) students may obtain a **Higher School Certificate**, which is gained without examination. For those who do not sit or are unsuccessful in the Bursaries or Scholarship Examinations, the Higher School Certificate serves to verify that they have attended school for 1 year beyond form 6.

Entrance to university is gained in 1 of 3 ways:

Before 1986, form 6 students could obtain the **University Entrance Certificate**, either by accreditation or by examination, which granted entry to university.

From 1986 students who enter university at the end of form 6 must apply for provisional entrance to a specific university and course of study. Provisional entry will be granted on the basis of performance in the Sixth Form Certificate, and other considerations.

Entry is also gained by achieving a minimum of 160 marks in 4 subjects in the **University Bursaries Examination** (form VII).

New Zealand

Technical/vocational secondary/further education

Vocational and technical education is largely provided by 12 technical institutes.

Part-time courses leading to the **New Zealand Certificates** in engineering, draughting science, building, quantity surveying, commerce and statistics take 5 years. The examinations for these certificates are organized by the awarding body, the Authority for Advanced Vocational Awards. The courses are conducted in the technical institutes, in 12 specially selected secondary schools and 5 government training institutions (e.g. the Forestry Training Centre). Members of the Technicians Certification Authority include representatives of the Department of Education, the technical institutes, the universities and sectors of industry and commerce. Academic standards required for a pass in most of the subjects taken in the first and second year of these 5-year part-time courses are generally considered comparable to those attained in the School Certificate and Sixth Form/University Entrance Examination Certificate respectively. Students who have gained satisfactory passes in relevant subjects at these examinations are granted credit towards the **New Zealand Technicians Certificate**. The certificate is not awarded unless the candidate, in addition to passing the examinations, has been employed in related work for at least 3 years. 4 community colleges offer similar training.

Apprenticeship training generally takes over 5 years, although a reduction may be given to those who have gained the School Certificate or passed trade examinations. Apprentices must pass written and practical examinations, set by the New Zealand Trades Certification Board. The Board also awards **Advanced Trade Certificates**, on examination, after completion of a post-apprenticeship year in specified trades. Some apprentices who have gained an Advanced Trade Certificate may enter the third year of the 5-year course of technician training.

Technical Institutes offer a wide range of part-time and full-time courses in technical subjects, as well as some aspects of WEA (Workers' Education Association) type adult education. Some of these institutions are called polytechnics, but the standard is not considered as high as that of polytechnics in Britain.

Community Colleges are virtually technical institutes, though with a wider range of WEA-type adult education.

HIGHER EDUCATION

The University of New Zealand was the only such institution until 1961. The university had constituent colleges which were subsequently split into the autonomous Universities of Otago, Canterbury, Auckland and Victoria. In 1964 the number of universities increased to 6, with the establishment of Massey and Waikato Universities. The universities offer diploma, degree and postgraduate courses in most disciplines.

The type of degree most commonly awarded is the 3-year Pass degree, requiring 8 or 9 'units' (a 'unit' being a year's work in a subject) in at least 2 subjects, and study at all 3 levels or stages. Since 1973 the universities have laid more emphasis on smaller units of academic value - e.g. credit points - and continuous assessment.

On average, 108 credits are required for an Ordinary degree, gained not less than 3 years from matriculation. A system of credit transfer exists between the universities so that students can move from one to another.

Honours degrees last at least 4 years, except in the case of students admitted to the second year of a course, due to outstanding performance in the Entrance Scholarships Examination.

Some degrees, mainly professional in character, are preceded by an intermediate course of 1 year.

Master degrees comprise 1-2 years study beyond the Bachelor degree. They may be awarded with Honours or Distinction and may involve course-work, thesis, or both.

The Ph.D. takes the form of supervised research for a minimum of 2 years.

Lincoln College is an autonomous agricultural college, awarding Canterbury University degrees.

TEACHER EDUCATION

Kindergarten

Courses for kindergarten teacher-training are provided at the state teachers' colleges, and entrance qualifications are the same as for primary teacher-training. A **New Zealand Free Kindergarten Teachers' Diploma** is awarded to students who successfully complete the 2-year course.

Primary

The basic primary teachers' college course lasts 3 years, plus an additional year of probation, and is known as Division A. The total course may extend to 5 years if it includes full-time university study. Some students undertake part-time university study in each year of the course, or take a B.Ed. course taught jointly by the college and the neighbouring university. The minimum entry qualification is the Sixth Form Certificate.

Students who have already completed a degree take a 1-year course of further training at a teachers' college. Students who have a minimum of 5 units towards a degree take a 2-year course of full-time teacher training. Each college awards its own diploma. The **Trained Teachers' Certificate** is awarded on satisfactory completion of the 1-year probation period.

The Trained Teachers' Certificate and the Kindergarten Teachers' Diploma are not cross-qualifications.

Secondary

To train as a secondary school teacher, a student must be eligible to enter university, and undertake up to a 3-year Division B course of concurrent study at a teachers' college and a university. Those already holding a degree take a 1-year course at a teachers' college. To obtain the Trained Teachers' Certificate, they must then complete a year of teacher training. On completion of 2 years teaching, students obtain a **Diploma in Teaching**.

New Zealand

Training for woodwork or metalwork teaching takes place partly at a teachers' college and partly at a technical institute. A **Technical Teachers' Certificate** is awarded after 2 years of satisfactory teaching in a state secondary school, intermediate school or manual training centre.

Technical institutes

Tutors and Instructors require professional qualifications in their subjects, but apart from a 3-month induction course during the first 2 years of service there is no formal training in methodology.

Teachers' colleges

There is no formal training for tutors; a degree is preferable but not necessary. Experience in teaching in primary or secondary schools is a prerequisite.

DISTANCE EDUCATION

The Correspondence School provides academic primary and secondary courses for children as well as adults who want a second chance to pass school examinations.

The Technical Correspondence Institute provides a full range of trades technician training by correspondence, linked with periodic face-to-face practical instruction.

Massey University offers a range of degree and diploma courses by correspondence, including annual face-to-face short residential courses.

The Advanced Studies for Teachers Unit provides professional courses for teachers to upgrade their Trained Teachers' Certificate to a Diploma in Teaching.

Nicaragua

Republic of Nicaragua

The medium of instruction is Spanish.

The academic year runs from March to December.

EVALUATION IN BRITAIN

School

Bachillerato en Ciencias y Letras - generally considered to compare to GCE O-level standard.

Higher

Licencia/Licencitura - may be considered to compare to British Bachelor degree standard.

MARKING SYSTEMS

School

Marking is on the scale 1-10 (maximum), with 6.5 as the minimum pass mark.

9.51-10	excellent
8.51-9.5	very good
7.51-8.5	good
6.5-7.5	average

The Bachillerato is only awarded if the grade 'good' is obtained.

Higher

Percentage scale; 70% is the minimum pass.

Nicaragua

SCHOOL EDUCATION

Primary

This covers 6 years.

Secondary

This covers 5 years, culminating in the examinations for the Bachiller en Ciencias y Letras.

FURTHER EDUCATION

The <u>Instituto Politecnico</u> is a private institution which awards professional qualifications after courses lasting 2-3 years.

HIGHER EDUCATION

There are 2 universities, one of which is private, founded by the Society of Jesus in 1960.

The entrance requirement for degree courses is the **Bachiller en Ciencias y Letras**, and an entrance examination is necessary for the faculties of engineering, veterinary medicine and humanities. Students of medicine and nursing may enter university after 3 years of high school.

A **Licencia/Licenciatura** takes 4-5 years. Professional qualifications vary between 1 and 7 years.

Medicine - the title of **Doctor** takes 7 years to obtain.

TEACHER EDUCATION

Primary

A 5-year secondary level course on completion of primary education, consisting of years general education followed by 2 years specialization, leads to the qualification of **Diploma de Maestro de Educacion Primaria**.

Secondary

Teachers are holders of the Licenciatura awarded with the **Titulo de Profesor de Ensenanza Media**.

Niger

Republic of the Niger

Niger gained independence in 1960. There is a strong French influence on the educational system.

The medium of instruction is French.

The academic year runs from October to June.

EVALUATION IN BRITAIN

School

Baccalaureat/Diplome de Bachelier de l'Enseignement du Second Degre - generally compared to GCE O-level standard.

Higher

Licence - generally considered slightly above GCE A-level standard.

MARKING SYSTEMS

School and Higher

Marking is on a scale of 0-20; minimum pass is 10.

16-20	very good
14-15	good
12-13	quite good
10-11	average

Niger

SCHOOL EDUCATION

Primary

This covers 6 years.

Secondary

This covers 7 years, divided into a 4-year lower general cycle followed by a 3-year upper cycle, during which pupils may specialize. On completion of the 3-year academic cycle, pupils take the examinations for the **Baccalaureat/Diplome de Bachelier de l'Enseignement du Second Degre**. The Baccalaureat is available in a variety of series/options.

Series A (options A1-A5)	philosophie-lettres	philosophy and social sciences
Series B	sciences economiques et sociales	social and economic sciences (available since 1976 but abolished in 1984)
Series C	sciences mathematiques et physiques	agriculture, mathematics, medicine, natural science, pharmacy, technology, veterinary medicine, and dentistry
Series D	sciences mathematiques et naturales	agriculture, mathematics, medicine, natural science, pharmacy, technology, veterinary medicine, and dentistry

Until 1972 the examinations were administered by the University of Abidjan in the Ivory Coast; since then they have been administered by the University of Niamey.

Technical secondary

On completion of a technical upper secondary course, pupils take the examinations for the **Baccalaureat/Bachelier Technicien** in Series F or G:

F1	construction mecanique
F3	electrotechnique
F4	genie civil
G1	administration technique
G2	business

HIGHER EDUCATION

There is one university, the <u>University of Niamey</u>, established in 1971 as the Centre d'Enseignement Superieur and upgraded to university status in 1973. The entrance requirement is the Baccalaureat plus a special entrance examination.

After 2 years study students obtain the **Diplome Universitaire d'Etudes Litteraires** (**DUEL**) in arts or the **Diplome Universitaire d'Etudes Scientifiques** (**DUES**) in mathematics or sciences. A further year leads to the **Licence** and yet a further year to the **Maitrise**.

TEACHER EDUCATION

Primary

The <u>Ecoles Normales</u> train teachers for primary schools.

Secondary

Teachers for first-cycle secondary schools are trained by the <u>Faculte de Pedagogie</u> of the <u>University of Niamey</u>. A 2-year programme leads to a professional diploma, the **DAP/CEG**. The Faculty also trains Inspectors and Advisers. Second-cycle teachers are trained at the Faculties of the University. Training forms part of the Licence programmes.

Nigeria

Federal Republic of Nigeria

In the early 1970s the Federal Government formulated a new National Policy on Education, with the aim of providing universal primary education, expanding facilities at secondary level and enabling the more even development of facilities throughout the country.

At present no cycle of education is compulsory.

The medium of instruction is usually the local language for the first three years of primary education, and English is used thereafter, although there is no official policy.

EVALUATION IN BRITAIN

School

West African GCE O-level - grades 1-6 are considered to equate to pass grades at GCE O-level (A, B, C).

West African Higher School Certificate - grades A-E are considered to equate to the same grades in GCE A-levels; a subsidiary pass would be compared to a pass at GCE O-level.

Further

Ordinary Diplomas - generally considered below BTEC National Diploma (formerly OND).

Higher Diplomas - generally compared to BTEC National Diploma (formerly OND).

Nigerian National Diploma - generally compared to BTEC National Diploma (formerly OND).

Higher

Bachelor degrees - generally considered to compare favourably to British Bachelor degrees.

Nigeria

Teacher

Grade III Teacher's Certificate - generally considered to be below GCE O-level standard.

Grade II Teacher's Certificate - has been known to be compared to GCE O-level standard, although it represents 1 year less of academic study than the course for the West African School Certificate.

Grade I Teacher's Certificate - generally considered to be between GCE O- and A-level standards.

Nigerian Certificate of Education - approximates to GCE A-level standard.

MARKING SYSTEM

School

West African GCE O-level:

1	excellent
2	very good
3	good
4-6	credit
7-8	pass
9	fail

West African Higher School Certificate:

A-E	pass
F	fail
O	subsidiary pass

Higher

Bachelor degrees

1st class	70-100%
2nd class upper division	60-69
2nd class lower division	50-59
3rd class pass	40-49

SCHOOL EDUCATION

Primary

This is now being standardized to cover 6 years, from age 6, although in some states it may still be up to 8 years. In the northern states it was 7 years from age 5.

Nigeria

On completion of this cycle pupils take the examinations for the **Primary (First) School Leaving Certificate** (P(F)SLC).

Secondary

Entry is based on results obtained in the Primary School Leaving Certificate. Pupils must also pass:

National Common Entrance Examination administered by the West African Examinations Council - for federal government-owned secondary-level institutions

or

State Common Entrance Examination administered by the individual State Ministry of Education - for state-owned secondary-level institutions.

Grammar schools offer a 6-year course, made up of a 3-year lower and a 3-year higher secondary cycle, leading to the examinations for the **West African GCE O-level**; students who wish can stay on for a further 2 years in the sixth form. At the end of the upper sixth, pupils take the examinations for the **West African Higher School Certificate**.

The limited number of secondary modern schools are being phased out but at present offer 2-3 years post-primary education.

Technical secondary

Secondary commercial schools offer 5-year courses including academic subjects and specialization (e.g. in book keeping, business studies and typing). At the end of the course, pupils may take the examinations for the **West African School Certificate** or of the **Royal Society of Arts**.

Junior Craft Schools, Trade Centres and **Technical Institutes** offer a variety of courses, some only from the level of the Primary School Leaving Certificate. Most courses lead to a qualification of the **City & Guilds of London Institute**, usually only **Part 1/Intermediate**. In 1966 it was suggested that national examinations should be set in certain subjects, and a new board for technical and craft education was established to assume overall responsibility; but the City & Guilds of London Institute has continued to provide the question papers. Joint certification only occurs in certain subjects where certificates are awarded to successful candidates by the West African Examinations Council in collaboration with the City and Guilds of London Institute.

FURTHER EDUCATION

In the late 1960s/early 1970s, 10 Colleges of Science and Technology were established at: Auchi, Calabar, Enugu, Ibadan, Ilorin, Kaduna, Maiduguri, Makurdi, Port Harcourt and Yaba. Further colleges have recently been established at Idah, Sokoto, Kano, Ikeja, Bida and Warri (the latter run by the Nigerian National Petroleum Company). Since 1976 the Colleges at Calabar, Ilorin, Maiduguri, Port Harcourt, and Sokoto have been upgraded to universities. In 1979 the colleges offered a 4-year course (including 1 year of practical training) from GCE O-level, leading to the **Nigerian National Diploma**. Until that date the colleges offered 2-year post-GCE O-level **Ordinary Diplomas** and 2-year **Higher Diplomas**. Many colleges offer the 2-stage diplomas in place of the Nigerian National Diploma.

The colleges also offer various certificates in technology which may be obtained after 1, 2 or 3 years.

HIGHER EDUCATION

The usual entrance requirement to Bachelor degree courses at Nigerian universities has been 5 GCE O-level and 2 A-level passes. Since 1977, admission has been centrally arranged by the Joint Admissions and Matriculation Board (JAMB).

Students who obtain good grades in the West African School and Higher School Certificates qualify for 'direct entry' to a 3-year degree course.

Students who held only the West African School Certificate or obtained only poor grades in the West African Higher School Certificate were able to take the concessional entrance examinations conducted by individual universities until 1977. Students who passed these examinations were able to proceed to a 1-year preliminary course, before embarking on the degree course.

When the JAMB was established, the responsibility for setting and administering the matriculation examination passed from the individual university to the Board. The JAMB now conducts a competitive entrance examination for admission to the preliminary course for those universities which do not have their own school of basic studies. The examination is in 2 parts:

Part 1   the use of English

Part 2   the candidate is required to answer questions in 3 subject areas related to the intended course of study.

The University of Ahmadu Bello runs its own Interim Joint Matriculation Board Examination.

The Universities of Benin and Nigeria have incorporated the usual content of a preliminary course in their 4-year degree courses and admit students with O-level qualifications.

Courses leading to a Bachelor degree normally last 3 years, except for those in medicine and veterinary medicine (5 years) and architecture (4 years).

Students may take either a single-subject Honours degree course or combined Honours. In the former, students study 3 subjects in the first year, 2 in the second year and 1 in the third. In the combined Honours course students take 3 subjects in the first year and 2 subjects in both the second and third years.

Postgraduate facilities exist at most institutions with courses available leading to **Diplomas** and **Master degrees**.

Until 1972 both federal and state governments were able to establish institutions of higher education and indeed each region planned its own university. With the creation of the 12-state structure in 1967, the regional universities (i.e. Ibadan, Nigeria

Nigeria

(Nsukka campus), Lagos, Ahmadu Bello at Zaria and Ife) continued to cater specifically for their own states as established out of the old regions. In 1972 the federal government took over sole responsibility for higher education throughout Nigeria, in an attempt to develop more evenly the facilities for higher education throughout the country. In 1976 the campus of Ibadan University at Jos, and the Calabar campus of the University of Nigeria became universities in their own right, and new universities were established at Sokoto and Maiduguri (upgraded and enlarged from the previously existing college of science and technology). Bayero College of Ahmadu Bello University became a university college, and university colleges were also established at Ilorin and Port Harcourt, but all 3 were immediately upgraded into full universities.

It is important to note that the civil war of 1967-70 had far-reaching effects on the educational facilities; the Nsukka campus of the University of Nigeria had to be rebuilt after the war.

TEACHER EDUCATION

Primary

2 years post-primary study at a grade 3 teacher-training college leads to a **Grade 3 Certificate/Elementary Teacher's Certificate**. These colleges are now being phased out.

4 years (sometimes 5 in the north) post-primary study at a grade 2 teacher-training college leads to a **Grade 2 Certificate/Higher Elementary Teacher's Certificate**. Holders of the old Grade 3 Certificate may take an upgrading course to become grade 2 teachers.

Secondary

Holders of the **Grade 2 Certificate** may also teach in lower secondary schools. Secondary-level teachers are normally trained in universities (on a **B.Ed.** course), advanced teachers' colleges or grade 1 teachers' colleges. The entrance requirement for both types of college is the West African School Certificate or a Grade 2 Certificate. Grade 1 teachers' colleges offer 2-year courses during which students study education and 2 teaching subjects and on successful completion obtain a **Grade 1 Certificate**. However most students prefer to study for 3 years at an advanced teachers college for the **Nigerian Certificate of Education**, which also qualifies them for university admission. Holders of the **Grade 2 Certificate** may be admitted to this course or to the 1-year course leading to the **Associate Certificate in Education**.

Technical

The National Technical Teachers' Colleges offer 3-year courses in technical or commercial fields leading to the **Nigerian Certificate of Education**, and a 1-year diploma course for technical teachers already qualified in their subject.

Norway

Kingdom of Norway

The significant feature of the Norwegian education system is its centralization and control by the state of all aspects, including syllabuses and timetables. The aim is to ensure equality of standards and of opportunity throughout the country. Various reforms have been introduced, mostly at the level of school education.

There are two languages - Bokmal and Nynorsk. Both are taught in schools, although Bokmal prevails.

The academic year runs from August to June.

EVALUATION IN BRITAIN

School

Realskole-Eksamen (before 1959) - generally compared to overall GCE O-level standard.

Avgangseksamen (since 1959) is taken by all the pupils at the end of the compulsory 9 years of basic school. The leaving certificate also includes marks for overall achievement in each subject.

Examen Artium (before 1981) - and **Vitnemal: Den Videregaende Skole** (since 1982 replaces Examen Artium for general subjects and for administration and commerce) - may be considered to satisfy the general requirement of universities and polytechnics.

Higher

Candidatus Magisteri - generally compared to British Bachelor degree standard.

Candidatus Realium, Candidatus Philologiae, Magister Artium - generally compared to a British Master degree by research.

Licentiatus, Doctor - generally compared to British Ph.D.

Norway

MARKING SYSTEMS

School

Before 1968:

Examinations at Gymnasium and Examen Artium/matriculation examinations were marked as follows:

4	excellent	saerdeles tilfredsstillende (S.tf.) (not used for oral examinations)
3	very good	meget tilfredsstillende (M.tf.)
2	good	tilfredsstillende (Tf.)
1	fair	noenlunde tilfredsstillende (Ng.tf.)
-2	poor	matelig (not used for oral examinations)
-3	fail	ikke tilfredsstillende (Ik.tf.)

This system was last used in:

1968 for subjects finished in the first year of upper secondary school (Gymnasium)

1970 for subjects finished in the second year

1970 for subjects finished in the third year.

After 1968:

Marking is on the scale 6 (maximum) - 0, with 2 as the pass mark.

This system was first used in:

1969 for subjects finished in the first year of upper secondary school (Gymnasium)

1970 for subjects finished in the second year

1971 for subjects finished in third year.

Deltatt

Where the student has taken optional subjects but has chosen not to be given a mark in a particular subject, the word 'deltatt' (has followed the teaching) appears instead of a mark.

Teknisk Hogskoler

Marking is on the scale 1.0 (excellent, almost never awarded), 1.5, 2.0, 3.0, 3.5 (lowest passing average), 4.0 (lowest passing mark), 4.5, 5.0, 6.0.

Distriktshogskoler/regional colleges

Marking is on the scale 1.0, 1.5, 2.0, 3.0, 3.5, 4.0; failure marks are not recorded.

Norway

Higher

1.0-1.5	laudabilis prae ceteris (maximum)
1.6-2.5	laudabilis
2.6-3.2	haud illaudabilis
3.3-4.0	non contemnendus (lowest passing grade)

When grading each subject only one decimal point is used, the final grade of a degree has 2 decimal places.

For general linguistics and general phonetics only 'passed' is used.

Teacher

<u>Pedagogiske Hogskoler</u> - 4 (maximum) to 1 (lowest passing grade).

SCHOOL EDUCATION

Kindergarten (Barnehager)

Facilities are available at this level for some children between the ages of 3 and 6-and-a-half. It is not compulsory.

Primary

Until 1959, primary schooling (Folkeskole) was compulsory for 7 years from age 7. The 1959 Primary Schools Act established 9 years of compulsory education (Grunnskolen) divided into 6 years elementary (Barneskole) and 3 years secondary (Ungdomsskole). By the academic year 1970/1 this increased period of compulsory education had been established more or less throughout the country.

The curriculum at <u>Barneskole</u> includes religious instruction, Norwegian, arithmetic, writing, arts, geography, history, music, handiwork, physical education, natural science, English (introduced in grade 4), social science, home economics, study of local history and folklore.

Lower secondary

Before 1959:

On completion of the 7-year primary course, pupils proceeded to the 3-year course at a <u>Realskole</u>. The syllabus of the first and second years was the same as that of the first 2 years of the 5-year Gymnasium course. The final certificate obtained on completion of the second year of the 3-year course was the **Realskole-Eksamen**. Pupils could then stay on for an additional year or transfer to a Gymnasium (see below).

After 1959:

Under the system of 9 years compulsory education pupils proceed to a 3-year course at an <u>Ungdomsskole</u> (comprehensive school) on completion of the elementary school. There is no entrance examination to these courses and no streaming.

At the end of the ninth year, pupils may exceptionally stay on for a tenth year to improve their marks or to consolidate their studies before going out to work or to begin at the Gymnasium/Videregaende Skole.

Norway

In grade 7 the curriculum includes Norwegian, mathematics, religious instruction, social studies, natural science, English, music, physical education, art and home economics. In grades 8 and 9 there is also some possibility for specialization. However, besides the obligatory subjects, certain topics must be covered: traffic training, alcohol, drugs, tobacco, environment, careers, school council, family life, consumer education, nutrition, first aid, dental health, and sex education.

On completion of grade 9, the leaving examination is taken, **Avangseksamen**, usually in 4 subjects, to include 2 from Norwegian, mathematics, English and science, which, together with teachers' assessments, produce a final mark (vitnemal).

Upper secondary

Before 1975:

These offered a 3-year course, generally culminating in the **Examen Artium**, for pupils who until 1959 had completed 2 years of Realskole, and after that date for those who completed the course at Ungdomsskole. Pupils would already have studied English.

Before 1976, 6 'Linjer' (areas of specialization) were available, although not all may have been available in one school.

Real-Linje	physics and mathematics
Latin-Linje	classical languages
Engelsk-Linje	modern languages with English as the main subject
Norron-Linje	Norwegian history and language
Naturfag-Linje	biology and chemistry
Okonomisk-Linje	economics

Regardless of the specialization taken, all pupils studied Norwegian, English, German, French, history and civics, geography, biology, chemistry with physiology, mathematics, physical training, and singing. More time was devoted to particular subjects, depending on the specialization. Both official Norwegian languages were compulsory.

The final examination, the **Examen Artium**, consisted of written and oral tests in Norwegian, English, German, mathematics, physics (only the science line) and Latin (only the Latin line), and a series of oral examinations in other subjects. Pupils had to pass in all subjects to matriculate. The results were analysed by the Council of Secondary Education, to ensure that the grading was uniform in all parts of the country. The full examination could be gradually built up by sitting the necessary individual examinations over a longer period of time, and certain subjects could be examined in the penultimate year.

Handelsgymnasia (commercial secondary schools)

These offered a 3-year course from completion of the second year of Realskole (before 1959) or the leaving examination of an Ungdomsskole. The course offered was similar to the Okonomisk-Linje of the Gymnasia (before 1976), and prepared the pupil for higher education.

Landsgymnasia

These were regional secondary schools offering a 4-year course on completion of 7 years primary education and a 6-month continuation course.

Norway

After 1976:

The 1974 New Curriculum Plan included a reform of the upper secondary school and introduced an all-round school system (i.e. combining academic upper secondary, gymnasium, and vocational) - <u>Videregaende Skole</u>. The new system was established formally from 1 January 1976, and fully operational from 1 August 1979.

The upper secondary school consists of 8 study courses. 2 are courses previously taken at the Gymnasia - the General Studies option and the Administration and Commerce option. The others are vocational: aesthetics, fishing and maritime studies, handicraft and industry, physical education, home economics, and health and social subjects. The vocational courses are job-orientated, whilst the general studies course leads on to academic study.

Obligatory subjects in the General Studies and Administration and Commerce options are:

Norwegian
English - language A
Modern languages - language B (begun in the lower secondary school in addition to English) and language C (begun in the upper secondary school - usually French and German)
Social studies (i.e. geography, history/civics), mathematics, natural science, physical education and religious education.

In the second and third years of General Studies, pupils may specialize in 1 of 4 branches:

Natural science - based on 2 or more of physics, chemistry, biology, mathematics

Social studies - based on 2 or more of law, history, mathematics, social studies, social economics, business administration and economics

Language - based on 2 or more of linguistics, English, Latin, Old Norse, languages B and C (usually German and French)

Music (few schools) - based on theoretical and practical studies of music.

There are also optional subjects covering two 15-week periods over 3 years. (The number depends on how many periods are covered in the subjects in the chosen specialization in years 2 and 3.) These optional subjects may be additional courses from the chosen specialization, fine or performing arts courses, or vocational courses such as typing.

On completion of the 3-year Allmennfag course pupils take the examination for the **Vitnemal: den Videregaende Skole**/Certificate of Upper Secondary Education.

The Videregaende Skole offers 1- to 2-year basic courses (grunnkurs) and advanced courses (videregaenderkurs). The general studies option normally lasts 3 years.

<u>Folkehogskoler</u> (folk high schools)

These offer courses of general education lasting up to 2 years to students aged at least 17. No examinations are taken.

Norway

Technical secondary

Before 1976:

Technical schools (Tekniske Skoler) offered 2-year courses, lengthened in the early 1960s to 3 years. The entrance requirement is the Realskole-Eksamen plus 1 year of practical experience, or the Ungdomsskole final examination and the corresponding practical experience. The qualification obtained, **Ingenior** (technician) had the same standing as the Examen Artium and admitted to university. Students entering the course already holding the Examen Artium did not need the practical experience.

Today the qualification of Ingenior is awarded only after a 2- to 3-year post-secondary course.

The <u>Tekniske Fagskoler</u> were more practically based and their 2-year course led to the qualification of **Tekniker**. They had the same academic requirements as the Tekniske Skoler but required additionally 2 years of practical experience.

Specialist vocational schools offered basic education and specialist training in a variety of fields through courses lasting between 6 months and 3 years. Most courses required, for admission, completion of the Realskoler or Ungdomsskoler.

<u>Verkstedskole</u> offered basic vocational training before beginning an apprenticeship, lasting about 1 year, sometimes up to 3.

<u>Laerlingskole</u> were part-time schools for apprentices.

After 1976:

The Videregaende Skoler have offered courses at further education level in all areas.

HIGHER EDUCATION

This is offered at a variety of institutions: universities and university-level national colleges, regional colleges (Distrikthogskoler), teacher-training colleges (Pedagogiske Hogskoler) and advanced vocational institutions (of engineering, social services, music and advanced nursing.) Some of these institutions offer courses which in Britain may be considered further education.

Entrance to higher education is based on Vitnemal: der Videregaende Skole (General Studies or Administration and Commerce), although for certain university faculties which are heavily over-subscribed (i.e. medicine and technology) a system of numerus clausus (restricted entry) is in operation.

There are 4 multi-faculty universities and 8 state colleges. The University of Tromso is the newest, founded in 1972 to provide an infrastructure of higher learning north of the Arctic Circle. The University of Trondheim was established in 1969 by 3 major educational and scientific institutions already in existence: Der Kongelige Norske Videnskabers Selskap (Royal Norwegian Society of Science), the Norges Laererhogskole (State College for Teachers), and the Norges Tekniske Hogskole (Norwegian Institute of Technology).

Norway

There is no strict time limit set for the completion of studies for a degree, and students present themselves for examination when they think they are ready. All students (except at Norges Tekniske Hogskole) must complete a preliminary course (normally about 6 months), leading to the **Examen Philosophicum**. The average length of study for Norwegian degrees is 5-7 years and they are acquired by accumulating subjects at subsidiary (grunnfag), minor (mellomfag) and major (hovedfag) levels.

In the Humanities Faculty of the University of Oslo, in addition to the courses at grunnfag, mellomfag and hovedfag which are on average calculated to last respectively 2, 3 and 4 semesters, there are now courses lasting half a semester (halvsemesteremner), 1 semester (semesteremner) and 4 semesters, the same length as hovedfag, but having a different structure and entitled 'storfag'. The storfag can be used as a preparation for hovedfag but will probably be most important as a self-contained post-experience course.

Students of liberal arts, social sciences and natural sciences usually read for a **Cand. Mag. (Candidatus Magisterii)** which is obtained by accumulating subjects at the subsidiary and minor levels, usually after a minimum of 4-5 years. Higher degrees, awarded after 2 years further study and/or research at the major hovedfag level, include the degrees of **Cand. Philol. (Candidatus Philologiae)**, and **Cand. Real. (Candidatus Realium)** in the humanities and sciences respectively.

In some fields of study, a **Licentiat** degree is offered on the basis of research to those already possessing a regular higher degree. There are a few courses preparing for the **Doctoral** degree e.g. the Doctor Ingenior of Trondheim. The Universities of Oslo and Bergen now offer higher degrees within the science faculties which will gradually replace the existing Cand. Real. and Doctorate grades. The structure is tripartite:

3-and-a-half years	Cand. Mag.
1-and-a-half to 2 years	Cand. Scient.
2 years	Dr. Scient.

Most Doctoral degrees however are awarded after dissertations of original research have been examined by a Committee of Specialists and after the candidate has defended the work in 2 public lectures. Engineering graduates of the Norwegian Institute of Technology obtain the qualification of **Sivilingenior** after approximately 4-and-a-half years. (Note the difference between this and the qualification of Ingenior, obtained before 1976 after a course of technical secondary education, and since then after a 3-year Examen Artium course.)

Law:

The **Cand. Juris (Candidatus Juris)** is obtained after a course of 5-6 years, leading on to courses for the **Licentiatus Juris** and **Doctor Juris**.

Medicine:

The **Cand. Med. (Candidatus Mediciniae)** is obtained after a course of 6-7 years, leading on to the course for the **Doctor Mediciniae**.

Dental science normally takes 4 years; Veterinary Science takes 6 to 6-and-a-half years.

Norway

Architecture:

The State College of Architecture offers a 5-year course leading to the qualification of **Arkitekt**.

Agriculture:

The State College of Agriculture offers a 5-year course leading to the qualification of **Cand. Agric.**

Folkeuniversitet (FU)

This is the national body into which Friundervisningen's (adult education) branches are grouped. The oldest organisation was founded in Oslo in 1864 to encourage university students to teach working-class adults. There are over 300 local branches of the Folkeuniversitet, which offer academic and vocational courses.

There are 12 colleges of engineering (Ingeniorhogskoler) which offer 2- and 3-year full-time courses from the level of the Examen Artium, leading to the status of **Ingenior**.

Distriktshogskoler

There are also a number of district colleges (Distriktshogskoler), the first of which was created in 1969. These provide courses of higher education of shorter duration than those offered by the universities, often vocational or based upon the particular needs of the region and built on an interdisciplinary approach. Courses last 1-3 years from the level of the Examen Artium. Students are awarded the qualification of **Hogskole Kandidat** after courses lasting 2 years. Courses are generally broader and more innovative than those of the non-university colleges of engineering, social work, etc.

Some Distriktshogskoler teach courses which the universities have validated and recognized as being grunnfag and (in fewer cases) mellomfag levels. Recent developments have led the Distriktshogskoler (and the other advanced vocational institutions) to award the degree of **Cand. Mag.** to those who accumulate the appropriate number of subjects at grunnfag and mellomfag levels.

TEACHER EDUCATION

Before 1973:

Folkeskole, Barneskole, Ungdomsskole - Prospective teachers undertook at a Laererskole a 4-year course on completion of Realskole/Grunnskole, or a 2-year course if they entered with the Examen Artium. Both courses led to the status of **Laerer**.

After 1973:

The new Law on Teacher Education (1973) changed the name of the Laererskoler to Pedagogiskerhogskoler, and these now offer a 3-year course from the level of the Examen Artium.

Norway

The title of **Adjunkt** is obtained either by a further 1 year's approved study in the case of a Laerer, or in the case of university graduates holding a lower degree (e.g. Cand. Mag.), by completing a 6-month course covering educational theory and teaching practice at a Pedagogisk Seminar.

Lektors, the majority of whom work in Videregaede Skoler, have either obtained a higher university degree and taken the 6-month course at the Pedagogisk Seminar or have completed approved studies at hovedfag level (see HIGHER EDUCATION) lasting a minimum of 2 years after the award of Adjunkt and 3 years after receiving the title Laerer.

Oman

Sultanate of Oman

Until 1970 there were very few facilities for education. Since then there has been considerable development, and it is believed that most children, male and female, start primary school. The drop-out rate still gives cause for concern but the general picture is one of continuing improvement, with particular attention being paid to development outside the capital area. The education of women is encouraged by the government, though their enrolment in school is still only between thirty to forty per cent of the total.

Education is not compulsory.

The medium of instruction in all government schools is Arabic; the teaching of English begins in the fourth year of primary education.

The school year runs from September to May, with a short break in February.

EVALUATION IN BRITAIN

Secondary School Leaving Certificate - generally considered to approximate to GCE O-level standard if marks of at least 50% (regardless of pass mark) have been obtained in subjects which can be taken in the GCE examinations, except English language. However, emphasis is given to rote learning and any student entering the British educational system would require at least a year to adjust to a more analytical approach.

MARKING SYSTEM

Secondary School Leaving Certificate is marked on a percentage scale.

SCHOOL EDUCATION

Primary

This covers 6 years, generally from age 6. Students sit examinations at the end of each year on the results of which they qualify for promotion to the next year. This system extends through to the end of the preparatory level. The drop-out rate in 1977/8 was about 25% for both boys and girls.

Preparatory/intermediate (secondary)

This was established in 1971/2. It covers 3 years at the end of which is a national examination, the **Preparatory Certificate**. The results of this examination determine whether a student proceeds into the academic stream at secondary school, attends a job-oriented institute, or goes straight into employment. The curriculum at secondary school includes religion, Arabic, English, mathematics, history and geography, general science and health, arts and crafts, and sports.

Secondary (2nd cycle)

In 1984/5, there were 9,151 secondary students in 38 secondary schools (some share premises with preparatory schools), 2 of which were for girls. The secondary (2nd cycle) course is for 3 years with specialization in the arts or the sciences in the second and third years. The drop-out rate at this stage for 1977/8 was 25% for boys and 13% for girls.

Technical/vocational secondary

Instead of going to a general secondary school, at the end of preparatory level, pupils can attend one of the following specialist schools:

Commercial School (one each for boys and girls)

Secondary Technical School (boys only, at Sohar)

Agricultural College (boys only, at Nizwa)

Vocational Training Institutes (9 institutions run by the Ministry of Social Affairs and Labour, teaching engineering craft and commerce courses)

The Vocational Training Institutes (VTIs) began in 1985, a process of upgrading to convert them from preparatory-level to secondary-level institutions.

A number of Ministries have training centres, usually at craft level, that give specialized training to employees. Examples are the General Telecommunications Organisation, the Roads Division of the Ministry of Communications, the Banking Sector. Petroleum Development Oman, the oil company, has a joint scheme with colleges in the UK leading to BTEC qualifications.

FURTHER EDUCATION

There is one further education college in Oman, **Oman Technical Industrial College**, teaching British-style curricula to approximately **BTEC National Diploma** level. It opened in 1984 and the subjects covered are civil, mechanical and electrical engineering, science and instructor training; computing is planned.

HIGHER EDUCATION

In September 1986, Oman opens its first higher education institution, **Sultan Qaboos University**. The university, built on a 180,000 m site, 40 km from the Capital area, will first offer an 18-month foundation course in English and science to about 500 undergraduates. They will then move into 1 of 5 faculties - science, engineering, medicine, agriculture and education/Islamic studies - for their main course. Men and women will be segregated in the circulation, and residential areas, but will be taught in the same classes. The first graduates are expected in 1991.

TEACHER EDUCATION

There are 3 teacher-training colleges - one each for men and women in the Capital area and one for men only in Salalah. They were upgraded in 1984 to post-secondary colleges and run 2-year courses for prospective primary (with some preparatory) teachers.

Pakistan

Islamic Republic of Pakistan

This chapter covers West Pakistan from the 1960s until the present day and East Pakistan until 1971 when it became the independent state of Bangladesh.

Although there was and still is a Federal Ministry of Education, each province (Punjab, Sind, North West Frontier and Baluchistan) has its own education administration.

In theory, education is compulsory up to grade (year) 10.

English is still widely used as the medium of instruction after grade 10 (matriculation).

EVALUATION IN BRITAIN

School

Matriculation/Secondary School Certificate - generally considered to be below GCE O-level standard.

Intermediate/Higher Secondary School Certificate - generally considered to approximate to GCE O-level standard if marks of over 50% have been obtained, regardless of the pass mark in each subject.

Diploma of Faculty of Arts/Science (FA/FSc) - generally considered to compare to GCE O-level standard.

Higher

Bachelor of Arts, Science or **Commerce** (obtained after a 3-year course) - generally considered to compare to GCE A-level standard, if awarded in the 1st or 2nd class.

Bachelor of Engineering/Bachelor of Science in Engineering - generally considered to approach British Bachelor degree standard.

Master degree - generally considered to compare to British Bachelor degree standard.

Pakistan

MARKING SYSTEMS

School

Secondary School Certificate	A	70-100%
Matriculation	B	60-69
Higher Secondary Certificate	C	50-59
Intermediate Certificate	D	40-47
Bachelor degree (until 1977)	E	minimum pass

The Board of Intermediate Education, Karachi, have a grade A1 which refers to marks above 80%.

Higher

Most universities operate the following marking system:

Division I	60+%
Division II	45-59.9
Division III	33-44.9
Fail	below 33

Alternatively some universities may use:

A excellent
B good
C satisfactory
D average

SCHOOL EDUCATION

Primary

Primary education covers grades 1-5, normally from age 5. In most schools Urdu is the medium of instruction, although in some the vernacular may be used for the first 3 years.

Secondary

This sector is divided into 2 cycles; 3 years middle school and 2 years high school. On completion of this second cycle students take the **Matriculation** examinations, external examinations conducted by the Boards of Intermediate and Secondary Education, of which there are 6. This examination is now more often called the **Secondary School Certificate** examination. Pupils are examined in 9 subjects: Urdu, English, Pakistan and Islamic Studies, Islamiyat, a vocational subject, and either 4 science subjects or 4 general subjects (including general science and general mathematics or home economics). Pupils may leave school with this qualification.

Pakistan

Pupils may study for a further 2 years at a higher secondary/intermediate college, specializing in science or arts. At the end of this period (first year inter-science/arts, second year inter-science/arts) pupils take the examinations for the **Intermediate Certificate**; these consist of papers in Urdu and English with either 4 science or 4 subjects from a social sciences/general group. There are many degree colleges offering a full course of higher education and facilities for the Intermediate Certificate course, which in certain circumstances may form the first 2 years of a 5-year degree course.

The Secondary School Certificate is an adequate entry qualification for the 2-year course leading to the **Diploma of Faculty of Arts/Science** (FA/FSc) at a university/degree college.

Students may also take the **Cambridge Overseas Examinations**; after 11 years the **School Certificate** and after a further 2 years the **Higher School Certificate**.

Technical secondary/further

Technical institutes and vocational schools offer (normally) 2-year courses from grade 9 leading to a Certificate qualification.

Courses in the government training centres are normally 18 months long, including up to 3 months supervised training within industry.

Technician training is offered at the Colleges of Technology during a 3-year course, usually covering grades 11, 12 and 13. The minimum requirement is successful completion of grade 10; however a few students enter with the Intermediate Examination Certificate (i.e. completion of grade 12).

Under the 1972-80 Education Act, polytechnics become Colleges of Technology. Although the courses leading to the qualifications of Certificate and Diploma are expected to continue, students who complete a 3-year Diploma course will be encouraged to undertake industrial training for 2 years before an additional 1-year course leading to the B.Tech. degree.

HIGHER EDUCATION

There are now 19 universities including Quaid-e-Azam University at Islamabad (graduate only); University of Baluchistan, Quietta; Gomal University, Dera Ismail Khan; Bahaudin Zakirya University, Multan; Islamiya University, Bahawalpor; Azad Jammu and Kashmir University, Muzaffarabad; Allama Iqbal Open University, Islamabad; Karachi; Peshawar; Sind, Hyderabad and Punjab, Lahore. There are also 3 agricultural universities, 3 universities of engineering and technology, the new International Islamic University at Islamabad, and the Agha Khan Medical University, Karachi.

There are also many degree colleges. The universities of Karachi, Peshawar, Sind and Punjab are affiliating institutions, i.e. the affiliated colleges depend on the university to which they are attached for their courses, examinations, and approval and award of qualifications. Affiliated colleges normally only provide courses leading to Pass or Ordinary degrees, whereas universities offer courses leading to Honours degrees.

Pass degrees are normally obtained after a course of 2 years, and **Honours degrees** after 3 years, except in engineering (4 years) and medicine (5 years).

A **Master degree** requires 2 years study after a Pass degree or 1 year after a Bachelor (Honours) degree. The B.Ed requires 1 year of study beyond a Bachelor degree in Arts or Science.

The **LL B (Bachelor of Law)** is a postgraduate qualification and entry to the 3-year course is by Bachelor degree in any other subject.

TEACHER EDUCATION

Primary

Entering with the matriculation examination qualification, students undertake a 2-year course at a teacher training school.

Middle School

Courses are taken at teacher training college/normal school.

Secondary

Graduates undertake a 1-year course of training leading to a B.Ed. degree.

Panama

Republic of Panama

The American system of education is dominant.

Education is free, universal and compulsory between ages six and fifteen.

The official medium of instruction is Spanish.

The school year runs from early April to December, except in rural areas where school timetables follow planting and harvesting times.

EVALUATION IN BRITAIN

School

Bachillerato - generally considered to compare to GCE O-level standard.

American High School Graduation Diploma - generally considered to compare to GCE O-level standard.

Higher

Licenciatura - may be considered to compare to British Bachelor degree standard.

MARKING SYSTEMS

School

Marks are usually given on a scale 1-5, the top mark being 5 and minimum pass mark 3.

Higher

Marks are given on a percentage basis, the minimum pass mark being 61%.

A	100-91%	sobesaliente	excellent
B	90-81	bueno	good
C	80-71	regular	average
D	70-61	minima de promocion	lowest passing grade
F	60- 0	fracasado	fail

Panama

SCHOOL EDUCATION

Primary

This lasts 6 years, though few of the rural primary schools offer the full course.

Secondary

This is divided into 2 cycles. The first cycle (ciclo comun) covers 3 years of general education. The second cycle (ciclo academico) consists of 3 years of more specialized study. The last 2 years of this cycle lead to the **Bachillerato de Ciencias** or **de Letras**.

FURTHER EDUCATION

The Department of Literacy and Adult Education offers Adult Education courses. The Institute for Training and Utilization of Human Resources offers comprehensive training courses for adults.

HIGHER EDUCATION

Higher Education is offered at the Universidad de Panama and the Universidad de Santa Maria la Antigua and the Universidad Tecnologia de Panama. The Universidad de Panama is an autonomous state university. The Universidad Santa Maria la Antigua is a private university. The Universidad Tecnologia de Panama is an autonomous university with 7 regional centres.

The Bachillerato de Ciencias and success in a university entrance examination gives access to the science faculties. For matriculation to an arts faculty, success in the university entrance examination and the Bachillerato de Letras are required. The Bachillerato de Letras allows admission to all other faculties.

TEACHER EDUCATION

Primary

Primary school teachers are trained in Escuelas Normales. The Secondary School Leaving Certificate (also called the **Certificado de Maestro Normal**) is awarded at the end of the last 3-year cycle of secondary education in a teacher institution (Escuela Normal). The certificate gives access to the same university faculties as a Bachillerato de Letras.

Secondary school teachers are trained at the Universidad de Panama.

Papua New Guinea

The education system is extensively decentralized with important powers being vested in provincial Educational Boards.

Education is not compulsory.

The medium of instruction is English.

The school year runs from January to December, the university year from March to November.

EVALUATION IN BRITAIN

Secondary School Leaving Certificate - generally considered to be below GCE O-level standard.

Higher School Certificate - generally considered to be between GCE O- and A-level standard.

Bachelor (Pass) degree - generally considered to compare to British Bachelor (Pass) degree standard.

Bachelor (Honours) degree - generally considered to compare to British Bachelor (Honours) degree standard.

MARKING SYSTEMS

Higher

Bachelor (Honours) degrees are classified:
Class I
Class II   division A
Class II   division B
Class III

Papua New Guinea

SCHOOL EDUCATION

Primary

This lasts 6 years, normally from age 7. Primary schools are now called community schools and cover grades 1-6.

Secondary

This lasts a possible 6 years. Grades 7-10 are undertaken in Provincial High Schools, culminating in the **Secondary School Leaving Certificate**. Selected pupils may then proceed to grades 11 and 12 at National High Schools, which culminate in the **Higher School Certificate**. This latter qualification is the entrance qualification for university degree courses.

FURTHER EDUCATION

There are 9 Technical Colleges, several Vocational Centres and various specialized institutions which offer courses of varying length.

HIGHER EDUCATION

The University of Papua New Guinea was established in 1965 by the Australian government. Although the normal entrance qualification is the Higher School Certificate, students may enter with the Secondary School Leaving Certificate and undertake a 1-year preliminary course before beginning the degree studies. All students then follow a foundation course of 1 year.

The University offers **Bachelor degree** courses in Arts, Sciences and Education over 4 years, with an additional year for Honours, and 5-year degree courses in Medicine and Law. The University has adopted a credit system for the Arts and Science degrees: each course runs for half an academic year, and progress towards a degree is achieved by accumulating passes in credit courses until 90 credit points are obtained. Credit points are valued at 4 points for Part I courses, and 6 points for Part II courses. Students normally begin Part II courses in their fifth semester.

The University of Technology was founded in 1973 and offers various degree and diploma courses. Some degree courses start as 2-year diploma courses followed by a further 2 years for a degree, i.e. accountancy, business studies, surveying, cartography and land management. Some degree courses last 4 years, i.e. forestry and engineering, and some 5 years, i.e. applied chemistry, mineral technology and food technology. There are also diploma courses aimed at the technician level, i.e. a 5-year diploma in applied physics.

Postgraduate courses are available at both universities leading to **postgraduate diplomas**, **Master** degrees and **Ph.D.s**.

TEACHER EDUCATION

Primary

There are 9 community teachers colleges, which train primary school teachers over a 2-year course. The minimum entrance requirement is now completion of grade 10.

Secondary

Teachers are trained at Goroka Teachers College (now part of the University of Papua New Guinea) in a 3-year **Diploma** course, following 4 years secondary education, or at the University of Papua New Guinea where they can obtain a Bachelor of Arts or Science degree with an option in education after 4 years study, or a **Postgraduate Diploma in Education** after a further year of study.

Paraguay

Republic of Paraguay

Education is free, universal and compulsory from ages seven to fourteen.

The medium of instruction is Spanish.

The school year runs from March to November.

EVALUATION IN BRITAIN

School

Bachillerato - generally considered to compare to GCE O-level standard.

Higher

Licenciatura - may be considered to be below British Bachelor degree standard.

MARKING SYSTEMS

School

Two grading systems are used in Paraguayan Secondary Schools: 1-5 and 0-10.

5	10	sobresaliente	excellent
4	8	muy bueno	very good
	9		
3	6	bueno	good
	7		
	3	aceptable	
2	4	regular	average
	5	suficiente	

Paraguay

1	1	aplazado	failed
	2	no aprobado	
	0	insuficiente (given only in cases of cheating)	

Higher

Grading is on a scale of 1-5.

5	sobresaliente	excellent
4	distinguido	very good
3	bueno	good
2	regular	average
1	reprobado	fail

SCHOOL EDUCATION

Primary

This lasts 6 years.

Secondary

This lasts 6 years and is divided into two 3-year cycles, the first being a general course known as Ciclo Basico and the second a specialized course known as Colegio.

Students who have completed Ciclo Basico may choose to enter either a vocational course or an academic/technical course.

Secondary school courses of 6 years lead to the **Bachillerato**. This satisfies matriculation requirements in Paraguay. In 1973 a law was passed to introduce curriculum reform to secondary education, the aim being to prepare graduates for employment as well as higher education.

Other specialized schools offer Bachillerato courses i.e. the Military School, the Police School and the Telecommunications School.

The Diversified Cycle has been divided into different tracks.

Old system:	Science and letters	Bachiller Diploma
	Commerce	Bachiller en Comercio
	Normal school	before 1960 Contador Publico (public accountant)
New system:	Humanities and science	Bachiller en Humanidades y Ciencia
	Commerce	Bachiller en Contables
	Technical - Industrial	Bachiller en Industria Technica
	Agriculture	Bachiller de Agronomo

Paraguay

Vocational

2 main centres for vocational training operate under the Ministry of Education: the Escuela Tecnica Vocacional and the Instituto Presidente Carlos Antonio Lopez. They provide vocational training for adults who have completed primary school and offer courses which last up to 3 years. Examinations are graded on a 0-10 scale. Students who successfully complete a course with an average of 6 or above are awarded a Diploma. Students with an average below 6 receive a **Certificate of Attendance**.

Technical

A technical Bachillerato which satisfies university matriculation requirements has recently been introduced. The first certificates of the **Bachiller Tecnico-Industrial** were awarded in 1979.

The Escuela de Tecnicas Industriales (School of Industrial Techniques) offers a 6-year course divided into 2 cycles: the Ciclo Basico and the Ciclo Profesional. Graduation from the Escuela de Tecnicas Industriales is not recognized for university admission.

Other technical courses are offered at a variety of schools run by different Ministries.

Agricultural

Before the new reforms, agricultural education at secondary level was offered at the Colegio Nacional de Agricultura. After a 4-year course students were awarded a **Certificado de Agronomo** (Agronomist). Graduates are eligible to enter the Faculties of Agriculture and Veterinary Science.

HIGHER EDUCATION

Paraguay has 3 institutions of Higher Education: the Universidad de Asuncion - under state control; the Universidad Catolica 'Nuestra Senora de la Asuncion' - under private control; the Instituto Superior de Educacion (Higher Education Institute) - under state control.

The entrance requirement to these 3 institutions is the Bachiller Diploma.

TEACHER EDUCATION

Under the old system students completed 5 years of a post-primary study to receive a diploma as **Profesor de Ensenanza Primaria** (primary school teacher) and 7 years post-primary study to obtain a diploma as **Profesor de Ensenanza Secundaria**.

After 1972 teacher education changed from secondary school level to post-secondary level. The entrance requirement for all teacher training courses is a Bachiller in Humanities or Science.

Paraguay

Primary

Teachers follow a 2-year course to receive the qualification of Profesor de Ensenanza Primaria.

Secondary

Teachers follow a 4-year course and receive the qualification of Profesor de Ensenanza Secundaria. Teaching diplomas are not recognized as equivalent to university degrees in Paraguay, although the entrance requirement and course duration are similar.

Peru

Republic of Peru

The education system is highly centralized, which includes control of the curriculum at school level. Important reforms of the system were initiated following the General Education Reform Law of 1972, although their implementation is not yet complete, and the democratic government elected in 1980 is reversing some of the changes implemented.

Until 1971, only primary education was compulsory, but since then education has been compulsory from ages six to fifteen.

The medium of instruction is Spanish.

English as a foreign language is introduced in state schools when pupils reach age twelve and continues until they leave school. There is an average of about three hours a week of English, though the level of instruction is not high. Private language schools abound.

The academic year runs from March to December.

EVALUATION IN BRITAIN

School

Certificado de Educacion Secundaria Comun Completa - generally considered to compare to GCE O-level standard.

Higher

Licenciatura or **Professional Title** - may be considered to compare to British Bachelor degree standard.

MARKING SYSTEMS

School and Higher

Marking is on a scale 0-20 (maximum), 11 being the minimum pass mark. There is no classification of degrees.

Peru

SCHOOL EDUCATION

Pre-primary

Some facilities are available for children between ages 3 and 6.

PRE-1972 REFORMS (but still the prevalent system)

Primary

This lasts 6 years from age 6 and includes a 1-year transition class between kindergarten or family and formal primary education. At the end of each year throughout their schooling, pupils have to pass a final examination to enter the following grade. If they fail, there is an opportunity to follow holiday classes and try again in March; failure then means re-doing the year. In practice, there are few second failures.

Secondary

This covers 5 years divided into 2 cycles, the first covering 3 years of general studies and the second covering 2 years of specialization. In the second cycle pupils choose from academic, commercial, industrial or agricultural branches. In the academic branch, pupils may choose between the arts or science section. Pupils who fail more than 4 subjects in their annual examinations must repeat the whole year. On successful completion of the second cycle, pupils obtain the **Certificado de Educacion Secundaria** (not the Bachillerato, as with most other Latin American countries), which in Peru is not in the form of a qualification, but a transcript of marks of the student's secondary education. Subjects studied include: Spanish language and literature, history, geography, religion, mathematics, chemistry, biology, physics, English, and art.

Although pupils may take the university entrance examination directly after their final examinations at secondary school, many first undertake a 1-year course of study (curso preparatario), often at a private school (academia).

POST-1972 REFORMS

Primary and secondary

Basic education is as follows:

First grade to sixth grade (primary)
First media to fifth media (secondary)

The curriculum covers language, mathematics, natural sciences, art, physical education, vocational education and religion.

Technical secondary

On successful completion of the second cycle of secondary education in the agricultural, commercial or industrial branch, pupils obtain the **Diploma de Aptitud Profesional**.

FURTHER EDUCATION

The <u>Escuelas Superiores de Educacion Profesional</u>, which have been established since 1975, offer courses from the level of grade 9. These last 6-8 semesters in a variety of specializations leading to the qualification of **Titulo Profesional** (in social work, nursing, journalism, etc). The courses also contain an element of general education (i.e. courses in Spanish, English, natural sciences, physics, religious education, history and geography).

The qualifications obtained do not admit the holder to university in Peru. A system of credits is being used, and certificates are awarded throughout the courses so that students may leave and take up employment before completing their studies.

HIGHER EDUCATION

Students wishing to enter a course of higher education at one of the 25 state universities or 17 private institutions must hold the **Certificado de Educacion Secundaria Comun Completa** and pass the competitive entrance examination. Students may only apply for one faculty of one institution at a time.

The first 2 years at university are devoted to general studies. Students need to obtain a particular number of credits to enter the faculty for their specialization. The period of specialization is 2-5 years, and leads to the **Bachillerato**. Successful submission of a thesis leads to a **Licenciatura** (or a professional title) which normally takes 6 months to a year. Most courses leading to the Licenciatura take about 5 years in total.

In law and medicine the professional qualification is obtained 3 and 5 years, respectively, after the award of the Bachillerato.

Certain universities award the **Doctorado** on successful submission of a thesis at least 2 years after obtaining the professional title/Licenciatura.

TEACHER EDUCATION

Primary

A 3-year upper secondary course on completion of the 3-year lower secondary course, leads to the title of **Maestro Normal**.

Secondary

Teachers at this level (**profesores**) must have completed a university course.

Philippines

Republic of the Philippines

In 1954 the National Board of Education (NBE) was established as the highest policy-determining body in education.

There are many private institutions offering courses of further and higher education. These have to obtain specific authorization from the NBE before they can grant certificates, diplomas or degrees.

Education is compulsory from age seven to twelve.

The media of instruction are Filipino and English. In accordance with the 1972 Constitution, the NBE declared a policy of bilingualism in schools. Filipino only is used as the medium of instruction in social studies/social science, character education, health education, physical education, music and art. Science, mathematics and technology are taught in English.

The medium of instruction in all schools at all levels is English, except in public (government) elementary schools where Filipino is widely used in the first 2 years of study.

The academic year runs from June to March.

EVALUATION IN BRITAIN

School

Secondary School Leaving Certificate - generally considered to be below GCE O-level standard.

Higher

Bachelor degree - generally considered to compare to GCE A-level standard.

Bachelor degrees awarded by the University of the Philippines, Ateneo de Manila, De La Salle and University Santo Tomas may be considered to compare to a standard approximately 1-year above GCE A-level.

Philippines

MARKING SYSTEMS

Marking systems vary amongst institutions. A, B, C grades and percentages are found at all levels.

Higher

The University of the Philippines and some other institutions use:

1	excellent
1.25, 1.5, 1.75	very good
2.0, 2.5	good
3.0	fair
5.0	fail

Marks are sometimes expressed:

A	1.00	97-100%
A-	1.25	94-96
B+	1.50	91-93
B	1.75	88-90
B-	2.00	85-87
C+	2.50	80-84
C	3.00	75-79
D	4.00	failed

SCHOOL EDUCATION

Primary

This usually lasts 6 years (for government schools) and 7 years (for private schools) from age 7. Progression to secondary education is by passing the final examinations at the end of each year. A diploma or certificate is awarded at sixth or seventh year.

Secondary

Secondary education usually lasts 4 years. Compulsory subjects include English, Filipino, science, social studies, mathematics, practical arts, Youth Development Training (YDT) and Citizen Army Training (CAT). The course culminates in the examinations for the **High School Diploma**.

FURTHER EDUCATION

Community colleges offer 1-year post-secondary courses in advertising, bookkeeping, clerical studies, co-operatives, food services, general office practice, office management, skills development, retail merchandizing, secretarial studies, etc.

Philippines

Colleges of Agriculture offer 1-year certificate courses in farm mechanics.

The qualification of **Graduate Nurse** and **Bachelor of Science in Nursing** BSN is obtained after 2 years of pre-nursing study at a college or university followed by 2 years plus 1 year practice in a hospital school of nursing. Before 1976 the course consisted of 1 year pre-nursing study plus 3 years of study in a hospital school of nursing.

HIGHER EDUCATION

Entrance to universities and other institutions offering courses of higher education is dependent on (a) possession of a high school diploma, (b) for elite institutions, a pass in the university's own entrance examination and (c) a pass in the **National College Entrance Examination** (NCEE).

The NCEE was held for the first time in November 1973. From the school year 1974-5 any student seeking admission to any post-secondary academic or professional degree course of a minimum of 4 years study at any institution (regardless of whether private or public) must pass this examination. This examination is a general scholastic aptitude test to regulate the entry of high school graduates to college.

In general, degree courses last 4 years full-time.

Pharmacy, Engineering and Architecture: the course is generally 5 years.

Law: a degree often takes up to 8 years to obtain. Before 1961 the course consisted of 2 years pre-law followed by 4 years law; since then students must already have obtained a Bachelor degree in another subject or have spent a number of years on a course of higher education before beginning the actual course in law.

Dentistry: before 1955 the course lasted 4 years, but since then it has taken 6 years (2 years pre-dentistry and 4 years dentistry).

Veterinary medicine: the course leading to the qualification of **Doctor of Veterinary Medicine** lasts 6 years (2 years basic science and 4 years veterinary medicine).

Medicine: before 1970 the qualification of **Doctor of Medicine** was obtained after a course consisting of 2 years pre-medicine and 5 years medicine. Since then students must first obtain a Bachelor degree in another relevant subject before beginning the 3-year course on medicine, followed by 1 year of clinical clerkship.

A minimum of 124 units is required for the award of a Bachelor degree, but the total is usually 144-164. One unit accounts for about 17 hours of tuition.

Master degrees normally require a further 2 years (in architecture 4), with a further 3 (minimum) for a **Ph.D.**

In most institutions it is possible to obtain an **Associate Degree/Certificate** after the first 2 years of a course. Junior colleges only offer courses lasting 2 years.

A variety of courses in philosophy and theology are offered by Catholic and Protestant Seminaries.

Philippines

TEACHER EDUCATION

Teachers at any stage must be university graduates, having completed 1 of the following courses:

B.Sc. in Elementary Education (minimum of 156 units)
B.Sc. in Industrial Education (171-180 units) to prepare vocational and industrial teachers for trade schools
B.Sc. in Education (minimum of 156 units) to teach in secondary schools.

Poland

Polish People's Republic

Since World War II, there have been periodic reforms at all levels of the education system in Poland. The main features of early reform have been the attempts to equalize opportunities for all children, the importance of education in the industrialization of the country and the consequent inclusion of scientific and technological subjects as an important part of every child's education.

Under the 1919 Decree on Compulsory Education, children had to attend school for seven years from age seven. The 1961 Law on the Development of Education increased this to eight years. Under the 1978 reforms, the period of compulsory school education was increased, to embrace one year at kindergarten and ten years of subsequent schooling, but the implementation of these reforms has been halted and it is unlikely that the programme will be completed as envisaged.

The medium of instruction is Polish.

The academic year runs from September/October to June.

EVALUATION IN BRITAIN

School

Matura/Swiadectwo Dojrzalosci - may be considered to satisfy the general requirement of universities and polytechnics.

Diploma (from a Technikum) - generally compared to BTEC National Diploma standard (formerly Ordinary National Diploma).

Higher

Magister - generally compared to British Bachelor degree standard but often translated on a certificate as Master degree.

Doktor - generally compared to British Ph.D. standard.

Poland

MARKING SYSTEM

School and Higher

bardzo dobry	very good
dobry	good
dostateczny	satisfactory/pass
niedostateczny	unsatisfactory/fair

SCHOOL EDUCATION

From 1932 to 1948/9 a 12-year course of schooling was available. This was lowered in the academic year 1948/9 to 11 years. In 1961 the Law on the Development of Education proposed complete reorganization of the school system including reform of the syllabuses and an increase in the length of the course to 12 years. The reorganization was not fully implemented until 1967/8. In 1978 further far-reaching reforms were introduced mainly stemming from the report of the Committee of Experts on the State of Education under Professor Szczepanski. It had been hoped to complete these reforms within 5 years but further implementation has now been suspended.

Before 1948/9

Elementary/primary: 6 years compulsory education from age 7; in villages usually only the first 4 grades were available.

Secondary: 6 years, divided into a lower cycle of 4 years general secondary schooling at a Gimnazjum, followed by 2 years specialization at a Liceum.

1948/9-61

Pre-school/kindergarten (przedszkole): optional for children aged 3-6.

Elementary/primary: 7 years compulsory schooling from age 7.

Secondary: 4 years education.

1961-78

Pre-school/kindergarten: optional for children aged 3-7.

Elementary/primary: 8 years compulsory schooling from age 7.

Poland

From the academic year 1973/4 there was automatic promotion to the next grade during grades 1-4. Promotion in grades 5-8 was on the basis of class performance, homework and tests during the year. On completion of grade 8, pupils obtain a certificate of completion of elementary school (**Swiadectwo Ukonczenia Szkoly Podstawowej**) which is necessary for admission to secondary education.

Under this system, grades 1-8 are referred to as the basic school (Szkola Podstawowa). It offers a general curriculum, with Russian being introduced in the fifth year and English, German or French from the sixth year. The reorganization of this period of schooling including the increase in number of grades (years) was completed by 1967/8.

Secondary:

The reforms for this sector under the Education Law of 1961 began in 1967/8 and were completed by 1970/1 when the twelfth year of schooling was introduced for all pupils. The 4-year secondary course could be taken at a general education lyceum (Licea Ogolnoksztalcace/Szkoly Ogolnoksztalcace), a secondary technical, secondary vocational or basic vocational school (for the latter 3 types of school see below). The main aim of the general education lyceums was to prepare pupils for university studies. Compulsory subjects throughout the 4-year course are Polish, Russian, English or French or German, history, mathematics, physics, technology, and physical education and social education; chemistry and geography are compulsory during the first 3 years and biology for the last 3. The syllabus includes non-academic subjects, e.g. national defence, hygiene and astronomy. Optional subjects include a second West-European language or Latin. In the fourth year a measure of specialization is introduced, allowing specialization in humanities, mathematics-physics, biology-chemistry, geography-economics, foreign languages, teaching and other professional areas.

On completion of the fourth year pupils took the examinations for the **Matura**, which were the only externally set examinations at school, being set at provincial level. Under a regulation passed in 1971 pupils were allowed to decide whether or not to take the examinations; those who did not, received a Certificate of Completion of Secondary Schooling (**Swiadectwo Ukonczenia Szkoly Sredniej**) or Certificate of Completion of the General Education Lyceum (**Swiadectwo Ukonczenia Liceum Ogolnoksztalcacego**). This certificate does not entitle holders to apply for admission to higher studies.

To obtain the **Matura** of the general education lyceums (**Swiadectwo Dojrzalosci Liceum Ogolnokstalcacego**) pupils had to pass a final written examination in mathematics and Polish, and an oral examination in 2 subjects chosen by the student from: foreign languages, social science, biology, physical and chemical sciences, technology, astronomy, philosophy, art and music. From 1973, pupils were able to undertake a project instead of one oral examination. Besides the examination marks, teachers' gradings for another 6 subjects are included on the certificate. Pupils may take the examination up to 4 years after completing high school, and may retake the full examination twice if they fail any part.

Since 1978

Pre-school/kindergarten: optional between ages 3 and 6; the last year of the 4-year course available is compulsory.

Basic school (i.e. elementary/primary and secondary):

Poland

Under the 1978 reforms, 10 years education is compulsory in addition to the 1 year at kindergarten. The 10-year basic school course is intended to cover the same ground as the previous 8-year elementary/primary/basic course and 4-year secondary course. The course is divided into 2 cycles: grades 1-3 (initial phase), and grades 4-10 (systematic phase). During the initial phase pupils are taught reading, writing, elementary mathematics, physical education and manual skills; during the systematic phase compulsory subjects are Polish, Polish history, biology, social development, and basic technology. In addition pupils must take subjects from at least 1 optional group: languages, biological sciences, technology, mathematics, economics, and history and aesthetics. The degree of specialization is increased in the later years of the phase. The **Matura** examinations will be taken on completion of grade 10.

Graduates of the 10-year basic school course, who wish to proceed to higher education, go to 'Further Schools' which offer 2-year courses within the student's intended speciality. These schools are divided into the following subject areas:

physical sciences and technology
medical sciences, biology and agriculture
social sciences and humanities
others

Basic-school leavers who have excelled during 2 years of military training or 2 years work experience may then sit the university entrance examination immediately.

Olympiads are country-wide examinations open to all pupils. In each subject (mathematics, physics, chemistry, biology, Russian and Polish) there is a written and oral examination, taken at the same time as the examinations for the Matura. Winners of the Olympiads are entitled to university entrance in their winning subject at the university of their choice. Under the new (post 1978) system winners of the Olympiads will be able to go direct to university, bypassing the 2-year course at a 'Further School'.

Technical secondary (1948-78)

On completion of the 7-year (until 1961) or 8-year primary course, pupils could proceed to a general education lyceum or to some form of technical secondary education; most attended a technical school.

Technical schools/technikum (Szkoly Techniczne) and vocational schools (Szkoly Zawodowe) offered a 5-year course to all pupils who had completed primary school, and a 2- or 3-year course for pupils who had also completed general secondary education. All students took chemistry, mathematics, military training, physics, Polish, Russian, and social sciences (geography and history). On completion of the course pupils took the Matura examinations.

Basic vocational schools (Zasadnicze Szkoly Zawodowe) still exist. They are open to pupils who completed elementary school and do not go on to a general education lyceum or a technical or vocational school. These schools offer 2- or 3-years training for agricultural or industrial trades. The schools are often attached to factories or state farms to enable the students to obtain practical experience. Some time is spent on civics, chemistry, mathematics, physics, Polish and Russian. On completion of the course students receive a Certificate of Completion of Basic Vocational School **(Swiadectwo Ukonczenia Zasadniczej Szkoly Zawodowej)**. They may then continue their education at a technical or vocational school, depending on the skill acquired, for a course lasting up to 3 years.

Poland

Technical/secondary (since 1978)

Under the new system pupils who complete the 2-year course at a Further School, where they may take a vocationally-oriented specialization, may sit the university entrance examination. The vocational schools offer courses of between 6 months and 2-and-a-half years, with the aim of training technicians and skilled craftsmen. There will also be a network of training centres providing 1-year courses to give basic-school leavers basic trade skills.

FURTHER EDUCATION

1948-78

Post-lyceum schools (Szkoly Pomaturalne/Szkoly Policealne) offered a 2-year course during which students could specialize and which led to a diploma. Students had to hold the Matura to be admitted to these schools although the schools are considered to be secondary in level. Courses are available in such subjects as librarianship and nursing.

HIGHER EDUCATION

Admission to university and other courses of higher education is on the basis of the Matura and success in a competitive entrance examination. The latter is marked on a points basis, with extra points being given to specific social groups (e.g. children of peasants or workers). Students may not normally choose their university, but must apply to one covering their province (voivodship) or town; exceptionally gifted students (e.g. Olympiad winners) are allowed to choose. However a student who has obtained a high enough standard in the entrance examination to indicate ability but still fails to obtain a place (or the local university does not offer a chosen course) may apply to a university other than the local one.

Institutions of higher education tend to specialize more than the British counterparts in a range of courses. Hence the universities (Uniwersytet) do not normally have departments of engineering, applied science and architecture, as these subjects are taught by the technical universities (Politechnika). The latter have the same status as the universities.

The universities cover sciences (applied aspects of the sciences are taught only at the technical universities), social science, languages and humanities. Apart from the universities and technical universities there are a number of academies and higher schools of particular specialization. Research and teaching are often divorced, in that research is largely undertaken by the Polish Academy of Sciences.

Most institutions of higher education (except the private Catholic University of Lublin and the Academy of Catholic Theology in Warsaw) are supervised by the Ministry of Science, Higher Education and Technology which lays down the syllabuses; the Ministry of Health supervises Medical Academies and the Ministry of Culture supervises institutions of Fine Arts etc.

Poland

The first qualification to be obtained is the **Magisterium/Magister**. From 1948-54 students spent 5 to 5-and-a-half years studying towards this qualification. The time was divided into 2 cycles: 3 to 3-and-a-half years training for a skilled job, followed by 2 years general schooling. During 1954-6 the course was shortened to 4 years. Since then the course has lasted 4 or 5 years. The first 2 years are now spent on generalized basic studies, and specialization occurs during the remaining 2-3 years. The final semester is spent preparing a dissertation which is the result of a supervised project in the final year. In addition to the subjects related to a student's chosen topic of study, each student must take 5 or 6 subsidiary subjects, some of which are compulsory (e.g. a foreign language); military training used to be included here. Credits (i.e. signatures) are received for the courses attended. A Diploma of Completion of Higher Studies (**Diplom Ukonczenia Studiow Wyzszych**) and the title of specialist is obtained on completion of a course in a particular professional field:

dental medicine	Lekarz-Dentysta	5 years
law	Magister-Prawa	4 years
medicine	Lekarz	6 years
veterinary medicine	Lekarz Weterynarii	5 years
engineering technology agriculture	Magister Inzynier	4-and-a-half years

Students must complete the course and graduate within the specified period.

In 1973/4 the duration of courses at the polytechnics/technical universities was shortened from 5 to 4-and-a-half years. At the same time more emphasis was laid on laboratory and other forms of practical training, and the variety of specializations drastically reduced. The aim was to provide students with a broader professional education.

A number of postgraduate courses are available, usually lasting 2 semesters, with the aim of updating the academic training of graduates who have been in employment for some time.

There are 2 types of doctoral degree:

Lower degree - **Doktor (dr)**. This may be obtained after 2-3 years study from the level of the Magister and the presentation of a dissertation. A total of 7 years is the maximum allowed to obtain this qualification.

Higher degree - **Doktor Habilitowany (dr hab.)**. This is conferred on the holder of a doctorate whose work (which is unsupervised) represents an original contribution to the development of a given scientific discipline. The research undertaken should be published. This qualification is necessary for any university teacher wishing to advance beyond the level of lecturer.

Folk universities

These provide part-time courses for 5 months of the year in country districts and 7 months in towns. The courses are comparable to adult education courses in Britain.

Poland

TEACHER EDUCATION

Pre-school/kindergarten

Before 1973, teacher education consisted of a 5-year post-primary course at a pedagogical lyceum (Liceum Pedagogiczne).

Since 1973, it has been a course lasting 12 semesters (6 years) for pupils who have completed the 8-year course at an elementary school; or a course lasting 4 semesters (2 years) for students who have completed the secondary course at a general education lyceum.

These courses are offered at study centres for pre-school teachers (Studia Wychowania Przedszkolnego - SWP). Students from the former pedagogical lyceums could continue their studies at the SWPs at the next higher grade level following the grade level completed in the pedagogical lyceums at the time of their transformation into SWPs. Graduates of pedagogical lyceums after 1 year of teaching practice in pre-schools can complete the required additional studies through part-time, evening or correspondence courses and by passing the final diploma examination which is considered to be comparable to the Matura.

Elementary

Teachers for this level are now required to complete a 4-year course at the higher education level. The 5-year secondary pedagogical lyceums which used to train teachers for grades 1-4 were phased out by 1970 (i.e. the last students qualified in 1970), and the 2-year post-secondary teachers' schools (Studia Nauczycielskie - SNs) which still trained some elementary school teachers for grades 5-8 were completely phased out by 1975.

Secondary

Universities, higher schools of pedagogy (Wyzsze Szkoly Pedagogiczne - WSP) and the higher teachers schools (Wyzsze Szkoly Nauczycielskie - WSN) train secondary school teachers on a 4-year degree course.

In 1974/5 it was decided that the teaching profession should be graduate entry only for all levels. By 1980 all teacher-training schools were phased out, and all courses now comprise 4 years university study from the level of the Matura and lead to the qualification of **Magister Pedagogiki** in a particular specialization. Teacher training for vocational schools, however, continues to be carried out in higher schools of engineering, economics, agriculture, etc., with education as a compulsory subject.

Portugal

Portuguese Republic

Education is under the strict control and supervision of the Ministry of Education, which is entirely responsible for its organization and curricula.

In 1971 the Lei Organica do Ministerio da Educacao Nacional led to a revision of the educational system at all levels. A draft for a new 'Basic Law' was presented in 1980 but was not passed. However, there have been many changes at all levels in the last few years.

Education was compulsory for three years until 1968 when it was increased to six years. In 1986 it was increased to nine years, age six to fifteen.

The medium of instruction is Portuguese. English is taught optionally in years five to eleven.

The academic year runs from September to June.

EVALUATION IN BRITAIN

School

Certidao do Curso Geral do Ensino Secundario/Curso Geral Nocturno/Curso do Ensino Unificado - generally considered to be below GCE O-level standard.

Certidao do Ensino Secundario/Curso Complementar (Nocturno)
Certidao do Decimo Segundo Ano - may be considered to satisfy the general requirement of universities and polytechnics.

Higher

Licenciatura - generally compared to British Bachelor degree standard, but has been known to be compared to a Master degree.

Mestrado - generally compared to taught Master degree standard.

Portugal

MARKING SYSTEMS

School

Marking is on a scale 0-20 (maximum); 10 is the minimum pass mark. Since 1974, some schools have used a scale of 0-5.

Higher

Marking is on a scale of 0-20 (maximum).

SCHOOL EDUCATION

Pre-1971 reforms

Pre-primary/kindergarten: No facilities available.

Primary: 3 years education was compulsory for children aged 7-10.

Secondary:

There was a selective entrance examination for pupils wanting to attend a liceu (high school). The first stage of secondary education comprised a 5-year course; after the first 2 years pupils could specialize. The second stage comprised a 2-year course preparing students for university entrance.

Post-1971 reforms up to 1980

The old system was almost completely phased out.

Pre-primary:

Some facilities were available at this stage, although they were only in private schools and for children aged 4-5.

Primary:

This comprised 4 years.

Upper primary/preparatory cycle:

This was a 2-year course - escola preparatoria. French was compulsory during this cycle, but English was optional.

Secondary:

This was divided into 2 cycles:

Portugal

3-year course - curso geral do ensino secundario

2-year course - curso complementar do ensino secundario

Courses at this level could be taken at liceus (high schools), escolas tecnicas (technical schools) or escolas polivalentes (comprehensive schools) until 1974.

In the curso geral do ensino secundario the following subjects were compulsory:

arts stream - Portuguese, French, English, history

science stream - geography, natural science, physics with chemistry, mathematics, technical drawing.

The certificate obtained on successful completion of the second cycle is the **Certidao do Ensino Secundario** or **Certidao do Curso Complementar**. Until 1974 this certificate entitled the holders to university admission if they had obtained an average of 14 marks out of 20. If they did not reach this average they had to take an additional university entrance examination. As from 1974 on completion of the second cycle of secondary education, students wishing to proceed to university had to undergo a 1-year orientation course, which replaced the university entrance examination. The course included civic service and a number of introductory courses, and was referred to as the **ano propedeutico**.

From 1980/1 to 1986

Pre-primary:

Non-compulsory and intended for children aged 3-6.

Basic education:

Compulsory for 6 years between the ages of 6 and 14. This period is divided into 2 cycles - 4 years primary followed by 2 years preparatory (5th and 6th year of schooling). On completion of the second cycle pupils obtain the **Certidao do Segundo Ano do Ensino Preparatorio**.

Secondary:

Non-compulsory and consisting of 6 years (7th to 12th years of schooling). It covers academic and technical subjects and is divided into:

General unified course (7th, 8th and 9th years of schooling). On completion of the 9th year pupils obtain the **Certidao do Curso do Ensino Unificado**.

Complementary course (10th and 11th years of schooling). Subjects include Portuguese, philosophy, foreign language and physical education. On completion of the 11th year pupils obtain the **Certidao do Curso Complementar**.

Twelfth year of schooling (pre-university year). This year is initially aimed at students intending to enter university and offers 2 curricular options: academic and vocational.

Portugal

The academic option develops into 5 courses according to the area of studies attended in the 10th and 11th years of schooling. It provides sufficient qualifications for admission to university higher education. The vocational option provides adequate information and training in a wide range of technological areas. It offers a great variety of more specifically oriented courses and provides sufficient qualifications for entry to polytechnic institutions. On completion of the 12th year a **Certidao do Decimo-Segundo Ano** is obtained which ensures access into higher education or integration into working life.

Changes introduced by the new 1986 legislation

Pre-school

No changes.

Basic education

Compulsory for 9 years between the ages of 6 and 15. This period is divided into 3 cycles - the first with 4 years, the second with 2 years and the third with 3 years. A diploma is awarded on completion of the basic education period.

Secondary education

Non-compulsory and lasting for 3 years. It may consist of courses with a technical or professional slant. A diploma is awarded on completion of the secondary education period which may be substituted by a technical or professional diploma.

FURTHER EDUCATION

Evening courses are intended for students over 14 and include:

The evening general course (9th year of schooling) - on completion the **Certidao do Curso Geral Nocturno** is obtained

The evening complementary course (11th year of schooling) - on completion the **Certidao do Curso Complementar Nocturno** is obtained.

Holders of the latter certificate are eligible to enrol in any of the 2 curricular options of the 12th year of schooling.

Technical and vocational education is at present being developed and offers pupils courses of professional training upon completion of the 9th year of schooling. Two kinds of course may be followed: the 1-year technical course with a 6-month training period; the 3-year technical-professional course leading either to working life or higher education.

Portugal

HIGHER EDUCATION

Higher education is offered by the universities and a number of public and private institutions. The 4 traditional universities are Coimbra, Oporto, Lisbon and the Technical University of Lisbon. The new universities and university institutes established since 1973 are the Universidade Nova in Lisbon, the Universities of Minho, Algarve, Aveiro, Evora and the Azores, the University Institute of Beira Interior, and the University Institute of Tras-os-Montes e Alto Douro.

In 1976/7 the system of numerus clausus (limited admission) started to operate for studies in medicine and veterinary medicine, but has now been introduced in all university courses.

From 1972 to 1980, the first qualification to be obtained after 3 years study in arts and science subjects at the Universities of Lisbon and Coimbra was the **Bacharelato**. This qualification has been discontinued at the universities.

University studies lead to the degree of **Licenciatura** after a 4- to 6-year course. In some subjects (engineering, agriculture, veterinary medicine and medicine) a year of practical training is also required before the Licenciatura is awarded. Most holders are called doctor by tradition and use the initials dr.

The **Mestrado** is a postgraduate qualification open to holders of a Licenciatura and is obtained after 1-2 years study.

The **Doutoramento** is open to holders of a Licenciatura or Mestrado and is obtained mostly by part-time study, as the students are generally also employed. The minimum period taken to obtain the doutoramento is 1-2 years (including the preparation and submission of a thesis), even if taken after full-time study. The holder of a doctorate uses the full title doctor as opposed to using the initials dr (see Licenciatura).

University higher education is also available in schools or higher education institutes of engineering, fine arts, dentistry, business management, accountancy and administration.

Non-university higher education

This is provided mainly in the recently created <u>polytechnic institutes</u> which offer 2-3 year courses which lead to a **Bacharelato**. Polytechnic institutes offer courses mainly in education and agriculture.

Non-university higher education also provides courses in fine arts, music, dance, drama, cinema, architecture, engineering, accountancy and administration.

Private higher education

This sector comprises the Catholic University, the Universidade Livre, three higher institutes of social services, one higher institute of applied psychology, one higher institute of languages and administration and one institute of new professions. Degrees conferred by the Catholic University and the Universidade Livre and some of the courses offered in other private institutes of higher education are recognized by the Ministry of Education.

Portugal

TEACHER EDUCATION

All teacher training colleges were closed down until 1968.

Primary

Teachers for this level are trained for 2 years at teacher training institutes (Escolas do Magisterio Primario) with a further 1 year teaching practice. Entry requirements are the **Certidao do Curso Complementar**.

Secondary

Teachers for this level have to hold a university qualification and up to now have had their training on the job under the supervision of a more senior teacher. This is now changing and secondary school teachers will be trained in the new polytechnic institutes.

The title of **Agregado** is conferred on university lecturers who successfully pass the state examination at the end of 2 years teaching since obtaining the Licenciatura.

Puerto Rico

There is a strong American influence on the eduction system, as shown by the use of the credit-unit system at school and higher education levels.

The medium of instruction is Spanish, apart from the faculties of dentistry and medicine at the University of Puerto Rico, where it is English.

The academic year runs from August to May.

EVALUATION IN BRITAIN

School

High School Graduation Diploma - generally considered to compare to GCE O-level standard.

Higher

Bachelor degree - generally considered to be below British Bachelor degree standard.

MARKING SYSTEMS

School

A credit-unit system is used. Pupils must earn 20 units from grades 9-12 to graduate.

Higher

A credit-unit system is used; it is usually explained on the transcript of marks.

Puerto Rico

SCHOOL EDUCATION

Primary

This covers 6 years.

Secondary

This covers 6 years divided into two 3-year cycles. In the second cycle, pupils can specialize in general/academic or technical. Regardless of the specialization, all pupils take mathematics, English, Spanish, natural science, and the social sciences. On completion of this period, pupils take the examinations for the **High School Graduation Diploma**.

HIGHER EDUCATION

There are 6 state institutions - 1 university and 5 regional technical colleges - and 5 private accredited institutions. The technical colleges were established in the 1960s and were originally intended to offer 2-year courses only; however, they now offer **Certificate**, 2-year **Associate degree** and transitional courses for those going on to degree courses at the university.

Entrance to degree courses is on the basis of the **High School Graduation Diploma** and an entrance examination.

The institutions are run on the American pattern - credit-unit system. **Bachelor degrees** take 3-6 years, the average being 4. An **Associate degree** can be obtained in some fields after 2 years. **Master degrees** take a further 1-2 years.

Law - students have to hold a **Bachelor degree** in another subject before beginning this course.

Medicine and dentistry - students have to undertake 3 years preparatory study before beginning the degree course.

Honours courses may be taken by better students.

TEACHER EDUCATION

Teacher training is at higher education level, and students may take a 2-year **Associate degree** course or a 4-year **Bachelor degree** course.

Qatar

State of Qatar

The modern education system dates from 1956. It is free at all levels for both sexes.

English is introduced as a subject at the fifth grade of primary level and continues through to the end of secondary.

The academic year is divided into two terms and runs from September/October until the end of May with a break in January/February.

EVALUATION IN BRITAIN

School

Secondary School Leaving Certificate - considered to approximate to GCE O-level on a subject-for-subject basis where marks of at least 50% have been obtained (regardless of the pass marks) in subjects which may be taken in the GCE examinations, except English language.

Higher

5-year BA/B.Sc. - generally compared to a British Bachelor (Ordinary) degree standard, but has been accepted for postgraduate study.

MARKING SYSTEMS

Secondary School Certificate is marked on a percentage scale.

SCHOOL EDUCATION

Primary

Primary schools normally enrol children at age 6 for a 6-year course. There is an evaluation of progress at the end of year 3 and a standardized examination at the end of the sixth grade.

Qatar

Preparatory

This is a 3-year course, at the end of which pupils take an examination administered by the Ministry of Education.

Secondary

Grades 10-12 cover this 3-year course. As in other Arab countries, grades 11 and 12 are divided into scientific and literary streams. At the end of grade 12 pupils take the **Secondary School Leaving Certificate** examinations.

Technical/vocational secondary

Vocational training is available for boys at the intermediate and secondary levels in the 6-year course at the vocational school.

Special vocational courses are available for adults to enable them to find employment. A 2-year course at the intermediate level allows adults with primary education to compress the usual 3 years into 2 by emphasizing the vocational subject matter and placing less stress on Arabic, religion and social studies than in the normal vocational curriculum.

A <u>regional vocational training centre</u> was established in Doha in 1970 to train Qataris in a variety of manual skills for employment in various industries during a 2-year course in building, mechnical and electrical trades. A number of **City & Guilds Part I** courses are also taught.

HIGHER EDUCATION

The <u>University of Qatar</u> was founded as twin Faculties of Education (male and female) in 1973. It acquired university status in 1977. By 1984 some 3,120 students had graduated from the University, which is a member of the Association of Arab Universities and the International Association of Universities. It has 6 faculties:

Education
Humanities and Social Science
Science
Islamic Studies
Engineering
Administration and Economics

together with Associated Institutes:

Educational Research Centre
Documentation and Humanities Research Centre
Scientific and Applied Research Centre
Research Centre for Sirra and Sunni Studies.

All students must first undertake a 4-year **Bachelor of Education** course. Students who succeed in this examination may continue for a fifth year, leading to a **BA** or **B.Sc. degree.**

Qatar

English is the medium of instruction only in the English language and literature courses and the English language methodology course offered by the English Language Unit of the University.

TEACHER EDUCATION

Teacher training for all stages, including the primary, is conducted by the Faculty of Education of Qatar University. While unqualified teachers are being upgraded on compulsory programmes at the Faculty, the courses available are: BA in Primary Education, General Diploma in Education and a Special Diploma in Education.

Romania

Socialist Republic of Romania

Education is organized and controlled by the state. All education is free.

The National Council of Science and Education (Consiliul National al Stiintei si Invatamintului) and the Ministry of Education and Instruction (Ministerul Educatiei si Invatamintului) are responsible for the implementation of the education policy of the Party and State. The Education and Instruction Act of 1978 provides the unitary legal frame of the organization, operation and development of education.

Compulsory education, since 1969, is ten years (ages six to sixteen).

The medium of instruction is Romanian. Use of mother tongue at all levels of education is ensured to each nationality within the country.

The academic year according to level of education, is thirty-four to thirty-eight weeks, from September to July.

EVALUATION IN BRITAIN

School

Diploma de Baccalaureat - may be considered to satisfy the general requirement of universities and polytechnics.

Higher

Diploma de Stat (State Diploma) - generally compared to British Bachelor degree standard.

MARKING SYSTEMS

Marking is on a scale of 1-10, with 5 as the minimum pass mark, except for the higher education graduation examination in which 6 is the minimum pass mark.

Romania

SCHOOL EDUCATION

Pre-school (invatamintul pre-scolar)

Widespread facilities are available in creches (Crese) for children aged 1-3 years, and in nursery schools (Gradinite de Copii) for children aged 3-6 years.

Primary and middle

The 8-year basic education (scoala generala) is composed of 4 years primary (forms I-IV), beginning at age 6, plus 4 years middle school at Gymnasium (forms V-VIII). Schools at this stage are unstreamed. To develop students' abilities, groups with additional music, fine arts and choreography programmes can be organized. Promotion to the next grade is by continuous assessment.

Secondary

Day high school (Liceul) comprises 2 levels, each lasting 2 years. High school evening classes are organized only at the upper level and last 3 years. There are 2 stages of high-school education: lower (forms 9 and 10), and upper (forms 11 and 12, eventually 13).

Admission to form 9 depends on successful completion of form 8. Lower high school is an integral part of the 10-year compulsory education acquired in the middle school. It provides training in a trade which enables students to take a job as a probationer, to enrol in vocational school or to enter upper high-school.

Admission to upper high school is by entrance examination.

The syllabuses are differentiated by high school type and specialization. They are unitary for every specialization and contain fundamental scientific disciplines, general education and social-political disciplines, specialized disciplines as well as training in industry.

There are the following types of high school: industrial, agricultural-industrial, forestry, economic, sanitary, mathematics and physics, natural sciences, philology and history, pedagogy and arts.

High-school studies end with a school-leaving examination (Examen de Bacalaureat). Candidates who pass receive a **Diploma de Bacalaureat** (School Leaving Diploma) and a **qualification certificate** which entitle them to go in for the entrance examination in any higher education establishment or to take a job.

Vocational

Vocational schools train for the basic trades of the national economy. They admit graduates of the 10-year compulsory education. The day and evening classes last 1 to 1-and-a-half years. The curricula are differentiated by trade, and include in addition to practical training, specialist subjects and subjects and activities meant to contribute to the political, ideological and civic education of pupils. Admission is by competitive examination. The course culminates in a practical test submitted by the candidate in the relevant trade. Graduates are granted a graduation diploma which entitles them to take a job.

Admission to foremen schools is by competitive examination, consisting of written papers in mathematics, technical design and the technology of the respective trade. The candidates can be qualified workers, or secondary or vocational school graduates with 8 years work experience in an industrial enterprise. The studies last 1 to 1-and-a-half years in the day school and 2 years in the evening classes. The course ends with a school-leaving examination which consists of defending a design, or a diploma paper on a given subject agreed on jointly with the enterprises for which the students are trained. Graduates are granted a graduation diploma which entitles them to work as foremen.

HIGHER EDUCATION

Higher education (invatamintul superior) is provided in universities, polytechnics, technical colleges, and conservatories, organized by faculties and departments.

Admission is by competitive entrance examination (Examen de Admitere) open to those holding a School-Leaving (Diploma de Bacalaureat) Certificate. Evening and extramural courses may be attended only by people in employment. The conditions for enrolling, the disciplines, tests, organization and carrying out of the entrance examination are laid down by the Ministry of Education and Instruction. Studies extend over 3-6 years; evening and extramural studies last 1 year longer than ordinary ones.

The nomenclature of types and specializations for day, evening and extramural courses, duration of studies and the intake figures are sanctioned by a State Council Decree (Decret al Consiliului de Stat) at the proposal of the Ministry of Education and Instruction.

Studies end in a graduation paper (Examen de Diploma). Those who pass are awarded the **Diploma de Stat**, which enable them to receive posts in production under the provisions of the law.

Postgraduate courses are available in economics, science, technology and culture for graduates of a higher education establishment who have completed (at least) 4-year day courses or 5-year evening or extramural courses. These postgraduate courses are organized by higher education establishments, usually on an extramural basis. Graduation is through examinations and defending a graduation paper.

The **Doctoral** (Doctorat) degree is the highest form of specialist training in various branches of science, technology and culture. It is organized by higher education establishments, academies of sciences and central research institutions.

The conditions for training for a Doctoral degree, the training stage and the conditions for obtaining the Doctoral degree are established through a State Council Decree.

Romania

TEACHER EDUCATION

School

Nursery school teachers (educatoare) and primary teachers (invatatori) graduate and take the school-leaving examination in a pedagogical high-school.

Middle-school teachers (profesori) graduate from and take the diploma examination in a higher education establishment (3- or 4-year courses).

High-school teachers (profesori) graduate from and take the diploma examination in a higher education establishment offering at least a 4-year course.

Vocational school teachers graduate from and take the diploma examination in a higher education establishment offering at least a 4-year course, or in a school for middle-grade engineers.

Teachers in foremen schools graduate from and take the diploma examination in a higher education establishment offering at least a 4-year course.

Higher

Higher education teaching staff consists of assistant lecturers (asistenti), lecturers (senior lecturers, lectori), readers (conferentiari) and professors (profesori) who graduate from and take the diploma examination in a higher education establishment offering at least a 4-year course.

The position of reader and professor requires a Doctoral degree.

In-service

In-service training of teaching staff is organized by the Ministry of Education and Instruction, through the educational and scientific research units. Annual and long-term plans elaborated by the Ministry are as follows:

For teaching staff in pre-school and primary education, refresher courses are organized, alongside periodical methodological-scientific activities, conferences and exchanges of experience, as well as training activities with a view to obtaining tenure and teaching grades.

For higher education teaching staff, further training is organized through the Doctoral degrees, postgraduate courses, training periods in production and design units, short-term periodical seminars, specialized conferences and scientific debates. Participation in all courses is compulsory.

Training the personnel who hold managing, guidance and control positions in pre-school, primary and middle school education is organized by school inspectorates. For those teaching in high, vocational and foremen schools, in higher education institutions or working in school inspectorates, training is organized by the Ministry of Education and Instruction.

Rwanda

Rwandese Republic

This chapter covers the period since independence in 1962. Before then the territory was the Belgian-administered trust territory Rwanda-Urundi.

Education is compulsory in theory until age fifteen but few children actually stay on until then. Since 1964/5 children have been able to begin their schooling at age six.

EVALUATION IN BRITAIN

School

Certificat des Humanites - generally compared to GCE O-level standard, except for English language.

Higher

Bachelier - generally considered to be between GCE A-level and British Bachelor degree standards.

MARKING SYSTEMS

School

90%	plus grande distinction
80	grande distinction
70	distinction
50-69	satisfaction

Higher

As above.

Rwanda

SCHOOL EDUCATION

Primary

This covers 6 years divided into 2 cycles. The premier cycle (literacy cycle) lasts 4 years during which teaching is in Kinyarwanda and is intended to give children a basic knowledge of arithmetic, geography, history, civics, religion and reading. On completion of this cycle pupils take an examination, success in which gives admission to the deuxieme cycle. This lasts 2 years, teaching is in French, and it culminates in examinations in French, arithmetic and civics, success in which gives access to secondary school. Pupils who are not able to enter an academic secondary school (as there is only a limited number of places, a high passing score is set) may stay at primary school for a seventh year (septieme complementaire) during which home economics and farming methods are taught.

Secondary

This covers 6 years divided into two 3-year cycles:

1st cycle - tronc commun d'orientation
2nd cycle - in modern or classical humanities (sections moyennes generales).

On successful completion of the 2nd cycle pupils are awarded the **Certificat des Humanites**.

There are also junior seminaries where many boys take courses based on Greek and Latin.

Technical secondary

There is a variety of 2-year courses to train aides in crafts and trades for pupils who have completed 2-3 years of academic secondary, although pupils could also enter directly from primary school.

The Official Trade School (Ecole Officielle de Metiers) in Kicukiro, Kigali, offers a 4-year post-primary course in carpentry, cabinet-making, mechanics, automechanics, electricity and welding.

The Groupe Scolaire in Butare (established in 1929 by the Roman Catholic Order of the Brothers of Charity) offers 4-year courses for students to train as medical, agricultural and veterinary assistants, business administrators or nurses.

HIGHER EDUCATION

The <u>National University of Rwanda</u> was established at Butare in 1963. Admission to degree courses is based on successful completion of the second 3-year cycle of academic secondary education.

Rwanda

The first stage of higher education leads (in most subjects) to the **Bachelier** after 3 years; Bachelier es Sciences, Bachelier es Lettres or Bachelier es Sciences Economiques et Sociales depending on the subject. In medicine the qualification of Doctor is obtained after a 7-year course; 1 year of general studies in the Faculty of Science and 2 years general study in the Faculty of Medicine, followed by 4 years specialization.

TEACHER EDUCATION

Ecoles de Moniteurs Auxiliares (for boys) and Ecoles de Monitrices Auxiliares (for girls) offer 2-year post-primary courses to train aides for primary school teachers.

Ecoles Normales Inferieurs train primary school teachers on 5-year post-primary courses (the first 3 years cover the same ground as the first cycle of general secondary education) followed by 2 years pedagogical training.

Ecoles Normales Moyennes used to train teachers for the first cycle of general secondary education on a 7-year post-primary course (5 years general secondary followed by 2 years teacher training).

The Institut Pedagogique National provides teacher training in conjunction with the University's faculties of letters and science. Students who successfully complete the 3-year course culminating in the **Agregation de l'Enseignement Secondaire Inferieur** may teach in the lower secondary cycle. Students who successfully complete the 5-year course culminating in the **Agregation de l'Enseignement Secondaire Superieur**, may teach in the upper secondary cycle.

Saudi Arabia

Kingdom of Saudi Arabia

Education for males and females is completely separate in the areas of administration, facilities and instruction. Private schools must conform to the curricula laid down for state schools. There are many international schools modelled on the British or American systems.

Education is free and voluntary at all levels.

Arabic is the medium of instruction, except in most of the faculties of science and medicine, where tuition is English.

The academic year runs (approximately) from October to July.

EVALUATION IN BRITAIN

General Secondary Education Certificate - may be considered comparable to GCE O-level standard.

Higher

A **Bachelor degree** from a Saudi Arabian university is unlikely to be considered comparable to a British Bachelor degree.

MARKING SYSTEMS

School

Students must obtain at least 50% of the total maximum in the intermediate examinations to enter secondary school. If they wish to pursue natural sciences at secondary school, they must obtain at least 50% of the maximum marks available in mathematics and science as well as passes in physics and chemistry.

Higher

All universities grade first degrees as follows:

Saudi Arabia

1. excellent
2. very good
3. good
4. pass
5. poor (fail)
6. very poor (fail)

The College of Engineering operates a grading scale of 1-100, with 50 as the minimum pass mark.

SCHOOL EDUCATION

Although male and female pupils are strictly segregated, they follow the same basic 6-3-3 pattern of education. In elementary and intermediate schools, both sexes follow the same curriculum. At the girls' secondary schools physical education is replaced by home economics. The same yearly examinations are taken throughout the school.

Primary

This covers a 6-year cycle (ages 6-12). At the end of each year, students take examinations. Success in every subject is essential for promotion to the next grade. If a student fails a subject he/she must retake the entire examination after the summer holidays. Failure on this occasion means that the pupil must repeat the entire year. At the end of the sixth-year examination, successful students are awarded the **General Elementary School Certificate**. This grants access to the intermediate school.

Intermediate

This covers a 3-year period (ages 12-15) and prepares students for general secondary education, teacher training and technical education. Students take yearly examinations. At the end of the ninth year, those who pass the final examination are awarded the **Intermediate School Certificate**. This grants access to secondary school education.

Secondary

Students can choose between general secondary school, vocational education and teacher training.

General

In the first year students share a common curriculum. At the end of this year, they are divided into the scientific and literary streams. A student scoring 60% in all the first-year subjects may choose between the scientific and literary streams. A student scoring less than 60% must opt for the literary stream. At the end of the third year, students sit for the **National Secondary Examination (Tawjihiyah)**. The results of this contribute 70% towards the **General Secondary Education Certificate**; classroom performance makes up the other 30%.

Saudi Arabia

Vocational

All technical and vocational training is handled by the General Organisation for Technical Education and Vocational Training (GOTEVOT) operating under a council of members of different government agencies and chaired by the Ministry of Labour and Social Affairs.

The vocational training centres offer 15 different courses, each lasting 18 months. Students must complete a minimum of 5-6 years in primary education and pass a written examination to qualify for entrance. The course consists of 25% theoretical instruction and 75% practical instruction. On completion students undergo 6 months of practical training before they are awarded the **Vocational Training Centre Certificate**.

Industrial training institutes

These provide technician training at secondary level. They offer 3 areas of specialization: mechanics, automation and electricity.

After the first 2 years, selected students can continue for 2 extra years. Students who successfully complete the 4-year course may continue to a Higher Technical Teacher Training Institute or apply to Colleges of Applied Engineering.

Commerce institutes

These secondary-level institutes come under the supervision of the Ministry of Education and offer 3-year courses. A Higher Institute for Financial and Commercial Sciences was set up in Riyadh in 1975 and offers 2-year courses.

Agricultural institutes

The agricultural institutes offer 3-year secondary-level courses.

FURTHER EDUCATION

Two Higher Technical Institutes and 3 Higher Commercial Institutes offer 2-year post-secondary courses. A selected number of students from Riyadh Higher Technical Institute may take the 3-year course to enable them to teach in the vocational secondary schools.

HIGHER EDUCATION

There are 2 kinds of establishment offering higher education: the traditional Islamic colleges and the Western-oriented colleges.

Admission to higher education is based on success in the General Secondary Education Certificate examinations. An average of 60% is required for admission to the science faculties, an average of 50% for admission to the arts faculties. Some faculties also provide entrance examinations. Part-time students are accepted.

Saudi Arabia

The normal length of a **Bachelor degree** course is 4 years, apart from pharmacy and medicine (4 years plus hospital training) and engineering (5 years). Courses mostly operate on the American credit system. Every course represents a certain number of hours, credits or points generally corresponding to the number of class-hours offered each week. The average student takes approximately 30-35 credits during the academic year; undergraduates must complete a minimum of 120 credits to graduate.

Women are admitted to university in Saudi Arabia on the same terms as men, but their studies are completely segregated. Women have separate facilities, are admitted to classes at different times from the men, or attend classes broadcast over closed-circuit television.

All universities and many faculties now offer **Master degrees**, or plan to.

All universities have plans to offer **Ph.D.s** and, at the University of Petroleum and Minerals (UPM), King Said University (KSU) and King Abdul Aziz University (KAAU), they are already underway in some faculties.

TEACHER EDUCATION

Primary

Before 1974:

Intermediate school graduates could take a 3-year (previously 2-year) training course in secondary-level training institutions to enable them to teach in elementary schools.

After 1974:

Teachers must now have the General Secondary Education Certificate, since the Intermediate Teacher Training Institutes were upgraded in 1975/6 to Secondary Teacher Training Institutes. To persuade more women to become elementary school teachers, the Girls' Education Administration offers 3-month post-secondary courses. There are also 11 Junior Colleges offering 2-year courses for women leading to a **Certificate of Education** enabling graduates to teach at primary/elementary and intermediate level schools.

Intermediate and secondary

Men:

The traditional method of becoming an intermediate or secondary level teacher is to take a **Bachelor of Education Degree** at university. Graduates who did not study education in their degree courses are generally sent abroad to follow 1-year teaching courses.

Saudi Arabia

Women:

There are 11 Colleges of Education for girls throughout the kingdom providing 4-year courses leading to a **BA or B.Sc. in Education**. Graduates are qualified to teach in secondary schools. Three of these colleges: <u>Jeddah</u>, <u>Riyadh</u>, and <u>Dammam</u>, provide post-graduate training for women interested in specialization.

Science and mathematics:

The Ministry of Education has established 2 centres for training and retraining science and mathematics teachers for work in intermediate schools. Trainees must be graduates of the Teacher Training Institutes or holders of the General Secondary Education Certificate. A preliminary remedial science course is followed by a 3-year course which leads to a **Teacher Proficiency Certificate**.

Fine arts and physical education:

There are separate fine arts institutes for men and women. Only men are allowed to teach physical education. Women can enter the fine arts institutes on the basis of the Elementary Education Certificate.

NON-FORMAL AND ADULT EDUCATION

Trade schools

The curricula of these schools provide basic vocational trade skills. The Centre for Short Term Vocational Training in Riyadh trains unemployed adult Saudi workers in selected basic skills by short-term (3-9 months) training courses.

Other non-formal training

Many institutions run training centres for their Saudi employees, offering courses which suit their needs. Examples are the Arabian American Oil Corporation (ARAMCO), which has a full range of training facilities; the Royal commission for Jubail and Yanbu, which runs human resources development centres in Jubail and Yanbu; Saudi Arabian Basic Industries Corporation (SABIC) whose 13 associated industries all run training centres; the Military Sector, covering the armed service; the National Guard, the Police Force, and other security service, who all run extensive training services; and all Ministries have training sectors and most run training centres, e.g. the Ministry of Health runs a series of nursing and technician training centres all over the country.

Senegal

Republic of Senegal

Formerly a French colony, Senegal became a member of the French Community in 1958. It was a part, together with Sudan, of the Federation of Mali from January 1959 to August 1960. On 20 August 1960, it became a fully independent state known as the Republic of Senegal.

There remains a strong French influence on the educational system. However, the 1969-73 Plan envisaged basic structural changes in the school system, and further reforms aimed to make the courses more practical. A new impetus for change was provided when Abdou Diouf succeeded President Senghor. In January 1980 he summoned an assembly (Etats Generaux de l'Education) to propose further reforms.

There is no compulsory period of education.

The medium of instruction is French.

The academic year runs from October to July.

EVALUATION IN BRITAIN

School

Diplome de Bachelier de l'Enseignement du Second Degre/Baccalaureat - generally compared to GCE O-level standard.

Higher

Licence - generally compared to a standard between GCE A-level and a British Bachelor degree.

Senegal

MARKING SYSTEMS

School and Higher

Marking is on a scale 0-20 (maximum); 10 is the minimum pass mark.

16-20	tres bien	very good
14-15	bien	good
12-13	assez bien	fair
10-11	passable	pass

SCHOOL EDUCATION

Pre-primary

Very limited facilities.

Primary

This covers 6 years, from age 6, leading to the **Certificat d'Etudes Primaires Elementaires (CEPE)**.

Secondary

There is a special entrance examination, akin to the former 11-plus examination in the UK. Secondary education lasts 7 years, divided into 4 years lower secondary and 3 years upper. The years are numbered in reverse order, i.e. the first year is classe sixieme through to the seventh year, classe terminale.

Lower:

This cycle (also called 'middle') can be studied at a College d'Enseignement General (CEG), which offers lower secondary education only, College d'Enseignement Moyen Secondaire, College d'Enseignement Moderne (CEM), College d'Enseignement Secondaire (CES), or a Lycee. The cycle ends in the examinations for the **Brevet d'Etudes du Premier Cycle (BEPC)**, now known as the **Diplome de Fin d'Etudes Moyennes (DFEM)**. Unsuccessful pupils may proceed only to teacher training or a technical/vocational course. Successful pupils may choose whether to proceed to an academic or technical lycee for upper secondary education.

Upper:

The 3-year academic course ends in the examinations for the **Baccalaureat de l'Enseignement du Second Degre**, which may be taken in 1 of 5 series, depending on the specialization taken in the last 2 years:

A	philosophie-lettres (sub-options A1-A5)
B	economique et social
C	mathematiques et sciences physiques
D	mathematiques et sciences de la nature
E	mathematiques et technique

Senegal

Technical secondary

Primary school leavers may undertake:

3-year courses at Centres de Formation, leading to the qualification of **Certificat d'Aptitude Professionnelle**

or

4-year courses at Ecoles d'Agents Techniques leading to the qualification of **Diplome d'Agent Technique de** (e.g. l'Agriculture).

On completion of lower secondary education, pupils (i.e. holders of the BEPC/DFEM) may take a 'short' course (2 years) leading to the qualification of **Brevet d'Agent Technique**, or a 'long' course (3 years) leading to the qualification of **Baccalaureat Technique**, whether at Lycees Techniques or Ecoles Nationales. Since 1974 the **Baccalaureat Technique/Diplome de Bachelier Technicien** may be taken in one of a variety of options:

F1 - F8   formation industrielle:

F1	fabrications mecaniques
F2	electrotechnique
F3	mecanique auto
F4	chaudronnerie et tuyauterie industrielles
F5	ouvrages metalliques
F6	chimie (since 1975)
F7	sciences biologiques (since 1975)
F8	genie civil et batiment (since 1976)

G   formation commerciale:

G1	techniques administratives
G2	techniques quantitatives de gestion

HIGHER EDUCATION

The Baccalaureat is the entrance requirement for degree courses at the university, although students also have to sit a special entrance examination:

examen A   arts, humanities and social science

examen B   mathematics, medicine, dentistry, veterinary medicine, pharmacy, and natural sciences.

There are 2 universities: the University of Dakar, established in 1957, and the University of Gaston-Berger (in the final stages of construction). There are also **Grandes Ecoles**, which are similar to those in France and offer specialized courses.

Senegal

At the universities all students take a multidisciplinary course for 2 years, leading to the **Diplome Universitaire d'Etudes Litteraires (DUEL), Diplome Universitaire d'Etudes Scientifiques (DUES), Diplome d'Etudes Juridiques Generales (DEJG)** or **Diplome Universitaire de Technologie (DUT)**, depending on the student's specialization.

A further year of specialization leads to the **Licence** (**d'Enseignement** in teaching subjects, and **de Recherche** in linguistics, psychology and sociology).

Students holding the Licence may undertake a 1-year postgraduate course leading to the **Maitrise**; in science subjects this takes 2 years. A year's research leads to the **Diplome d'Etudes Approfondies (DEA)**, and a further 2 years to the **Doctorat de Troisieme Cycle**. With either qualification, students may undertake a minimum of 2 years research in pharmacy, law, economics, arts and science, leading to the **Doctorat d'Etat**. This qualification is necessary to teach in higher education.

The **Doctorat d'Universite** is obtained by successful submission of a short thesis on completion of a minimum of 2 years research after the Licence. Holders of this qualification are not entitled to teach.

Law: students may enter the universities, without the Baccalaureat, for a 2-year course leading to the qualification of **Capacite en Droit**. They may then enrol on the 3-year law degree course.

Medicine: the first qualification is the **Doctorat d'Etat en Medecine** obtained after 7 years.

Pharmacy and dentistry: the first qualifications, obtained after 5 years, are the **Diplome de Pharmacien** and **Doctorat d'Etat en Chirurgie/Dentaire** respectively.

TEACHER EDUCATION

Primary

Holders of the BEPC/DFEM undertake a 1-year course at a Centre Regional de Formation Pedagogique (CFP) leading to the **Certificat Elementaire d'Aptitude Pedagogique (CEAP)**, and the position of instituteur/institutrice adjoint (i.e. assistant teacher).

Teachers (instituteurs) take a 3-year course of upper secondary education at an Ecole Normale culminating in the **Baccalaureat** or **Brevet Superieur de Fin d'Etudes Normales**, and a **Certificat d'Aptitude Pedagogique**.

Secondary

pre-1971

Lower:

Teachers for the Colleges d'Enseignement General (CEG) were trained at the Ecole Normale Superieure (ENS) on a 2-year course from the Baccalaureat, leading to the **Certificat d'Aptitude a l'Enseignement dans les Colleges d'Enseignement General (CAPCEG)**.

Senegal

Upper:

Teachers had to be graduates. If they held the Licence they took a 1-year course leading to the position of adjoint d'enseignement (assistant teacher). Holders of the Maitrise took a 1-year course leading to the **Certificat d'Aptitude au Professorat de l'Enseignement Secondaire (CAPES)**.

Since 1971

In 1971 the Ecole Normale Superieure was partly integrated into the University of Dakar. Holders of the Licence now take a 1-year course leading to the **Certificat d'Aptitude a l'Enseignement (CAEM)**; holders of the Maitrise take a 1-year course leading to the **Certificat d'Aptitude a l'Enseignement Secondaire (CAES)**.

The **Agregation** is a competitive examination taken by qualified secondary school teachers which leads to an increase in salary and prestige.

Seychelles

Republic of Seychelles

Education in the Seychelles has been in a state of transition since 1977, when the present Socialist government came to power.

Education is compulsory from age six to fifteen.

The medium of instruction is Creole from age six to ten. Then it changes to mainly English, but in some subjects Creole or French may be used as well.

EVALUATION IN BRITAIN

School

Cambridge Overseas School Certificate (before 1982 and after 1984) - grades 1-6 are equated to GCE O-level (grades A, B or C).

Cambridge Overseas Higher School Certificate - grades A-E passes are equated to GCE A-level.

Seychelles National Certificate of Education (1982-4) - not recognized in Britain.

MARKING SYSTEMS

School

Cambridge Overseas School Certificate (COSC) is graded 1 (maximum) - 9:

1-2	very good
3-6	credit
7-8	pass
9	fail

Seychelles

Cambridge Overseas Higher School Certificate (COHSC):

A-E	pass
S	subsidiary pass
F	fail

SCHOOL EDUCATION

Pre-primary

Pre-school education is carried out from age 4 to 6, although attendance is voluntary.

Primary

This is conducted in 28 schools from age 6 to 15+. Children study Creole, English, French, mathematics, science, social sciences, art and crafts and agriculture. There is an examination at the end of the ninth grade.

Secondary

National Youth Scheme:

All young people are encouraged to leave home at the end of primary education to go to camp for 2 years. The National Youth Scheme is compulsory for those who wish to go on to further education. Their training is based on acquiring life skills, undertaking community projects and looking after themselves. At the end of 2 years students sit the **Seychelles National Certificate of Education**. This is an internal examination based in some areas on the Cambridge Overseas School Certificate.

The Polytechnic:

Those wishing to continue with further education take courses at the Polytechnic. This is an amalgamation of several previous colleges of further education. There are colleges of agriculture, art and design, business studies, construction, education, engineering, health studies, hotel and tourism, humanities and social sciences, maritime studies, mathematics, sciences and media studies. Courses are mainly 2 years. Students may also take O- and A-levels.

HIGHER EDUCATION

There are no institutions of higher education. Generally, those wishing to continue their education do so in the UK or elsewhere.

Seychelles

TEACHER EDUCATION

In-service courses are run in vacations and in the evening.

Teachers train for 3 years after the National Youth Scheme to teach at the creche, lower primary and middle primary levels. Students leaving the Polytechnic with at least 1 A-level may take a 4-year course, involving 2 years study in Australia, to teach upper primary classes. Students may also take courses in the UK to become graduate teachers.

Sierra Leone

Republic of Sierra Leone

There is no compulsory period of education.

Medium of instruction is English.

The academic year runs from September/October to July.

EVALUATION IN BRITAIN

School

West African School Certificate (WASC) and Cambridge Overseas School Certificate (COSC)	- grades 1-6 are generally equated to GCE O-level (A, B, C)
West African Higher School Certificate (WAHSC) and Cambridge Overseas Higher School Certificate (COHSC)	- generally equated to GCE A-level standard.

Higher

Bachelor degree

Ordinary degrees are generally compared to British Ordinary Bachelor degrees

Honours degrees are generally compared to British Honours degrees

However students graduating at the University of Sierra Leone may be required to undertake a qualifying year at a British university before being admitted to a taught Master course.

MARKING SYSTEMS

School

West African School Certificate and Cambridge Overseas School Certificate	- graded 1 (maximum) to 9 (fail)

Sierra Leone

West African Higher School Certificate and - graded A, B, C, D, E, O (subsidiary
Cambridge Overseas Higher School Certificate   pass), F (fail)

Higher

Njala University College

A	5	excellent
B	4	good
C	3	fair
D	2	bare pass
F	1	fail

Fourah Bay College

A	70-100%	
B+	60-69	
B	50-59	
C+	45-49	
C	40-44	
D	35-39	fail
E	below 35	fail

SCHOOL EDUCATION

Pre-primary

Limited facilities available.

Primary

This covers 7 years from age 5 (although many children start later).

The curriculum covers: English; mathematics; science; music; health and physical education; history; geography and current events; arts and crafts; home economics; and religious instruction. The local language is often the medium of instruction in at least the first 2 years, even though the official medium is English. On completion of the 7 years, pupils take the **Selective Entrance Examination** set by the West African Examinations Council. If pupils obtain 50% or above, they may continue to secondary education.

Secondary

This covers 7 years, divided into 5 years lower and 2 years upper (sixth form).

On completion of lower secondary, pupils take the examinations for the **West African School Certificate**/GCE O-levels. If successful, they may proceed to the sixth form and take the examinations for the **West African Higher School Certificate**/GCE A-levels.

Technical secondary

2 <u>Technical Institutes</u> (Kenema and Freetown) offer a variety of courses leading to qualifications of the **City and Guilds of London Institute**, OND and OTD (in building and engineering). They also offer lower-level craft certificates (from the end of form III) and qualifications of the **Royal Society of Arts**.

2 <u>Trade Centres</u> offer 3-year courses in various fields from the end of form III.

Sierra Leone

HIGHER EDUCATION

The University of Sierra Leone consists of 2 colleges - Fourah Bay and Njala. In 1960 Fourah Bay College became University College of Sierra Leone and, in 1966, it became a constituent college of the University of Sierra Leone along with Njala University College (since 1964), at which time it reverted to the title 'Fourah Bay College'. Until 1967 the University awarded degrees by the University of Durham.

The entrance requirement to **Bachelor degree** courses is normally 5 O-levels; general degrees take 4 years, honours degrees 5 years. With good A-levels the degree courses will be reduced by 1 year each, students starting in year 2. With poor A-level results students start on a par with O-level entrants.

A 1-year course on completion of an Honours degree may lead to a **Master degree**, but this is not available in all departments.

A minimum of 3 years research after the Bachelor degree leads to a **Ph.D.**

The university also offers a large number of undergraduate certificates and diplomas.

TEACHER EDUCATION

Primary

A 3-year course from GCE O-level standard is offered at a teacher training college.

Holders of 3 GCE O-level passes may take a 2-year course.

Secondary

Lower: a 3-year course from GCE O-level leading to a **Higher Teachers' Certificate** at Milton Margai Teachers College.

Upper: a 4-year **Bachelor of Education** degree at Njala University College or a 1-year **Postgraduate Diploma** in education after a Bachelor of Arts/Science at Fourah Bay College.

In 1972 the Institute of Education became a constituent institution of the University.

Singapore

Republic of Singapore

This chapter covers the period from 1950 to the present; Singapore became an independent state in 1965.

Singapore's education system has undergone a major revision as a result of a report in 1979 produced by Dr Goh Keng Swee, first Deputy Prime Minister and the then Minister of Defence but later Minister for Education.

There are four official languages: Chinese (Mandarin); Malay (the national language); English; and Tamil. At the primary and secondary stages the government provides facilities for instruction in each of the languages and parents are free to choose. In non-English-medium schools the second language is always English. At the tertiary level, English is the medium of instruction.

There is now a great focus on language learning and the streaming of pupils at various stages of the system to place them in a course best suited to their abilities. There has been a steady shift from Chinese/Malay/Tamil-medium schools to English-medium schools as more and more parents have opted to send their children to English-medium schools. (Ninety-three per cent of students enrolled in Primary 1 in 1984 were in English-medium schools.) To preserve cultural roots a policy of bilingualism has been vigorously pursued for all but the lowest in ability.

The academic year is divided into four terms (two semesters) from January to November.

EVALUATION IN BRITAIN

School

Government Senior Middle 3 **Government Secondary 4**	- generally considered to be below GCE O-level standard.
Cambridge Overseas School Certificate	- grades 1-6 are equated to GCE O-level (grades A, B or C).
Federation of Malaysia Certificate **Singapore/Cambridge GCE O-level**	- generally compared to GCE O-level standard on a subject-for-subject basis where marks of 1-6 have been obtained.
Cambridge Overseas Higher School Certificate	- grades A-E are equated to GCE A-level.

Singapore

Singapore/Cambridge GCE A-level — generally compared to GCE A-level standard if grades A-E have been obtained.

Further

Technician Diploma (from Singapore Polytechnic and Ngee Ann Polytechnic, 3 years full-time) - may be considered comparable to BTEC Higher National Diploma (formerly HND) however, a minimum of grade C is required for entry to a university.

Technician Certificate (4 years part-time) - generally compared to a Technician Diploma of the City & Guilds of London Institute.

Industrial Technician Certificate (Industrial Training Board/Vocational and Industrial Training Board) - generally compared to the Final Technician Certificate of the City & Guilds of London Institute.

Higher

Bachelor degrees (from the National University of Singapore) - generally considered to compare to British Bachelor degree standard. Degrees awarded by the former Nanyang University have been known to be accepted for postgraduate study in Britain.

MARKING SYSTEMS

School

Cambridge Overseas School Certificate
Singapore/Cambridge GCE O-level — graded 1 (maximum) - 9 (fail)

Cambridge Overseas Higher School Certificate
Singapore/Cambridge GCE A-level — graded A (maximum) - F (fail)

Higher

Honours degrees are classified as follows:

class I
class II division i
class II division ii
class III

Hons (I or II) are awarded for the degrees of B.Eng., B.Acc., B.Sc. (Building), B.Sc. (Estate Management).

Hons (unclassified) are awarded for degrees of B.Arch., BDS, and MB BS.

Singapore

SCHOOL EDUCATION

Pre-primary/kindergarten

Approximately 40% of children receive formal pre-school education through private registered kindergartens, People's Association kindergartens and children's centres operated by the Ministry of Community Development.

Primary

This lasts 6 or 8 years, divided into 2 cycles, from age 6. The study of a second language is compulsory at this stage, but English is the medium of instruction in most schools. At the end of the Primary 3 cycle pupils are streamed in 3 ways: normal, completing their primary education after 6 years; extended, completing after 8 years; and monolingual, in which pupils are not normally expected to complete until age 14. At the end of the cycle, pupils take the **Primary School Leaving Examination** (PSLE), an achievement test in the first and second languages, mathematics and science. The results of the PSLE determine the streaming group of the pupil in secondary school and the choice of secondary school. Pupils who fail the PSLE may stay in Primary 6 and take the examination until they pass it. If they have still not passed by age 14 or are in the monolingual course, they may go on to take a 2-year course run by the Vocational and Industrial Training Board (VITB) which may lead to further training by the same body.

Secondary

This is divided into 4 or 5 years secondary and 2 or 3 years higher secondary/pre-university. Since 1969 the first 2 years of secondary education have been based on a common curriculum. At the end of the second year, aptitude tests decide whether a pupil continues in the science, commerce, arts or technical stream, or leaves to take a course at a vocational institute. Since 1980 there has been an 'express' stream in which pupils are expected to complete their secondary education in 6 years.

Until 1971 various school-leaving certificates could be obtained on completion of the 4-year courses at the various media schools. In English-medium schools pupils took the **Cambridge Overseas School Certificate** (COSC).

The **Singapore-Cambridge GCE O-level** examination was established in 1971. The examination is conducted by the University of Cambridge Local Examinations Syndicate in conjunction with the Singapore Ministry of Education; the Cambridge Syndicate is the examining authority for subjects examined in the medium of English, and the Ministry of Education is the examining authority for subjects examined in Chinese, Tamil or Malay. A pass in a second language is needed to obtain the certificate.

The **GCE N-level** course lasts 4 years. Pupils who do well study for a further year before taking GCE O-level. The others enter direct employment or join the VITB for vocational training.

Until 1973, the **Cambridge Higher School Certificate** (Malay medium), the **Government Higher School Certificate** (Chinese), the **Cambridge Higher School Certificate** and the **Higher School Certificate** (Commerce) examinations were held at the end of the 2-year pre-university courses. The Government Higher School Certificate (Chinese) and the Higher School Certificate (Commerce) were local examinations, whereas the others were conducted by the University of Cambridge Local Examinations Syndicate in collaboration with the Universities of Singapore and Malaya. After 1973, students were able to take the Singapore/Cambridge GCE A-levels in English or Malay. The Government Higher School Certificate (Chinese) and the Higher School Certificate (Commerce) was replaced by the **Singapore GCE A-level** (Chinese) and (Commerce) examinations respectively. The current practice is to take the Singapore/Cambridge GCE A-levels, but students may take a limited number of subjects in Chinese, Malay and Tamil.

Eleven junior colleges offer 2-year pre-university courses in arts and science in the English medium. The syllabuses are the same as those used at the upper-secondary stage of normal secondary schools. Pupils generally offer 4 A-levels, and there is a compulsory A/O paper in English (General Paper).

Technical secondary

Some schools provide 4-year courses offering specialization in woodwork, metalwork, mechanics and technical drawing, with the possibility of taking examinations at the end of the course for the GCE O- or N-levels.

One secondary commercial school prepares pupils for the **London Chamber of Commerce examinations**.

The **Secondary Vocational Certificate** may be obtained after a 2-year vocational secondary course, enabling the pupil to embark on artisan/trade courses conducted originally by the Industrial Training Board, but now by the Vocational and Industrial Training Board, set up in 1979. These courses are provided at vocational institutes established in 1967/8; 4 vocational schools were upgraded to industrial training centres in 1969, and 4 new vocational institutes were established. The industrial training centres were renamed as vocational institutes in 1971. There are now 15 vocational institutions under the Vocational and Industrial Training Board. Each institute specializes in craft/artisan/apprentice-level courses in its own sector of the metal, building, electrical and motor vehicle trades. A **Trade Certificate** may be obtained after a basic preparatory course designed to train people for industrial careers at the skilled level. A 1-year course is available for pupils who left at the end of Secondary IV or Technical Secondary IV, and 2-year courses are available for those who completed Secondary II, Secondary III or Technical Secondary III. The Trade Certificate in manual or applied arts is obtained after a 2-year course; the course in manual arts is for those who have at least completed the primary school course, while the course in applied arts is for those who have reached GCE O-level. The artisan courses, usually 6 months are for primary school leavers.

FURTHER EDUCATION

The main institutions offering instruction at this level (apart from certain courses at the vocational institutes run by the Industrial Training Board, now the Vocational and Industrial Training Board) are the Ngee Ann Technical College and the Singapore Polytechnic.

Singapore Polytechnic was established in 1954, but teaching did not actually begin until 1958. The medium of instruction is English. The Polytechnic offers 2-year **Certificate Courses** and 3-year **Technician Diploma** courses. Most students enter for the 3-year Diploma course after O-level, the minimum requirements being passes in English language, mathematics and an appropriate science or technical subject. Students with A-levels can enter the second year of the Diploma course if they have a pass in English language at O-level and A-level passes in mathematics and a suitable science subject.

Ngee Ann Polytechnic - like the Singapore Polytechnic, also offers 3-year post O-level diploma and 2-year post A-level diploma courses. It was founded in 1963 as the Ngee Ann College. The 1967 Ngee Ann College Act altered the status of the institution from a private to a public body, and the 1968 Ngee Ann Technical College Act altered the title. This change in name reflected the change in the level and nature of courses offered by this institution. Until 1967 the College offered 4-year degree courses in telecommunications, industrial chemistry, Malay language and literature, and accountancy. In that year it accepted and implemented the recommendation that it should become an institution of higher learning offering courses in engineering and commerce at sub-degree level to meet the growing needs of industry and commerce in Singapore. The Institution has functioned as a polytechnic since then. However, it was only early in 1982 that it was formally renamed Ngee Ann Polytechnic.

HIGHER EDUCATION

Until 1979

There were 2 universities: the University of Singapore and Nanyang University. Degrees from both institutions were given equal status and many of the external examiners for both institutions were from Britain.

University of Singapore. In 1949 the King Edward VII College of Medicine and Raffles College were amalgamated to form the University of Malaya, situated in Singapore, but serving the needs of Singapore and the Federation of Malaya. In 1959 it was reorganized into 2 largely autonomous institutions of equal status, one in each country, and the University of Malaya in Singapore was formally established in 1959. On 1 January 1962 the 2 institutions separated and became the national universities of the countries in which they are situated.

Nanyang University. This institution was established in 1953 to provide facilities for higher education in the Chinese medium. Teaching actually began in 1956. Instruction became more and more English-oriented until 1975, when it became completely English medium.

From the academic year 1978/9 the joint campus scheme was in operation, whereby students could take courses at either institution with common syllabuses and examinations. The degrees were awarded jointly by Nanyang University and the University of Singapore.

From 1980

In August 1980 the University of Singapore was designated the National University of Singapore (NUS). Nanyang University has become the Nanyang Technological Institute (NTI). By special arrangement with the University Senate, all NTI engineering students undergo a common first-year course at the University's Faculty of Engineering.

Singapore

Pass degrees are usually obtained on completion of 3 years study, and students who obtain very good grades may study for an additional year to obtain **Honours**. A new direct Honours course for students in the Faculties of Arts and Social Sciences and Science, which enables them to obtain an Honours degree after 3 instead of 4 years of study, was introduced in 1982. This course was introduced in parallel to the existing Honours degree course and is aimed at outstanding students in these 2 Faculties. **Bachelor degrees** in dentistry, law, engineering, building and estate management are taken over 4 years, in architecture 4-and-a-half years (to register as an architect students must also complete 2 years of practical office experience), and in medicine 5 years.

Students who are taking an arts course must take a subsidiary course in science, and those taking a science course must take a subsidiary course in arts.

Courses of 1 and 2 yeras are available for **postgraduate diplomas**; a minimum 1-year course is available for a **Master degree**, with a minimum of 2 years for a **Ph.D**.

The academic year runs from July to February.

TEACHER EDUCATION

The Teachers' Training College was established in 1950 and originally offered courses only in English. In 1954 it began to offer courses in Chinese, and in 1957 also in Malay. The College was renamed in 1973 the Institute of Education. It is the only institution offering training for teachers at the primary and secondary (including technical secondary) stages. A 2-year **Certificate** course is available for students who have obtained GCE A-levels, and there is a 1-year **Diploma** course for graduates of the University. Postgraduate courses are available leading to the **M.Ed.**, and facilities are offered for research leading to a **Ph.D**. The Institute also provides for the continuing education of qualified practising teachers through the provision of the full-time **Further Professional Certificate in Education** (FPCE) programme and other (shorter) in-service courses.

Solomon Islands

Education in the Solomon Islands is a Government responsibility; before 1946 this responsibility belonged to the Church.

There is no compulsory education.

The main languages spoken are Melanesian, Pidgin English and English.

The university academic year runs from February to November, in other institutions from January to November.

EVALUATION IN BRITAIN

School

Solomon Islands School Certificate - generally considered to compare to GCE O-level standard.

Higher

Bachelor degrees from the University of the South Pacific - generally considered to compare to British Bachelor degree standard.

MARKING SYSTEMS

Higher

Degrees from the University of the South Pacific are unclassified.

SCHOOL EDUCATION

Primary

This lasts 6 years, formerly 7 years, covering standards 1-6.

Solomon Islands

Secondary

There are 12 provincial secondary schools, at Vonunu, Pawa, Aligegeo, Tangarare, Siota, Luesaleba, Kamaosi, Honiara, Rokva, Allardyce, Avu Avu and Choiseul Bay.

The length of attendance at these schools is 3 years.

These provincial schools are situated in rural areas and were designed to promote self-sufficiency and contribute towards improvement in rural life. The schools grow much of their own food and the core curriculum of English and mathematics is allied to skills and occupations relevant to the area in which the school is situated. During the third year all secondary school students undergo a **Form III Assessment** which is English and mathematics based.

Completion of form III represents the end of school education for most students; a few transfer to form IV in a national secondary school. Others continue their education at the Solomon Islands College of Higher Education. Those leaving full-time education qualify for a **Form III Leavers' Certificate**.

There are 8 national secondary schools which offer academic courses (forms I-V) leading to the **Solomon Islands School Certificate**.

Su'u, Goldie, Tenaru, Selwyn, Betikama and Kukudu are church or independent schools; the King George VI school at Honiara and Waimapuru School on Makira Island are government secondary schools.

FURTHER EDUCATION

Betikma Adventist High School has a small sixth form intake of students from the Seventh Day Adventist faith. The National Sixth Form is situated at King George VI School and draws pupils from all National Secondary Schools. Satisfactory completion of the sixth-form course (either science or arts based) enables students to go on to either the University of the South Pacific or the University of Papua New Guinea.

Solomon Islands College of Higher Education (SICHE) is an autonomous body opened in 1984. It replaced 4 government training institutions and the first students were registered in 1985.

The College has 6 schools: Education and Cultural Studies, Industrial Development, Finance and Administration, Nursing and Paramedical Studies, Marine Studies, Natural Resources.

The College accepts students with the Form III Leavers Certificate or with the Solomon Islands School Certificate. Each student follows a 1-year **Foundation Programme** and then a **Certificate** or a **Diploma** course.

Solomon Islands

HIGHER EDUCATION

Students enrol at the University of the South Pacific in Fiji, or at the University of Papua New Guinea.

The universities run 2 pre-degree programmes each lasting 1 academic year which provide the basis for further study.

Preliminary programmes (in either science or social science) are for students entering university from regions where there are no sixth-form studies. They may then proceed to the Foundation programme.

Foundation programmes are for students with **New Zealand University Entrance examination** or equivalent sixth-form studies.

Admission to first degree courses is based on satisfactory completion of the foundation year or other studies comparable in standard to a 1-year post New Zealand University Entrance course.

The University of the South Pacific offers 3-year **BA, B.Ed., B.Sc.** and **B.Agr.** courses, and 4-year **BA** and **B.Sc.** courses with a **Graduate Certificate in Education**.

2-year **Diploma** courses are available in most disciplines for students satisfactorily completing the Foundation programme.

Postgraduate courses are available in some disciplines for students who have satisfactorily completed a degree course.

TEACHER EDUCATION

Courses may be taken at the Solomon Islands College of Higher Education leading to the **Solomon Islands Teaching Certificate** for primary teachers or a **Diploma of Education** for provincial and national secondary school teachers.

Courses are also available at degree level at the University of the South Pacific or the University of Papua New Guinea.

South Africa

Republic of South Africa

Following the implementation of the new constitution in September 1984, education in South Africa (excluding the 'independent' and 'non-independent' homelands) is controlled as follows:

Each 'Own' Affairs Section (the House of Assembly for Whites, the House of Delegates for Indians, and the House of Representatives for Coloureds) has its own Education Department, all known as the Department of Education and Culture, which deals with the education of the specific race group.

African affairs including African education are not considered to be an 'Own' Affair. The Department of Education and Training continues to administer African education within the Republic of South Africa; each of the ten (four independent, six non-independent) homelands has its own education department and administers its own education.

The Department of National Education is now considered a 'general' affair and deals with matters which affect all race groups; it sets norms and standards for educational running costs, for salaries and conditions of employment of staff, for the professional registration of teachers, for syllabuses and examinations, and for the certification of qualifications.

The academic year runs from January to November/December, but exact dates vary from province to province and from system to system.

Compulsory education for White children is from age seven to sixteen; for Coloured children from seven to sixteen; and for Indian children from seven to fifteen. Compulsory education for Black children is gradually being introduced into those schools where the School Committee has requested it.

English and Afrikaans are the 2 official languages. The medium of instruction at school/further education level is as follows:

White - English or Afrikaans, depending on the mother tongue, but both subjects are compulsory

Black - the vernacular until standard 2, English/Afrikaans thereafter

Coloured - Afrikaans and English

Indian - English.

South Africa

At the higher education level English is used as the medium of instruction at the following universities: Cape Town, Natal, Rhodes and Witwatersrand; Afrikaans is used at the universities in Orange Free State, Pretoria, Rand Afrikaans, Stellenbosch and Potchestroom. Port Elizabeth University and the University of South Africa (UNISA) are bilingual. The medium of instruction at the ethnic universities is mainly English, and in the new University of Vista it is entirely in English.

EVALUATION IN BRITAIN

School

The overall standard of the **Matriculation Certificate** (South African Joint Matriculation Board), showing the matriculation standard in English language and 4 other subjects, and the **Senior Certificate**, giving exemption from the matriculation certificate examination, is generally considered to compare to a standard between GCE O- and A-levels.

On a subject-for-subject basis, subjects passed at the marks of A-D at both the 'higher' and 'standard' grade would generally be compared to GCE O-level. Subjects awarded marks of E or F at either grade are unlikely to be accorded O-level status.

Some institutions in Britain are willing to consider students holding only one of these certificates for entrance to a Bachelor degree course, but most would require at least successful completion of the first year of a South African degree course or, alternatively, GCE A-levels.

Higher

The **Bachelor (Honours) degree**, obtained on completion of a 4-year course, is generally considered comparable to a British Bachelor (Honours) degree. A Bachelor degree awarded on completion of a 3-year course is likely to be compared to a British Bachelor degree.

The 4-year Ordinary engineering degree may be compared to a British Bachelor (Ordinary) degree, while the 4-year Honours engineering degree may be compared to a British Bachelor (Honours) degree.

Individuals holding a 4-year Honours degree from South Africa may be accepted for post-graduate study in the UK.

MARKING SYSTEMS

School

Marking may be alphabetical or expressed as a percentage; in standard 10 it is alphabetical.

South Africa

Senior Certificate/Matriculation

A	80-100%	
B	70-79	for both standard and higher-grade
C	60-69	subjects in the Matriculation and
D	50-59	Senior Certificates
E	40-49	
F	33-39	

The pass mark in all higher-grade subjects is 40% except in Afrikaans second language higher grade and English second language higher grade. The pass mark in all standard grade subjects is 33%.

The aggregate pass mark for matriculation is 45%; until 1960 it was 40%.

Higher

Honours degrees are classified:

1st class	75-100%
2nd class division 1	70-74
2nd class division 2	60-69
3rd class	50-59
fail	below 50

SCHOOL EDUCATION

Pre-primary

Limited facilities for all race groups.

Primary

Until 1967 this covered 7 years for all children from age 5, except those in the Black sector who had to complete an extra year, learning English and Afrikaans.

The present system covers 6 years for White and Indian children, 7 years for Black children. It consists of grades 1 and 2 and standards 1-5.

The curriculum covers English, Afrikaans, arithmetic, history, geography, nature study, hygiene, RI, art and crafts, PE and woodwork/homecraft.

Until the mid-1970s students took tests for the **Primary School Leaving Examination Certificate** on completion of standard 6. In Black schools, since 1976, examinations leading to the **Higher Primary Certificate** have been taken at the end of standard 1.

Secondary (standards 6-10)

The curriculum is centrally prescribed by the Committee of Education Heads, consisting of members of the national education departments and the Joint Matriculation Board. In standard 6 it covers the first and second languages, mathematics, history, geography, and general science; in standards 6/7 and 7/8, industrial arts/housecraft and an optional subject are added.

South Africa

Students in most schools are streamed from standard 6, into ordinary and practical courses. The practical courses have a more vocational bias, and the syllabuses are not parallels of the ordinary courses. It is possible for students to transfer from a practical to an ordinary course if their performance warrants this. Students who complete the full practical course, to standard 10, are awarded the **Standard 10 (Practical) Certificate**.

On completion of standard 8, pupils in Black schools sit the external examinations for the **Junior Certificate**.

In the senior secondary cycle of education, students may study subjects either at the higher or standard grade, the higher-grade syllabuses covering more material.

Until 1976 only languages were offered with 2 levels of syllabus. In some education departments, they were designated as higher and lower, in others as A and B.

For the award of the Senior Certificate, the first or second official language must be passed, either at the higher or standard grade.

The candidate's choice of study courses is limited by regulations laid down by the various authorities responsible for racially segregated education and by the courses the schools themselves are able to offer.

Examination subjects leading to the Senior Certificate (standards 8-10) have been divided into 6 groups:

English and Afrikaans (official languages)
Maths
Natural sciences
Third languages
Human sciences
Additional subjects (e.g. commercial arts).

On completion of standard 10, students sit the external **Senior Certificate** examination, set by one of the examination boards appointed by the Joint Matriculation Board, and consisting of tests in 6 or 7 subjects.

Each education authority has its own system of Senior Certificate Examinations but admission to university is controlled by the Joint Matriculation Board, which represents all universities in the RSA, and it conducts its own Matriculation examination for this purpose. However, Senior Certificates are recognized for university admission if they conform to the requirements of the Joint Matriculation Board for Matriculation exemption. In general, these require a candidate to:

1. Offer at least 6 and no more than 7 subjects from the 6 groups.

2. Pass in at least 5 subjects in one sitting.

3. Attain an aggregate mark of at least 45.

4. Pass at the higher grade in at least 3 subjects from the first 5 groups with at least 40% in each.

5. Pass in both official languages, at least one at the higher grade.

6. Offer at least one subject from each of 4 of the groups, provided no more than 4 languages are offered.

South Africa

Students who do not meet the requirements for the Senior Certificate may retake some or all of the examinations, or have some of their higher grade marks converted into standard grade. Under certain conditions, students may retake one or more subjects at a supplementary examination, provided they have passed at least 3 subjects at a minimum of 40% at the first sitting. They may not, however, use this opportunity to retake a standard-grade subject as a higher grade.

A **Secondary School Certificate** may be awarded if the result is not good enough for a Senior Certificate.

Students at private schools wishing to proceed to university may take the **Matriculation Examination** administered by the Joint Matriculation Board. Those who pass the examination obtain the **Matriculation Certificate**.

It is not possible to accumulate passes for the Matriculation Certificate, but the whole examination may be retaken. The Joint Matriculation Board also grants partial exemption: a student who has passed 2 of the 3 higher grade subjects has 5 years to make up the deficient higher grade subject.

Technical secondary

At the secondary school level, technical education is available through technical centres, vocational schools and technical high schools.

The technical high schools offer a course leading to matriculation, by means of which entry to universities and technikons is available.

Vocational schools offer artisan training in courses lasting 2-4 years, plus a period of practical training. Trainees may then take a standardized government trade test, success in which awards full artisan status. Trainees usually enter technical courses on completion of standard 8. After a 4-year course, a qualification may be gained which is considered comparable to the Standard 10 Certificate.

FURTHER EDUCATION

At the pre-tertiary and tertiary levels, there are technical colleges and technikons (other types of institution have largely been phased out or are going to be).

An essential distinction should be made between apprentices, who are trained to become artisans mainly on a pre-standard 10 level of education, and technicians, whose training is based on a post-standard 10 level of education.

Apprenticeship training for technicians is offered by technical colleges. The entrance requirement is standard 6, 7 or 8, depending on the trade. Apprentices study for the **National Technical Certificate** during their training, which consists of 3 parts, N1, N2 and N3, each part lasting 1 year. At least 3 subjects must be passed at each level. When part N3 is supplemented by passes in English and Afrikaans it may be considered equivalent to the Senior Certificate for entry to tertiary-level **National Certificate** courses.

The technikons are autonomous institutions, subsidized by the Department of National Education, and they provide training at the post-Senior Certificate level; courses lead to the **National Diplomas** and **Certificates**, not degrees.

South Africa

Some technical colleges offer tertiary-level training, but most training in technical colleges is at pre-Senior Certificate level. Training at both types of institution is offered through sandwich courses, part-time courses and short release courses.

The Department of National Education controls official courses offered at technical colleges and technikons; it draws up the syllabuses and is the examining body. Most of these institutions, however, also offer courses which are not controlled by the Department of National Education. The admission qualification for all courses offered by the technikons is the Senior Certificate, generally including passes in mathematics and science.

The first level of qualification is that of the **National Certificate** and **National Certificate for Technicians.** The courses leading to the National Certificate for Technicians are almost always sandwich courses. Following the reorganization of technical education in 1967, the subject content of the courses was altered and subjects were designated T1, T2, T3 and T4. The pass level in each subject is 40%. The final grade for each course is calculated on the basis of 75% examination mark, 25% work performed during the year. Students may be exempted from some subjects on the basis of previous study. Subjects for which a student has obtained exemption are recorded on the certificate. A student may enrol for courses in individual subjects, not necessarily for the whole course leading to the National Certificate. In this case a statement showing successes in the individual subjects taken is awarded. The examinations and pass requirements are set by the Department of National Education for all population groups, but the Certificates are awarded by the various departments responsible for the education of the different population groups. The National Certificate for Technicians is generally awarded when the student has been registered for at least 3 trimesters, has passed at least 4 T1, 4 T2 and 4 T3 subjects, and has submitted evidence of at least 2 years in-service training. The **National Higher Certificate for Technicians** is awarded after a further trimester of study and success in 4 T4 subjects.

Courses leading to the **National Diplomas** cover the same subjects but at an advanced level. For entry to all courses, students must hold the Senior Certificate, but for some courses students must already hold the National Certificate either in the same or in a related field.

Students may obtain the **National Diploma for Technicians** (previously the **National Engineering Diploma**) if they have been registered for at least 6 trimesters, pass at least 6 T1, 6 T2, 6 T3 and 6 T4 subjects, and have undertaken at least 2 years in-service training. An **Intermediate Diploma for Technicians** may be awarded on completion of half the requirements for the full diploma. A **National Higher Diploma for Technicians** may be awarded after a further period of training (no definite duration). Courses may be taken in individual subjects. Statements are awarded, showing success in these. A student on a National Certificate course who obtains 50% in all subjects may transfer to the course leading to a National Diploma and need only supplement the missing subjects and laboratory work. A National Certificate may be awarded to a student who has not reached the pass mark of 50% in individual subjects for the National Diploma, but has satisfied the requirements for the National Certificate.

South Africa

HIGHER EDUCATION

Admission to courses leading to a Bachelor degree at South African universities is controlled by the Joint Matriculation Board, originally created as an examining body for the universities and responsible for setting the Matriculation examination. Gradually it has become responsible for co-ordinating the Senior Certificate examinations of the racially segregated education authorities.

The Joint Matriculation Board grants exemption from the Matriculation examination to holders of a Senior Certificate with sufficient marks in a particular combination of subjects.

The University of South Africa (UNISA) offers tuition by correspondence only, either in English or in Afrikaans, for Bachelor degrees and postgraduate qualifications. Course work is structured in modules, with students registering for papers in a unit/credit system, and a maximum of 10 years is allowed to obtain a Bachelor degree, 3 years for postgraduate qualifications, and 4 years for a doctorate. The degrees are considered in South Africa to be equivalent in standard to those awarded by other universities.

With the exception of UNISA, other universities have been organized on the basis of racial segregation. Non-Whites were barred from entering 'White' institutions except with the permission of the responsible Government minister, given in cases where the subject of study is not available at institutions already open to the applicant.

However, since early 1986, the position has been that White universities are free to admit students of all races who satisfy their admissions criteria without reference to the responsible minister. Technically, there is still a quota system in operation, which restricts the number of non-White students who may be admitted to White institutions, but the numbers have never been specified and the system has not actually been implemented.

Institutions established along racial lines in recent years include:

Fort Hare
The University of Zululand
The University of the North
The University of the Western Cape
The University of Durban-Westville
MEDUNSA (for the training of black doctors, veterinarians, dentists and paramedics)
The University of Vista for Urban Blacks.

Courses leading to the award of a Bachelor degree last 3-6 years:

humanities, commerce, science (3 years)
agriculture, law, engineering, and pharmacy (4 years)
veterinary medicine and architecture (5 years)
dentistry (5-and-a-half years)
medicine (6 years).

Students of the humanities, commerce and science, who are awarded a Bachelor degree after 3 years of study, are required to take an Honours degree, which can be awarded after a further year's study, before they can proceed to a Master degree.

South Africa

A **Master degree** generally requires a minimum of 1-2 years research after the award of an Honours degree.

A **Doctorate** requires a minimum of 2 years research beyond the Master degree.

Bachelor degrees in theology, law and education are considered to be postgraduate qualifications, in that applicants must already hold a Bachelor degree in another subject.

TEACHER EDUCATION

White

3- or 4-year **Diploma** courses, qualifying their holders to teach in primary schools, are run by provincial training colleges and certain universities. The general admissions requirement for Diploma courses is a Senior Certificate with pass marks in both official languages, one of which must be at the higher grade, with one other subject besides a language on the higher grade, and certain other specified subjects.

Degree-level courses for secondary school teachers are run by most White universities; for admission, a Matriculation Certificate or a Senior Certificate with Matriculation exemption is required.

Black

All pre-standard 10 and 2-year teacher training courses at teachers colleges run by the Department of Education and Training were phased out in 1982; they have been replaced with a variety of 3-year post-standard 10 primary and secondary school teachers' Diplomas.

Teacher training is offered at the universities for Blacks; courses offered include 4-year integrated education degrees for which a Matriculation Certificate or Matriculation exemption is the entry requirement.

Coloured

Primary and junior secondary school teachers are trained over a 3-year course for which a Senior Certificate is the entry requirement.

The University of the Western Cape trains teachers at undergraduate and postgraduate levels for all academic secondary school subjects; the entry qualification is a Matriculation Certificate or Matriculation exemption.

Indian

3-year courses leading to Diplomas in primary and junior secondary education, for which a Senior Certificate is the entry requirement, are run by colleges of education and the University of Durban-Westville.

The University also offers a 4-year integrated degree and a 1-year postgraduate higher Diploma in education for secondary school teachers; a Matriculation Certificate or Matriculation exemption is the entry requirement to these courses.

Spain

Spanish State

There is a central Ministry of Education and Science and a Secretary of State for Universities and Research.

The administration of education is currently being devolved to the seventeen autonomous communities that now constitute Spain. The extent and nature of Ministry of Education and Science control varies widely in these autonomous communities. Six autonomous communities (Catalunya, Basque country, Galicia, Andalucia, Valencia and the Canaries) have full competence over educational matters. The others will follow shortly. In the future the Ministry will maintain control of general policy, national inspectorate, recognition of qualifications, and curriculum development in primary and secondary education.

In 1984, a new Education Act was passed (LODE: Ley Organica del Derecho a la Educacion-Right to Education Act) under the new Socialist government. The LODE is the Ministry of Education and Science's statutory provision for the development of principles referring to educational matters laid down in the 1978 Constitution. LODE lays down certain rights and responsibilities for students, teachers, parents and government concerning education. It also sets out the general school categories and makes provision for each category - state schools, private schools, special agreement schools (private schools which are maintained with public funds and give free education) and non-maintained schools (private, no public funds, fee paying). Reform of the 1970 Education Act which introduced major changes both in school and higher education is currently being discussed.

Up to 1964 only six years schooling was compulsory; since then it has been increased to eight years, starting at age six. There are now plans to make education compulsory up to the age of sixteen and to reform EGB (higher) and BUP into a single programme with a later division (i.e. at sixteen) between academic and technical/vocational training.

The academic year runs from October to July.

EVALUATION IN BRITAIN

Bachillerato Unificado y Polivalente (BUP) - generally compared to GCE O-level standard.

Spain

Curso de Orientacion Universitaria (COU) - may be considered to satisfy the general requirement of universities and polytechnics.

Licenciado, Titulo de Ingeniero, Titulo de Arquitecto - generally compared to British Bachelor degree standard.

MARKING SYSTEMS

School

10	matricula de honor	distinction
9-9.9	sobresaliente	outstanding
7-8.9	notable	good
5-6.9	aprobado	satisfactory
below 5	suspenso	fail

The aggregate mark ('calificacion global') on a certificate is on a scale of 9.

9	sobresaliente
7-8.9	notable
6-6.9	bien
5-5.9	suficiente
2-4.9	insuficiente muy deficiente

Higher

10	matricula de honor
9-9.9	sobresaliente
7-8.9	notabable
5-6.9	aprobado
below 5	suspenso

Doctorate

Apto: Awarded by the tribunal, before which the student has to defend a doctorate thesis.

No Apto: This is awarded when it is not satisfactory.

Cum Laude: An excellent marking for the thesis, which may be awarded by the tribunal.

Spain

SCHOOL EDUCATION

Primary

Before the 1970 Education Act:

The first cycle of primary education was the Periodo Elemental, lasting 4 years (ages 6-9 inclusive). Pupils proceeded either to advanced primary or to the first cycle of secondary education.

The second cycle of primary education was the Periodo de Perfeccionamiento and lasted 4 years (ages 10-13 inclusive). The leaving certificate was the **Certificado de Estudios Primarios**. Holders could take an examination entitling them to enter the third year of the Ciclo Elemental of Ensenanza Media; pupils who did this were 2 years behind those who went straight from the Periodo Elemental to Ensenanza Media.

After 2 years of the Periodo de Perfeccionamiento a pupil could begin vocational training (at age 12).

Before 1964, the second cycle of primary education lasted only 2 years and the primary certificate examination was taken after the 11th birthday.

Since the 1970 Education Act:

Educacion General Basica (EGB: basic general education)

EGB is provided in Centros de Educacion General Basica; state schools are called Colegios Publicos. The introduction of the new system following the 1970 Education Act was begun in 1971/2 and completed in 1974/5.

The Primera Etapa (first stage) of EGB lasts 5 years, age 6-10. The Segunda Etapa (second stage) lasts 3 years, to age 13. On satisfactory completion of the Segunda Etapa, pupils are awarded the title **Graduado Escolar** which gives access to upper secondary schools (Centros de Bachillerato). Pupils who fail to attain the required standard receive the **Certificado de Escolaridad** (Certificate of Scholarity) which gives access to vocational training centres.

Secondary

Before the 1970 Education Act:

Ciclo Elemental de Ensenanza Media (first cycle secondary)

Pupils who had completed the first cycle of primary education could, at age 10, begin Ensenanza Media. The course lasted 4 years, to age 13, and led to the **Bachillerato Elemental** certificate.

Ciclo Superior de Ensenanza Media (second cycle secondary)

Admission was on the strength of the Bachillerato Elemental. The Ciclo Superior lasted 2 years and led to the **Bachillerato Superior**, obtained at age 15.

Spain

Curso Pre-Universitario (PREU: pre-university course)

Pupils who wished to go to university took the 1-year Curso Pre-Universitario after obtaining the Bachillerato Superior. On completion of the Curso Pre-Universitario, students took the **Prueba de Madurez** which gave access to university. During the PREU, pupils had a choice of specialization in either classics or science.

Since the 1970 Education Act:

Holders of the Graduado Escolar can be admitted to Centros de Bachillerato to follow a 3-year course leading to the **Bachillerato Unificado y Polivalente** (BUP) or upper secondary school leaving certificate obtained at age 16. The course includes Spanish, a foreign language, social science, natural science, mathematics, art and music, religion and physical education.

These subjects are compulsory. Pupils also study 1 of industrial technology, agriculture, commerce and home economics. Evaluation is by continuous assessment; each pupil has a Libro de Calificacion Escolar, a booklet giving a record of progress.

Curso de Orientacion Universitaria (COU: university preparation course)

Pupils holding the Bachillerato can be admitted to the COU. This course lasts 1 year and includes 3 compulsory subjects of study (Spanish, a foreign language and mathematics), as well as 3 optional subjects, and classes in religion, civics, careers guidance and study techniques. The course aims to strengthen knowledge of basic subjects and to provide guidance in the choice of university course.

The COU is organized and supervised by a university but can be taught in establishments of secondary education. Students are assessed by continuous assessment. The certificate is issued by the Ministry of Education and Science.

Holders of the **COU Certificate** are qualified for admission to university. They have completed 12 years of education, from age 6 to 17 inclusive.

Selectividad

This is a university entrance examination set by each university. Candidates must have successfully completed COU. Selectividad consists of 6 tests.

Vocational and technical secondary

Before the 1970 Education Act:

Aprendizaje y Maestria Industrial (apprenticeship and foreman)

Before beginning an apprenticeship, a student had to complete 2 years of advanced primary education (Periodo de Perfeccionamiento, see above) i.e. a total of 6 years of education to age 11. A 2-year course was then taken, full- or part-time, of Iniciacion Profesional, to age 13, followed by an Aprendizaje (apprenticeship) of 3 years, either full- or part-time, to age 16. The certificate awarded on completion of Aprendizaje was of **Oficial Industrial** (skilled workman) in a particular specialization.

Holders of the Oficial Industrial certificate could go on to a full-time 2-year course at a Centro de Maestria Industrial, to obtain the **Maestria Industrial** certificate (Foreman's Industrial Certificate) at age 18. This qualification gave access to further education.

Spain

Courses leading to the Bachillerato Tecnico (upper secondary technical leaving certificate)

Before 1967, pupils who had completed the Periodo Elemental of primary school (at age 9) could, on passing an entrance examination, enter the Curso Elemental of technical schools. The Curso Elemental lasted 5 years and led to the **Bachillerato Tecnico Elemental**, obtained at age 15. This certificate gave access to Escuelas Superiores de Magisterio (primary teaching training schools), Escuelas de Commercio (commercial schools), and Escuelas de Ayudantes Tecnicos Sanitarios (schools for medical technical assistants), and to the Curso Superior of technical secondary schools.

After 1967, pupils wanting a technical education had to continue their general education until they had completed 4 years of primary education plus 4 years of lower secondary education at age 13.

To enter the Curso Superior (second cycle) of technical secondary education, a pupil held the Bachillerato Tecnico Elemental up to 1967, and the Bachillerato Elemental between 1967 and 1970. The Curso Superior lasted 3 years, to age 17, and culminated in the award of the **Bachillerato Tecnico Superior**. This qualification gave access to the 1-year Curso Pre-Universitario and thence to higher education (see above).

Courses leading to the Bachillerato Laboral (upper secondary school vocational leaving certificate)

Vocational secondary schools of many types (e.g. Escuelas Medias Laborales, Institutos Laborales, Centros de Ensenanza Media y Profesional, Universidades Laborales) were open to students who had completed compulsory education. Courses were offered in agriculture, industrial or commercial studies, fisheries, etc. The first part of the course lasted 5 years and led to the **Bachillerato Laboral Elemental**. The second part lasted 3 years and led to the **Bachillerato Laboral Elemental**. This would admit the holder to higher education, subject to success in the Curso Pre-Universitario (see above).

Escuelas Tecnicas de Grado Medio (intermediate technical schools preparatory course)

Up to 1965, students who held the leaving certificate of the first cycle of secondary education (either the Bachillerato Tecnico Elemental or the Bachillerato Elemental, both obtained at age 13) were eligible for admission to the 1-year preparatory course at an Escuela Tecnica de Grado Medio. Holders of the Oficial Industrial (skilled workman) certificate were also qualified for admission to the preparatory course.

Between 1965 and 1970 the preparatory course was discontinued. Holders of the Bachillerato Elemental were no longer admitted to Escuelas Tecnicas de Grado Medio.

Selection course

Until 1965, holders of all types of secondary school leaving certificates or equivalent (including the Maestria Industrial, Foreman's Industrial Certificate: see above) were eligible for admission to the selection course, or adaptation course, at an Escuela Tecnica de Grado Medio. This course lasted 1 year.

Between 1965 and 1970 the selection course was open only to holders of the Bachillerato Tecnico Elemental.

Spain

Perito course

Until 1965, students who had successfully completed the selection course were admitted to the 3-year course leading to the **Perito** diploma.

Between 1965 and 1970, holders of secondary leaving certificates or equivalent were admitted direct to the Perito course.

Escuelas Tecnicas de Grado Medio prepared students for the qualification of **Perito** (technician engineer). Courses normally lasted 3 years full-time, but could also be followed in evening classes. Fields of study included aviation, agriculture, work supervision, industry, mines, waterways and forests, maritime studies, public works, telecommunications, textiles and topography. In each case, the holder of the Perito certificate was called by a specific title e.g. Perito Agricola (agricultural technician engineer), Perito Industrial, Perito de Telecomunicacion. The term 'Aparejador' (expert) is sometimes used in place of 'Perito'. The holder of a Perito certificate would have completed a minimum of 14 years of education, and be aged approximately 19.

The Perito qualification gave access to Escuelas Tecnicas Superiores (higher technical schools) and could lead to university studies and to teaching in technical and vocational schools.

Since the 1970 Education Act:

The transition to the reformed system was completed by the academic year 1976/7.

Centros de Formacion Profesional Industrial

Courses are provided at 3 grades, grades 2 and 3 for students of post-secondary and post-university level respectively (see below: FURTHER EDUCATION).

Primer Grado, Iniciacion Profesional (first grade)

This grade is open to holders of the Graduado Escolar certificate, or the Certificado de Escolaridad, both obtained at age 13. The Primer Grado is a 2-year full-time course, compulsory for pupils who are not continuing with academic study. The course is made up of a 6-month period of lessons called 'Introduction to the World of Work' followed by training in a trade or occupation such as agriculture, commerce, art, catering.

Escuelas de Arte y Oficios Artisticos (art schools), Escuelas de Ceramica

These schools provide vocational training for pupils who have completed 6 years of school (at age 11). The 5-year full-time course is divided into 2 parts: the first 3 years provide a common course of general and vocational studies, while the last 2 years are devoted to one specialization. The final certificate is in a particular specialization (such as decoracion y arte publicitario: decoration and advertising art; or artes aplicables al libro: book crafts or in art teaching.

Escuelas Periciales de Comercio (commercial schools)

Pupils aged 14 who hold the Graduado Escolar or Certificado de Escolaridad, and have passed an entrance examination, can enter these institutions to follow a 3-year full-time commercial course. Evening classes are also offered. The leaving certificate is the **Perito Mercantil**.

The proposed new act (LOSE) will probably change this in 1987.

Spain

FURTHER EDUCATION

Before the 1970 Education Act

Escuelas Profesionales de Comercio (vocational commercial schools)

These provided 3-year full-time courses for holders of the secondary school leaving certificate, the Perito Comercial Mercantil, or equivalent. The course led to the **Profesorado Mercantil** (Commercial Teacher Certificate) which enabled the holder to teach at Escuelas de Comercio. This certificate also gave access to higher education.

Similar courses were available in a variety of specializations.

Since the 1970 Education Act

Centros de Formacion Profesional Industrial

The first grade is described above.

Segundo Grado, Nivel Medio (second grade, intermediate level) provides full-time courses of a maximum 2 years for students who hold the Bachillerato, aged 16 or 17, or for those who have completed the Primer Grado of Formacion Profesional Industrial (also aged 16 or 17). The course provides training relevant to employment in specific areas such as agriculture, commerce, administration.

Tercer Grado, Nivel Superior (third grade, higher level) courses last for a maximum of 2 years full-time. These courses are for people who have completed the 3-year first cycle of university, or who have completed a complementary course after following the Segundo Grado course. The courses aim to provide a transition between study and work: areas of specialization are the same as in the Segundo Grado.

People who have completed both the Tercer Grado of Formacion Profesional and the first cycle of university receive the title of **Diplomado** and are qualified in one of a variety of fields e.g. teacher of Educacion General Basico; vocational guidance auxiliary; dietetic technician; computer programmer.

Escuelas de Ingenieria Tecnica (schools of technical engineering)

These institutions are the successors of the final 3 years of the course given at Escuelas Tecnicas de Grado Medio leading to the Perito qualification. These new Escuelas de Ingenieria Tecnica are incorporated in the university schools, and the course corresponds to the 3-year first cycle of university.

HIGHER EDUCATION

Before the 1970 Education Act:

Escuelas de Bellas Artes, Conservatorios Superiores de Musica, Escuelas Superiores de Arte Dramatico (schools of fine art, conservatories of music, higher schools of drama)

Spain

The institutions offered courses lasting 5 years following a preparatory year. The entry requirement was the secondary school leaving certificate plus an entrance examination.

Escuelas Tecnicas Superiores (higher technical schools)

These provided a 5-year course leading to the professional title of Engineer or Architect.

Before 1965, holders of the Bachillerato Superior plus the Prueba de Madurez (i.e. university entrance standard), or a Perito certificate in an appropriate field, or other equivalent qualifications, were admitted to a 1-year guidance course. Successful students proceeded to a 1-year introductory course before embarking on the course of study proper, lasting 5 years.

In 1965 the guidance and introductory courses were discontinued and students began immediately on the course proper.

The Titulo de Ingeniero or Arquitecto entitled the holder to practise the profession. A further 2 years of study beyond this, during which the student prepared a thesis, led to the degree of Doctor.

Universidades (universities)

The admission requirement for university entrance was the Bachillerato Superior or Bachillerato Tecnico Superior, plus the Prueba de Madurez; holders of the Bachillerato Laboral Superior plus the Prueba de Madurez were restricted to Faculties of Science. Holders of the primary school teaching certificate (who did not have the Bachillerato Superior) could enrol in the pedagogic section of a Faculty of Philosophy and Arts.

The **Licenciado** (first degree) was obtained after a course lasting 5 years in Ciencias; Ciencias Politicas, Economicas y Commerciales; Derecho; Filosofia y Letras (Science; Political, Economic and Commercial Science; Law; Philosophy and Arts). The first year of the course in Filosofia y Letras was a common course to all students in the faculty. The Licenciado was obtained after a 7-year course in Farmacia; Medicina; Veterinaria (Pharmacy, Medicine, Veterinary Medicine); the first year of the course was selective.

Examinations were held about 3 times a year throughout the Licenciado course. In some cases the results obtained determined whether a student would continue with a particular subject. The final examinations included oral as well as written papers.

After obtaining the Licenciado a student could proceed to the **Titulo de Doctorado**: undertaking rigorous written examinations as well as a thesis. The minimum duration of studies for the Doctorado was 1 year (2 years in medicine) but the work was rarely completed in this time.

Since the 1970 Education Act

Music, drama and dance studies

Conservatories offering music, drama and dance depend on the Ministry of Education and Science (or autonomous community where education powers have been devolved). The Ministry has a Subdireccion General de Ensenanzas Artisticas. There are Conservatorios

Spain

Elementales, Conservatorios Profesionales (which offer **Titulo de Grado Medio** previously also called Grado Profesional), Conservatorios Superiores (which offer **Titulo de Grado Medio** and **Titulo Superior**). Children can attend from age 8 having passed an entrance examination. Children accepted by conservatories follow their normal education in state schools and do specific courses in the conservatories at the same time. They have to have completed the relevant EGB/BUP courses to obtain qualifications from the conservatories.

Fine Arts degrees are studied at the university Faculties of Fine Arts.

Universidades (universities) and Universidades Politecnicas (polytechnic universities)

These now incorporate higher technical colleges (Escuelas Tecnicas Superiores) of engineering and architecture. Polytechnic universities were formed where there were groups of Escuelas Tecnicas Superiores e.g. Madrid, Barcelona, Valencia and Las Palmas. The Escuelas Tecnicas Superiores have very high standards. The polytechnic universities also incorporate the former Escuelas de Formacion Profesional, Tercer Grado (schools of professional training, third grade) and Escuelas Universitarias Tecnicas (university technical schools).

Entrance for universities and polytechnic universities is the same, except that the Curso de Orientacion universitaria has a more technical emphasis for entry into the polytechnics.

The structures of the degree courses are the same for universities and polytechnic universities: 5 years for the first degree and a further 2 years minimum for the Ph.D.

Courses are divided into 3 cycles:

Primer ciclo, ciclo basico (1st cycle, basic course)

Admission is on the basis of the Bachillerato Unificado y Polivalente plus the Curso de Orientacion Universitaria. (People aged over 25 who do not have the Bachillerato can enter university on the basis of an entrance examination.)

The Primer Ciclo lasts 3 years and is devoted to the study of basic disciplines. Students may continue to the Segundo Ciclo of university, or leave after the Primer Ciclo and enrol on a Tercer Grado (third grade) course at a Centro de Formacion Profesional to obtain the qualifications of Diplomado after 2 years of study (see FURTHER EDUCATION).

Primer Ciclo courses are taught not only in universities but also in institutions such as university schools which offer no facilities beyond this level (e.g. Escuelas de Ingenieria Tecnica).

Secundo ciclo, ciclo de especialisacion (2nd cycle, cycle of specialization)

To enter the Segundo Ciclo, a student must have: completed the Primer Ciclo of university; or graduated from a university school; or graduated from an Escuela de Ingenieria Tecnica.

The Segundo Ciclo provides a 2-year course of specialization. The degree awarded is the **Licenciado** in most fields, the **Titulo de Ingeniero** in Engineering and the **Titulo de Arquitecto** in Architecture. To obtain the Titulo, engineers and architects must complete an end-of-course project (Projecto Fin de Carrera).

Spain

Tercer ciclo, ciclo de especialisacion para la investigacion y docencia (third cycle, specialization for research and teaching)

To enter the Tercer Ciclo a student must hold the Licenciado or Titulo de Ingeniero/Arquitecto. Students study a number of special courses (curcos monograficos de doctorado) during the first 2-years on which they are examined. They do research which may take a year or more longer and have to defend a thesis before a tribunal to obtain the **Titulo de Doctorado** (Ph.D.).

Escuelas Universitarias were envisaged as professional short courses of 1 cycle (under the Education Act of 1970) which has been modified by the University Reform Act, making it easier to go into second cycle studies.

The 1983 University Reform Act (LRU - Ley de Reforma Universitaria) gives each university autonomy. The state lays down the minimum requirements to obtain degrees but universities have a great deal of flexibility beyond this. The 1970 Education Act laid down that the Ministry of Education and Science accorded titles and degrees; LRU has modified this so that any university titles are awarded by the rector of the university in the name of the King of Spain.

TEACHER EDUCATION

Before the 1970 Education Act

Primary

Escuelas Superiores de Magisterio (primary teacher training schools)

Before 1965, holders of the Bachillerato Elemental (aged 14) could begin teacher training. After the 3-year course students obtained the **Maestro de Primera Ensenanza** (Primary School Teacher's Certificate).

From 1965 to 1970 the Bachillerato Superior (obtained at age 15) was the entrance requirement for teacher training. The course now lasted 2 years. After obtaining the Teacher's Certificate, successful students attended an 8-month practical course to obtain the title of **Magister**.

The Maestro de Primera Ensenanza qualified students for admission to university Pedagogical Faculties. If the pre-university course had also been followed, a student could enter any university faculty.

Escuelas Superiores de Magisterio provided special courses for teachers of upper primary classes, of special schools for handicapped children, and of nursery and pre-primary schools; and for aspiring head teachers of Escuelas Nacionales (state schools) with 8 or more classes.

Spain

Secondary

Escuelas de Formacion del Profesorado (secondary school teacher training colleges)

To teach in secondary schools a university degree was required. The 2-year course of teacher training was concurrent with the final years of the degree course, and consisted of an introduction to general pedagogy and didactics followed by a year of practical training provided in the form of teaching practice in secondary schools. The certificate awarded was the **Certificado de Aptitud Pedagogica** (CAP) which entitled the holder to enter a competitive examination for certification.

There were various categories of teacher:

Catedraticos Numerarios (certificated teachers): holders of the CAP who had passed the certification examinations; or teachers who did not hold the CAP but had taught for 2 years and then passed the certification examinations.

Adjuntos Numerarios (assistant teachers): they did not hold the teaching certificate, but had obtained the CAP.

Ayudantes (assistants): they were not qualified as teachers and had no direct teaching responsibilities.

Instituciones de Formacion del Profesorado del Ensenanza Laboral (technical teacher training colleges)

Training for technical teaching in technical secondary schools (for pupils aged 15-17 taking the Bachillerato Tecnico Superior or Bachillerato Laboral Superior) was provided at these institutions. The Perito qualification was the admission requirement, and courses lasted 1 year. After 5 years teaching, teachers sat a competitive examination to confirm their appointment.

Higher

University teachers and teachers in Escuelas Tecnicas Superiores: Catedraticos Numerarios (full professors, with chairs) had to hold a doctorate and have a minimum of 2 years university teaching or research. They were appointed for life (retirement at 70) and had the same status as civil servants. They were responsible for the teaching of the subject for which they held the chair, but did not themselves work full-time.

Encargados de Catedra Vacante (temporary professors) could hold a vacant chair until a permanent appointment was made. They had the same qualifications and performed the same functions at Catedraticos Numerarios.

Profesores Agregados (associate professors) had the same qualifications and functions as Catedraticos Numerarios but were head of a single department only. They were obliged to exercise their functions full-time. They too were of civil servant status.

Profesores Adjuntos (assistant professors) had to hold a doctorate. Appointment was for a period of 4 years, renewable. They could occupy a vacant chair, but their main duty was to conduct tutorials; they taught full-time.

Encargados de Curso (lecturers) were appointed for 1 year. Most held a doctorate but some only a Licenciado. They taught subsidiary subjects.

Ayudantes (assistant lecturers) held the Licenciado. They were appointed for 1 year, and assisted professors and lecturers in practical classes.

Spain

Since the 1970 Education Act

Primary and lower secondary

<u>Escuelas Universitarias de Formacion de Profesorado</u> (primary and lower secondary - EGB - teacher training schools)

Since 1970, the former Escuelas Superior de Magisterio have become Escuelas Universitarias (university schools). Admission requirements are as for any university course (see above). The teacher training course forms the Primer Ciclo of university studies, and lasts 3 years.

Training, both theoretical and practical, is provided under the supervision of Institutos de Ciencias de la Educacion (Institutes of the Sciences of Education). The qualification of **Diplomado** is obtained when a student has successfully completed 3 years at university plus 1 year at a Centro de Formacion Profesional (see above). Students who have received good marks throughout their training are immediately qualified teachers; others have to take further examinations.

Holders of the Diplomado are qualified to teach in pre-schools and Educacion General Basica (i.e. children from 4-13).

Upper secondary

Teachers in upper secondary schools (Centros de Bachillerato) must hold a university degree (Licenciado) or equivalent. It is possible to combine pedagogic studies with a degree course; students who have not done this receive training at an Instituto de Ciencias de la Educacion. Prospective teachers have to pass a competitive examination.

Centros de Formacion Profesional

Training for teaching in the Primer Grado (pupils aged 14-16) is provided in the Segundo Grado of the same institutions. The course lasts 2 years, and the pedagogic element is organized by the Instituto de Ciencias de la Educacion.

Teachers for the Segundo Grado (pupils aged 16/17 and 17/18) must hold a university diploma obtained after the 3-year Primer Ciclo. Pedagogic training is organized by the Instituto de Ciencias de la Educacion.

Teachers for the Tercer Grado (pupils have completed 3 years of higher education) must hold a university Licenciado (degree); pedagogic training is in the form of an intensive course provided by the Instituto de Ciencias de la Educacion. Students whose degree course included pedagogy are exempted from this.

Higher

Teachers in university schools (Escuelas Universitarias) must hold a Licenciatura or equivalent; unless the degree course included pedagogic training, prospective teachers must attend an intensive course run by an Instituto de Ciencias de la Educacion.

Since 1970, there have been fewer official categories of university teacher.

Catedraticos Numerarios (professors who hold chairs) must have a doctorate plus pedagogic training.

Profesores Agregados (associate professors) have the same qualifications as Catedraticos Numerarios.

Spain

Profesores Adjuntos (assistant professors) must have a doctorate plus at least 1 year's experience as an Ayudante or of research with the Higher Scientific Research Council.

Visiting professors may also be appointed. Both Profesores Adjuntos and Visiting Professors are appointed to perform specific duties.

Profesores Ayudantes (assistant lecturers) must have at least a Licenciado or equivalent. They are appointed for 1 year with the possibility of renewal for a maximum of 4 successive years.

Extraordinary professors may be appointed for a limited period of time, and very occasionally for an indefinite period. They can never receive civil servant status.

Only about 10% of university teaching staff has a permanent appointment.

Sri Lanka

Democratic Socialist Republic of Sri Lanka

Education is compulsory from age five to fourteen and free from kindergarten to university level in state institutions. There are also fee-levying private institutions up to university level.

At school level, Sinhala and Tamil are the media of instruction. English is taught as a secondary language from year IV but is not compulsory for Sri Lankan O-levels, nor for university entrance. At university-level, Sinhala, Tamil and English are the media of instruction, depending largely on the subjects studied. Lectures in the Arts and Social Sciences Faculties are usually held in Sinhala and/or Tamil; Medicine, Engineering and Architecture are generally taught in English; and all the other subjects are initially taught in Sinhala and/or Tamil with an increasing use of English towards the end of the degree course. Answers for the university examinations can be written in Sinhala, Tamil or English.

The school year is divided into three terms and starts in January; the university year starts in October.

EVALUATION IN BRITAIN

School

National Certificate of General Education (introduced in 1975 and abolished in 1977) - generally considered to be below GCE O-level standard.

Sri Lankan O-levels - generally accorded GCE O-level status for grades of Credit and Distinction.

Sri Lankan A-levels - generally accorded GCE A-level status for grades A, B or C.

Higher

Sri Lankan Special degree (4 years) - generally considered to compare to British Bachelor degree (Honours) standard.

Sri Lankan General degree (3 years) - generally considered to compare to British Bachelor degree (Ordinary) standard.

Sri Lanka

MARKING SYSTEMS

School

Sri Lankan GCE O-levels are graded as follows:

75-100%	D	distinction
50-74	C	credit
35-49	S	pass
0-34	F	fail

Sri Lankan GCE A-levels are graded as follows:

75-100%	A	distinction
65-74	B	very good pass
55-64	C	credit
40-54	S	ordinary pass (simple pass)
0-39	F	fail

Higher

The grading system for first degrees is as follows:

75-100%	A
55-74	B
40-54	C
30-39	D
0-29	E

For a First-Class degree, candidates must obtain an average of at least 70%, with A grades in at least half the papers and a minimum grade of C in the remaining papers.

An Upper-Second requires an average of at least 60%, with A or B grades in at least half the papers and a minimum grade of C in the remaining papers.

A Lower-Second requires an average of at least 55%.

A Pass requires an average of 40% or more, with a minimum grade of C in all papers.

SCHOOL EDUCATION

Educational reforms 1972-7

A new school system, introduced in 1972, aimed to provide a general education better suited to modern needs which would allow greater equality of opportunity. It was organized in 3 stages:

Sri Lanka

Stage	Duration (years)	Grade	Approximate age on entry
Primary	5	I-V	6
Junior secondary	4	VI-IX	11
Senior secondary	2	X-XI	15

2 new examinations were introduced, the **National Certificate of General Education** (NCGE), taken at the end of junior secondary (grade 9), and the **National Certificate of Higher Education** (NCHE), taken at the end of senior secondary (grade 11).

The **National Certificate of General Education** was not an examination that candidates passed or failed; instead, each candidate received a certificate, indicating performance in the different subject areas on a 5-point scale: a, b, c (pass), d and e. School assessment also contributed to the final grades.

The first NCGE examination was held in December 1975 and the second in 1976. The first NCHE examination was to have been held in April 1978. The old system (i.e. GCE O- and A-level examinations) which was to have been phased out in 1979 ran concurrently with the new system.

1977-84

The government elected in 1977 decided to revert to the GCE O- and A-level examinations, and the NCGE and NCHE examinations were cancelled. Candidates preparing for the NCHE examination sat for the 'Interim Syllabus' in 1979. Those who took the NCGE were allowed an extra year at school to sit O-levels if required.

As the NCGE was taken 1 year earlier than the Sri Lankan GCE, it is normally considered to be below GCE O-level standard.

From January 1985

Primary

This covers a 6-year course (years I-VI) with entry at 5+ years.

Junior secondary

This is compulsory up to age 14 (school-leaving age). It consists of a 2-year course (years VII-VIII).

Senior secondary

This lasts 3 years from age 14 (years IX-XI). At the end of year XI (in December) pupils sit for **Sri Lankan O-levels**.

Collegiate

This course lasts 2 years (years XII-XIII) from age 17. At the end of year XIII (in August) pupils sit for **Sri Lankan A-levels**.

In February 1986 a new national examination in English language was held, the **National Certificate in English** (NCE).

The level is rather above the Sri Lankan O-level and it is hoped the certificate will provide a language profile of use to employers.

Technical/vocational

This covers engineering, commerce/business studies and crafts. There are 22 technical institutes, at 2 levels: Polytechnical Institutes and Junior Technical Institutes. These offer courses lasting 1-4 years at the levels of **National Craft Certificate, National Certificate, National Diploma** and **Higher National Diploma**. The minimum age for admission is 17. Entrance to the more elementary courses requires successful completion of at least the eighth year of education, while entrance to Certificate courses requires GCE O-levels and entrance to Diploma courses GCE A-levels. Courses in engineering and allied fields and technician level courses in commerce, as well as some craft courses, are offered at Polytechnical Institutes; the Junior Technical Institutes offer mainly craft and certificate-level courses. (The distinction between the 2 grades, however, is no longer strictly maintained).

FURTHER/NON-FORMAL EDUCATION

Further and non-formal education is available mainly in youth work, technical training and rural development.

Youth work

Government-sponsored youth schemes include: agricultural projects designed for youth settlement, practical farm schools, young farmers' clubs, and programmes of the Department of Small Industries. Some non-government organizations are involved in youth work, notably SARVODOYA, a national secular movement which runs youth farms and youth leadership courses.

Technical

Technical courses are provided at the Ministry of Labour's vocational training centres, at the Ministry of Education's Technical Units, and by the National Apprenticeship Board.

Rural development

This work is organized by the Rural Development Department, which offers on-the-job training (through its network of rural development officers) and residential courses for officials of local groups.

HIGHER EDUCATION

With the implementation of the Universities Act, No. 16, of 1978, on 1 January 1979, the University of Sri Lanka was replaced by 6 universities and a university college. A second university college was started in Batticaloa in 1981.

Entrance to university is GCE A-level standard. The full spectrum of higher studies is covered. **General Bachelor degrees** involve 3 years study. **Special Bachelor degree** courses last 4 years; **Master degree** courses last 2 years full-time or 3 years part-time.

Sri Lanka

External candidates can study law at the University of Colombo and arts and science subjects at the University of Peradeniya.

Distance education

The Open University of Sri Lanka was established in 1980; it offers **Foundation** and **Certificate** courses in various subjects and, since 1983, **Degree** courses.

TEACHER EDUCATION

The minimum qualification for teaching was GCE O-level passes in 4 subjects. However, since December 1981, the minimum entry qualification for teacher education has been 6 GCE O-level and 2 GCE A-level passes. The prospective teacher serves a probationary period of up to 2 years in a school before becoming eligible for entry to a teacher-training college. In-service teachers who have never undergone teacher training can take a Ministry of Education examination after a specified number of years in service to qualify as certified teachers. The Government does, however, put a high priority on teacher training.

The main types of teacher training are:

1-year courses for graduates leading to a postgraduate Diploma in Education offered by the Faculty of Education of the University of Colombo and the University of Peradeniya.

2-year courses at teacher-training colleges for teachers specializing in English, science, mathematics, agriculture, etc. Teachers who qualify in these courses are designated 'trained teachers'.

2-year courses at teacher-training colleges for those who specialize in primary education.

3-year courses leading to a **Trained Teacher's Certificate** for non-teachers with 3 GCE A-level passes.

At university level, **B.Ed.** and **MA Ed.** courses as well as a **Certificate** course consisting of part of a degree programme with some study of educational subjects.

A **Postgraduate Diploma in Education** by correspondence (the content of which is currently being revised) offered by the Open University.

Distance-education courses for teacher-training in science, mathematics and primary education conducted during weekends and holidays.

In 1972 a technical teacher-training centre was established to provide a 1-year full-time day course.

The Sri Lankan Education Project has been set up under the Ministry of Education.

Sudan

Democratic Republic of Sudan

The medium of instruction in schools in northern Sudan is Arabic. English is a compulsory subject from the intermediate stage. The medium of instruction in the south at secondary level is English. There are Arabic and vernacular primary and intermediate schools.

The school year normally runs from July to March in the north; March to December in the south.

EVALUATION IN BRITAIN

School

Secondary School Certificate (formerly called the Sudan School Certificate or Higher Secondary School Certificate) - normally accorded GCE O-level status on a subject-for-subject basis, provided that marks of at least 50% are obtained in subjects which can be taken in the GCE examinations.

Higher

A Sudanese **Bachelor degree** is unlikely to be considered fully comparable to a British Bachelor degree.

MARKING SYSTEMS

School

The Sudan Secondary School Certificate is marked on a scale of 1-9, with 8 as the lowest pass mark:

1	outstanding
2	very good
3	good
4	
5	pass with credit
6	

7   pass
8

9   fail

Higher

The marking system for the third and fourth years at the University of Khartoum is as follows:

66-100	A	Div. I
50-65	B	Div. II
45-49	C	Div. III
0-44	F	fail

SCHOOL EDUCATION

Primary

This course of basic education lasts 6 years.

Intermediate

This lasts 3 years. Success in a competitive examination at the end gives access to secondary school.

Secondary

Academic:

The academic secondary schools offer a common course which leads to the **Secondary School Certificate.** The Cambridge Overseas Examinations Syndicate was involved in administering the Sudan School Certificate. Formal collaboration ended in 1962, but the same pattern is followed.

In the first and second years, pupils follow a common course, but in the third year they choose to enter literature, mathematics or biology streams. At most schools the mathematics/science streams are merged.

Technical:

The technical secondary schools grew out of the intermediate trade schools discontinued in 1967/8. They include industrial, commercial and agricultural schools for boys and 2 home economics secondary schools for girls. Courses last 4 years so that students can cover the full academic course as well as the technical subjects.

National industrial:

The Ministry of Education has established national industrial schools. These offer a primarily vocational 2-year terminal post-intermediate course. Specialization includes: woodwork, metalwork, leatherwork, shoe making, carpet-making, and furniture-making.

Sudan

FURTHER EDUCATION

A wide range of facilities for learning exists outside the formal education system. The National Literacy Programme 1975-9 offered courses lasting 9 months, with 4 one-hour sessions per week. The certificate awarded on completion of the course is considered equivalent to the standard of the fourth year at primary school.

The Workers' Education Corporation offers 3-6 week in-service courses.

Khartoum Polytechnic offers evening craft classes to primary school leavers and a wide range of City and Guilds and ONC-type courses, plus more specialist courses.

The Sudan Council of Churches provides vocational training courses and plans to establish 'village polytechnics' to teach technical skills to young people. Boys' Centres will run vocational technical courses.

The Sudan Council of Churches also has schemes geared to the needs of southern Sudan. In May 1975 the Ox-Plough Training Centre opened, offering 6-month agricultural courses for farmers.

A multi-service training centre, opened in 1973 in Juba, provides training in basic skills. It offers a variety of courses, including 3-month upgrading courses for government employees. The rural training centre at Amadi runs 9-month courses in farming, among others.

The FAO also runs educational projects in the south. It sponsors a rural primary school project near Rumbek and an agricultural college in co-operation with the Regional Ministry of Agriculture. The College offers 2-year courses to secondary school graduates.

HIGHER EDUCATION

4-year **General degrees** and 5-year **Honours degrees** are offered by the University of Khartoum, University of Gezira, University of Juba, Islamic University of Omdurman, and the University of Cairo (Khartoum branch), which offers Cairo University degrees. Ahfad University College for Women offers 4-year degree courses, diploma and certificate courses. Khartoum Polytechnic offers **3-year diploma** courses in a variety of technical subjects as well as a B.Tech.

Other colleges offer courses in medicine, engineering, commerce, nutrition, education, the arts, agriculture and nursing.

TEACHER EDUCATION

Primary

Originally the primary teacher-training institutes accepted intermediate school graduates for a 4-year course. Most institutes operate under the new system, which admits secondary school graduates for a 1-year course.

Intermediate

There are 3 National Institutes for training intermediate school teachers: 1 for men at Bakht er Ruda; and 2 for women at Omdurman. There are also 3 regional Intermediate Teacher Training Institutes. Courses last 2 years and applicants are normally secondary school graduates with several years teaching experience.

Secondary

Secondary school teachers are taught at the Faculties of Education of the Universities of Khartoum, Gezira and Juba. Graduates are awarded a B.Ed. degree. There is also a special 1-year course for unqualified teachers.

ISETI

The In-Service and Educational Training Institute (ISETI) was established with Unicef support, to upgrade in-service unqualified primary teachers. This has since expanded to include in-service training of junior secondary teachers. ISETI is based in Khartoum with branches throughout the regions; those in southern Sudan are for primary teachers only.

Suriname

Republic of Suriname

The education system is based on that of the Netherlands. There are numerous private institutions recognized by the state. The information in this chapter refers specifically to the situation until 1975. It has not proved possible to obtain information on the current situation, although we understand several reforms have been implemented.

Education is compulsory from age seven to twelve.

The medium of instruction is Dutch.

EVALUATION IN BRITAIN

School

VWO - generally considered to be between GCE O- and A-level standard.

MARKING SYSTEM

School

10	uitmuntend	excellent
9	zeer goed	very good
8	goed	good
7	ruim voldoende	quite good
6	voldoende	satisfactory
5	bijna voldoende	not satisfactory
4	onvoldoende	unsatisfactory
3	gering	low
2	slecht	poor
1	zeerslecht	bad

Suriname

SCHOOL EDUCATION

Pre-primary (Kleuterschool)

There are limited facilities for children aged 4-6.

Primary/elementary (Gewoon Lager Onderwijs/GLO)

This lasts for 6 years and the curriculum covers Dutch, history, geography, natural history, singing, drawing, needlework, reading, writing, arithmetic, physical education; English is introduced in the fifth year.

Extended elementary (Uitgebreid Lager Onderwijs/ULO)

This covers 2 years for children who have completed 6 years primary and will have no further schooling. The curriculum is the same as in the primary school, plus some commercial subjects (e.g. bookkeeping).

Secondary

All children who wish to continue their education undertake an orientation year (brugklas). At the end of this year, pupils are directed to a form of secondary education according to their ability.

Lower secondary/extended elementary (Meer Uitgebreid Lager Onderwijs/MULO):

This is a more academic form of ULO. Pupils obtain a diploma after 3 years (i.e. orientation year plus 2) or may stay on for an extra year to prepare for a course of further education or teacher-training. During the course, pupils may specialize in Section A (commercial subjects and foreign languages - English, French and Spanish) or Section B (mathematics, physics and foreign languages - English, French and German).

Upper secondary:

Pupils may proceed after the 3- or 4-year course, to the Algemene Middelbare School (AMS) for a 3-year course. Compulsory subjects are English and Dutch; pupils may choose to specialize in economics and commerce, economics and mathematics, mathematics, or courses designed for entry into higher teacher-training. Successful pupils in this cycle may proceed to university in the Netherlands.

Pupils who show particular promise during the orientation year may be directed towards a cycle of schooling leading to completion of a full course of secondary education:

Hogere Burgerschool (HBS) - covers 3 years general education followed by 2 years of science, commercial subjects or preparation for the higher teachers' training course (MO.B).

Regular secondary schools - on completion of the orientation year, pupils spend 2 years studying Dutch, English, mathematics, biology, history, geography, drawing, religion, and physical education. Depending on the results of an end-of-year examination, pupils are then selected to follow 1 of 3 courses:

Suriname

1. <u>Hogere Algemeen Voortgezet Onderwijs</u> (HAVO) - 2-year course. Compulsory subjects are English and Dutch; in addition, pupils must choose 4 other subjects, depending on their specialization (i.e. business, science and mathematics, language, or preparation for teacher-training), from mathematics, physics, chemistry, biology, Spanish, French, German, geography, history and commercial science. On completion of the course, pupils take an examination in 6 subjects, and must pass in all 6 to obtain the **HAVO Certificate**. Holders of the HAVO certificate may enter higher technical schools, higher teacher-training courses, and certain university courses. On completion of first-year students may obtain the **MAVO Certificate**.

2. <u>Gymnasium</u> - a 3-year course, during which pupils may specialize in humanities (Gymnasium A) or science (Gymnasium B). Compulsory subjects for both specializations are Dutch and English. In Gymnasium A, pupils also study Latin, history, another classical language, and 2 from Spanish, French, mathematics, geography, and commercial science. In Gymnasium B, pupils also study Latin, mathematics, 1 science and 2 from another classical language, mathematics II, an additional science, and commercial science. On completion of this cycle, pupils obtain the **VWO Certificate**, and are eligible for university entrance.

3. <u>Atheneum</u> - a 3-year course with a more general bias than that offered by the Gymnasium. Compulsory subjects are Dutch and English. Pupils may again specialize in humanities (Atheneum A) or science (Atheneum B). In Atheneum A, pupils also study a modern language, history or geography, and commercial science in the first year of this 3-year course, and a modern language, history or geography, mathematics, and commercial science II in years 2 and 3. In Atheneum B, pupils also study mathematics and 2 sciences in the first year of this cycle, and a language, mathematics II, 2 sciences, and history and geography or commercial science in years 2 and 3. On completion of this cycle, pupils obtain the **VWO Certificate** and are eligible for university entrance.

Technical secondary

Technical secondary courses are available for pupils who have completed ULO or the 3-year MULO course.

FURTHER EDUCATION

Pupils who have completed a course of upper secondary education may undertake a 3-year course which includes a year of practical training. No qualification is obtained on completion of the course, but pupils may transfer to a technical university in the Netherlands.

HIGHER EDUCATION

Until 1971, pupils wishing to go on to a course of higher education normally went to the Netherlands, except in the fields of law and medicine, for which facilities were available. In that year the existing faculties of law and medicine became the <u>University of Surinam</u>. There are still no other faculties.

Suriname

Medicine – 3 years pre-medical and clinical work leads to the **Candidaatsexamen**; a further 2 years clinical work leads to the **Doctoraal**; after a further 2 years training as an assistant, students go to the Netherlands to take the **Artsexamen** (professional state examination).

Dentistry, pharmacy and law – this course leads to the title of **Meester** (mr.) on passing the **Candidaatsexamen**; the **Doctoraalexamen** takes 5 years.

TEACHER EDUCATION

Primary
Teachers are trained at secondary level in a <u>Kweekschool</u>:

3 years for pupils who have completed 3 years MULO, 2 years for pupils who have completed 4 years MULO/MAVO/HAVO.

After a further year the teachers may also teach in a ULO school.

Secondary

Lagere Onderwijs (LO) Akte

This 2-year part-time course ensures the ability to teach in ULO, MULO and MAVO schools.

Meer Onderwijs (MO) Akte

MO.A – a 3-year course from MAVO, or 2 years from LO, to ensure the ability to teach in the first 3 years of regular secondary schooling.

MO.B – a course which prepares students to teach at any level: secondary school and <u>Kweekschool</u>.

Swaziland

Kingdom of Swaziland

Swaziland was linked with Botswana and Lesotho until 1975 through the University of Botswana, Lesotho and Swaziland, and the Examinations Council of the University, which was responsible for conducting the Junior Certificate and Cambridge School Certificate examinations throughout the three countries.

There is no compulsory period of education.

EVALUATION IN BRITAIN

School

Cambridge Overseas School Certificate - grades 1-6 are generally equated to pass grades at GCE O-level (A, B, C).

Higher

Part 1 (i.e. the first 2 years) of a degree course at the University of Botswana, Lesotho and Swaziland or the University of Botswana and Swaziland - generally considered to compare to GCE A-level standard.

Part 2 (i.e. the remaining 2 years) - generally considered to be between GCE A-level and British Bachelor degree standards.

MARKING SYSTEMS

School

Cambridge Overseas School Certificate is graded:

1	excellent
2-3	good
3-6	credit
7-8	pass
9	fail

Swaziland

Higher

Before 1967:

A	pass with distinction
B	pass
C	fail

Since 1967:

Examinations at the end of Part 1 and Part 2 are classified:

A	80-100%	excellent
B	70-79	very good
C	60-69	good
D	50-59	pass
E	40-49	fail, but student can take a supplementary examination
F	below 39	complete fail

Bachelor degrees are classified:

1st class   B average
2nd class first division   C average
2nd class lower division   D average
pass   E,F average
fail

SCHOOL EDUCATION

Primary

This used to last for 8 years, divided into 2 cycles of 6 years and 2 years respectively; now 7 years covering standards 1-7, or grades 1 and 2, standards I-V. On completion pupils obtain the **Primary School Certificate**.

Secondary

This covers 5 years, forms I-V. On successful completion of form III pupils obtain the **Junior Certificate**, and on completion of form V the **Cambridge Overseas School Certificate**.

TECHNICAL/FURTHER EDUCATION

The Swaziland Industrial Training Institute (SITI) was founded as a trade school in 1946; it then became the <u>Swaziland College of Technology</u> (SCOT).

Swaziland

It offers craft courses for people holding the Junior Certificate and technician courses for those holding the Cambridge Overseas School Certificate. All craft and technician courses are based on the syllabuses and examinations of the **City and Guilds of London Institute**.

The Swaziland Trade School offers 3-year courses for a **Craft Certificate** for those who have satisfactorily completed primary school. They may then proceed to a 2-year apprenticeship, and take the examinations for a qualification of the **City and Guilds of London Institute**.

Similar types of course are offered by Mburluzi Clerical Training Centre.

The Swaziland Agricultural College has developed into a centre of agricultural training for Botswana, Lesotho and Swaziland.

HIGHER EDUCATION

The University of Botswana, Lesotho and Swaziland (UBLS) which was established in 1964 at Roma in Lesotho covered higher education in Swaziland. In 1966 the Swaziland Agricultural College became associated with the University and was renamed the Swaziland Agricultural College and University Centre (SACUC). In 1971 teaching for courses in Part 1 of the degree courses began at SACUC. A new campus of UBLS was opened in 1973 in Swaziland. Students then completed the first 2 years (i.e. Part 1) of their degree course there and transferred to the campus at Roma for the final 2 years (Part 2). Students now undertake the whole of their course at the campus in Swaziland. When Lesotho withdrew from the arrangement in 1975, Botswana and Swaziland continued their co-operation, and the university became the University of Botswana and Swaziland, with campuses at Gaborone (Botswana) and Kwaluseni (Swaziland). In July 1982 the 2 constituent colleges of the University of Botswana and Swaziland became the University of Swaziland and the University of Botswana.

Courses leading to the **BA** and **B.Sc.** generally last 4 years, divided into two 2-year cycles, Part 1 and Part 2. The normal entrance requirement is the Cambridge Overseas School Certificate in first or second division, with credit in English language. Students holding 2 or more relevant passes at GCE A-level or in the Cambridge Overseas Higher School Certificate may be admitted directly into the second year of the course.

There are no facilities for studying engineering, architecture, medicine, pharmacy, dentistry or veterinary medicine.

Courses are available leading to the award of an **MA**, **M.Sc.**, or **M.Ed**. A wide range of undergraduate certificate and diploma courses is also offered.

Swaziland

TEACHER EDUCATION

Primary

Until 1969 prospective primary teachers obtained the **Elementary Vernacular Certificate** after a period of study. This course was then discontinued and replaced by a 3-year part-time upgrading course to bring teachers to the level of the Primary Lower Certificate. This upgrading course was discontinued in 1978.

The normal courses of study were the 2-year course for the **Primary Lower Certificate**, for students who had completed forms I and II, and the 2-year course leading on from the Primary Lower Certificate for the **Primary Higher Certificate** for those holding the Junior Certificate.

In the early 1970s these 2 courses were condensed into a 2-year course for the **Primary Teachers' Certificate** for holders of the Junior Certificate. The Ngwane Teachers College which runs primary courses is about to implement an entry qualification of Cambridge Overseas School Certificate rather than Junior Certificate but it remains to be seen whether it will attract sufficiently qualified candidates.

Secondary

A 2-year course for holders of the Cambridge Overseas School Certificate leads to the **Secondary Teaching Certificate** obtained from the William Pitcher Primary and Secondary Teacher Training College.

The University of Botswana, Lesotho and Swaziland also offered **BA** and **B.Sc.** degrees with education components, and a **Postgraduate Certificate of Education (PGCE)**.

Sweden

Kingdom of Sweden

Since the early 1950s education reforms have been introduced at all levels. It is difficult to divide the system into the usual sectors of school (primary and secondary), further, higher and teacher, as the only clear divisions are school (comprehensive and upper secondary gymnasium) and higher. The reforms give more emphasis to continuous assessment and the 'development of personality' than to examinations. The extreme centralization of the system has been altered since the end of the 1970s. Decision-making powers have been increasingly delegated to individual municipalities and schools, allowing greater scope for local curriculum development and teacher-pupil influence. The 1977 Higher Education Act has decentralized decision-making powers and created a unified higher education system (Hogskola).

Education is compulsory for nine years from age seven.

English is compulsory from grades 3 or 4 to 9.

The academic year runs from mid-August/September to May/June.

EVALUATION IN BRITAIN

School

Realexamen - overall standard generally compared to GCE O-level.

Grundskola Certificate - overall standard generally compared to GCE O-level if grades of 3 or above have been obtained.

Studentexamen/Avgangsbetyg - may be considered to satisfy the general requirement of universities and polytechnics.

Slutbetyg (from the Teknisk Linje) - as above, but more likely to be compared to BTEC National Diploma (formerly OND).

Higher

Filosofie Kandidatexamen/Fil.Kand./FK - generally compared to British Bachelor degree standard.

Filosofie Licentiatexamen/Fil. Lic./FL - often compared to Master degree standard, but has been compared to a Ph.D.

Sweden

MARKING SYSTEMS

School

Grundskola Certificate is graded 1-5 (maximum). The marks are relative, i.e. they refer to the average national level of achievement in each subject. There is no fail grade.

Avgangsbetyg is graded 1-5 (maximum).

Teacher

Teaching certificates were earlier awarded with 3 grades in teaching skill:

3 (highest) earned by	15%
2	25%
1 (average)	60%

Since 1982 only grades approved or failed are awarded.

Higher

	Before 1969	Since 1969
laudatur	3 units	60 points
approbatur	2	40
cum laude approbatur	1	20

SCHOOL EDUCATION

Pre-primary/kindergarten

There are extensive facilities for day-care at this level. It is optional and available for children aged 1-6. Municipalities must offer a year of pre-school to 6-year-olds, but it is optional for families to take advantage of this.

Primary/secondary

Before 1962:

From the late 1930s to 1950, 7 years education was compulsory from age 7, with 8 being compulsory from 1950. The period of compulsory education was referred to as <u>Folkskola</u>.

For those who did not wish to proceed to higher education, the 7 or 8 years were composed of 6 years (primary) and 1 or 2 years at continuation school (see section on **Technical secondary**). Pupils wishing to further their academic education proceeded to a <u>Realskola</u>. Courses usually lasted 5 years for pupils who had completed 4 years primary education, and 4 years if they had completed 6 years primary education. On completion of the course at a Realskola pupils took the **Realexamen**. Success in this examination was a pre requisite for entry to one of the types of Gymnasium.

Sweden

The academic Gymnasia were divided into 3 branches: classical, natural sciences and general studies. Each branch was again subdivided, the classical branch into pure classical (Latin and Greek) and semi-classical (Latin and French), the natural sciences into mathematics, physics, chemistry and biology, and the general studies into social studies (history, civics and mathematics) and modern languages (3 languages). Courses usually lasted 3 years, but some pupils who had left the <u>Realskola</u> at the end of the second highest form took courses lasting 4 years. At the end of both courses, students took the **Studentexamen**.

Since 1962:

The 1950 Education Law introduced a reorganization of the education system below the level of the Gymnasium. The basic principle was to incorporate the primary schools and Realskola into <u>Enhetsskolor</u> (comprehensive or unitary schools). Experimental comprehensive schools were set up between 1952 and 1962 when an Act of Parliament formally established the 9-year compulsory course of comprehensive education. The course at the Enhetsskolor is divided into 3 stages, each of 3 years: junior (<u>Lagstadium</u>) covering grades 1-3, middle (<u>Mellanstadium</u>) covering grades 4-6, and senior (<u>Hogstadium</u>) covering grades 7-9; all 3 comprising <u>Grundskola</u>.

During grades 1-6 all pupils take the same subjects: Swedish, mathematics, music, physical education, religious instruction, and local studies, in grades 1-3; handicrafts and English are added in grade 3. In grades 4-6 drawing, civics, history, geography and nature study are added. In grades 7-9 there are common subjects (as in grades 4-6, physics, chemistry and biology being taken instead of nature study) but with the possibility of some specialization.

There is no streaming in the comprehensive schools. There are no formal external examinations, and a pupil's performance is judged by continuous assessment, based partly on standardized tests which are centrally prepared and locally marked. The result is intended to be related to average performance throughout the country.

On completion of grade 9, there is selective entrance to the Gymnasia. In 1966 the new model Gymnasium was introduced; it provides facilities for study not only of academic subjects but also of commercial and technical subjects. The Gymnasium has 5 'lines': humanities (modern languages); social sciences (civics and psychology); economics (business economics and law - this is a vocational course which confers the title of Gymnasium economist); natural sciences (mathematics, physics, chemistry and biology); and technology. The 'lines' are subdivided into branches, accounting for about 120 variations. Courses are normally 3 years, although pupils studying in the technology 'line' can stay on for a fourth year and become Gymnasium engineers.

From July 1977 all upper secondary courses (provided students have studied 2 years of English and 2 of Swedish at this level) qualify the student for higher education, although extra qualifications may be necessary for certain courses. A system of selective admission (numerus clausus) operates in the faculties of medicine, dentistry, pharmacy, engineering and technology. An average of 2.3 in the final certificate or Studentexamen is generally required for university admission. There is no final school-leaving examination; in their last term, pupils are given a leaving certificate which states their average mark per subject. The **Slutbetyg** certificate may be obtained on completion of the full 9 years of comprehensive education and the **Avgangbetyg** is obtained on completion of a 2- or 3-year course at a Gymnasium.

Scholastic performance in the Gymnasia is controlled by the National Board of Education using a more or less continuous series of centrally administered tests. Pupils are automatically promoted to the next grade.

Sweden

Outside the upper secondary school system but more or less on the same level are the 'folk high schools' (Folkhogskolan). Most of these schools are subsidized by the state and run either by the counties or are attached to organizations. The schools have great freedom to decide their curricula, and special attention is paid to education in good citizenship. There are no formal examinations.

Technical secondary

Pre-1962/3 reforms:

On leaving the Folkskola pupils could attend one of the following:

<u>Verkstadskola</u> (full-time) or <u>Aftonskola</u> (part-time) which offered a course combining general education and basic technical training

after some practical experience, a <u>Kommunal Tekniska Skola</u> which offered courses lasting approximately 1-and-a-half years, leading to the qualification of **Tekniker**

<u>Tekniskt Institut</u> which admitted pupils to a course leading first to the qualification of **Tekniker**, and then after a further year to that of **Institutsingenjor**.

Students who had passed the Realexamen could proceed to a technical school. There were 2 types:

<u>Tekniska Gymnasia</u> which provided a similar 3-year course to those offered by the general/academic Gymnasia but with a much greater emphasis on technical subjects. A minimum of 2 months practical experience was required before beginning the course. The qualification obtained was that of **(Gymnasie) Ingenjorsexanen**, which entitled the holder to enter a technical university.

<u>Tekniska Fackskolor</u> which were generally specialized technical schools providing training for a particular branch of industry. 2 years practical work experience was required before beginning the course. The usual 2-year course led to the qualification of **Fackskoleingenjor**. This did not in itself give access to a technical university, but by additional private study could be brought up to the level of the Ingenjorsexamen. These schools also provided a variety of evening courses lasting up to 5 years.

1962/3-1971:

Pupils holding the **Grundskola Certifikat** obtained on completion of 9 years compulsory education could enter:

<u>Tekniskt Gymnasium</u> for the 3-year course leading to the qualification of (Gymnasie) Ingenjor. In practice few students were admitted to university after the 3-year course; the 1963 reforms thus increased the course to 4 years with the aim of increasing the time spent on general subjects. The Tekniska Gymnasium was now divided into 4 lines: mechanics, electricity, construction and chemistry.

<u>Fackskola</u>. The courses were more specialized, with less time given to general subjects. Courses are taken in 1 (or more) of 3 areas: technical, social, and economic. Studies are often completed on a part-time basis, but in total are equivalent to 2 years full-time study. Courses in the economic and social fields could lead on to a further course of training (e.g. in nursing or a service profession), whereas the technical courses prepared students directly for employment. The technical courses were

available in mechanics, electricity, construction and chemistry. Students who entered the course with the **Grundskole Certifikat** had to undertake 1 year's training in industry before the final examination could be taken (normally completed between years 1 and 2). Students who completed skilled-worker training were also eligible to take the course and did not need to undertake additional industrial training. Students who did particularly well on the course were able to transfer (on completion of the course) to the second year of the Gymnasium.

Verkstadskola. These offered courses lasting 2-4 years, giving training for a skilled trade.

The Teknisk Fackskola also tended to take over the courses offered by the Tekniska Skola leading to the Tekniker qualification and the courses at the Tekniskt Institut, leading to the qualification of **Institutsingenjor**, which become the teknisk-kurs and fackkurs respectively, leading to the same qualifications.

Secondary (since 1971)

In July 1971, it was decided to merge the 3 existing types of post-secondary institution, i.e. vocational schools (Yrkesskola), Gymnasia and Fackskola, into a single upper secondary school (Gymnasium). The admission requirement is the Grundskola Certifikat, and courses vary between 2 and 4 years. The vocational courses generally last only 2 years. Compulsory subjects throughout are: Swedish, introduction to working life, and gymnastics. Students must choose at least 1 additional subject from: English, civics, religion, and mathematics.

HIGHER EDUCATION

Like all sectors of education in Sweden, this area has also undergone reforms.

Before 1969 the following qualifications could be obtained at universities or institutes of university status:

Filosofie Kandidatexamen/Fil. Kand./F.K./FK
Filosofisk Ambetsexamen/Fil. Mag./F.M./FM
Filosofisk Samhallsvetenskaplig Examen/Fil. Pol. Mag./F.P.M./FPM
Juridisk Samhallsvetenskaplig Examen/Jur. Pol. Mag./J.P.M./JPM
Filosofie Licentiatexamen/Fil. Lic./F.L./FL
Filosofie Doktorsgrad/Fil. Dr./F.D./FD

The method of obtaining a qualification was based on the units system. The minimum requirement to obtain the first degree (the **Fil. Kand.**) was 6 units in at least 2 subjects (i.e. 2 major fields of study), 2 units in each of 3 subjects, or 2 units in each of 2 subjects and 1 unit in each of 2 other subjects. A degree would not be awarded on the basis of 1 unit in each of 6 subjects, or 2 units in 1 subject and 1 unit in 5 other subjects.

Sweden

The usual period required to obtain the **FK** and **FM** (primarily intended for prospective secondary school teachers) was 3-5 years. The **FPM** and **JPM** were more specialized qualifications, and students had to obtain 7 units to be awarded the degree. For admission to the course leading to the **FL**, students had already to hold an **FK** or **FM**. They could study for the **FL** in the subject or 1 of the subjects in which they already had 3 or 4 units. The course usually lasted 3-5 years and qualified the holder to teach in the highest teaching posts in secondary schools. To obtain the **FD**, students had to undertake advanced research after obtaining the **FL** and to publish, and defend publicly, a thesis. Depending on the grade obtained, this could qualify the holder for a university teaching post (usually that of docent).

Students who began their studies before 1969 were able to continue under the new system, and the courses already completed were equated with the terms of the new system. A special certificate was awarded explaining the arrangement.

The qualifications **Fil. Mag.** and **Fil. Lic.** were abolished in 1970. The **Fil. Pol. Mag.** and **Jur. Pol. Mag.** have disappeared.

Since the 1977 Higher Education Act most undergraduate education has been organized into about 100 general studies programmes, established by Parliament, which vary from 1 to 5-and-a-half years. Each programme consists of courses varying in length and instruction and is designed to meet vocational training requirements of a permanent and general nature. Each may be classified within 1 of the following 5 vocational training sectors: technical; administrative, economic and social welfare; medical and nursing; teaching; and cultural and informational.

There are also local study programmes. Like the general study programmes, these vary in length. The difference is that a local study programme is normally aimed at local needs and conditions. A third type of specialization is the individual study programme, intended to fulfil the wishes of one or more students for a particular educational programme. Both local and individual study programmes are established by the governing board of each institution of higher education.

Separate single-subject courses are short-cycle study programmes designed to meet the need for further education or advanced professional training. Separate single-subject courses, too, are established by the governing board of each institution of higher education.

The study programme is measured using a point system. 1 point is equivalent to 1 week of full-time study. 1 academic year thus consists of 40 points, and the year is divided into 2 terms.

Marks are given on a 3-level scale: fail, pass and pass with distinction. Some courses use only a 2-level scale. On completion, the student receives a diploma. When these studies have comprised a full study programme, the diploma indicates the name of the degree earned. Each includes the Swedish word examen (degree), regardless of the time required to complete the study programme. The name of the degree also indicates the field of studies or the occupation involved.

Since 1986 the **Fil. Kand.**, **Jur. Kand** and **Teol. Kand. examen** have been reintroduced. Students must hold 120 points with at least 60 points in 1 subject, and apply to their respective institution for the title.

Sweden

Postgraduate

Admission is based on the following criteria: a student must hold at least 80 points from a general or local study programme, or at least 120 points from a single-subject course. The student must have at least 60 points in the subject to be studied at postgraduate level and within these there must be advanced courses including an independent work with a major paper. The **Filosofie Doktorsexamen** is obtained after 4 years study in 1 subject and successful defence of a dissertation. The **Filosofie Doktorsgrad** is a higher standard qualification than the Doktorsexamen.

Medical qualifications

Medicine Kandidatexamen (Med. Kand./MK) is obtained after a 2-year pre-clinical period of theoretical studies followed by a preliminary medical examination.

Before 1969, the **Medicine Licentiatexamen** (Med. Lic./ML) qualification was obtained after 4-and-a-half years study after **MK** and entitled the holder to practise medicine in Sweden. Completion of a thesis then led to the **Medicine Doktorsgrad** (Med. Dr./MD). The MD was kept until 1 July 1971 although on 1 July 1969 the new **Medicine Doktorsgrad** was introduced as the only qualification to be obtained at this stage.

Free and directed faculties

There is an important distinction in Swedish universities between 'free' faculties and 'closed/directed' faculties. In the 'free' faculties (theology, law, philosophy, the arts, some social sciences and natural sciences), students are given little supervision, and are free to present themselves for examination subject-by-subject when they consider themselves to be ready; 3 attempts are allowed at each subject. Students thus often take longer than the average period to complete their degrees.

In the 'closed' faculties (medicine, dentistry, engineering, pharmacy, economics, and agriculture) the requirements and sequences of courses are such that most students complete their first degree in the normal period. The courses have a structured curriculum, usually with some compulsory lectures.

Within the system of higher education (Hogskola) there are specialist colleges, notably those of social work, public administration, journalism, agriculture and forestry. These institutes have full university status:

Karolinska Institutet, Stockholm (medicine and dentistry)
Royal Institute of Technology, Stockholm
Chalmers Technical Institute, Gothenburg (engineering and technology)
Handelshogskolan i Goteborg - Gothenburg School of Economics and Business Administration
Handelshogskolan i Stockholm - Stockholm School of Economics
Lantbrukshogskolan - Sveriges Lantbruksuniversitet, Uppsala
Skogshogskolan - Skogshogskolan, Umea
Veterinarhogskolan - Sveriges Lantbruksuniversitet, Uppsala

Sweden

TEACHER EDUCATION

Before the introduction of compulsory comprehensive schools, primary teacher education for teachers of the first 2 classes of preparatory schools courses lasted 2 years, and only admitted women. The entrance requirement was the Realskola certificate.

2 courses were available to teachers trained for teaching in primary schools: a 2-year course for students with the Studentexamen, or a 5-year course for students with the Realexamen.

Students undertaking the 2-year course had to have the Studentexamen in the subjects they wished to teach. The course mainly covered practical training and instruction in pedagogics, psychology, etc. Students undertaking the 5-year course had to study to Studentexamen-level, the subjects they wished to teach in elementary schools.

Secondary school teachers normally took the university course leading to the **Fil. Mag.**, followed by a 4- to 6-month course on pedagogics and teaching practice.

From 1962 (approximately) to 1977:

Teachers in comprehensive schools were trained as follows:

Lower stage. Infant school teachers were trained in special sections of the general teacher-training colleges. Students holding the Realexamen took a 3-year course, and students with the Studentexamen took a 2-year course.

Middle stage. Teachers were trained at teacher-training colleges on 2-year courses if they already held the Studentexamen, or on 4-year courses if they held only the Realexamen.

Higher stage. Teachers were graduates (i.e. with the **Fil. Mag., Fil. Lic.** or **Fil. Dr.**) and were trained by older teachers during a probationary period of 6 months to 1 year. Teachers with the Fil. Mag. were called adjunkt, those with the Fil. Lic. or Fil. Dr., were called lektor.

Higher stage. Those who have taken a Doctor's degree with Honours are called docents, and this title confers the right to teach at a university.

From July 1977:

Teacher training was integrated with the universities in the regional Hogskola institutes. The basic qualification for teaching at the junior and middle levels of comprehensive schools is obtained after a 3-year course. A 1-year postgraduate course is available for those going on to teach at the third stage of comprehensive schools or Gymnasia.

Switzerland

Swiss Confederation

Switzerland is a confederation of twenty-six cantons and half-cantons. Education is primarily the responsibility of the individual cantons, so the system in operation for each area varies. (It is suggested that enquirers contact the National Academic Recognition Information Centre regarding qualifications which do not seem to fit the general pattern outlined here).

There is no federal ministry of education, but there are federal regulations for studies, training and certification in medical and paramedical fields (medicine, veterinary medicine, dentistry and pharmacy). Nursing is a cantonal responsibility. Vocational training (in industrial fields, handicrafts, commerce, agriculture and home economics) is under federal control to ensure that it is uniform and that the qualifications obtained are valid throughout Switzerland. There is also a Federal Maturity Certificate which gives admission to all institutions of higher education. The two Federal Institutes of Technology are under federal control.

In 1970 the Concordat on School Coordination was agreed, and has been endorsed by twenty-one cantons. Under this agreement certain standards were established: uniformity of age of entry to school (six years); duration of compulsory schooling to be nine years; and the length of study to be undertaken by pupils who take the maturity examination (minimum twelve years, maximum thirteen). Vital differences remain between the Italian, French and German-speaking cantons and between cantons in these linguistic regions.

There are international schools, particularly in the French-speaking region, which may offer the courses and qualifications offered by the national schools but are run predominantly on American or British lines and offer American or British qualifications.

There are many private institutions, both at school level and at further education level, and some of these enjoy federal or cantonal recognition.

Until 1970, compulsory education varied from seven to nine years from age six or seven, depending on the canton. Since 1970 the period has been nine years throughout Switzerland.

The media of instruction are principally German, French or Italian, depending on the language of the region.

The academic year ran from August-October to June for cantons in central and French-speaking Switzerland, and April to March in most German-speaking cantons. After the 1985 referendum it was agreed that the Swiss school year would begin uniformly in the autumn.

Switzerland

Cantons and half-cantons

Canton	Main language(s) spoken
Aargau	German
Appenzell is divided into the half cantons of:	
Appenzell-Ausser Rhoden	German
Appenzell-Inner Rhoden	German
Basel (Basle) is divided into the half-cantons of:	
Basel-Landschaft	German
Basel-Stadt	German
Berne	German (French)
Friebourg	French (German)
Geneve (Geneva)	French
Glarus	German
Graubunden	German (Italian) Romansch
Jura	French
Luzern (Lucerne)	German
Neuchatel	French
Schaffhausen	German
Schwyz	German
Solothurn	German
St Gall	German
Thurgau	German
Ticino	Italian (German)
Unterwalden is divided into the half-cantons of:	
Nidwalden	German
Obwalden	German
Uri	German
Valais	French (German)
Vaud	French
Zug	German
Zurich	German

Switzerland

EVALUATION IN BRITAIN

School

Maturitatszeugnis (German-speaking cantons), **Certificat de Maturite** (French-speaking cantons, except Vaud), **Baccalaureat** (Vaud), **Attestato di Maturita** (Italian-speaking canton of Ticino) - may be considered to satisfy the general requirement for universities and polytechnics.

All diplomas of this designation, issued by the Confederation, different cantons and even private schools (with the mention 'according to the ordinance of the Federal Council concerning the recognition of the **Maturite** certificate of 22 May 1968') can be considered federally recognized and controlled; that is, their standards of assessment are practically equal.

Higher

Diplom, **Staatsdiplom** (German-speaking cantons); **Lizentiat, Licence, Diplome d'Etat** (French-speaking cantons) - generally considered comparable to British Bachelor degree standard.

Doctorate - generally compared to British Master degree standard.

MARKING SYSTEMS

School and Higher

Different scales are used:

1-6 (maximum); minimum pass 4 (most frequently used)
1-10 (maximum); minimum pass 6
6-1 (maximum); minimum pass 6.

10	6	1	sehr gut/tres bien/molto bene	very good
9	-	-		
8	5	2	gut/bien/bene	good
7	-	-		
6	4	3	mittelmassig/suffisant/sufficiente	fair
5	-	-		
4	3	4	unbefriedigend/insuffisant/insufficiente	poor
3	-	-		
2	2	5	schlecht/schwach, sehr schwach/mauvais/ molto debole (nullo)	fail
1	-	-		

Switzerland

SCHOOL EDUCATION

Pre-primary

Some facilities are available for children aged 3-7 at <u>kindergartens/ecoles enfantines/case dei bambini</u>.

Primary

The period of schooling varies according to canton from 3 to 6 years for children from age 6 (until 1970 from 6 or 7, depending on the canton) - see below. In cantons where primary education covers 6 years, this period is generally divided into a 3-year lower and a 3-year upper cycle. During the lower cycle (of the 6-year course) or the full 4- or 5-year course, pupils study their mother tongue, reading, writing, arithmetic, physical education, singing and the environment.

In cantons where primary education covers only 4-5 years, the next cycle is characterized as middle/lower secondary, and courses are taken at 1 of the following:

<u>Realschule/Mittelschule/Progymnase/Sekundarschule/College Cantonal/Ecole Secondaire/ College Moderne/Ginnasio/Scuola Maggiore</u>.

During this cycle and the upper cycle of the 6-year course, the study of the second national language or a second modern language is compulsory; in the French-speaking cantons it is German, in the German-speaking cantons French, and in Ticino it is French or German.

There are 3 types of lower secondary school: basic, intermediate and academic. For entrance to the last 2 types, pupils must pass an entrance examination. The curriculum of the basic type covers: native language, mathematics, elementary science, drawing, geography, history, industrial arts or domestic science, physical education, singing and writing. The intermediate lower secondary schools offer the same curriculum, but at a more advanced academic level. Pupils who complete the course at a basic or intermediate secondary school normally proceed to vocational school or general education continuation school or take up an apprenticeship. Pupils who complete a course at an academic lower secondary school can proceed to an academic upper secondary school (Gymnasium).

In a small number of cantons this cycle of education is called the cycle d'orientation and contains the various types of lower secondary (and upper primary) education in a course offered by a comprehensive school. The cycle lasts 3 years in Geneva, Valais and Fribourg and 4 years in Neuchatel and Ticino.

Pupils do not normally obtain a qualification on completion of this cycle of education, but sometimes a **Certificat d'Etudes** or **Certificat Secondaire** is awarded.

Upper secondary

This lasts 3-5 years, or 3-4 years at a post-compulsory level, depending on the canton, and is undertaken at <u>Gymnase/Gymnasium/Lyceum/Lyzeum/Lycee/Liceo/Istituto/Kollegium/ College Classique</u>. Before the agreement of 1970, schools offered a grade 14, but this now only exists in the canton of Valais for pupils taking the specialization A or B. Under Swiss law all pupils preparing the maturity examination have to complete 6 years of preparatory (secondary) work.

Switzerland

Since 1973 there has been the opportunity for pupils to specialize in 1 of 5 options - before that only options A, B and C were available:

A   Latin/Greek
B   Latin/modern languages
C   mathematics/science
D   modern languages
E   economic science

Of the 11 subjects in the curriculum, 9 are compulsory throughout the cycle and common for all pupils: 2 national languages (i.e. 2 of French, German or Italian), history, geography, mathematics, physics, chemistry, natural sciences, drawing or music. In the maturity examinations, pupils must include, as a minimum, 2 national languages, mathematics and 1 of the specialist subjects of their option. These subjects plus history must be studied during the final year. Specialist subjects per option are:

A   Latin and Greek
B   Latin and a third national language or English
C   descriptive geometry and a third national language or English
D   English and third national language or Spanish or Russian
E   economic law and third national language or English

Depending on the canton, there may be additional compulsory subjects.

On completion of this cycle, pupils may take the examinations for the Federal Maturity Certificate and/or the Cantonal Certificate. The first of these certificates was originally established to regulate entry into a course of training for the health professions. The specializations for which it provides a leaving qualification have now been increased, and pupils from any of the 5 specializations may take the examinations for this certificate - **Maturitatszeugnis/Certificat de Maturite/Attestato di Maturita**. A pupil who has studied at a non-federally recognized school may take the examinations for this certificate at one of the annual general testings.

Pupils may also take examinations for the Cantonal Maturity Certificate - **Kantonale Maturitat/Maturite Cantonale/Maturita Cantonale**. Each canton has its own regulations for these examinations, which in general follow the outline of the federal examinations, though sometimes a little less rigorous. The examinations are usually offered in the same 5 subject options, but not all options may be available at all schools in each canton. The Cantonal Maturity Certificate only gives admission to selected faculties of the university in the same canton, and may be accepted at other universities if there is an intercantonal agreement or at a university's discretion. In the French-speaking cantons pupils may receive both a Federal Maturity Certificate and the Cantonal Certificate, but this does not mean that the pupil has undertaken any additional work.

The school system in years per canton:

	Primary	Secondary	
Aargau	5	+ 4	+ 4
Appenzell:			
Appenzell-Ausser Rhoden	6	+ 3	+ 4
Appenzell-Inner Rhoden	6	+ 3	+ 4
Basel (Basle):			
Basel-Landschaft	5	+ 4	+ 4
Basel-Stradt	4	+ 5	+ 3
Berne	4	+ 5	+ 4
Friebourg	5	+ 4	+ 4

Switzerland

Geneve	6	+ 3	+ 4
Glarus	6	+ 7	
Graubunden	6	+ 3	+ 4
Jura	6	+ 5	+ 4
Luzern	5	+ 7	
Neuchatel	5	+ 4	+ 3
Schaffhausen	6	+ 2	+ 4
Schwyz	6	+ 7	
Solothurn	5	+ 4	+ 4
St Gall	6	+ 3	+ 4
Thurgau	6	+ 3	+ 4
Ticino	5	+ 4	+ 3
Unterwalden:			
Nidwalden	6	+ 7	
Obwalden	6	+ 7	
Uri	6	+ 7	
Valais	6	+ 1	+ 4/5
Vaud	4	+ 5	+ 3
Zug	6	+ 7	
Zurich	6	+ 6	

Vocational secondary

On completion of primary schooling and/or basic/middle school, pupils may opt for a full-time vocational secondary course or an apprenticeship (which includes part-time attendance at school).

Full-time vocational courses at schools are available in agriculture and technology, but mainly in commerce and artistic fields. Courses normally last 3-4 years. At the full-time commercial schools (**Handelsschulen/Ecoles Superieures de Commerce/Scuole di Commercio**) pupils may take the examinations for the **Handelsmaturitat/Maturite Commerciale** as well as for the **Federal Certificate of Capability (Fahigkeitszeugnis/ Certificat de Capacite/Attestato di Capacita)** on completion of the 4-year course.

Apprenticeships may be undertaken either by:

in-service training with a firm/factory/office, with part-time attendance (minimum of 1 day a week) at a vocational continuation school (**Gewerbeschule/Gewerbliche Berufschule/Ecole Professionnelle/Scuola Professionale**)

in-service training, with the general education given in a teaching workshop (**Lehrwerkstatte/Ecole de Metiers/Scuola Cantonale d'Arti e Mestiere**), such full-time schools being run by industries or the cantons to train apprentices for particular vocations

in-service training, with the general education given in a workshop school (**Werksschule/Ecole Atelier**), such schools usually being run by large companies to train future employees.

Training, normally lasting 2-4 years, from the minimum age of 15, is subject to federal regulations which determine the designation of the profession, length of apprenticeship and organization of examinations. On completion, pupils take a final examination (**Lehrabschlussprufung/Examen de Fin d'Apprentissage/Esame di Fine Tirocino**) conducted by the cantonal authority. Success leads to the qualification of **Federal Certificate of Capability (Fahigkeitszeugnis/Certificat de Capacite/Attestato di Capacita)** and the status of skilled worker. The certificate does not normally state the length of training, but it is usually possible to obtain a transcript of marks.

Switzerland

Since the 1970s higher vocational schools (Berufsmittelschulen/Ecoles Professionelles Superieures/Scuole Medie Professionali) have been established. These offer academic instruction beyond the compulsory minimum. Pupils have to study 2 languages (their own plus the second official language or English) and contemporary history. They still only receive the Federal Certificate of Capability, although in certain circumstances a **Berufsmittelschuldiplom/Baccalaureat Technique** may be obtained.

There is also a small number of general education continuation upper secondary schools (Diplommittelschule/Ecole de Culture Generale/Scuola Cultura Generale) which offer 2-3 years of general subjects for pupils who have completed compulsory schooling. The diploma awarded is rarely accepted for university entrance, but since 1970 it has been recognized throughout Switzerland.

FURTHER EDUCATION

Higher technical and commercial schools (Hohere Technische Lehranstalt (HTL)/Ecole Technique Superieure (ETS)/Scuola Tecnica Superiore/Technikums und Hohere Wirtschaftschulen) offer courses lasting 3-4 years. For some courses, students are admitted directly on completion of compulsory schooling (i.e. 9 years study), whereas most students will have completed their apprenticeship or attended a craft school. Students have to sit an entrance examination in mathematics, drawing and their own national language. Students who have completed a course of academic upper secondary education have to undertake practical training before beginning the course proper.

HIGHER EDUCATION

Courses are offered by 7 universities, which are under cantonal control: 3 in the French-speaking cantons (Geneva, Lausanne, Neuchatel), 3 in the German-speaking cantons (Basel, Berne, Zurich), and 1 using both French and German for its medium of instruction. There is no university in the Italian-speaking region. There are 2 Federal Institutes of Technology (Zurich and Lausanne), and 1 graduate school specializing in business, economics and public administration, but there is no federal university.

The Federal Maturity Certificate (Maturitatszeugnis/Certificat de Maturite/Baccalaureat/Attestato di Maturita) forms the admission requirement to degree courses. The Cantonal Maturity Certificate gives admission to restricted facilities - (see under SCHOOL EDUCATION, Upper secondary). The Cantonal Certificates do not give admission to courses in dentistry, medicine (as well as veterinary medicine) and pharmacy, for which until 1982 the Federal Maturity Certificate has been required. There is no numerus clausus (system of restricted entry) for any courses of higher education.

In general, the first degree obtained after a minimum of 4 years, is the **Licence/Lizentiat/Diplom**. In pharmacy and architecture, courses last 4-5 years; in veterinary medicine and dentistry, 5-6 years; and in medicine, 6-and-a-half years (13 semesters). In many courses students take an examination on general studies and basic work in their subject at the end of the first year: **Vordiplomprufung I/Propedeutique I/Examen** year: **Vordiplomprufung II/Zwischenprufung/Propedeutique II/ Examen Preliminaire II.**

Switzerland

On some courses at the universities in the French-speaking cantons a **Demi-Licence** may be obtained after the first part of the course (2-3 years). Although a minimum period of study is stipulated for a degree, most students take longer. Students sometimes move from university to university during their studies, but they must spend a minimum of 6 semesters at the same university. For courses in certain professional fields it is not possible for students to move to another university during their studies, as the courses are more structured.

At the <u>Federal Institutes of Technology</u> the first qualification may be obtained after 7-8 semesters - **Diplome d'Etat/Staatsdiplom**.

The qualification obtained on successful completion of a course of higher education does not automatically entitle the holders to practise their profession, e.g. medicine, law, architecture. They must pass a state examination officially set by their cantonal authorities - in medicine this is a federal examination.

A minimum of 8 semesters study after the award of the first degree may lead to the award of the **Doctorate**. Shorter postgraduate taught courses (often part-time) are also available, and referred to variously as **l'Etude de Troisieme Cycle/Nachdiplom/Postgraduierten Studium**.

TEACHER EDUCATION

The requirements for prospective teachers vary greatly from canton to canton, except for technical teachers, where there are federal requirements.

Primary

Except for the cantons of Geneva, Basle, Neuchatel, Aargau and Vaud, training is undertaken over 4-5 years at a <u>Lehrer</u> (innen) <u>Seminar/Ecole Normale/Scuola Magistrale</u>, after completing 9 years compulsory schooling. In the German-speaking cantons it is usually a 5-year course divided into:

Unterseminar - 3 to 3-and-a-half years of secondary-level general education

Oberseminar - 1-and-a-half to 2 years of pedagogical training.

In most cantons the duration will be prolonged in the future.

Students holding the Maturity Certificate may enter the oberseminar cycle of training directly.

In the cantons of Basle, Neuchatel, Aargau, Geneva and Vaud training is only open to holders of the Maturity Certificate (either federal or cantonal). This lasts 2 years in the first 3 cantons and 3 years in Geneva.

Both types of course lead to the qualification of **Primarlehrer-Diplom/Patent/Fahigkeitszeugnis fur Elementarlehrer/Lehrerpatent/Wahlfahigkeit als Lehrer/Certificat d'Aptitude a l'Enseignement Primaire/Brevet d'Enseignement Primaire/Patente di Maestro di Scuola Elementare**.

Switzerland

In the canton of Aargau there are also 2 <u>Pedagogical-Social Gymnasiums</u> (PSG). On completion of the 3-year course, students may obtain the Cantonal Maturity Certificate, going on to the <u>Hohere Padagogische Lehranstalt</u> (HPL) for a 2-year course leading to the qualification of **Wahlfahigkeit als Lehrer der Aargauischen Primarschule**. Pupils who attend an academic upper secondary school (Gymnasium) and then obtain the Federal Maturity Certificate must undertake a 4-year course at the HPL to obtain the teaching qualification.

Secondary

This includes the training undertaken for the basic or middle cycle in those cantons where primary education lasts no longer than 4-5 years.

The distinction in training for lower- and upper-secondary school teachers is made only in the German-speaking cantons and Neuchatel. There are no teacher-training courses for prospective secondary school teachers in Ticino.

Lower secondary/basic/middle-students holding the Maturity Certificate may sit the university entrance examination and if successful undertake a course lasting 5-8 semesters (depending on the canton), leading to the qualification of **Mittellehrerdiplom/Sekundarlehrerpatent/diplom/ Fahigkeitsprufung fur Sekunda Lehrer/Fachlehrer auf Sekundarschulstufe**. Students who hold the primary teachers' certificate may:

take a course at a teacher-training college lasting 1-4 semesters, leading to the qualification of **Bezirkslehrerdiplom/Mittellehrerdiplom/Oberschullehrerdiplom/Reallehrerdiplom/Sekundarlehrerdiplom**

undertake the university course (as above) if they pass the university entrance examination.

In Neuchatel, prospective teachers undertake a 6-semester course from the entrance level of the Maturity Certificate, leading to the qualification of **Brevet pour l'Enseignement du Degre Secondaire Inferieur**; if the prospective teacher already holds a Licence, the course leads to the **Certificat d'Aptitude Pedagogique**.

In the other French-speaking cantons, prospective teachers must undertake 1-2 years of pedagogical training beyond their Licence, leading to the qualification of **Brevet d'Aptitude Pedagogique/Certificat d'Aptitude a l'Enseignement Secondaire/Brevet d'Enseignement Secondaire/Certificat d'Aptitude Pedagogique**.

Upper secondary teachers must complete a degree course.

In most German-speaking cantons the universities offer degree courses aimed specifically at prospective teachers; they therefore require little or shorter training in pedagogical subjects. The qualification obtained is the **Diplom fur das Hohere Lehramt/Gymnasiallehrerdiplom/Patent fur das Hohere Lehramt/Oberlehrerdiplom**.

In Basel and Zurich, as well as in the French-speaking cantons, prospective teachers must undertake pedagogical training (1 year in Vaud, Neuchatel, Basel and Zurich, 2 years in Geneva) beyond their degree (Licence), leading to the qualification of **Diplome de Maitre de Gymnase/Oberlehrerdiplom** or **Gymnasial-lehrerdiplom**.

Syria

Syrian Arab Republic

Education is universal, free and compulsory up to age fourteen (the end of the preparatory cycle).

The medium of instruction is Arabic but both French and English are taught as second languages in the preparatory and secondary cycles.

The school academic year runs from September to May and the university academic year from October to June.

EVALUATION IN BRITAIN

Al Shahada Al Thanawiya (Syrian School Leaving Certificate) or **Baccalaureat** - generally compared to GCE O-level standard.

Licence (4-year) or **Bachelor degree** - is considered to be below a British Bachelor (Honours) degree in academic standing, but may be compared to British Bachelor (Ordinary) degree standard.

MARKING SYSTEMS

School

Marks in the literary Baccalaureat are out of a maximum of 240; minimum pass mark 102.

Marks in the scientific branch of the Baccalaureat are out of a maximum of 260; minimum pass mark 104.

University

Marks are based on a percentage system; minimum pass mark 50%.

100-90	honours	Martabet al Sharaf (rarely awarded)
89-80	excellent	Momtaz
79-70	very good	Jayed Jeddar
69-60	good	Jayed
59-50	pass	Makboul
49- 0	fail	Raseb

Syria

SCHOOL EDUCATION

Primary

This lasts for 6 years and children enter school at age 6. During the first 3 years pupils must repeat the year if they receive more than 2 unsatisfactory markings (Daief) in reading, writing and arithmetic. In the fourth, fifth and sixth years pupils must repeat the year if they receive more than 2 unsatisfactory markings in grammar, dictation or writing and in reading and comprehension.

Preparatory/lower secondary

This lasts for 3 years and is free. Pupils study foreign languages, science and political studies. At the end of grade 9 pupils sit an examination for the Preparatory School Leaving Certificate known as **Al Kafa'a**. Maximum marks in the Al Kafa'a are 290; minimum pass mark 122. Pupils must pass in Arabic to obtain the certificate.

Secondary

This lasts 3 years and covers grades 10-12 (ages 15-17). Students may enter either the general or technical branches although entry is selective and based on the Al Kafa'a examination taken at the end of grade 9.

General:

The first year is introductory, after this pupils enter 1 of 2 streams: literary or scientific. At the end of the 3-year course pupils sit for the Secondary School Leaving Certificate known as the **Baccalaureat** or **Al Shahada Al Thanawiya**, which is the only qualification that gives automatic access to higher education.

Technical:

All technical secondary schools are run by the government. Technical secondary education is divided into 2 streams: industrial and commercial. In the industrial schools the boys receive instruction in different engineering trades while the girls receive training in electricity and electronics. At the end of the course pupils take the **Technical Baccalaureat**. This offers only limited opportunities in the field of further education, such as entry to the Institute of Technical Education in Aleppo.

Secondary education courses in home economics and nursing do not lead to the Baccalaureat.

Agriculture:

The Ministry of Agriculture runs various secondary agricultural schools, two of which offer special training (one in veterinary science in Damascus, the other in farm machinery in Al-Hassaka).

Other:

Home economics and nursing courses at secondary level are available for those girls who do not opt for general or commercial education. (Few girls opt for the industrial schools as only 4 admit women, compared to 20 industrial schools for boys).

Syria

Religious:

Religious education is free and run by the Awkaf Ministry. It provides a 6-year course parallel to the preparatory and secondary cycles in the secular system.

FURTHER EDUCATION

Various technical and vocational institutes, known as Intermediate Institutes, operate in Syria and offer 2-year post-Baccalaureat courses. The entry requirement is the Baccalaureat. Most courses are 2 years although some are longer. Some of the institutes grant **degrees**.

HIGHER EDUCATION

There are 4 universities: Damascus University, Aleppo University, Tishrine University (formerly the University of Latakia) and Al-Baath University (founded in 1979).

Degree courses in Syria last 4-6 years and the medium of instruction is Arabic.

Certain faculties in Damascus and Aleppo Universities provide 1-year **Postgraduate Diploma** courses and 2-year **MA and M.Sc.** courses by instruction. Very little research is done.

TEACHER EDUCATION

Primary

Until 1966/77 primary teachers underwent 1 year of post-secondary study or 4 years post-preparatory. The 1-year course is now 2 years and the 4-year course has been phased out.

Preparatory

Holders of the **Baccalaureat** attend a 2-year training course. Graduates may teach without special training.

Secondary

Some graduates attend the Faculty of Education at the universities. For subjects where there is a teacher shortage, preparatory school teachers are trained in 2-year courses at an intermediate institution.

Syria

Vocational

Holders of the **Technical Baccalaureat** follow a 2-year course at an intermediate institute studying additional subjects. A new teacher training institute for vocational teachers is being established.

In 1972 the Unesco/Unicef field centre in Amman initiated a programme of in-service training for primary school teachers. The long-term aim was to encourage every teacher to attend a 1-week orientation course, a 2-hour weekly seminar during the school year and a 2-week course at the end of the school year once every 5 years.

Unrwa schools

The United Nations Relief and Works Agency (Unrwa) runs 110 schools at primary and preparatory levels only for Palestinian refugees. English is the only foreign language taught in these schools. Unrwa also provides teacher training at its Development Unit (formerly the Institute of Education) and runs a Vocational Training Centre at Mazzeh, Damascus for holders of the Preparatory School Leaving Certificate (Al Kafa'a) and the Baccalaureat.

Taiwan

Taiwan, Province of China

Education is compulsory from age six to fifteen.

The medium of instruction is Chinese.

The academic year consists of two semesters and runs from August to July.

EVALUATION IN BRITAIN

School

Taiwan High School Leaving Certificate - generally considered to compare to GCE O-level standard.

Higher

Bachelor degree - generally considered to be below British Bachelor degree standard.

MARKING SYSTEMS

A numerical grading system by percentages is in use at all levels:

A   80-100%
B   70- 79
C   60- 69

SCHOOL EDUCATION

Primary

The Constitution provides for free elementary education for all children aged 6-12. In 1968 the Nine Year Basic Education Programme was introduced. This extended the scheme of free education to include the 3-year period of junior middle school education (grades 7-9). The junior middle school entrance examination was abolished.

Secondary

Before 1968 secondary education was provided by the junior middle school and senior middle school. Pupils attended either academic or vocational schools within this system. After the introduction of the Nine Year Basic Education Programme in 1968, all country, city and Taipei municipal junior high schools were renamed public junior high schools. Private secondary schools must conform to the syllabus of the public junior high school.

All students must study English during the first and second years of junior high school. Successful graduates receive a certificate and may proceed to the senior secondary schools or the 5-year junior colleges.

Senior secondary school

Senior secondary education is offered by the senior high school and the vocational high school. Graduates of the junior high school must take the **Senior Secondary School Entrance Examination** to be admitted to a senior secondary school.

Senior high school

Students may choose to specialize either in natural sciences or in social sciences. English is a compulsory subject throughout senior high school. Students can attend either for a 4-year full-time period or for a 4-year evening-class period. Students are selected for 1 of these divisions on the basis of their performance in the **Senior School Entrance Examination**.

Senior vocational high school

The senior vocational high schools are divided into 6 categories: agricultural, industrial, commercial, marine products, nursing, and home economics. As at senior high school, students attend either during the day or in the evening. Owing to the nature of their studies, students from these schools are unlikely to proceed to a 4-year college or university. Successful graduates can continue their education in the 2-year junior colleges. (These are being phased out and will be replaced by 3-year junior colleges.)

Normal schools

These secondary-level schools trained elementary school teachers. They have now been converted into junior normal colleges.

HIGHER EDUCATION

Higher education in Taiwan is covered by junior colleges and 4-year colleges and universities.

Junior colleges

The junior college system aims to teach applied sciences and train technicians. There are 3 kinds of junior college: 5-year; 3-year; and 2-year.

Taiwan

Five-year junior college

This college takes junior high school (grade 9) graduates who have been successful in the 5-year **Joint Junior College Entrance Examination**.

Five-year normal colleges (see TEACHER EDUCATION)

Two-year and three-year junior colleges

These colleges accept successful graduates of the senior vocational high schools who have passed the 2-year **Joint Junior College Entrance Examination**. Senior high school graduates who need an extra year of technical education take the 3-year Joint Junior College Entrance Examination.

Students follow a course designed to provide skills and training suitable for employment.

Successful graduates of junior college courses receive a **Diploma**. Only 4-year colleges and university graduates receive degrees.

Four-year colleges and universities

Entrance to the 4-year colleges and universities is based on the results obtained in the **Joint Four-Year College and University Entrance Examination**.

Most **Bachelor degree** courses involve 4 years study. The exceptions are medicine (7 years), dentistry (6 years), veterinary medicine (5 years) and education (5 years).

TEACHER EDUCATION

Primary

The 5-year course at the normal junior college is open to graduates of the junior high school (grade 9). Students must complete a minimum of 300 semester hours.

Secondary

Prospective secondary school teachers must obtain a **Bachelor of Education** degree. This is a 5-year course.

Tanzania

United Republic of Tanzania

This chapter covers the period from 1961, when Tanganyika became independent. In 1964 Zanzibar was united with the mainland and became known as Tanzania.

There is central control of school curricula, and since 1973 the National Examinations Council of Tanzania has administered the main school examinations.

Education is compulsory from age seven for seven years (standards 1 to 7).

The medium of instruction is Swahili in primary schools and English in secondary schools, colleges and at the university.

The academic year runs from:

July - University of Dar es Salaam and most other further education establishments

January - Sokoine University of Agriculture

January - primary and secondary schools.

EVALUATION IN BRITAIN

School

Cambridge Overseas School Certificate (COSC), East African Certificate of Education (EACE) - grades 1-6 are equated to GCE O-level standard (grades A, B, C).

National Form IV Examination - grades A, B and C are generally compared to GCE O-level standard.

Certificate of Secondary Education - grades A, B and C are generally compared to GCE O-level standard.

Cambridge Overseas Higher School Certificate (COHSC), Advanced Certificate of Secondary Education, National Form VI Examination - grades A-E are equated to GCE A-level.

Tanzania

Higher

Bachelor degree - generally compared to British Bachelor degree standard.

MARKING SYSTEMS

School

Cambridge Overseas School Certificate   - these are graded 1 (maximum) - 9 (fail)
East African Certificate of Education

National Form IV Examination - graded A-F, where E and F are fail grades.

A candidate gets the Certificate of Education for achieving, at one sitting, a pass at least at grade D in Kiswahili and a pass at grade A, B or C in any other subject. Candidates who fail to meet this requirement but obtain at least 2 passes at grade D in any 2 subjects will be awarded a statement of results.

Certificate of Secondary Education:

A	excellent
B	very good
C	good
D	satisfactory
E	poor

Cambridge Overseas Higher School Certificate (COHSC) - graded A, B, C, D, E, O or S
East African Advanced Certificate of Education (EAACE) (both subsidiary pass grades), F (fail).

National Form VI Examination is graded A, B, C, D, E (principal level), S (subsidiary pass), F (fail). A candidate obtains the certificate for achieving at least 3 subsidiary passes, 2 of which must be in subjects offered at principal level. Candidates who do not qualify but obtain at least 1 pass at subsidiary level in a subject offered at principal level and a pass in a general paper will be awarded a statement of results.

Higher

Degrees are classified:

1st class Honours
2nd class Honours (upper)
2nd class Honours (lower)
Pass

SCHOOL EDUCATION

Pre-primary

There is no state provision for this, although a policy is being prepared.

Tanzania

Primary

This covers 7 years, divided into lower (covering grades 1-4) and upper (grades 5-7). It culminates in the **Primary Certificate Examination (PCE)**.

Secondary

This covers 6 years, divided into 4 years lower followed by 2 years upper. From form II, pupils are streamed into arts or science. Since 1973, secondary education has been oriented towards vocational subjects and all are designated technical, agricultural, commercial or home economics.

Until 1969 pupils normally took the Cambridge Overseas School Certificate and London GCE O-level examinations at the end of form IV and the Cambridge Overseas Higher School Certificate and London GCE A-level examinations at the end of form VI.

From 1970 to 1973 pupils took the East African Certificate of Education examination at the end of form IV and the East African Advanced Certificate of Education examination at the end of form VI, both examinations being run by the East African Examinations Council. However, in 1971 Tanzania announced that it was withdrawing from the East African Examinations Council and would run its own national examinations. In the past, all form IV pupils sat an internally set examination, called the Regional Form IV Examination, in August. The results were used to select those pupils who would begin in form V the following January, as the results of the COSC or EACE were not available until March or later. This initial selection was subsequently changed in accordance with the COSC or EACE results, once these were known. With the development of the National Form IV Examination, taken in November, which was first set in 1974, the Regional Form IV Examination was scrapped. In the National Form IV Examinations pupils must take political education, Kiswahili, English language, mathematics, history, geography and biology, and a maximum of 3 optional subjects. The **Certificate of Secondary Education** has now replaced National Form IV.

Pupils take the National Form VI Examinations, now called the **Advanced Certificate of Secondary Education**, at the end of form VI.

Technical secondary

As indicated above, some secondary schools are technically biased, and although students in these as in others undertake a core of common subjects, the emphasis is on technical subjects. Students successfully completing the CSE may continue their studies at <u>Technical Colleges</u> which offer certificate- and diploma-level training.

Lower-level vocational training can be obtained at centres run by the National Vocational Training Division, offering full-time (4 years) and part-time basic craft training.

FURTHER EDUCATION

There are many institutions (over 300) offering specialist training at post-form IV (or form VI) level leading to certificates or diplomas at the semi-professional level in a wide variety of disciplines. The institutions are the responsibility of the relevant government ministry under which they fall e.g. Ministry of Agriculture and Livestock Development Agricultural (MATIs) and Livestock (LITIs) Training Institutes, Ministry of Health and Social Welfare Nurse Training Schools and Medical Assistants Training Centres, and Ministry of Finance Dar es Salaam School of Accountancy.

In addition there are several specialized training centres, designed primarily for form VI leavers. These include Institute of Finance Management, National Institute of Transport, Ardhi Institute and Institute of Management Development (previously IDM). These offer **3-year Diploma courses** in subjects related to their speciality, and the qualification obtained is regarded as a near-degree equivalent.

HIGHER EDUCATION

There are 2 universities. The University of Dar es Salaam, established in 1970 was originally founded in 1961 as the University College of Dar es Salaam and became a constituent college of the University of East Africa in 1963. Sokoine University of Agriculture, located in Morogoro and launched in July 1984, was created from the former Faculty of Agriculture, Forestry and Veterinary Science of the University of Dar es Salaam.

Admission to degree courses is based on passes in the Certificate of Secondary Education plus passes in the Advanced Certificate of Education. However since 1975/6, students who meet the academic requirements have not been entitled to direct admission to degree courses. Preference is given to applicants who have a number of years of work experience and are supported by their employer. The academic requirements are 2 passes at principal level, 1 at subsidiary level in the form VI examination, and 5 passes in the National Form IV Examination.

Bachelor degree courses last 3 years, except for veterinary science and engineering, which takes 4 years, and medicine, which takes 5 years. A further 1-3 years study leads to a **Master** degree. A minimum of a further 2 years original research leads to a **Ph.D**.

TEACHER EDUCATION

Primary

The **Grade C Certificate** entitles the holder to teach in the first 2 grades of primary education. The course lasts 3 years from the end of standard VII.

The **Grade B Certificate** is obtained by promotion or by successfully completing a 4-year course at a teacher-training college after standard VII.

The **Grade A Certificate** is obtained on successful completion of the 2-year course from the end of form IV and allows the holder to teach in all 7 grades of primary education.

Tanzania

Secondary

Lower:

A 2-year Diploma course at the Colleges of National Education from the National Form VI Examination is required.

Upper:

Teachers for this level should be graduates.

Thailand

Kingdom of Thailand

The education system is highly centralized. The National Scheme of Education (1977) laid down the essential principles of the present system.

Until 1961, four years of primary education was compulsory for children between the ages of eight and fifteen. The National Scheme of Education (1960) and the Primary Education Act (1962) made provision for seven years. In 1978 this was reduced to six years.

The medium of instruction is Thai, and English used to be compulsory from grade V.

The academic year runs from mid-May to the end of March.

EVALUATION IN BRITAIN

School

Mathayom Suksa 3 (before 1984) and **Maw 3** (after 1984) - generally considered to be below GCE O-level standard.

Mathayom Suksa 5 (before 1984) and **Maw 6** (after 1984) - generally considered to compare to GCE O-level standard on a subject-for-subject basis where there are counterpart subjects in the GCE examinations (except English language).

Higher

Bachelor degree - generally considered to be below British Bachelor degree standard.

MARKING SYSTEMS

School

Mathayom Suksa 5 (MS5)

1960-75 - percentage system; pupils required to obtain at least 500 marks out of 1,000; English can account for up to 240.

Thailand

1976-81 (although still in use until 1983) - credit system; pupils required to obtain 100 credits of which 34 must be from the compulsory subjects. The remaining 66 credits allow pupils to choose from elective subjects; a maximum of 40 credits for English can be chosen.

Maw 6 (M6)

Since 1981 - the unit system was introduced (adopted from the American system of Carnegie Unit). The first pupil to complete M6 on the unit system did so in 1984. Pupils are required to complete 75 units for graduation from M6; of these 75, 36 units must come from compulsory subjects consisting of 24 units of general subjects (Thai, social studies, science, and physical and health education), and 12 units of vocational core subjects. The remaining minimum of 39 units are for elective subjects where the maximum of 31 units of English can be chosen.

Higher

Credits and grade-point average are awarded; an explanation is usually given on the transcript of marks.

SCHOOL EDUCATION

Pre-primary/kindergarten

This is voluntary, and is available for children aged 3-5.

Primary

Although officially beginning at age 7, some children begin at 6. There were 2 cycles: <u>lower prathom</u> (grades I-IV) and <u>upper prathom</u> (grades V-VII). In 1978 the latter was shortened to cover grades V-VI. There is now 1 cycle covering grades I-VI.

On completion of primary education pupils take the **Primary School Leaving Examination**.

Secondary

Pupils take the secondary school entrance examination for entry to this stage which is again divided into 2 cycles.

Before 1978 these were:

lower (grades VIII-X/Mawsaw I-III) leading to the leaving examination MS3, and the entrance examination 6

upper (grades XI-XII/Mawsaw IV-V) leading to the final school leaving examination, the MS5.

A new system was introduced in the 1978-9 academic year: secondary education now covers 6 years, divided into two 3-year cycles: lower M1-3, and upper M4-6.

The terminology is now being changed from Mawsaw to Maw; from 1984 the leaving examination will take place in the sixth year at M6.

Thailand

In 1963 the upper secondary cycle was subdivided into arts, science and general (vocational) branches. Compulsory subjects at this stage are the Thai language, social studies, science and physical and health education.

A credit was assigned to a theoretical subject requiring 1 period of class time per week for 1 term, or to a practical subject requiring 2 periods of class time per week for 1 term. Until the post-1981 unit system, a unit corresponded to 2 periods of study per week per semester; 1 period covered 50 minutes.

During the mid-1960s comprehensive schools were established, which offer both academic and vocational education.

Since 1951 the Thai government has recognized the vocational schools as equal to academic schools. From 1960 courses have been available varying in duration from 1-6 years.

There are a number of private secondary schools run by missionary societies and Chinese and Muslim groups. The 1954 Private School Act stipulates the minimum standards required in buildings, teaching and equipment, and also how many hours of study are permitted in a language other than Thai (e.g. Chinese).

School equivalency

The School Equivalency Programme offers a variety of courses for people who need equivalency certificates for employment purposes (i.e. to bring them up to a recognized grade in the school system). Instruction is provided at 5 levels which are compared as follows:

Level 1 - primary grades 1 and 2
Level 2 - primary grades 3 and 4
Level 3 - primary grades 5 and 6
Level 4 - lower secondary (M1-3)
Level 5 - upper secondary (M4-6).

FURTHER EDUCATION

The Institute of Vocational Technology was established in 1974 to provide 2-year courses for students who have completed a course at a vocational college, and leads to a **Bachelor in Technology** (including vocational teacher training, engineering, business, home economics, fine arts and agriculture). The Institute has now been renamed the Institute of Technology and Vocational Education (ITVE), and also provides general trades teaching courses leading to a **Diploma** qualification (technician level). The Institute comprises a large number of constituent technical and business institutes, higher education and agricultural colleges.

A number of vocational agricultural colleges offer courses leading to a Higher Certificate in Agriculture. The Institutes of Agricultural Technology offer 2-year **Degree courses in Agricultural Technology**.

Thailand

HIGHER EDUCATION

This is provided by universities and private colleges. Most of the colleges have been established since 1969 and the passing of the Private College Act. Some universities have developed from training schools or colleges established originally by one of the various ministries, e.g. Thammasat University was originally the Law School of the Ministry of Justice.

The College of Education has been redesignated Sri Nakharinwirot University. Ramkhamhaeng University was established in 1972 as an open-access university which admits all qualified applicants. In 1978 Sukothai Thammathirat Open University was created by Royal Charter. It is empowered to award its own degrees. High school graduates or holders of Grade X Certificates, over 20 years of age, who have at least 5 years work experience are eligible for enrolment without any entrance examinations. In most other institutions some form of selective entry operates.

There is a common entrance examination for admission to all universities, and all institutions require a pass in English language. The common entrance examination is taken soon after the examinations for the M6. Since 1963 all applications have been dealt with by a Central Clearing House.

English is a compulsory subject for the first 2 years of university study, but not thereafter except in a few disciplines. **Bachelor degrees** are normally obtained after 4 years study, with 5 years for architecture and pharmacy and 6 for medicine and veterinary medicine. 2 years preparatory study are required for students wishing to study medicine, dentistry and pharmacy. An **Associate degree** may be awarded at the end of the first 2 years of a degree course.

Most institutions have facilities for postgraduate study. A minimum of 1 year's study is required to obtain a **Master degree**, with a minimum of a further 2 years for a **Doctorate**.

A credit system (comparable to that of the United States) was initiated in 1957 at this level and is now more or less nationwide, 144 credits being required for the award of a Bachelor degree. Examinations are given at the end of each semester and a cumulative grade-point average of not less than 2.00 is required to be able to continue on the course.

TEACHER EDUCATION

There are 3 types of teacher training institute:

Teacher Training Colleges offer 2- and 4-year courses but will eventually offer 4-year courses only from M6. The 2-year courses lead to the **Higher Certificate** which entitles the holder to teach at the lower secondary level. Since 1975 most colleges have been given degree-granting status and the 4-year course leads to a **B.Ed**. Certain colleges offer specialized courses (e.g. physical education, nursery teaching).

Sri Nakharinwirot University (formerly the College of Education) offers 4-year (from M6) and 2-year (from the Higher Certificate) courses leading to the **B.Ed**.

University faculties of education offer 4-year **Bachelor degree** courses, and a variety of postgraduate courses.

Togo

Togolese Republic

Education in Togo is centrally administered by the Ministry of Education and the Ministry of Technical Education and Professional Training. Educational standards are considered in West Africa to be high.

Education is compulsory to age sixteen.

The official medium of instruction is French although two local languages, Ewe and Kabiye, are being introduced into primary education. English is a compulsory subject throughout secondary education.

EVALUATION IN BRITAIN

School

Baccalaureat - generally considered to be between GCE O-level and A-level standards. For entry into higher education the host institution may require GCE A-levels.

Higher

Licence - generally compared to British Bachelor (Ordinary) degree standard.

MARKING SYSTEM

School

Baccalaureat is graded: mention passable, assez bien, bien, tres bien (highest).

Higher

Each faculty has its own system of examining, although grading is usually on a scale of 0-20 (maximum). Students are normally given the option of being evaluated on the basis of continuous assessment or by examination. Students whose performance is evaluated on the basis of continuous assessment and thereby pass or obtain an average of 10/20 in all major subjects during the school year are not required to take the written examinations in June. Those students who do not obtain a minimum pass in classwork during the year in all major subjects or those who have not been graded in all subjects for any reason, sit for the formal examinations in June. The results of major subjects are multiplied by a coefficient of 2:

16-20	tres bien
14-16	bien
12-14	assez bien
10-12	passable

SCHOOL EDUCATION

Primary

Children begin school at age 6 or 7. Primary schooling lasts 6 years, at the end of which pupils are awarded a **Certificat de Fin d'Etudes du Premier Degre** (CEPD)

Secondary

Pupils are streamed at the end of primary schooling for entry to the first cycle of secondary education. This cycle of lower secondary education lasts 4 years (6ieme, 5ieme, 4ieme, and 3ieme) after which students take the examinations for the **Brevet d'Etudes du Premier Cycle**.

Students are then streamed again and oriented into vocational or training institutes, or enter the university preparatory cycle at a lycee. This second cycle lasts 3 years (2ieme, 1ieme and terminal). On completion of this cycle pupils take the examinations for the **Baccalaureat** administered by the Office du Baccalaureat de l'Enseignement du Second Degre. The Baccalaureat can be taken in any of 5 options:

A humanities and philosophy
B economics
C mathematics and physical sciences
D applied sciences and mathematics
E science and technology.

English is an obligatory subject in the Baccalaureat, and at this stage all students will have completed 7 years of English study at school.

Students who do not pass the examinations at the first sitting in June may resit in September/October. A supplementary oral test may be taken after the written examinations.

The **Certificat de Fin d'Etudes Secondaires** is not the equivalent of the Baccalaureat, although it may be obtained at the same time. It represents class attendance in the last year of secondary school. If a student presents this, it often means that the student was not successful in passing the Baccalaureat examination.

Students may not be able to produce a transcript of marks for the Baccalaureat (the livret scolaire) as this is not generally given to the student, but can be obtained direct from a school.

Technical secondary

On completion of the 4-year cycle of lower secondary, students may go on to a 3-year cycle of technical secondary education culminating in the examinations for the Baccalaureat Technicien in option F (engineering and science) or G (business and commerce).

HIGHER EDUCATION

Until 1977 the university academic year ran from October to July; it now runs from September to June. It is rare for students to go straight through secondary school without repeating any year, and many students do not then go straight on to university. Most students do not begin their university studies until the age of about 22. All students who pass the Baccalaureat have the right to enter university and study the subject of their choice, although there is a special entrance examination for those who do not hold the Baccalaureat.

The Centre d'Enseignement Superieur was established in 1962 with buildings in Dahomey and Togo under an agreement between the governments of the 2 countries and the Government of France. In 1970 Dahomey decided to create its own national institution. The University of Benin was then established in Togo to replace the former Togolese part of the Centre. The University is French orientated and modelled on similar French institutions. In 1972 major reforms were put through affecting the curriculum and structure of courses.

The degree structure varies:

Faculte des Sciences et Faculte des Lettres:

The first cycle of 2 years study leads in the Science Faculty to the **Diplome Universitaire d'Etudes Scientifiques** (DUES), and in the Arts Faculty to the **Diplome Universitaire d'Etudes Litteraires** (DUEL). A further year of study leads to the qualification of **Licence**.

The Institut National des Sciences de l'Education (INSE) has recently been created and offers compulsory courses to be taken throughout the 3-year course leading to the Licence. In addition INSE offers a course leading to a Licence. Entry is generally based on the DUEL or DUES, although students from other faculties who have completed 2 years of undergraduate study are also admissible.

Ecole Nationale Superieure d'Administration et des Carrieres Juridiques

On completion of the first 2-year cycle students who have not performed outstandingly well in the earlier part of the course obtain the **Diplome Universitaire de Techniques Juridiques** (DUTJ), which is generally a terminal qualification. Those students who are proceeding to the second 2-year cycle do not normally obtain this qualification, and go on to take the examinations for the Licence.

Togo

Ecole Superieure de Techniques Economiques et de Gestion

A 4-year course leads to the Licence en Techniques de Commerce et Gestion or the Licence en Techniques Economiques.

Ecole Superieure de Mecanique Industrielle (ESMI)

This institution was established in 1972 to train engineers at 2 levels; Ingenieur de Realisation and Ingenieur de Conception. The short cycle lasts 3 years and leads to the qualification of Ingenieur de Realisation (advanced technician). Students wishing to obtain the Diplome d'Ingenieur de Conception are usually streamed out of the second year of the short cycle and then proceed to a further 3 years of study.

Ecole Superieure d'Agronomie (ESA)

This institute follows the same pattern of courses as the ESMI.

In 1975 the university began to offer postgraduate courses. In humanities, students on courses leading to the **Maitrise** have first to hold a Licence. They then have to obtain a second Certificat de Maitrise and submit a short thesis. In science the Maitrise is often obtained without candidates holding a Licence. The **Diplome d'Etudes Superieures** (DES) or the **Diplome d'Etudes Approfondies** (DEA) represents completion of a further 1 or 2 years of academic study beyond the Licence. Persons holding the **Doctorat de Specialite de Troisieme Cycle** will have completed 1 or 2 years study beyond the Maitrise or DES.

TEACHER EDUCATION

Primary

A 3-year course at the upper secondary level can be taken at a teacher-training college.

Secondary

A 1-year course at post-secondary level taken at a teacher-training college (Ecole Normale Superieure) leads to a professional qualification and entitles the holder to teach at lower secondary level.

Teachers of upper secondary education are trained in the school of arts, where they obtain a **Licence d'Enseignement** and a **Certificat d'Aptitude au Professorat de l'Enseignement du Second Degre/Secondaire** (CAPES) or the **Certificat d'Aptitude Pedagogique**.

Higher

Teachers at this level must hold the Doctorat du Troisieme Cycle.

The **Agregation de l'Enseignement du Second Degre** and the **Agregation de l'Universite** are certificates of outstanding proficiency in teaching and are obtained by examination before a committee. The agregation is _not_ in itself a degree, and requires no specific course or research qualifications.

Tonga

Kingdom of Tonga

Education is compulsory between the ages of six and fourteen.

The medium of instruction is Tongan, with English taught as a second language.

The academic year runs from January to December.

EVALUATION IN BRITAIN

School

Higher Leaving Certificate - generally considered to be below GCE O-level standard.

Tonga School Certificate - generally considered to be below GCE O-level standard.

SCHOOL EDUCATION

Primary

This covers 6 years, at the end of which pupils take entrance examinations to **Tyson College** and **Tonga High School**.

Secondary

This covers a possible 7 years. On completion of 4 years of secondary education, pupils take the **Higher Leaving Certificate**. Some schools go on to prepare pupils for the **New Zealand School Certificate** in the fifth year. Both these examinations will be replaced in 1987 by the **Tongan School Certificate** which will be taken in form 5. This Certificate is based on the New Zealand School Certificate.

The Higher Leaving Certificate will continue to be available in non-government schools.

Tonga High School prepares pupils for the **New Zealand University Entrance Examination**. Tyson College prepares pupils for the **Victorian Intermediate and Leaving Certificate** examinations (Australia). Pupils sit the **New South Wales Higher School Certificate** at 1 of the secular non-government schools.

Tonga

FURTHER EDUCATION

The Hango Agricultural College offers a 2-year course in agriculture, for those intending to become farmers/farm managers. The entrance requirement is the Higher Leaving Certificate, but candidates may be accepted without this.

HIGHER EDUCATION

Atenisi University (secular, non-government) runs degree courses.

The University of the South Pacific runs extension courses in Tonga.

Most students go to Australia, New Zealand, Fiji, Papua New Guinea and Samoa to pursue their studies.

TEACHER EDUCATION

There is 1 teacher-training college at Nukualofa. It offers a 3-year course leading to a **Diploma of Education** for teachers of primary and secondary schools. Until 1986, primary school teachers took a 2-year course.

At present, the entry requirement for the teacher-training college is the New Zealand School Certificate, but this may change in the future.

Trinidad and Tobago

Republic of Trinidad and Tobago

The education system is based on the British model.

Compulsory education is from age six to twelve.

The medium of instruction at all levels is English.

The academic year runs from September to June.

EVALUATION IN BRITAIN

School

GCE O- and A-levels - of the same standard as GCE O- and A-level examinations taken in Britain.

Caribbean Examinations Council Secondary Education Certificate - grades 1 and 2 at the general proficiency level have been equated to GCE O-level (grades A, B or C).

Higher

Bachelor degree - generally considered to compare to British Bachelor degree standard.

MARKING SYSTEMS

School

GCE O- and A-levels are marked as in Britain.

Trinidad and Tobago

Caribbean Examinations Council Caribbean Secondary Education Certificate subject examinations are taken at 3 proficiency levels:

basic proficiency
general proficiency
technical proficiency.

The 5 grades awarded have been defined as follows:

I	comprehensive working knowledge of the syllabus
II	working knowledge of most aspects of the syllabus
III	working knowledge of some aspects of the syllabus
IV	limited knowledge of a few aspects of the syllabus
V	insufficient evidence on which to base a judgement.

Higher

Bachelor degrees are awarded with the following classifications:

first-class honours
second-class upper division
second-class lower division

If the performance has been insufficient for Honours, the degree is awarded as a Pass.

SCHOOL EDUCATION

Primary

This covers 6 years (generally from age 5), culminating in the **11+ examinations**, which are being phased out.

Secondary

This covers a possible 7 years.

Until 1971 the first 5 years were served by the 5-year secondary schools, all-age schools, and the junior forms (i.e. junior streams) of the general secondary schools. Since 1971 a number of junior secondary schools have been established; these have expanded to become 5-year secondary comprehensive schools. The comprehensive and traditional academic secondary schools existed side-by-side for a time, but all education is being transformed into the comprehensive system. The latter culminates in the examinations for the GCE O-levels and, more recently, in the examinations of the **Caribbean Examinations Council** (see Appendix), on completion of 5 years, and for the GCE A-levels on completion of 2 years in the sixth form.

Under the comprehensive system there is a common curriculum for the first 3 years: agriculture; arts and crafts; electives; English; general science; industrial arts or home economics; mathematics; music; physical education; religious instruction; social studies; and Spanish. In the final 2 years offered by the comprehensive schools, there are 3 streams: academic, pre-technician or craft. The core subjects for all 3 streams are: English, mathematics, science, social studies, and Spanish. In the academic stream, pupils take more courses in mathematics, chemistry, physics, biology and English OR language arts (English, literature, Spanish and French) OR social studies (history, geography, economics and English).

Technical secondary

The Technical Institute offers technical and vocational courses in: business studies, engineering, surveying, home economics, and graphic and applied arts. Craft-level courses do not require O-levels for admission; they lead to the **National Craftsman Certificate**. Technician courses are from GCE O-level standard, and lead to the **National Technician Certificate**. Both Certificates are awarded after success in examinations by the National Examinations Council for Technical and Vocational Education of the Ministry of Education and Culture of Trinidad and Tobago.

FURTHER EDUCATION

The John Donaldson Institute in Trinidad offers high-level technician courses in engineering, business studies, and teacher training.

The Caribbean Union College was established in 1927 by the Seventh Day Adventists; it offers secondary-level courses leading to examinations for GCE O- and A-levels as well as a variety of post-secondary courses, including teacher training.

HIGHER EDUCATION

A campus of the University of the West Indies is based at St Augustine in Trinidad, where it opened in 1960. The campus houses the University's Faculties of Agriculture, Engineering and Law (first year only). It has facilities for education, natural science, social science, arts and general studies. The university became an independent degree-granting institution in 1962, although under its affiliation to the University of London it offered external degrees of that university until 1963.

The normal minimum entrance requirements for **Bachelor degree** courses are 5 GCE passes, 2 being at A-level. There is a lower matriculation level of 5 GCE O-levels; students who enter with this level take 4-year degree courses, the first year leading to the preliminary/NI examination. Bachelor degree courses normally last 3 years.

Facilities are also available for study leading to **Master** and **Doctorate** degrees.

A professional Law School is also sited near the University campus. It trains students for professional competence in both branches of the legal profession. Admission to the School is on the basis of the LLB degree.

Tunisia

Republic of Tunisia

Tunisia was a French protectorate from 1881 to 1956. The education system was originally modelled on the French pattern and only now is beginning to evolve a more specific Tunisian form.

Primary education is compulsory.

The medium of instruction in the primary school is Arabic, with French taught as a foreign language in the last three years. At secondary school, the humanities are taught in Arabic and the sciences and mathematics in French. English is the most common second foreign language (the first being French); it is introduced in the fourth year. The medium of instruction in the university is French, except in the department of Islamic studies, where it is necessarily Arabic, and the departments of foreign languages, where the medium is usually the language studied.

The academic year runs from mid-October to the end of June.

EVALUATION IN BRITAIN

School

Baccalaureat - generally considered to lie between GCE O- and A-level standards. For entry into higher education, the host institution may require British GCE A-levels in addition.

Higher

Tunisian university qualification, awarded with high average marks and obtained after 4 years university study - may be compared to a British Bachelor degree.

MARKING SYSTEMS

School
Marks are on a scale 0-20 (maximum); 10 is the pass mark.

16-20	tres bien	very good
14-15	bien	good
12-13	assez bien	fair
10-11	passable	pass
0- 9	fail	fail

The overall result of the **Baccalaureat** is determined by a system of co-efficients, varying between the main streams, applied to the subject scores.

Higher

The marking system used is as above. Tres bien is rare.

SCHOOL EDUCATION

Primary

The present primary course lasts 6 years, leading to a competitive secondary entrance examination. The Sixth Development Plan (1982-7) envisages the extension of basic education to 9 years, which will include an element of technical training, and of preparation for working life.

Secondary

The secondary system offers a short course of 3 years, mainly technical training, leading to a **Brevet de l'Enseignement Secondaire Professionel**; or long courses of either 6 years leading to a **Diplome de Technicien**, or 7 years leading to the **Baccalaureat** and so to university entrance. In the last 4 years of the Baccalaureat course, students specialize in Lettres, Sciences Mathematiques, or Sciences Techniques. A very few continue from the 6-year courses into a special seventh year, also leading to the Baccalaureat.

HIGHER EDUCATION

Tunisian institutions of higher education are under the supervision of the Ministry of Higher Education, or of the Ministry most appropriate to their speciality (e.g. Agriculture). All these institutions offer university-level qualifications, but usually only those under the Ministry of Higher Education are regarded as making up the <u>University of Tunis</u>. There is no overall university structure outside the Ministry of Higher Education.

University-level study is divided into 3 cycles of 2 years each; it is necessary to complete both the first and second cycles to achieve what in Britain would be regarded as a university degree. The actual title of the qualification awarded is no guide to the level reached, which should be assessed by the number of years, excluding repeating, spent in university studies.

Tunisia

The commonest qualifications awarded are:

Diplome (DUES, DUEL)	after the first 2-year cycle
Maitrise **Licence** (law, economics, theology) **Diplome d'Ingenieur** (agriculture)	after the second 2-year cycle
Diplome de Recherches Approfondies Diplome d'Etudes Approfondies Diplome Superieur	after the third 2-year cycle
Doctorat de Specialite Doctorat en Medecine Doctorat d'Etat	after 6 or more years

In some disciplines there is also a Tunisian form of **Agregation**, achieved by competitive examination.

TEACHER EDUCATION

Primary

Prospective primary school teachers attend secondary level Ecoles Normales.

Secondary

Secondary teachers are trained at the Ecole Normale Superieure or the Ecole Normale Superieure de l'Enseignement Technique, both of which have a structure similar to that of the regular university faculties, including a postgraduate cycle.

Turkey

Republic of Turkey

There is a centralized system of education in Turkey. The Education Law of 1973 led to radical reforms, including increased compulsory education (from six to eight or nine years). Implementation of this law, commencing in urban areas, began in 1982.

The medium of instruction is Turkish, except at the Middle East Technical University and Bogazici University, where it is English.

The academic year for schools, runs from September to June; and for academies and most universities, from November to June.

EVALUATION IN BRITAIN

School

Devlet Lise Diplomasi (State High School Diploma) and **Lise Bitirme Diplomasi** (Private High School Finishing Diploma) - sometimes considered between GCE O- and A-levels, but generally compared to GCE O-level standard on an individual subject basis where there are counterparts in the GCE syllabus and marks of over 50% have been obtained in individual subjects (except English language).

Devlet Lise Diplomasi (State Technical 4-year High School Diploma) and **Devlet Meslek Lise Diplomasi** (State Vocational or Trade High School Diploma) - have been considered on a similar comparative level.

Higher

On Lisans Pre-Licentiate Diploma - awarded on successful completion of a 2-year course at university, or from 1982, the new Yuksek Egitim Okulu (Higher School of Education). The former are available on a very limited number of subjects. Candidates must have chosen to enter these institutions on their entry form before taking the selection and placing university examinations at the end of their secondary education.

Lisans Diplomasi (Bachelor degree) - generally compared to British Bachelor degree standard.

Turkey

MARKING SYSTEM

School

From the time a pupil enters primary school up to the end of schooling he or she must pass in every subject in the class examinations outlined below to go on to the following year.

Elementary (primary-middle)

Primary section is marked on a scale of 1-5 maximum, with 2 as the minimum pass mark.

Middle section is marked on a scale of 1-10 maximum, with 5 as the minimum pass mark.

Pupils move on to the next class only if they have passed in every subject in the class examinations with a high enough average of their end-of-term average marks. Class examinations are set in the same way as for secondary school (see below) but with 2 written and 1 oral per subject per term.

Secondary

Marking is on a scale of 1-10 maximum, with 5 as the minimum pass mark.

3 written class-examinations and 1 oral per subject per term are set. To go on to the following year, a pass in every subject, whether or not connected with the pupil's stream, is necessary. An average is taken of the four marks in each subject at the end of each term; at the end of the second term, both terms' average marks in each subject are averaged once more. Examinations may be re-taken in June and/or September.

Failure means the pupil must prepare externally for the examinations.

9-10	A	pek iyi	very good
7-8	B	iyi	good
5-6	C	orta	average
3-4	F	noksan	fail
1-2	F	pek noksan	fail

Further

As for higher education, but there is a probationary period of 1-2 years for graduates of the Yuksek Egitim Okulu (Higher Education School). Marking is on a scale scale of 1-10, with 5 as the pass mark.

Higher

Undergraduates:

This varies from one university to another: numerical scale 1-10 (maximum), where 5 is the minimum pass mark; alphabetical scale A (maximum), B, C, D (minimum pass) and F (medicine and dentistry); grade-point average scale 0-4 (maximum). There is in some universities (e.g. Middle East Technical University) a credit-system for which the marking scale is 1-5, with minimum pass 2.60.

Master (by instruction):

Similar to undergraduate; credit system also followed.

Turkey

Doctorate:

As well as the usual 'research', candidates must pass examinations on their knowledge of a foreign language - in most cases English, closely followed by French and German. There are taught courses to be followed for a Ph.D., as in the American university system. A pass in all sections is stipulated before a candidate presents a thesis.

Docentship (post-doctorate):

Similar to the system for Doctorate. Candidature is not limited to those in normal university hierarchy but can be entered by professionals holding doctorates and giving lectures in their professional area at evening, or part-time university courses.

SCHOOL EDUCATION

Before 1973

Pre-primary

Limited facilities are available in urban areas for children aged 3-6 in nursery schools (Cocukokul) and kindergartens (Anaokul).

Primary (Ilkokul)

This covered 5 years, divided into 2 cycles of 3 and 2 years respectively, for children from age 6. The curriculum covered Turkish reading and writing, elementary arithmetic, geometry, drawing and handicrafts, music, physical education, history, geography, natural science, and religious instruction. On completion of the second cycle, pupils obtained the **Primary School Leaving Diploma**.

Before 1954

Secondary

This covered 7 years, divided into 3-year and 4-year cycles; then covered 6 years, divided into 3 years middle school (Ortaokul) followed by 3 years high school (Lise).

Middle school (Ortaokul)

The curriculum at the academic middle schools covered: Turkish, a foreign language (English, French or German), geography, history, mathematics, natural science, agriculture, commerce, art, music, physical education, handicrafts (for boys)/sewing and home economics (for girls). On completion of this cycle, pupils obtain the **Middle School Leaving Diploma**.

Turkey

High school (Lise)

Pupils who obtained the Middle School Leaving Diploma, could be admitted to the academic high school (Lise). The first year was common for all pupils and the curriculum covered: Turkish, a foreign language (English, French or German), mathematics, chemistry, physics, geography, history, and physical education. In the second and third years, pupils could specialize in science and arts. Subjects common to both specializations were: a foreign language, Turkish, chemistry, mathematics, physics, geography, history, and physical education. In 1973, civics and logic were added. Pupils taking the arts specialization also studied philosophy; those who took the science option also studied geology. Astronomy was added to both streams in the final year.

On completion of the second cycle, pupils took the examinations for the **Lise Diplomasi**. The examinations were taken in a minimum of 6 subjects and a pass in each subject was necessary.

Technical Secondary

At the Technical Institute (Sanat Enstitusu) pupils took a common first year with pupils from the academic Lises. Compulsory subjects taken from the first year included: bookkeeping, accounting, commerce, mechanics, materials and technical drawing. These were studied alongside the particular techniques of the chosen specialization. Courses lasted 3-4 years. Workshop practice increased after the first year. Pupils took examinations for the **Sanat Enstitu Diploma** on conclusion of the course.

Evening schools

From 1958 to August 1982 students could study at evening schools at middle school, high school, vocational and further education level. The duration was 1 year more than for day-school. However, this was stopped in 1982.

Higher

The 'Academies' of the 1970s became universities under the new Education Law of 1982.

From 1982

Pre-primary

Limited facilities are available in urban areas for children aged 2-5 in nurseries and kindergartens. What used to be pre-school year has now been added to the elementary or basic education period - in urban areas, and is to be 'phased in' gradually in other regions.

Elementary (basic education)

Primary section:

Pupils begin at age 5. The curriculum is as before, but no Diploma is granted at the end of this part of the first cycle.

Turkey

Middle section:

The curriculum is now: Turkish language and literature, mathematics, science, national geography, national history, citizenship, history of the Republic and Ataturk's Reforms, a foreign language (English, French or German), religious culture and civics, art/handicrafts, physical training and music. In 1983 this was expanded to include, in urban areas, compulsory training in playing a musical instrument (flute, recorder or mandolin).

On completion pupils obtain the **Basic Education Diploma**. The system of examination is the same as used for **Lise Diploma**.

Secondary

This covers the 1-4 year cycle at a high school (Lise). Pupils are granted the **Lise Diploma** on obtaining pass marks in all subjects in their classes examinations (see under MARKING SYSTEM).

Special state Lises (Anadolu Lises) and private high schools (Ozel Lises) covering the 'middle section and second cycle', offer instruction in some subjects (particularly science and mathematics) in a foreign language.

From 1984, 2 new types of state semi-English medium schools were established - Anadolu Technical High Schools and Anadolu Commercial High Schools (Teknik and Ticaret respectively). Entry to all of these special schools is highly competitive and by state examination.

There are also foreign schools, particularly American, and schools operated by and for religious and ethnic minorities.

Technical secondary

There are a few state technical high schools (<u>Teknik Lise</u>) with entry either from middle school - the last 3 years of basic education - or at high school level. Entry to either cycle is by state examination. Courses at middle school level may prepare for a specific skilled trade, or lead on to the second cycle of technical secondary education.

Subjects common to these and the academic high schools are: Turkish, a foreign language, geography, history, mathematics; subjects related to the pupil's craft or trade are also studied. Along with the subjects studied in common with the first year of an academic Lise are: bookkeeping, accounts, materials and technical drawing, and industrial equipment. On completion of the foundation year, pupils take 3 years specialization in one of the following areas: electrical techniques, electronics, communications, carpentry/woodwork, accounting, home economics, fashion, and decorative arts. On completion of the course, pupils obtain a qualification as a craftsman or technician in the field of specialization.

Since 1970, pupils who successfully complete the course at a technical Lise have been granted the right to sit the university examinations to compete for places (preferably at technical institutions) appropriate to the pupils' fields, but from 1985, in all subjects.

Turkey

State secondary vocational schools (Meslek Lises)

These run courses consisting of 2 cycles (3 + 3 years from the end of primary education/the end of the first cycle basic education) in: agriculture, fine arts, health, printing, religious instruction (which also has a course of 3 + 4 years cycles), tailoring, social services, and textiles. Pupils who successfully complete the second cycle have recently gained the right to sit the university higher education examinations for places closely related to the branch they have studied so far.

Trade schools (Endustri Meslek Lises)

These were established in 1969 to train workers in basic skills. They have 2 cycles, each of 3 years. Students at both types of Meslek Lise follow the same foundation year as in the Technical Lises and may continue at the latter providing they have very good marks.

Evening School

Since 1985, evening classes for secondary level have been 'phased in' again. The first year of the 4-year programmes began in October 1985; from 1986 there will be first and second year.

HIGHER EDUCATION

State universities

Holders of the Lise Diplomasi are entitled to take the state university entrance examination; those from technical or Meslek Lises may also compete for places in technical subjects. From 1955 to 1961 the universities each set their own entry examination. In 1962, entrance was centralized under the National Admissions policy (whereby all students from an academic Lise wanting to go on to a university course took the Inter-University Student Selection Examination, OYSM). This has been extended to include those from technical and vocational (Meslek) Lises. Up to 1981, there was only one general examination, the second being the placing examination. The examinations are highly competitive; the first includes tests in social sciences, languages and science. Placing is dependant on the student having the necessary marks in the area appropriate to the subject(s) the student has selected on the application form. A student who does not gain sufficient marks to enter the university and study the subject of first choice, may be relegated to another university to study another subject.

Courses, lasting 4 years, lead to the **Lisans Diplomasi/Bachelor degree** (at Middle East Technical University). Courses in dentistry, veterinary medicine, architecture and engineering generally last 5 years, with 6 years in medicine. At the technical universities a qualification in engineering takes 4-6 years to obtain. At the English-medium universities, Middle East Technical University and Bogazici University, where direct-course instruction is in English, students take an English language test on entrance to the university, which decides whether they can proceed directly to their degree studies or enter the 'Prep School' or preparatory year of English. This is also the case for medical studies at Hacettepe and Marmara universities, and dentistry at Hacettepe. The latter faculties are English-medium within Turkish-medium universities.

Turkey

A further 1-2 years lead to the **Yuksek Lisans Diplomasi/Master degree** (Middle East Technical University). At the other technical universities, students obtain the **Yuksek Muhendis Diplomasi/Higher Engineer's Diploma**. It is now compulsory for a candidate to hold a Master degree before going on to do research towards a Doctorate which consists of a 2-year instruction period plus 1 year of research.

<u>Schools of Higher Learning</u> offer 2-4 year courses of post-secondary professional training in commerce, tourism, and technical education. Students have to take the university admission and placing examinations to enter.

All institutions of higher education have been state institutions since 1971, when all private institutions were declared illegal. One important consequence was that Robert College, American in origin and previously run on American lines, became the State University of the Bosphorus (Bogazici University). The medium of instruction is still English.

<u>Private universities</u>

A decree has just been passed permitting the founding of private universities with the proviso that they should be Vakiflar, i.e. Special Foundations, run and founded. The first of these, the Bilkent University (set up and funded by the Hacettepe Foundation), had had its first intake of students in the 1986/7 academic year.

It has Faculties of Engineering, Computer Sciences/Engineering, Health (including those supplementary to medicine), Fine Arts, and part of the present Faculty of Fine Arts at Hacettepe University will be transferred here. There will also be a Department or School of Foreign Languages. There will be 2-year courses towards **On Lisans** as well as the normal 4-year degree courses in the fields of Computing and Health.

TEACHER EDUCATION

Primary

Until the early sixties, on completion of primary education in rural areas and lower secondary education in urban areas, pupils could work for 1-3 years as probationary teachers. They then took a course of training lasting 3 years. Until 1973, training consisted of a 3-year cycle at secondary level after 8-9 years of education (primary and intermediate). Between 1974 and 1980, it was increased to 5 years at a higher school of education.

From 1982 under the new education system, teachers of the new first-cycle (basic education - primary and intermediate: 9 years) must have completed 2 years at a Higher School of Education (Yusek Egitim Okulu) and 1-2 years as probationer teachers; they may also teach pre-primary level. Entry is via the university selection and placement examination.

Pre-school

From 1982:

Pupils must complete the Children's Development and Education Stream of the Girls Vocational Lise, Ankara; or the Girls Technical High School Education, Ankara.

Turkey

Secondary

Until 1982:

There was 3 years training at secondary level on completion of 9 years basic education. Students then took a 2-year course at a teacher-training school or a 3-year course at a teacher-training institute. After 1982, the old teacher-training institutes were abolished by YOK (Higher Education Board), and replaced by the new Faculties of Education in the universities.

From 1982:

On completion of 12 years education at school (primary, intermediate and high), students follow a 4-year course in a Faculty of Education, entrance is through the university selection and placement examinations. They are awarded a **Bachelor of Education** (B.Ed.) which is a recognized teaching qualification for secondary school teachers.

Before 1984 graduates of other Faculties could teach their subject at intermediate and high school by taking a Diploma or Master in Education at the Faculties of Education. However, this practise was abandoned in 1984 and all school teachers must now graduate from the Faculties of Education.

Uganda

Republic of Uganda

Until 1970, pupils took the examinations of the University of Cambridge Local Examinations Syndicate. In 1967, the East African Examinations Council (EAEC) was established, with Kenya and Tanzania as co-members. Collaboration with the University of Cambridge Local Examinations Syndicate in the administration of the East African Certificate of Education and the East African Advanced Certificate of Education continued until 1974. In 1971, Tanzania withdrew from the EAEC, and in 1980 Kenya withdrew. The Uganda National Examinations Board then took over the conduct of all examinations previously run by the EAEC, and also the Primary Leaving Examination formerly conducted by the Ugandan Ministry of Education.

There is no period of compulsory education.

The medium of instruction is English.

The school year runs from January to December, and the university year from July to March.

EVALUATION IN BRITAIN

School

Cambridge Overseas School Certificate East African Certificate of Education Uganda Certificate of Education	grades 1-6 are generally equated to GCE O-level (grades A, B, C)
Cambridge Overseas Higher School Certificate East African Advanced Certificate of Education Uganda Advanced Certificate of Education	grades A-E are generally equated to GCE A-level

Higher

Bachelor degree - Ugandan degrees are generally considered comparable to British Bachelor degrees.

Uganda

MARKING SYSTEMS

School

Cambridge Overseas School Certificate (COSC)　　　graded 1 (maximum)-9 (fail)
East African Certificate of Education, (EACE)
Uganda Certificate of Education (UCE)

Cambridge Overseas Higher School Certificate (COHSC)　graded A-F (fail)
East African Advanced Certificate of Education (EAACE)
Uganda Advanced Certificate of Education (UACE)

Higher

Bachelor degrees:

class I
class II i
class II ii
pass
fail

SCHOOL EDUCATION

Primary

This consists of a 7-year course for children mainly aged 6-14 years. At the end of 7 years pupils sit for the national examination, the **Primary Leaving Examination (PLE)**, which serves both as a terminal examination and a qualifying test for post-primary institutions.

The curriculum consists of: religious education, languages (English and vernacular), handwriting, numbers (maths), science (nature and health), art and crafts, music, PE and social studies.

Secondary

Until 1961: this covered 6 years plus 2 years in form 6.

Since 1961: it has covered 4 years plus 2 years in form 6. The curriculum covers English, general science, geography, history, home economics and needlework (girls), civics, metal science and woodwork (2 of these 3 for boys), mathematics, physical education, religious instruction, singing, arts and crafts. Languages, commerce and political education. Agriculture is compulsory in all secondary schools.

Until 1970: pupils could take the examinations for the **Cambridge Overseas School Certificate** (COSC) at the end of form 4 and for the **Cambridge Overseas Higher School Certificate** (COHSC) at the end of form 6.

From 1968 to 1980: pupils could take the examinations for the **East African Certificate of Education** (EACE) at the end of form 4 and, from 1969 to 1980, for the **East African Advanced Certificate of Education** (EAACE) at the end of form 6.

Uganda

Since 1980: when the Uganda National Examinations Body took charge of all school examinations, pupils have taken the examinations for the **Uganda Certificate of Education (UCE)** at the end of form 4 and for the **Uganda Advanced Certificate of Education (UACE)** at the end of form 6.

Technical secondary

Technical schools offer 3-year courses to pupils who successfully pass the Primary Leaving Examination. All technical schools offer full-time courses in the following: carpentry and joinery, brick-laying and concrete practice, plumbing, pottery, electrical installation work, leather tanning and shoe-making, tailoring, motor vehicle maintenance, tropical agriculture. Students sit for the **Uganda Junior Technical Certificate** examination. Qualifying students who do very well may join the Technical Institutes.

FURTHER EDUCATION

Uganda College of Commerce offers a 2-year course in business studies for pupils holding the COSC/EACE/UCE.

Technical Institutes offer 2-year courses leading to the **Uganda Technical Institute Certificate**. Students are usually selected from secondary school leavers who have obtained the Uganda Certificate of Education with credits in mathematics, physics and technical subjects.

Technical Colleges offer 2-year courses leading to the **Ordinary Technicians Diploma**. A further 2-year course leads to the **Higher Technicians Diploma**. The intake base is students with A-level certificates with at least 1 principal pass in physics, and a subsidiary pass in mathematics, or vice versa.

HIGHER EDUCATION

There is one university, Makerere. This was founded in 1922 as a technical college, became a university college with a special relationship with the University of London in 1950, part of the University of East Africa in 1963, and an independent university in 1971.

Admission to degree courses was similar to that in Britain, a minimum of 5 GCEs, 2 being at the Advanced level, but there is now a minimum of 5 GCE O-levels plus 1 or 2 GCE A-levels.

Courses leading to the award of a **Bachelor degree** in arts, science, agriculture and law last 3 years, with 4 years in veterinary science and technology and 5 years in medicine (the award of the title of Medical Doctor takes another 3 years, including the preparation of a thesis).

Bachelor of Philosophy degrees take 1 further year of study, and **Master degrees** a further 18 months. Research leading to a **Doctorate** lasts a minimum of 2 years after the award of the Master degree.

Certain certificate and diploma courses leading to various professional awards are also offered.

TEACHER EDUCATION

Primary

Lower: 4-year course for pupils who have completed a full course of primary education, leading to the **Grade III Teachers Certificate**.

Upper: 2-year course for holders of the COSC/EACE/UCE, leading to the **Grade IV Teachers Certificate**.

Secondary

The National Teachers' Colleges run 2-year courses for holders of the COHSC/EAACE/UACE, leading to a **Grade V Teachers Certificate**. There is also a 3-year up-grading course for grade IV teachers, leading to the Grade V Teachers Certificate. To teach in the sixth form, teachers must hold a **Bachelor of Education degree**.

Union of Soviet Socialist Republics

The main features of the education system are central control and the emphasis on uniformity throughout the USSR. The system is developed in accordance with the aims and guidelines of the National Five Year Plans. The main reforms have been:

1958 Law on strengthening the links of the school with outside life and further developing the system of public education ('Krushchev reforms'), which amounted to a reform of the entire system, with the emphasis on polytechnic and labour training;

1964 revisions of changes instituted under the Krushchev reforms, including decreasing emphasis on polytechnic education;

1966-70 measures for the further improvement of the work of the general secondary education school;

1973 Basic Law on Education, which consolidated previous changes, but did not include radical reforms.

Under the Krushchev reforms compulsory education was extended from seven to eight years. This was further increased in 1970 (under the Ninth Five Year Plan) to ten years.

The medium of instruction is Russian, although classes do exist in the other national languages.

The academic year runs from September to June.

EVALUATION IN BRITAIN

School

Attestat o Srednem Obrazovanii (Certificate of Secondary Education) - generally compared to GCE O-level standard, and is awarded on completion of grade 10.

Higher

Diplom ob Okonchanii Vysshego Uchebnogo Zavedeniya (Diploma Specialist) - generally compared to British Bachelor degree standard.

USSR

Diplom o Srednem Spetsialnom obrazovanii (Diploma of Specialized Secondary Education) - no British equivalent; awarded to technician personnel graduating from technical and medical colleges.

MARKING SYSTEMS

School and Higher

Marking is on a scale 1-5 (maximum), with 3 as the minimum pass mark. Marks of 1 and 2 are almost never awarded.

SCHOOL EDUCATION

Pre-primary

There are limited facilities for children aged 3-7 in kindergartens.

Basic/incomplete

This section of school education is sometimes referred to as incomplete, as pupils may stay on at school for a further 2-3 years 'secondary' education. Until 1959/60 this covered grades 1-7, divided into 2 cycles of 2 and 4 years respectively.

In 1960 it was extended to cover grade 8, the extra year being added to the first cycle. In 1964 the extra year was dropped, but basic and compulsory education was increased to cover grades 1-10 (including the previous period of 'secondary' education), and is sometimes now referred to as 'complete' secondary education; pupils may choose, however, to follow a course of specialized technical/vocational education for the final 2 years. Compulsory subjects are: Russian, mathematics, physical education and labour training in grades 1-10; literature and history in grades 4-10; a foreign language (usually English) in grade 5. More emphasis is given to science subjects in the final years. On completion of grade 10, pupils take the examinations for the **Attestat o Srednem Obrazovanii** (Certificate of Secondary Education).

Secondary

Until 1959 this covered 2 years; from 1959 to 1964 it was 3 years, and since 1964 it has covered 2 years but is now included in the period of basic and compulsory 10-year education. The curriculum covers Russian language and literature, history, the Soviet constitution, economic geography, mathematics, physics, chemistry, biology, astronomy, mechanical drawing, and general technical or agronomical education.

Special language and mathematics schools were established on an experimental basis in the 1950s, and since the mid-1960s they have become more widespread. For the mathematics schools, pupils are selected from age 15 on the basis of Olympiads (examinations). The curriculum covers general education and the advanced study of mathematics. There are no special entrance tests for the language schools, which children may enter at age 7. They begin to learn a foreign language in the second class. In the upper years, pupils study some subjects of the general education syllabus (e.g. history and geography) in the language of their specialization.

Technical secondary

Secondary specialized schools

On completion of 4 years education, pupils may enter one of these schools. They offer 3-year courses, including both general and vocational education, with the emphasis on the vocational elements (training in a great variety of occupations, including highly skilled technical and clerical jobs, nursing, library work, etc). Pupils who have covered 10 years (complete) education may take such a course in 2 years. On completion of the course, pupils may take the examinations for the **Attestat o Srednam Obrazovanii** (Certificate of Secondary Education), and are eligible to apply for a course of higher education.

Vocational technical schools

These are much more specialized, with emphasis on learning a trade. Before the 1958 reforms, there were a number of different types of course for pupils who completed 5-6 years elementary education. After the reforms, the courses were recognized and offered solely by vocational-technical schools for skilled workers; pupils could enter on completion of 8 years basic education. Since 1970, pupils have been able to enter the schools on completion of 10 years basic education, although some schools still offer courses for pupils completing only 8 years. Courses last between 6 months and 3 years and lead to a Diploma in a particular trade. Pupils may go on to a course of higher education with this Diploma by studying part-time (evenings or correspondence) at a Young Workers' School.

General secondary and secondary specialized education are also available part-time (evenings/correspondence) at Young Workers' Schools/Schools for Working Youth and Young Farmers' Schools/Schools for Rural Youth. This form of education is intended for young people who did not continue with full-time education after age 15. The curriculum covers essentially the same subjects as the full-time courses, and pupils who take and pass the examinations for the certificate of secondary education are considered for entry to higher education alongside pupils from the full-time courses. As the 10-year basic/complete courses become more fully implemented, so these schools will decline in importance.

Reform of General and Vocational Schools

From 1986

Under the guidelines for Reform of General and Vocational Schools, full secondary general education will last 11 years, instead of 10, with an additional year being introduced at the primary level. Schooling will begin at age 6, instead of 7. The transition to the new system will take several years. Practical measures are being introduced to suit the school system to the needs of the economy. There will be more emphasis on manual skills, starting at primary level.

The new structure is:

Primary school (including 1 year preparatory) - forms 1-4

Incomplete secondary school - forms 5-10

General secondary and vocational school - forms 10-11

USSR

After form 9 of secondary general education, pupils may continue education at:

General secondary school

Courses last 2 years. One day per week will be devoted to training in a production job appropriate to the area.

Vocational secondary school

The different types of vocational skills which exist presently are being reorganized to form one type, which has different departments offering training in skilled jobs and trades. The courses will generally last 3 years. There will also be 1-year courses for graduates of the eleventh year secondary general schools.

Secondary special educational colleges

These train middle-level technical personnel (nurses, technicians, etc.)

HIGHER EDUCATION

A variety of institutions offer courses at this level: universities (mostly in human and theoretical sciences), polytechnic institutes (specializing in engineering, science and technology), and specialized institutes. All institutions are administered by the state, and admission requirements, courses, etc., are standard throughout the USSR. Study fields are dictated by the National Plan, and quotas of study places available are laid down annually.

Admission is on the basis of success in a competitive entrance examination and possession of the Secondary School Leaving Certificate obtained on finishing a course of 'complete' education or its equivalent. Under the reforms of 1958, pupils who had finished secondary schooling were required to spend 2 years in productive work before they could be admitted to a course of higher education, and men were required to spend 2-4 years in military service. By 1966 the work requirement was more or less abandoned, but as the number of applicants exceeds the number of places available each year, many students will have obtained some work experience before beginning their course of higher education.

The first qualification, that of **Diplom ob Okonchanii Uchebnogo Zavedeniya** (Diploma Specialist) is normally obtained after a course lasting from 4-5 and-a-half years. The courses are lecture-intensive, with the emphasis on general education for the first 2-3 years, followed by intense specialization for the latter part of the course. Thus a degree would not be in civil engineering, for example, but in industrial construction. Students choose their specialization at the beginning of the course, and although they may change midway through the course, this rarely happens. There is a background of basic culture throughout the course; all students take compulsory courses in a foreign language, history of the Communist Party in the USSR, Marxist-Leninist political economy, and dialectical and historical materialism.

Students do not normally proceed directly to postgraduate studies, but this is possible. Admission to this period of study (aspirantura) is based on possession of the Diploma of Specialist and on success in the entrance examinations (subject of specialization, 1 foreign language, and the history of the Communist Party). The course lasts a minimum of 3 years, and the qualification obtained on successful completion of the course (including an examination) and submission of a thesis is the **Kandidat Nauk (Candidate of Science)**.

Until 1956, students could then obtain the **Doktoratura** on successful submission of a doctoral thesis. Since that time the only higher qualification to be obtained, the **Doktor Nauk**, has been awarded not on the basis of a formal course of study but in recognition of advanced original work.

The Patrice Lumumba People's Friendship University was founded in 1960 by the Soviet Government jointly with the Soviet Afro-Asian Solidarity Committee, the Union of Soviet Societies for Friendship and Cultural Relations with Foreign Countries, and the All-Union Central Council of Trade Unions, and offers courses for students from developing countries. Graduates receive a special diploma, the **Magister**, rather than the diploma awarded to students at other Soviet institutions of higher education.

TEACHER EDUCATION

Teaching at basic school level requires:

first cycle - originally 2 years increased to 4 years in the early 1960s at a Pedagogic Institute.

second cycle (grades 4/5-10/11) - Diploma of Specialist from a university.

United Arab Emirates

The United Arab Emirates (UAE) is composed of seven states: Abu Dhabi, Dubai, Sharjah, Ajman, Umm al Quywain, Ras al-Khaimah and Fujairah. The Federal UAE Ministry of Education came into being in 1972. Education follows the general 6-3-3 pattern.

The medium of instruction and examination is Arabic.

The school and university academic year runs from early October to mid-June.

EVALUATION IN BRITAIN

School

UAE Secondary School Certificate - may be compared to GCE O-level standard when marks of at least 50% (of the maximum marks in each subject) are obtained in subjects which have counterparts in the GCE syllabus (English language is not acceptable).

Higher

The 4-year UAE **Bachelor degree** is likely to be compared to a standard between GCE A-level and the British Bachelor degree. Students graduating with high grade point averages might be considered for postgraduate study in the UK, but may be required to do a qualifying year for admission to a research degree.

MARKING SYSTEMS

School

The UAE Secondary School Certificate shows the name of the subject studied; alongside this are four columns of marks (maximum, minimum, score obtained, and retake score). Subjects have different maximum or minimum scores, according to their weighting as regards the Certificate.

United Arab Emirates

Higher

The University of the United Arab Emirates at Al'Ain uses the following grading system (percentages):

90-100	A	4
80-89	B	3
70-79	C	2
60-69	D	1
0-59	E	0

The minimum pass grade is D (60-69%). Students must normally obtain approximately 120 credits for the award of the Bachelor degree.

SCHOOL EDUCATION

Primary

This is compulsory and lasts 6 years, generally from age 6. English is introduced at the fourth grade.

At the end of the primary education cycle pupils must sit an examination to proceed to the next cycle. The various subjects in the curriculum are given a certain weighting in the examination by means of different maximum and minimum marks.

Preparatory

A 3-year intermediate course with the same type of curriculum as at the primary level.

Intermediate secondary

A 3-year course consisting of a common first year followed by specialization in science or arts. At the end of the twelfth year students take the examinations for the **Tawjihiyya (Secondary School Certificate)** set by the Ministry of Education's Inspectorate, but eventually to be the responsibility of the Faculty of Education at the University of the UAE.

Technical/vocational secondary

After Independence, the 3 trade schools at Sharjah, Dubai and Ras al-Khaimah were upgraded from schools offering only a preparatory (intermediate) cycle to Technical Secondary schools offering both intermediate and secondary cycles. All students must take Islamic studies, Arabic, English and mathematics. In addition, in the intermediate cycle, courses are offered in general science, social studies, physical education, technical drawing, fitting, fabrication, electrical and woodwork. In the secondary cycle, courses are offered in physics, chemistry and engineering drawing, with 18 periods a week of machining, welding, automotive and electrical engineering for the first year and specialization in machining or welding or automotive or electrical engineering or electronics in the second and third years.

The intermediate cycle provides an engineering course for the introduction and acquisition of basic skills, leading to the **Intermediate Certificate** examination. At the end of the secondary cycle, a **Technical Secondary Diploma** is awarded.

There is an <u>Agricultural Secondary School</u> at Ras al-Khaimah which offers secondary (i.e. post-intermediate) courses of varying lengths in horticulture, animal husbandry, agro-engineering, general agriculture, canning industry, agro-economics, plant diseases and product marketing; all students also follow courses in Islamic studies, Arabic, English, mathematics and science.

The former Dubai trade school housed a commercial section which has since become an independent institution - the <u>Commercial Secondary School</u>. All students follow courses in Islamic studies, Arabic, English, economic geography, economic history, bookkeeping in Arabic and English, business accounts, government accounts, economics, secretarial training (in Arabic and English), business communications (in English) and typing in Arabic and English. Like the agricultural school at Ras al-Khaimah, the Commercial Secondary School only admits students who have passed through the preparatory (intermediate) cycle.

HIGHER EDUCATION

Courses started at the <u>University at Al-Ain</u> in 1977 in 4 faculties: Arts, Science, Administrative and Political Sciences, and Education. In 1978, the Faculty of Sharia and Law was added and in 1980 the Faculties of Agriculture and Engineering opened; a Faculty of Medicine is scheduled to open in 1986. Some postgraduate work started in 1983 and a postgraduate **Diploma in Gulf Studies** started up in 1984. There is also a Department of Higher Education, a Department of Student Affairs, and a Faculty of External Tutorial Studies which offers tuition to external students by means of centres in each emirate. In the student entrance procedure, UAE nationals are favoured in being required to achieve only a 55% pass mark in the final secondary school examination for admission to most faculties (although Administrative and Political Sciences still require 65% and Engineering 75%); other students must achieve 65-90% depending on area of study and nationality. Nationals below the minimum percentage can still be admitted after successful completion of a 1-term course in remedial studies.

TEACHER EDUCATION

Until the establishment of the University of the UAE in 1977 only 2 teacher-training institutes existed at secondary level. On completion of training, teachers could teach only in the elementary/preparatory cycle, as a university degree was required for teaching at a higher level.

United Arab Emirates

Teacher training has now become the responsibility of the Faculty of Education at the University, which concentrates on training secondary school teachers, and of the Federal Ministry of Education, which concentrates on in-service training at that level and pre-service training for primary school teachers. Efforts by the latter, however, have not been sufficient to cope with the need to train UAE nationals to replace the many foreign teachers in the country. Accordingly, a recent decree ordered an enquiry into the need for additional teacher training institutes.

United Kingdom

United Kingdom of Great Britain and Northern Ireland

Education is compulsory for children in the United Kingdom between the ages of five and sixteen, and about 95% of the school population attend a school maintained by public funds. The other 5% attend independent schools where the fees are paid by the child's parents. Education for children under five is not compulsory but may be provided by either maintained or independent nursery schools.

MARKING SYSTEMS

England and Wales

There are 2 secondary school certificates in England and Wales - the **General Certificate of Education** (GCE) and the **Certificate of Secondary Education** (CSE). From 1988 onwards the GCE (O-level) and CSE will be replaced by the **General Certificate of Secondary Education** (GCSE).

The GCE is conducted at 2 levels, Ordinary (O) and Advanced (A). There are no compulsory subjects at either level.

O-level candidates are awarded one of 5 grades (A-E), or are ungraded, in each subject. Grade E is the lowest level of attainment adjudged to be of sufficient standard for recording.

At A-level there are 5 official pass grades A-E, with 'A' as the highest grade, although a candidate not achieving the required standard may be eligible for N grade, from 1987 onwards, instead of a compensatory O-level pass. There are no absolute standards of grading at either O-or A-level. When marking has been completed, the chief examiners determine the grade boundaries in such a way that similar quality of work is awarded similar grades in successive years. The new examinations will have a new grading system.

The Certificate of Secondary Education (CSE) was introduced in 1965. Like the GCE, it is a single-subject examination. There are 6 grades ranging from 1 (the highest) to 5 (the lowest) and U (ungraded). Grade 1 is usually recognized as equivalent to a pass at GCE O-level grades A-C.

United Kingdom

From 1988 onwards the GCE O-level and CSE will be replaced by the new examination system, the General Certificate of Secondary Education (GCSE). This will be administered by 5 examining groups comprising GCE and CSE Boards. GCE A-level will continue. Courses for the GCSE were introduced in autumn 1986 for first examination in summer 1988.

Grading will be on a 7-point scale, A to G. Grades A to C will reflect standards at least as high as GCE O-level grades A to C, and grades D to G will correspond to the present CSE grades 2-5. A major difference between the old system and the new is that the GCSE will provide a more objective assessment of students. They will need to demonstrate specific levels of skills, knowledge and understanding. Subjects will be taught to reflect the different abilities of students and the assessment of a pupil's ability and achievement by the teacher will play a major role.

The government has further announced the introduction of **Advanced Supplementary** (AS) levels as part of the new examinations structures. These are designed to broaden the curriculum for A-level students. They are to be taken alongside A-levels over 2 years. They are to cover at least half the ground covered by an A-level in the subject concerned but demand the same intellectual standard. Two passes at AS level will be considered equivalent to one GCE A-level pass. The grades will be linked to A-level standards.

The counterpart in Scotland of the GCE is the **Scottish Certificate of Education** (SCE) examinations, which are conducted at 2 levels, Ordinary and Higher. The grading system at Ordinary level is as follows:

A	70% or more
B	60-69
C	50-59
D	40-49
E	30-39

The SCE Ordinary grade is being replaced by the new SCE Standard grade. The Standard and Ordinary will be equivalent grades operating in parallel for a transitional period until the latter disappears. The standard awards are based on a 7-point scale with grade 1 the highest and grade 7 the lowest. The award for each subject is an aggregate grade, representing the combination of the grades awarded for different elements within the subject. It has been decided that, at least for the transitional period, the minimum attainment for grade 3 will be equivalent to the minimum required before 1986 for an award of band C in the subject.

The Higher grade represents 1 further year of study and is taken commonly at the age of 17+ or 18+.

The grading system at higher grades is as follows:

A	70% or more
B	60-69
C	50-59

In addition there is a **Certificate of Sixth Year Studies** (CSYS) which may be taken by a pupil who is normally in the sixth year of secondary schooling (18+) who already has a Higher grade pass in the subject. In the CSYS there are no pass or fail grades, just 5 grades from A (highest) to E. Candidates can take a minimum of 3 subjects.

United Kingdom

In Northern Ireland, candidates may take the Northern Ireland GCE or the Northern Ireland CSE, which are equivalent to those examinations in England and Wales. From 1988 onwards they will take the Northern Ireland GCSE which is also equivalent to its counterpart in England and Wales.

SCHOOL EDUCATION

Schools maintained by the Local Education Authorities (LEA), of which there are 105 in England and Wales and 5 in Northern Ireland, may be divided into primary and secondary (2-tier system), or into first, middle and upper schools (3-tier system).

Pre-primary

There is no compulsory schooling for children under 5 in the United Kingdom. Many LEAs provide facilities for pre-school/nursery education, and these are staffed by qualified teachers and nursery assistants. Many children attend pre-school groups that are organized, independent of the LEA, by parents and voluntary organizations. Pre-school education is generally aimed at the 3- to 4-year-old age group, although it is not uncommon to find younger children in a nursery class/pre-school group.

Primary

Primary schools cover education from age 5 to 11, or, in Scotland and a few parts of England, up to 12 years. The age of transfer to secondary school may vary between 11, 12 and 13, or even 14, according to the individual LEA's policies. Primary schools are usually co-educational and have no centrally prescribed curriculum. Within the overall policy of the LEA, the headteacher of the school is free to devise the type of education best suited to the pupils in the school.

Secondary

These schools cover education from age 11 or 12 to a minimum school-leaving age of 16. Pupils can stay on, if they wish, for up to 3 years longer - about 9% of pupils in the maintained sector do so. There are 3 types of secondary school:

1. The comprehensive school caters for children of all abilities in the age group, allowing a wide variety of subjects in the curriculum (about 85% of secondary pupils in maintained schools attend comprehensive schools).

2. The grammar school provides a mainly academic course for pupils selected on the basis of their academic ability from age 11 to 18, or 13 to 18 in areas where there are middle schools.

3. The secondary modern school provides a general education with a practical bias up to age 16.

Maintained schools are predominantly day-schools, but some LEAs provide boarding facilities.

In 1965 LEAs were asked by the then Secretary of State for Education to draw up plans to reorganize all secondary schools along comprehensive lines. However, after the change of government in May 1979, sections of the Education Act relating to comprehensive education were repealed in the Education Act of 1979.

United Kingdom

The GCE O-level is taken by 15-16-year-old pupils at the end of their fifth year in secondary education. It can be seen as a school-leaving examination for those starting employment or as a guide to suitability for further study. The CSE is also taken by 15-16-year-old pupils in their fifth year of secondary education. It is designed to measure the attainment of 16-year-olds within the top 60% ability group, while the GCE O-level aims at the top 20%. The GCSE, which replaces both of these, is not intended for any particular portion of the ability range, but for all candidates who are able to meet the standards required for the awards of particular grades, in each subject.

Under the present system, no pupil need take either CSE or GCE examinations before leaving school at age 16.

GCE A-level is usually taken at the end of 2 years study in the sixth form, between ages 17 and 19. From September 1987, GCE AS levels will also be available over the same period.

In 1982 the Government announced plans to introduce a new examination at 17+. The **Certificate of Pre-Vocational Education** (CPVE) is intended for pupils with modest - or no - grades at the 16+ examination, who have taken a 1-year course with a practical bias.

FURTHER EDUCATION

Broadly, further education is the name given to all post-school education except courses leading to a degree or a teaching qualification. The further education sector includes both academic courses below degree level and training courses for those who wish to become craft workers and technicians for industry. Institutions offering further education include polytechnics, colleges of higher education, colleges of commerce and other colleges specializing in a particular field such as agriculture, building and nautical studies. In Scotland there are over 60 centres of further education, 14 central institutions and 9 colleges of education.

The entrance requirements vary according to the level of the course.

Vocational

The British education system offers facilities for obtaining all types of vocational education and training and is notable for providing alternative routes to higher qualifications for those unable to continue full-time education after leaving school. Many broadly vocational courses are available at the polytechnics and the 800 or so further and higher education colleges, while some university courses, such as medicine and engineering, are also vocational.

There is a great variety of courses for young people, leading to appropriate qualifications in many trades and occupations, ranging from lower-level courses which have few or no entry requirements, to courses of near degree level.

The City and Guilds of London Institute (CGLI) offers examinations at operative, craft and technician level. Most of the schemes offered are designed for students who work in industry and study part-time at technical colleges under day-release arrangements.

United Kingdom

The main body responsible for awards in technical and business studies is the **Business and Technician Education Council** (BTEC), which was formed by the merger of the Business Education Council (BEC) and the Technical Education Council (TEC) in 1983. The corresponding bodies in Scotland, the Scottish Business Education Council (SCOTBEC) and the Scottish Technical Education Council (SCOTEC), were likewise merged in 1985 under the title **Scottish Vocational Education Council** (SCOTVEC).

Many further education colleges offer courses in shorthand, typing, book-keeping and office studies. More advanced level work, however, is available in polytechnics or other colleges with a department of business studies. Management studies take place in polytechnics and other colleges.

A comprehensive guide to further education in the United Kingdom, the <u>Directory of Further Education</u>, is published annually by the Careers Research and Advisory Centre.

HIGHER EDUCATION

There are 46 universities in the United Kingdom, including the Open University. There are 30 polytechnics in England and Wales, 16 central institutions in Scotland, and a number of colleges and institutions of higher education.

Universities are empowered by Royal Charter to award their own degrees. In the polytechnics and other institutions, courses are validated and degrees awarded by the **Council for National Academic Awards** (CNAA), which has its own Royal Charter, or by universities. The use of external examiners ensures that comparable degree standards are maintained in different institutions and in different parts of the higher education sector.

Admission to degree courses

The usual minimum qualifications for entry to a first-degree course are passes either in 5 approved subjects, including 2 at GCE A-level, or in 4 approved subjects, including 3 at A-level. A student who holds an **International** or **European Baccalaureate** will be considered for admission by all universities and polytechnics. These qualifications, whether obtained in the United Kingdom or in another country, do not automatically entitle the holder to a place in a university or polytechnic. Entry is competitive, and the final decision on admission is made by the individual institution. Nor is there any automatic granting of credit for studies already completed, either in the United Kingdom or elsewhere.

First degrees

Most first degrees are called **Bachelor of Arts** (BA) or **Bachelor of Science** (B.Sc.). but there are also **Bachelor of Education** (BEd) **Bachelor of Engineering** (BEng) and so on. However, at Scottish universities, first degrees in arts are generally called **Master of Arts** (MA) though this practice is not followed by CNAA in Scotland, which awards Bachelor degrees.

United Kingdom

At the universities, first-degree courses in arts and science are of 2 main kinds: those in which students specialize in 1 or 2 subjects and those which allow study of a wider field. The former kind is usually called a **degree with Honours** and is awarded with the classifications first, upper or lower second and third. The term **joint** or **combined honours** degree is sometimes used for degrees with specialization in 2 (or more) subjects. Degrees obtained at the end of the less specialized type of course are usually unclassified. The title of a first degree does not necessarily indicate the subject studied; some institutions award a **Bachelor of Arts** in almost every discipline, including science and engineering.

First-degree courses in arts and sciences normally last 3 or 4 years, except those in medicine, dentistry and veterinary science, which take 5 or 6 years.

Postgraduate degrees

Postgraduate degrees are of 2 kinds: higher degrees by examination and higher degrees by research. There are also postgraduate certificates or diplomas offering vocational training or a professional qualification. These usually require 9 months of full-time study. They can be qualifications in their own right, or they may be integrated within a Master degree programme.

A **Master** degree is usually awarded after at least 1 year's study which may include some research. This can be either a **Master of Arts** (MA) (arts, social science) **Master of Science** (MSc) (science, technology) **Master of Education** (MEd) (teacher education) or **Master of Business Administration** (MBA) (business, management). The **Master of Philosophy** (MPhil) is a research degree obtained by thesis, which normally takes 2 years. In some institutions **Bachelor of Philosophy** (BPhil) or **Bachelor of Literature** (BLitt) may be awarded for postgraduate work. Cambridge graduates, after a specified number of years, can obtain an MA from their university without any further study, on payment of a fee.

The degree of **Doctor of Philosophy** (PhD or DPhil) is awarded after at least 2 years' research and indicates a higher level of achievement than a Master degree in the same subject. The Ph.D. thesis is expected to be an original work and to make a definite contribution to knowledge. Other doctorates, for example, **Doctor of Letters** (D.Litt.) and **Doctor of Science** (D.Sc.), are conferred only upon scholars distinguished by outstanding contributions to knowledge, usually graduates of the university concerned. Senior doctorates are awarded to established scholars, most often on the basis of their published work.

The Open University

The **Open University** provides part-time first-degree courses, mainly for UK residents, using a combination of television and radio broadcasts, correspondence texts and summer school, together with a network of study centres which provide counselling and tutorial help. No formal academic qualifications are required to register for these courses and credit exemption is given to students who held certain qualifications. Its degrees are comparable in standard to those of other universities. The first degree (BA) is a general degree awarded on a system of credits for each course completed. The Open University admits full-time postgraduate students to read for higher degrees.

United Kingdom

The Polytechnics: CNAA

These were created between 1969 and 1973 by the amalgamation into new institutions of major colleges of technology, of commerce and of art and design, many of which had a long history of teaching at degree level. Their purpose is inherent in the title polytechnic which means 'many arts, many skills' - they encompass courses in the sciences, technology, business studies, accountancy, law, architecture, fine art, fashion, librarianship and the humanities. They provide a wide spectrum of education. Their emphasis is vocational.

First degree courses are studied by over two-thirds of the full-time and sandwich students in polytechnics. These courses are usually three years in duration for full-time courses and four years for sandwich courses in which full-time attendance at the polytechnic is combined with interspersed periods of training related to the course. Usually there is a total of about one year for the training element of the course - this may be arranged as a complete year (usually between the second and final years) or as two or three shorter periods. Many polytechnics offer degrees with a modular structure which enables students to choose from a wide variety of subjects and to study some unusual combinations. Some degree courses offered, such as in Surveying, Tourism, Art and Design and Sports Studies, are little taught in the universities. These degrees, awarded under the aegis of the **Council for National Academic Awards** (CNAA), are comparable in standard with degrees granted and conferred by the universities and are validated and reviewed thoroughly each five years. A number of the polytechnics are now able to validate their own courses under special Institutional Agreements with the CNAA.

Polytechnics also provide courses in a wide range of scientific and technological subjects and in business studies which lead to the **Higher National Certificates** and **Diplomas** of the **Business and Technician Education Council** (BTEC). In many polytechnics these schemes give students the opportunity to transfer, at appropriate stages, to a degree course or another degree-level course. While BTEC Higher award courses normally follow on from lower level BTEC courses, there is usually provision for entry direct from school with appropriate GCE passes (including one 'A' level) or equivalent qualifications.

The Colleges and Institutes of Higher Education

The colleges and institutions of higher education emerged from the reorganisation of higher education in Britain in the 1970s to form a sector of higher education alongside the polytechnics and universities. A total of 55 colleges of higher education and institutes have developed from varied origins - some are former colleges of education which continue to offer teacher training courses only while others are colleges of education which have added general higher education courses to their programmes.

The colleges and institutes offer courses at certificate, diploma, first degree and postgraduate degree levels - the majority of awards are validated externally by universities, the CNAA or BTEC. The training of teachers remains one of the main functions of many of the colleges and institutes of higher education. Minimum entry qualifications to courses are the same as for admission to the polytechnics or universities.

Professional bodies

In the United Kingdom, professional bodies set standards in such fields as accountancy and engineering. Degrees in a particular subject may give exemption from the academic requirements laid down by a professional body for admission to a particular level of membership. Often these bodies conduct their own examinations, but preparation for them is offered by polytechnics, central institutions and other colleges. Some Business and Technician Education Council (BTEC) National and Higher National Awards are also accepted for partial or complete exemption.

A comprehensive guide to British educational, technical, professional and academic qualifications, British Qualifications, is published annually by Kogan Page.

TEACHER EDUCATION

Pre-primary

It is necessary to have an approved teaching qualification to teach in a pre-school group or nursery school. This can either be the same qualification required for primary and secondary teaching (see below) or a specialist qualification from the **National Nursery Examination Board** (NNEB). An NNEB qualification will also enable the holder to teach in day-nurseries and hospitals for young children. In nursery schools, an NNEB holder would work to a qualified teacher.

Primary and secondary

All teachers in maintained schools in England, Wales and Northern Ireland must have qualified teacher status, which they gain after they have satisfactorily completed a 1-year probationary period in a school.

There are now 2 main routes to qualified teacher status. At undergraduate level, there are courses at universities, polytechnics, colleges and institutes of higher education and other non-university institutions leading to the **Bachelor of Education** (B.Ed.) degree, either after 3 years without Honours or after 4 years with Honours. Alternatively, those who already hold a first degree may undertake a 1-year course leading to the **Postgraduate Certificate in Education** (PGCE) in a university, polytechnic or other higher education institution.

There are exceptions to this general pattern:

> A few institutions, mainly universities, offer concurrent courses (normally of 4 years) leading both to a degree (other than a B.Ed.) and to a teaching qualification.

> People with relevant qualifications below degree level and with practical experience in business studies, music and craft, design and technology may qualify to teach by taking a 1-year non-graduate **Certificate in Education** course. In music the last year of entry to such courses was the academic year 1983/4.

More recent graduates in mathematics and some sciences have until now been able to enter teaching in secondary schools without undertaking professional training, because of shortages of teachers in these subjects. The Government announced its intention to withdraw this general exception with effect from 31 December 1983 and since this date such candidates have been nominated by LEAs for exceptional recognition as qualified teachers in individual cases where this is justified on supply grounds.

Graduates who obtained their degrees before January 1974 may teach in secondary schools without having taken a course of professional training, and those who graduated before 1 January 1970 may teach in primary or special schools.

United Kingdom

For those who have not decided on a teaching career, a new type of higher education course, lasting 2 years and leading to a **Diploma of Higher Education** (Dip.HE) has been introduced. The Dip.HE is a qualification in its own right, but at some colleges it is possible to transfer from a Dip.HE course to the third year of a degree course. Some colleges also allow transfer from a BA or B.Sc. to B.Ed., or vice versa, at some stage during the first 2 years.

Normal minimum entry requirements to a B.Ed. course or for a Dip.HE course are 2 GCE A-levels plus 3 GCE O-levels (grade C or above) or CSE grade 1s (or an equivalent qualification).

In line with the policy of improving minimum standards in the teaching profession, evidence of competence in English language and mathematics is required from those who completed teacher training at the end of the 1983/4 academic year or thereafter. For school or college leavers or graduates this means having grade Cs or above in mathematics and English language at GCE O-level (or their equivalent) for entry to a training course.

There is no upper limit for entry to training or teaching, but mature entrants will have to satisfy the college authorities that in English language and mathematics their competence is comparable to the requirement already mentioned.

The following qualifications are still accepted by the Department of Education and Science (DES):

2-year Certificate of Education (Cert.Ed.): the last entry on these courses was September 1959

3-year Certificate of Education: the last entry was September 1979. This was introduced in September 1960 following the extension of the Certificate from 2 to 3 years.

SPECIAL EDUCATION

To teach blind or deaf children, or children with partial hearing, in special schools, teachers must have additional specialist qualifications. To teach children handicapped in other ways, whether in a special or ordinary school, specialist qualifications are not obligatory. Some further education establishments offer courses for teachers of children with special educational needs.

NORTHERN IRELAND

In Northern Ireland teacher training takes place in the education departments of the 2 Universities, in 3 colleges of education and 1 technical college. The principal courses are the Certificate (3 years study) and the Bachelor of Education (4 years) but there are also 1-year courses for graduates or holders of other appropriate qualifications.

United Kingdom

SCOTLAND

Teachers in Scotland are required to be registered with the General Teaching Council for Scotland. To be eligible for registration it is necessary to hold a teaching qualification awarded by a Scottish college of education or an equivalent qualification approved by the Council.

The following are the 3 main routes to teaching in a Scottish primary school:

- 3-year course for non-graduates at a college of education
- university degree followed by a 1-year course at a college of education
- 4-year course at a college of education, leading to the award of the degree of Bachelor of Education, in which academic studies and professional training are taken concurrently.

From the beginning of the 1984/5 academic session, admission to the 3-year course for non-graduates or to the existing B.Ed. degree courses ceased. A new 4-year degree course for primary teachers was introduced. Candidates seeking a qualification to teach an academic subject at secondary level must hold an appropriate university degree or an equivalent qualification and must undertake a 1-year course at a college of education. Most Scottish colleges of education also offer 4-year courses leading to the B.Ed. degree. Candidates seeking a qualification in a practical or aesthetic subject may take one of a wide variety of courses. Some of these are concurrent courses of education and training provided by colleges of education; others are provided by institutes of higher education and must be followed by a 1-year course at a college of education. It is not always necessary for teachers in the independent section to have a teaching qualification.

United States

United States of America

There is no federal ministry of education in the United States to regulate standards or oversee the establishment of institutions. Education is the responsibility of the individual states.

In most states education is compulsory from age six to sixteen.

The school year runs from September to June.

EVALUATION IN BRITAIN

School

High School Graduation Diploma - generally accorded GCE O-level status, when an average grade of at least C is obtained in subjects which have their counterparts in the GCE syllabus, and have been studied for 3-4 consecutive years at high school.

US students are usually required to have studied for 1 or 2 years at a college/university before being considered eligible for entry to British degree courses. However Scottish universities and the Joint Matriculation Board of the Universities of Manchester, Liverpool, Leeds, Sheffield and Birmingham will consider high school graduates whose qualifications include a satisfactory performance in the Scholastic Aptitude Test and Achievement or Advanced Placement Tests.

Higher

The American system of education lays emphasis on breadth of study. A typical undergraduate may not devote more than a third of the studies for his or her degree to the main subject of specialization (major). American graduates holding Bachelor degrees, awarded with good grade-point averages by accredited institutions, are considered for postgraduate study in Britain. The courses completed are taken into consideration, with particular reference to the major, and the quality and reputation of the American institution is also taken into account.

The Associate degree (2 years) is generally compared to GCE A-level standard. Courses of a more vocational nature may be compared to the BTEC National Certificate/Diploma, formerly ONC/OND.

In terms of specialization, the American Master degree is often compared to the British Bachelor degree (Honours).

United States

MARKING SYSTEMS

School

The High School Diploma is awarded on the basis of continuous assessment, during which the student must obtain 14-16 credits or units over 4 years. To earn a credit/unit the student must study a subject for 1 year, pass the prescribed tests and complete written assignments.

The grading system used is as follows:

A	excellent
B	good
C	average
D	pass
E	fail

Students entering higher education in the United States would generally need an average of grade C or better in the High School Diploma.

Higher

Institutions of higher education use the credit system. This means that each course earns a specified number of credits/units/hours depending on the work involved. The course grades or marks constitute the basis for evaluating the student's academic performance:

A	excellent	4.0
B	good	3.0
C	average	2.0
D	pass	1.0
E	fail	0

Students should maintain an average of C or better to remain in good academic standing.

Academic achievement is measured by grade-points. On the 0-5 point scale, each credit hour with a grade of A earns 4 grade-points, B earns 3, C earns 2, D earns 1, and F earns no grade-points. The student's **grade-point average** (GPA) is calculated by dividing the total number of grade-points (reached by multiplying the grade-point for each course by the credit hours of the course) by the total number of credit hours of enrolment. Students must normally maintain a minimum GPA of 2.0 to remain in good academic standing.

Accreditation

There is no central body in the United States which ensures that educational institutions maintain high academic standards. This work is carried out by the 6 regional accrediting associations: the Middle States Association of Colleges and Secondary Schools, the New England, the North Central, the North West, the Southern, and the Western. Accreditation is the process whereby an agency or association grants public recognition to a school, institute, college, university or specialized programme of study, which meets certain established qualification and educational standards. This

United States

is determined through initial and periodic evaluations. The essential purpose of the accreditation process is to provide a professional judgement on the quality of the educational institution or programme. Universities and colleges may also acquire professional accreditation for the courses they offer (e.g. engineering, business), awarded by the responsible professional bodies in the United States.

SCHOOL EDUCATION

Elementary

Children normally enter grade 1 at age 6, after an optional year in kindergarten, and attend elementary school for 6 years.

Junior high

Students normally attend junior high school for 3 years.

Senior high

Students normally attend senior high school for 3 years (grades 10-12). By the beginning of grade 10, they must decide whether to take an academic course, a vocational course or a general course, consisting of both options. All courses lead to the High School Graduation Diploma, awarded to students who have successfully completed 14-16 credits with an average of grade D.

Some school districts may follow an 8-4 year pattern, rather than the 6-3-3 pattern.

The credits/units which make up a High School Diploma are recorded on a transcript, which will indicate the grades earned for each course. If so instructed by the student, the school will send copies of transcripts to anyone who needs to see them. A typical academic (College Prep.) Diploma might consist of 4 years for English, and 3 years for mathematics (algebra I and II and geometry), with the remaining 8 or 9 units spread over foreign languages, social sciences and natural sciences.

Tests

College/university admission tests

In addition to the High School Diploma, many universities require admission tests. The most frequently used is the College Board Admission Testing Program (CB/ATP), consisting of the **Scholastic Aptitude Test** and **Achievement Tests**. Some universities may ask students to take the **American College Test** (ACT).

Scholastic Aptitude Test

This 2-and-a-half hour test consists of five 30-minute timed sections, testing verbal and mathematical ability. The score reports show sub-scores for each section of the test, percentile ranks (to show how the student scores in relation to the other students taking the test) and scaled scores, which run from 200 to 800, in each section. A combined score of around 1,300 or above is usually required for entrance to prestigious universities. Students often quote one total score by adding the two scaled scores together.

United States

700 +	excellent
600 +	very good
450-550	average
200-400	generally unacceptable

Test of Standard Written English (TSWE)

This is also included in the administration and examines knowledge of the mechanics of written English. This test is used by colleges primarily for placement purposes.

Achievement Tests

These are 1-hour, multiple-choice tests which measure knowledge in specific subjects. There is a choice of 15 subjects and most colleges which require Achievement Tests ask for 3.

American College Test (ACT)

This consists of 4 tests, each lasting 35-40 minutes in English, mathematics, social studies and natural sciences.

Score range		
	1-33	English
	1-36	mathematics
	1-34	social studies
	1-35	natural sciences

The average of these scores is called the composite score.

Advanced Placement Tests

These tests are set by the College Entrance Examination Board and offered annually to gifted high school students to demonstrate university-level achievement. In the examinations, students answer essay questions, having followed a prescribed syllabus which is intended to compare to the standard of the first year of a Bachelor degree. The grading system used is on a 1-5 (maximum) scale. Students achieving scores of 3, 4 or 5 may be placed in the second-year courses for a given subject.

Some 29% of secondary schools offer this course to 16% of their university-bound students. The number of students sitting these exams has increased tremendously in the past few years. In 1983, 182,000 sat Advanced Placement Tests; in 1986 this number had nearly doubled to 350,000.

Essays ('free-response' sections) are graded by a national group, comprising school and university teachers, overseen by a chief reader. Multiple-choice questions are graded separately by the Educational Testing Service in Princeton, New Jersey. Many tests incorporate both formats. In 1986, the mean grade was 3.10, with 14.2% achieving 5.

English proficiency tests

Students whose mother tongue is not English normally have to take the **Test of English as a Foreign Language** (TOEFL). This consists of a 2-hour, multiple-choice test, involving listening comprehension, reading comprehension/vocabulary and structure/written expression. Scores range from 20 to 80. The overall score for the entire test ranges from 200 to 800. Most American universities and colleges require an overall score of 550+.

United States

FURTHER EDUCATION

Associate degree

Community and junior colleges provide courses for vocational, technical and academic study, leading to an Associate degree after 2 years of study as well as shorter certificate courses. A 'terminal' Associate degree tends to be vocational or technical training, while a 'transfer' programme provides the core curriculum preceeding the final 2 years of a Bachelor degree. In some states, notably California, 'articulation' agreements exist, whereby a student who successfully completes a prescribed curriculum can automatically transfer to a state university to complete the final 2 years of a Bachelor degree. Many students also transfer to private colleges.

Community colleges are usually locally controlled and publicly financed for the benefit of the nearby population. This option is attractive to students because of the low fees for tuition and the ability to commute from home.

General Education Development (GED) Tests

Adults who did not acquire a High School Diploma while at school, foreign students, etc., may take GED tests, which are set nationwide and consist of 5 multiple-choice tests. These are designed to investigate correctness and effectiveness of expression, interpretation of reading materials in the social sciences, interpretation of reading materials in the natural sciences, interpretation of literary materials, and general mathematical ability. Students who achieve an average GED score of 45 may be awarded a **High School Equivalency Diploma** by the State Department of Education concerned. Many American universities will accept the GED in lieu of the High School Diploma, provided average scores of 50 are obtained.

HIGHER EDUCATION

Degree courses are offered by universities and colleges. Universities and colleges are of equal academic standing, but colleges mainly award undergraduate qualifications. Liberal arts colleges (originally entitled liberal arts and sciences colleges) were founded to provide academic rather than professional education, although all now offer some professional courses. Training for some professions, e.g. medicine and law, is undertaken at postgraduate level only.

The Bachelor degree involves 4 years of academic study:

First year - freshman
Second year - sophomore
Third year - junior
Fourth year - senior

Courses taken in the first 2 years are referred to as 'lower division courses' and those in the last 2 years as 'upper division courses'.

United States

The degree has 3 components: core courses (general education in various fields); the major field; and electives or options. During the first 2 years students will take their core courses, introductory courses to their major fields, and some electives. During the last 2 years they concentrate on courses in their major field and also take some electives which may complement or support the major.

A typical undergraduate will enrol in 4 or 5 courses each term, representing 12-18 credit hours. The semester system, used by most colleges and universities, consists of two 14- to 18-week terms each academic year. Normally a student must complete 120 semester credit hours or 8 semesters for a Bachelor degree, and maintain a minimum grade-point average of 2.00 to remain in good academic standing.

Honors degrees

Universities may offer various academic honours. The terms 'cum laude', 'magna cum laude' and 'summa cum laude' indicate that the student may possibly have graduated within the top 20%, 10% or 2% of that year. Each university designates different percentages. Alternatively, some may use a fixed grade-point average instead of a percentile curve.

The term 'Honors program' generally means that the student took a particularly rigorous academic programme, but did not take additional course-work. It may indicate the submission of a special 'Honors' thesis.

Higher degrees

The Master degree involves 1-2 years of full-time academic study. A thesis is often an option. This degree is the entrance requirement for several professions, including teaching in secondary schools and junior colleges.

The Doctor of Philosophy (Ph.D.) usually involves 4-5 years study/research beyond the Bachelor degree. Candidates must complete taught courses lasting up to 2 years, which culminate in a qualifying examination, and may include proficiency in 1 or 2 languages. Students then embark on their doctoral thesis.

TEACHER EDUCATION

Teacher education in the United States is offered exclusively at the higher education level by universities, state colleges, liberal arts colleges and special schools. The minimum requirement for teaching at elementary or secondary level in any of the 50 states is the Bachelor degree, while almost half of the states require teachers to obtain a postgraduate degree within a given period.

In-service courses and workshops are available to serving teachers.

United States

ADULT EDUCATION

This sector has expanded more rapidly than any other during the last 15 years. The motivation comes from 2 sources. The universities/colleges themselves wish to make economic use of their plant and facilities outside normal academic terms, while state authorities have increased certification requirements in many fields, particularly health and education. The unit system which forms the basic structure of American higher education makes it flexible and easily adaptable to part-time study.

At least half the universities in the United States offer part-time courses, specially designed for mature students, through weekend, evening and summer courses, but also through correspondence.

In addition to degree-granting institutions, community colleges have always played an extensive part in adult education. Co-operation with industry to complement on-the-job-training, and 'distance learning', through the use of audio-visual equipment to link work-places with colleges is fairly common.

Uruguay

Eastern Republic of Uruguay

Education was compulsory for six years until 1972, but is now for nine years.

The medium of instruction is Spanish.

The academic year runs from March to November.

EVALUATION IN BRITAIN

School

Bachillerato - generally considered to compare to GCE O-level standard.

Higher

Licenciado - may be considered to compare to British Bachelor degree standard.

MARKING SYSTEMS

School and Higher

Marking is on the scale 0-12 (maximum), with 3 as the minimum pass mark.

12	sobresaliente (S)	excellent
11	sobresaliente (SMB)	
10	muy bueno sobresaliente (MBS)	
9	muy bueno (MB)	very good
8	muy bueno bueno (MBB)	
7	bueno muy bueno (BMB)	
6	bueno (B)	good
5	bueno regular (BR)	
4	regular bueno (RB)	
3	regular (R)	average
2	regular deficiente (RD)	
1	deficiente regular (DR)	
0	deficiente (D)	

Uruguay

SCHOOL EDUCATION

Pre-primary

This is available from age 3 to 5.

Primary

This covers 6 years, from age 6 to 7.

Secondary

Until 1978:

This covered 6 years divided into a 4-year lower cycle and a 2-year higher cycle. Final-year pupils could specialize in law, agricultural science, architecture, economics, engineering or medical science.

The Reform Plan introduced, into a limited number of schools, the pattern of 6 years divided into 5 years (again subdivided into 3 plus 2) plus 1 year; this system is being phased out.

Since 1978:

Under the Reform Plan of 1976 schools are now operating on the system of 3-year ciclo basico followed by a 3-year ciclo diversificado. The curriculum of the ciclo basico covers Spanish, mathematics, French, biology, history, moral and civic education, geography, physical education, and manual arts. The first year of the ciclo diversificado is divided into 2 specializations: humanities and science; the second year into 3: humanities, science and biology; the third into 6: law, economics, architecture, engineering, agronomy, and medicine. On completion of this cycle pupils take the examinations for the **Bachiller**.

Some schools also offer a ciclo preparatorio, specifically for university entrance.

Technical secondary

Until 1978 pupils could specialize in a technical field during the final 2-year cycle of secondary education. The reforms of 1976 increased this to 4 years and holders of the Bachiller from the ciclo tecnico may now go on to university. In the first year there are 8 specialiations, increasing to 12 in the final year.

HIGHER EDUCATION

There are 3 universities: the Universidad de la Republica (State University); the Universidad del Trabajo (Technical University of Uruguay); and the Universidad Catolica del Uruguay Damaso Antonio Larranaga (private and recently opened Recognized by the Uruguayan authorities in 1985).

The first qualification obtained is the **Licenciado**, generally after a course lasting 4 years. Postgraduate courses lead to the **Doctorado**.

Uruguay

The first qualification may be obtained after a course lasting 7 years for medicine, 5 for dentistry, and 6 for law and social science.

3-year courses offer professional training in engineering, medicine and administration.

Taught postgraduate courses are available in: economics, odontology, chemistry, veterinary science, psychology and medicine. There are no research facilities.

TEACHER EDUCATION

Primary

Until 1955:

Teachers were trained on a 7-year course, which consisted essentially of the 4-year secondary course followed by 3 years teacher training, leading to the qualification of **Maestro de Primer Grado**, with which teachers could teach children in grades 1-4. To teach grades 1-6, holders of this qualification had to pass an additional examination leading to the title of **Maestro de Segundo Grado**.

1955-early 1970s:

Teachers were trained on an 8-year course consisting of the 4-year academic secondary course followed by 4-year teacher training at an Instituto Normal. The course led to the qualification of **Maestro**, with which the holder could register in some university faculties.

Since the 1970s:

Teachers are trained on a 3-year post-secondary course leading to the title of **Maestro de Educacion Primaria**. The course is to be extended to 4 years from 1986.

Secondary

Teachers are trained at higher education level on a course lasting approximately 4-years until 1976 and now 3 years, leading to the title of **Profesor**.

Vanuatu

The Anglo-French condominium of the New Hebrides became the independent Republic of Vanuatu on 30 July 1980.

Before independence, dual French and English education systems were in operation. Since independence the systems have been unified under one Ministry of Education, Youth and Sports, even though the media of instruction continue to be either French or English and the curricula at present are different.

Education is not compulsory and is free at primary level.

The country is developing a common curriculum for all schools at both the primary and the secondary level and eventually there will be common examinations. The national language, Bislama, is used as an official language along with French and English, but it is not used as a medium of instruction in the schools.

EVALUATION IN BRITAIN

School

Year 10 Leaving Certificate or **Brevet de Fin du Premier Cycle** - generally considered to be below GCE O-level standard.

Cambridge Overseas School Certificate - grades 1-6 are equated to GCE O-level (grades A, B or C).

Baccalaureat - see the chapter on France.

Higher

Bachelor degrees from the University of the South Pacific - generally considered to compare to British Bachelor degree standard.

Vanuatu

MARKING SYSTEMS

School

Cambridge Overseas School Certificate is graded 1 (maximum) - 9

1-2	very good
3-6	credit
7-8	pass
9	fail

Higher

Degrees from the University of the South Pacific are unclassified.

SCHOOL EDUCATION

Primary

In both the English and the French sectors this lasts 6 years.

Formerly English sector: classes 1-6

French sector:
- classe d'initiation de francais
- cours primaire
- cours elementaire 1
- cours elementaire 2
- cours moyen 1
- cours moyen 2

At the end of the 6 years, pupils take the **Certificate of End of Primary Studies** or the **Diplome de Fin d'Etudes Primaires**, the basis for selection for the secondary cycle. At present there are separate examinations with a common certificate (printed in the 2 languages). It is planned to have a common examination in the 2 languages by 1992.

Secondary

Secondary education in both English- and French-medium schools consists of 2 cycles of 4 years and then 3 years.

First cycle - years 7-10
Second cycle - years 11-13

formerly	English medium	French medium
	form 1	6eme
	form 2	5eme
	form 3	4eme
	form 4	3eme
	form 5 lower	2de
	form 5 upper	1ere
	form 6	terminale

Vanuatu

In the English-medium junior secondary cycle, pupils study a core curriculum of English, French, mathematics, social science and basic science and agriculture.

On completion of these 4 years, students sit for the **Year 10 Leaving Certificate**.

In the French-medium cycle, pupils study a core curriculum of French, English, mathematics, geography, history and science. At the end of the first cycle they sit the **Brevet de Fin du Premier Cycle**. This examination is assessed by accredited staff and moderated by the University of Dijon.

It is planned to have a common curriculum for both French and English and a national examination at the end of the first cycle by 1989.

In the second cycle, English-medium students embark on a 1- or 2-year course leading to the **Cambridge Overseas School Certificate**.

Those successful in the Cambridge Overseas School Certificate may continue into years 12 and 13 in preparation for tertiary education specializing in arts or science. An internal examination is set.

Under the French system, the student studies from year 11-13 and then sits the Baccalaureat, which is set and marked in France and moderated by the University of Grenoble.

It is planned to have a common examination at the end of year 13. Its recognition will be negotiated with France and Britain, so that Vanuata students have access to higher education overseas.

HIGHER EDUCATION

Students who have followed the French system tend to go to mainland France, but students intending to pursue undergraduate studies may enrol at the University of the South Pacific in Fiji. The main campus, Laucala, is at Suva, Fiji, and the Alafua campus, consisting of the School of Agriculture, is in Western Samoa.

The university runs a pre-degree programme, the **Foundation** course, for students with the **New Zealand University Entrance Examination** or equivalent.

Admission to first-degree courses is based on satisfactory completion of the foundation year or other studies comparable in standard to a 1-year post New Zealand University Entrance course.

The University offers 3-year **BA, B.Ed.** and **B.Sc.** courses; a 4-year **Bachelor of Agriculture** which includes practical experience; and four-year **BA** and **B.Sc.** courses with a concurrent **Postgraduate Certificate in Education**. A wide variety of certificate and diploma courses is available. Postgraduate studies for **MA** and **Ph.D.** are offered for a limited number of students.

The University Extension Services Department provides credit courses through correspondence and satellite radio links, as well as a range of continuing education programmes: in this way it is like the British Open University.

Vanuatu

TEACHER EDUCATION

Primary

There is now a common course for English- and French-medium students at the recently established <u>Institute of Education's Teacher Education Centre</u>.

The Centre offers a 3-year **Certificate** course with the minimum entry requirement of a Form Ten Leaving Certificate. The course is 2 years full-time study followed by 1 year supervised internship in school.

Secondary

There are no courses at present for secondary teachers in Vanuatu. Students are trained at the University of the South Pacific or in other overseas institutions.

Venezuela

Republic of Venezuela

Since democracy was introduced, education in Venezuela has undergone enormous expansion, encouraged by the increased revenue from oil and the importance placed on producing technically trained personnel to assist industrial growth.

Education is free and compulsory from ages seven to sixteen (grades 1-9).

The medium of instruction is Spanish.

The school year runs from September to July and the university academic year runs from January to December, or in some cases from September to July.

EVALUATION IN BRITAIN

School

Bachillerato - generally considered to compare to GCE O-level standard.

Higher

Licenciado - may be considered to be below British Bachelor degree standard.

MARKING SYSTEMS

School

Most institutions of intermediate education, in both the common and diversified cycles, employ yearly grades. Examinations are not nationally set but are designed by individual schools under the supervision of the Ministry of Education.

Grading is on a scale of 20-1, with 10 as the minimum pass mark.

Venezuela

Each academic year is divided into 3 or more periods. A grade is given for each period. At the end of the year the grades of each period are averaged to form a previa grade. This makes up 60% of the pupil's final mark. If an overall grade of 10 in the final examination and in the combination of the previa and the final examination is not obtained, the pupil must resit in September.

Higher

Examinations are graded on a 20-0 scale, with 10 as the minimum pass mark. 2 or more partial examinations are taken during each marking period. The average of all the partial examinations yields 40% of the final grade and must be 10% or above for the student to take the final examination.

Institutions of higher education differ in the grading scales they use. Some use both a percentage scale and a 9-1 scale:

9	91-100%	excelente	excellent
8	81-90	sobresaliente	outstanding
7	71-80	distinguido	very good
6	61-70	bueno	good
5	50-60	satisfactorio	average
4	37-49	deficiente	failure
3	25-36	deficiente	
2	13-24	muy deficiente	
1	1-12	muy deficiente	

SCHOOL EDUCATION

Pre-primary

This is voluntary for children aged 4-6. The Ministry of Education has been active in expanding the provision of places at this level.

Until 1981:

Primary

This was free and compulsory from age 7-13 (grades 1-6). Promotion from one grade to another was based on the teacher's assessment and was generally automatic. In the last year pupils had to take an examination set by the teacher of the sixth grade. Successful pupils were awarded a **Certificado de Educacion Primaria** (Certificate of Primary Education) which granted access to secondary education.

Secondary

This lasted 5-6 years. It was made up of 2 cycles - a basic common cycle of 3 years followed by a diversified cycle of 2 or occasionally 3 years.

Venezuela

Basic common cycle:

This covered 3 years providing a general course of education. Promotion from one year to the next was dependent on the average marks obtained during the year and on the results of the end-of-year exams (in July). Successful completion of the basic common cycle gave access to the diversified cycle. Students did not receive a certificate but graduated with a grade record.

Diversified cycle:

This is still in operation and offers 3 specialized branches of study - academic, technical and normal (pedagogic). All 3 branches offer 2- to 3-year courses leading to the **Bachillerato** which gives access to higher education. Before 1972 only the academic branch led to the Bachillerato and therefore to higher education. The title of **Bachiller** is now awarded in industry, commerce, agriculture, primary school teaching, and social work, as well as science and humanities. Students can also choose 1 of 38 special options in their chosen branch of Bachillerato studies.

All students follow basic subjects during the first year of this cycle. These are Spanish language and literature, mathematics, Venezuelan history and geography, English, and physical education.

Academic branch - both the science and humanities courses normally last 2 years. Successful students receive the title of **Bachiller** in **Sciences** or **Humanities**.

Technical branch - students who opt for this can study 1 of 4 subjects (commerce, social work, agriculture or industry). The commercial courses last 2 years. The average length of course in the remainder is 3 years.

Normal or pedagogic branch - this provides teacher training at primary level. Courses generally last 3 years and students specialize in the second year. Successful students obtain the title of **Maestro** at the end of the course; this is considered equivalent to a Bachillerato in primary school teaching.

Since 1981:

Basic primary

In 1981, basic primary education became free and compulsory from age 7-16 (grades 1-9). Final-year students take an examination set by the teacher of grade 9 and if successful are awarded a **Certificado de Educacion Basica** which grants access to secondary education.

Secondary

This now lasts a minimum of 2 years and is called the diversified cycle, which remains the same as the pre-1981 diversified cycle.

Vocational

The *Instituto Nacional de Cooperacion Educativa* (INCE) was founded in 1959. It operates 54 centres throughout the country and mobile units servicing the rural areas. INCE provides free courses and course materials and assists students when necessary.

Apprenticeship programmes last up to 3 years. Apprentices must have completed primary school. Special courses are available for those who have not reached the required standard to begin their training programmes.

Venezuela

Full-time vocational training is available from age 16 to 26.

HIGHER EDUCATION

The Bachillerato entitles the student to a place in higher education and the demand has led to the rapid growth of traditional universities. Entry is not normally dependent on selection procedures. There are 19 universities. The oldest of these, the Universidad Central de Venezuela, was founded in 1721. Universities created since 1958 are termed 'experimental'. They operate selection procedures and offer technological courses geared to industrial development. In the 1970s the government created 5 University Institutes of Technology (IUTs), 2 Junior Colleges (Colegios Universitarios) and 3 University Polytechnic Institutes (IUPs). One IUP already existed at Barquisimeto. Most degree courses take 4-5 years.

University Institutes of Technology (IUTs)

These were intended to provide the technical courses between graduate and school level required for industrial development and to relieve the pressure on university places. They offer shorter 3-year courses with practical bias involving short industrial attachments which lead to the qualification **Tecnico Superior**. This period of education can be credited as a 3-year study towards a 5-year degree course. Junior Colleges are similar to IUTs but offer a broader range of subjects.

University Polytechnic Institutes (IUPs)

The first IUP opened in 1953 and offered 4-year **Tecnologo** courses closely tailored to the requirements of industry. This qualification is no longer offered. The IUPs now offer 5-year degree courses, comparable to university engineering courses though not as theoretical. The new IUP in Caracas allows students to leave after 3 years with the qualification of **Tecnico Superior**.

Military Academies

All the Military Academies offer 4-year academic courses leading to the degree of **Licenciado**.

The basic entry requirement is completion of 5 or 6 years intermediate-level education. The basic degree is awarded in Military Arts and Sciences. There is also an option (mencion) in a university-type field.

Naval Academy

The Escuela Naval offers a degree in Naval Sciences (**Licenciado en Ciencias Navales**).

TEACHER EDUCATION

Primary

Primary school teachers are trained within the secondary school system in normal (pedagogical) schools. In future, primary teacher training will occur within the higher education sphere although the courses may last only 2 years.

Venezuela

Secondary

Secondary school teachers are trained in Institutos Pedagogicos, teacher training institutes, and Universities or Junior Colleges. The teacher-training institutes operate outside the university system but are officially accorded equal status.

In-service training for teachers is offered at 2 special training centres - the Centro Interamericano de Educacion Rural and the Centro de Capitacion Docente El Macaro.

The Instituto de Mejoramiento de Profesores (literally the Institute for the improvement of teachers) offers correspondence courses to allow unqualified practising teachers to obtain the teacher's certificate.

ADULT EDUCATION

The Division of Adult Education is largely responsible for non-formal education, assisted by bodies such as INCE, IAN (Instituto Agrario Nacional) and the individual municipalities. A presidential decree in 1969 called for the establishment of educational training facilities for adults within the existing education system. Adults can now follow a shortened period of schooling (4 years primary and 5 years secondary) at night school, ordinary school or through radio, television and correspondence courses. Various vocational adult courses are held in conjunction with primary school training.

Viet Nam

Socialist Republic of Viet Nam

Educational facilities were severely affected by the hostilities in the 1950s, late 1960s and 1970s. Many educational documents and certificates were lost or left behind during this time, and thus it may not be possible to obtain evidence of qualifications held.

There was a strong French influence in the area from the beginning of this century, and until the late 1970s four almost separate education systems: Vietnamese, Franco-Vietnamese, French, and 'foreign' (e.g. American, Chinese); the last three only in southern Vietnam.

Education is compulsory for children aged six to fifteen.

The medium of instruction is now Vietnamese.

The academic year runs from September to June.

EVALUATION IN BRITAIN

Before 1975

School

Vietnamese Baccalaureat Part II (obtainable until 1970) - generally considered to compare to GCE O-level standard.

Higher

Licence (obtainable until 1970) - generally considered to be below British Bachelor degree standard.

For all other qualifications enquirers are advised to contact the National Academic Recognition Information Centre.

Viet Nam

After-1975

School

On completion of secondary schooling, pupils now obtain the **Tot Nghiep Pho Thong**.

Higher

Diplomas are awarded on successful completion of 5-year courses.

Details of the education system are given below for the period before 1975 (in the Democratic Republic of Vietnam and in the Republic of Vietnam) and after 1975.

Before-1975

DEMOCRATIC REPUBLIC OF VIETNAM

The education system was centralized in all respects, and schools were offered a Vietnamese curriculum only.

Primary

For children from age 7, this covered 4 years in level I of general education.

Secondary

This covered 6 years, divided into two 3-year cycles in levels II and III. The curriculum covered national literature, political education, mathematics, and foreign languages, with an introduction to physics and chemistry in grade 8. On completion of grade 11, pupils took the examination for the **Vietnamese Baccalaureat Part I** and, on completion of grade/year 12, for the **Baccalaureat Part II**.

Technical, vocational and adult education

Vocational and technical secondary courses were available for pupils lasting 2, 2-and-a-half and 3 years, from the end of level II.

There was an extensive programme of adult education for the working population (to bring their education up to levels I and II). Basic subjects taught were Vietnamese history and geography, simplified arithmetic and science, and civics.

Further

Many specialized institutions offered this type of education.

Higher

There was 1 university, the University of Hanoi, which suffered heavy losses after 1954. It was re-founded in 1956. Admission was by competitive examination on successful completion of a full course of secondary education. Studies lasted 4-5 years, leading to a **Diploma** in the particular field of study. Students also undertook practical work in agriculture and industry.

Viet Nam

Teacher

Primary — a 3-year course at a secondary-level teachers' college was provided for pupils who had completed level I.

Secondary — a 1-year course at a secondary-level teachers' college was provided for pupils who had completed grade 7, enabling them to teach level II.

— some colleges also offered a 3-year course for pupils who had completed level II, enabling them to teach level III.

REPUBLIC OF VIETNAM

Primary education was compulsory, but in practice limited facilities prevented this in some areas.

The medium of instruction for general education varied according to the type of school:

Vietnamese schools - Vietnamese throughout

Chinese schools - usually Mandarin, but required to teach 6 hours of Vietnamese per week

French schools - French, but required to teach Vietnamese as a subject

International schools (American and English) - English and Vietnamese.

At the higher education level French was used, but in the 1960s Vietnamese gradually replaced French in the Humanities.

Primary

From age 6, this covered 5 years. The curriculum included Vietnamese, moral education, civics, history, geography, science, and arithmetic. On conclusion of this cycle, pupils took the examination for the **Certificat d'Etudes Primaires** (CEP).

Secondary

Until 1952, this covered 6 years; it was then increased to 7 years. Admission was gained by the CEP and by success in a competitive entrance examination. From 1965 until 1975 there were 4 branches: general; technical and vocational; agricultural; and comprehensive. In the general branch, studies were divided into a 4-year followed by a 3-year cycle. In the first cycle, pupils studied history, geography, French, English, Chinese, physics, chemistry, and mathematics, and could obtain the **Brevet d'Etudes du Premier Cycle** (BEP) on conclusion of this cycle.

Pupils could then choose which specialization they wished to take in the second cycle: experimental science, mathematics, modern literature, classical literature.

Viet Nam

Until 1973, pupils took the national **Baccalaureat I/Bang Tu-Tai I/Bang Tu-Tai Nhut/ Bang Tu-Tai Mot** on completion of year 11. Pupils had to obtain one of these qualifications to proceed to grade/year 12. The examinations were abolished in 1972/3. On completion of year 12 pupils took the examinations for the **Baccalaureat II/Bang Tu-Tai Hai** (until 1973) and for the **General Education Baccalaureat Diploma/Tu Tai Po Thong** (1974/5).

After 1965 the comprehensive branch was available in a limited number of 'model' schools established under American auspices, which operated the American high school system.

Pupils were also able to study for the Vietnamese **Baccalaureat** examinations by home study/correspondence.

A number of schools teaching through the medium of French operated on the French system until 1975. Examinations were set for the **Brevet d'Etudes du Premier Cycle**, and **Baccalaureats I** and **II** (the last two until approximately 1972; after that the **Baccalaureat de l'Enseignement Secondaire** was awarded), with papers and examiners being sent annually from France (administered by the Service Culturel Francais).

Technical and vocational

Until 1973, admission to this branch was by a competitive examination at the end of grade 7 (i.e. 5 years primary followed by 2 years of general technical education). The course lasted 5 years, divided into 2 cycles of 2 and 3 years respectively. On completion of grade 11 pupils took the **Technical Baccalaureat I**, and at the end of grade 12 **Technical Baccalaureat II** examinations.

During 1973-5, admission to the course was on completion of grade 9, and it lasted 3 years. The **Technical Baccalaureat I** was abolished, but pupils could obtain the **Technical Baccalaureat** on successful completion of grade 12.

Agricultural

Until 1973, this lasted 7 years, divided into 2 cycles of 4 and 3 years respectively for pupils who were successful in an entrance examination at the end of grade 5. From 1973 the course lasted 3 years from completion of grade 9. On completion of grade 12, pupils did not take the examinations for the Baccalaureat, but if they met the course requirements they were awarded the **Agricultural Baccalaureat Diploma (Bang Tu-Tai Canh-Nong)**, and the status of agricultural technician.

Further

Community colleges were established in 1972-3, offering 2-year courses to train middle-level technicians. A few specialist institutions also offered courses at this level.

Higher

The University of Saigon was established in 1954, and the Universities of Can Tho and Hue in the 1960s. There were also private universities established by religious groups.

Viet Nam

University admission was on the basis of the **Baccalaureat II/Bang Tu-Tai Hai** until 1972, when it was replaced by the general education **Baccalaureat Diploma/Tu-Tai Po Thong**. Some institutions also administered entrance examinations (**Thi Tuyen**).

Courses lasted 4-5 years, leading to the **Licence/Cu Nhan/professional qualification**:

architecture	6 years
dentistry	5
law	3 until 1964/5, then 4
medicine	7
pharmacy	5

A further 2 years study led to the **Advanced Diploma of Higher Education (Bang Cao Hoc)**. A minimum of 2 years further research led to the **Doctorate (Tien Si)**. At the University of Saigon the **Doctorat de Troisieme Degre** could be obtained on successful completion of 3 years research after the first university qualification, and the **Doctorat d'Etat** after 5 years.

Teacher

Primary:

Until 1962, prospective teachers were trained on a 3-year course at an Ecole Normale, from the admission requirement of the **Brevet d'Etudes du Premier Cycle** (completion of lower secondary education) plus success in an entrance examination.

From 1962, teachers were trained on a 2-year course at an Ecole Normale (until 1972), College Normale (from 1973) from the admission requirement of the Tu-Tai Po Thong/Baccalaureat I. The qualification obtained was the **Certificat d'Aptitude Pedagogique/Certificate of Kha-Nang Su-Pham Cop Bo-Tu**.

To ease the shortage of teachers, some teachers were trained on a 1-year post-BEP course.

Secondary:

Prospective teachers were trained at the higher education level, from the admission requirement of **Baccalaureat II** plus success in an entrance examination. From 1959 until 1963 the course lasted 3 years, with a preparatory year added in 1963/4. Until 1962, teachers were trained at the Higher School of Pedagogy, which then became the Faculty of Education of the University of Saigon. On successful completion of the course, students obtained the **Diploma of Graduation/Tot-Nghiep Dai-Hoc Su-Pham**.

Viet Nam

After-1975

Pre-primary

<u>Creches</u> are available for infants from 2 months to 3 years old.

<u>Kindergartens</u> for ages 3-5. They are the responsibility of the Ministry of Education, but are directly run by agricultural co-operatives, factories and state farms. Semi-boarding kindergartens are beginning to appear in rural areas.

Basic general

There are 9 grades from ages 6-15, split into 2 levels. Level 1 = grades 1-5, are taught by one class teacher; level 2 = grades 6-9, are taught by subject teachers.

Secondary general

This covers grades 10-12 and prepares pupils for further education. The school year is divided into 2 terms of about 4 months each.

The syllabus at both basic general education schools and secondary general education schools includes: civic duties, ethics, history, geography, literature (Vietnamese and World), and 1 foreign language; maths, physics, chemistry and biology; drawing, music, physical culture, sport and basic military training. Pupils are also taught general skills for industry and agriculture.

Exams are taken at the end of each term, and there are special exams for the selection of majors, and entry examinations.

Marks are awarded according to a 10-point scale. General evaluation in term exams is rated:

excellent
good
fair
bad.

Pupils who fail may be allowed to resit.

Pupils who get 5 or more (without any 3s) will automatically pass. Those who average 4-5 but who get no zeros and who have been rated 'excellent' or 'good' at school will also be passed.

Basic general school exams are the responsiblity of the provincial education services. Secondary general school exams are the responsibility of the Ministry of Education.

Study of work schools

This is run on an experimental basis. Pupils attend classes for 4 hours a day, and work 3-4 hours a day in factories or on state farms.

Complementary education

This began in 1945 and is open to all adults. There are 2 main types: in-service training for people who are studying whilst employed, and classes for adult literacy, basic maths, basic agricultural skills, and hygiene.

Viet Nam

Since 1945, mass literacy has been an educational priority, together with replacing French by Vietnamese as the main medium of instruction.

Job training

There are now 366 schools set up to train pupils in technical skills. Entry is usually from basic general education schools, although 40 only accept secondary general school graduates. Training courses last 1-3 years.

Higher

There are now 84 universities and other institutions of higher education in Vietnam. Many Vietnamese study at undergraduate and postgraduate level in the USSR.

There is a growth in post-university research centres in Vietnam.

Teacher

Teacher-training classes are run by the Ministry of Education for graduates of secondary general schools. 4- to 5-year courses are offered for teaching subjects at secondary school level.

Provincial and municipal administrations run 3-year courses for graduates of secondary general schools to teach 1 main subject plus 1 subsidiary subject at a basic general education school (level II).

2-year courses are available to enable teachers to teach at basic general education schools (level I).

2-year courses exist for kindergarten teachers.

University training is provided to train teachers for teacher training-schools.

All teacher-training courses include 4 months of practical training. Follow-up training for teachers is also provided.

West Bank

This chapter covers the period since 1967; for information on the system before that, see the chapter on Jordan. The system described is that of the West Bank, including East Jerusalem.

Primary and preparatory (lower secondary) education is compulsory.

The medium of instruction is Arabic, with the exception of a few private schools that prepare students for the GCE.

The academic year runs from September to May.

EVALUATION IN BRITAIN

School

Secondary School Certificate (Tawjihi) - generally compared to GCE O-level standard on a subject-for-subject basis provided marks of at least 50% have been obtained in subjects which can be taken in the GCE examinations, except English Language.

Higher

Associate degree (Birzeit University) - generally compared to GCE A-level standard.

Bachelor degree - generally compared to British Ordinary degree standard.

MARKING SYSTEM

School

The system varies according to subject, but is clearly marked on the certificate.

West Bank

Higher

The grading system used is:

Grades		Grade points
A	excellent	4.0
B	good	3.0
C	average	2.0
D	pass	1.0
E	fail	0

Students must normally maintain an average of 'C' or better to remain in good academic standing.

SCHOOL EDUCATION

Pre-primary

Limited facilities.

Primary/elementary

This covers 6 years from age six. The curriculum includes: Arabic, religion, arithmetic, civics, history, geography, science, drawing, embroidery (for girls), music, and physical education. English is taught from grade 5.

Preparatory

This covers 3 years and includes some vocational training. The curriculum includes: Arabic, religion, English, mathematics, social studies, science, art, and physical education. Each boys' school has to offer 1 of 3 vocational courses: agricultural, industrial, or commercial. The girls' schools offer courses in home economics.

Secondary

This covers 3 years. In grade 10 (first year), all pupils follow the same course. In grade 11, pupils are placed in 1 of 2 streams, either arts or science, depending on their performance in the previous year's work. The common curriculum includes: Arabic, religion, English, mathematics, drawing, vocational education and physical education, with those in the arts stream also taking general science, history, geography, economics and extra Arabic; and those in the science stream taking biology, physics, chemistry and additional mathematics. On completion of grade 12, pupils take the examinations for the Jordanian General Secondary Education Certificate.

Technical secondary

The entrance requirement is 6 years elementary, 3 years preparatory, and 1 year secondary education. The main subjects studied are building, surveying, electrical and automechanics.

There is also a number of vocational training centres, some being private, run either by the government or by Unwra (see Appendix). They offer courses in various trades including automechanics, electricity, welding, carpentry, surveying, building, plumbing.

West Bank

Nursing training is offered at various levels, but graduate, registered or qualified nurses are mostly trained on a 4-year course. Bethlehem University and the Arab College of Medical Sciences offer a 4-year course in nursing leading to the award of a B.Sc.

FURTHER EDUCATION

<u>Hebron Technical Engineering College</u>, previously known as Hebron Polytechnic, offers 2-year courses leading to various technical **Diplomas**, after the completion of 70 credit hours.

HIGHER EDUCATION

In 1967 there was no university education on the West Bank, but since then 4 higher institutions have been opened or developed from lower-level schools: Birzeit University, Bethlehem University and An Najah National University at Nablus, and Hebron Islamic University.

<u>Birzeit University</u> was first founded in 1924 as a high school; in 1961 it became a junior college and in 1972 began offering Bachelor degree courses. Arabic is the official language, but English is the main medium of instruction. Courses are organized on the credit system, and in general Bachelor degrees take about 4 years.

<u>Bethlehem University</u> was established in 1973 and has links with Laval University in Canada. Courses are organized on the credit system. The media of instruction are Arabic and English.

<u>An Najah University</u> began in 1965, as a college, to offer 2-year teacher-training courses. In 1977 it was inaugurated as a university and now offers courses at both undergraduate and postgraduate level. The medium of instruction is Arabic.

<u>Hebron Islamic University</u>, founded in 1971 as Al Sharia College, became a university in 1980 when an Arts Faculty was added. Preparations are being made for the construction of a Science Faculty.

Entrance to all 3 institutions is on the basis of the General Secondary Education Certificate.

Other degree-awarding institutions include:

<u>College of Science and Technology, Abu Dies</u>, established in 1981, which awards B.Sc. in Science and Technology (135 credits required).

<u>Arab College of Medical Professions</u> established in 1979 as a nursing college; in 1980 a medical technology course was introduced and since then the college has become a degree-awarding institution.

<u>Arts College for Women</u> evolved from Der Al Tifl College for Women which awards **BAs** in TEFL and Teaching of Arabic Languages.

West Bank

TEACHER EDUCATION

Primary/preparatory

Prospective teachers undertake a 2-year course at a teacher-training institute from General Secondary Education Certificate level.

Secondary

Teachers for this level are generally graduates and should have undertaken a Graduate Teaching Diploma at one of the 3 universities.

Yemen

Yemen Arab Republic

The development of education in Yemen has been recent and rapid. At the time of the revolution against the Imamate in 1962 there were only four government secondary schools in the country. By 1985/6 the number had risen to 164. The greatest part of this development has taken place since 1970 when the civil war ended. Schooling is based on the 6-3-3 (primary, preparatory and secondary) system recommended by the Arab League in 1957. The curriculum has been adopted from Egypt which also supplies a large number of teachers for the secondary schools.

With the exception of certain courses (e.g. medicine) at Sana'a University the language of instruction is Arabic.

The academic year runs from September to June.

EVALUATION IN BRITAIN

General Secondary Certificate (Al Thanawiya) - normally accorded GCE O-level status.

A **Bachelor degree** from the University of Sana'a is unlikely to be considered comparable to a British Bachelor degree.

MARKING SYSTEMS

School

The General Secondary Certificate examination is graded out of 700 as follows:

over 630	excellent
561-630	very good
491-560	good
421-490	fair
350-420	pass

Yemen Arab Republic

University

A score of at least 75% in the Thanawiyyah is required for admission to the Faculties of Medicine and Engineering at Sana'a University. For Science, Agriculture and Commerce the requirement is 65-70% and for Law, Education and Arts around 50-60%. Precise entry requirements may vary from year to year.

University degrees are graded according to the following percentages:

88-100	excellent
78-87	very good
63-77	good
48-62	pass

SCHOOL EDUCATION

Primary (6 years)

This is in theory compulsory and schools are now distributed widely throughout the country. The total enrolment in 1985/6 was roughly 55% of the children of primary school age.

Preparatory (3 years)

Enrolment represents about 10% of the children of preparatory school age, of which about 10% were girls.

Secondary (3 years)

Enrolment in 164 schools in 1985/6 was around 22,000 of whom 13% were girls. This reflects the progress of girls education and the motivation for girls to continue their education once they have made the transition to preparatory school. Secondary education is divided, after the first year, into scientific and literary streams. The **Thanawiya** examination is taken at the end of the third year.

FURTHER EDUCATION

There are some technical secondary schools, 3 Vocational Training Centres, a Veterinary Training School, a Health Manpower Training Institute and a few agricultural secondary schools. In addition there are religious institutes concentrating on Islamic education. Plans are currently being implemented for a general strengthening of technical and vocational education and for the establishment of a polytechnic in Sana'a.

Yemen Arab Republic

HIGHER EDUCATION

Higher education is provided by the University of Sana'a, founded in 1970. Although it was originally intended as a teacher training college it is expanding into a national institution of higher education.

Admission is limited to students scoring at least 205-210 in the general secondary school examination.

TEACHER EDUCATION

Teachers for the primary and preparatory schools are trained at a total of 76 Teachers Training Institutes (15 of which are Women's TTIs). Trainee teachers follow either a 5-year post-preparatory course or a 3-year post-secondary course. Total enrolment in 1985/6 was 10,500 of whom 3,000 (28%) were girls.

Teachers for the secondary schools are trained by the Faculty of Education at Sana'a University. Although the Faculty was the 'mother college' of the University when it was established in 1970, enrolment has tended to remain low at around 10% of the total student body.

Democratic Yemen

People's Democratic Republic of Yemen

This area covered the Crown colony of Aden until 1967 when it became independent.

The medium of instruction is Arabic, although certain private schools use English. In the area around the city of Aden, Arabic is used for primary and intermediate education, and English for secondary.

EVALUATION IN BRITAIN

School

Cambridge Overseas School Certificate - grades 1-6 are equated to GCE O-level (grades A, B, C).

Thanawiya/General Secondary Education Certificate - generally compared to GCE O-level on a subject-for-subject basis where marks of at least 50% have been obtained in counterpart subjects, except English language.

Higher

Bachelor degree - generally considered to be between GCE A-level and British Bachelor degree standards.

MARKING SYSTEM

School

Cambridge Overseas School Certificate - marking is on a scale of 1 (maximum) - 9 (fail).

Thanawiya (General Secondary Education Certificate) - marking is on a percentage scale.

Higher

No information available.

Democratic Yemen

SCHOOL EDUCATION

Pre-primary

Limited facilities are available.

Primary

Until 1967:

This consisted of 7 years, divided into 4 years lower plus 3 years intermediate for children from age 6 or 7, except in Aden where it covered 8 years divided into two 4-year cycles.

Since 1968:

Primary education has covered 6 years. The curriculum covers Arabic, Islamic religion, mathematics, science and health, art, physical education, and music, with history and geography from grade 2, and English from grade 5.

Secondary

Until 1967:

Secondary education covered 4 years.

Since 1967:

It now consists of 3 years preparatory and 3 years secondary. The curriculum of the preparatory covers Arabic, Islamic religion, mathematics, English language, science, history, geography, civics, art, and physical education.

The first year of secondary education is common for all pupils and covers Arabic, religion, English, mathematics, physics, chemistry, natural history, history, geography, local society, physical education, and military. At the end of this grade pupils may choose whether to specialize in either the literary or scientific stream. The compulsory subjects for both are religion, Arabic, English, mathematics, economics, Arab society, physical education, and military training. The specialist subjects in the literary branch are: general science, history, geography, sociology and local society; and for the scientific branch: physics, chemistry and natural history.

Until 1970 pupils generally took the examinations for the Cambridge Overseas School Certificate or the General Certificate of Education at Ordinary level of the London Board on completion of their secondary course. Since then pupils have taken the examinations for the **Thanawiya**, administered by the Yemeni Ministry of Education. Since 1974 pupils must pass all subjects to obtain the Certificate.

A few institutions offer 2-year courses leading to the examinations for GCE **A-levels**.

Technical secondary

The Technical Institute offers full- and part-time courses leading to qualifications of the **City & Guilds of London Institute, Royal Society of Arts**, and GCE **O-level** examinations of the Associated Examining Board.

Democratic Yemen

HIGHER EDUCATION

The University of Aden was established in 1973, incorporating colleges founded between 1970 and 1973. Higher education courses are also offered by the Nasser College of Agriculture, College of Administration and Economics at Crater and the Malla Technical Institute (medium of instruction is English).

Bachelor degree courses generally take 4 years from the entrance qualification of the Secondary School Certificate.

TEACHER EDUCATION

Primary/elementary

A 2-year secondary-level course is provided.

Intermediate

A 2-year post-secondary diploma course is provided.

Secondary

A 4-year Bachelor degree course is provided.

Yugoslavia

Socialist Federal Republic of Yugoslavia

The education system is to a large extent decentralized; the basic policy and guidelines are laid down at federal level, and each republic and province implements this policy in its own way and at its own pace. Regular meetings of the education secretaries of each province and republic ensure a degree of parity for the standards.

Major reforms of the system followed the promulgation of the General Law of Education in 1958 (a period of eight years primary and lower secondary education became the unit of basic education) and the reform of secondary and tertiary education in 1970 (still not complete). Higher education was further reformed with the General Law on Universities in 1954 and the General Law on Universities and Faculties in 1960. All the republics and autonomous provinces have passed laws regulating higher education (1970-80).

All educational institutions are state-run.

Compulsory education covers the period of basic education; that is, eight years between age seven and fifteen. Before 1952 it covered seven years (from age seven).

The medium of instruction is Macedonian, Serbo-Croat or Slovene, depending on the republic in which the institution is situated. (There is besides, Albanian at the University of Pristina, and Hungarian at the University of Novi Sad.)

The academic year runs from September/October to June.

EVALUATION IN BRITAIN

School

Matura (before 1980 from the <u>Gymnazija</u>/academic upper secondary course) **Secondary School-Leaving Diploma** (before 1980 from a technical secondary school) - may be considered to satisfy the general requirement of universities and polytechnics.

Secondary School-Leaving Diploma (obtained since 1980) - generally compared to BTEC National Diploma (formerly Ordinary National Diploma) and may be considered to satisfy the general requirement of universities and polytechnics.

Further

Qualifications obtained from Vise Skole - generally compared to BTEC National Diploma (formerly Ordinary National Diploma).

Yugoslavia

Higher

Vise Obrazovanje (First-level degree obtained on completion of a 2-year course) - generally considered to be between GCE A-level and British Bachelor degree standard.

Visoko Obrazovanja (Second-level degree obtained on completion of a 4-year course) - generally considered comparable to British Bachelor degree standard.

Magistar - generally compared to British Master degree standard.

MARKING SYSTEMS

School

Marking is on the scale 1-5 (maximum), with 2 as the minimum pass mark.

Higher

Slovenia and Croatia	1-5 (maximum), 2 (minimum pass)
Bosnia and Herzegovina, Montenegro, Macedonia, Serbia, Kosovo, Vojvodina	5-10 (maximum), 6 (minimum pass)

SCHOOL EDUCATION

Pre-primary

Limited facilities are available in creches (<u>Decje Jaslice</u>) for children to age 3, and kindergartens (<u>Decji Vrtici</u>) for children aged 3-7.

Primary, basic, elementary

This period of schooling (at <u>Osnova Skole</u>) covers 8 years from age 7, but in some republics children may be admitted from age 6. The period is divided into 2 distinct stages: classes 1-4, and 5-8. Classes are unstreamed and based on the comprehensive system. Pupils begin studying foreign languages in the fifth year and may usually choose 1 of English, Russian, German or French.

Secondary

Until 1980:

(The terminology used for denoting this cycle varies from republic to republic.)

Selective entrance tests decided what form of secondary education pupils could enter. The academic cycle covered 4 years at a <u>Gymnazija</u>, of which the first year was common to all pupils. They could then choose to specialize in science/mathematics or humanities/social studies and languages. The final examination was the **Matura**.

Yugoslavia

Technical and vocational secondary

Before 1980:

Technical secondary education covered a variety of fields. On completion of the 4-year course, pupils took examinations for the **Matura** and a vocational qualification.

Vocational schools offered courses lasting 3 years, including a period of practical instruction. Apprentice schools offered training courses lasting 2-3 years, leading to the qualification of skilled worker.

Since 1980:

All forms of secondary schooling now contain an element of vocational training and instruction. The course still covers 4 years, of which the first 2 cover a common-core syllabus. Compulsory subjects are the mother tongue and its literature, the majority language in the given republic, a foreign language, art, Marxism, self-management, history, geography, mathematics, physics, chemistry, biology, physical and medical education, defence, and initiation in production and technology. During the second cycle of 2 years (usemreno obrazovanje - 'directed' education) pupils may undertake some specialization. Admission is by competition. The vocational diploma obtained on completion of the second cycle is based on continuous assessment rather than examination.

FURTHER EDUCATION

There are many post-secondary schools (<u>Vise Skole</u>) which offer 2-year courses in professional and technical education.

HIGHER EDUCATION

Entry to a course of higher education is on the basis of a Secondary School Leaving Certificate regardless of whether it was obtained on completion of an academic or technical course; whereas the former will admit to all faculties, the vocational/ technical diploma gives admission only to certain faculties. Holders of a qualification from a professional school/apprenticeship may have to sit entrance examinations. A system of numerus clausus (restricted entry) operates in some universities.

Before 1959

There was only 1 degree, obtained after a course lasting 4-6 years (depending on the subject).

Since 1960

Within the organization of higher education, 3 stages for 'degrees' can usually be identified:

Yugoslavia

First stage, covering 2-3 years, leading to the **Vise Obrazovanje** (Diploma of Higher Education) with a professional title (Strucni Naziv) - e.g. engineer (Inzenjer), lawyer (Pravnik)

Second stage, covering a further 2-3 years, during which students specialize, leading to a **Visoko Obrazovanja** (Diploma of Higher Education) with a professional title (Strucni Naziv) - e.g. graduate engineer (Diplomirani Inzenjer), graduate lawyer (Diplomirani Pravnik)

Third stage, postgraduate studies, covering 2 years research, leading to the academic degree (akademski stepen) of **Magistar** or 1-year advanced specialization leading to the advanced specialist diploma of **Specijalist**.

A **Doctorate of Science** may be obtained after a further approved period of research and defence of a thesis.

Higher education courses are offered by university faculties, specialist institutes (e.g. art academies), and high schools (Visoke Skole). These offer only limited facilities for postgraduate study.

Note: 'high' schools offer courses of higher education, whereas 'higher' schools offer lower-level courses. (See under FURTHER EDUCATION.)

Workers' (Radnicki)/People's (Narodni) Universities (Univerziteti)

These offer a great variety of courses lasting from only 2 weeks to 2 years. They do not award degrees, but offer special courses leading to a particular vocational qualification and are used mainly to supplement earlier deficiencies in a person's education, for example by preparatory courses for adults wishing to enter a course of higher education.

TEACHER EDUCATION

Primary

Teachers are trained in Vise Skole (further education establishments) for 2 years.

Secondary

Teachers are university graduates. Courses last 4 years.

ADULT EDUCATION

Basic schools for adults (Osnovne Skole za Odrasle) offer the course of basic education (normally taken over 8 years) over only 4 years. The certificate awarded at the end is of the same value as that awarded at the end of the normal 8-year course.

Secondary schools for adults (Srednje Skole za Odrasle) offer the normal course of secondary education, but it may be undertaken through part-time study (e.g. in the evening), correspondence, or, in the case of workers, on full-time paid leave.

Zaire

Republic of Zaire

This chapter covers the period since independence was gained in 1960. The area was previously administered by Belgium as the Belgian Congo; and on independence this became the Democratic Republic of the Congo. It changed its name to Zaire in 1971.

The medium of instruction is French.

The academic year runs from October to June.

EVALUATION IN BRITAIN

School

Diplome d'Etat d'Etudes Secondaires du Cycle Long - generally compared to GCE O-level standard.

Higher

Licence - generally considered between GCE A-level and British Bachelor degree standards.

MARKING SYSTEMS

School

Marking is on a percentage scale, the minimum pass mark is 50%.

For the Diplome d'Etat, pupils must obtain at least 50% in each subject. Course-work accounts for 25% of the final mark.

Zaire

Higher

Marking is on a percentage basis.

90-100%	la plus grande distinction
80-89	grande distinction
70-79	distinction
50-69	satisfaction
50	minimum pass

An attestation is given at the end of each year confirming whether a student has been successful and noting the mention (grade) obtained.

SCHOOL EDUCATION

Primary

This covers 6 years and is referred to as premier cycle. The classes are numbered in reverse order: classes 12-7.

The curriculum includes: French, arithmetic, moral and religious instruction, physical and natural sciences, history and geography, civic instruction, physical education, art, and African languages. Until 1961, primary education was taught in the vernacular.

A **Certificat d'Etudes Primaires** is awarded to pupils who do well in the examen de fin de cycle.

Secondary

Pupils have to sit the **examen selectif**, which determines admission to secondary education. There are 2 cycles, the lower lasting 2 years and the upper 4 years. The lower cycle is referred to as the orientation cycle/cycle inferieur/CO. It covers general education; the curriculum includes: French, mathematics, history, geography, science, technology, African sociology, civic instruction, and physical education. On completion of class 2, pupils take an examination and successful performance leads to the **Brevet du Cycle d'Orientation**.

There are 2 types of course in the cycle superieur: cycle long and cycle court.

Cycle court - this consists of technical secondary and professional training courses lasting 2 to 3 years. This leads to the **Diplome de Fin d'Etudes Secondaires** in technical fields and the **Brevet de Fin d'Etudes Secondaires** in professional areas.

Cycle long - this lasts 4 years. Pupils may specialize in 1 of the following options: Greek - Latin - humanities/Latin - mathematics/Latin - science/modern science A or B/ modern economics. The following subjects are common to all options - religion and civics, French, English, history, geography, and mathematics. Until 1967, pupils took school examinations and were awarded diplomas by the individual school at the end of class 6. In 1967 the examen d'etat was established as the final examination. In that year, pupils were awarded a **Diplome de Fin d'Etudes Secondaires**, but from 1968 to 1971 the final certificate awarded on successful performance in the examen d'etat was the **Diplome d'Etat de l'Enseignement Secondaire**. Until 1970, if pupils obtained marks of no more than 40-50%, they were awarded a **Certificat d'Etat**. Since 1972 the final certificate has been the **Diplome d'Etat d'Etudes Secondaires du Cycle Long**. Pupils wishing to go on to higher education take the epreuve d'orientation, in which they must obtain 45% in their subject of specialization. The examination includes tests in general subjects plus the desired subject of specialization and leads to the **Certificat du Jury d'Enseignement Secondaire**. Pupils who fail this examination may undertake a preliminary year - propedeutique.

Homologation - legalization of a certificate by the Commission d'Homologation. The Commission ensures that the course of studies has followed the state teaching course or a course approved by the Ministry of Education. Before the introduction of the examen d'etat in 1967, the Commission also homologated the school diplomas issued by the individual schools.

FURTHER EDUCATION

There are technician-training institutions affiliated to the university - e.g. Ecole Superieur de Commerce. They offer 3-year courses for students who have completed secondary school, and lead to the qualification of **Gradue**.

HIGHER EDUCATION

Since 1971 there has been 1 university, the National University of Zaire (UNAZA). The 3 existing universities were integrated into 1 institution following the 'nationalization' of education, and they now make up the 3 campuses:

Kinshasa - formerly the University of Lovanium; founded in 1954 under the auspices of the University of Louvain (Belgium) in Kinshasa (formerly Leopoldville), as a Catholic institution

Lubumbashi - formerly the Official University of the Congo; founded in 1956; affiliated to the University of Brussels in Belgium at Lubumbashi (formerly Elisabethville) as a state institution

Kisangani - formerly the Free University of the Congo; founded in 1963 as a Protestant institution as Kisangani (formerly Stanleyville).

Entrance to degree courses is with the Diplome d'Etat d'Etudes Secondaires du Cycle Long, and success in the epreuve d'orientation. Students who do not hold sufficiently good school qualifications to be admitted to university or whose course is not homologated, may take an examination leading to the **Certificat du Jury Universitaire**. Students who fail the epreuve d'orientation may undertake a preliminary year - propedeutique - which is also often undertaken by students intending to start on a science course.

Zaire

Until 1971, courses generally followed the Belgian pattern of premiere candidature (year 1), deuxieme candidature (year 2), premiere annee de licence (year 3), and deuxieme annee de licence (year 4). Since then the first 2 years have consisted of broadly based studies leading to the qualification of **Gradue** - in medicine and law this stage lasts 3 years. The examinations at the end of the first, second and third years are the first, second or third candidature. A further 2 years leads to the **Licence**, or 3 to 4 years to a professional qualification. The examinations at the end of each year are called first, second or third Licence.

Medicine - the title of **Docteur en Medecine** is obtained after 6 years, including 1 year internship.

In arts, philosophy and science, individual research lasting a minimum of 3 years leads to a **Doctorat**. There are no Master degrees.

Theology - the **Baccalaureat** in theology is obtained after 1 year of university study. The Doctorat is obtained 1 year after the Licence on successful submission of a thesis.

Law - the **Baccalaureat** is awarded after 1 year of university study. The Doctorat is obtained after at least 1 year of study after the Licence; students must obtain the Diplome d'Etudes Speciales and then present a thesis.

TEACHER EDUCATION

Primary

There are 2 levels of course taken in:

Cycle court - a 3-year course consisting of 2 years general education followed by 1 year's in-service teacher-training (stage pedagogique), leading to the qualification of **Brevet d'Instituteurs**

Cycle long - a 4-year course followed by 1 year of in-service teacher-training, leading to the qualification of **Diplome d'Instituteurs**.

Secondary

Lower - a 3-year course for holders of the Diplome d'Etat at the Ecole Normale Moyenne, leading to the qualification of **Gradue en Enseignement**.

Upper - holders of the Gradue en Enseignement may undertake a further 2-year course at the Institut Pedagogique National or Institut Superier Pedagogique (both affiliated to the Ecole Normale Superieur), leading to a **Licence d'Enseignement**. Holders of the Diplome d'Etat may take a 3-year course leading to the **Licence d'Enseignement**. Students who take degree courses in subjects other than education may obtain the **Agregation de l'Enseignement Secondaire Superieur** if they pass a paper in education and undertake some teaching practice.

Zambia

Republic of Zambia

The education system is centrally controlled but certain aspects of education administration are now being decentralized. The Ministry of Education and Culture conducts examinations through its examinations section, but the awarding body is the Zambian Examinations Council, which at present conducts the grade VII, IX and XII examinations.

Primary education is compulsory.

The official medium of instruction has been English since 1965 (confirmed by the Education Act of 1966).

The academic year runs as follows:

Schools	-	January-December
Teacher training colleges	-	June-March
University	-	October-July

EVALUATION IN BRITAIN

School

Zambian School Certificate - grades 1-6 are generally compared to GCE O-level standard.

Further

DTEVT Advanced Certificate - may be compared to BTEC National Diploma (formerly OND) level standard.

Higher

Bachelor degree - generally compared to a standard between GCE A-level and British Bachelor degree.

Zambia

MARKING SYSTEM

School

Zambia School Certificate is graded 1-9, where 9 is fail.

Higher

Course-work:

86% and above	A+	distinction
76-85%	A	distinction
66-75%	B+	meritorious
56-65%	B	very satisfactory
46-55%	C+	definite pass
36-45%	C	bare pass
35% and below	D	fail

Overall mark:

The overall mark is obtained by averaging the course-work percentages and is described in the same way as the course-work. Thus an overall mark of 66-75% would be B+ meritorious.

SCHOOL EDUCATION

Pre-primary

Limited facilities available.

Primary

This has covered 7 years from age 7 since 1974; before then it was from age 5. The period is divided into 2 cycles:

lower - grades I-IV
upper - grades V-VII

The curriculum includes English, mathematics, science, social studies, practical subjects, Zambian languages, religious instruction, home economics, music and physical education. On completion of grade VII, pupils take an examination which has been known by a variety of names: Primary School Leaving Certificate Examination/Grade VII Leaving Certificate Examination (LCE)/Grade VII Composite Examination/Secondary School Selection Examination (SSSE) now known as the **Composite Examination/Secondary School Selection Examination**. The examinations consist of 5 papers - English, mathematics, science, social studies amd Zambian languages, plus 2 special papers consisting of non-verbal intelligence tests. There are plans to extend the basic cycle to grade IX for all pupils.

Zambia

Secondary

This covers 5 years, divided into:

Junior - grades VIII and IX
Senior - grades X-XII

Junior: All pupils take English, mathematics, science, religious education, civics, history, geography and agricultural science. Options include French, art, music, woodwork, metalwork, technical drawing, typewriting, office practice, bookkeeping and homecraft. The cycle culminates in the **Junior Secondary School-Leaving Examination**; to obtain the certificate, pupils must pass English and 5 other subjects.

Senior: On completion of this cycle pupils take the examinations for the **Zambia School Certificate**.

It is possible to study for London GCE A-levels through private correspondence colleges and some state-run evening classes, but there is no counterpart to this examination within the Zambian school system.

Technical secondary

The Department of Technical Education and Vocational Training (DTEVT), originally established as a Commission in 1969 responsible for the restructuring of technical education in Zambia, now operates 14 institutions offering over 90 full-time programmes. Present enrolment is over 5,000 students. DTEVT is part of the Ministry of Higher Education. Its awards are issued under the approval of the Examinations Council of Zambia and are divided into 4 categories - Diploma, Advanced Certificate, Certificate and Craft Certificate. A fifth award, 'The Record of Achievement', is issued to those who successfully complete short courses of at least 12 months duration, not normally considered as full programmes. Broadly speaking DTEVT administers 2 types of institution: trades training institutes and higher institutions.

There are 7 Trades Training Institutes. A further 3 are planned. The minimum entry requirement is grade IX. The institutes' trade/ craft programmes last for 2 years at the end of which an interim **Craft Certificate** is awarded. Students then need to obtain 1 year's working experience before the final Craft Certificate is given.

FURTHER EDUCATION

The minimum entry requirement for almost all courses at these institutions is grade XII.

The Zambia Institute of Technology (ZIT) offers a variety of courses within the following 6 training departments:

Academic and Industrial Science
Business Studies
Construction
Electrical, Electronics, Telecommunications and Instrumentation
Mining
Extension Studies

Zambia

Students who successfully complete the 2-and-a-half year technician course receive an **Advanced Certificate**, while those pursuing the 3-and-a-quarter year technology course receive a **Diploma** awarded by DTEVT.

<u>Northern Technical College</u> (NORTEC). The 3 training departments of the College are:

Mechanical Engineering
Automotive Engineering
Electrical Engineering

The courses offered by these departments are full-time and lead to DTEVT's own qualifications. There are evening and part-time commercial and office practice courses leading to a variety of external qualifications. GCE A-level courses in mathematics and physics are also offered.

<u>Zambia Air Services Training Institute</u> (ZASTI) offers Diploma and Certificate programmes in commercial aviation, aviation electronics, aircraft maintenance, air traffic control, meteorology, telecommunications and fire services.

<u>Evelyn Hone College of Applied Arts and Commerce</u> offers Diploma and Certificate courses in a variety of commercial and vocational subjects. For example, business studies, personnel management, secretarial studies, journalism, printing, hotel and catering and paramedical subjects. Awards of the **City & Guilds of London Institute** may also be obtained.

Nursing

Zambia state-registered nurses undertake a 3-year course. The entry requirement is a Cambridge School Certificate with passes in 5 subjects. Zambia state-enrolled nurses follow a 2-year course for which minimum entry is grade XI. There is also a 1-year post-registration course in midwifery conducted at Schools of Midwifery.

Agriculture

At the lowest level are the farmer training centres in each district for training subsistence farmers. Above these are the farm institutes - one in each province - that run a variety of short courses mainly for extension workers.

There are 4 <u>Farm Colleges</u>. Minimum entry requirement is usually grade VII and courses last up to 3 years.

The 2 <u>Colleges of Agriculture</u> (one at Monze and the other at Mpika) run identical 2-year Certificate in General Agriculture courses. Minimum entry is grade IX and the following subjects are studied: agricultural science (first year only but students must pass it), animal husbandry, crop husbandry, farm management, farm engineering (girls study home economics instead), and extension methods (which also covers human nutrition).

<u>The National Resources Development College</u> in Lusaka offers 3-year Diploma courses in agriculture, agricultural engineering, agricultural education and nutrition. Agriculture students can major in their third year in animal science, crop science or business management.

Zambia

HIGHER EDUCATION

There is one university, the University of Zambia (UNZA). The entrance requirement to Bachelor degree courses is 5 GCE O-levels. Passes at GCE A-level may exempt students from part of the course. All students enter the School of Natural Sciences, School of Humanities and Social Science, or the School of Education, for the first year. They may then move from the School of Natural Sciences to the faculties of engineering, medicine, agricultural science or mines, and from the School of Humanities and Social Science to the Faculty of Law. **Bachelor degree** courses in Arts, Science and Law take 4 years (in all) and 5 years in Engineering and Agriculture. There is no division into Ordinary and Honours degrees.

Master degrees take 1 further year.

Facilities for **doctoral study** were introduced in the late 1970s.

The university also offers various **Certificate** and **Diploma** courses.

Medicine - the degree course lasts 7 years, but after the first 4 years students are awarded the Bachelor of Science in Human Biology.

Dentistry and pharmacy - there are no facilities to study these subjects.

TEACHER EDUCATION

There are 12 primary Teachers' Colleges of which 1 is for teachers of the handicapped; and 3 secondary colleges of which 1 is for technical and vocational teachers.

Primary

There is a 2-year certificate course for which the minimum entry qualification is the Junior Secondary School Leaving Examination. Increasingly students who have studied to grade XII are applying.

Secondary

Junior: a 2-year diploma course for which the minimum entry requirement is the Zambia School Certificate. The Technical and Vocational Teachers' College comes under the DTEVT. The examinations and curriculum of the other 2 colleges are moderated by the university.

Senior: teachers for grades IV and V come not from the Teachers' Colleges but from the School of Education at the university. The School of Education awards the degrees of BA (with education) and B.Sc. (with education).

Zanzibar

United Republic of Tanzania

Zanzibar and Tanganyika were united in 1964 to form the United Republic of Tanzania. Zanzibar however retained its own Ministry of Education and its own system of education which has never been fully integrated into that of the mainland, although pupils take the Tanzanian National Examinations. For higher education courses pupils have to go to the University of Tanzania on the mainland.

Education is free and compulsory for eleven years from age 6 (standards 1-8 and forms I to III).

Swahili is the medium of instruction for standards 1 to 8, and English for forms I and above.

EVALUATION IN BRITAIN

As for Tanzania.

MARKING SYSTEMS

As for Tanzania.

SCHOOL EDUCATION

Nursery is optional from age 3 to 6. There are government nursery schools in 9 towns (5 in Zanzibar, 4 in Pemba).

Primary

This lasts 8 years (standards 1-8) and covers similar subjects to those studied on the mainland, but includes Arabic and Islamic studies.

Zanzibar

Secondary

This covers 6 years. At the end of form III pupils take Zanzibar examinations to determine who continues to form IV. A number of different colleges offer the form IV course leading to the National Form IV Examinations.

Lumumba and Fidel Castro secondary schools offer the form IV course and the 2-year course leading to the National Form VI Examinations.

FURTHER EDUCATION

<u>Karume Technical College</u> offers the National Form IV Examinations and a 3-year course leading to the full **Technicians Certificate**.

TEACHER EDUCATION

<u>Nkrumah College</u> offers a 2-year teacher-training course to post-form IV students which enables them to teach up to standard 8. This course is also offered to untrained teachers already teaching at primary level. The College also offers a 2-year course leading to the **Diploma in Education** for teachers already holding the Primary Teacher's Certificate.

<u>Institute of Kiswahili and Foreign Language</u> teaches Swahili to foreign and local students. A Diploma is offered to local post-form IV students after 4 years of study of Swahili and other academic arts subjects, including 2 foreign languages. The course also includes an education component and can lead to further study at the University of Dar es Salaam or employment in government posts. The Institute also conducts research into oral literature and the Swahili language and its dialects.

Zimbabwe

Formerly Southern Rhodesia, the Republic of Zimbabwe gained independence in April 1980.

Primary education is free but secondary education is not compulsory. However, there are, for example, charges for general purposes and building levies. Secondary education is available to O- and A-level standards.

The medium of instruction is English.

The school year runs from mid-January to early December and is divided into three terms. The university year, for most faculties, runs from March to November.

EVALUATION IN BRITAIN

School

Cambridge Overseas School Certificate - equated to GCE O-level (grades A, B, C) when grades of 1 (maximum) to 6 are awarded.

Cambridge Higher School Certificate - equated to GCE A-level.

M-level - one year above GCE O-level and one year below GCE A-level.

The Associated Examining Board (AEB) and the University of London conduct **GCE O-** and **A-level** examinations in Zimbabwe.

The M-level examination is also conducted by the AEB.

Higher

A **Bachelor degree** from the University of Zimbabwe may be compared to a British Bachelor degree.

Zimbabwe

MARKING SYSTEMS

School

The Cambridge Overseas School Certificate is marked on a scale of 1 (maximum) to 9. The Cambridge Higher School Certificate is marked on a scale of A to F.

Higher

University examination papers are set by lecturers and approved by the heads of departments. Papers are marked by the lecturer and also by an external examiner. The papers are marked on the scale: first, upper second, lower second, third, fail.

SCHOOL EDUCATION

Background

Before 1979, 2 separate systems of education operated in Rhodesia: one for Africans, and one for Europeans, 'Coloureds' and Asians. For the Africans, schooling was not compulsory; for the rest, it was compulsory between the ages of 7 and 15 but places were not always available.

The 1979 Education Act

The 1979 Education Act, passed by the transitional government, abolished compulsory education and classified schools into 3 groups: private schools; community schools; and state government schools.

A new **National Certificate of Education** replaced the Rhodesia Junior Certificate of Education, and a scheme of 'Distance Schooling' was introduced.

Independence, 1980

After Independence the new Ministry of Education and Culture, now the Ministry of Education, introduced free primary education for all children from grades 1 to 7, and secondary education was extended. Areas of expansion have included: improved facilities in the rural areas, greater government participation, mass literacy and numeracy campaigns, increased vocational and technical education and a non-formal education sector for adults.

The 2 African national languages, Shona and Ndebele, are now subjects in former European schools, with English still the main medium of instruction.

Primary

In primary schools, grades 1 to 7 lead to a national grade 7 examination.

Zimbabwe

Secondary

From grade 7 there is automatic entry to form 1 at secondary level. Within the secondary system there is only 1 stream. All pupils take the **Zimbabwe Junior Certificate** at the end of form 2 but the purpose of this examination is not to weed out pupils. All continue through to form 4 at the end of which **O-levels** are taken. Most pupils then leave school. This system whereby all pupils pass automatically from primary to secondary school and all secondary school pupils take O-levels is currently under discussion. From 1987 there will probably be radical changes to the system. Pupils with good GCE passes in 5 subjects may go on to the lower sixth form to follow a 2-year **A-level** course. Approximately 10.5% of all O-level pupils progress to A-level courses. The **M-level** exam of the Associated Examining Board still available in the former Group A secondary schools (previously for whites only), is due to be phased out completely in 1987. The M-level had been for white students who wanted to go to South African universities.

FURTHER EDUCATION

Agricultural

Agricultural education is offered at 3 levels:

Agricultural Institutes

There are 4 agricultural Institutes offering 2-year courses leading to a **Certificate in Agriculture**. The minimum entry requirement is the Zimbabwe Junior Certificate but O-level entry is becoming more widespread.

Colleges of Agriculture

There are 2 Colleges of Agriculture. The entrance requirement is 5 passes at GCE O-level which must include English, maths and a science. The 2-year course leads to a **Diploma in Agriculture**.

Faculty of Agriculture, University of Zimbabwe

The entrance requirement is 5 GCE passes of which 2 must be at A-level; both must be science subjects. The course lasts 3 years and includes various practical-work assignments. The faculty also offers **M.Phil.** and **D.Phil. degrees** by research.

Technical/vocational

Responsibility for technical and vocational education lies with the Ministry of Labour. Various courses are offered leading to skilled worker, technician and apprenticeship qualifications. Apprenticeships last 3-4 years. During this period the apprentice is exposed to practical and theoretical training. The latter is undertaken at one of the technical colleges, usually on block release. Level of study at the college is determined by secondary school qualifications.

The ministry runs the following types of institution:

Zimbabwe

Technical Colleges
Regional Vocational Training Centres
National Vocational and Training Development Centre (Harare)
Management Training Bureau (Harare)
Vocational Technical School (Harare)

In the private sector there are about 80 institutions offering a wide variety of vocational courses.

Bachelor of Technology courses were introduced at Harare Polytechnic in October 1985.

HIGHER EDUCATION

The University of Zimbabwe was founded in 1957 as the University College of Rhodesia and Nyasaland and later became the University of Rhodesia before assuming its present title at Independence.

Entrance is generally comparable to university entrance in Britain, i.e. 5 passes at GCE, of which 2 must be at Advanced level. All students must have GCE O-level English language. The University offers 3- to 4-year **Bachelor degrees**, **Special Diplomas** or **Postgraduate Certificates**, 2- to 3-year **Master degrees** and 3- to 4-year **Doctorate** programmes.

TEACHER EDUCATION

There are 8 primary and 3 secondary teachers colleges. They are affiliated to the Associate College Centre in the Faculty of Education at the University of Zimbabwe. The entry requirement for all the colleges is 5 passes at GCE O-level, including a language. The course lasts 4 years and is administered on a 'year-in year-out' basis. The course leads to a **Certificate in Education of the University of Zimbabwe**.

The Faculty of Education at the University of Zimbabwe offers a 3-year part-time B.Ed. course. The course is for in-service teachers who already hold a Certificate of Education and have subsequently acquired the necessary A-levels. B.Ed. graduates normally teach at senior secondary levels but are trained to teach at any level within the secondary system.

The Zimbabwe Integrated National Teacher Education Course (ZINTEC) is a government programme aimed at reducing the number of untrained primary teachers with minimum loss of teaching capacity while students are in training. It starts with an intensive 16-week residential course of lectures, tutorials, practical work and teaching practice; this is followed by 10 terms of supervised teaching and in-service training by correspondence work and vacation courses. There is a final residential course of 16-weeks at a regional teacher-training centre. At the end of the 4-year cycle, students who are successful in the final examinations and receive adequate assessments are awarded 'standard-trained' status.

Appendix 1

Cambridge Overseas School Certificate
Cambridge Overseas Higher School Certificate

The examinations of the University of Cambridge Local Examinations Syndicate are taken in many overseas countries.

Countries which have taken the Syndicate's examinations in the past, and the years in which they last did so, are as follows:

Fiji	1974
Ghana	1961
Guyana (British Guiana)	1964
India	1976
Kenya	1973
Nigeria	1963
Tanzania (including Zanzibar)	1970
Uganda	1973

The countries in which the **School Certificate** and **Higher School Certificate** examinations are taken at present are:

Bangladesh
Botswana
Brunei   - pupils take only the GCE examinations
Lesotho
Malawi
Mauritius
Nepal
Pakistan
Republic of Singapore   - pupils take only the GCE examinations.
Swaziland
Zimbabwe

Peninsular Malaysia)   students now take the examinations in English language
Sabah   )   (subject) only, other subjects being administered by the
Sarawak   )   Malaysian Syndicate. An Examinations Council has become
                        responsible for the Higher School Certificate since 1982,
                        but the Cambridge Syndicate continues to assist the local
                        body.

Appendix 1

Zambia	-	since 1981 the Ministry of Education in Zambia has assumed responsibility for the joint examination for the School Certificate and GCE. The Cambridge Syndicate continues to assist the local body.
Caribbean	-	Anguilla, Antigua, Bahamas, Barbados, Belize, Bermuda, the Cayman Islands, Dominica, Grenada, Jamaica, Montserrat, Nevis, St Kitts, St Lucia, St Vincent, Trinidad, Turks and Caicos Islands, British Virgin Islands.

The School Certificate was originally a group certificate, for the award of which pupils had to pass in a specified number of subjects. The Cambridge Syndicate then assisted a number of countries to develop their own examination system (eg in West and East Africa), and they now award School and Higher School Certificates and GCEs themselves. In the late 1950s, the Cambridge Syndicate introduced the joint examinations for the School and Higher School Certificates and General Certificate of Education (the School Certificate with the GCE at Ordinary level, and the Higher School Certificate with the GCE at Advanced level). Any student who passed the required number of subjects was awarded a School Certificate. A student who did not qualify for the School Certificate but passed in at least one subject at grade 6 or better was awarded a certificate showing the subjects in which he/she was deemed to have reached GCE 'O' level. These joint examinations are offered by eg the West African Examinations Council. In some countries only the examinations for the GCE are now offered - eg in the Caribbean countries listed above.

The Cambridge Overseas School Certificate has also been known as the Cambridge School Certificate and Cambridge Senior School Certificate. (The Cambridge Junior School Certificate used to be available at a stage 2 years before the Senior Certificate.)

EVALUATION IN BRITAIN

Cambridge Overseas School Certificate - grades 1-5 (until 1960), grades 1-6 (since 1961), A, B and C are equated to GCE O-level.

Cambridge Overseas Higher School Certificate - grades A-E are equated to GCE A-level.

MARKING SYSTEMS

The **School Certificate**/GCE Ordinary level examinations are graded:

Appendix 1

1)		) A	until 1960 only grades 3-5 were
2)	a, very good	)	considered as credit passes
3)		)	
4)	c, credit	) B	
5)		)	
6)		) C	
7)			
8)	p, pass (in the School Certificate only)		
9	f, fail		

Grade aggregate: the aggregate on which a candidate's **general performance** for the School Certificate is judged is obtained by adding together the best 6 subject-grades. With the exception of Mauritius and Zambia, School Certificates are classified as follows:

first division - for an aggregate not exceeding 23, with at least a 'credit' in 5 subjects (including English language), and at least a 'pass' in a sixth;

second division - for an aggregate not exceeding 33, with at least 'credit' in 4 subjects and at least 'pass' in 2 others (subjects passed to include English language);

third division - for an aggregate not exceeding 45, with either at least a 'credit' in one subject and at least a 'pass' in 5 others, subjects to include English, or at least a 'credit' in 2 subjects and at least a 'pass' in 3 others (subjects to include English language).

The **Higher School Certificate**/GCE A-level examinations are graded:

A)
B)
C) principal passes, considered as passes at GCE A-level
D)
E)

F   fail

O-level subsidiary pass - fail at GCE A-level, but considered as a pass at Ordinary level in that subject.

Appendix 2

London Chamber of Commerce and Industry

Examinations Boards

The examinations of the London Chamber of Commerce and Industry (LCCI) are generally available on demand in some 40 countries overseas, which include Singapore, Malaysia, Hong Kong, Guyana and the Caribbean, Nigeria, Ghana, Sierra Leone, Malta, Cyprus, Zambia, Zimbabwe and Mauritius as well as European countries.

There is a varying emphasis on subjects related to particular countries, for example: Hong Kong is particularly strong on accounting and bookkeeping; Greece has a particular interest in shipping and related insurance subjects; Malaysia and Singapore spread more generally over business studies and the secretarial field; in European countries, on the other hand, the emphasis is on English for commerce, spoken English for industry and commerce, and group secretarial awards.

The LCCI examinations available overseas are:

Business studies examinations

Higher Stage Group Diplomas in Accounting, Advertising, Auditing, Cost Accounting, Economics, Languages, Law, Management Accounting, Marketing, Public Relations, Selling and Sales Management and Shipping.

Higher Stage Diploma in Managerial Principles.

Single-subject examinations in Business Studies.

Elementary:

Arithmetic
Audio-typewriting
Bookkeeping
Elements of commerce
English for commerce
Foreign languages
Handwriting
Mathematics
Office practice
Shorthand (English and French)
Typewriting

Intermediate:

Arithmetic
Audio-typewriting
Bookkeeping
Business statistics
Cost accounting
Economics
English for commerce
Foreign languages
Mathematics
Office practice
Shorthand (English and French)
Structure of commerce
Typewriting
Word-processing

Appendix 2

Higher:

Accounting
Advertising
Audio-typewriting
Auditing
Business and industrial administration
Business computing
Business statistics
Commerce and finance
Commercial arithmetic
Commercial law
Cost accounting
Creative advertising
Economics
English for commerce
Foreign languages
Information processing
Law of business association
Legal institutions and principles
Management accounting
Marine insurance
Marketing
Principles of management
Public relations
Selling and sales management
Shipping
Shorthand (English and French)
Typewriting

Group secretarial and technology examinations

Secretarial Certificate
First Certificate in Office Technology
Private Secretary's Certificate
Second Certificate in Office Technology
Private and Executive Secretary's Diploma (available in UK, Singapore and Australia only).

For further information on these examinations, their content and standard contact:

London Chamber of Commerce and Industry
Examinations Board
Marlowe House
Station Road
Sidcup
Kent
DA15 7BJ

Appendix 3

City and Guilds of London Institute

The City and Guilds of London Institute, which is the largest technical examining body in Great Britain, offers examinations at operative, craft and technician level. Most of the schemes offered in the UK are designed primarily for students who work in industry and study part-time at technical colleges under day-release arrangements.

Many UK schemes are also available overseas; but teaching institutions are usually required to obtain the approval of the City and Guilds of London Institute in order to ensure that the necessary facilities and equipment are available and the qualifications and experience of the teaching staff are satisfactory.

City and Guilds UK schemes are available overseas in a wide range of subjects, providing for industries such as:

    Agriculture and agricultural engineering
    Chemical, metallurgical and allied industries
    Clothing, footwear and leather
    Construction
    Engineering and vehicles
    Furniture
    Hotel and catering
    Paper, printing and publishing
    Textiles

Schemes and qualifications are also available to meet the needs of those in professional, scientific and miscellaneous services such as:

    Computer programming and information processing
    Data processing for computer users
    Hairdressing and beauty therapy
    Quality control
    Science laboratory work

Where syllabuses for existing examinations, designed for conditions in the United Kingdom, are not appropriate in countries overseas because of climatic or environmental differences, a series of syllabuses has been specially prepared for use in those countries. They are designed to be equivalent in level to the corresponding courses and qualifications in Great Britain, but with differences in syllabus content to match special requirements overseas. They include craft courses in engineering, construction, motor vehicles, coal mining and food subjects. There are also Diploma courses, having a broader syllabus coverage and a more academic base than technician certificate courses. These are usually full-time, the principle ones being:

Appendix 3

Ordinary Technician Diploma in:

    Building and civil engineering
    Mechanical and electrical engineering

Higher Technician Diploma in:

    Construction
    Mechanical engineering
    Electrical engineering

EVALUATION

City and Guilds craft schemes are primarily of a technical nature: it is not normally possible to compare them with other British qualifications such as GCE. In the case of technician schemes, direct comparison is not easy, because City and Guilds syllabuses are vocational and intended to be the further education complement to the industrial training which people receive, whereas GCE and similar schemes are normally undertaken in full-time secondary education. However, syllabuses at Part 1 technician level are usually at least equivalent to GCE 'O' level. At Part 2 level in technician schemes, the technical content of the syllabuses is considerably beyond 'O' level and approximates to 'A' level.

A more appropriate comparison can be made with Ordinary National Certificates and Diplomas now BTEC National Certificates and Diplomas. The Part 2 Technician Certificate and the Ordinary Technician Diploma are broadly equivalent in level to ONC or OND. The Full Technological Certificate (awarded to those holders of Technician Part 2 and Part 3 Certificates who have appropriate industrial experience) and the Higher Technician Diploma are broadly equivalent in level to HNC or HND ie BTEC Higher National Certificate or Diploma.

Appendix 4

East African Examinations Council

The East African Examinations Council (EAEC) was established in 1967 and was abolished in 1980. The EAEC worked initially in conjunction with the University of Cambridge Local Examinations Syndicate in administering School examinations in Kenya, Tanzania and Uganda: the East African Certificate of Education (EACE) and the East African Advanced Certificate of Education (EAACE).

In Kenya the joint examination for the East African Certificate of Education and the East African School Certificate replaced the joint examination for the GCE and School Certificate of the University of Cambridge Local Examinations Syndicate in 1970. In Tanzania and Uganda the examinations of the Cambridge Syndicate were replaced by the East African Certificate of Education. In 1974 the EAEC assumed full responsibility for the conduct of the examinations, but the Cambridge Syndicate continued to assist in marking a proportion of the scripts. (In 1971 Tanzania withdrew from the EAEC to form its own Examinations Council; Kenya followed suit in 1980.)

The joint East African Certificate of Education and General Certificate of Education are awarded when pupils obtain at the same examination sitting 1 pass with credit and passes in 2 other subjects or passes in 3 subjects.

A pupil may take a maximum of 5 subjects at either principal or subsidiary level at one sitting for the East African Advanced Certificate of Education. Pupils also take a general paper. The EAEC does not administer any other examinations.

EVALUATION IN BRITAIN

East African Certificate of Education - grades 1-6 are generally equated to GCE O-level standard, grades A, B, C.

East African Advanced Certificate of Education - is generally equated to GCE A-level standard.

Appendix 4

MARKING SYSTEM

East African Certificate of Education is graded 1 (maximum) to 9 (fail).

1	
2	very good
3	
4	credit
5	
6	
7	
8	pass
9	fail

The joint East African Certificate of Education and School Certificate is classified:

first division	6-23 points (based on aggregate score of grades obtained in 6 best subjects)
second division	24-33 points
third division	34-44 points

East African Advanced Certificate of Education is graded A (maximum) to F (fail):

A	
B	
C	principal passes
D	
E	
O	subsidiary pass
F	fail

Appendix 5

West African Examinations Council

The West African Examinations Council (WAEC) was established in 1952 to determine the examinations required in the public interest in West Africa, to conduct such examinations in Ghana (the Gold Coast as it then was), Nigeria, Sierra Leone and The Gambia, and to award certificates comparable to those awarded by equivalent examining bodies in the United Kingdom. Liberia became the fifth member country in 1974. The Council is made up of representatives from all member countries.

In its early years, the Council acted as agents in administering examinations such as the School Certificate Examination of the Cambridge Local Examinations Syndicate and the General Certificate of Education Examinations of the University of London, and maintained a close relationship with these examining bodies. However, with the acquisition of the necessary expertise, the Council started taking on greater responsibilities, and in 1955 the Cambridge School Certificate, renamed the West African School Certificate (WASC), was awarded by the Syndicate in collaboration with WAEC.

Starting in 1960 with the School Certificate Examination of the West African Examinations Council (SC/WAEC), renamed the School Certificate/General Certificate of Education (SC/GCE) in 1963, the Council now independently develops and administers all its own examinations and administers others on behalf of (or in collaboration with) certain examining bodies. Currently, WAEC develops and administers the Joint Examination for School Certificate and GCE Ordinary-level and the GCE Advanced-level.

EVALUATION IN BRITAIN

West African School Certificate - grades 1 to 6 are generally equated to GCE O-level standard, grades A, B, C.

West African GCE A-level - is generally equated to GCE A level standard.

To check the validity of a certificate, contact:

The West African Examinations Council
Walkden House
10 Melton Street
London
NW1 2EJ.

Appendix 5

SCHOOL CERTIFICATE AND GCE O-LEVEL

For the award of the School Certificate, candidates must take a minimum of 6 and a maximum of 9 subjects from any 4 of the following subject groupings, English language being compulsory:

Group 1 - languages, including English language
2 - general, including literature in English
3 - mathematical
4 - science
5 - arts and crafts
6 - technical
7 - commercial and secretarial

Candidates must:

pass all subjects at the same sitting

reach a satisfactory standard in the aggregate of grades of the 6 best subjects

either pass in 6 subjects
or in 5 subjects with credits in at least 2
or pass with credits in 4 subjects.

To qualify for the award of GCE O-level, the candidate must either have entered the School Certificate and while failing to gain the Certificate should pass in at least 1 subject or have entered on a single-subject basis, securing a pass in at least 1 of them.

Interpretation of subject grades

The pass grades at School Certificate and the GCE O-level are equivalent. For purposes of comparison, passes at grade 6 and above are equivalent to the former GCE O-level. The interpretation of the subject grades in terms of the School Certificate is as follows:

Grade	School Certificate	West African GCE O-level
1	excellent	excellent
2	very good	very good
3	good	good
4	credit	good
5	credit	credit
6	credit	credit
7	pass	pass
8		
9	fail	fail

Appendix 5

Classification of the Certificate

Division I with Distinction

awarded to candidates who pass in 6 subjects chosen from any 4 or more of the subject groups, including English language, and either a Group 3 or Group 4 subject with 5 credits, yielding an aggregate score not exceeding 12 in their best 6 subjects.

Division I

awarded to candidates who pass in 6 subjects chosen from any 4 or more of the groups, including English language, and either a Group 3 or a Group 4 subject with 5 credits, yielding an aggregate score not exceeding 24 in their best 6 subjects.

Division II

awarded to candidates who pass in 6 subjects from any 4 or more groups, including English language with credits in at least 4 of the subjects, producing an aggregate score not exceeding 36 in their best 6 subjects.

Division III

awarded to candidates who obtain 6 passes or 3 passes plus 2 credits or 4 credits; the aggregate score from the grades of the subjects not exceeding 48 in their best 6 subjects.

HIGHER SCHOOL CERTIFICATE AND A-LEVEL

As with the School Certificate, the Council administered the Higher School Certificate Examination and also later the Advanced-level Examination on behalf of the Cambridge Syndicate and the University of London, respectively, from its inception until 1972, when WAEC began to develop and administer its own examinations at the advanced level. After 1974 the Council discontinued the Higher School Certificate examination and adopted the single-subject GCE A-level examination. Candidates for GCE A-level may offer up to 5 subjects.

Interpretation of grades on the GCE A-level certificate

There will be 7 grades in order of merit. The first 5, designated A, B, C, D and E, are grades of pass. The sixth grade is designated a subsidiary pass, defined as a standard below A-level and above O-level. The last grade represents a failure.

Appendix 6

Caribbean Examinations Council

The Caribbean Examinations Council (CXC) was established in 1972, and presently covers Anguilla; Antigua and Barbuda; Barbados*; Belize*; British Virgin Islands; Dominica; Grenada; Guyana*; Jamaica*; Montserrat; St Kitts/Nevis; St Lucia; St Vincent and the Grenadines; Trinidad and Tobago*; Turks and Caicos Islands.

(*See separate chapters for more information.)

The examinations offered by the CXC are criterion referenced with a large element of teacher assessment, and are designed for pupils who have completed 5 years of secondary school education. They are intended to offer greater flexibility and thus assist pupils with limited academic ability or interest in technical studies. Eventually these examinations will replace those offered by non-Caribbean examining authorities; in the meantime pupils may still take GCE O-level examinations in subjects not offered by the CXC.

The first examinations (in five subjects) for the **Caribbean Examinations Council Secondary Education Certificate** were offered in 1979. The Council now examines candidates in 29 subjects. Additional subjects are currently under consideration.

Candidates may offer subjects for examination under a general proficiency scheme and under a basic proficiency scheme. The **general proficiency scheme** is designed for students who intend to pursue further educational programmes and who therefore require an in-depth knowledge of the subject. This scheme is taken by pupils who would normally have taken GCE O-level examinations. The emphasis in the **basic proficiency scheme** is on the acquisition of skills, since it is intended that students who pursue this option will be preparing to enter the job market. Both examinations are offered to students who have completed five years of education at the secondary level. Students are encouraged to take a combination of basic and general proficiencies, since this allows them to broaden their knowledge of a number of subject areas.

There is also a **technical proficiency level** in certain fields.

The CXC has had assistance from examining bodies in America (e.g. Educational Testing Service of Princeton, New Jersey) and Britain (e.g. University of Cambridge Local Examinations Syndicate, University of London Examinations Council, Joint Matriculation Board, Metropolitan Regional Examinations Board, and Scottish Certificate of Education Examination Board) in developing its examination capability.

Appendix 6

EVALUATION IN BRITAIN

Caribbean Examinations Council Secondary Education Certificate - grades 1 and 2 at the general proficiency level have been equated to GCE O-level (grades A, B, C).

The Joint Matriculation Board will give individual consideration to candidates offering Grade 1 at basic proficiency level.

MARKING SYSTEM

There is no pass/fail mark.

Grade

1   comprehensive working knowledge of the syllabus

2   working knowledge of most aspects of the syllabus

3   working knowledge of some aspects of the syllabus

4   limited knowledge of a few aspects of the syllabus

5   insufficient evidence on which to base a judgement.

In addition to this overall grade the profile reports (for each subject which has been examined) provide information on the student's specific strengths and weaknesses. The profile report uses the following grades:

A   above average
B   average
C   below average
N/A   no assessment possible.

The Council is moving towards offering examinations beyond the CSEC level.

Appendix 7

College of Europe

The College of Europe was founded in 1949 in Bruges, Belgium, as a postgraduate institute specializing in the problems of European unity.

Teaching is offered in both French and English. Candidates for admission must hold a first degree which would generally be considered comparable to the British Bachelor degree or French Licence in economics, law, political science or social science. A limited number of students are admitted each year, chosen by selection committees in various European countries.

Students choose one area in which to specialize: economics, law, political science or European studies in society and civilization. Besides taking taught courses in their chosen specialization, students also take taught courses in multidisciplinary studies, intended to give them a rounded education.

The course lasts one year and there is an eliminatory examination in mid-December. The remaining 7 examinations are taken at the end of the academic year (October to May), and lead to the **Certificat de Hautes Etudes Europeennes/Certificate of Advanced European Studies.** Students who obtain the Certificate may go on to prepare and submit a thesis. If this is approved they are awarded a **Diplome d'Etudes Appronfondies/Master of European Studies.** Before the academic year 1978/9 the qualification obtained at this stage was the **Diplome de Hautes Etudes Europeennes/Diploma of Advanced European Studies.**

Appendix 8

European Baccalaureate

Diplome du Baccalaureat Europeen
Zeugnis der Europaischen Reifeprufung
Diploma di Licenza Liceale Europea
Europees Baccalaureaats Diploma

The European Baccalaureate may only be obtained by pupils from the small number of European Schools, the first of which was established in 1957, under an agreement signed by the then members of the European Community (EC). The United Kingdom, Eire and Denmark acceded to the statute in 1972/3, and an agreement modifying the regulations was signed in 1978 by the 9 member-states of the EC. The Baccalaureate is the final examination certificate of these schools, and generally enjoys the same status as the national final school leaving certificates of the member countries of the EC.

These schools provide nursery, 5 years elementary and 7 years secondary education, essentially for the children of EC officials. Each school offers a maximum of 7 language streams, (i.e. English, Danish, French, German, Dutch, Italian, and Greek).

At the end of the third secondary year, a limited degree of specialization occurs and pupils are required to select 1 of 5 options:

1. classics
2. Latin - modern languages
3. Latin - mathematics - science
4. modern languages - mathematics - science
5. economics and social science.

The following subjects are compulsory throughout years 4, 5, 6 and 7: mother tongue, mathematics, modern languages, history and geography (the last 2 are taught through the medium of a foreign language), and philosophy (years 6 and 7 only). In addition, it should be noted that

options 3 and 4 contain the advanced courses in mathematics, physics (years 4, 5, 6, 7 in both cases), chemistry (years 5, 6, 7) and biology (years 6,7)

option 5 involves courses in economics and sociology (both through the medium of a foreign language)

options 1, 2, and 5 contain an intermediate course in biology.

Certain changes of specialization are possible but not later than the end of the fifth year.

Appendix 8

A pupil may be a candidate for the European Baccalaureate only if he/she has followed at least the final 2 years of the course at a European School. The final examinations are taken at the end of the seventh secondary year, and standards are maintained by an examination board consisting of at least 2 qualified representatives from each Community country and headed by a university professor. All pupils must sit 4 written and 4 oral examinations, incuding a written and oral examination in the mother tongue, and an oral examination in the first foreign language, and either history or geography. The remaining written and oral examinations are determined by the specialization that the pupil has followed:

Latin - Greek	: written	- Latin, Greek and philosophy or first foreign language or mathematics
	oral	- biology
Latin - modern	: written	- Latin, first foreign language and languages philosophy or second foreign language or mathematics
	oral	- biology
Latin - mathematics	: written	- mathematics, physics and Latin or sciences philosophy, or first foreign language
	oral	- biology or chemistry
Modern languages	: written	- mathematics, physics and first foreign language mathematics - science, language or biology or philosophy
	oral	- chemistry
Economics and social	: written	- economics, mathematics/statistics and science sociology or first foreign language or philosophy
	oral	- biology

EVALUATION IN BRITAIN

European Baccalaureate - may be considered to satisfy the general requirement of universities and polytechnics.

More detailed guidance on comparability and on the factors to be taken into account in assessing the ability of holders to benefit from degree and other courses of higher education is provided by the Department of Education and Science in <u>The European Schools and the European Baccalaureate</u>.

MARKING SYSTEM

The final overall mark for the Baccalaureate is given as a percentage, made up of 3 elements:

Appendix 8

	% of total mark	
written examinations	36	
oral examinations	24	
continuous assessment throughout the final year	40	(half for tests - mostly short - and the other half for classwork)

The weighting of individual subject marks depends upon the course followed. Pupils must obtain at least 60% overall to be awarded the Baccalaureate.

Appendix 9

International Baccalaureate

The International Baccalaureate (IB) Programme is a 2-year pre-university course designed to:

facilitate the mobility of students

promote international understanding

provide a widely accepted university matriculation qualification (the IB Diploma examination)

The IB is offered in schools and colleges in 50 countries throughout the world. The schools have been individually assessed and approved by the International Baccalaureate Office (IBO) which is based in Geneva and administers the examination through an International Examining Board.

There is no formal entry requirement to IB courses but it is intended as a 2-year upper secondary programme. For example, in Britain, it is taken as a post GCE O-level course and provides a broader and more varied general education than the GCE A-level course.

Curriculum and examination

The curriculum consists of 6 subject Groups:

1. Language A (first language including the study of selections from World Literature.

2. Language B (second language) or a second language A.

3. Study of man in society: history, geography, economics, philosophy, psychology, social anthropology, organisation studies

4. Experimental sciences: biology, chemistry, applied chemistry, physics, physical science, experimental psychology

5. Mathematics: mathematics, mathematics and computing, mathematical studies, mathematics with further mathematics

6. One of the following options:

    Art/design, music, Latin, Classical Greek, computing studies

    A school-based syllabus approved by IBO.

Appendix 9

Alternatively a candidate may offer instead of a Group 6 subject: a third modern language, a second subject from the Study of man in society, a second subject from Experimental sciences.

To be eligible for the award of the Diploma all candidates must:

1   offer 1 subject from each of the above Groups

2   offer at least 3 and not more than 4 of the 6 subjects at Higher level and the others at subsidiary level

3   submit an Extended essay in 1 of the subjects of the IB curriculum

4   follow a course in the Theory of knowledge

5   engage in extra-curricular activities (CASS).

Candidates may also offer single subjects, for which they receive a Certificate.

Marking system and grades

At both higher and subsidiary level, each examined subject is graded on a scale of 1 (minimum) to 7 (maximum). The award of the Diploma requires a minimum total of 24 points and satisfactory completion of the Theory of knowledge course, the Extended essay and CASS.

Examples of IB Diplomas:

Higher	**Subsidiary**
Mathematics	English A
Physics	German B
Chemistry	History
French A	Mathematics
Arabic B	Biology
Economics	Art/Design

EVALUATION IN BRITAIN

The <u>full</u> **International Baccalaureate** may be considered to satisfy the general requirement of universities and polytechnics.

Further information may be obtained from:

International Baccalaureate Office
18 Woburn Square
LONDON
WC1H 0NS

Appendix 10

United Nations Relief and Works Agency

United Nations Relief and Works Agency for Palestine Refugees in the Near East (Unrwa) operates in five different areas: Jordan, Lebanon, the Syrian Arab Republic and the territories of the Gaza Strip and the West Bank, and mirrors the system of the host country, i.e. Jordan in the case of the West Bank, and Egypt in the case of the Gaza Strip.

SCHOOL EDUCATION

Unrwa offers 6 years primary/elementary education, followed by 3 years preparatory/lower secondary; 4 years in Lebanon. Some pupils are then able to go into state or private schools to undertake a course of upper secondary schooling.

VOCATIONAL TRAINING

Unrwa opened its first vocational training centre in 1953; there are now 8 centres. These cater for the needs of industry in the Middle East and aim to produce skilled craftsmen. Practical training takes place in workshops and is supplemented by theory, technical drawing, mathematics and general science. English is taught where it is necessary for trainees to read and understand technical terminology and literature written in the language.

Courses (mostly 2 years) at post-preparatory level include:

metal trades: instrument mechanic, machinist-welder, diesel and construction equipment mechanic, auto body mechanic, sheetmetal worker, blacksmith-welder, moulder, toolmaker, office machine mechanic

electrical trades: electrician, radio-TV mechanic, auto-electrician

building trades: builder/shutterer, plasterer-tilesetter, plumber, carpenter-woodmachinist.

vocational courses for girls: dressmaking, clothing production, hairdressing.

Appendix 10

Courses (mostly 2 years) at post-secondary level include:

technician: land-surveyor, quantity surveyor, construction technician, architectural draughtsman, telecommunication technician, engineering draughtsman, vocational training instructor, machine maintenance technician

commercial: business and office practice

para-medical: assistant pharmacist, laboratory technician, public health inspector

vocational courses for girls: secretarial, home and institutional management, infant leader.

TEACHER EDUCATION

Unrwa operates 4 teacher education centres: Jordan (1), Lebanon (1), and West Bank (2). The course is of 2 years and trains teachers for primary/elementary education.

Appendix 11

United Nations University

The United Nations University is jointly sponsored by the United Nations and Unesco to be 'an international community of scholars engaged in research, postgraduate training and the dissemination of knowledge'.

The charter of the university was approved by the General Assembly of the United Nations in December 1973 and the headquarters of the university became fully operational in September 1975 in Tokyo, Japan.

It is not a university in the normal sense of offering instruction on a main campus and it does not offer courses leading to a degree. Its objectives are rather to stimulate, support and co-ordinate research and advanced training in institutions throughout the world on the 'problems of human survival, development and welfare', with the three main areas of work being on world hunger, human and social development, and the use of natural resources.

Two types of institution are involved in the university's work:

Incorporated institutions. These are administered by the university itself. They may be actually established by the university, or be existing institutions for which responsibility is taken over by the university. New institutions are only established if no suitable institution exists to meet a particular programme need, or when a local/regional development need strongly justifies it.

Associated institutions. These are joint operations between the university and other institutions.